WOLFE TONE

Prophet of Irish Independence

'The great object of my life has been the independence
of my country. Looking upon the connexion with
England to have been her bane I have endeavoured by
every means in my power to break that connexion...to
create a people in Ireland...by uniting the Catholics
and the Dissenters. For a fair and open war I was
prepared; if that has degenerated into a system of
assassination, massacre, and plunder I do...most
sincerely lament it.'

Tone's trial speech, Dublin, 10 November 1798.

MARIANNE ELLIOTT

YALE UNIVERSITY PRESS
NEW HAVEN AND LONDON · 1989

FOR TREVOR

Designed by John Nicoll

Set in Linotron Bembo by Best-set Typesetter Ltd, Hong Kong
Printed and bound at The Bath Press, Avon, Great Britain

ISBN 0–300–04637–5

Library of Congress Catalog Number 89–36283

CONTENTS

VI REVOLUTIONARY (1794–1795)

VII MISSION TO FRANCE (1796–1797)

VIII FINAL DAYS (1797–1798)

ACKNOWLEDGEMENTS

One fine June morning in 1983, as we crossed the Irish border, returning north from a conference at Maynooth, my old friend, Tom Bartlett, suggested that I write a biography of Theobald Wolfe Tone. It was the link to those student days at Queen's University when we had both been fired to pursue research into Irish history by the seminars of Jim Beckett and Peter Jupp, and to Belfast itself, which has continued to exercise an influence on my thinking. Some weeks later, in Des Moines, Iowa, I met John Tone, the descendant of Tone's uncle who had settled in the United States in the eighteenth century. If I needed any further convincing about embarking on the project, this uncanny coincidence was it. My colleague at Iowa State University, Andrejs Plakans, added further encouragement. To him, and to my other colleagues and friends in Ames, Iowa, I owe more than I can ever repay. I was then embarked on the translation of Richard Cobb's *Armées révolutionnaires* and a frustrating two years ensued before I could commence work on the present book.

But my interest in Tone goes back to childhood, to traditions transmitted by my Kerry mother, Sheila (O'Neill) Burns, and my Belfast father, Terry Burns. My father died shortly before I embarked on the biography, but his influence is ever present in my writing. It was in my father that I first encountered that passionate interest in Irish history so noticeable among the Irish populace. I found it again in a stirring debate on Tone which occurred at Maughan's, Lacken, Co. Mayo, during the 1988 Humbert Summer School. I am deeply grateful to the people of Lacken and to the organisers of the Humbert Summer School, notably John Cooney, who made the occasion possible.

I have been assisted throughout by friends. Roy Foster, Tom Paulin and Sam Butler in particular have been a constant source of inspiration and support, and Roy Foster stepped in at a crucial moment to help rescue the project when it was flagging. Anne Laurence did likewise and I cannot easily repay their friendship during that trying time. I have benefited from frequent discussions with John Styles, who also introduced me to the wonders of computer writing. The sociability of Susan Paton, Janet McIver, Judy Wyatt, Judy Stone, Dominique Le Rambert, Roger Price, Peter

Jones, Penny Woods, Giti Paulin, Aisling Foster and Margot and Ciaran Fee lightened the long stretches of research away from home.

I have been particularly fortunate in the friendship of Tone's direct descendants in the United States. Mrs Katherine Dickason welcomed me into her family and her home, made the family papers freely available to me and shared with me family oral traditions. There was nothing hagiographic in those traditions and my knowledge of Tone has benefited considerably from the discussions with Mrs Dickason and with her grandson, David King, during frequent visits and in extended correspondence. Her friendship has been one of the most valued products of the research for this biography. The book is a tribute to that friendship.

In all the libraries and archives used, I have found the staff ever willing to lend assistance. In particular I would like to thank the staff of the Institute of Historical Research in London, notably Alice Prochaska, Anne Neary and Eamonn Mulally of the Irish State Paper Office, Miss McNeill of the Middle Temple Library, Jonathan Armstrong of the King's Inns Library, Trevor Parkhill of the Northern Ireland Public Record Office, Ríonach uí Ogáin of the Folklore Department, University College, Dublin, Mrs Reid of the Presbyterian Historical Society, Belfast, Bill Maguire and Noel Nesbitt, of the Ulster Museum, John Gray, of the Linenhall Library, Catriona Crowe of the Public Record Office, Ireland, Siobhán O'Rafferty, of the Royal Irish Academy, Oliver Snoddy, of the National Museum of Ireland, Felicity O'Mahony of Trinity College Dublin, and most of all Kevin Whelan, National Library, and Phil Connolly, Public Record Office, Ireland, who went beyond the common call of duty to help in the final checking before the book went to press, and the archivists of the Library of Congress, Washington, through whom I first met Katherine Dickason. Eoghan O Néill helped with research in the Department of Irish Folklore, and I am particularly grateful to Rudolf Dekker and Harm-Jan van Rees, Erasmus University, Rotterdam, for the assistance they afforded in locating the Dutch material. I would also like to thank the British Academy, the Nuffield Foundation and Liverpool University, who helped fund my research, Brian Walker, for sharing with me his unrivalled knowledge of local Ulster history, and Jakez Cornou who kindly made available to me some of the illustrations used in the preparation of his book: L'Odyssée du vaisseau "Droits de l'homme" (Quimper, 1988).

The book was written whilst I was a member of the academic staff at Liverpool, and latterly, at Manchester University. I am grateful to colleagues at both for their companionship and patience when faced with my insistent raids on their knowledge, particularly Judith

Brown, Brian Pullan and Peter Marshall (who kindly commented on the American chapter), at Manchester, and at Liverpool, Eve Rosenhaft, Alan Harding, Irene Collins, Chris Allmand, Elizabeth Danbury, Tony Ryan, Jennie Kermode, Edward Acton, Peter King, Paul Laxton, Richard Waller, Keith Mason—who likewise helped with the American chapter—and Brean Hammond, with whom I passed many pleasurable moments identifying Tone's literary allusions. My colleague at Liverpool, Michael de Cossart, died just as the book was going to press. His rare sense of wit and his companionship will be sorely missed. Liverpool University's library staff, particularly Bernard Jubb, afforded constant help. But without the patience and skills of Anne Rowland at inter-library loans, the book would never have been written.

Howard Brown applied his unique knowledge of the Directory to a critique of the French chapters, and Marion Treacy shared with me her specialist knowledge of *Belmont Castle*. But the debt I owe Christopher Woods and Sean Connolly would be difficult to repay. Both abandoned their own commitments to read the full text at high speed. No one knows more about Tone and Russell than Chris Woods and his generosity in sharing that expertise has made for years of lively conversations and correspondence. Sean Connolly applied an impressive range of knowledge to an overview of the topic and I made significant changes on his advice. I hope neither will be disappointed at the outcome.

The arrival of young Marc Elliott might have throttled the book in its final stage had it not been for the support of a remarkable team at Arrowe Park Hospital and in the Wirral health authority—notably Pauline Lynch, Janet Smyth, Belinda Thompson, Dr. Geoffrey Meyer, Devina Edwards, Anne Cooper and Doreen Johnson—of Sheila Jones and Margaret and David Rankin, Claire Vincent, but most of all of my dear friend Susan Paton.

I was able to call on the lifetime publishing experience of my father-in-law, Mr. C. Elliott, for help with proofing. My publisher, John Nicoll, and agent, Xandra Hardie, were more patient than I ever deserved, and Catharine Carver—undeterred by the experience of *People's Armies*—took on the task of copy-editing at short notice, ironing out the ragged edges and producing a more polished work than would have emerged without her dedication and experience. I am left wondering what I have done to deserve the array of friendship and help upon which I have been able to call over the past three years.

But my chief debt is to my long-suffering husband, Trevor Elliott. The dedication of this book to him is small recompense for the trials he has had to endure during its writing. I hope it will go some way towards refuting his frequent jest that no one mattered in the Elliott household but Wolfe Tone.

Cheshire, June 1989

NOTE ON QUOTATIONS AND DATES: I have adhered to the original MS spelling and punctuation in all quotations, only using *sic* in the case of blatant misspellings. Those from Tone's journals and autobiography cite the manuscript rather than the published versions. The correspondence between Gregorian and French Republican calendars has been made according to that set out in Martyn Lyons, *France Under the Directory* (Cambridge, 1975), 239–40.

Map of Ireland in the eighteenth century

Introduction

Theobald Wolfe Tone is the recognised founder of Irish republican nationalism. As such, his name and political ideas, the circumstances of his life and early death, became powerful political weapons in the hands of later nationalists and were incorporated into the very educational system of the new Irish state earlier in the present century.[1] Today his name still arouses heated passions. He is hailed as the first prophet of an independent Ireland, and nationalists of all shades go in annual pilgrimage to his grave at Bodenstown in County Kildare. However, it is the provisional IRA and Sinn Féin who celebrate the anniversary proper of his birth, and the apparent takeover of the Tone cult by the men of violence, the 'Irish Irelanders' and Catholics generally, has alienated the Ulster Protestants. Both are reacting to the myths which have developed over two centuries. They fail to recognise that the most powerful single influence on Tone's life and opinions was that of the Ulster Presbyterians; that militant Irish separation was more a product of Belfast than Dublin; that Tone was a deist who disliked institutionalised religion and sectarianism of any hue; that he had no time whatsoever for the romantic Gaelicism which has become part of Irish nationalism, and was far less dogmatic about England or the resort to arms than is commonly supposed. His central message was not that Ireland's abiding evil was England, but rather that her people were disunited. Resolve the one and the other would resolve itself naturally. This is why, nearly two hundred years after his death, Wolfe Tone is still a living force in Ireland.

These are not the only misreadings of Tone's life. The loss of the early journals, writings and letters has also given greater prominence to those written after he had become a republican exile.[2] The impact of the writings which have survived has been double-edged. Tone was a gifted writer. The personal journals have helped make him one of the most approachable of Irish historical figures and explain his enduring popularity. They are the outpourings of an extremely restless, sociable and loquacious young man, forced by exile and the nature of his later political activities into long periods of loneliness in cheap lodgings far from home, family and friends. He was a compulsive writer, as he was a compulsive talker, and the spontaneity, humour and the openness and sheer candour of the journals are the main reason for their lasting appeal. But they also distort, the very process of retrospective writing clarifying political ideas which were anything but clear at the time. Ultimately Tone did seek independence from England by force of arms, and his account of how he arrived at such a solution became the gospel of Irish republican nationalism. But he was never as clear about the means as later militant republicans liked to claim, and in his final public statement he distanced himself from the rebellion which tore through Ireland in 1798.

Tone was highly educated, and had a passion for books and learning; his ideas spanned Enlightenment and Romantic traditions, and, but for the times in which he grew to political maturity, he might have been remembered more as an eighteenth-century man of letters than as a revolutionary nationalist. By opponents and friends alike Tone was considered a man of considerable warmth, generosity and talent. I 'admired him for the brilliancy and great variety of his conversation, the gay and social cast of his disposition', wrote William Sampson, a fellow barrister,[3] and many political opponents came to regret the fate of a man whose company they had so coveted in the past. Loyalty to friends he elevated to a principle as important as any other in dictating his conduct. But he was impatient of humbug, cavil and unearned privilege, and his intellectual contempt for the country's rulers laid the ground for his active republicanism. He was quite fearless, sometimes to the point of folly, in pursuit of a principle. This, attached to a penchant for a life of adventure, made him an ideal revolutionary, if a negligent, though never unloving, husband and father. But he also had a number of blind spots which caused him to rush in regardless where others, more experienced, trod carefully. Notable among these was his underestimation of the depth of religious divisions in Ireland and his failure to appreciate that his own rational outlook was not always that of others. His shock at the outcome of the 1798 rebellion was genuine, if naïve. He was not to be the first revolutionary to fail to anticipate the abuse of his ideas.

No biography of Tone based on extensive research has ever been written. Frank MacDermot's *Theobald Wolfe Tone*, which first appeared in 1939, remains the only life of Tone which is not purely derivative, and was a milestone in its day. The multitude of brief lives and versions of his central political statements have all tended to be hagiographic and devoid of any explanation of the man's complex character or the context in which he operated.[4]

Tone was born in Dublin in 1763 into a middle-class Protestant family. His education—at a private classical school, at Trinity

College, Dublin, and finally at the Inns of Court in London—
groomed him for membership of Ireland's Protestant élite, with
good prospects of attaining legal and political office. His formative
years were those of 'Grattan's Parliament',[5] a period looked back to
by constitutional nationalists as one in which Ireland came close to
resolving peacefully its anomalous constitutional position. After
almost a century of insecurity, and grudging acceptance of England's
tight colonial control, the Irish Protestants had emerged in the 1780s
as confident, improving, deeply influenced by Enlightenment ideas
of reason and progress, and impatient at the impediments put in
the way of that progress by England's mercantilist hold on their
commerce, government and legislative process. A constitutional
opposition had won legislative independence for Ireland in 1782,
while retaining the connection with England through the crown and
executive.

The reality of that independence, however, remained a dead letter.
Necessary political reform did not follow because of Protestant fears
of restoring political rights to the Catholics. But the rhetoric of
reforming pamphleteers in the 1780s had created something new
in Ireland, public opinion. It was on the wave of this rhetorical
excitement that Tone emerged as a leading reformer, and it was his
discovery in the early 1790s that much of what had gone before was
simply rhetoric that set him on the road to republicanism. Analysing
why Irish political life remained as corrupt, unfree and unrepresentative after 1782 as before, Tone discovered the answer in 'the disunion of Irishmen' and Protestant fears of sharing political power
with the Catholic majority. The result was his first mature work: *An
Argument on Behalf of the Catholics of Ireland* (1791)—a pamphlet
which was to alter the course of Irish radical politics. Tone thought
institutionalised religion fostered ignorance and timidity, and he
never quite lost his belief that the Catholic masses were ignorant and
lacking in spirit. Behind his own lingering Protestant prejudices,
however, lay a growing conviction of the fundamental injustice of
excluding Irish Catholics from the political life of the nation.

Tone's *Argument* was the turning-point in his own life and indeed
in the development of Irish nationalism generally. His father's
sudden bankruptcy, his own lack of success at the bar, and urgent
domestic needs brought on by early marriage and the swift arrival of
a family, allied to exceptional abilities, made him restless for success.
As a political writer he found it. His works addressed controversial
issues with clarity and authority. They were written in plain-man's
English, knew how to target an audience and became best-sellers in
their time. They brought Tone to the notice of radical opinion and in
quick succession he was invited to Belfast to help found the Society

of United Irishmen (soon to become the first Irish republican movement), and was appointed agent to the Catholic Committee, then campaigning for total repeal of the penal laws against the Catholics.

For the next three years he acted as chief publicist for both movements, producing a flood of newspaper articles, propositions and petitions. Expectations of full emancipation for the Catholics and an extension of political rights generally ran high, and some, Tone included, spoke privately of the eventual possibility of full negotiated independence from England—though before 1795 this was never seriously contemplated, even by Tone.

However, war erupted between Britain and Revolutionary France in 1793. The execution of the French royal family and nobles sent a tremor through Europe's ruling élites. French subversion abroad made governments nervous of radical movements at home, and demands considered constitutional before 1793 became positively subversive thereafter. In Ireland war-induced panic produced a series of coercive measures which startled even Whitehall by their severity. The United Irish Society was suppressed, demands for Catholic emancipation and political reform rejected, and the sudden clampdown when expectations had been running so high left reformers of all hues stunned. The arrival of a French agent with offers of military assistance for the disenchanted radicals forced them to take a decision as to their future direction. Tone was asked to write a statement on Ireland's internal situation, despite his doubts about the advisability of doing so. Thereafter he was publicly associated with treason and was exiled in consequence. It was only at that point that his republican career commenced—a case of necessity as much as choice.

For the remainder of his life Tone acted as republican agent abroad, first in America, then from 1796 to 1798 in France, where he attained the rank of adjutant-general in the French army. In Ireland Tone had been considered likeable and talented, even by those of opposing views, but hardly dangerous. Of educated, even aristocratic tastes, finely featured, almost foppish in dress, and so open about his views that many felt he was being made the victim of his own candour, Tone did not have the appearance of a conspirator. His success in negotiating French military aid for Ireland is as surprising, with hindsight, as it was at the time. By 1796 the French government was hardened to minority foreign groups seeking help in effecting their revolutions. Yet Tone managed to convince the Directory that the Irish were different. He negotiated and sailed with a full-scale French invasion force to Ireland in 1796, with a Franco-Dutch venture in 1797, and on a last fateful expedition in 1798 which culminated in his own capture, conviction of treason and suicide in a Dublin prison.

By then the squabbling sectarian divisions, which he had so decried, had decimated the United Irish movement, alienated the French, and driven many of the movement's Protestant and Presbyterian supporters to seek protection in the unloved but increasingly necessary connection with England. Following the bloody and sectarian 1798 rebellion, the Irish Parliament was abolished, and the sectarian take-over of the extremes of loyalism and nationalism, by Protestants on the one hand and Catholics on the other, projected into the future a more deeply divided nation.

I

EARLY LIFE
(1763–1790)

1

Family and Education

Theobald Wolfe Tone, eldest son of Peter and Margaret Tone, was born in Dublin on 20 June 1763. The Tones then lived at 27 St. Bride Street, just behind Dublin Castle, the seat of Irish government.[1] Ireland was a dependency of England, governed by an English Lord Lieutenant and legislated for by the Westminster Parliament. But although Ireland's connection with the mother country was similar to that of America, until the legislative union with Britain in 1801, it was complicated by the existence of an Irish Parliament. Throughout the eighteenth century the Irish Parliament claimed considerable autonomy. It finally won legislative independence from England in 1782, though retaining the connection through the crown and executive.

Political power in eighteenth-century Ireland was held by a tiny group of landed Protestants, most of them descendants of those who had acquired land confiscated from Catholics in the seventeenth century. The Catholic populace, though comprising two-thirds of the population, was excluded from political rights and theoretically from landownership. The Dissenters too were excluded from corporations until 1780, and though not legally debarred from Parliament, only a handful of Dissenting MPs was ever returned. Protestant insecurities about their position among a dominant and potentially aggrieved Catholic populace applied a brake on their distrust of England. But it was a resentful dependence, and although the 1760s witnessed the beginnings of agrarian troubles, the quiescence of the Catholic populace helped create a novel confidence among the ruling class. Coupled with the explosion of the printed word from mid-century, it produced several decades of debate about Ireland's constitutional position and provided the backdrop to Tone's early years.

The world of Irish politics was small, highly personalised and centred within a few minutes' walking distance from the Tones' home in Dublin. The city was the centre of the country's government, politics, trade, military, professional and educational life. There was a sense of living at the hub of things, which was shared by a complete cross-section of society, and mob interference in municipal and national politics was common. The epidemic of new building which would open up the north-east quarters of the city to the spacious malls and squares of the affluent was just starting. In 1763, however, Dublin was still a crowded and tightly knit city, radiating out from the bustling river quays, with some 130,000–150,000 people packed into an area two and a half by two and a quarter miles across.[2]

The Tones soon moved to 44 Stafford Street, a better address north of the river, and a stone's throw from the newly developed and fashionable Sackville Mall. Here Tone was to spend his life until his mid-teens. Peter Tone, son of Jane Kinney and William Tone,[3] was a coachmaker by trade, as were his younger brothers, Thomas and Matthew. But there is no truth whatsoever in the nineteenth-century sneer that Tone's political development rested on 'the naked meanness of plebeian ambition.'[4] Although Peter Tone later fell on hard times, Tone was brought up in a family accustomed to such middle-class comforts as servants. The property in Stafford Street was substantial, comprising a newly built house, a coach-house, stable and other outbuildings. Peter Tone also had property interests on the outskirts of the city in Summer Hill and Drumcondra, and on the death of his father in 1766 he acquired the family's freehold property in Kildare.[5] Trade was not a social stigma and those engaged in it could and did rise to leading positions in the country's social and political life.[6]

Coachmaking was a prosperous and respectable line of business, involving some forty practitioners in Dublin by the end of the century. In these, the boom years of the Anglo-Irish Ascendancy, coaches were much in demand. Peter Tone was a member of the guild of saddlers, upholsterers, coach and coach-harness makers, one of the 25 Dublin guilds which dominated municipal government and had considerable political influence. The guilds were largely employers' associations and bastions of Protestantism against the rising Catholic middle classes.[7] Although Tone would later be in open conflict with the sectarianism of their representatives on the Dublin Corporation, he never showed any sympathy for the workers' combinations against which his father's guild fought for much of the century.

Tone's ancestors were Protestants from Gascony in France, the branch from which he was descended having settled in England at the end of the sixteenth century, then moved to Ireland early in the seventeenth century. Peter Tone was the second son in a family of eight. Why he should have acquired the family land, rather than his elder brother Jonathan, we do not know. But the litigation involved would later ruin him financially and severely damage his son's prospects at the outset of his professional career.[8]

Margaret Tone's maiden name was Lamport. Her father and grandfather had been involved in merchant shipping.[9] She was a Catholic, but formally adopted Protestantism in 1771.[10] Although detractors later attributed Tone's promotion of the Catholic cause to his parentage, Catholicism seems to have played no part whatsoever in his upbringing.[11] He was a member of the Established Church. But he was not a member of the so-called Protestant or Anglo-Irish Ascendancy (that narrow social élite which dominated the country's political and professional life). Although Irish Protestants had considerable legal advantages over Catholics and Dissenters, securing a toe-hold on the ladder of success was often as difficult and precarious for a middle-class Protestant in Ireland as it was for the middle classes elsewhere.

Margaret and Peter Tone had sixteen children, only five of whom survived to adulthood, and as Tone was starting his own family in the 1780s, he had an infant brother, Arthur, born 1782, and a sister, Fanny, born c. 1784. Fanny died of tuberculosis in 1792, an illness which plagued generations of Tones.[12] The entire family had a restless streak. William, born 1764, who most resembled Tone in temperament and appearance, ran away to London at the age of sixteen and enlisted under the East India Company. Matthew, born 1771, a quieter, more reflective boy than his older brothers, nevertheless had lived in England, America, the West Indies and latterly France before he reached twenty-five. Arthur, the youngest, was the most wayward of all, and went to sea at twelve. Mary, born sometime before Arthur, seems only to have been restrained by the limitations on her sex. Yet she accompanied her eldest brother to America and spent her own married years in Hamburg, Paris and Santo Domingo.[13] They were a close-knit family and there was genuine friendship among the siblings. Tone, as the eldest, had considerable influence over them and in adulthood assumed responsibility for their welfare when his parents could no longer afford to do so.

Although Tone's wife looked upon her mother-in-law with affection, Margaret Tone seems to have been a stern women.[14] But Tone came to recognise that she had good reason, and though he was closer to his father, he held him responsible for the family's declining fortunes. 'About this time [1776–7]...my father, who for some years had entirely neglected his business and led a very dissipated and irregular life, meeting with an accident of a fall downstairs, by which he was dreadfully wounded in the head, so that he narrowly escaped with life, found, on his recovery, his affairs so deranged in all respects, that he determined on quitting business and retiring to the country.'[15]

The lands in Kildare, which were held on freehold leases and said to have been worth about £300 per annum, were situated on the estate of Theobald Wolfe, a distinguished barrister and politician, Tone's godfather and name-sake.[16] The Kildare property consisted of over 200 acres at Cassumsize, Sallins, Whitechurch and Bodenstown. On leaving Dublin, the Tones took up residence in the family farmhouse just opposite Bodenstown churchyard. The old church, still such a feature today, was already a ruin in the 1770s and the Tone family rented the neighbouring glebe field. The lands at Cassumsize and part of those at Sallins were sublet and became very valuable when the Grand Canal was cut through them.[17]

I

Tone was a great favourite with his father, and when he showed early signs of ability, Peter Tone spared nothing on his education. The Tone children appear to have received their initial schooling at home, and since all (except Arthur) were highly literate, passable musicians and poets and steeped in current literature and drama, their parents had done well by them. At the age of eight or nine Tone was sent to the much-acclaimed school of Sisson Darling, a man of liberal views, whom Tone came to regard with affection and respect.

Studious application was not in Tone's nature. But even in adulthood failure before his friends was unimaginable, and the quarterly oral examinations in front of friends and family induced sufficient application for him to pass with credit. Indeed he was remembered as having 'pursued his classical studies with uncommon success' at school and 'evinced a degree of intelligence far above his years'.[18] Darling was sufficiently impressed to recommend a transfer to one of the city's classical schools which prepared pupils for entrance to Dublin University (Trinity College). He declared Tone 'a fine boy, of uncommon talents', and told his father 'that it was a thousand pities to throw me away on business', when he might aspire to a college fellowship. Darling was supported by the minister of their parish, Dr Jameson, who had been taking a keen interest in the boy's education.[19]

Tone was accordingly transferred to the more rigorous discipline of the Revd William Craig. Craig's school was in Henry Street, adjacent to Stafford Street, and with the knowledge of parental scrutiny, and a genuine liking for Greek and Latin, Tone progressed well. The 'drudgery' and 'disagreeable labour' of the classical schools was much criticised at the time, and Craig was described as 'a dull, plodding fellow' who gave his pupils the 'drilling' they required.[20] Despite the high standard of scholarship at such schools, the

curriculum was rigidly dictated by University entrance requirements. It included long lists of Greek and Latin texts, Latin translation, basic groundings in Greek and Roman history, English
composition and arithmetic.[21] Tone, however, was never one to
tolerate senseless drudgery. He liked the course, and retained a
facility in Latin and Greek for the rest of his life, a retentiveness not
usually associated with mere cramming. Tone's criticisms of Craig's
school were of a different order: low expectations on the part of
teachers and insufficient challenges for the better student. As at
Dublin University itself, teaching seems to have been aimed at the
average to below-average student.

The outcome of the family move to Kildare was that Tone was left
in lodgings to finish his schooling in Dublin, a freedom from
parental control which he admits did him no good whatsoever. With
his father's superintendence removed, and finding himself a free
agent in Dublin before he had reached the age of sixteen, Tone
calculated that he could use his time rather better; 'and as, at this
time,' he wrote in 1796, 'I am not remarkable for my discretion, it
may well be judged I was less so then.' He reckoned that Craig's low
expectations could be satisfied in two instead of five days. He
persuaded half a dozen of the brightest boys that they too could
easily pass the other three days in amusement, taking long walks into
the country or to the seaside, attending all the parades, field days,
and reviews of the garrison in the Phoenix Park.

Tone's passion for political societies and clubs emerged even this
early as he formed his friends into a debating society.[22] He was
popular among his schoolfellows and considered remarkably bright.
They remembered his irrepressible gaiety, his optimism and per-
suasiveness. There can be no doubt that he was the ringleader in the
'mitching' episodes. The future College Fellow, George Miller,
recalled that 'even in his schoolboy days he evinced the vivacity of a
Frenchman, with great acuteness'. He was never one to despair or be
discouraged 'for he was always ready for anything; having had a
great facility in quoting Shakespeare, and raising a laugh by a pun'.
But Miller remembered also 'a levity of character which disqualified
him for any continuous effort of attention'. It was a fact which Tone
admitted readily in his thirties and he regretted the time he had idled
at school and college.[23]

It was through these sorties that he first became enamoured of
military life. 'Being at this time, approaching to seventeen years of
age, it will not be thought incredible that *woman* began to appear
lovely in my eyes, and I very wisely thought that a red coat and
cockade, with a pair of gold epaulets, would aid me considerably in
my approaches to the objects of my adoration. . . . I began to look on

classical learning as nonsense; on a fellowship in Dublin college as a pitiful establishment'.[24] He formed his school friends into a military corps, and absented himself more and more from class to watch the recruits drill at Dublin Barracks.

At length Craig did what Tone claims he should have done long before and wrote to his father. A 'violent dispute' ensued, at which Tone declared his wish to enter the army. But his father won the battle of wills, for he would give him no assistance to carry through his ambition and Tone was too proud to follow William into the service of the East India Company. 'In consequence, I sat down again, with a very bad grace, to pull up my lost time', and succeeded in entering Trinity College in February 1781.

II

As a 'pensioner', paying annual fees of £15, Tone fell into the category of 'persons of moderate incomes'—the largest among the student body. Trinity College was a predominantly middle-class institution, with less than 10 per cent of the students entered as 'fellow commoners' or 'noblemen'. Both groups paid higher fees, £30 and £60 respectively. But they also had certain privileges, including the right to graduate in three rather than the normal four years, to dine at the Fellows' table and to wear a gown which in splendour outclassed even that of the Fellows—'as full of tassels as a livery servant's'. The type of gown worn was an indicator of one's social standing in and out of college.[25]

The lowliest student category was the 'sizars', the smallest grouping in college. These were bursary students, wearing gowns 'as plain as a parish sexton's, paying no fees, but, like the servitors in Oxford, having to perform certain menial duties such as serving at the Fellows' table. The experience left a bitter taste with some.[26] Many sizars were from clerical families and were no less middle class than the bulk of the student body. But privilege and status was inbuilt in the system, and if some sizars or pensioners benefited from the lavish spending and partying of a fellow commoner like Thomas Gould—one of Tone's friends and future Master in Chancery, said to have squandered some £10,000 'in rioting and entertainments' during his student days (1781–6)—the social distinctions accepted in youth would come to rankle in later years. Tone undoubtedly did exchange his much sought-after wit and sociability for favours in kind while a student. But it is no accident that Gould was to figure as the savage caricature of foppish wealth in Tone's first literary production: the *roman à clef*, *Belmont Castle*, written in 1788 with several student friends.

As a freshman in 1781, however, Tone was entering one of

Ireland's élite institutions. The gown itself was a status symbol, giving the wearer special privileges of entry into the gallery of the Irish House of Commons and recognised by the Dublin populace as conferring a certain social status. The very buildings of the college spoke privilege. The building craze which transformed eighteenth-century Dublin, first into a splendid Palladian city, then into one of the best examples of contemporary British neo-classicism, did not bypass Trinity. Almost all the buildings of the present college would have been new in Tone's day. In 1732 a magnificent library had been built and a library square laid out as the college's central feature. The library stock—estimated at some 146,000 volumes by Tone's day—had built upon Archbishop Ussher's outstanding seventeenth-century collection (the Book of Kells included), which Mazarin had tried to acquire for Louis XIV. An anatomical theatre, a laboratory and a printing house followed.

It was in the 1750s, however, that the Trinity which figures so prominently in Malton's celebrated views of Dublin was created. A great new façade, some 300 feet in length and 65 feet high, was planned by William Chambers. With its rigid classical proportions in the Corinthian order, it came straight out of *Vitruvius Britannicus*. A new quadrangle, laid out behind the façade, was named Parliament Square, in recognition of the source of funding which had enabled Trinity within a matter of years to alter its external appearance to suit its intellectual ethos of confident, optimistic enlightenment. A new dining hall, to encourage more students to attend commons, a new common room, which became the meeting place of the College Historical Society, and a new Provost's house (modelled on Burlington's designs for London's Piccadilly) completed the overall classical balance.

But building continued throughout the 1770s and 1780s, and the noise, mess and disruption which attends building projects was a feature of Trinity and Dublin generally in Tone's student years. A short walk from the college gates and the student would encounter buildings being pulled down on the instructions of the Wide Streets Commissioners, or to clear ground for the construction of the new frontage of the House of Lords. A jaundiced view of the internal appearance of the college behind its grandiose façade appeared in *Walker's Hibernian Magazine* for December 1793. Yet the description of the half-finished buildings and the mud and squelch under foot during autumn and winter was an accurate enough portrayal of a city which was trying to be grand, but whose selective splendour disguised considerable poverty, decay, dirt and inadequate paving and drainage.[27]

Trinity functioned as an élite finishing school for those who were

already part of Ireland's fashionable society—or those seeking entry
to it. In *Belmont Castle* the foppish finery of the young bucks—the
hero Belleville preening himself in his 'orange coat, with a blue cape
and mother of pearl buttons—a waistcoat of pea-green sattin—and
breeches of purple velvet'—is lampooned by the more mature
Tone.[28] But although time sorted out those with privileged
connections from those without, Tone remained part of that tiny
élite of university men to the end.

Tone's student days coincided with the splendours of the Rutland
viceroyalty in Ireland. Young and elegant, Charles Manners, 4th
Duke of Rutland (Lord Lieutenant from 1784 till his untimely death
in 1787), and his beautiful wife hosted dinners, balls and levees so
lavish 'that it was commonly remarked they might well have been
sovereigns of a rich and independent kingdom'. The popularity of
masked balls gave rise to a new industry in fantastic costumes and to
a new popular pastime as crowds milled about the carriages and tried
to guess the identity of their occupants. Hospitality was on a grand
scale and with upwards of 1,200 guests heading for masked balls
lasting till morning, pre-Union Dublin had such an air of unreal
gaiety that accounts thereafter breathe a sense of lost splendour.[29]
Tone was intimately acquainted with this world, and *Belmont Castle,*
with its savage satire of society frivolity, contains much autobiographical material and self-mockery.

College social life also reflected the rowdy, often irresponsible
pastimes of privileged Ireland in the late eighteenth century. The
college boys were notorious for their riotous behaviour. Jonah
Barrington—a student in the mid-'70s—tells of nightly rampages, as
students dashed along the streets in coaches, smashing windows,
throwing firecrackers into glass and porcelain shops, raiding
gambling dens and thrashing 'macaronis', the effete young men of
the day. Tone's friend, William Magee, was to find himself poacher
turned gamekeeper in the late 1780s, when, as lately elected Fellow
and junior Dean, he had to cope with the problem at first hand. 'I
was not two days in office,' he wrote, 'when I was obliged to sally
out at eleven at night, from a warm room, and under a heavy cold, to
put a stop to a battle between a body of our sanctified youths and a
body of the police. After plunging through the dirty streets on a very
wet night for more than an hour, I raked them all into the College;
some out of the watch-house, and some out of the kennel.'[30]

Nor did the students need to leave the precincts of the college for
such boisterous entertainment. There was something of a barrack-
room atmosphere within its walls, a noisy male companionship for
which Tone never lost his taste. The evening meal, or commons,
after which Tone was to court his future wife, was representative of

this. It was served in a cold, drafty, barn-like dining hall, where the older students paraded their worldly knowledge and wit. They would then descend to the beer cellar below, 'a damp wretched underground vault' where youths were to be found 'who in any other period of their lives would be the highest ornaments of the court or drawing room'. Heavy drinking was a characteristic of upper-class Irish society, though it was in decline in the closing decades of the century.[31]

The enticement of the pleasures of Dublin—already such an attraction to the adolescent Tone at Craig's crammer—increased dramatically during his college days. His freshman years coincided with the pinnacle of Volunteering and the campaign for legislative independence. The Volunteers were citizens' militia which had sprung to life in Ulster in 1778 to defend Ireland during the American war. But they quickly became a powerful element in the parliamentary Patriots' campaign to win greater political and economic independence from England. Largely middle-class in composition, though often gentry-led, the Volunteers evinced considerable civic and national spirit, and although they remained outside government control, many leading politicians were involved and in time they became one of the country's most applauded institutions.

During Tone's college days in Dublin, scarcely a week passed without a review of the Volunteers in St. Stephen's Green and College Green, or of the troops in the Phoenix Park. The sound of artillery or musket salutes added to the general hubbub of building, the chorus from the innumerable meat, poultry, fish and grain markets, and the shouting and horn-blowing as coaches left the hotels and post office for the provinces. The highlight of the Volunteer year was the celebration of William of Orange's birthday on 5 November. Not until the 1790s did the occasion become a symbol of sectarianism.[32] It was the kind of military display which Tone would not have missed. Dublin society would turn out in all its finery for Volunteer parades, and the Volunteering mania of these months—the splendid uniforms and raiment, and not least the admiration of the ladies—must surely have reacted upon Tone's dream of a military career at a time when he was becoming alienated from the torpor of Trinity's curriculum.[33]

It is of course too easy to be misled by views of Gandon's Dublin into thinking that the whole city presented the same vision of airy elegance which obtained in the centre and east of the city.[34] West and south-west of Trinity and the Irish Parliament lay the Liberties, so called because independent of the Lord Mayor's jurisdiction. Here lived a population of weavers, petty shopkeepers, labouring poor and beggars, densely packed into narrow streets and overcrowded buildings. The filth and stench of the area was legendary: 'the slaughter-houses, carrion houses, distilleries, glass houses, and lime kilns, with which this part of Dublin abounds', noted one near-contemporary, 'contribute not a little to render the air truly deleterious to its wretched inhabitants'. The streets were ill lit, ill drained and ill policed. They swarmed with beggars, prostitutes and footpads. Serious riots were sparked off in 1783 by a government scheme to set up working villages elsewhere in the country, with the object of dispersing the turbulent manufacturers from the Liberties, 'that hive of drunkenness, combinations, idleness and mobs'. Here too could be found the city's lustier entertainments: bull-baiting, cock-fighting and an astonishing array of taverns, gaming houses and brothels. It was on the fringes of this world that the many lodgings of the mature Tone were to be situated. He was no stranger to Dublin's less splendid sector. Indeed the college boys frequently participated in its brawls, including the pitched battles which raged for days between the weavers of the Coombe, in the Liberties, and the butchers of Ormond Quay, on the north side of the river Liffey, where Tone almost certainly resided during his first year at college.[35]

But Tone's development was not that of most youths in his position—youthful rebelliousness developing into later respectability. Quite the reverse. The young Tone was a social climber, possessing the social graces, confidence and wit, if not the fortune, to give him entry to a social world not normally open to the son of a businessman down on his fortune. Tone was considered and considered himself a gentleman, and the college gown would have marked him out as such in society. But although he would have mixed equally with those of higher social status, his particular friends at Trinity came from social backgrounds similar to his own, and were invariably among the college intellectuals. George Miller, son of a Dublin merchant and a companion of Tone at Craig's, became a College Fellow in 1789 and quickly won acclaim for his lectures on the philosophy of history.[36] William Conyngham Plunket, like Miller ahead of Tone at Trinity, though younger, was the son of a Presbyterian minister from Fermanagh, who had transferred to Strand Street meeting house in Dublin. The Plunket house in Jervis Street was a popular resort of the parliamentary Patriots, and remained so with Tone and his friends long after they had left Trinity. Plunket went on to a distinguished legal career, becoming Ireland's Solicitor-General, Attorney-General, and in due course Lord Chancellor. They were estranged as Tone's politics became more and more radical, but a *rapprochement* in 1795 reveals the depth of their friendship in former times.[37]

William Magee was another northerner and childhood friend of
Plunket in Fermanagh. But as the son of a Glasgow-educated
Dissenter, Plunket had been raised in the advanced liberal tradition
prevalent in the Scottish universities and throughout his life he
remained a staunch campaigner for Catholic emancipation. Not so
the Protestant Magee, who had been brought up 'with the hot no-
Popery blood of the Inniskilling Dragoons in his veins'. He entered
and graduated from Trinity at the same time as Tone, became a
Fellow in 1788, successively professor of mathematics and Greek,
and died as Archbishop of Dublin. Magee later renounced his
friendship with Tone because of political differences. But Tone's
friend through school and college, Charles Kendal Bushe (future
Solicitor-General and Chief Justice of the King's Bench) courageous-
ly defended him in Parliament after his exile as a suspected traitor.[38]

III

Despite Tone's reservations about his schooling, the tutor Craig had
chosen for him was the most popular and talented teacher among
Trinity's Junior Fellows. This was the Revd Matthew Young, then a
mathematician of some repute, future professor of physics (1786) and
Bishop of Clonfert (1798). In the 1780s almost the entire undergraduate teaching programme fell on the younger Fellows, and
Young's reputation brought him an unprecedented number of
pupils. He was a gifted scholar, with catholic tastes, and under such a
polymath Tone's education would have been wider than suggested
by the narrowness of the syllabus and examination system. As for
the formal syllabus, attendance at early-morning Greek and science
lectures and at weekly religious instruction was theoretically
compulsory. But the thin attendance registers at 'those comfortless
Greek lectures which are held at so early an hour as six o'clock', tell
their own story. They were not lectures in the normal sense. Rather
the prescribed text was circulated and each student required to
'scramble through' a portion of translation. Not surprisingly there
was little enticement to attend, particularly for students living
outside college—of whom Tone was one—and the bulk of the
teaching was conducted rather by one's tutor after chapel at 4 p.m.
The flexibility which this system permitted students and tutors alike
was considerable, as witnessed by the successful opposition mounted
in 1786 to the Provost's attempt to enforce attendance at evening
classes.[39]

That was just one in a long line of battles between the college and
its provost, the politician John Hely-Hutchinson. Though an able and
enlightened man, he was a notorious pluralist, with an insatiable
appetite for office. His appointment to the Provostship in 1774 had

been a political bribe to persuade him to step down from the Prime Sergeantship, and conflicted with college tradition and regulations in that he was neither a cleric nor celibate. It would have been one of Tone's earliest experiences of that central issue of eighteenth-century republican and reforming campaigns generally: the use of places and pensions to increase executive power. The celibacy requirement for Fellows was frequently contravened. But it was still on the statute books. It could be and was invoked against offenders, creating a furtiveness about wives living in college and a fund of student ribaldry.[40]

In Tone's day Hutchinson's influence on the college would have been most immediately evident in the dancing, fencing, riding and language classes which he had introduced to prepare the students for outside life. The innovations were scathingly dismissed by his enemies as tending to promote certain evils among the students, notably the fashion for duelling. Since most of Tone's particular friends were at odds with Hely-Hutchinson, we can assume that the shared the general dislike of the controversial Provost. But Hely-Hutchinson differed from other government men in his commitment to Catholic emancipation, and as in so many other instances, Tone's recognition of the Hutchinson family's liberalism marked his progressive estrangement from his former life and friends in the early 1790s.

Despite the Provost's efforts to broaden the Trinity syllabus, it remained dominated by the classics. Classes were conducted in Latin on a question-and-answer pattern. But Tone found the solid core of classics, mathematics, natural philosophy, logic and ethics very much to his liking. The syllabus had been modernised to bring it into tune with the spirit of the age and the general ethos of the college, which until the 1790s was one of liberal Whiggery. The influence of Newton, Locke and Cicero—together the dominant inspiration of the Enlightenment—was greatly expanded. Locke's *Two Treatises of Government* and *Essay on Human Understanding* were such student favourites that in the rebellion year of 1798 one of the Junior Fellows felt impelled to bring out a new edition of the latter, explaining how Locke differed from Paine, and warning against confusing the ideas of the two on who constituted 'the people'.[41]

Notable too was the prominence given to Demosthenes. The new editions of his *Orations* (1754) and *Life of Philip of Macedon* (1758) by Thomas Leland—Fellow of Trinity until 1781—became the staple diet for a host of future Irish orators. Such works emphasised the concepts of civic liberty and public virtue which suffused the Enlightenment and the Irish Patriot movement of the 1770s and 1780s. This admiration for the great advocate of Athenian freedom

was particularly attuned to the times in Ireland. Frustrated at the
increasing stranglehold of the English Parliament over Irish affairs
after the Glorious Revolution, polemicists like Swift had identified
with republican figures from the classics, and, like Leland, come
close to justifying regicide when liberty was threatened. Far from
being the dry dust of ancient history, the classical tradition in
eighteenth-century Ireland was a potentially revolutionary force,
which would take off in the 1780s with the heady oratory of the
Patriot politicians and that embodiment of active virtue, the
Volunteers.

Through his education at Trinity, Tone had entered the 'republic
of letters' in which Enlightenment thinking transcended national
boundaries. He spoke the same language as those Patriot and
Volunteer leaders who were pursuing the campaign for Irish legislative independence and parliamentary reform in the 1780s, the same as
the politicians of the newly independent American states, the same as
the future leaders of the French Revolution. It was a language
reflecting the same classical writers, the same Enlightenment values,
and it spoke of public virtue, military vigour, a fellow-feeling with
other men, a love of liberty and opposition to tyranny in every form,
a sense of political purity, practicality, and above all a secularism and
tolerance which, for a while, made educated men flinch at the blatant
intolerance of Irish society. Enlightenment optimism in man's ability
to change things for the better had already exhausted itself in many
other countries. But it was long in coming to Ireland and was at its
height when Tone arrived at Trinity. The Enlightenment was contemptuous of mere erudition. Its dominant value was active virtue,
taken from its favourite classical scholar, Cicero, and enshrined in his
De Officiis, 1.6, one of the prescibed texts for Trinity students in
Tone's day. Tone was part of an intellectual élite. It was this élitism
of the cultured man which was to make him intolerant of stupidity
and vulgarity in others, especially those with pretensions to power.

Tone entered on his academic career diligently enough, scoring
top grades in his first quarterly exams of 1781. But a middling grade
in logic—a subject which by his own admission he found a
struggle—lost him the premium to another student, Benjamin
Phipps, a fellow commoner from Cork, soon to become one of his
most intimate friends. Tone clearly felt some injustice had been
done, and injustices he remembered with a fervour. Writing fifteen
years later, he was still smarting from it. Edward Ledwich—author
of Antiquities of Ireland and founder member of the Royal Irish
Academy—who had been the examiner on this occasion, he
described as 'an egregious dunce...who instead of giving me the
Premium, which as best answerer I undoubtedly merited, awarded it

to another, and to me very indifferent judgements. I did not stand in need of this piece of injustice to alienate me once more from my studies.'[42] The competitive spirit which Trinity promoted in its students and the public nature of the examinations explains the intensity of disappointment felt by others besides Tone at failing to win a premium in the quarterly exams.

Such an exam-based syllabus is prey to exploitation by the able student, and Tone was nothing if not that. He took full advantage of the flexibility offered and (as with Craig) seems to have been fortunate in a tutor who recognised his abilities and allowed him free rein. His attendance record at lectures speaks for itself. His name appears on attendance lists for the early-morning Greek lectures in the Michaelmas and Hilary terms in 1781. But he was among those cautioned for lack of diligence, and he was in good company, sharing the censure with others later to hold high political or legal office.[43] The bright student would have found little stimulation in such an arid system of questions and answers, and it was dullness as much as injustice which alienated Tone from his studies.

Trinity examinations were 'strenuous viva voce affairs lasting for eight days', conducted in Latin before the entire college body, events of sheer endurance for fellows and students alike.[44] Even more strenuous were the Whitsuntide competitions for the few fellowships available, which had the reputation of being 'the most gruelling public examination in the world'. Little wonder that Tone soon abandoned his early ambitions for academic preferment. Leading public figures attended on such occasions, and students placed bets on front-runners. The examination hall would be packed with students, each examinee thereby exposed likewise to the verdict of his peers. Some of the best minds to emerge from Trinity had come up with Tone from Craig's school and his circle of talented acquaintances was growing. To crave the admiration and respect of one's peers is not unusual, but in Tone the craving was pronounced to a degree.

At the next quarterly examinations, Whitsuntide 1781, he was again pipped for a premium, this time by a student scoring the same grades. Tone never quite appreciated that the college authorities were looking for signs of diligence as much as brilliance. He was always one of the high flyers at exams, but the grades he scored were secured through short bursts of intensive study rather than consistent effort. 'I continued my studies at college, as I had done at school; that is I idled, until the last moment of delay; I then laboured hard for about a fortnight before the public examinations, and I always secured good judgements'. But although he completed his senior freshman year (1781–2), securing the coveted premium in the Hilary examination, and was one of the two highest scorers in his section in the Whitsuntide exams at the end of the academic year, he never returned to lectures after his second caution in Hilary term 1782, and does appear to have withdrawn entirely from college for the 1782–3 session.[45]

There was another reason for Tone's withdrawal. He was involved in a fatal duel. Duels were the very stuff of fashionable Irish society and the papers of the day are full of accounts of young fellows confronting each other through early morning mists on Donnybrook Fair Green, to the south of the city—a favourite duelling spot. 'A duel was indeed considered a necessary piece of a young man's education', according to Barrington, and Trinity students imitated their social elders in the 'duelmania' of the period, as they did in everything else. That Tone was not involved in more duels—indeed he became one of the sternest critics of the practice—may be attributed to the unfortunate circumstances of his initiation. Late in 1782 he went out as second to a young acquaintance named Foster in a duel with another lad named Anderson. They were close acquaintances—Anderson's second, William Armstrong, being Tone's 'most particular friend' since their school-days together at Craig's— and the reason for the encounter appears to have been sufficiently trivial to have been settled by a simple satisfaction of honour. But Foster shot Anderson through the head, and at a time when the College Fellows were up in arms at the invidious influence of Hely-Hutchinson's fencing classes, it was predictable that Tone, though not publicly prosecuted as Foster was, should have been temporarily barred from college.

Tone does not linger on the incident in his autobiography. He had grown up by 1796, when he wrote it, and lamented as a folly of his youth 'this unfortunate business' in which 'the eldest of us was not more than twenty years of age'. But it clearly had more important repercussions than his one-paragraph description suggests. A garbled account in the *Freeman's Journal* of November 1798 conveys some idea of the serious disciplinary repercussions and the importance to Tone of the Wolfe family, whose intervention secured his eventual return to college.[46] He returned in Michaelmas term 1783, considerably chastened, and his reputation as one of the college's outstanding products dates from then.

2
Sentimental Schooling

Tone's exile was spent acquiring a rather different education in the glittering society of Richard Martin (Patriot MP for Jamestown, County Leitrim) and his beautiful and well-connected wife, Elizabeth Vesey of Lucan, County Dublin. Her father's home was the first of the great mansions on the road west from Dublin to Kildare. With the return of Peter Tone to the family home in Kildare, Tone would have spent much of his student days in this, the prime area for country seats and aristocratic mansions.[1]

In Kildare the Tones' neighbour, the wealthy and public-spirited MP Richard Griffith of Millicent, was much impressed with young Tone's gifts and provided his entrée to Dublin society.[2] He was introduced to the Martins' social circle in fashionable Kildare Street and at their country seat of Dangan, on the shores of Lough Corrib, three miles from Galway town. Here Tone made three long visits during the years 1783–5. He shared the Martins' passion for amateur dramatics. Martin was also a celebrated duellist and must have sympathised with the young man's plight. Tone was invited to accompany them to Dangan as tutor to Martin's younger half-brothers.

There a new social world was opened to him. The Martins were well connected with the country's leading political families, on both 'government' and 'opposition' sides. But Richard Martin was genuinely reformist and many of the ideas which were to dominate Tone's political thinking would have been encountered first in Martins' company. Martin was a colonel of the Galway Volunteers, a believer in Catholic emancipation and an indomitable critic of corruption in politics. He had been supporter of Henry Grattan, the talented leader of the Patriot opposition in Parliament, but at the time of Tone's residence with the family he was undergoing an agonising conversion to the side of Henry Flood, Grattan's predecessor and rival.[3]

It is, however, as the cuckold that we encounter Martin in Tone's journal. The manuscript journal, that is, for in the published version all references to Tone's amorous adventures have been removed by his widow and son. Tone fell passionately in love with Eliza Martin, and was left a clear field during the long absences of her husband. He

accused Richard Martin of neglecting his wife, which was true. But
this was not unusual for eighteenth-century men, Tone included, and
judging from Eliza's later elopement with the English merchant, John
Petrie, Tone was blinded by his own passion into placing the wrong
entirely on the husband's side. It was a kind of self-justifying trip-
switch which would come into play again some years later to explain
away his liaisons in London. Eliza was a coquette, and the account of
her affair and elopement with Petrie in 1790 would grace the pages
of a novel by Fielding or Defoe. Yet Tone deluded himself into
thinking that it was he—his passion aroused by mock-amorous
encounters with Eliza in the Martins' theatrical productions—who
made all the initial running. It was perhaps as well for his self-esteem
that he retained his delusions; in reading the very extensive and
salacious press reports of the criminal conversation case brought by
Martin against Petrie in 1791, Tone still attributed Eliza's action
entirely to Martin's neglect.[4]

I

The two-year affair with Eliza Martin was an extension of the unreal
world of the theatre in which it had first developed. The Irish passion
for the theatre was then at its height. The day when the theatrical,
with the political, world was to decline into provincialism, and the
best actors and actresses be drawn ineluctably to London, was not far
off. But in the 1780s the Irish theatres still attracted the leading
names. Dublin was the first stop for London productions before they
went to Bath or Edinburgh. In 1783 the splendidly refurbished Crow
Street theatre, vying with its main rival in Smock Alley and the
recently opened Capel Street theatre, was attracting some of the
most famous actors and actresses of the day. Tone himself was
captivated by the beautiful and much-acclaimed young actress
Elizabeth Farren, in Dublin from Drury Lane for the 1784 season.
Kemble and Mrs Siddons played to packed houses, and the careers of
future legendary performers like Mrs Jordan were launched in the
Dublin theatre.[5]

However, the emotionalism of the Dublin audiences could with
equal passion be turned the other way, and an unpopular or weak
performer might be ordered by a howling gallery to 'die at once' in
the lingering death scenes which were a feature of the time. Riots,
frequently initiated by the young bucks of the city, were common,
and the Trinity students continued to be among the rowdiest of
theatre-goers. But Mrs Siddons was such a favourite with the
students that in June 1784 their élite debating society (with Tone
prominent among its members) voted a medal struck in her honour.[6]

Tone's lifelong passion for the theatre is a recurrent feature of his

writings, and it was probably in her role as Calista in Nicholas Rowe's
The Fair Penitent—one of the most frequently performed of all plays
in eighteenth-century Ireland—that Tone first came to appreciate the
acting abilities of Eliza Martin. In 1786 her performance in the role
caused the *Freeman's Journal* critic to pay her the giddy compliment
that 'she excelled Mrs Siddons, and every other woman in the world'.
Little wonder that the impressionable undergraduate was equally
captivated three years earlier. Calista, Rowe's heroine, has been
promised against her will to the dull but virtuous Altamont. But her
virtue and heart have been stolen by the villain, Lothario, who
abuses both, and she commits suicide to save the family honour. The
moral of the story is the traditional eighteenth-century one of the
nobility of true love. But a subsidiary theme complains of the inequality of the sexes and attacks the husband who neglects his wife,
thereby preparing his own fate as cuckold.[7] Tone was to become a
much sterner critic in later years of the kind of emotional melodrama
served up to the reading and theatre-going public of the day. But
even in Paris in 1796 he could still be captivated by a beautiful and
vivacious actress, and as a twenty-year-old student, possessed of
'an imagination easily warmed, without one grain of discretion to
regulate it', it was Eliza Martin as actress with whom he became
infatuated, and the Martins' passion for amateur dramatics which
brought them together.

In the atumn of 1782 the talented Irish actor, Robert Owenson,
arrived in Galway with his travelling troupe. He quickly secured
financial support from Martin to build a theatre in Kirwan's Lane in
Galway town. It opened on the evening of Friday, 8 August 1783,
with a double bill of John Home's popular historical tragedy, *Douglas*
and Isaac Jackman's farce, *All the World's a Stage*. The new theatre
was too small to accommodate a gallery, but a cleverly designed
sloping pit could seat a hundred people, and in expectation of a
packed first house, ladies were requested not to wear hoops. It was a
select audience, prices of 4s. 4d. for the pit and an exorbitant
£1. 2s. 9d. for a seat on stage being far in excess of charges for the
Dublin theatres. Rehearsals took place that summer, with at least one
private performance recorded at Lord Altamont's classical mansion,
Westport House. Playbills were printed by The Volunteer press,
Volunteer officers took most of the parts, and in Jackman's farce
Tone played the comic role of the dumb but melodramatic butler,
Diggery, clumsily failing in everything, even his own suicide.[8]

In contrast he took the male lead in *Douglas*, playing Lord
Randolph opposite Mrs Martin's Lady Randolph. Martin played the
murderous villain, whose advances are repulsed by the heroine. Set
in Scotland at the time of the Viking invasions, *Douglas* is a tale of

martial valour, nobility of spirit, virtue, true love and tragic death. Lord Randolph has married the beautiful and virtuous widow of the slaughtered Douglas, knowing that all he can expect is her respect, because of her love for her dead husband. Her son by that first marriage turns up, and the noble, but impressionable Randolph allows himself to be persuaded by the villain, Glenalvon, that the youth is his wife's lover. A challenge leads to the lingering and melo-dramatic death of young Douglas, the suicide of the heroine, and the doomed departure of Randolph to war in search of a similar fate.[9]

Lady Randolph is the exaggerated personification of the eigh-teenth-century ideals of virtue, sentiment, beauty and love. But Tone seems not to have made the distinction between the fictional character and the real Eliza, and the two continued in real life to act out the parts of their favourite characters. The 'particular situations' which he was 'daily thrown into with her both in rehearsals and on the stage', as he later described these events, aroused barely controllable passion in the young Tone, and the combined ecstasy and agony of this almost adolescent love affair is still evident in his recollections written over a decade later. 'I very soon became in love to a degree almost inconceivable. I have never met in history, poetry or romance a description that comes near to what I actually suffered on her account'. Certainly the resemblance between the fictional Douglas and Tone's real-life situation must have lent a particular edge to the Galway performances. 'Yet this distinguish'd Dame', runs Randolph's soliloquy on the absence of true love in marriage,

> Invites a youth, the acquaintance of a day
> Along to meet her at the midnight hour
> Her manifest affection for the youth
> Might breed suspicions in a husband's brain.

Tone adored Eliza, and no wonder. Her beauty and acting abilities were acclaimed by all who knew her. He had a low opinion of his own looks and describes himself rather as 'an interesting young man of twenty' at the time of the affair. Certainly the earliest portrait we have of him (painted some eight or nine years after these events) reveals a rather pallid, thin young man of unprepossessing appear-ance. Yet Lady Morgan claimed that females of the day who professed platonism, but sought conquest, 'prefer pale young men with dark eyes to ruddy men with light ones',[10] and women did find Tone attractive. He was five foot eight in height, and his slight frame created the overall impression of smallness. He had brown hair, a small, oval-shaped face, low forehead, deep-set dark eyes, sallow, pock-marked complexion—a common condition in the days before inoculation[11]—a nose rather too large for the small face, high cheekbones, very thin lips and small chin. He was a smart dresser, indeed even admitted an element of foppery. In the two portraits we have of Tone he wears his hair long and tied in a queue. But at some stage in the 1790s he wore it cropped, as was the fashion among French sympathisers, one contemporary remembering his 'forehead very low the hair cut close and growing up from it like the monkeys [sic]'[12]

Yet the still-life portraits give little idea of the fine features, lively eyes, and most of all the animation which male and female acquaintances alike single out in their pen portraits of Tone. Sir Philip Crampton—a student at Trinity in the 1790s—thought Catherine Tone's posthumous portrait an inadequate representation of the man.

> I am perfectly certain that the small grey glancing eye of the .original is not represented by the soft tranquil brown eye of the portrait. . . . According to my recollection of him he was a *very* slender, angular *rapid* moving man, a thin face, sallow and pockmarked, eyes small lively bright. . .laughed and talked fast with enthusiasm about music and other innocent things, so that one could not possibly suspect him of plots and treason—*wise* he could not be but he had not a foolish look—too lively and smart for that.[13]

Eliza Martin in 1783 was young, childless and carefree, and Tone put her on a pedestal. She combined that beauty of mind and body which he sought in the perfect woman and the description of his infatuation with her has an ethereal quality which raises the question of whether she became his mistress. *Belmont Castle* offers little illumination. Scudamore, the fictional embodiment of Tone, pursues his Eliza (Lady Clairville) relentlessly, resorting to his flute and the recitation of popular verses and ditties of the day for consolation, as Tone himself would have done. But the pursuit and eventual assignation are treated with such black humour and a sense of the ridiculous, that they seem more an exercise in mockery than a true reflection of the 'seraphic' nature of his affair with Eliza Martin.

The virtuous love of the hero of the novel, Belleville, is more favourably portrayed, though all the male characters are unstable in some way or another. It was common in eighteenth-century fiction and drama to depict the heroine as a pillar of virtue and steadfastness, and the epilogue of *Belmont Castle* closely resembles Rowe's popular play, *The Fair Penitent*.[14] *Belmont Castle* was a parody of contemporary romantic fiction. But it also contains a wealth of autobiographical detail on this relatively uncharted period of Tone's

life. His own belief in the primacy of virtue and purity in a woman
differed little from the romantic models he professed to ridicule—
which might explain why he was to elope with a sixteen-year-old
innocent beauty on the rebound from his affair with Eliza Martin.
'With regards to the delicacy and purity of women', he later
admitted, 'I entertain notions of perhaps extravagant refinement'.[15]

It is this romantic conservatism in his attitude towards women
which provides the key to Tone's youthful passion for Eliza Martin.
Richard Martin's biographer, Shevawn Lynam, suggests that Martin
suspected Tone to be the father of the Martins' first child, Laetitia,
born in Feburary 1785.[16] Lord Kenyon, pronouncing judgement on
the case brought by Martin against Petrie in 1792, likewise cast doubt
on the legitimacy of the Martin children. The *Freeman's Journal*
carried detailed reports on the case, and Tone was far too intelligent
not to have made the connection, had there been one.[17] His autobiography is so remarkably frank about his amours that, had there
been the remotest possibility of paternity, he would have alluded to
it. It is clearly at the back of his mind in his constant reference to the
virtuous nature of the liaison:

> I was the proudest man alive to have engaged the affections of a
> Woman, whom even now I recognise to have had extraordinary
> merit, and who then appeared in my eyes more divine than
> human. In this intercourse of sentiment, which alternately pained
> and delighted me almost beyond bearing, we continued for about
> two years, . . . without however in a single instance overstepping
> the bounds of virtue, such was the purity of the extravagant
> affection I bore her.

It is a disclaimer which accords entirely with Tone's sexual
romanticism. Yet the salacious details of Eliza's and Petrie's nights
together, given in evidence at the trial, and broadcast to the world in
1791–2, must have deeply wounded Tone. In his account of his
youthful affair (written in 1796) there is a niggling doubt that he too
may have been deceived. Had she simply been playing with his
affections? 'She supposed she might amuse herself innocently in
observing the progress of this terrible passion in the mind of an
interesting young man of twenty; but this is an experiment no
woman ought to make. . .it opened my eyes on many little
circumstances that had passed between her and me, and perhaps (as I
now think) had my passion for her been less pure, it might have been
not less agreeable.' Whatever her action in later years, Tone
persuaded himself of the genuine and virtuous nature of their mutual
affection in 1783–5.

The truth is I loved her with an affection of a seraphic nature; the profound respect I bore her, and my ignorance of the world, prevented my availing myself of opportunities which a man more trained than I was, would not have let slip.... I cannot regret that my inexperience prevented me from wronging a man to whom I was indebted for many civilities [a more mature reflection on the wronged husband than he was capable of a decade earlier], or from profiting, as I might have done, of the affections of a woman, at that time undoubtedly virtuous, whom I adored as a deity, and who, I am sure, returned my affection with an ardour equal to my own.

An incurable romantic with a puritanical attitude towards female virtue, Tone was not an irresponsible lover. He was to become a faithful, if negligent, husband and father, after he had grown out of his somewhat prolonged student flirtatiousness. Paternity is not at issue. The other worldly, 'seraphic' nature of the affair would not have survived the transformation of the 'deity' into a mortal mistress.

Tone's much-used excuse for his own liaisons—husbandly neglect—is a token of how his passion for the theatre interwove fact with fantasy in his own personal affairs. His published journals reflect his early theatrical grounding, with their happy-go-lucky refrains and ditties, picked up from popular musicals. The actor in Tone was instinctive. It explains the ease with which he could cast aside practicalities and assume the role of the romantic hero. His journal mingles serious moral purpose with ironic and frequently flippant humour. It was a characteristic of eighteenth-century writing which was lost on nineteenth-century readers when the journals were published.

Tone's lengthy association with the Martins ended abruptly early in 1785, when he refused to testify about a burglary at Dangan. Tone does not explain his reason for such a refusal. There may have been some element of fear of discovery by Martin, a noted duellist, whose successful encounters and readiness to 'blaze' at the slightest excuse had earned him the nickname 'hair-trigger Dick', and rivalry had bred in Tone a deep dislike for the wronged husband. Whatever his motives, the upshot was the sudden termination of his relationship with Eliza Martin. He never saw her again, but she left a deep and lasting impression, and his widow's suppression of that part of Tone's journal describing his youthful affair, understandable as her action was, did an incalculable disservice to historical understanding of his development. The affair shows him to have been a Rousseauistic romantic, but without Rousseau's anti-feminism. Mrs Martin had set a standard by which every subsequent female of his acquaintance was measured.

His sentimental education already well advanced, the Tone who returned to Trinity at the end of 1783 was a very different, more confident young man that the one who had withdrawn a year earlier, and in retrospect he acknowledged his debt to Eliza Martin. 'But if I suffered, as I did most severely, by this most unfortunate passion, I also reaped some benefit from it; the desire to render myself agreeable to a woman of elegant manners and a mind highly cultivated, induced me to attend to a thousand little things and to endeavour to polish myself in a certain degree, so that after the first transports of rage and grief at her loss had subsided, I considered myself as on the whole considerably improved.'[18]

II

On his return to college in Michaelmas term 1783, Tone had to drop a year, which in retrospect he accepted as entirely justified. But this he quickly made up, winning a second premium at Easter 1784, and a third the following year. That year too he became a scholar. Scholarships were awarded to the best students on the basis of a two-day exam in the classical authors. They carried with them the right to free commons, rent and cellar concessions, and an endowment of £4 per annum.[19]

But it was not through academic attainment that the young men of Trinity prepared their future reputations. Even the bar was not an all-graduate profession, though growing professionalisation would soon make it so. No, in Ireland those reputations, and the friendships and connections to sustain them, were first made in the College Historical Society. It was the first college debating society in the British Isles and was the training ground for almost all the leading political figures in the age of Grattan's Parliament. Founded by Edmund Burke in 1745, it had been re-established on a permanent basis and given rooms in college in 1770. It was not, however, a place for Trinity students simply to display their love of oratory— though certainly in Tone's time it was in danger of becoming such, a fact of which he was duly critical. Rather it was a place in which to learn the 'useful pursuits of oratory, history and composition'. disciplines quite separate from the college syllabus and designed to prepare the Society's members for public life. What was the use of emerging from college 'flushed with collegiate honors', asked the Society chairman in October 1784. Such honours provided 'certain proof of other diligence, but no infallible proof of their understanding'. Only in the College Historical Society would they 'take a rank that would set them high above their fellows, and send them well recommended to any of the learned professions'. Then, pointing to the example of William Pitt (the Society's hero), he spoke for the middling origins of most members and showed how eloquence and ability could raise even men 'born to no patrimony' to such heights.

Proceedings lasted from 6 p.m. to midnight each Wednesday, and members were fined for absence, lateness, failure to vote and non-observance of rules. The College Historical Society took itself very seriously. Sixty pages of history were set for study each week and members were questioned on them at the beginning of each session. Proceedings would then move on to debate a topic chosen two weeks previously by a committee selected each month for that purpose, and periodically members' compositions would be read and adjudged. Medals and merits were awarded in each section, and Tone took away twelve merits and three medals (one for history, two for oratory) during his membership.[20] Membership was open only to those of junior sophister (third year) level or higher; though an exception was made for nobles' sons, who by implication were already part of an élite for which the others were being groomed. Even then, admission was not automatic. New members were balloted for, and many applicants, later to become famous, were rejected.

At the time of Tone's initiation, Wednesday, 3 December 1783, the Society was meeting in the common room above the dining hall. With proper floor matting, green upholstered seats and an ante-room to which members adjourned in mid-evening for coffee, the surroundings were considerably more comfortable than the average undergraduate would have been accustomed to. An elected steward saw to members' material comforts, and the Society employed a porter, whose many duties included the ceremonial burning of members' works which offended the Society's patriotic leanings. It was one of the many ways in which the Society mimicked existing power politics, the parliamentary pretensions of its members being heightened by the attendance of large numbers of the general public, whose presence contributed to the excitement of meetings. The porter during Tone's membership, Samuel Bilson, was killed by a fall from the top of the Society room's stairs. Tone chaired a committee set up to aid Bilson's distressed children; it recommended an annuity of £4 for his daughter and set aside funds to apprentice the son when he reached the age of fourteen.[21]

The Society was a self-governing, self-financing, but elected élite, fully possessed of a sense of its own importance as such. Since membership did not cease at graduation, the attendance of MPs, professional men and college Fellows perpetuated the Society's self-image as a debating forum second only to the Irish Parliament itself.

As such it tended to reflect the prevailing political atmosphere of the day, and topics for debate generally reproduced the preoccupations of the Whig opposition. Thus were the right of 'the People...to send delegates to consider National Grievances, and lay them before Parliament' (19 May 1784) and the cause of America (1 December 1784, 7 December 1785) upheld, an absentee tax (9 June 1784) and the independence of the judiciary (28 January 1784) approved, and a poem deemed offensive to the Volunteers ceremonially burned (25 February 1784). Likewise the Society opposed restraints on the freedom of the press (28 April 1784, 11 January 1786), undue executive influence in Parliament (10 March 1784), a standing army in peacetime (12 May 1784), aristocratic control of government (26 May 1784), corruption in politics (12 March 1785), and the principle of a union with Britain. There was an overwhelming respect for the institution of monarchy and repeated criticism of Charles I's execution, but ambivalence when the rights of the 'people' were pitted against tyranny. Thus were the assassination of Caesar (2 November 1785) and the 'insurrection of the people of Ireland in the year 1641' (5 May 1784, 11 June 1785) excused. But these were distant events. There is a sense that in the 1780s they were living in freer times—with a constitutional monarchy and men of ability in Parliament—and a general Whiggish belief in the 'purity' and freedom enshrined in the 'British constitution'.

It is unlikely therefore that Tone's outlook would have been radicalised by the debates in the Historical Society, and voting patterns became more conservative later in the decade. But he would have received there his earliest grounding in the fundamental political principles of the age. The choice of Hume and Robertson as history texts followed contemporary taste for more disinterested and philosophical histories, and many students would have been introduced to Irish history for the first time. Tone's friend and the future United Irishman, Thomas Addis Emmet, recalled many years later how he first became aware of 'the falsehood of the history of Ireland...by the accident of having to take part in a college discussion on the Irish massacre and rebellion of 1641'. He discovered Curry's *Historical and Critical Review of the Civil Wars of Ireland* (1786), which sought to correct what Curry believed to be historical misrepresentations of the Irish Catholics. 'This made a mark on me', Emmet admitted, 'and much changed my life'.[22] Tone's evident pride in the Society and his scathing criticism of those who spoke without preparation are signs that he would have prepared his own contributions meticulously, particularly during his two periods as chairman in 1785.

His performance in the Society indicates total acceptance of its

almost pompous sense of its own importance. His first year, though
punctuated by absences from March to April, and again from
October to December, when he was undoubtedly at Dangan, and by
a number of small fines for breaches of the regulations, nevertheless
reveals a Tone who was a stickler for correctness. His early inter-
jections were all on procedural matters, when he was to be found
among a vociferous and critical minority which included his friends
Plunket and Magee. In June 1784 he was recommended for one of the
medals in oratory, and by the beginning of 1785 he was proposed for
one after another of the leading positions. In none of his motions or
questions is there any sign of his future radicalism. Rather these
continued to show an attachment to form and regulations and an
impatience with sloppiness and empty disputes. In debate he was
often found on the more conservative side, preferring octennial to
triennial parliaments, disputing a motion that the discovery of
America was of advantage to Europe, and, on 15 April 1789,
proposing an extra silver medal for the author of the 'best poetick
composition on the late happy recovery of his present Majesty'. He
fully shared his fellow members' reverence for monarchy and dislike
of factional politics.

By 1787 Tone had become one of the Society's most respected
members, constantly consulted on procedural matters and showered
with adulation. The Historical Society was above all a sociable club.
One needed wit, conviviality and above all the approval of one's
peers to enter. 'When we came into these walls', their chairman told
them in October 1784, 'we leave all the laborious parts of learning
behind us to converse only with liberal and pleasing objects . . . the
instruction of criticism without the pain of detection; and . . . the
animating applause of a judicious and favourable audience'.[23] By all
accounts Tone measured up well to the requirements. His manner
of speaking, devoid, on his own admission, of 'exalted ability or
splendid eloquence', nevertheless had a liveliness, penetration and a
sound grasp of subject matter. He impressed contemporaries, and
long after he became a rebel to everything Trinity stood for, former
friends and enemies alike paid tribute to the young man whose
friendship at college was so coveted. 'He distinguished himself in the
College Historical Society, whose object was the cultivation of
oratory, history and composition', reported the *Freeman's Journal* in
November 1798;

> in the first, with a weak voice and ungraceful manner, he
> succeeded in a wonderful degree; in the study of history, he found
> ample room for the exercise of a penetrating judgement and
> powerful memory; and some of his composition, both in verse

and prose, stood unrivalled in the collections of that society.... such a man could not remain unnoticed; his company was courted by every student of taste in the university, and so attractive was his conversation, that many young men of the first rank and fortune solicited his acquaintance and in return became his most useful patrons.[24]

III

It was in the Historical Society that Tone first met those friends who remained such an important influence on his life. Notable among them was Thomas Addis Emmet. The Emmet family was highly respected in Dublin circles, with a fine house on St. Stephen's Green and country residence at Casino. The head of the family, Dr Robert Emmet, was an eminent doctor holding the office of State Physician. The eldest son, Temple, who was lionised by the College Historical Society, was already making a name for himself at the Irish bar. The youngest, Robert—at this stage an infant of only three or four—was to become the most famous of all, with his rebellion and famous trial oration in 1803. But it was Thomas whom Tone came to regard as 'the first of my friends'. He was only a year Tone's senior, but like Plunket he had entered Trinity early and graduated in 1783. At the time of Tone's entry into the Historical Society, Thomas Emmet was a medical student at Edinburgh University. But, reeling from the premature death of his son Temple in 1788, Dr Emmet persuaded his second son to abandon a medical career and take up that of his late brother.[25]

Two other particular friends of this period were Whitley Stokes and Peter Burrowes, 'men whose talents I admire, whose virtues I reverence, and whose persons I love', wrote Tone in 1796. Burrowes, 'an honest but eccentric genius', as Plunket's son described him, had been one of the talents of the Historical Society in his student days, and continued to attend after his call to the bar in 1785. He was an early campaigner for Catholic emancipation, publishing a pamphlet on it while still a student at the Middle Temple. He was friendly with many leading parliamentary Patriots and with the Emmets, and was to maintain his friendship with Tone and Emmet long after others came to consider them traitors. It was a friendship which was to expose him to the ill favour of the authorities in the 1790s and considerably hamper his progress in the legal profession.[26]

Whitley Stokes likewise had graduated earlier than Tone, in 1783, though they were the same age. He became a Fellow of the College in 1788, but because of his liberal tendencies and membership in the United Irish Society he was passed over for more senior appoint-

ments, and in 1798 was publicly censured and barred from college
duties for three years. He was by all accounts a man of considerable
ability and eventually, in 1830, became Regius Professor of Physics.
His well-known and inflexible purity of principle landed him on the
wrong side of the authorities during the crisis of the late 1790s. But
that quality could equally well operate in the other direction. He
withdrew from the United Irish Society at an early date because of its
growing revolutionism, and was to publish an attack on Paine's *Age
of Reason* in 1795. For this he was thanked by the same college board
which three years later suspended him. His was an inflexibility
which, though he admired it, Tone came to regret. 'With regard to
Stokes,' he wrote, 'I know he is acting rigidly on principle, for I
know he is incapable of acting otherwise; but I fear very much that
his very metaphysical unbending purity, which can accommodate
itself neither to men, times nor circumstances, will always prevent
his being of any service to his country, which is a thousand pities, for
I know of no man whose virtues and whose talents I more sincerely
reverence.'[27]

Most of Tone's friends were no better off financially than himself.
Magee and Plunket had both sought sizarships, and Bushe spent his
early years at the bar paying off his father's debts. But Tone also
appears to have been friendly with others considerably wealthier
than himself. 'Wild Tom' Gould, the rich and gifted, if giddy, young
man from Cork, may also have been in their circle. Income aside,
however, it was their distinction in the Historical Society which
marked off Tone's circle of friends. They were the bright young men
of the day, much admired for their oratory and wit, and, Magee's
no-popery notwithstanding, they were all political liberals.

Plunket by all accounts was a serious lad, yet even he remembered
with regret the conviviality of those days. All the group were noted
conversationalists, wits and bon viveurs. Magee, even while embarked on the arduous route to a fellowship, was known to break off
his studies late at night for a ball. Burrowes too was said to have
danced all night after a forty-mile walk to Portarlington. Tom Gould
was described as 'the admirable Crichton, flirting for half a day in
Sackville Street with all his heart, and then giving half his heart and
half his head to study'. Bushe was remembered for his love of
'gentlemanly fun' and 'genial laughter' which made him 'the most
fascinating of companions'.

Throughout his short career Tone was to show a tendency for
personal attachment which frequently played a more important role
in dictating his career than did pure principle. To ignore the camaraderie which led men like Tone to found the Society of United
Irishmen is to misunderstand the accident which was Irish republi-

canism. Certainly the *esprit de corps* and camaraderie which Tone found in the College Historical Society kept him within a circle more than willing to promote his good. But it was a charmed circle in which talent rather than birth or fortune was the qualification, and it ill prepared him for the reverse in real life. Tone delighted in that *esprit de corps*. He displayed a passion for rules and regulations in the various offices he held in the society and a liking for barrack-room male company. Might he then have settled to a quite different career had his father allowed him to follow his youthful desire for a military life with the British forces in America? I think not. There was in Tone an impatience with empty bombast and sloppiness, and an intellectual contempt for those who did not measure up to his standards. He was incapable of deferring to those he did not respect—a trait which critics later misread as a desire to run the show himself. Yet he was happy to take a back seat to those he respected. He could make a good military subaltern, given a commander and a cause he believed in, and did so in France under Hoche. But the eighteenth-century British army did not produce generals such as Hoche, and I doubt if Tone would have succeeded any better in a military than a legal career. His republicanism was an accident of character as much as of timing.

IV

In 1785, however, he was an elegant and eloquent twenty-one-year-old, with a new confidence gained from a romantic entanglement which had introduced him into Irish high society. Sallying forth with friends after commons one spring evening, he was struck by the beauty of young Martha Witherington, sitting at a window in no. 68 Grafton Street, and determined to engineer an introduction. This was not difficult, since her elder brother, Edward, was Tone's near-contemporary at Trinity, and though he had graduated the previous year, Witherington would undoubtedly have felt complimented by the attentions of someone of Tone's rising reputation.[28] The latter's introduction to the household was finally gained through a mutual interest in music. Tone would accompany Edward's violin on the flute and soon became a great favourite with the family.

Grafton Street, where Swift had dined with Stella's friend, Mrs Dingley, was then declining as a fashionable residential area, as the gentry moved away from the congested older parishes.[29] But, with the adjacent St. Stephen's Green, it was still an area favoured by the leading politicians. The remnants of the Witherington residence are still visible today above the plate-glass windows of the modern shops. Even then Grafton Street was a busy shopping area. Martha was the daughter of William Witherington, a woollen draper.[30] But it was her grandfather, the Revd Mr Fanning, who was the patron of the family.

Tone and Martha became infatuated with each other, and after a courtship of but a few months they eloped. Setting out 'one beautiful morning in the month of July [1785]'—the 21st, to be precise—they swiftly covered the short distance to the parish church of St. Ann's in nearby Dawson Street, where they were married.[31] They then went off to Maynooth in County Kildare till the storm of discovery calmed, and, when forgiven, settled in lodgings close to Martha's home.

She was renamed Matilda by Tone—a rather heartless gesture, since it was the name of the character in *Douglas* played by Eliza Martin. Yet it was typical of Tone's theatricality that he should have chosen for his new love the name of Home's fictional ideal of woman, wife and mother: as in so many other respects, so in his family, fiction spilled over into real life. Matilda was but sixteen at the time of their marriage, and although elopement was a common occurrence at the time, it must have seemed to her family an appalling betrayal of trust by Tone. The truce did not last long. Matilda and her sister Kate would remain close. But a feud developed between the Tones and the rest of the Witherington family which raised such painful memories for Matilda, forty years later, that references to it were omitted from Tone's published journals.[32] Thus excluded from the kind of financial help they might have expected from the Witheringtons, Tone and Matilda moved in with his parents at Bodenstown, and from there he set about finishing his degree and acquiring some means of livelihood.

Had marriage brought with it a new sense of responsibility? Certainly Tone's performance at college suggests as much. In November 1785 he was elected auditor of the College Historical Society, its highest honour.[33] The journals reflect his scrupulous punctuality in attendance and active participation. In January 1786 he was awarded a medal for best answers in history and another for oratory. After taking his degree in February 1786, Tone resigned the auditorship and his name disappears from the Society's journals until 21 June.[34] In the interval Matilda had given birth to their first child, Maria.

We have little information on the early years of Tone's and Matilda's marriage, though it does appear to have been passed almost entirely at the Tone household at Bodenstown, since Tone's name appears only twice in the Historical Society journals during the 1786–7 session. On the first occasion, 1 November 1786, the Society was told of a dramatic robbery at the Tone house two weeks previously. Among the spoil the robbers had made off with the three medals awarded Tone by the Society. Plunket, lately returned from the Inns of Court in London, proposed supplying replacements 'as well as to testify our respect for so valuable a member as...to perpetuate those proofs of our own discernment'. The motion was seconded by Magee and carried unanimously.[35]

The incident referred to threw Tone's career plans into disarrary—for the robbers had also taken the money his father had set aside for his son's legal training. Tone looked again to Matilda's family for help, but received none. 'My wife's family, though they were in great affluence and well knew our embarrassments, refused to give us the least assistance'. He spoke harshly to Edward Witherington on several occasions about the matter, but was restrained from further action by Matilda's sensitivity.

The Bodenstown robbery had likewise caused such terror about the safety of his family that this is the only incident from this part of his life recounted in detail in his autobiography. 'Of all the adventures wherein I have been hitherto engaged, this undoubtedly was the most horrible—it makes me shudder even now to think of it.' It took place early on the evening of 16 October. Tone was in the courtyard when a gang of six robbers, armed to the hilt, their faces blackened, seized and bound him and proceeded to break into the house. For two hours he lay guarded by one of the robbers, listening to the destruction taking place within. China, glass and everything else which could not be carried off was smashed.

When the robbers finally left. Tone struggled to each of the windows in turn, but could see no one. 'I called, but received no answer; my heart died within me...it was horrible!—I set myself to gnaw the cords with which I was tied in a transport of agony and rage, for I verily believed that my whole family lay murdered within.' He was relieved of this 'unspeakable terror' by the return of Matilda to look for him. The family had managed to untie each other after the flight of the robbers. When they were at some distance from the house, Tone's absence was remembered, and Matilda insisted on returning alone, despite the risks involved.

It was, as Tone himself recognised, a remarkable act of courage. 'I can imagine no greater effort of courage; but of what is not a woman capable for him she truly loves?' It was a line depicting the selfless love of the ideal heroine which could have come from any of the theatrical productions of the day, a highly romantic conception, with a considerable element of double standard. A spirited Eliza Martin or a Calista would not have been Tone's ideal companion, and while there is no doubting his genuine love for Matilda, one suspects that his infatuation with this innocent sixteen-year-old was an unconscious recognition of that fact. Certainly in the coming years Matilda was to need that inner strength of character which this incident reveals.

Her own account of what happened in the house as Tone lay bound in the courtyard also tells us something of the strange codes of honour operating in eighteenth-century rural banditry. One of the robbers took the screaming Maria from her cradle and placed her beside her mother on the bed, where she lay bound with Mrs Tone and Mary. Two of the gang were taken in another robbery, some days later, and eventually hanged. The incident left Tone jumpy and aggressive. Throughout the ensuing winter every noise, every knock at the door after nightfall had him rushing out with pistols kept in readiness under his pillow, and for years afterwards he would challenge highwaymen and footpads, rather than submit to their threats—foolhardy, but in the event successful.[36]

V

In January 1787 Tone left to begin his law terms in London. On 24 January he called in briefly at the Historical Society, where he would have received a convivial send-off from his many friends who were still members. It is a token of his attachment to the Society that it was also his first port of call on his return to Ireland in December 1788. He was by then regarded as one of its most esteemed senior members, and the Society presented him with three medals for 'his exertions in oratory...and best answering of history on former periods.'[37]

But Tone had changed, as indeed had his beloved Society, and when called upon to close the 1789 session with a speech from the chair, 'the highest compliment which that society is used to bestow', as he later described it, he delivered a swingeing attack on its declining standards. Gone were the days when the Historical Society was considered 'the brightest star in the constellation of literature'. Instead its members had become 'a mob of gladiators', turning the Society into 'a theatre of war and tumult', and disgracing its sessions with a 'vindictive spirit of sanguinary personal resentment'—Tone hated bickering. 'Shall the laws of the country be insulted', he asked, 'the discipline of the university contemned [sic], and disorder, and misrule, and anarchy be let loose on us, at the will of any hot-headed, giddy young man, who may choose these walls as the scene of his riotous valour, and turn the seat of science into a field of blood?' The attendance of these men at history was thin and unprepared, their skills at oratory non-existent, as personal abuse became confounded with eloquence. 'Let such look to the low scurrility of a Demosthenes against an Aeschines, the pitiful sarcasms of a Cicero against an Antony, the contemptible ribaldry of a Grattan against a Flood, and see how those mighty geniuses fall into contempt and ridicule when, with a hand able to grasp the thunderbolt, they descend to the infamy of wielding a dungfork!' Barrington was right. Tone was no orator. As for composition, he continued, 'silence is mercy—this is not your era for composition', and in prophetic strain, he warned that the very existence of their institution was under threat.[38] The speech is one of the first testimonials we have to that irritation at unprofessionalism, inefficiency and disloyalty, which would surface time and time again throughout Tone's life.

The attack seems to have been entirely justified, even if its tone is one of almost adolescent hyperbole. The Society had lately been rebuked by the Provost and fellows for its comments on 'modern politics'; the library was in disarray; members were negligent about fulfilling duties which in Tone's day were considered an honour, and on several occasions during that 1789 session, Tone himself had served on emergency committees to select questions for debate when those officially chosen had reneged on their duty. There were irregularities in ballots for officers and several elections were declared void; the records of the Society for this period show nothing of the earlier efficiency and regularity.[39] There is an element of the elder statesman in Tone's speech from the chair—a standing which was indeed accorded him in the final years of his attachment to the Historical Society.

Everything augured well for a glittering legal career. Trinity was, after all, an élite institution, recognised as the nursery of leaders, whose 'vigorous shoots of genius' would later grow 'high in the estimation of their country' attaining 'the highest honours of their professions'. The words are Tone's, but the sentiment was generally accepted, and Tone to all appearances had passed with distinction the first stage towards a promising public career. He was now part of a brotherhood of talent which in time saw Plunket, Burrowes and Bushe reach the height of the Irish legal profession. His career in the Historical Society had marked his transformation from the rebellious and star-struck youth into the impatient, confident and much-admired figure of 1789–90. He had long repented of that wilful rebelliousness which had almost denied him his university experience. 'I look back on my College days with regret,' he wrote in 1796, 'and I preserve, and ever shall, a most sincere affection for the University of Dublin.'[40]

But it is ever the experience of the king-pin student that he rejoins the outside world at the bottom. Coming from the heights of acclaim, where fortune had mattered little and where ability and companionability counted for all, it came as a shock to Tone when he encountered a world where the balance of ability and fortune or connections was reversed. Barrington claimed that Tone's abilities at college were overrated. If this was so the disappointment at unfulfilled expectations would have been all the greater. Tone had been bred to gentility without the family fortune to sustain it. He had neither the connections nor the patience required to succeed in a legal career. He was not well advised in embarking on it.

3
Middle Temple

Many barristers practising at the end of the eighteenth century had nothing but contempt for the bar as a profession. In this, as in much else, Tone was typical of his time. Why then did so many fathers continue to channel their ambitions for their sons in this direction? The answer is simple. In an age when the landed class automatically occupied the plum positions in most walks of life, the bar alone held open the opportunity for high office, wealth and reputation to those of humbler origins. More peerages were awarded to members of the legal profession than to any other, and a seat in Parliament was not an unreasonable expectation.[1] Nearly all Tone's college companions who embarked with him on a legal career were to attain eminence either in the legal or the political world. Above all the bar was a 'gentlemanly' profession. It conferred a certain social status on all who were called, and although Tone's private fortunes were in decline, in public he was about to become a member of a powerful élite. Buoyed up by the acclaim of his contemporaries in the Historical Society, Tone had reason to feel optimistic about his future. His last call-in at the Historical Society on the evening of 24 January 1787 would have ensured a rousing send-off, and he left for England a day or two later to prepare for the bar at the Inns of Court in London.

Tone's two years as a law student in London are often cited as part of the tantalising image of the irresponsible rake later to turn sober (or equally irresponsible, depending on one's viewpoint) rebel. It is a tempting image, but a false one; the truth is far more mundane. Tone was too romantic to be a rake. His life-style in London was nothing out of the ordinary, and his abbreviated account singling out the highlights, the more pleasant moments, was part of that common mental process which retrospectively blots out the bad times. Behind the façade, however, there is a sense of frustrated boredom, an increasing discomfiture in a social position for which his own financial standing did not equip him—though he always 'contrived to maintain the appearance of a gentleman'— and a developing middle-class obsession with money amidst the feckless spending of his better-off companions, which would later land one of them in debtors' prison. The middle classes do not amass debts. There is a penny-counting in Tone's *Life*, an appreciation of the value of money and a dread of going without. The Middle Temple account books show him scrupulously obeying the rules and paying promptly. In contrast, the thoughtless splendour of fashionable London society seems to have set the tone for his reaction against aristocratic values generally.

I

Tone landed at Liverpool in the last week of January 1787, after a stormy crossing in which the boat nearly foundered. The experience gave rise to a fear of the sea which came to haunt him later in France. Liverpool, with a population of 41,000 and a tangle of narrow streets just starting to give way to a major rebuilding programme, was small by Dublin standards. But the town's port and dock were already among the busiest in the country. A mail coach to London had been operating since 1785. The journey cost £3. 13s. 6d., took thirty hours, and was a test of endurance. Stops were made only to change horses and drivers and take refreshments at the coaching inns, and sleep was well-nigh impossible. Tone was a bad traveller, and he did not make the return journey home during his two years at the Temple.[2]

John Philpot Curran, the famous liberal barrister, who would later defend most of the United Irishmen (Tone included), had entered the Middle Temple in the previous decade. He arrived in London on a summer's evening and was struck by the vast number of steeples, the magnificence of the public buildings, 'the gaudy display of wealth and dissipation' and the 'hurry of business that might make you think this the source from which life and motion are conveyed to the world'.[3]

Since the early part of the century fashionable London had been moving west from the more populous districts to Cavendish Square, Hanover Square, Grosvenor Square and New Bond Street. They left behind a densely populated world of courts, alleys, tenements, rookeries and 'the dangerous districts' generally situated in the City (where the Inns of Court were located). It was an area which had developed without proper planning in the sixteenth and seventeenth centuries, and was crumbling rapidly by the eighteenth. Derelict houses filled up with beggars, and a notable feature of this period was the regular collapse of crumbling buildings. Everyone, even the rich, dwelt in cramped conditions, and most lived out their lives outside the home, in the taverns, alehouses, clubs or coffee-houses with which London abounded. The eighteenth century had witnessed a vast increase in the number of places of amusement, and successive generations of magistrates complained of the bewildering assortment of gaming houses, night cellars and brothels which mushroomed around the many new theatres springing up to supply the contemporary taste for theatricals. Such resorts, reported the Middlesex Grand Jury in May 1788, were the cause of 'that general spirit of dissipation and extravagance which so particularly distinguishes the present times'. London in the 1780s was living as if there was no tomorrow, and the Fleet prison, a few minutes' walk from the Temple, was filling up with debtors of all classes.[4]

Indeed the mingling of social ranks in such lustier amusements was a feature of the age. On a visit to a tavern in Covent Garden, the law student hero of Thackeray's *Pendennis* finds men of all sorts and conditions.... Healthy country tradesmen and farmers...squads of young apprentices and assistants...rakish young medical students, gallant, dashing, what is called "loudly" dressed, and...somewhat dirty...young University bucks...handsome young guardsmen, and florid bucks from the St. James's Street clubs; nay, senators English and Irish—and even members of the House of Peers.'[5] Tone would have had plenty of opportunity for observing the behaviour of his social betters at close quarters. He would also have participated automatically in the most popular pastime of the period: drinking. Drinking was seen by everyone but the moral and social reformers as a social virtue, a prerequisite in this most convivial of centuries. 'Drunkenness was a common habit some fifty or sixty years ago when all ranks got drunk', wrote Francis Place in 1829, reflecting back on his youth in the area of the Inns of Court.

Place lived and served his time as an apprentice breeches-maker in the Temple Bar area during the same years that Tone kept chambers in the Middle Temple. They would have been neighbours, even if from different social classes, and they may well have crossed paths in the many public houses of the Temple Bar and Fleet Street area, 'frequented principally by the more dissolute sort of barristers, attorneys, and tradesmen of what were then called the better sort'. Place gives us a vivid description of the dissipation of the times, the loose family and sexual morals and the lack of hygiene at every social level. The streets swarmed with prostitutes, thieves, crimping agents and press-gangs, and on weekly market days people went in fear of their lives, as maddened bullocks were chased through the streets in one of the more tumultuous popular pastimes. The dissipation of the capital in the late eighteenth century is well documented, and Tone's preference for the intimate company of a few friends seems positively prudish by comparison. Social convention would have demanded such frequentation of taverns. But Tone was a more private person than tradition allows. The noise of London bothered him, and the sound of the bells in the numerous churches surrounding the Temple made him wish that he was in some Mohammedan country. He disliked taverns, disapproved of the morals and materialism of London, and was becoming increasingly dependent on the intimate friendship of a few. It was a signpost to that preference for private society which so marks the nineteenth century off from the eighteenth.[6]

The eighteenth-century legal world was centred on Temple Bar, sinister memorial on which the heads of those convicted of treason earlier in the century had been impaled and still the scene of riotous assemblages of young apprentices. Here London's most important legal buildings were concentrated in an area of some two square miles: two of the four Inns of Court (the Middle and Inner Temple) adjacent to Temple Bar, a third, Lincoln's Inn, a few minutes' walk up Chancery Lane, and the fourth further along at High Holborn. Westminster Hall, home of the common law courts, was conveniently located and in Tone's day was the scene of the greatest box-office attraction of the period: the trial of Warren Hastings, former Governor-General of India.

Although Tone visited the public gallery of the House of Commons, he had little interest in English affairs. The lurid details of the Hastings trial filled the newspaper columns with irritating monotony. But Tone seems to have devoted more attention to the lighter society columns, with their reports of levees, balls, masques, and their theatrical reviews. If he needed any further reason to ignore the trial of the century, his old Trinity friend John Wharton was on hand to provide it. Now a member of the exclusive Whig club, Brooks's, and courting an English parliamentary seat in the Foxite Whig interest, he would have conveyed to Tone something of the Foxites' irritation with Burke's relentless and single-minded persecution of Hastings.

As he passed through the great gates of the Middle Temple, with their lamb and cross standard of the Knights Templar, Tone would have entered another world, which was steeped in tradition, inward-looking, and self-governing. The sweeping walks, opening on to the river Thames, and the closed courtyards delimiting the Temple area on the Fleet Street side accentuated its sense of other-worldliness. The Inns of Court provided no legal training, and the law student might find himself sharing chambers with a variety of people, each category with its own pecking order on the staircase. The ground floor was reserved for successful barristers or politicians—Pitt and Flood had chambers in Lincoln's Inn in Tone's day. A successful writer might occupy rooms on the next floor up—and the Middle Temple was known more for its resident writers, of whom Cowper,

Goldsmith, Sheridan and Fielding were the most notable, than its great legal minds. Rooms might also be let out to respectable tradespeople, peruke-makers, hatters, tailors, etc. But the cheaper rooms at the top invariably housed students, as like as not sharing with one or more friends.[7] Young Pendennis has chambers in the Temple up three pairs of stairs, a 'nasty black staircase', leaving his uncle's valet to wonder 'how a gentleman could live in such a place'. The uncle is similarly unimpressed when he goes to visit:

> When Major Pendennis reached that dingy portal...he was directed by a civil personage with a badge and a white apron, through some dark alleys, and under various melancholy archways into courts each more dismal than the other [Tone lived in one of these, Hare Court], until finally he reached Lamb Court. If it was dark in Pall Mall, what was it in Lamb Court? Candles were burning in many of the rooms there—in the pupil room of Mr Hodgeman, the special pleader, whose six pupils were scribbling declarations under the tallow; in Sir Hokey Walker's clerk's room,...the clerk...was conversing in a patronising manner with the managing clerk of an attorney at the door [attorneys were despised by the bar]; and in Curling the wig-maker's melancholy shop...large sergeants' and judges' wigs were looming drearily.... Two little clerks were playing at toss-halfpenny [in the court].... A laundress in pattens passed in at one door, a newspaper boy issued from another. A porter, whose white apron was faintly visible, paced up and down. It would be impossible to conceive a place more dismal, and the Major shuddered to think that anyone should select such a residence.[8]

The women who attended chambers, or 'laundresses', were usually elderly, and many were Irish. The Grecian coffee-house in Devereux Court was a favourite haunt with students, who would shuffle down in slippers, nightcap and dressing gown to read the newspapers.[9] Indeed it was at no. 8 Devereux Court that Tone first had lodgings, possibly shared with two Irish friends, Robert James from Monaghan, and Richard Fortescue Sharkey from Westmeath. James would remain as a practising barrister in London; Sharkey was called to the Irish bar in 1788, and later became MP for Dungannon. They were older than Tone: James was thirty-three, Sharkey thirty-two. Both had been Trinity students in the 1770s, and though they were entered at the Middle Temple in 1781 and 1785 respectively, they spent much of their time in Dublin, and the three would almost certainly have met at the Historical Society.[10]

There was a network of Irish at the London Inns, ready to receive newcomers. Many were Trinity products, and they tended to stick together, handing on friends and lodgings alike.[11] It was thus that another friend came Tone's way, a friend with considerable family connections. This was the son of Lord Northland, the Hon. George Knox, from Tyrone in Ulster. Knox's political future was assured by the family's connection with the powerful Abercorn interest, and in London he associated with leading Irish political figures such as Flood and Sir Laurence Parsons, both seeking English parliamentary seats at the time. A graduate of Oxford, he had been entered at Lincoln's Inn in 1782, where he became a close friend of Plunket. Knox was receiving a more aristocratic grooming than many of his student friends, and it was in between journeys of his Grand Tour that he befriended Tone. Despite social differences, he was in outlook typical of Tone's circle of friends and was to remain one of the foremost champions of Catholic emancipation after taking his seat in the Irish Parliament. Knox was one of the friends who did not abandon Tone when his republicanism put them in opposite political camps, and in exile in 1796 Tone recalled their friendship as something 'of which I am as proud as of any circumstance of my life. He is a man of inappreciable merit, and loved to a degree of enthusiasm by all who have the happiness to know him'. Knox does indeed seem to have been an extremely warm and talented man, who acted with considerable integrity during the harrowing events of the 1790s, even at the expense of his own political career.[12]

Another friend was James Walkinson Bell of Lucan. He and Tone had entered the Middle Temple on the same day and went bail for each other. He was almost certainly the model for the love-struck hero, Belville, of *Belmont Castle*, who 'To a good person...unites an elegant, though melancholy, languor of countenance, which bespeaks a heart of the kindest susceptibility; whilst his eyes, enlightened by a peculiar fire, give an irresistible force to his animated conversation. The patrimony of a younger brother of a younger branch being insufficient for his support, he has determined on the profession of the law.'[13]

We get a glimpse at the importance of these friendships in Tone's life in London in a rare letter from this period, dating from the summer of 1787. Bell was called to the bar on 22 June. Knox and Sharkey too were gone, and there is a sense of the futility of keeping terms in London, which shortly would turn Tone, like so many other law students, to writing.

My Dear Sharkey,
I cannot with any justice pretend to reprove you for not writing earlier, being myself so villainously slow in my answer, but I presume the same cause, may serve for an excuse for us both—the

fact is that I have been in a state of stagnation mental and corporal, ever since you left London—when Geo. Knox was gone I consoled myself in your society but now...'I am like a tree in the forest shorn of its crown...'. It is with great satisfaction I acquaint you that James was called the last Friday of last term and that in consequence I dined with him—We sat till very late over our claret and parted not very like a company of stoics—he becomes his wig and Bar gown prodigiously.

And in an early indication of an exaggerated sensitivity and quickness to sense a slight, Tone adds: 'Give my sincere and affectionate regards to Charles Knox [one of the "young men of station" Tone mentions as having been his friends in London: no relation to George Knox], he promised to write to me but no more of that—perhaps he may when he goes to Ireland'.[14]

Tone had also renewed an old college friendship with John Hall from Fermanagh. He had entered Trinity as a fellow commoner the same year as Tone, and had recently inherited a large estate in Yorkshire on the death of his aunt, Margaret Wharton, whose name he then assumed. Tone visited the estate and thought Yorkshire 'the finest part of England'. Through his Yorkshire interests, Wharton also acquired important political connections with the opposition Whigs, notably the political patronage of the county's leading landowner and Lord Lieutenant, Earl Fitzwilliam. He was accordingly entered at the exclusive political club, Brooks's, married into the Durham Whig family, the Lambtons, and groomed for the seat of Beverley in Yorkshire, which he won in 1790. Wharton was a reformer in Parliament, supporting the abolition of the slave trade, constitutional reform, and, significantly, Catholic emancipation. As a person, he seems to have been typical of the quick-witted, fun-loving and companionable group with which Tone had associated in Dublin and again in London. 'He is young, gay, lively, a little volatile, little known and, of course, of no great weight in the town...', wrote one Whig colleague in opposition to his candidacy for Beverley. The following year, however, the colleague had to admit his error, when Wharton proved so popular with the voters that he destroyed the government interest in a landslide victory and returned the seat to the Whigs.[15]

Richard Jebb, brother to the more famous theologian and bishop, John Jebb, Thomas Radcliffe and Benjamin Phipps had likewise been contemporaries of Tone's at Trinity. They had entered Lincoln's Inn early in 1785 and were already well established in London when Tone arrived. The Middle Temple had been more fashionable with Irish students before the 1780s. But fashions change. By 1785

Lincoln's Inn had overtaken it in popularity, and it may well have been on the advice of Richard Griffith that Tone was entered instead at his old Inn. But soon Tone's social life was revolving around the more fashionable Lincoln's Inn, where Phipps 'kept a kind of bachelor's house, with good wine, and an excellent collection of books (*not law books*) [for which Tone was already displaying an insatiable appetite] all which were as much at my command as his... he had a great fund of information, particularly of political detail, and in his company I spent some of the pleasantest hours which I passed in London'.[16]

Soon Tone's younger brother, William, joined him in London. After almost eight years of service with the East India Company, William had all the address of a military man and a good deal more sense than his elder brother. He scarcely needed the mother-hen-like guardianship of Tone, who months before William's arrival was trying all manner of strategems to set his brother on the road to a more steady career. It is one of the many indications of Tone taking seriously his role as eldest sibling. 'I am determined to strain every nerve to bring my brother, of whom I spoke to you, to the bar', he wrote to Sharkey in July 1787; 'will you therefore on your annual take on yourself the arrangement of putting his name on the Inns of Court. You can be his bail, I dare say, and it will oblige me extremely.... When you write let me know candidly what you think of him [William was then in Ireland]—he cannot be informed, from circumstances, but from his letters I think he must have capabilities—at any rate he is my brother and please reason if it be possible I will extricate him from a situation so foreign to his feelings as I know the present one to be'.[17] Tone came to an agreement with his friend Magee—then preparing for a fellowship at Trinity—to the same purpose. Magee was to enter his own name at the Middle Temple and William would attend the qualifying dinners in his place. It would have been easy enough to execute, since law students simply signed chits of paper to signify their attendance. In the event Hely-Hutchinson made implementation of the scheme impossible. Magee had opposed the Provost's son's candidacy for one of the college's parliamentary seats, and paid the price. The Provost in revenge invoked the all-but-obsolete requirement that Fellows take orders, and the Church rather than the bar became Magee's fate.[18] It is perhaps worth noting that nepotism does not figure in Tone's later complaints about political corruption.

In the event William came to join Tone as companion rather than fellow student, arriving about March 1788. William had been only sixteen when they last met and Tone was apprehensive as to what he would find in the twenty-three-year-old. He was pleasantly surprised. Despite 'such execrable society as the troops in the Company's service...I was much surprised...to find him with the manners of a gentleman, and a considerable acquaintance with the best parts of English literature; he had a natural turn for poetry [which William's compositions bear out].... He was a handsome, well made lad, with a very good address, and extremely well received among the women, whom he loved to excess.'[19] Together they moved into rather better chambers on the first floor of no. 4 Hare Court—still one of the more attractive of the Temple courts, closed to through traffic from Fleet Street, yet open and bright in aspect.[20] Reminiscing in 1796 on 'the happy hours' he, William and Phipps spent together, though 'often without a guinea', Tone can barely contain his emotion. 'It fills me now with a tender kind of melancholy...to recall the many delightful days we three have spent together and the walks we have taken, sometimes to a review; sometimes to see a ship of war launched; sometimes to visit the India men at Deptford', the other two carried along by William's 'invincible gaiety' and 'inexhaustible fund of pure Irish humour'. It was sorties such as these which bred in Tone a healthy respect and admiration for England's military might, and much as he applauded the spirit of the French army, he thought French soldiers sloppy by contrast. The brothers made frequent visits to the ballet and theatre. They travelled to well-known beauty spots such as Llangollen in Wales, and Tone was much impressed at the neatness of English villages and estates. They visited Westminster Abbey, St. Paul's (which Tone later thought infinitely superior to Soufflot's Panthéon in Paris) and Hampton Court. Tone hated palaces, not so much because of his republicanism as for their wanton lavishness and he would find Henry VIII's palace positively modest beside Versailles.[21] His general impression of London was not unfavourable. He was particularly struck by the prosperity which commerce brought and was an enthusiast for capitalist developments in the economy.

II

Tone also had relationships with several females in London, details of which were omitted by his widow and son when publishing his autobiography. The ideal in a woman is set out in *Belmont Castle* as 'beauty, taste and accomplishments', 'nature and education' contending for 'pre-eminence',[22] and by all accounts Tone was not disappointed by those he met in London.

At the age of four and twenty, with a tolerable figure and address and in an idle and luxurious capital, it will not be supposed I was without adventures with the Fair Sex. The Englishmen neglect their wives exceedingly in many essential circumstances; I was totally disengaged, and did not fail to profit, as far as I could, of their neglect, and the Englishwomen are not naturally cruel. I formed in consequence several delightful connections in London, and as I was extremely discreet, I have the satisfaction to think that not one of those, to whom I had the good fortune to render myself agreeable, ever suffered the slightest blemish in her reputation on my account. I cherish yet the memory of one charming woman to whom I was extremely attached, and I am sure she still remembers me with a mutual regard.[23]

There is a cool detachment in this description of his liaisons in London which compares unfavourably with the emotional agony caused by recollections of Mrs Martin. Certainly one of the flirtations may have started out as a swaggering wager with friends. Tone wrote to Sharkey in July 1787: 'I call often at Chancery Lane and am as well received as ever but I do not find "Caroline" [a popular contemporary love story] advancing a step which "*makes me uneasy*".'[24] There are none of protests of virtue as in his description of his love for Mrs Martin, and we can be sure that some of these 'adventures' in London were affairs in every sense of the word. Yet the signs are that Tone was inept as a rake, and his tendency to become totally enraptured by the object of his passion is mocked by his friend Radcliffe in the Scudamore character of *Belmont Castle*.

Belmont Castle was written during this period in London by the three friends, Radcliffe, Jebb and Tone, and was 'intended to ridicule the execrable trash of the Circulation Libraries'.[25] But as the friends joked about the scheme, reading out frivolous passages from the *Morning Post* for possible inclusion, they got carried away, and the novel contains exaggerated portraits of themselves, their friends, and of fashionable society generally. The intended 'burlesque novel' became a *roman à clef* in which some of the characters are barely disguised. This was surely the reason for their failure to get it published in London, for all the booksellers operated in the area where the fictional characters conduct their liaisons, and the identity of many would have been immediately recognisable. A Covent Garden play by Lady Wallace—*The Ton; or Follies of Fashion*—was withdrawn in 1788 for this very reason. *Belmont Castle* was finally published in 1790 by Tone's publisher in Dublin, Patrick Byrne.[26]

The writing of *Belmont Castle* can be fairly precisely dated because of its use of contemporary material from the London newspapers of winter–spring 1788. The story is one of virtuous and illicit love. The heroine, Georgiana Blandford, is being forced to marry a villainous aristocrat, Colonel Neville, instead of the penniless but honourable

Belville. An elopement is arranged, but discovered and thwarted by the nefarious Neville, who rapes the heroine, causing her to die of guilt and sorrow, upon which Belville commits suicide. The sub-plot—an illicit affair between Belville's friend, the Hon. Charles Fitzroy Scudamore, and Lady Eliza Clairville, who is neglected by a faithless husband—ends with the lover's death at the hands of the jealous husband, and Lady Clairville's Ophelia-like suicide. The entire work is a kitsch pastiche of stock themes of the romantic novels and plays of the day: the glorification of true love and female virtue, denunciation of the arranged marriage and the negligent husband, the conspiratorial role of servants, the value of a good heart, disciplined by prudence (of which Scudamore, and by implication Tone, is totally devoid), and the whole written in the epistolary form so popular at the time. Few of the characters are credible, and when in danger of becoming so, the authors contrive to introduce an element of the ridiculous. All of them, the men included, are subject to inexplicable fainting fits. Belville, perhaps the most credible of all the characters, nevertheless casts animals over fences to defend his loved one; while his suicide is so prolonged that he has time to write a lengthy description of the clothes he has chosen for the death scene. Scudamore's death by the sword of Lord Clairville is likewise dragged out through three letters to his friend.

But it is the character of Scudamore, the hopeless and hapless romantic, which tells us most about Tone. Scudamore has fallen madly in love with Lady Clairville, and the relationship is nurtured through music as Scudamore accompanies her pianoforte on his 'German flute'. Tone was a good musician, and, as with the Witheringtons, his ability to participate in drawing-room duets would have been a social asset in London. But Scudamore is a ridiculous character, terrifying the object of his love by exaggerated proclamations of his passion and by his indiscretions. Even when success is close, and he engineers a rendezvous at a masquerade in Oxford Street, he becomes so lost in dreams that he gets into a fight, is pick-pocketed, and turns up at the masquerade with a black eye. Scudamore eventually chooses for the assignation a place in Soho of such ill repute that all romance is lost, and he is forced out of bed and killed by the offended husband.

The caricature of Tone is unmistakable: the exaggerated emotions, the tendency to melodrama and impetuosity, the habit of speaking in quotations and in verse and of finding some kind of solace in detailed descriptions of food and drink. 'His feelings, tho' strong and rapid, were not deep', wrote Plunket's son of his father's friend, 'and his spirits were seldom in the same state for any length of time: now playful and buoyant, the next moment melancholy and depressed.'[27]

The comparative coolness of Tone's description of these liaisons in London may well have been brought about by the recollection of his friends' good-humoured mockery of their emotional comrade. Tone was an incorrigible flirt, but was not always sure how to handle things when flirtation developed into something more serious, and he was to run for cover from his landlady's advances in Paris.[28]

The setting of *Belmont Castle* is the fashionable Grosvenor Square, Wimpole Street, Portland Place and Harley Place areas of London, and there are detailed descriptions of interiors and of major social occasions which suggest personal involvement. Tone's Paris journal shows that he was familiar with expensive London hotels like the Adelphi and fashionable meeting places like the Bedford coffee-house. The aristocratic connections of Wharton, Knox and Radcliffe would have afforded a natural introduction to such society, and contributed to Tone's self-image at the time as a young man of fashion. Indeed by definition the young men at the Inns of Court were regarded as gentlemen, and Daniel O'Connell, a student at Lincoln's Inn seven years later, was no stranger to such fashionable gatherings or indeed to the rough-and-tumble hazards the streets held for the likes of Scudamore.[29]

Yet there is a growing discomfiture in Tone's account of his London days. The experience of the middle-class man, participating in the world of high society but never truly belonging to it, was not untypical. Arthur Pendennis has quickly tired of the 'dulness and sameness' of society parties and balls, and 'the dandified pretensions, and fine-gentleman airs which he has contracted, among his aristocratic college acquaintances', and turns instead to 'the rough pleasures and amusements of a London bachelor.' His pleasures now consist of a 'long morning's reading, a walk in the park, a pull on the river, a stretch up the hill to Hampstead, and a modest tavern dinner; a bachelor night passed here or there, in joviality, not vice...; a quiet evening at home with a friend...and a humble potation of British spirits...'—a description which would have fitted Tone's routine just as well in his second year at the Middle Temple.[30]

There is little mention of his wife and baby girl in all this, but the few insights we have into his thinking for this period suggest a sense of guilt. He urged Sharkey to go and see them when he arrived in Ireland. 'I will ensure a welcome—write to them a couple of days before that having lately left me in good health you purpose doing yourself the honor etc. and be sure if you go to give me a large character.' In the next sentence he could switch over to talk of his female friend in Chancery Lane.[31] Nevertheless his changed circumstances nagged at him throughout his stay in London, and, like Pendennis, he was always short of money. After the robbery at their home, Peter Tone could give his son little with which to sustain himself in London. Initial outgoings—a £4 admission fee and food and lodging—would have been moderate, for Tone was not billed for chambers and commons till the following year, and tavern food was wholesome and inexpensive. Moveover, his better-off companions were only too glad to bail him out—Wharton in particular lending £150 'at a time when I was under great pecuniary difficulties'. But he was not accepting such generosity with the same alacrity as in his student days, and there is a nagging sense of financial disadvantage in his account of these times.[32]

III

Like so many other law students, Tone now turned to writing to earn a living. Sharkey had been encouraging his obviously gifted but strangely self-effacing friend to do so. At first he was reluctant. 'As to Monsieur l'Inca,' he replied, 'I thought you had known me better than to suggest any thing whatever, and it is but little that I can do by way of execution, I can originate nothing—I could as soon carry St. Paul's on my back, or swallow the monument as write a single paragraph in the style you mention—observation is not my forte.'[33] Yet Tone was soon to became a compulsive writer, his initiation occurring shortly after the above exchange in reviews commissioned by the *European Magazine*. Reviews and articles were unsigned, but Tone was responsible for some of those attacking the many trashy romantic novels of the day and almost certainly for a review of Andrew Keppis's *Life of Captain James Cook*.[34]

Tone dismissed these early literary efforts as 'poor performances enough' though 'in general as good as those of my brother critics'.[35] But for *Belmont Castle* he retained a soft spot, not so much for its literary merit—of which it had little, except as an accurate enough synthesis of the style and theme of the popular romantic novels of the period—but as a token of the friendships of which it was a product. It was one of the few books he took to France in 1795–6, from his by then extensive library, and it was captured with him on his last voyage to Ireland in 1798.[36]

It is a token of Tone's emotional attachment to things of his youth, that his other major writing venture of the period—his Sandwich Islands project—remained a firm favourite for the rest of his life. The Enlightenment had given rise to a passion for information on remote places and people, and Tone, his brother and Phipps spent the summer of 1788 reading up on recent voyages of discovery. A memorial proposing the establishment of a British military colony on the newly discovered Sandwich Islands, as a counterweight to Spanish overseas power, was at length drawn up by Tone and delivered by hand to no. 10 Downing Street on 10 August 1788. Thirteen days later, having received no acknowledgement, Tone wrote a second memorial, which likewise went unacknowledged. Pitt had been a great hero with the Trinity students and Tone was hurt by such neglect.

The tone of the 10 August memorial is one of youthful effervescence, at times of verbose pomposity, punctuated nevertheless by moments of self-doubt as the writer apologises for his excessive enthusiasm. Most of all there is an almost fawning reverence for Pitt, an admiration felt by many for the youthful Prime Minister who had saved the country from the ill-favoured Fox–North coalition five years earlier. Tone writes as an enthusiastically loyal subject: 'if ever colony promised great and sudden advantages to the Mother Country, *this* is that colony; if power and unanimity and peace and wealth at home be indispensible previous requisites, *this* is the period, for England is mighty; if wisdom and virtue...in the Government can ensure success, *this* is the period, for You are the Minister.... I am in common with millions, your much obliged and grateful admirer, THEOBALD WOLFE TONE'.

The 1788 proposal already shows signs of that facility with words which would shortly make Tone one of the most fêted political writers in Ireland. But it shows little comprehension of current politics. British foreign policy in 1788 was more concerned with northern and eastern Europe than with Spain. It also shows a continuing mesmerisation with the military vigour of ancient Rome, mingled with a garbled Rousseauistic romanticism about the 'noble savage'. Tone proposes the establishment of the kind of military colony perfected by ancient Rome, to be serviced from California. The 'savage ferocity' of the natives, tempered by 'the mild precepts of the Christian religion', would be harnessed to its defence, and for their bravery they would be rewarded with grants of land. In another version of the project, written in 1790, Tone is more realistic in recognising that initial coercion and confiscation of land would be inevitable, though he takes the Lockean view that ultimately the ownership of land and property would have a stabilising and civilising role. There is a spirit of buccaneering adventurism in the memorials, and Tone and his companions were perfectly willing to embark immediately for the Pacific, had the plan been approved.

There is an element of bandwagoning in these memorials, unconscious certainly, but indicative of a personality never content to flourish in backwaters or side-tracks. Interest in the Pacific was riding high in London after the acclaimed stage production, *Omai, or A Trip Around the World*, which had opened at Covent Garden the year before Tone's arrival. It celebrated Cook's three voyages of discovery, employing exotic scenery and costumes to tell the story of Omai brought back by Cook from his voyages of the 1770s—the first Polynesian ever to visit Britain. Dignified and striking in appearance, Omai became the living symbol of Rousseau's noble savage, uncorrupted by civilisation.[37]

But it was for their 'political advantage' rather than as objects of 'philosophical curiosity' that Tone looked to Cook's discoveries. He read all the leading works on the subject: Narborough's *Account of Several Late Voyages and Discoveries to...the South Seas* (1694), Ulloa's *Voyage to South America* (translated from the Spanish, 1758), Woodes Rogers's *A Cruising Voyage Around the World First to the South Sea* (1712: the inspiration for Defoe's *Robinson Crusoe*, and above all Anson's *Voyage Round the World* (1748), Dampier's *A New Voyage Around the World* (1697) and the most recent editions of Cook's voyages in the 1770s. All these works were bestsellers in the eighteenth century, the latest edition of Dampier (Tone's favourite) appearing in 1785. It was this most recent version that Tone used. Details are accurately transcribed, even if they are voiced more confidently by Tone than in the original text.

Dampier was one of the leading figures in the classic buccaneer era of 1690–1700. The buccaneers were indeed pirates, but with a difference, for they also presented the world with some of the earliest studies of the navigation, anthropology and natural history of the South Seas. Their services were much sought after by merchants and navigators, and, having set themselves up as free-lance protectors of English interests against Spain, many were employed by the various colonial governors in a semi-official capacity. The buccaneers had become national heroes, their savagery forgotten in the romantic image of the camaraderie and egalitarianism said to have operated in their ranks. They were the direct models for the kind of expedition Tone had in mind, and the more ambitious recommendations of the 1790 memorial for a buccaneering-type expedition against the Spanish Empire were prefigured by the 1740s mission which had helped raise the one-time buccaneer, Anson, to the dizzy heights of First Lord of the Admiralty. Most of the works cited above propagated the belief that the Spanish Empire was collapsing from within, Spanish rule having sapped the vigour of the native populations.[38]

If Tone was not unrealistic in his recommendations, however, he was so in his belief that an unknown like himself would be sponsored in such a venture. Tone's self-confidence was a leftover from Trinity days. But his heightened sensitivity never let him forget a slight—or a good turn, for that matter—and his later republicanism was to supply him with a plausible rationalisation for his youthful sense of

grievance against the English Prime Minister. Tone resented being
talked down to: 'Men in high station ought not to speak short to men
who do not deserve it', he wrote at a later date.[39] This did not
necessarily make him a republican, and he was to criticise it as much
in French Revolutionary leaders as in English politicians. But it did
give rise to a deep contempt for conventional politics which was the
basis for that republicanism.

Too much, however, should not be read into his youthful sense of
rejection by Pitt. It did not prevent his resubmitting the proposal
two years later; by then he was realistic enough to submit it through
normal ministerial channels, rather than going straight to the top. He
also came to recognise that not everyone could be expected to share
an enthusiasm generated among his coterie of friends. 'Every man
has a corner to go mad in,' he would write to Matilda in 1797, 'and
you know my folly in regard to the Sandwich Islands.' Yet his early
passion for voyages of adventure and discovery was as strong as
ever, and he mused on how in a different age 'instead of planning
revolutions', he might have been 'carrying on a privateering war...
on the coasts of Spanish America.'[40]

IV

But Tone surely had come to London to read for the bar, not to write
reviews, romantic novels and political memoranda. By the end of his
two years he admitted to knowing as much about the law as of
necromancy. 'I was...amenable to nobody for my conduct; and in
consequence, after the first month I never opened a law book nor
was I ever three times in Westminster Hall.'[41] Few have been able to
write about this period in Tone's life without a twinge at his apparent
irresponsibility. Signs of pure ordinariness in Tone would later
be reviled by critics and brushed aside with embarrassment by
admirers.[42] But this is to extract him from his times and to measure
him against unrealistic standards of greatness. The legal historian of
the eighteenth century will recognise Tone's London experience as
typical. Like Grattan, Curran and O'Connell, Tone read his law
books assiduously enough at the outset. But Grattan soon found the
galleries of the English Parliament more interesting; Curran's biographer doubts he maintained his early labours, and O'Connell's
reading matter consisted almost entirely of contemporary literature.[43]

The only formal requirement of the Inns of Court was to eat
dinners in hall—which was no great hardship, for 'an excellent
wholesome dinner of soup, meat, tarts, and port wine or sherry'
could be had for a most moderate price. There was no formal
supervision. Everything was left to the student's own devices. The
Inns had become little more than professional clubs, serving the

needs of established barristers, young heirs to estates who never
intended making a living from the law, and attorneys attempting to
pull themselves into the more respectable branch of the legal
profession the hard way, rather than via the more gentlemanly route
of the universities. Not all law students had degrees in Tone's day,
but increasingly a university education was seen as the dividing line
between 'a scholar and a gentleman' and the common run of
attorney. A university degree, followed by a spell at the Inns of
Court, was a stamp of social status, and qualified people like Tone,
Curran and Grattan to hold their place with the highest in the land.
For Tone and his like the chief function of the Inns of Court was the
'social as well as the intellectual education and training, which their
common life and activities...gave to their inmates'.[44]

As to law books, 'what should he do with law-books?' asks the incredulous servant in Fielding's *Temple Beau*, when visited in
chambers by the rakish law student's father.[45] Ignorance of the law
was a deterrent to promotion in the bar, but it was no deterrent to
becoming a barrister in the first place. Most English Templars could
simply travel up from Oxford, or from their families' London homes
to eat dinners.[46] But for the middle-class American or Irishman,
compelled to reside in London, the wastefulness of the system cannot
have failed to be apparent. The warm memories of friendship aside,
what comes through most in Tone's sketchy account of his years in
London is his 'uneasiness of mind' at 'the extreme uncertainty' of his
financial situation. There is a sense of being peripheral to a world of
privilege, whose absurdity was still dictating the lives of people like
himself—and that world was an English one. Although Tone found
many things to admire about England, he would at times have found
himself treated as a provincial in London, and in time such
patronising fed an increasingly sensitive national identity. However,
the culture shock on first encountering the reserved individualism of
English society has been a common one for Irish people throughout
the centuries. Tone did not stay long enough in England to
overcome that culture shock, and whilst it would not have generated his republicanism, retrospectively it did become one of its
justifications.

It was financial worries, brought on by early marriage and the
deteriorating family fortunes, which increasingly eroded the carefree
disregard for practicalities of Trinity days. Shortly after the
foundering of his Sandwich Islands project, Tone suffered another
blow to a spirit naturally inclined to extremes of mood. His father
wrote of his own financial worries, complaining no doubt of the
extra burden of catering for Tone's family. It came at a time when
Tone's own affairs were 'exceedingly embarrassed, and...my mind

was harassed and sore with my own vexations', and his remedy was to end such worries by enlisting as a soldier in the East India Company's service. William pleaded with him to reconsider such a drastic solution, but agreed to accompany him when he persisted in his resolution, and the two set off for India House in Leadenhall Street, just east of St. Paul's. It was a location William knew all too well, for it was here that he had enlisted eight years previously after running away from home. The two had all the appearance of gentlemen, and the clerk was taken aback by their request to enlist. But in September and October no Indiamen sailed; 'the season was passed', they were told, 'but if we returned about the month of March following, we might be received'. 'Thus were we stopped', adds Tone, 'and I believe we were the single instance, since the beginning of the world, of two men, absolutely bent on ruining themselves, who could not find the means—desperate as were our fortunes, we could not help laughing at the circumstance that India, the great gulph of all undone beings, should be shut against us alone'.[47]

The need to earn a living was becoming an obsession with Tone and he felt that Matilda would fare better with the husband her family so disliked out of the way. Tone may have criticised other men for neglecting their wives, but, ever a man of his times, he did so himself in the grandest of manners. The incident is a telling one. It shows an impetuousness and a willingness to embark on the most unrealistic of ventures with scarcely a thought for the consequences, a tendency to brush aside the sensible cautions of those who knew better, and perhaps most dangerous of all, an ability to take those people with him. 'The genius of Wolfe Tone', writes Plunket's son, was accompanied by its full share of eccentricity. His mind, powerful and impulsive, rushed at its object without looking to consequences, and foiled in one direction charged with double energy in another.'[48]

But a way out of the hopelessness which had prompted such action soon presented itself. Tone had kept all but one of his terms at the Middle Temple—it was, after all his only duty—and that one could be remitted by simple payment of commons fees, which he duly paid.[49] An application to Matilda's grandfather produced a promise of £500 and a request for his return. He and William accordingly set off for Ireland, arriving in Dublin on 23 December 1788. He was now eligible for a call to the Irish bar and could expect within a few months, and with a little more legal learning than he had acquired in London, to be called to the most prestigious profession in Ireland.

4

Gentleman of the Law

The standing and influence of the Irish bar in the eighteenth century was out of all proportion to its intrinsic merits. Tone's dismissive references to his career as barrister are often taken at face value and this part of his life dealt with in a perfunctory fashion. However, Tone was still practising as a barrister on the eve of his exile from Ireland in 1795, and felt himself very much a part of the legal fraternity. Moreover, it was through his experiences at the Irish bar that his sense of alienation from the landed establishment was fully developed. It was the natural doorway to a political career for those prepared to wait. But the Irish bench and courts were packed with placemen, and to an ambitious but struggling young barrister the need for social and political connections to succeed soon became painfully apparent.[1] Tone was too impatient to wait, too proud to defer, and he was not alone. The Irish bar also introduced him to a body of like-minded men, unwilling to follow the hierarchical route through years of docility to preferment. These were the men who would dominate the Dublin Society of United Irishmen. Tone was about to become part of that process of fracturing élites which was producing revolution all over Europe.

I

Tone and William landed at Dublin on 23 December and reached the family home in Kildare on Christmas Day. With Maria only three, Arthur seven, Fanny about five or six, Mary fourteen and Matthew seventeen, the house was filled with young voices that Christmas. But a severe winter and anxiety about their future had taken their toll of Matilda's health. Tone was shocked at how delicate she looked. Matilda fretted when Tone was away, and his two years in London cannot have been an easy time for her. Estranged from her own family, she was to develop a warm attachment to Mrs Tone.[2]

Early in the new year Tone effected a reconciliation with the Witheringtons and took his family back to Dublin. The Revd Mr Fanning paid over the promised £500 and the Tones took lodgings nearby in Clarendon Street. Clarendon Street backed on to Grafton Street, which was fast replacing Dame Street as booksellers' row.

Bookshops then sold tobacco, cosmetics, patent medicine, stationery and lottery tickets, as well as an ever-increasing assortment of pamphlets, reprints of all the main books published in London, and growing numbers of foreign-language titles to satisfy the mania for French books in particular. It seemed but justice that Grafton Street should have become the literary centre of Dublin, for its famous English Grammar School had already trained an impressive list of actors, actresses, playwrights and poets. Here too the Dublin Society and the Royal Irish Academy—between them responsible for most of the antiquarian, scientific and literary scholarship of the period— were operating in Tone's day. Competition among booksellers was keen, some producing short-lived literary magazines to supply a demand still escalating in 1789, but going into sharp decline after 1795.[3]

Tone took out a subscription to the new *Universal Magazine*. He also wrote reviews for it.[4] In content it was similar to the *European Magazine*. The latest books were reviewed and extracted, there were pen portraits of leading world figures, digests of Irish, English and foreign news, rounded off with the perennial births, deaths and marriages. But it also provided particularly full coverage of developments in the French Revolution, and the important French writings of the period. Overall it was reformist and nationalist in tone. The opposition case against the government is supported, the Volunteers applauded, Montesquieu and Paine serialised, Mary Wollstonecraft praised, Burke criticised, and in Ireland the developing campaign for repeal of the penal laws fully reported. It was published by Patrick Byrne, a Catholic and one of the more successful Dublin booksellers, who had moved his shop from College Green to no. 108 Grafton Street in 1784. Excluded from many of the rights of his profession by the penal laws, Byrne became a prominent supporter of parliamentary reform, Catholic emancipation, and ultimately of the United Irishmen. He was to publish *Belmont Castle* and Tone's major political pamphlets, and to act as printer to the Catholic Committee and to the United Irishmen. As in France, revolution in Ireland was not made by the great treatises of the Enlightenment, but by the Grub Street sub-culture of pamphlets and hand-bills. Tone's work occasionally reached a higher plain, but in essence it falls largely into this category, and disgruntled booksellers like Byrne played a vital and much underestimated role in popularising the revolutionary ideas of the few.[5]

Immediately west of Clarendon Street lay the Liberties, with their restless population of struggling weavers. These were the years of increased combining and strikes to resist the introduction of machinery. The declining silk trade filled the newspapers with tales of distress. Pitched battles between silk weavers and the more prosperous linen weavers brought increasing numbers of troops on to the streets even before the war-induced troubles of the mid-1790s. The Police Act of 1786, replacing the old city watch with a Dublin police force, was designed to combat escalating disorder. Instead it was denounced by factious city politicians as another source of government corruption and increasing disorder and attacks on the police were thereby legitimised. Spiralling levels of crime continued to give cause for concern. It was said that 20,000 members of the female population were involved in prostitution and begging, and a particularly adept group of female tricksters frequented Grafton Street. Increased employment opportunities on the Grand and Royal Canals were enticing more people from the country, bringing customary rural pastimes like bull-baiting with them and predictably adding to the clashes with the authorities. The thin line that divides popular entertainment from riot and crime in proto-industrial societies was stretched to breaking point in Ireland by developments at the end of the eighteenth century.[6] The lower strata of Dublin society were ripe for the incursion of Defenderism. The Defenders was a secret organisation of lower-class Catholics, which developed from sectarian disturbances in South Ulster in the 1780s and spread rapidly to adjacent provinces during the crisis of the 1790s.

But Tone in 1788 was still being groomed for the élite. One of his first acts on returning to Dublin after Christmas was to renew his links with the College Historical Society. His name reappears on its attendance register for 31 December. It was the same night that John Sheares of Cork took his seat, a future president of the United Irish Society and a far more militant republican than ever Tone was. Tone was treated like a returning hero, awarded two medals for past oratory and voted on to most of the important committees.[7] It would have underscored his developing sense of Irishness in contrast to his recent frustrating English sojourn.

Society affairs had fallen into disarray since his departure. The increasing polarisation of Irish politics was bringing the ever-Whiggish Society into conflict with Hely-Hutchinson, the government's appointee as College Provost. The senior members tried to placate the authorities—Tone himself proposing an extra silver medal for the author of 'the best poetick composition on the late happy recovery of his present Majesty', after the illness which had produced the regency crisis of 1788–9.[8] But it was the petty internal bickering which most provoked Tone. A particularly vindictive conflict between two members on the night of 25 April 1789 led to an attempted duel the next day and a scurrilous campaign in the press. It was incidents such as this which were the backdrop to Tone's blister-

ing speech from the chair on 1 July 1789.[9] Nearly all his old friends
turned out to hear him: among them Burrowes, Radcliffe and Jebb,
now members of the Irish bar, and Miller, recently raised to a
College Fellowship.[10]

The questions which Tone helped choose for debate that year
reflect both his own developing interest in current politics and early
signs of a radicalism in the Society which would soon involve it
deeply with the United Irishmen. In November the small committee
he chaired returned the following questions: 'Should property be
esteemed a necessary qualification in a Member of Parliament?'
'Whether the establishment of a free constitution in France, would be
prejudicial to England?' 'Whether a Union with England would be of
advantage to this country?' 'Whether exiles are justified in bearing
arms against their country?'—a reference to the revolts which were
beginning to dismantle the old order on the Continent, and one of
prophetic significance for Tone himself. All were directly associated
with current political issues, after the Society had been rebuked by
the college authorities for motions 'relating to modern politics'. The
vote on the French issue shows a significant increase in sympathy for
France since the debate in June on a similar motion (though the
number of abstentions suggests more indecision that anything else).
But the last two questions were hotly debated, every member
present voting one way or the other—which was unusual. The union
proposal was overwhelmingly defeated, the right to arm against
one's country carried with a similar majority.

On 8 December Tone was again asked on to an emergency committee to draw up questions for the following month's debates. It
returned with topics questioning the right of Britain to tax the
American colonies, and asking if Ireland could subsist independently
of any other nation—a case pleaded by Tone's friend and a future
United Irishman, Whitley Stokes.[11] It would of course be stretching
a point to attribute responsibility for such topics to Tone alone,
particularly since the trend towards increasing politicisation in the
Society was already under way before his return from London. But
given his recognised seniority in the organisation, and its tendency to
accept his advice in other areas, his role on the committees would
have been significant. More importantly, preparation for Society
debates was in itself an education and Tone's reading matter in these
days would have been a far cry from the trashy romantic novels or
buccaneering books of his London days. After attending regularly
throughout 1789, Tone's participation in the Historical Society fell
off sharply. In part this reflects growing commitments elsewhere.
But long after he had become thoroughly disenchanted with the
world of privilege, Tone's loyalty to the Historical Society remained
undiminished.

II

Tone's formal association with Trinity College continued until spring of 1789.[12] He had set aside £100 of the Revd Mr Fanning's £500 to purchase a law library, and after a characteristic burst of work, he took his Bachelor of Law degree that spring. The exam was scarcely taxing: little more was required than 'some slight knowledge of Latin and a minimum of inventiveness and presence of mind', and Tone was called to the Irish bar in the summer of 1789. Conditions for admission to the King's Inns in Dublin had recently been tightened up—a degree and eight terms' residency at an English Inn being standard requirements. Candidates likewise had to take certain oaths, designed to keep out Catholics,[13] present a testimonial of non-involvement in any trade or business, supply sureties from two persons for £160 each, and lodge a certificate from the English Inn testifying to the required eight terms' residency. The bar was an exclusive profession, and a further requirement that candidates should not have practised as an attorney or solicitor, or even worked as a clerk in the office of one, ensured that it would remain so.

Many of the Inns' records were lost in 1802 in transit to their present site in Henrietta Street and only three of the five documents required for Tone's admission have survived. His Middle Temple certificate states that he had kept all but one of the eight terms (the one remitted on payment of commons), and paid all fees and dues. The 'Memorial to be admitted to the degree of barrister', written by himself, declares: 'That your memorialist's father and mother are Protestants of the Church of Ireland as by law established, and that your memorialist is also a Protestant. That your memorialist has never been bred to or followed any trade business or occupation whatsoever'. It is certified by an old college friend, Marcus Beresford—a barrister of three years' standing and son of one of the most powerful political figures in the country. On the morning of 4 May 1789, Tone attended the Court of Common Pleas in Christ Church Lane and took the oaths of adjuration and allegiance as set down by acts of 1704, 1710 and 1766, designed 'to prevent the further growth of popery'.[14]

At the centre of Irish law were the Four Courts in Christ Church Lane. It was a narrow street in the Liberties, close to the Cornmarket and Tholsel, Dublin's town hall—a massive seventeenth-century building in Skinners Row, where quarter sessions also were held. The Law Courts area was a scene of incredible bustle, particularly in term time, during sessions and on market days. It was also the area where the city's jewellers, gold- and silversmiths had their shops. In 1789, however, the Law Courts were a sorry sight. Work had already started on Gandon's showpiece, the Four Courts on Inns Quay—still today the most breathtaking remnant of Georgian

Dublin—and plans were envisaged for their opening in 1793. In the meantime the old courts were falling into disrepair and had become desperately overcrowded.

The new barrister would have attended the Law Courts regularly, for this was where all legal contacts were made, not least with 'messieurs the attorneys', who introduced him to potential clients. The entrance hall was a general social concourse. In addition to the barristers and attorneys, laymen on business trips to town would call in, as did those seeking all manner of political gossip. Booksellers, fruit vendors, flirtatious young ladies setting their caps at the junior bar—for a counsellor was considered quite a catch—and a general throng of the Dublin populace made up the remainder of those milling about. The hall itself was long and narrow and dominated by an octangular cupola. The entrance was through a door in a gloomy passage, ten feet below ground level, commonly referred to as 'Hell' because of the carved image of the devil dominating its entrance. However, 'Hell' opened into Christ Church Yard, home of the city's toyshops, firework shops, as well as its taverns, snuggeries and 'lodgings for single clerical men'. This was where children were taken for treats, where clerics conversed and counsellors drank claret and argued with the attorneys.[15]

Once inside the hall of the Law Courts, judges sitting in the Courts of Exchequer, Chancery, Common Pleas and King's Bench could be seen simultaneously, for no doors separated the courts from the general mêlée in the hall. Unlike their English counterparts, Irish barristers practised in all four courts, and the frequent need to dash between courts in mid-session added to the general confusion of the place. The same laws operated in England and Ireland, and legal precedent cited was more often English than Irish. But the Irish courts were popular theatres, witnesses and defendants alike entering into battles of wit with counsel, and crowds cheering on rival barristers. Some of Tone's friends, notably Bushe, and the colourful Tom Gould, attracted huge audiences. English appointees to Irish legal office found such noisy scenes undignified.[16] The different nature of offences in Ireland also contributed to the level of noisy popular participation. Outside Dublin, many offenders were sturdy peasants rather than hardened criminals, in court for 'insurrectionary' or agrarian crimes. Such defendants knew the value of a clean suit and shirt on the day of the trial, and many were acquitted because of their apparent respectability. They knew too how to value legal counsel, and a barrister might be forced to refund his fee if a plea was unsuccessful.[17]

The bar was hard-living and ostentatious and plunged many of its members, even the most successful, into financial ruin. Flights of flowery oratory were as much valued as legal knowledge and 'truth and nature were too frequently sacrificed to effect'. Duels were commonplace, and in the admittedly arid post-Union years, lawyers reflected nostalgically back on 'the morning of whiskey, the noon of duelling, and the nights of claret', which characterised the Irish legal system at the end of the eighteenth century.[18]

But it was the political corruption of the Irish bar of which Tone and many others complained most. The bar and the judiciary were increasingly used to provide places for government supporters after 1782–3. Then 'a class of persons without legal qualifications, had pushed themselves into business by the mere force of vulgar, bustling activity, which would not be tolerated at present'. Thus reflected Tone's old friend Bushe in 1826, after he had himself reached the bench.[19] The Union of 1801 had improved the quality of the bar by removing the dead weight of placemen'for which it was so attacked in the 1780s and 1790s. Before the Union progress at the bar was almost entirely dependent on political connection, to an extent unparalleled in England. Of the 33 judges appointed to the Irish bench between 1760 and 1800, 30 sat in the House of Commons, 19 belonged to those landed families who had controlled Irish political life for much of the century, and others owed their elevation to the favour of the same families. Not all were slavish government supporters, though one of the judges on Tone's first circuit (Alexander Crookshank) most certainly was. But Tone was soon to discover that the favours of the parliamentary opposition were likewise in the gift of a small clique of landed families, and his experience at the bar was to give added edge to the term 'aristocracy', dislike for which was the incubator of his republicanism. He noted with disgust the number of mediocre lawyers attaining high office and the mental enfeeblement induced in the junior bar by such dependence on political favours for professional advancement.[20]

Nor were his criticisms as jaundiced as Frank MacDermot suggests.[21] They were voiced by many others. Even George Knox, with all his political connections, found 'the competition at the bar...formidable. It is filled with protégés from all the great interests, besides a number of adventurers, to whom I must yield the superiority in talents and knowledge', he complained to Lord Abercorn.[22] Sheil remembered the peculiar head-wagging tendency of his fellow barristers in court, as they feigned approval for every word from the bench.[23] Lord Earlsfort (John Scott, the future Lord Clonmell, Chief Justice of the King's Bench) was indeed 'ignorant' and 'corrupt'—as Tone described him in his first year at the bar. Earlsfort was notorious for his naked ambition and his personal vindictiveness towards defendants. A celebrated case in 1789–90, in

which he relentlessly pursued the editor of the *Dublin Evening Post*
for libel, shocked others besides Tone and deeply influenced the
latter's verdict on the corruption of the Irish bar. John Egan, another
of Tone's targets, had no talent but a political seat, and Bushe felt he
would not have earned half a crown a year as a barrister after the
Union. Michael Smith—shortly to become Baron of the Exchequer,
and one of the most distinguished members of the bar—Tone
allowed had considerable merit.[24]

In his early assessment of how the leading figures of the Irish bar
had attained such heights Tone reserved most space for John
Fitzgibbon, future Earl of Clare, Lord Chancellor, and the most
powerful legal figure in the country. Son of a former Catholic,
Fitzgibbon had already had a distinguished legal and political career,
acquiring all the right political connections, when he was plucked
from the outer bar to the Attorney-Generalship in 1783. The political
connection which had won him such rapid promotion was his sister's
marriage into the powerful Beresford family—undeniably one of the
most important political-interest groups in late eighteenth-century
Ireland. They dominated the governing process; every English Lord
Lieutenant, bar one (Fitzwilliam), accepted the need to placate them
as part of the natural order of things, and they were credited with
bringing about the downfall of Fitzwilliam for his blatant insensi-
tivity to such long-accepted conventions. Fitzgibbon did have
considerable legal talent—which Tone conceded. His elevation to
the Lord Chancellorship in 1789, just as Tone was starting out on his
legal career, was widely acclaimed, not only because he was the first
Irishman to fill the post in that century, but also because of his
reputation for efficiency. It was a quality which many hoped would
end the interminable proceedings in the Chancery courts, where vast
fortunes were made and lost and litigants on both sides impoverished
by the legal fees incurred. In this expectation they were not
disappointed, and Tone himself makes no complaint about the
conduct of his father's case in Chancery in December 1789 which he
lost so disastrously. Fitzgibbon is a much-hated figure in Irish
history, best remembered as a violent defender of the Protestant
interest and the English connection, a virulent anti-Catholic and
prime mover of the Union. But even his detractors gave him credit
for legal knowledge, and a personal rectitude which revealed itself in
some remarkable instances of clemency towards the United Irish
leaders in the 1790s. Nor should it diminish the merit of such actions
to recognise that this was Fitzgibbon acting in his most characteristic
role as defender of the Ascendancy, even of its wayfaring members.
His stand on Ascendancy principles was outmoded in the 1790s; but
he was far from being a government slave, and Tone always gave

him credit for consistency in his principles, however much he abhorred them.[25]

But it was Fitzgibbon's tendency to let virulent personal animosity cloud his judgement which Tone noticed most. With such a man at the head of the legal profession, there could be little hope of a career open to talent. 'Fitzgibbon's want of temper and undoubted partiality', wrote Tone in his journal for 21 June 1789, 'will let in his resentments and his affections to bias his decision'.[26] The most famous case of this was the Lord Chancellor's dispute with the barrister John Philpot Curran, leading opposition MP and later friend to the radicals. The war between the two was waged in the courts, in Parliament and in a celebrated duel, and kept Curran from the most lucrative Chancery cases.[27] All of which was most unfortunate for Tone, for Fitzgibbon was also Matilda's cousin. He and Tone would have met at the Witherington house and been on nodding terms in the hall of the Four Courts. Fitzgibbon took family ties seriously and in different circumstances might have afforded Tone a powerful legal and political connection. That no such help was forthcoming suggests that Fitzgibbon shared the Witheringtons' dislike for their son-in-law, and though blood ties might explain the clemency with which Tone was treated in 1794–5, they also explain the unusual attention paid by Fitzgibbon to Tone's developing radicalism. The two men were obsessed with each other, as worthy enemies always are.

Tone's early fragmentary notes on the Irish bar, however, suggest not so much disillusionment—that came retrospectively—as an ambitious young barrister analysing the means by which others had reached the top: Tone was nothing if not ambitious. So considerable were the dignities and rewards attaching to the profession that 'the highest families in the kingdom rushed to share them'.[28] The very title 'counsellor' commanded instant respect. But rewards did not come automatically. The bar was considerably overstocked with aspirants, with an estimated 711 barristers practising in Ireland in 1793, against only 604 for the whole of England.[29] Ruin, or at best mediocrity attended many. Without the right connections one was nobody. Tone's very nature needed success and acclaim, and in the legal profession the cards were stacked against him.

The main source of income for most barristers was the twice-yearly circuits, and Tone duly left Dublin on his first circuit in July 1789. He had—as was usual at the time—chosen his home circuit, that of Leinster. But although he could scarcely have done otherwise, it was an unfortunate choice; the closest to Dublin, it was therefore the most popular and attracted many of the great legal names of the day.

The first circuit would have taken him to Wicklow (23 July), Wexford (27th), Kilkenny (1 August), Carlow (7th), his home county, Kildare (11th), Queen's County (14th), King's County (19th). It was a gruelling timetable, in an unusually wet summer, and a more experienced barrister left Dublin for circuit duty with a heavy heart, anticipating the 'useless expense, and discomfort in a thousand forms.'[30]

Earlier in the century the entry into an assize town by the judges, barristers, attorneys and witnesses, in a great 'legal caravan', was an occasion of great pomp. Much of the extravaganza had gone by the end of the century. But those attending the circuit judges were showered with attention by the country people. Waiters, landlords and coachmen would bow and scrape, and 'country belles receive them with their choicest smirks'—many a struggling barrister falling foul of the attorneys for paying insufficient attention to their daughters. The young barristers' livelihood depended upon the attorneys putting clients their way, and Tone admits that part of the reason for his own lack of success was his failure to curry favour with them.[31]

Yet Tone did rather well on his first circuit and there is a feeling of importance in his description to Sharkey of the specially crested bridle which he had used on the occasion—not for Tone 'the modern degeneracy of slinking into a circuit-town, in the corner of the Dublin mail', so much criticised by Curran.[32] In truth he could not have afforded the coach fares, and the horse was borrowed. But he nearly cleared his expenses on his first circuit—a flying start, since the main expense was in one's first year of practice.[33] He was already a popular figure with his fellow barristers and showed great promise. Thomas Prior (an undergraduate at Trinity in 1789, at a time when Tone was still frequenting the Historical Society), remembered him as 'a young lawyer in great estimation...highly esteemed for his moral qualities'. But Jonah Barrington, who was on the same circuit as Tone, thought his early promise overrated. 'He was not worldly enough, nor had he sufficient common sense for his guidance'[34]

Though written with hindsight, this was probably a fair assessment of Tone's career as a barrister. He had embarked on that career with all the handicaps fledgling barristers were warned to avoid. He had no connections and no private money to see him through the many years before the law would yield an income, and, in a profession where patience and physical stamina were needed for the endless dull slogging required to succeed, he had neither. His voice was too weak, his temperament too emotional for the expert pleader, and worst of all he had a wife and family to support. What was needed was staying power; sheer perseverance often raised those without talent to the highest positions. But Tone was in a hurry. He would have seen other, perhaps more senior, barristers mocked for their lack of success. Judges and politicans were merciless in this respect and the not entirely accurate description of Tone himself 'strutting briefless in the hall of the Four Courts', was to become a damning catch-phrase in the mouths of his detractors.[35]

The amount of time and work required before one started to earn a living in the law was proverbial. It took William Saurin—future Attorney-General and Chief Justice of the King's Bench—thirteen years before he got anywhere. Barry Yelverton, Isaac Corry, Curran (to mention but a few) had similar experiences. Even the right connections did not ensure success, and the early failures of the future Lord Camden were such that all his early earnings went on horse-flesh, as one nag after another died under him on circuit. Such stories were common in legal circles, and Tone's earliest journal entries show a painful awareness of their truth. Reflecting in 1790 on the downward swing of the Tone family fortunes, he noted how long it had taken even men as eminent as Sir Michael Smith and Judge Downes to make a living at the bar.[36] His search for some additional channel of income starts shortly after this and was an important reason for his move into political journalism.

III

This desperate need for a regular income was brought about by his father's bankruptcy. In December 1789 Peter Tone lost all his property after the judgement in a lengthy dispute with his brother went against him. On what terms Jonathan Tone held the family lands in Kildare, from the time of his father's death in 1766 until Peter gave up his business in Dublin, we do not know. But Tone considered them rightfully his uncle's and in several passages omitted from the published *Life* was highly critical of his father.[37] Jonathan in fact appears to have been the elder by two years, which might explain the conflict over who was rightful heir. He was a likeable though hapless man, with no financial acumen whatsoever. He was always borrowing, he neglected the lands in Kildare and failed to fulfil whatever terms he had made with Peter about their occupancy. Accordingly Peter distrained for rent and had his brother thrown into debtors' prison at Naas for non-payment. Conditions for debtors in prison were very often worse than for ordinary criminals. Jonathan suffered considerably and under duress secured the terms of his release. Peter would pay his debts if Jonathan returned the lands and left the country. Jonathan agreed and sailed from Ireland in 1785 to take up a new career in the East India Company. On board ship he borrowed £5 from a young man destined to become Tone's closest friend, Thomas Russell. From Liverpool Jonathan wrote asking Peter to honour this new debt, which Peter agreed to do, but issued a stern warning that he would pay no further bills.[38]

Jonathan did well in India, returning with a commission as lieutenant in the Grenadiers of the 22nd Regiment. He cut a romantic military figure, with which Tone clearly identified. Certainly from what we know of him, Jonathan was never cut out to be a farmer, but did well in active service. Tone resembled the uncle more than the father, and in the dispute between the two he thought his father 'undoubtedly in the wrong'. Although Tone always speaks of his father in terms of filial respect, there are hints throughout of strained relations. In contrast he remained on good terms with his uncle, even after the 1789 decision. We find him watching with concern over Jonathan's last illness in 1792, and he was the only member of Peter Tone's family mentioned among the beneficiaries of Jonathan's will.[39]

In 1789 Tone 'obstinately refused to take any part [in the dispute], not thinking it decent to interfere where the parties were so nearly allied to me'.[40] It may be that his father was pushing him to plead the case personally and in the end he appears to have agreed. He wrote jocularly to Sharkey, 'I have been drafting *Chancery pleadings*! Think of that Master Brooke.'[41] For a novice, with but one circuit behind him, it was indeed something which would surprise his friend. He was technically qualified to plead Chancery cases. But the Court of Chancery was a minefield for the inexperienced barrister. A silk gown was almost a prerequisite for getting the case heard, the good will of the Lord Chancellor for its success. Knowledge of the Chancellor's displeasure might destroy for good a barrister's opportunities for employment in this most lucrative field of the law, and since the Lord Chancellor also had the power to bring lawyers from the outer to the inner bar as King's Counsellors, Tone acted unwisely in exposing his ignorance before his wife's critical kinsman.[42]

The case came on in Michaelmas term, Fitzgibbon's second as Lord Chancellor. It opened on 6 November with the ceremonial procession from the Chancellor's house in Ely Place, just east of St. Stephen's Green, to the Four Courts. Nearby in College Green a mock cavalcade set off simultaneously, pursued by rag women, apple women, basket boys and porters, offering enormous sums in bail for make-believe defendants. Fitzgibbon had opened his Chancellorship with orders for extensive alterations and the decoration of the Court of Chancery—a visible token of the new régime which hoped to dispose of tedious Chancery cases in one term instead of the normal three, and make justice speedier and less costly.[43]

Peter Tone, however, was not to be among the beneficiaries of the new broom. Jonathan, being in 'actual possession' of the lands in Kildare, won the case. Tone tried to save what little was left to his father, investing much of what remained of Fanning's £500 in the process. In July Peter Tone had assigned two properties, in Stafford Street and Summer Hill, to his son, for payments of £140 and £151. 11s. 8d. respectively. The former sum was nearly 40 per cent in excess of the value of the property and we can assume that the payment was a temporary expedient by Tone to help his father financially. But to no avail. The two properties were sold off within the next nine months, 'much under their value, to men who took advantage of our necessities as is always the case'—one of the buyers was Patrick Byrne, Tone's future publisher.[44] It would have taken the entire proceeds to pay the legal costs, and Peter Tone was destroyed financially. He secured a small post with the Paving Board shortly after the disaster, which kept him in a moderate living till his death in 1805. The affair jaundiced Tone's relations with his father. 'I had not even the satisfaction to see that my Father was content with the efforts I made on his behalf, though they were in fact far beyond my abilities; but I have always observed that money transactions are fatal to friendship, and even to natural affection.'[45]

The Witherington-Fanning lifeline was also removed that year, because of a quarrel with Matilda's brother Edward, in which he, according to Tone, was the aggressor. As old Fanning's affection grew for his granddaughter—indeed even for Tone himself, 'notwithstanding my irregular introduction into the family'—Edward 'contrived by a thousand indirect means to sow feuds and dissensions between us',[46] almost striking Matilda one day when he met her in the street. William was staying with Matilda while Tone was in the country—almost certainly on his third circuit. He demanded an apology from the brother and threatened a duel if it was not forthcoming. By all accounts Edward Witherington was a spineless character. Not only did he deliver the required apology, dictated to him by William, but meekly accepted such abuse from William as Tone felt 'no officer, or gentleman ought to have submitted to'. There was still some chance of a reconciliation when the matter was raised in a chance encounter between Tone and Edward shortly afterwards. But Edward would not recant and honour and pride dictated a complete rupture. We do not know the cause of the quarrel, and whilst there does seem to have been some truth in Tone's suggestion that it was a ploy to cut Matilda out of any legacy from the aged grandfather, there was considerable inflexibility on both sides. The Revd Mr Fanning died shortly afterwards. Tone was called in for the reading of the will and suffered the indignity and disappointment of seeing Matilda passed over. The incident still pained Matilda in 1826, and was left out of the published *Life*.[47]

By 1790 the misfortunes on both sides of the family had combined to create the conditions for Tone's premature launch into politics. Many who were admitted to the Irish bar viewed it primarily as a springboard to a career in politics, and a number from origins more humble than Tone's had raised themselves to political eminence. But the acquisition of the necessary connections and patronage for a career in conventional politics took time. Time was something Tone did not have. He was in a hurry, and the rapid growth of radicalism in the wake of the French Revolution instantly opened up a career in unconventional politics, ideally suited to his talents and temperament.

II

POLITICS
(1790–1791)

5
Whig

The year 1789 was a turning-point in Irish politics, not because of the French Revolution—its dramatic impact on Ireland came later—but because it saw the emergence of something like an Irish parliamentary opposition. Opposition to government had hiterto been an affair of individuals and interest groups—the so-called 'Patriot' party not-withstanding. Politics in practice were little more than 'a competition between a few great families' for the spoils available, and even after 1782 governments continued to be able to buy off opposition with places.[1] This was the Protestant Ascendancy proper, 'a narrow social and political élite', in Anthony Malcomson's now standard definition, 'defined along social and political, rather than ethnic lines...comprising those who themselves sat in the Irish Parliament or who exercised significant influence over the return of 300 members to the House of Commons'.[2] It was recognition of this truth—that opposition and government men were alike part of one privileged oligarchy—which turned Tone away from conventional politics. But it was a home truth which was concealed for some time by the vituperative attack of government supporters on their opponents, and by the nationalistic gloss given to the campaign against increasing executive influence. The conflict between opposition Whigs and government acquired a personal vindictiveness which pulled the press, the courts and the Dublin populace into the affray. Given Tone's personal ambitions, his circle of friends, and his participation in a highly politicised profession, his involvement was predictable.

The pinnacle of Patriot and Volunteering achievement had been the so-called 'constitution' of 1782. It declared the independence of the Irish Parliament and denied the right of the English Parliament to legislate for Ireland. By leaving the executive sufficient power to dictate its will to the Irish Parliament, however, the settlement proved a grossly defective answer to the problems besetting Anglo-Irish constitutional relations. Over the next two decades crown (or executive) influence increased in the supposedly independent Irish Parliament while it was declining at Westminster itself. It was the only way an executive responsible to London could carry its business through Parliament. Successive administrations needed the support of the great family connections to manage Parliament effectively, since some 214 of the 300 parliamentary seats were controlled by one or two individuals or a tiny clique. After 1782 the gap widened between the Irish executive (representing England's interests *in situ*) and the Irish Parliament. 'Management' of Parliament through pensions, peerages and patronage became more difficult and more costly. In coming years, when unanswered demands for parliamentary reform and Catholic emancipation were alienating many from conventional politics altogether, the quest for responsible government remained the touchstone of parliamentary 'patriotism'.[3] Government and opposition Whigs played a cat-and-mouse game on Ascendancy rules and old issues as the country drifted into revolution.

I

The relative political calm of the late 1780s was broken dramatically in the winter of 1788–9 by news of George III's 'insanity'. The crisis which developed over the next few months convinced Pitt that Union alone would preserve the connection. The dispute was not who would be regent—the Prince of Wales was the natural choice—but when and how he would assume power. Because of the Prince's friendship with the Foxite Whigs and his antagonism towards his father, Pitt's ministry thought a regency bill would play for time until the King recovered. The English Whigs, however, scenting a chance at office under their friend the Prince, called for a regency by address and the corresponding assumption of full regal powers. These expectations communicated themselves to their relatives and allies in the Irish Parliament, and for a time there was a risk that the Prince would assume full regal powers in Ireland but not in England. The possibility of this resulted in a remarkable scuttling of support away from the Dublin government. The 'four great rats', the powerful borough patrons Leinster, Ponsonby, Shannon and Loftus—all then in office—deserted to the opposition and many others became lukewarm. Only Fitzgibbon stood fast in his support for the government, and warned that those who proposed an independent Irish crown were proposing separation.[4] Neither Pitt nor the King ever forgot Fitzgibbon for his steadfastness during the crisis, just as they never forgot those who had voted in opposition.

Yet Irish politicians in the eighteenth century had traditionally adhered to the constitutional fiction of separate crowns for Ireland and England, even though held by the same person. For Ireland to follow England's line on the regency would, claimed Grattan, be 'injurious to your independence' and 'deprive the Monarchy of Ireland of his authority'.[5] The 1782 'constitution' accordingly became the rallying point for the diverse group taking the Whig line. Tempers were frayed after several late-night sittings. The address inviting the Prince to assume full powers as Regent of Ireland was voted. But the Lord Lieutenant refused to transmit it and continued in office, despite parliamentary censure. It was a classic example of how empty was the independence of the Irish Parliament under the 1782 constitution, when the executive could continue to operate in defiance of it. A delegation of leading government opponents set off to deliver the address to the Prince in person. But scarcely had they reached Holyhead when news of the King's recovery came through, and the ensuing audience with the Prince in London was deeply embarrassing. Tone at this stage was not yet the young Whig careerist he was to become later in 1789, and could appreciate Fitzgibbon's maliciously humorous depiction of the delegation as a troupe of travelling players, with their retinue of monkeys, bears and tricksters.[6]

This triumphing in the government camp continued for years afterwards. The press echoed with headlines about 'turn-tail rats', 'aristocratic combination[s]', 'faction[s]' and accusations that the stand on 1782 and Ireland's parliamentary independence disguised personal careerism. Certainly the nakedly ambitious role of the Ponsonby–Shannon faction compromised men like Grattan, and he was never allowed to forget it.[7] The main outcome of the affair, however, was to unite the shifting sands of Irish opposition, forced together by the awful truth that there was now no chance of office while Pitt remained Prime Minister and George III King. The arrival on 5 January 1790 of a new Lord Lieutenant, in the person of the young John Fane, 10th Earl of Westmorland, restored some kind of *modus vivendi* with Dublin Castle. But the leading culprits, the Ponsonbys, Shannons and Leinsters, were out for good and a potentially formidable opposition arose led by the powerful political combinations on which the Castle had once relied.

That opposition emerged from the crisis with a party label—the Irish Whigs—a programme, and an organisation based on a number of Whig Clubs—the first of which was established in Dublin on 26 June 1789. Its membership presented an impressive array of the leading political families in the country and its 'Resolutions and Declarations', issued on 19 August, were the basis for the new party's programme. A month after the fall of the Bastille, they seem strangely quaint. Tracing their lineage back to the constitution of 1688 as 're-established in Ireland in 1782', the Irish Whigs proclaimed '"the King of Ireland and the Lords and Commons thereof"...the only legislature of this realm'. Any hint of separatism is avoided by a declaration of support for 'our connection with Great Britain' and frequent references to the 'King of Ireland' and 'the Imperial Crown in this Realm', as if the two things were different.[8]

The programme was the traditional Whig one of combating 'undue [crown–executive] influence' through demands for place and pension bills, the disqualification of revenue officers from serving in Parliament, and the abolition of that other recently created source of government corruption, 'the extravagant, ineffectual and unconstitutional police of the city of Dublin'. The Police Act of 1786 was an answer to the very real problems of growing crime in the metropolis. But it also had political motives and sought to undermine the position of the Volunteers. Moreover, since 7 aldermen acting as Police Commissioners had the power to appoint 700 constables, it was seen by the Whigs as a new source of government patronage and a means of increasing executive control over Dublin politics.[9] Despite intermittent references to the 'sacred rights of the people', the Whig Club was concerned only with the internal reform of Parliament, and parliamentary reform in its traditional sense of extending the franchise and regulating electoral practices was not taken up as an opposition measure until 1793. By that stage the Whigs had already lost a base of popular support in the country.[10]

II

Such Whiggish obsessions were the subject of Tone's first political scribblings.[11] But it was another, related case—then going through the Dublin courts—which particularly attracted his attention. This was the case of John Magee, editor of the racy and scurrilous pro-Whig newspaper, the *Dublin Evening Post*, who was sued for libel by the manager of the Theatre Royal and the editor of the rival *Freeman's Journal*, Francis Higgins. The case came up in June 1789 before Lord Chief Justice Earlsfort (shortly to be elevated as Lord Clonmell), who set such a ridiculously high bail that Magee languished in prison for the next six months, prompting Tone's impatient outburst against the biased judge. The case was tried just before Christmas amidst riotous scenes both at the Four Courts and at Earlsfort's country residence. Magee was found guilty, but his case was taken up by the Whigs in Parliament, where, to a packed public gallery (now frequented by Tone), they argued effectively against Earlsfort's conduct of the case.[12]

Tone's admiration for the Whigs had been growing throughout 1789.[13] He looked back on this early attachment with some embarrassment: 'I was very far from entirely approving the system of the Whig clubs and much less their principles and motives; yet seeing them at the time the best constituted political body which the country afforded, and agreeing with most of their positions, tho' my own private opinions went infinitely further, I thought I could venture on their defence [his pamphlet on the 1789 parliamentary session] without violating my own consistency'.[14] This claim to more advanced ideas than those of Whiggery is highly debatable— even if there are hints of some very un-Whiggish opinions in this his first pamphlet. The Whigs in fact were his first instructors. The atmosphere of 1789–90 in Dublin was electric, as the aggressive new Whig machinery mobilised for the 1790 election, and in a landslide victory they snatched the city from the government for the first time since the mid-century.

Much of the excitement was generated by the interplay between events inside and outside Parliament. The last session of the old Parliament had been a heated one, opening with the regency debate, moving through the opposition's first attempts to see place, pension and responsibility bills passed, to the turbulent hearings of a disputed mayoral election and the Magee case. Virulent personal abuse was exchanged across the floor of the House of Commons and the whole issue of executive power and the nature of the connection with England was aired in a way that sparked off Tone's train of thought as he listened from the public gallery. The gallery of the Irish House of Commons had recently been altered to accommodate some 280 persons, and afforded an unrestricted view over the entire chamber. It was not cleared for divisions as in the English House, and the intensely Whig sentiments of the public attending in the spring of 1790 so disturbed the Speaker that he ordered it cleared during the hearing of Magee's case.[15]

It was during this session that Tone heard the famous speech of Sir Laurence Parsons, which he later claimed had been one of the formative influences on his own republicanism.[16] A disciple of Flood, Parsons had pursued a fiercely independent line since he entered Parliament in 1782 and was a particular critic of corruption in government. Tone thought him 'one of the very, very few honest men in the Irish House of Commons'. He had become acquainted with Parsons in the College Historical Society towards the end of 1789, at a time when Parsons's parliamentary star was rising rapidly. He remained independent on the regency issue, underscoring the naked party ambitions of the opposition by pointing to the sheer unconstitutionality of their actions. He never joined the Whig Club and objected in principle to an organised opposition. His speeches were devoid of empty party rhetoric and carried considerable weight. At the close of the 1789–90 session—whose debates had indeed uncovered the extent of increased government corruption since 1782—he made a devastating attack on the whole system of privilege in Ireland and appealed for serious consideration to be given to

popular demands for reform. On 1 February 1790, at the close of
a debate on a motion to create yet more government offices, he
warned government that the failure to listen to the demands of the
people threatened the very connection itself. The corruption of the
Irish government since 1782 rendered the freedom they had won
then meaningless.

Two weeks later he returned to the attack with a devastating
speech on George Ponsonby's motion against pensions and places.
Ponsonby had spoken of government as 'a trust from the people' and
criticised ministers for abusing the King's confidence. But this was
normal opposition rhetoric and the Whigs were always careful to
avoid any imputation of treason by separating the King as a person
from the crown as executive power in the persons of his ministers.
But this was the very issue confronted by Parsons on 15 February.
He again warned of the dangers of alienating public opinion by so
corrupting Parliament as to prevent the passage of popular bills. 'The
people of this island are growing more enlightened every day, and
will soon...know and feel their power. Near four millions of people
in a most defensible country, ought, perhaps, to be courted, but
certainly ought not to be insulted with the petty, pilfering, jobbing,
corrupting tricks of every deputy of a deputy of an English minister
that is sent over here.' Dublin Castle deflected criticism by boasting
of Ireland's prosperity. Yet what was Ireland asked Parsons, 'but a
secondary kingdom? An inferior member of a great Empire, without
any movement or orbit of its own?...we are scarcely known beyond
the boundary of our shores. Who out of Ireland ever hears of Ireland?
What name have we among the nations of the earth? Who fears
us? Who respects us? Where are our ambassadors? Are we not a
mere cypher...? All these...sacrificed to the connection with
England.... A suburb to England, we are sunk in her shade. True,
we are an independent kingdom; we have an imperial crown distinct
from England; but it is a metaphysical distinction'. Ireland was still
governed by English ministers, and though the connection brought
great advantages with it, ministerial corruption was not one of them.
Such ministers were acting as if they ruled over an inferior people, an
unwise tendency, for the Irish 'have the feelings of men, they suffer
like men, and they may be found to resist like men'. They had
looked to 1782 to provide them with better government; their anger
would be great when they discovered they had been deceived. 'Let
ministers then beware of what conclusions they may teach the
people, if they teach them this, that the attainment of everything
short of separation will not attain for them good government....
Where, or when, or how is all this to end? Is the Minister of

England himself sure that he sees the end? Can he be sure that this system, which has been forming for the coercion of Ireland, may not ultimately cause the dissolution of the Empire?'[17]

Lecky thought these two speeches put forward ideals which were later taken up by the United Irishmen.[18] The claim is undeniable, seeing the deep impact they had on Tone. Yet Parsons was no revolutionary and he possessed that exaggerated notion of popular passions so common to his class. He did, however, sense a changing mood in Ireland and gave vent to a frustration at the traditional play of factional politics which ignored it. In his private journals Parsons admitted his own fear of embracing reform at the time. But he felt 'that things cannot remain long as they are, and that timely and radical change will prevent sudden and violent convulsion'.[19]

It was this heated parliamentary session and the public interest generated by it which was the occasion of Tone's first sortie into political pamphleteering. *A Review of the Conduct of Adminstration During the Last Session of Parliament* was dashed off by Tone before he left on the Lent circuit on 18 March 1790, and published by Byrne in the first week of April. It is an essay in political journalism, a rag-bag of the issues occupying Dublin at the time. 'To speak candidly of this performance', Tone admitted in 1796, 'it was barely above mediocrity, if it rose so high'[20] Even this was a generous assessment in someone normally so self-critical. The exaggerated and at times ridiculous imagery reveals none of the controlled argument and the background preparation of his Sandwich Islands memorials. Rather it transposes the atmosphere, preoccupations and language of the parliamentary session on to paper, including huge chunks from Grattan's speeches and the flowery language so in vogue in the Irish Parliament. Despite Tone's subsequent disclaimers, it is very much a party pamphlet. It applauds the public-spiritedness of the Whigs, identifying their cause with that of the people against a corrupt government, and ends with a volley trumpeting 1782 as having liberated Ireland 'from foreign usurpation'.[21]

It was as a party pamphlet that it was received at the time, the *Freeman's Journal* attacking the opposition 'habit of hiring pamphleteers' and singling out Tone's *A Review* as a prime example.[22] As a party pamphlet too it has been dismissed by modern writers. But this is too simple a view. That Tone was bandwagoning in search of some introduction into politics is as undeniable as it was natural for someone in his position and profession. Nor does he deny it. That he was utterly convinced of the justice of the opposition's case against government corruption is equally undeniable, and the bubbling enthusiasm and tone of naïve shock that government supporters could admit the increase in places and pensions lends credence to his claim to have written the pamphlet on 'honest principles'.[23]

Over half the work surveys the case against Magee with a competence and fluency which belies Tone's self-professed ignorance of the law and contrasts sharply with the amateurishness of the pamphlet's political sections. These are a jumble. But they are already creating questions which would become central to Tone's thinking in succeeding years. He does not go as far as Parsons in his discussion of the future of the connection with England, nor does he question the role of the King. But the confusion between the crown as person and the crown as government influence is glossed over less easily then in Whig rhetoric. That was the kind of humbug which the mature Tone could not tolerate, and it would soon go (even if he never entirely lost a sneaking respect for royalty). He also highlights the nonsense of Ireland's supposed independence when its revenue is totally at the disposal of English ministers. 'Not one Irishman concerned. . .unless, perhaps, the clerk who reckons out the guineas'. It was perhaps taking up Parsons's criticism of English ministers treating the Irish as inferiors. But Tone's native sensitivity on this issue needed little prompting.

More interestingly, there are the beginnings of an enquiry into the location of political power, which would be further developed in his unpublished writings of this period and emerge in a commitment to popular sovereignty even before the appearance of Paine's Rights of Man in 1791. Tone was a distiller of ideas rather than an original thinker. The example of America had given rise to demands for a more representative political system, particularly in Dissenting circles. His friend Peter Burrowes had already identified the people outside Parliament as the real focus of authority, in a forceful pamphlet published six years earlier (which Tone had clearly read)[24]— as had Parsons, in his speeches of February 1790. Although the intention of A Review was to convince the electorate to vote Whig in the forthcoming election, its final appeal was to 'the great body of the people, who have no suffrage. . .[to] come forward, and speak their determination'.

Tone's first pamphlet is very much a late Enlightenment document, in its classical references, its glorification of honour and public virtue, which it sees as being sapped by corruption, and in its faith in man's ability to improve his lot. But even this early, Tone is picking up the more revolutionary aspects in the various strands of eighteenth-century political thought. Locke had less influence on English thinking than once supposed and the profoundly revolutionary nature of his Two Treatises of Government was misinterpreted.

In Ireland, however, it was quite the reverse. The full implications of the contract theory were rehearsed in a celebrated pamphlet, *The case of Ireland Being Bound by Acts of Parliament in England, Stated*, published in 1698 by Locke's friend, William Molyneux.[25] Though putting the case of Ireland's Protestant Parliament, it spoke in terms of the Irish people and nation and was later used, not least by Tone himself, to justify separatism. Tone's writings reveal a total familiarity with Locke's arguments. However, when campaigning after 1791 for the restoration of political rights to the Catholics, he rejected Locke as being essentially undemocratic—Locke's doctrine of tacit consent and virtual representation binding future generations and all but denying popular participation in government after the initial 'contract'.[26] Given the importance of Locke in Irish political thought in the eighteenth century, Tone's rejection represents a break with contemporary political philosophy far more fundamental than that of the philosophical radicals in England, with whom Tone otherwise had much in common. It was a denial of the right of the past to bind future generations which would figure prominently in Paine's *Rights of Man*. But Tone found it first in Molyneux.

Interestingly, Tone's *A Review* sees government as a trust from the people. This was potentially more revolutionary than the idea of a contract between government and the governed since it assumed a one-sided agreement with ultimate power located in the people. Locke does discuss the concept of a trust,[27] but Tone seems to have taken it from elsewhere. It was central to seventeenth-century republican thought in England—Cromwell was one of Tone's heroes—and to eighteenth-century Rational Dissent, which deeply influenced Tone's developing thought. Indeed Joseph Priestley, its leading exponent, thought well of Tone's work.[28] Tone may not yet have been 'republican' in the Irish nationalist and separatist sense of the word, but he was certainly republican in its eighteenth-century reading.

Like Tone's own thinking, republicanism was an amalgam. From the seventeenth-century commonwealth tradition it took its dislike of overpowerful and corrupt officials; from the older classical republican tradition its promotion of virtue in public life; and from Rational Dissent its demand for an opening of public life to the middle classes and for religious toleration. But republicanism was not necessarily a revolutionary ideology. It sought to reform the existing system, not to overthrow it; the creation of a meritocracy, not a democracy, and an equality of opportunity, not of property.[29]

Tone had chosen well in the timing and content of his pamphlet. It was taken up by the Whigs as an election statement, reprinted in a shorter version and distributed by the newly created Northern Whig Club, and used to great effect in the Antrim and Down elections that year.[30] The Northern Whig Club was less aristocratic, more reformist in sympathy than its Dublin parent. It omitted from its foundation resolutions the proposal that the connection with Britain was 'sacred and inviolable', on the grounds of Britain's 'infamous' and 'ruinous' treatment of Ireland. It objected to 'the growing power of the crown and of the aristocracy', and preferred the term 'legal commonwealth' to 'limited monarchy', as more accurately reflecting the club's wish to establish 'the majesty of the people'. In an unusually tetchy letter to Lord Charlemont, the club's founder, its secretary—the Belfast Presbyterian Dr Alexander Haliday—rejected his friend's phrase 'the King's most excellent majesty' as 'hackneyed', 'productive of much slavish principle', and flying in the teeth of 'that better majesty of the people'. Haliday went on to deny any 'republican ideas'.[31] But such statements fed the growth of those ideas, and when forced to retreat from this rhetoric over the next few years, the Whigs disintegrated, having nothing else to offer but the old cry against executive influence. Moreover, they were fatally divided on Catholic emancipation and parliamentary reform, the two issues which alone offered any alternative to the growing pull of republicanism. It was on the Catholic issue that the Northern club encountered the heaviest attack from its Dublin parent, and a year later Haliday was among those whose misgivings about the Catholics delayed the formation of the Belfast Society of United Irishmen.

III

In 1790, however, Tone was enamoured of the Whigs and began to visualise a future in association with them. The pamphlet had brought him to the notice of their parliamentary leader, George Ponsonby, whose family headed the most powerful and most aristocratic political grouping in the Irish House of Commons. The contact was made through a fellow barrister, who aroused in Tone inflated expectations about his future. Nor were those disappointed in the short term, for he was engaged as counsel for the Ponsonby interests in a disputed election petition, brought by the outgoing member for Dungarvan in County Waterford.

Election petitions were a lucrative source of legal income and much coveted by the profession. Dungarvan—a small seaport, inhabited mainly by fishermen—was a household or potwalloping borough, in the gift of the Devonshire and Waterford (Beresford) interests. Chambre Brabazon Ponsonby and Tone's friend, Marcus Beresford, were returned for the two-member constituency—the latter with a slim majority secured through blatant exercise of his father's revenue patronage, whereby a host of revenue officials were supplied with 40s. freeholds for the occasion. Tone would soon become a fierce critic of such malpractice. But if his defence of it in 1790–1 caused him any qualms, he does not say so. The petition was laid before the House of Commons on 2 July 1790, but not considered until the following February, when the petitioners, the sitting members, their counsel and agents were called before the bar of the House to discuss the case. The decision in favour of Ponsonby and Beresford finally came through on 18 February 1791. Tone's disillusionment with the Whigs accordingly came later than suggested in his journal. He was paid the princely fee of £79. 12s. 6d. His detailed list of how it was spent gives a telling insight into his parlous financial state. Most of it went to repay small loans to friends, payments to his mother and sister, a subscription of 11s. 4d to the Catch Club and the purchase of stockings.[32] But he was also assured that other political business, if not indeed a parliamentary seat, would be put his way—which must surely have been behind the ease with which he allowed the degrading Witherington link to disintegrate.

Certainly his mind 'had now got a turn for politics'.[33] His notebooks for these months are full of flourishing signings of his own name. Yet his political jottings of that winter laid the ground for a less elevated view of Irish parliamentary politics. 'My idea of political sentiment in Ireland', he wrote, 'is that in the middling ranks and indeed in the spirit of the people is a great fund of it but stifled and suppressed as much by the expansive depravity and corruption of those who from rank and circumstances constitute the legislature. Whatever has been done has been by the *people* strictly speaking who have not often been wanting to themselves when informed of their interests by such men as Swift, Flood, Grattan etc. etc'.[34] And later we find a note added to his thoughts on the mooted war between England and Spain: 'nonsense of waiting for the interference of the legislature in cases where the spirit, wisdom and virtue of the people are of themselves sufficient'.[35] As published in the *Life*, these draft essays give the impression of a steady move that winter towards republicanism. In the manuscript journals, however, they are interspersed with continuing worries about his legal career and political references which show him still very much a Whig in principle.

The jottings about the spirit of the people seem to have been inspired by the support of the Dublin populace for the parliamentary opposition, rather than by any populist notion. Tone was opposed to social turmoil, but events such as the triumphal procession by the Dublin populace on 12 May 1790 to celebrate the return of Grattan and Lord Henry Fitzgerald in the Whig interest would have disguised the underlying mobocracy. The triumphal car of the victorious candidates was drawn through the streets by representatives of the Dublin Corporation and the 'working manufacturers' of the city, carrying banners proclaiming *'vox populi est vox Dei'*, 'Liberty', 'Magna Carta', 'Bill of Rights', banners supporting the various Whig causes, and two large green silk ones portraying Grattan and Fitzgerald as 'the agents of the people'. Like disgruntled political élites elsewhere in Europe, the Irish Whigs were enlisting the crowd in their cause and educating it in the process. But the other side of such joyous celebrations was the riots which they produced in the volatile world of the Dublin trades—already in a turmoil of combinations, strikes and depression in the silk industry. As usual, the butchers and tailors of the Liberties took opposite sides in the political campaigning, and faction fighting raged in the days leading up to the election. The night of the victory celebrations, the crowd turned its attention on the ill-fated police, its violence legitimised by Whig attacks on the institution. Three rioters were killed when police opened fire on them and the military were called in to quell the ensuing disturbances.[36]

At the height of such ill feeling against the police, the Board of Aldermen elected as Lord Mayor the unpopular government candidate, Alderman James—who had the misfortune also to be Police Commissioner. The city's Common Council, spurred on by two veteran demagogues in city politics—James Napper Tandy and John Binns—elected its own candidate, Alderman Howison, and issue was joined on the police connections of the opposing contender. The campaign on both sides became hysterical, the Common Council, according to the admittedly biased *Freeman's Journal*, spouting pure 'French anarchy'. The parliamentary opposition clashed with government on the issue, Curran and Ponsonby pleading the Dublin Commons's case before the Privy Council on 7 June. Fitzgibbon presided, and Curran used the rare opportunity of confronting his enemy outside his own court to deliver an unusually sarcastic speech. The decision in James's favour was as predictable as the mobilisation of the city politicians and the Whigs against it. Tandy became increasingly inflammatory and was seconded by a fellow Whig Club member and future United Irishman, Archibald Hamilton Rowan.

The Whig Club too joined in the fray, which was coloured by long-standing personal disputes. On 24 July Fitzgibbon made a caustically dismissive attack on the Club, describing its members as 'a horde of miscreant traitors professing peace but practising corruption' and as 'persons of the grossest ignorance'. The whole was prefaced by a brilliant piece of innuendo, the Whig Club being

dismissed as 'a porter club', its business confined to dining and
drinking sessions—which was partly true, for the business was
conducted entirely at weekly dinners in Derham's tavern. The press
took up the charge and had a field day, and the club felt obliged to
issue a 'Vindication'. It identified the Whig cause with that of the
people. In attacking it the Lord Chancellor had insulted the nation,
and when 'ministers of the crown...attack the rights of the people,
we shall always be forthcoming—uniting with our fellow subjects
in common defence and common danger'. Most of the document
belabours the legal case of the mayoral election, closing with a
reiteration of the Whig programme against places, pensions and the
Dublin police.[37]

Tone was on circuit when the 'Vindication' appeared. Party spirit
was riding high in the towns of the Leinster circuit. The Kildare
assizes opened at Athy on 3 August. Wogan Browne, a Whig Club
member and High Sheriff of Kildare, sent the 'Vindication' to the bar
room for approval by the attending barristers. Tone took it up
enthusiastically, but of 14 others present only 2—one of them his old
friend Peter Burrowes—supported his resolution: 'That the Leinster
Bar, in common with the Whig Club...felt the warmest indignation
and abhorrence of the late unconstitutional proceedings of the Privy
Council, in the election of Alderman James—proceedings no less
formidable to the liberties of the capital, than alarming to every city
in the kingdom, as forming part of a system subversive of their
franchises, whether established by custom, charter, or the statute
law of the land'. Thus far had Tone become obsessed with Irish
Whiggery! The incident shows that he had sufficient standing with
the outer bar to secure a hearing, and indeed to receive a written
response to his resolution—even if the lukewarm nature of the
response angered him. He had also assumed the mantle of Whig
apologist, and in October 1790 was still being singled out by
government press as 'the little counsellor who promised to write
essays *gratis*' for the Whig Club.[38]

IV

Early that summer Tone latched on to yet another of the controversies of the moment in his developing career as political pamphleteer. He had returned to the public gallery of the House of Commons
on 2 July 1790 to hear a special session on supplies for a threatened
war with Spain. Spain had seized several British merchant ships off
the North American coast at Nootka Sound. On 4 May 1790 a
general impressment of seamen had been ordered in Britain and
the implications for Ireland of a war were hotly debated in the Irish

press.[39] Tone contributed to the general discussion with his pamphlet. *Spanish War!: An Enquiry How Far Ireland is Bound, of right, to Embark on the Impending Contest on the Side of Great Britain.*

Tone later claimed that his *Spanish War!* 'advanced the question of separation, with scarcely any reserve much less disguise but the public mind was by no means so far advanced as I was, and my pamphlet made not the smallest impression'.[40] In fact the pamphlet says no more about separation than Parsons and many others were saying at the time, and protests from government supporters about its treasonable nature were as predictable as they were inaccurate. The debates in the Irish Parliament questioned what benefits Ireland could expect in return for her support in the war and objected to the trade disadvantages under which the country still suffered. Supplies of £200,000 were nevertheless voted, Ireland's and Britain's interests declared identical, and the automatic involvement of Ireland in England's wars went unquestioned.[41]

It was between this sitting on 3 July and the next on the 19th that Tone wrote his pamphlet and addressed it to the members of both Houses of Parliament, urging them to think again. From someone still trying to make a career in politics, *Spanish War!* was an outspoken and radical statement which flew in the face of current Whig policy.[42] It demonstrates well both Barrington's and the younger Plunket's assessments of Tone's character. Tone had little sense of caution and was pulled into republicanism by the implications of his written words, which, though set down at a time when he was not a separatist, nevertheless presented ideas otherwise only whispered in drawing rooms.

Spanish War! is Tone's first mature work as a political pamphleteer. As with his Sandwich Islands project, it was carefully researched. It is cogently and lucidly argued, and is devoid of the exaggerated rhetoric of his *A review*. It objects to the automatic entry of Ireland into England's wars on four grounds. Firstly, that of 'right': the Irish legislature as 'separate and independent' is not bound by a British act declaring war. Secondly, on the grounds of 'expediency': the quarrel is an English one, all the benefit accruing to England in the event of victory, Ireland receiving no recompense for lost trade, 'treasure spent', 'gallant sons fallen'. Thirdly, he confronts the 'moral obligation' claim: '*the good of the empire*, the honor of *the British flag*, and *the protection which England affords as*'. The word 'empire' he sees as a gloss for 'England', who 'would reap the entire profit', since Ireland would be fighting for rights to trade from which she was excluded.[43] On the topic of the honour of the national flag, Tone asks: 'where is the national flag of Ireland?. . .such a badge of inferiority, between the two kingdoms, is a serious grievance. Is the bold pride of patriotism nothing? Is the ardent spirit of independence nothing? Is national rank nothing?...We are compelled to skulk under the protection of England...contented to be the subaltern instrument in the hands of our artful and ambitious and politic sister'. As for 'gratitude for the protection which she affords us', look to her 'narrow jealousy' in not allowing us a navy, docks or arsenals. 'Have we, then, forgotten the memorable protection of the last war'—a sore point with all sides in Ireland, which had been denuded of troops for the American war and forced to raise the Volunteers as a substitute.

Most of Tone's arguments were irrefutable and would be raised by others during the French war after 1793. But any discussion of foreign policy and defence touched on the delicate nature of the interregnal connection. Irish politicians stayed well clear of such issues, accepting them as an English preserve. Tone was treading on dangerous ground, but he does not carry through his arguments to their natural conclusion—that the so-called crown of Ireland, distinct from that of England, was a fiction. He still speaks of the 'Crown of Ireland' and of 'our own King' as accepted facts, and the pamphlet is remarkable not so much for any republican undertones, as for its prickly sense of national identity which breaks away from the work's otherwise measured tones in a flourishing finale. Here there is a sense of the wastage war would inflict on Ireland's limited resources and a crusading call for her to look to her own needs, 'to foster and cherish a growing trade', 'cultivate and civilise a yet unpolished people', 'obliterate the impression of ancient religious feuds', and 'watch...the cradle of an infant Constitution', 'We should spurn the idea of moving, an humble satellite round any power, however great, and claim at once...our rank among the primary nations of the earth. Then should we have, what, under the present system, *we never shall see*, A NATIONAL FLAG, and spirit to maintain it. If we then fought and bled we should not feel the wound, when we turned our eyes to the Harp waving proudly over the ocean'. Take a stand now, he urges Parliament, by 'fixing the rank of your country among the nations of the earth'.[44]

The day after publication, Tone stood in Byrne's shop 'listening after my own reputation'. Sir Henry Cavendish entered, 'a notorious slave of the House of Commons', Tone wrote long after he had rejected the Irish Parliament altogether. Cavendish in fact was a founder member of the Whig Club. He threw Tone's pamphlet on the counter, and fumed, '*Mr Byrne, if the author of that work is serious, he ought to be hanged*'. The next caller predicted soaring inflating should the principles of the 'abominable work' spread. He was a bishop, 'an English doctor of divinity, with five or six thousand a

year, *laboriously* earned in the church'—thereby uniting two of
Tone's greatest bugbears: unearned privilege and the appointment of
Englishmen to plum Irish positions.[45] They were also common
themes in Swift, whom Tone was only then discovering.

The fact that men in prominent positions had bought and read
such a pamphlet within a day of publication, is a reflection of the
quick reputation which might be made from political pamphleteering. Tone had entered the field for purely careerist reasons, only
to emerge converted by his own arguments. He already showed
much aptitude for the genre, spotting a controversy and proving
adept at self-promotion. The *Spanish War!* is a shock-horror title at a
time when rumours of war were rife. Shock-horror too is the
preface, designed to lure the browser with the prospect of forbidden
fruit. It warns that 'cautious men' will find the ideas inside
'extraordinary' and 'too hardy', claims a degree of novelty, and
flatters the 'reason' and 'spirit' of prospective readers in assuming
their agreement with its conclusions.

The same promise of shock-horror is held out in Tone's letter
from a 'Liberty weaver' to one of the Dublin newspapers—a favourite promotion tactic of his, employed likewise for *Belmont Castle*.
The letter opens with the feigned shock of the weaver on reading
such 'high treason' and 'abominable heresy', then takes an ironic tone
as the 'poor weaver' sets about demolishing 'the prejudice of the
greater folk'. In practised hyperbole the weaver lists the miseries
suffered by the ordinary folk in the last war, and just as eighteenth-
century writers frequently used symbols of innocence to criticise
accepted values, Tone uses the political naïvety of the poor weaver to
question accepted arguments in favour of the English connection.
The letter also has a Panglossian ring in its absurd portrayals of cause
and effect.

> Now, to say that it is a *necessary consequence* of our connection with
> England is to say that we should be involved in every war *her
> Ministers* shall wage for her *pride*, or her *power*, or her *profit*, I hope
> and believe a most foul *calumny* upon that *connection*. Devoted to
> the connection, as I am, it would grieve me to the heart, to think
> that such a *curse* was to be the consequence of it. And, therefore, as
> an honest and loyal, though poor subject of his Majesty, I set
> out. . . with here solemnly disclaiming, as a most *abominable heresy*
> against his Crown and Government, the most *pernicious* and
> *dangerous* doctrine, that *Ireland* is to be involved in every war
> which it shall please the Minister of England to make; and that *our
> King* has not a *right* to make terms of peace and neutrality for us.

There is a self-conscious rejection of the élitist learning of the 'great
lawyers', some early signs of Tone's developing thought on the

unrepresentative nature of Parliament, a clear identification with
the problems of this family breadwinner, and the first signs of a
reverence for Swift's political writings.[46]

Spanish War!, however, did not make the splash Tone had every
right to expect it would, and he suspected Byrne of having suppressed the entire print run for fear of prosecution. Certainly some
such action appears to have been taken.[47] Even the *Freeman's Journal*,
ever watchful for a chance to pounce on Tone as the Whig Club
scribe, did not notice it. The Magee case was a living warning of
the perils facing the indiscreet printer. A Catholic bookseller in
particular had every reason to be cautious. The criticisms and premature fate of his pamphlet notwithstanding, Tone thought it 'a
good one', and he was right. But it was unrealistic to think that
England could tolerate the presence of enemy vessels in the ports of a
neutral Ireland, or to suggest that the King could act differently in
England and Ireland, when to do so would be so obviously against
English interests. On both issues Tone was simply carrying further
opinions already aired by others, any originality lying rather in his
uninhibited expression of what others thought but dared not express.
More than anything the pamphlet underscores the absurdity of the
nature of the connection after 1782, with two independent kingdoms
sharing a common monarch and expected to act together, when
more often than not their interests diverged. Although a full
recognition of the constitutional absurdity is not yet apparent, it is
so obvious in the pamphlet's conclusions that Tone could not fail to
recognise it.

6
Radical

It was in the process of forming a new and powerful friendship that Tone's ideas (and indeed personality) grew to maturity. In the public gallery of the Irish House of Commons during the July 1790 sittings, Tone met and befriended Thomas Russell. Several years his junior, Russell was a foil to Tone in every way. He was everything Tone was not. An officer on half-pay, he had recently seen active military service in India and had a commanding military presence, his huge dark eyes and thick black hair offset by fine, almost aristocratic features. His good looks and 'stately' bearing commanded attention from men and women alike. Even the order for his arrest in 1803 is complimentary: 'a tall, handsome man', of 'dark complexion, aquiline nose, large black eyes, with heavy eye-brows, good teeth, full-chested, walking generally fast and upright, and having a military appearance...speaking fluently, with a clear distinct voice, and having a good address'.[1] Mary Ann McCracken—an early feminist and one of the few women to have a significant impact on the United Irishmen—remembered Russell as: 'A model of manly beauty..., more than six feet high', 'majestic [in] stature' and 'martial in his gait and demeanour...the classic contour of his finely formed head, the expression of almost infantine sweetness which characterized his smile, and the benevolence that beamed in his fine countenance, seemed to mark him out as one, who was destined to be the ornament, grace and blessing of private life'.[2]

Deeply religious and introspective, Russell's seriousness and self-flagellation for his own failings prompted the friendly raillery of the more flippant and gregarious Tone. In contrast to the male companionship of Tone's education, Russell (youngest of five children by many years) had been educated at home by his father, a former clerical student turned soldier. Russell emerged with a good knowledge of the classics, science and modern languages, but most of all of scripture and morals—unlike Tone, whose knowledge of the Bible was so inadequate as to suggest that he had neglected scripture classes at Trinity as he did so many others.[3]

Russell's journals reveal a complex personality. After the publication of his *Life* in 1826, Tone was bitterly attacked by Russell's nephew for misrepresenting his friend as a womaniser and heavy drinker.[4] In fact both traits are well documented and Matilda was far more critical of Russell in these respects than was her husband.[5] Yet no one knew better than Tone the moral torture poor Russell went through because of human weaknesses which Tone accepted as natural. He was torn between a heightened sexuality (with frequent resort to prostitutes and casual partners), and such an idealisation of pure love that when he finally encountered the beautiful Eliza Goddard his difficulty in communicating that love was such that he lost her entirely. 'Such is man or at least such I am,' he wrote disconsolately after one of his casual encounters, 'so vicious, so imperfect, with wishes and desires for virtue and a firm belief in revelation and yet lapsing into vice on the slightest temptation. I do not improve.'[6] His drinking bouts, often with Tone as companion, occasioned the same soul-searching, and a visit to a Moravian settlement in County Antrim elicited an impressive journal entry on the Enlightenment dilemma of the conflict between reason and passion in human motivation. His passionate admiration for France was to crumble on the discovery of old-world corruption among her officials.[7]

Russell was much less worldly than Tone and his failure to take the most basic of financial precautions was a source of concern both to himself and his friends. It resulted in several incidences of foolhardy generosity which threw his sister and himself on the charity of others. 'I am much interested for this seemingly unfortunate young man, Russell', wrote Martha McTier, William Drennan's sister, in November 1793; 'he seems very poor, is very agreeable, very handsome and well informed and possess'd of most insinuating graceful manners—his dress betrays poverty and he associates with men every way below himself, on some of whom I fear he mostly lives'.[8] Quite apart from his own moral suffering, Russell's depth of sympathy for the lower orders gives a substance to his attack on the ruling classes which is not always evident in Tone. He was also one of the few United Irishmen to believe in the equality of the sexes, both in terms of mental ability and opportunity.[9] Never as fluent as Tone, he has left only one published pamphlet, a handful of newspaper articles, and a more substantial body of scribblings, journals and letters, so nearly illegible that many historians have simply ignored them. This, and a congenital inability to spell (there are even signs of dyslexia), was a further cause of teasing by his friends and family. His contribution to the development of Irish republican nationalism has been grossly underestimated. Only one full biography of him has ever been written, and that in Irish. Yet for a while the Dublin government regarded Russell as a more dangerous revolutionary than Tone. His journal reveals ideas complementary to Tone's, and frequently more advanced, and the two had an intellectual relationship little short of symbiotic.

Such was the many-sided character of the handsome twenty-two-year-old who was to become Tone's closest confidant for the remainder of his life. Tone's pet name for Russell was 'P.P. [parish priest] clerk of this parish'. It was a take-off on Swift's *Memoirs of P.P. Clerk of This Parish*—the story of a pious young man, led astray by pleasure and women—and gently mocked Russell's moral dilemma.[10] It was typical of their friendship, and Russell returned the compliment by calling Tone 'John Hutton', after a leading Dublin coachmaker of the day—a reminder of his family background in trade. But Russell suffered more from the raillery than Tone, and it was something Tone agonised about during his lonely exile in Paris, haunted by the recognition of how much Russell had meant to him.[11]

Russell's father—Lieutenant John Russell, a veteran of the battles of Dettingen and Fontenoy—held a position at the Royal Hospital in Kilmainham. His brother, Ambrose, a captain in the 52nd Regiment, who had fought in the American war, had been ordered to India in March 1783. Russell also enlisted as a volunteer in the regiment. The two Russells took part in the attack on Tipoo Sahib at Cannanore, where Thomas helped carry the wounded Lieutenant-Colonel Henry Barry—Tone's future patron—from the field. It was also during his Indian campaign that Russell established friendly links with the Knox family of Tyrone, through Colonel John Knox, George Knox's elder brother. It was as if he and Tone were destined to be friends.[12]

At the time of their first meeting, Russell was on half-pay of £28 per annum and living with his father at the Royal Hospital, after following in his father's footsteps with an abortive attempt to train as a minister in the Established Church. It was almost certainly the day of Fitzgibbon's attack on the Whig Club (24 July) that the two met. At first they argued about the Whigs, Tone, as he later claimed, having already lost faith in them. But judging from Tone's attempt to whip up support for the Whigs during the Kildare assizes in August, the two men's Whiggery was about equal. The dispute was of short duration. They dined together the following day and the friendship deepened over the next few weeks.

Thus began a friendship of unusual and moving intensity. Their journals speak almost with one voice, using the same code words, quotations and popular songs of the day, each written very much with the other in mind. 'You know how exactly our humours concurred,' wrote Tone from America five years later, 'and that particular style of conversation which we had framed for ourselves and which to us was so exquisitely pleasant; those strained quota-

tions, absurd phrases and extravagant sallies'.[13] In Paris in 1796 Tone
reflected on that friendship as:

> a circumstance which I took upon as one of the most fortunate of
> my life... There cannot be imagined a more perfect harmony, I
> may say identity, of sentiment, than exists between us; our regard
> for each other has never suffered a moment's relaxation from the
> hour of our first acquaintance, and I am sure it will continue to the
> end of our lives. I think the better of myself, for being the object of
> the esteem of such a man as Russell;... and if I am ever inclined to
> murmur at the difficulties wherewith I have so long struggled, I
> think on the inestimable treasure I possess in the affection of my
> wife, and the friendship of Russell, and I acknowledge that all my
> labours and sufferings are overpaid.[14]

I

Tone returned from the Kildare assizes to find Matilda distressed
after the dispute with her brother. It was not a pleasant summer to be
in Clarendon Street. Continuous rain made it one of the wettest in
memory. The war scare had filled Dublin with recruiting parties and
press-gangs were seizing men from ships on the quays. The
attendant crowd of prostitutes milling about College Green and
Dame Street produced a police clamp-down in August. The
demagoguery of the city politicians rumbled on, taking a different
turn in July, with Tandy and Rowan promoting a new breed of
Volunteers. Sporting national cockades and voicing threats against
the members of the Privy Council for their decision in the mayoral
election, these new Volunteers prompted considerable press hysteria
about 'French anarchy' and the consequences of whipping up the
rabble.[15]

Matilda's health continued to give cause for concern and she may
well have been pregnant with their second child, born the following
April. At length she was ordered to bathe in salt water. Tone hired a
little box of a house on the sea at Irishtown', where they spent the
remainder of the summer. Irishtown, situated to the south-east of the
city, offered magnificent views north towards Howth Head, the hills
of County Louth and in the distance the Mountains of Mourne.
It was not a fashionable resort and was rather too near the continuing
work on the Grand Canal and the squalid village of Ringsend. Here
shipping entered the busy port of Dublin, an area described by one
English visitor as one of those 'waterside excrescences comparable to
Rotherhithe and Wapping'. This may explain the availability of the
little house at such short notice, for at the end of the eighteenth
century bathing was popular and in summer the roads to the seaside

resorts would have been choked with carriages and holiday-makers.

Tone remembered these days at Irishtown as the happiest of his life. The cottage was frugally furnished, but the twelve chairs bought for its dining room speak for themselves, and the house was filled with friends and family. Russell spent most of August with them. His father and elder brother, John Russell, and William and Matthew Tone were regular visitors. Mary Tone was living permanently with them, possibly because of Matilda's ill health. Their time together was spent composing poems, verses and political squibs, conducting long political discussions during afternoon walks and rivalling each other in 'the humour, indigenous in the soil of Ireland'.[16] A booklet of their writings that summer has survived—'Fugitive Pieces by William Tone (and others) 1790'. It is a handwritten collection of ballads, ditties, elegies and poems, many sending up contemporary styles, much in the manner of *Belmont Castle*.[17]

Tone's account of this holiday provides a rare insight into the domestic life of the Tone family. There is an element of role differentiation: a refraining from 'ribaldry and indecency' in conversation as unsuitable to female company, and a suggestion that children are a female concern. On the other hand there is a surprising willingness in Tone to participate in domestic duties and a total involvement of the women in discussions, political and otherwise. 'I recall with transport the happy days we spent together during that period', Tone wrote later in his autobiography,

> the delicious dinners, in the preparation of which my wife, Russell and myself, were all engaged, the afternoon walks, the discussions we have had, as we lay stretched on the grass. . . . These were delicious days. The rich and great, who sit down every day to the monotony of a splendid entertainment, can form no idea of the happiness of our frugal meal, nor of the infinite pleasure we found in taking each his part in the preparation and attendance. My wife was the centre and the soul of all—I scarcely know which of us loved her the best. . . . In short, a more interesting society of individuals, connected by purer motives, and animated by a more ardent attachment and friendship for each other, cannot be imagined.

In September Russell finally got a posting to Belfast, and came to Irishtown '"*all clinquant, all in gold*"', as he reported to his friends. But he was not to be let off with such pomposity, feigned though it was, and Tone and Matilda set him to work in the kitchen, notwithstanding his 'very fine suit of laced regimentals.'[18]

Later reflections on the summer of 1790 show a new-found

happiness in the marriage, not evident in the earlier years. Tone admitted as much to Matilda some years later: 'You know I dote upon you with a degree of fervour and animation which at our earliest union I did not feel.' He was embarrassed by excessive sentiment and there is a conscious effort to avoid sentimentality in his letters to Matilda. It was an effort which at times went too far, and in this respect Matilda compared him unfavourably with Russell.[19] Matilda was emerging as someone of considerable strength of character. One poem in the family compilation, 'The Rose and the Myrtle, a Fable addressed to Mrs T.W. Tone', is of particular interest. It is a more serious piece than the others, a lengthy poem in rhyming couplets about a rose asserting its superiority over the flowerless myrtle. But your bloom will wither, replies the myrtle; mine as an evergreen will endure.

However, it was the blossoming of his friendship with Russell which Tone most remembered from that summer. 'Russell and I were inseparable, and, as our discussions were mostly political, and our sentiments agreed exactly, we extended our views and fortified each other in the opinions, to the propagation and establishment of which we have ever since been devoted.' The most important outcome of their long discussions was the formation of a political club during the following winter. Russell's very person had revived Tone's fascination with military life. Their summer retreat was mockingly named 'Garristown'. Tone's notebooks for the period are dotted with sketches and doodles of soldiers, shields and swords,[20] and their main preoccupation was a refinement of Tone's youthful Sandwich Isles project to suit the more favourable climate of 1790.

II

Tone's second memorandum on the Sandwich Islands was written at the height of the Nootka Sound crisis, when Britain's dispute with Spain over trading rights off the north-west coast of America brought the two powers to the brink of war.[21] Tone unearthed all the old notes from his London days and with Russell revised the original memorandum. The final product was sent to the Master of the Ordnance, the Duke of Richmond, on 20 September. It drew heavily on Cook's third voyage, pointing to the wealth of natural resources and the natural harbour facilities found on the island of Oaha.[22] Once again the main advantage of such a colony was seen as strategic rather than commercial, and the buccaneering influence is still strong. The island would serve as a base for launching 'a predatory and incursive war' along the South American coast, tying down Spanish forces and disrupting Spain's trade in the Pacific. The problem of native interests is again largely ignored. But there is an assumption that those living under British rule in this new settlement would be a free people governed by consent, in contrast to the Spanish colonies, where the absence of freedom sapped the vigour of the natives and weakened the colonies from within.

It was this theme which was taken up in a third memorandum, when Richmond replied with advice to re-submit the memoir to the Secretary of State for Foreign Affairs, Lord Grenville. By the same post as he sent an effusive, almost fawning reply to Richmond, expressing his delighted surprise at the great Duke's interest, Tone re-submitted his memoir to Grenville. A polite note arrived some weeks later which he 'looked upon as a civil rejection' and he determined 'to think no more of it'. Yet on 12 November Tone wrote again to Richmond, expanding his limited project into a full-blown plan for the emancipation of South America.

The change indicates the influence Russell was already exercising over Tone's thinking, for although the Sandwich Islands project had originated with Tone, the proposal for a war of liberation in Spanish America did not. Rather it came from a new friend Russell had made in Belfast. This was the veteran American, Thomas Digges, one-time representative of the Colonies in London, who would eventually prove a false friend to the two young men now captivated by his experience in matters of secret diplomacy. Tone, at Russell's behest, had submitted all his papers on the project to Digges. Digges exposed the narrowness of Tone's project and pointed to the Mexican uprisings against Spanish power over the last three decades. He warned of the inevitable failure of expeditions bent on conquest or plunder. Only those mounted in support of 'liberty or freedom', by engaging the internal support of the natives, would be sure of success, and what is more would have the tacit support of the United States. A similar argument had been urged on Pitt by the South American revolutionary, Francesco Miranda, earlier that year and would be taken up by successive British ministers after 1796. But after revolution in her own colonies, and faced with revolution in France, Britain was nervous of encouraging foreign subversion and fell back on the old policy of conquest, with disastrous results. Digges, rogue that he was, was right in his analysis, for it was the emancipationist school of thought which dominated other memoranda of the period.[23]

Influenced by Digges, Tone wrote again to Richmond and Grenville with a plan for liberating South America from Spanish control, which touched upon such issues as freedom, natural rights and the recommendation of a republic as a form of government. Tone offered to come to London. But Grenville replied on 17 December politely declining to take up the project, though assuring

Tone that 'under different circumstances, many of the considerations
mentioned by you would be highly deserving of attention'. 'My
unfortunate plan...is, now, deceased,' wrote Tone in his notebook,
'and peace to its ashes.'[24] He remained convinced, however, that he
was right and that time would prove him so—as indeed it did. Nor
was the project ever laid to rest. He kept all the papers, and he would
return again to this one of his more enduring passions.

The dating and contents of these latest projects are significant.
They show the fleeting nature of the nationalistic fervour into which
Tone had whipped himself in *Spanish War!* Once again the incident
highlights that trait in Tone's character which could launch him with
such utter conviction into the passion of the moment, and permit
him to turn to something else when the moment passed. Once again
his passion for military adventure would have sent him willingly to
the other side of the world. Once again he was ready to leave Matilda for a venture with uncertain prospects, and since she was
pregnant, one must wonder about Tone's temperamental suitability
to domestic life.

The family had moved back to town shortly after Russell's
departure in September, to the less fashionable Longford Street, just
behind the Castle. By this stage things were quiet, if not downright dull, in town. The theatre season was not due to start until
November—when the gentry came back to town for the Michaelmas
legal term—and parliamentary sittings would not resume until the
following February. Novels seemed to offer one of the few diversions, and the press was lamenting their destructive influence on
female virtue. Ever responsive to prevailing fashion, Tone prepared
Belmont Castle for press. It was advertised by Byrne at 3s. 3d. on
13 November, in time to catch the interest of fashionable people
spilling back into town from their country seats. Both the advertise-
ment and a review in the *Universal Magazine* (almost certainly
written by Tone himself) cleverly appealed to the prurient scandal-
mongering of the day.[25] There is no sign that Jebb and Radcliffe
were reinvolved, and since both were then making their uneventful
progress through the Irish bar, they would hardly have been enthusiastic. The novel had a moderate success. Tone's increasingly
restless pen was now in search of new subjects, and in the winter of
1790–1 he produced a spate of essays from which more mature
political ideas were to emerge with dramatic effect some months
later.

III

Tone returned with the rest of the legal fraternity to the Four Courts
for the opening of Michaelmas term, hoping that those hints of

preferment, held out by the Whig barrister the previous spring, would materialise. But since the Dungarvan petition would not be heard until February 1791, when his abilities would be tried, this was an unrealistic expectation. However, the Ponsonbys did think of him as on some kind of retainer (which he undoubtedly was, given the extended time-scale of the petition hearings), as did the government press which attacked the 'petty barristers' trying to win their way by means other than legal talent.[26]

In the winter of 1791–2, when Tone was acquiring a reputation in another field—as a leader of the United Irish Society, and champion of the Catholics—the Whig barrister called on him again, this time to express his surprise at the new direction of Tone's politics. He 'insinuated pretty directly, though with great civility, that I had not kept faith with the Whigs, with whom he professed to understand I had connected myself, and whom, in consequence, I ought to have consulted before I took so decided a line of conduct'. There followed a harangue by Tone, which he recounts in some detail. He was stung by the imputation that he was some kind of hack for the Whigs, and by the implied accusation of duplicity, and he admits his irritation that the Whigs expected the benefits to flow one way only. 'I spoke rather haughtily in this affair, because I was somewhat provoked at the insinuation of duplicity, and besides I wished to have a blow at Mr George Ponsonby, who seemed desirous to retain me as a kind of pamphleteer in his service, at the same time that he industriously avoided any thing like communication with me...and as I well knew he was one of the proudest men in Ireland, I took care to speak on a footing of the most independent equality.'[27]

It was another of those incidents of the great talking down to their inferiors which so rankled with Tone. He was, moreover, incapable of playing the kind of waiting game the great family connections required of people like himself, and was irritated at the docility induced in the junior bar by the long trek towards preferment. In his autobiography Tone accepts that his youthful expectations were over-inflated, and admits that the Whig barrister genuinely wanted to help him and scarcely deserved the treatment meted out to him.[28] Like any man of letters in the eighteenth century, Tone had accepted patronage as a necessary evil. But it was the paltry nature of the patronage which most upset Tone, and he admits as much. 'George Ponsonby is, on a sudden, grown vastly civil and attentive,' he wrote to Matilda at the end of 1791. 'He got me a guinea yesterday as a retainer against the next assizes—I wonder did he think I would sell myself for a guinea?—be that as it may I kept the money as I shall all that comes *honorably*.' Matilda clearly thought it had not and suppressed the entire passage in the published letter. Tone thought such a pitiful fee insufficient to retain him as the Ponsonbys' scribe, but it did in some measure justify Whig irritation and Tone felt they were out to punish him thereafter.[29]

All of this scarcely amounts to a positive rejection by the Whigs, for Tone was considered in their junior camp and continued to wear the Whig Club uniform even after the foundation of the United Irishmen. It was certainly an element in the process of his alienation from the world of privilege. But more than anything it reveals Tone at one of the turning-points of his life. Restless as ever, and having won some recognition for his writing abilities, he was mentally closing a door on one part of his life and launching himself through another. The new life, moreover, was peopled by equals rather than superiors.

IV

His restlessness revealed itself initially in the revival of his early passion for founding clubs. In November and December 1790 he was attending Historical Society debates again,[30] and it was from here that the members of his club were picked. They included John Stack, a recent candidate for the chair of astronomy at Trinity, Whitley Stokes, Peter Burrowes, William Johnston, future judge of the King's Bench, and Thomas Addis Emmet. Thomas Russell was a corresponding member, and two noted reformers and polemicists, the barrister Joseph Pollock and the physician William Drennan—both Ulster Presbyterians—were also members.

They were talented writers, and Tone set about preparing a book of essays on a wide range of topics, including religious toleration and Catholic emancipation, these to be written by Russell. Only four essays survive, however, all written by Tone, all touching on the connection between Ireland and England. The manuscript essays are rough, heavily scored drafts, not yet ready for publication. Nevertheless they do reflect a considerable change in attitude on the constitutional issue since *Spanish War!*, and were the outcome of Tone's lengthy discussions with Russell. Russell himself produced nothing more substantial than jottings—pointing up the difference between the two friends.[31] Russell was a man of advanced and informed ideas—Tone clearly thought so—but he had difficulty reproducing them on paper. Even so, his influence on Tone was profound and many of his ideas on Catholic emancipation were to find their way into Tone's influential *Argument on Behalf of the Catholics*.

Although Pollock and Drennan contributed nothing formally to the club, Tone continued to consult them informally. Pollock's reputation as the 'Irish Rousseau' had been won the previous decade, largely through the impact of his *Letters of Owen Roe O'Neill* (1779). This remarkable treatise on Irish independence was a work much admired by Tone, and key phrases from it appear in his draft essays of this winter.

But, after Russell, it was Drennan who exercised most influence on Tone at this stage. He was eight years Tone's senior and the two men made strange companions. Even Drennan's friends found his cold manner off-putting. He 'might have passed, in appearance, for the demure minister of some remote village-congregation of the Scotch kirk', wrote Lady Morgan, and a certain pedantry and secretiveness in his character would later lead to clashes with Tone and Russell in the United Irish Society.[32] Drennan too had made a reputation as an advanced thinker during the 1780s. His best-known work was his *Letters of Orellana* (or Helot Letters), published in 1785 in reaction to the failure of the Volunteer reform campaign. Ireland, having won independence from a foreign tyranny in 1782-3, Drennan now saw as suffering from a home-grown aristocratic one. Public spirit was better represented, he argued, in the kind of extra-parliamentary conventions and committees organised by the Volunteers. It was the same glorification of the Volunteers and the anti-parliamentarianism which in 1791 would produce the United Irish Society

The ideas of Pollock and Drennan, Tone soon made his own, and in his four draft essays we see him working through and beyond his initial Whiggish principles to a much more positive anti-Englishness than appears in either of the other two. In an emotional outburst, he points to the position of Ireland before 1782: 'sunk to the subordination of an English county,...We had ceased to remember that we were a nation'. The American example had allowed the Irish in 1782 to break 'the manacles' of 'British ambition', and Ireland's 'imperial crown' was rescued from 'the felonious custody of arbitrary and jealous domination'[33]

There is nothing very novel in all this. Much of it derived from Molyneux's *Case of Ireland's Being Bound by Acts of Parliament in England*, an 'almost inspired volume', as Tone termed it, which he had only recently discovered. Molyneux's claim that Ireland and England were two separate kingdoms helped fortify Tone's rising Irish nationalism and what emerges most from these early essays is a romantic attachment to things and people Irish. Secondly there is a resentment at Ireland's inferior status. Echoing Parsons, Tone depicts Ireland's nationhood as unrepresented and unrecognised abroad, her government controlled by 'some insignificant English nobleman, who presides, some obsequious tool of the British Minister, who proposes, and a rabble of the most profligate of our countrymen,

who execute his mandates'. Finally there is a growing anti-Englishness, based on the 'arrogance' with which he (and a good many
others) felt England treated Ireland, and a recognition that the location of the monarchy and centre of government in England would
always see 'the interest of the Government and the [Irish] nation drag
different ways'. There are hints of separation as the only real solution, but they are more accidental than designed.

In paired essays comparing Ireland's situation in 1720 and 1790, it
is again England's 'lust for power', 'pride' and arrogant presumption
towards dependent peoples which comes in for the strongest attack.
Tone accepts that there was little political spirit in Ireland until revived by the American war. But at the suggestion that there is something in the Irish character which induces 'laziness, and dishonesty',
and 'stifles all tendency to improvement, and will for ever keep us a
subordinate nation of hewers of wood, and of drawers of water', his
hackles rise. The 'ignorance and poverty' of Ireland (which he does
not deny), he attributes rather to 'misrule' and 'oppression', and he
dismisses as blasphemous the suggestion of 'innate and immovable
depravity' in 'millions of God's creatures'. There is a deism in these
essays, with their belief in an approachable and humane providence
and an unflinching faith in mankind's propensity for self-improve-
ment. It is 'public virtue and wisdom' which will reform Ireland's
corrupt 'Senate'. It is as if Tone is reproducing all the clichés of the
Enlightenment but recognising how inapplicable they are in existing
circumstances. And indeed the essays mark the point at which Tone,
the Enlightenment man, comes up against Tone the modern
nationalist. There is nothing cosmopolitan about Tone's Enlightenment precepts. Rather the belief in qualities common to all mankind
leads back to the local situation of Ireland and to his 'great discovery':
that 'the English Government here was founded, has been supported,
and now exists. . .in the disunion of Irishmen'.

This is the conclusion of the last of his essays, 'on the Necessity of
Domestic Union'. Drennan had confronted the problem of religious
divisions in Ireland on several occasions. But he thought the issue of
Catholic emancipation divisive, and was prepared to drop it in the
interests of political reform.[34] Tone, however, soon decided that
political reform was impossible without Catholic emancipation. His
discovery was not new, except to himself, and the impact it made on
him was so startling that he remembered it as a Pauline conversion.[35]
Certainly that conviction introduced a new purpose and clarity into
his writings. Tone at last had found his mission.

His essay on domestic union starts off from the obscure and erudite
stance of the classical scholar, arguing from Hesiod to prove the
whole greater than the part. As the essay develops, however, there is

a visible transformation of the scholar into the publicist and populariser of radical ideas. Tone argues that the 'whole people' of Ireland, the Catholics, Presbyterians and Protestants, is greater than any one of the sects individually. Yet because the parties were absorbed in 'watching each other'—the one becoming 'contemptible' because of the exertion of 'power unjust', the other 'cowed and rebuked' so long 'that they appear to have lost their spirit'—the Irish government, and through it England, had been able to carry out its 'insidious acts' unmolested. Meanwhile, as they continue this 'destructive struggle,... men [are] sent from England, to do the business of England', to monopolise the 'honors, the emoluments, the sword and the purse of Ireland'. Disunity, in other words was the illness, English monopoly the symptom.[36] It was in his club writings that Tone made this discovery, and still in the context of the little club that his most refined and most famous statement on separatism was to emerge in a much-leaked personal letter to Russell of July 1791.

Russell had asked Tone to draw up founding resolutions for a society to be inaugurated during Belfast's celebration of the French Revolution on 14 July 1791. The resolutions will be discussed later.[37] But the covering letter shows that by 1791 Tone privately considered separation from England as no bad thing. He voices his belief 'that the bane of Irish prosperity is the influence of England' and 'that influence will ever be exerted while the connexion between the countries continues'. And though he agreed that such an opinion was, for the moment, 'too hardy', nevertheless he was confident it would be universally accepted before long. 'I have not said one word that looks like a wish for *separation*, tho' I give it to you and to your friends as my most decided opinion that such an event would be a *regeneration* for this country.'[38] Yet Tone was no revolutionary in 1791. Like other advanced reformers of the period he sought a regeneration of the political system to take account of other forms of property besides the landed variety—notably to accommodate the social leaders of the Catholics and the middle classes generally.[39] However republican his 1791 statements might appear, they were expressed by others at the time.[40] Tone was quite prepared to work within the existing constitution to achieve radical reform, and nothing he wrote in these years suggests otherwise.

The letter and accompanying resolutions immediately fell into government hands. How this happened is a mystery. When the discovery became public in 1793 Digges was assumed to be the culprit.[41] He had been given the letter by Russell to copy. But since it had been transcribed by a Castle clerk and was sent to London by Westmorland on 11 July as one of the 'two [the other being Drennan's] very dangerous papers in secret circulated in this country', this seems unlikely. It would not have had time to make the journey to Belfast by then. It was typical of Westmorland's conspiratorial mentality— on which London had frequently to caution him—that he should have elevated a private letter to the level of an inflammatory handbill. But the text of the London copy is truncated and the last paragraph, which would have revealed Tone's identity, omitted.[42] It looks as if Fitzgibbon, into whose hands the letter had fallen, may intentionally have withheld the author's identity. Tone after all was a kinsman and a member of a privileged élite. It would not be the first time a way-ward member was protected by his political enemies.[43] But Fitz-gibbon took particular exception to members of the bar who strayed from the fold and Tone's continuing radicalism ensured a suffocating vigilance from the Lord Chancellor. Certainly something like a battle of wills developed between the two men. The letter was to become Fitzgibbon's main evidence in his contention that Tone and the United Irishmen had been militant separatists since 1791—a charge which Tone totally denied.

Tone continued to practice at the bar over the next few years, but with growing reluctance. Nevertheless his membership in the ex-clusive legal fraternity brought his radical activities under the kind of scrutiny from those in power which others more revolutionary than he did not automatically attract. It was such attention which marked him out as a dangerous republican when he was nothing of the kind. Fitzgibbon was not alone in considering him a 'viper in the nest' which had nourished him, and in 1791 he was about to betray one of the Ascendancy's most sacred of cows, its Anglicanism, by taking up the cause of the Catholics and the Northern Presbyterians.

III

ACROSS THE RELIGIOUS DIVIDE
(1791)

7
Anti-Popery and the Rise of Presbyterian Radicalism

It is not republican separatism that Tone considered his most important contribution to the history of Ireland, but his effort to heal its religious divisions. The land confiscations and plantations of the sixteenth and seventeenth centuries, the penal laws of the eighteenth and the triumph of Orangeism have contributed to the long-accepted image of a besieged Protestant minority amidst an aggrieved and hostile Catholic majority. The Catholic populace was not poised to overturn the Protestant land settlement and state during the eighteenth century. But a Protestant siege mentality was undeniable and it was the heightened sectional identities of the Protestants and the Ulster Presbyterians which dictated Tone's Catholic mission. Catholic emancipation was the most heated issue of the day and it was as a Catholic campaigner rather than a United Irishman that Tone was considered dangerous by the authorities.

I

Although their Catholicism sat lightly on the mass of the Gaelic-speaking populace, it was seen by Protestants as a traitorous creed, subject to an external power in Rome, which upheld the Jacobite cause until 1766 and reputedly counselled the killing of heretics and the dethroning of heretic kings. To Protestants the Glorious Revolution symbolised the defeat of this foreign Catholic conspiracy. Protestantism became synonymous with liberty, Catholicism with slavery and poverty, a view which the Irish Catholic population, consisting overwhelmingly of peasants, served to underscore. The idea that popery also enslaved the mind was instinctive with Irish Protestants and is evident even in Tone and Drennan, the Catholics' most outspoken champions.[1]

This intense distrust of Catholicism and the belief in the essential inferiority of its adherents has long been underestimated as a factor in framing the eighteenth-century penal code. Political and economic considerations, deemed at one time the dominant motivation for the penal laws, were indeed vital. The seventeenth-century land settlement, whereby huge tracts of land and the political power which went with them were transferred to Protestant ownership, required protection. In this the penal laws were entirely successful, and the proportion of land under Catholic ownership had declined to 5 per cent by 1776.[2] However, only a small number of people actually owned land in eighteenth-century Europe and few Catholics were directly affected by such dispossession. Lease-holding was the norm, even for Irish Protestants, and the 31–year leases of the penal laws gave rural Catholics more security than they had experienced previously. Peasants throughout *ancien régime* Europe would normally have been excluded from political power, and the Catholic peasants of Ireland were just as far removed from the Catholic gentry as their French counterparts.[3] The Irish penal laws were closely modelled on those affecting English Catholics, and the idea that those laws were somehow a tool of England's colonial subjection of Ireland has no foundation. The Catholic Church as an institution suffered considerably less in Ireland than at the hands of contemporary Catholic monarchies elsewhere in Europe.[4]

However, the penal laws gave rise to tensions which increased rather than diminished with time. They helped create flash-point areas such as south Ulster and Wexford, where the end-of-century crisis erupted, and they fostered a sense of oppression which was used to good effect by middle-class radicals. The facts that the penal laws were not always applied or that the Catholics learnt to evade them should not disguise Protestant perception of them as a symbol of their own supremacy, fostering a triumphalism even among lower-class Protestants. The powers of magistrates to search Catholic houses for arms—Catholic possession of which was forbidden under one of the earliest (1695) of the penal laws—were extended as late as 1775, and a proposed relaxation in the 1790s met with particularly fierce opposition from Protestants of every social class. This was not simply for reasons security. It was rather the threatened loss of a visible symbol of Protestant superiority. The right to bear arms was associated with freeman status, and in the 1780s and '90s the sight of Catholics carrying arms sparked off serious sectarian troubles in Ulster.[5] Moreover, Catholic leaders were expected to adopt a deferential, almost servile, manner in presenting their case for relief. It was a servility no longer acceptable to the burgeoning Catholic middle class which was to promote Tone as its prophet.[6]

The Catholic gentry had spent much of the century trying to prove their loyalty, and the event endorsed their claims. The Irish Catholics remained quiet during the Jacobite rebellions of 1715 and 1745 and there was no political content in the Whiteboy disturbances of the 1760s. Even during the American war the Catholic Committee supported British arms, whereas Protestants and Dissenters generally

took the American side.[7] It was against the backdrop of the American
crisis that a major English Catholic Relief Act in 1778 led to pressure
to introduce similar legislation in Ireland.[8] Gardiner's 1778 Catholic
Relief Bill for Ireland was a cautious measure, permitting Catholics
to hold leases for 999 years, disposing of the invidious inheritance
clauses of the 1704 act, but retaining prohibitions on actual ownership. It nevertheless stirred up a hornets' nest, provoking an emotional and confused outcry in the Irish Parliament, which mingled
worries about the Protestant land settlement with deeper concerns
about popish principles. The same paranoia greeted another English-
sponsored Relief Act in 1782. Catholics finally gained the right to
own and bequeath land, but they were still debarred from owning
land in parliamentary boroughs, and the 1782 act represented a considerable whittling down of the concessions England had been
prepared to grant.

II

The Catholic Committee, which had been in existence since 1760,
maintained a low profile throughout these proceedings. But the mood
in the country changed dramatically in the 1780s and started to push
the position of the Catholics to the forefront of a heated reform debate. Foremost in the debate was the Volunteer movement. Yet that
movement was aggressively Protestant and however advanced it
might be on the political front, it shared the Ascendancy's anti-
popery. Those corps which opened their ranks to Catholics tended
to be in towns, with sizeable Catholic mercantile communities. In
1779, when Tone was at the height of his schoolboy passion for the
Volunteers, his future friend, Joseph Pollock, urged the Volunteers
to abandon their religious exclusiveness and admit Catholics to their
ranks. In the absence of Volunteer leaders like Lord Charlemont,
who opposed further Catholic relief, the Ulster Volunteer Convention, meeting at Dungannon in September 1783, passed a resolution
calling for a limited extension of the franchise to Catholics.[9]

The Belfast Dissenters had dictated the pace of the Convention.
But a national Volunteer reform convention, meeting in Dublin two
months later, refused to discuss the Catholic issue.[10] The Volunteer
reform bill, divested of any reference to the Catholics, was nevertheless defeated in Parliament that November. After years of seemingly
unstoppable victory, the Volunteer delegates seemed utterly directionless. The twenty-year-old Tone watched them spilling from the
Rotunda in apparent disarray and recalled the scene many years later:

I had the misfortune to see them on the day of their disgrace,
when the great bubble burst, and carried rout and confusion, and

dismay, among their ranks; when *three hundred* of the first gentlemen of Ireland, girt with swords, the representatives of the armed force of the kingdom, who, by giving independence, had given to their Parliament the means of being virtuous, fled like deer to their counties, to return no more, after making a foolish profession of their pacific intentions;...and I wondered then, like a young man, why such men, so circumstanced, with the eyes of Europe upon them, should submit, quietly, to treatment, which a few years experience has shown was inevitable; they were disgraced, because they were unjust; through them the honor of their country was wounded, her name sunk, her glories forgotten, and from the last day of the Convention, there has been *no people in Ireland.*

They had failed, Tone thought, because in rejecting the Catholics 'they built on too narrow a foundation....From their failure we are taught this salutary truth, that no reform can ever be obtained which shall not comprehensively embrace Irishmen of all denominations. The exclusion of the Catholics lost the question under circumstances that must have otherwise carried it against all opposition'.[11]

At the time of the Volunteer defeat Tone's future friends, Peter Burrowes and William Todd Jones, had reached the same conclusion. In 1784 Jones, a country gentleman and MP for Lisburn in Ulster, anticipated Tone's *Argument on Behalf of the Catholics of Ireland* when he proclaimed the interdependence of political reform and Catholic emancipation in his influential *Letter to the Electors of Lisburn.*[12] Burrowes's *Plain Arguments* of the same year criticised the tiny electorate on which Parliament rested. Only unity among the people and the enfranchisement of the Catholics would 'subdue that aristocratical phalanx which thrives on their division'. The claim that popery would then become pre-eminent was a 'mere bugbear', 'idle hobgoblin rumours' to keep the nation divided. Like Tone later, Burrowes could reconcile his instinctive anti-popery with the call for Catholic emancipation by claims that the Catholics themselves had changed: 'they live in a period of liberation—[and] have caught the love of freedom from yourselves...popery is decaying and likely to decay all over Europe...in our country it will wear out...unless we prop their superstition...and keep their prejudices alive by maintaining our own'.[13]

It was an argument for the decline of popery and superstition within Catholicism which helped reforming Protestants overcome their anti-popery. The French Revolution, with its attack on institutionalised Catholicism, gave the argument new substance and permitted the campaign for Catholic emancipation to take off in the

1790s. But in the 1780s such sentiments were not yet widely shared. The reform campaign split on the Catholic issue. Charlemont's opposition helped erode the nascent alliance in Ulster between Presbyterian and Catholic. Even Drennan thought the Catholic issue should be dropped. He considered the Catholics at an inferior stage of civilisation. But in time this would be corrected through the prosperity generated by a reformed Parliament, and by association they would acquire the Protestants' habits of industry and public spirit.[14]

It is doubtful if the abandonment of the Catholic issue would have materially altered the outcome of the reform campaign. With Belfast defiantly proclaiming its right to instruct its parliamentary representatives, even moderate reformers thought these extra-parliamentary congresses and conventions were beginning to usurp the place of Parliament. The reform congress which met in Dublin in October 1784 accurately reflected the widening gulf between the Patriot politicians and extra-parliamentary radicalism. The response had been poor. Forty delegates failed to attend. Only two of the northern counties sent representatives. Caution prevailed. The Catholic issue was not mentioned. The reform plan which emerged was moderate. An address was issued advising the people to respect the laws, the 'dignity of the legislature' and their attachment to Great Britain, and the congress went quietly out of existence in April 1785. Reform bills were defeated in both the English and Irish Parliaments and the issue was effectively shelved for the remainder of the decade. The frustration of the advanced reformers at this whimpering demise of their campaign erupted in a public questioning of the benefits to Ireland of the connection with England, and there was even talk of armed resistance.[15]

The growing fissure on the reform and emancipation issues in the mid-1780s laid the lines of demarcation for the dramatic developments of the next decade. Unlike the political underground in England during the 1790s, in which working-class leaders were often unfamiliar to the authorities, the revolutionary movement in Ireland developed within the same urban élites which had dominated the reform campaign a decade earlier. Prominent Dublin politicians like Tandy and country gentlemen like Rowan belonged to the same world as the government supporters who moved against them, and several brushes with the authorities in the 1780s (notably with Fitzgibbon) left to the United Irishmen a dangerous legacy of old personal scores.[16] Nearly all these radical reformers were Volunteers. Many felt betrayed by the movement's aristocratic and parliamentary leaders and shocked at the dismissive treatment meted out to their conventions and reform congress.[17] A hallowed tradition survived of the Volunteers and their conventions as symbols of active public spirit.

Nor was the Catholic issue easily laid to rest. A tithe war of the late 1780s produced a flood of pamphleteering.[18] Rowan entered into a lengthy correspondence on the issue with his old tutor at Cambridge, the noted Unitarian and radical John Jebb. The Protestants need have no fear of the Catholics, Jebb assured him. Their clergy were naturally inclined to authority and if only propertied Catholics were enfranchised the balance of power would remain with the Protestants. A reform of Parliament should be the reformers' first object, 'but I fear that none can be obtained, unless the honourable and worthy of all persuasions cordially unite in the attempt'.[19] It was the same argument which was to launch Tone's political career six years later and there was good reason why both men should see Ulster as the reformers' main hope.

III

Ulster came to represent for Tone the classical ideal of martial vigour and independent public spirit. Home of the Volunteers, it had pushed their reform campaign aggressively and sustained it when it foundered elsewhere after 1785. It also contained Ireland's largest concentration of Presbyterians. Ireland underwent a process of rapid transformation in the seventeenth century, and nowhere more so than the nine counties of Ulster. From being the most Gaelic, most underpopulated, most inaccessible and most underdeveloped province at the beginning of the seventeenth century, Ulster had, by the end of the eighteenth, become the most Protestant, most populated and industrialised of all. It was, however, the most explosive. Much of Ireland had experienced land forfeitures, confiscations and plantations, but none as radical as those which occurred in Ulster after 1609, when plans were implemented for settling six counties (Armagh, Tyrone, Fermanagh, Derry, Donegal and Cavan) with English and Scottish tenants.

The history of the Presbyterians in the east of the province, however, was different from that of the settlers in the planted counties. They had already settled heavily in the non-plantation counties of Antrim and Down before 1609, and a massive influx of Scottish Presbyterians in the second half of the seventeenth century made Presbyterianism the dominant element in Ulster Protestantism.[20] The Presbyterians were generally better off, less dependent on the Protestant gentry, and, because concentrated in non-plantation counties, less exposed to the tensions created by dispossession and less afraid of the economic threat posed by Catholics. Most important of all, their very religion, with its democratic church structure, anti-authoritarianism and doctrine of a direct covenant between God and man, put them out of step with contemporary patterns of authority and deference.

Fundamental to Presbyterianism was the Calvinistic belief in a direct communion between God and man, unimpeded by intermediaries in either church or civil government. Translated into political terms, such beliefs could be profoundly revolutionary, for although the monarch was considered God's representative on earth, Presbyterians did not recognise any civil authority in which the Church was not sovereign. They were seen by successive governments as the most volatile element in Irish society, more dangerous even than the Catholics. From as early as 1649 they were deeply antiparliamentary, and state discrimination throughout the seventeenth and eighteenth centuries intensified their sense of persecuted purity and alienation from an infidel state. The outcome was an ingrained dislike of the entire hierarchical system of prelacy, aristocracy and authoritarianism in government, a notorious lack of deference towards landlords and politicians alike, and a tendency to resist as a matter of religious principle. There was too in Presbyteranism a sense of intellectual superiority which was to manifest itself in contempt for Catholic passivity. Throughout the history of the Volunteers and the United Irishmen the Presbyterians' self-image was one of the northerners leading their slavish countrymen to salvation.[21] It was an image which Tone fully endorsed.

Anti-popery, however, was at the very heart of Presbyterianism, enshrined in its key doctrinal statement, the Westminster Confession of Faith.[22] The notion that popery and authoritarian doctrine enslaved men's minds, inducing mental and material impoverishment, remained strong, even among the advanced radicals, and was to introduce a fatal weakness into the United Irish movement. Certainly governments of the day found the notion of the Presbyterians sponsoring Catholic emancipation difficult to credit.[23] Although latitudinarianism came to dominate Ulster Presbyterianism by the end of the eighteenth century, anti-popery remained strong and by no means all Presbyterians supported the novel Catholic emancipationism which swept through this highly politicised religion in the early 1790s. It was not that the reformers' anti-popery had declined. Rather a series of events gave rise to the belief that Catholics were becoming more like Protestants and might, in time, be safely entrusted with political rights. These events provide the backdrop to the rise of advanced radicalism in east Ulster and the espousal of Catholic emancipation as a necessary ingredient of reform.[24]

The Belfast Volunteers came to recognise the connection after the rejection of reform proposals in 1783. Several Presbyterian ministers,

including the Revds William Bruce of Belfast and Samuel Barber
of Rathfriland in County Down, played prominent roles both in
preparations for the 1784 reform congress and the anti-tithe campaign. Yet most still felt the extension of the suffrage to Catholics
should be gradual and the Protestant nature of government preserved.[25] While most Protestants argued that danger to property was
their main objection to readmitting the Catholics to political rights,
for Presbyterians it was the lingering fear of popish authoritarianism
and mental enslavement.[26] The Catholics should renounce 'those
political elements of their religion', one radical Presbyterian advised
a Catholic friend, their 'adherence to a foreign power in temporals,
as well as spirituals...and all the other scandals kept up to degrade
your persuasion'. Even then, he feared the Catholics would always
treat and temporise. 'Your people are not as enlightened as ours and
alas ignorance is the most durable of all Empires'.[27] The French
Revolution and Tone's celebrated *Argument on Behalf of the Catholics
of Ireland* temporarily calmed such doubts, though enough remained
to create persistent suspicions of their new Catholic allies among
many United Irishmen.

IV

News of the French Revolution was generally well received in
Ireland. Bastille hats became one of the many peculiar fashions of the
time and by early November 1789, *Gallic Freedom; or, The Destruction
of the Bastille* was drawing crowds at the Theatre Royal in Dublin.
But it was the sight of Europe's most Catholic nation sharing power
with Protestants which attracted most attention. The spotlight was
turned inwards on Ireland's own lamentable record in religious
toleration. The traditional claim that the Catholics were 'unfit' for
liberty was dismissed, and England and Ireland were urged to follow
France's example by granting them political rights.[28]

At first Belfast—so recently the torch-bearer for Catholic rights—
did not make the connection. The spirit which had moved its
Volunteers to open their ranks to Catholics and march to mass in
Belfast's first Catholic chapel in 1784 seemed entirely dead.[29] By
1790, however, events in France began to erode the strange torpor
which had descended on Belfast since the days of the Volunteers. At
Charlemont's prodding it finally mobilised in support of the Whig
Club by founding an Ulster branch in March 1790. Though still
dominated by aristocratic names, the Northern Whig Club had a
larger middle-class membership than the parent body. Among its
members were the Belfast cotton manufacturer and owner of the
Belfast News Letter, Henry Joy; Drennan's brother-in-law, Sam Mc-
Tier (clerk to the Ballast Office); the Lisburn radicals Dr Alexander

Stewart and Todd Jones; and the linen merchant William Sinclair, who had been a prominent participant in the Volunteer reform campaign of 1784–5.[30] The result was an internal tension which had not existed in the Dublin club. At a meeting on 1 March 1790 to discuss the foundation resolutions, the Catholic issue produced a heated debate and was dropped in deference to the 'gentlemen of superior rank and fortune'. Even this did not satisfy Charlemont, who thought religion should not have been introduced at all, and the issue was studiously avoided at future meetings.[31] The continued weight of aristocratic influence in the club was dissatisfying to the mercantile element. A second more middle-class club, the Whig Club of Belfast, was founded alongside it and Sinclair even tried to form one among the tradesmen.[32]

The French Revolution caused many Belfast Dissenters to view the Catholics in a new light. They noted too the changing character of the Catholic Committee and the rise of an aggressive middle-class element within it. Drennan in his *Letters of Orellana* had given voice to the belief that the assumed brutishness of Irish Catholicism derived as much from the absence of 'men of weight and estimation. . . in the middle ranks of life; who gently instil into the minds of those beneath them, the milk of human nature', as from religious principles.[33] Certainly the document issuing from a meeting of Belfast Whigs in October 1790 indicates that a number of Presbyterians were prepared to confront and denounce the continuing fears of Catholic reforms. The meeting resolved:

That freedom is the indefeasible birthright of Irishmen derived from the Supreme Author of their being, and which no power on earth has a right to deprive them.

That the glorious spirit of the citizens of France in forming and adopting the wise system of a republican government, and abrogating that enormous power and abused influence which the clergy of that kingdom had for years past usurped, is a bright example for enlightened citizens of every country to imitate. . . .

That the Protestant Dissenters, and Roman Catholics of this kingdom, being compelled to pay tithes, and yield up their property for the exercise of sacredotal functions. . .is become an insufferable grievance, and calls for national address.

That the Protestant Dissenters, fully convinced of the constitutional principles of their brethren the Roman Catholics, and of their zeal to support and defend the Liberty of their country, will on all occasions support their just claim to the enjoyment of the rights and privileges of freeborn citizens, entitled to fill every office, and serve in whatever station their country may think proper to call them to.[34]

Presbyterian anti-authoritarianism, belief in a direct compact between God and man, ideas coming in from France and America and a middle-class identity of grievances against the hated 'aristocracy' were beginning to produce that unusual conjunction of Dissent and Catholicism which would lead to the formation of the United Irishmen.

8

Argument on Behalf of the Catholics

It was developments in England which revived the Catholic campaign in 1790. The English Catholics had renewed their petitions for relief in 1788. The outcome was Mitford's bill of 1791, opening up the professions to English Catholics and removing many of their remaining disabilities. The petitions and debates were reported in the Irish press, recognition of 'the enlightened philosophy of the present age' highlighting the outmoded nature of the Irish penal laws. The Irish Catholics were as loyal as any other subjects, proclaimed the *Freeman's Journal*. They might hold the same religion as the Pope, but they were hardly 'papist'; 'they laugh at his temporal authority and have no opinions repugnant to a free constitution'. Yet the paper spoke for the majority of liberal Protestants in seeing emancipation as a gradual process and recommending a total repeal of the penal laws only after Catholic loyalty had been established through 'long experience of. . . rectitude of conduct. . . temperance, moderation, and a studious disregard of political strifes'.[1] The Irish government likewise warned Pitt of the repercussions in Ireland of concessions to the English Catholics, and those on offer in Mitford's bill were scaled down accordingly.[2]

However, the urban middle-class Catholics in Ireland—particularly those on the Catholic Committee—were growing restive. Notable among them was John Keogh, a wealthy Dublin silk merchant. Employment in trade was despised in eighteenth-century Europe generally, and the penal laws contained only minor restrictions. Some Catholics made great fortunes. Keogh was one of them. He had worked his way up from apprenticeship to retire a rich man in 1787. By then he had also acquired extensive landed interests in Sligo, Leitrim, Roscommon and Dublin, where his mansion at Mount Jerome was to become a centre for Catholic mobilisation in the early 1790s and a favourite haunt of Tone's. Keogh was a blunt, no-nonsense man of fifty-two when Tone first began working with him in 1792. His abilities, and his antagonism to the aristocratic domination of the Committee, had brought him to government attention as early as 1784, when a clumsy and unsuccessful attempt to dissuade him from co-operation with the Dissenters marked him out as leader of the democratic party within the Committee. But although he became involved with the United Irish Society in its early years he withdrew in 1794–5 and was more shrewd, cautious and altogether more mature politically than the young men who took it forward thereafter. It was his cautiousness, and a tendency to go for immediate benefits rather than hold out for full emancipation, which periodically set him at odds with Tone. But Keogh had longer experience in handling the sensitive Catholic issue, and Tone came to respect him for it. He proved a formidable leader of the Catholics and was feared as such by the authorities long after the crisis of the 1790s had passed.[3]

Richard McCormick and Edward Byrne were also typical of the new breed of Catholic leaders. McCormick was a successful Dublin poplin merchant, and like Keogh an active Volunteer. He was later to become a member of the United Irish executive and was the man Tone most esteemed on the Catholic Committee.[4] Byrne had made a fortune in distilling and sugar and was reputedly the wealthiest man in Ireland.[5]

In 1790–1 the Catholic Committee decided that the time was ripe to campaign for a repeal of the penal laws. New elections were organised and for the first time urban representatives considerably outnumbered those from the country. They included the attorney Edward Lewins, his uncle, the Dublin merchant Thomas Braughall, the physician William James NacNeven, the prominent Catholic pamphleteer, Dr Theobald McKenna, his and Tone's printer, Patrick Byrne, the brewer John Sweetman, the barrister Dominic Rice, Edward Byrne's partner, Randall McDonnell, the cotton manufacturer Thomas Warren, and, from Ulster, Dr Christopher Teeling. Almost all were shortly to become prominent members of the United Irish Society.[6]

The returns reflected the urban Catholics' impatience for relief, and their determination surfaced at the first meeting of the new Committee on 10 February 1791. McCormick was elected secretary for three years, and a committee of eight—all but one future United Irishmen—was appointed to consider the resolutions sent up from the town committees, calling upon their representatives to demand a redress of their grievances. The tone was loyal and respectful, but the new impatience was unmistakable and a sub-committee of twelve, which included Keogh, Byrne, McCormick, McDonnell, Braughall, Sweetman and McKenna, was appointed to carry the recommendations into effect.[7]

The Irish administration was averse to further concessions, and its insistence on old habits of submissiveness rankled with the new breed of Catholic leaders.[8] At first the sub-committee sought the support of the leading Catholic aristocrats, Lords Kenmare and Fingall, in presenting their petition and resolutions to the Irish Parliament. Kenmare prevaricated, then disowned the resolutions in an audience on 14 March 1791 with Chief Secretary Hobart. The split in the Committee, which would lead to the formal withdrawal of 68 Kenmarites by the end of the year, was actively encouraged by Hobart and leave to present the petition withheld.[9] Not even Grattan, or the Independent MP for County Antrim and a leading reformer of the 1780s, Sir John O'Neill, would agree to present it. The Catholic Committee then turned to the country, published the petition in the press, and gave its sub-committee free rein to adopt whatever measures it saw fit to secure a repeal of the penal laws.[10] Having been rebuffed by the Castle, the Committee now looked instead to Whitehall, and Keogh travelled to England during the summer recess. They had finally broken with the game of 'domineering' by the authorities and the 'tardiness' and 'melancholy... accommodating temper' of past committees.[11]

I

These events were the immediate background to Russell's commission to write essays on the Catholics for Tone's political club. They remained unfinished. But the points raised closely resemble those covered in Tone's *Argument* some months later. Russell's notes also marked yet another step in their alienation from the Whigs. If an MP of John O'Neill's stature could not be encouraged to come forward, wrote Russell, what hope was there of the others?[12]

Awareness of the issues involved was sharpened by the success of Paine's *Rights of Man*, Part I. First advertised by Byrne in March, and selling at 2s. 2d., a private subscription from the Whigs of the Capital—a less exclusive offshoot of the Whig Club—allowed the price to be dropped to sixpence and ensured wide circulation. It was a move sponsored by the club's radical wing, dominated by Tandy and other future United Irishmen like the iron-founder Henry Jackson, and the booksellers Randall McAllister and John Chambers.[13] Soon eleven booksellers were stocking it. By mid-May all 10,000 copies of the three Dublin editions were sold out and it was being serialised in four newspapers. In Belfast it had the largest circulation of any pamphlet and Russell returned there in April to find his friends already full of it.[14] Apart from his glowing and romanticised account of the French Revolution, it was Paine's attack on 'the old aristocratical system' and on religious intolerance which most struck home.

The dissatisfaction of Tone and Russell with the Whigs was shared by most reformers in Dublin and Belfast, and the establishment of an alternative body was much discussed.[15] Drennan wrote to Sam McTier on 21 May suggesting some form of 'Brotherhood' or 'benevolent conspiracy' for 'the greatest happiness of the greatest number', the real independence of Ireland and an end to bigotry and prejudice. It would be a total break from Whig clubbery, he said, and would have no attachment to party or aristocracy. It would not simply affect the language of patriotism, or concern itself with 'speculative plans of reform', but would be a practical organisation, concerned with the '*means* of accomplishment' through publication and communication. Privately Drennan saw 'the democratic part' of the Catholic Committee as allies, and tried to rescue his old friend Bruce from his anti-popery by representing the Catholics as more enlightened and less priest-ridden than Bruce imagined. Separation from Britain alone would produce reform and Drennan thought there were many people of like opinion.

Drennan's ideas are far more militant than anything Tone was writing at the time, and both Tone and Russell were to disagree with his proposal for a secret society. McTier showed Drennan's document to a number of people in Belfast and found most favourably disposed. This was the society for which Tone was asked by Russell to draw up the founding resolutions. The new society, whose inauguration was planned to coincide with Belfast's 14 July celebrations, was being organised jointly by the Volunteers and the Northern Whig Club. Drennan was asked by McTier to compile an appropriate declaration. A piece of grand rhetorical prose, typical of Drennan, was duly sent on 2 July. It rejoiced in the French Revolution, spoke of the human race as bound in a 'brotherhood of interest', of government as a trust and of civil obedience as conditional. The Catholics were not mentioned specifically (an omission which Drennan later sought to remedy) except in the expression of a general desire for an end to religious intolerance. Yet even this statement caused problems, and the Northern Whig Club withdrew its agreement to meet jointly with the Volunteers. But Drennan's Catholic amendment was adopted by the First Belfast Volunteer Company, which would go on to found the United Irish Society.[16]

The respective roles of Tone, Drennan and others in the foundation of that Society have been a source of contention.[17] The idea of Tone as sole founder of the United Irish Society is so firmly established in Irish tradition—indeed was so even in the 1790s—that some clarification is desirable. Political clubbery was in fashion and a club of its kind had been on the cards for some time. Tone, Russell and William Sinclair had kept in touch through that summer. Talk of an alliance between Dissenters and Catholics was rife, intolerance was depicted as unfashionable and reformers in Dublin and Belfast were involved in a frantic campaign to translate such sentiments into action.[18] Tone was no great initiator of ideas. But he was often the person who pulled them into shape. So it was with the United Irishmen. He was only one of the founding team. But he enabled the event to take place when it did, he coined the Society's name and proclaimed its principles with the clarity which gave them such effectiveness at the time and has provided the stuff for republican legend ever since.

Drennan had already sent off his declaration for the 14 July celebrations when a request arrived for resolutions as well. Drennan replied in ill humour. They should have made their plans a month ago, for now he could not oblige. Instead he recommended Tone. 'Tone will probably be able to throw off some address to the people or to mould his resolutions into that shape. He has a ready and an excellent pen'.[19] Tone received the request for resolutions on the 7th and the fact that an elegantly written document was on the mail coach to Belfast by the 9th amply justifies Drennan's confidence in his writing ability. It also speaks volumes about the state of his own legal career.

Tone's resolutions proclaimed English influence the ruin of Ireland. The remedy proposed was a 'more equal representation of the People in Parliament' and a union of all her people. The document, and the more famous accompanying letter, quickly fell into the hands of the Castle, as we have seen, and was sent with Drennan's declaration to Whitehall on the 11th. But the anti-English sentiments went unremarked at the time. They did so because in 1791 they were unexceptional. It was rather as 'an alarming Catholic paper' that it caused such a stir, for Tone's third resolution called for 'a complete internal union' of all Irishmen. It lamented 'the mistaken policy which has long divided them' and resolved to promote measures 'tending to the abolition of distinctions'. The word 'Catholic' appears nowhere in the document. Yet it was this last proposition which was rejected by the Belfast Volunteers.[20]

Looking back on these events from his Paris mission of 1796, Tone considered the rejection as the turning-point in his political career.

> Russell wrote me an account of all this, and it immediately set me on thinking more seriously than I had yet done on the state of Ireland. I soon formed my theory, and on that theory I have unvaryingly acted ever since.
>
> To subvert the tyranny of our execrable government, to break

the connexion with England, the never-failing source of all our political evils, and to assert the independence of my country— these were my objects. To unite the whole people of Ireland, to abolish the memory of all past dissensions, and to substitute the common name of Irishman, in place of the denominations of Protestant, Catholic and Dissenter—these were my means.[21]

But these words were written when Tone was an exile, a committed revolutionary negotiating military aid from France. At the time the rejection turned him into 'a red hot Catholic', not a revolutionary republican—even if the government made little distinction. The 'means' of uniting the people, now became the main 'object' in itself. The immediate outcome was Tone's most celebrated work, and, Paine aside, the most important polemical pamphlet of the period.

II

Tone's *Argument on Behalf of the Catholics of Ireland* was written by 1 August 1791 and published by Byrne at a shilling three weeks later. Though addressed to Protestants generally, it was aimed specifically at those Ulster Dissenters who, while radical in politics, were squeamish about the Catholics. It laments the disgraceful inferiority of Ireland among the nations of the world, identifying 'our evil Government' as the immediate cause, 'our own intestine division' the remote one. Remove the latter and reform of the former would inevitably follow. The 1782 'revolution' Tone dismisses as a 'bungling, imperfect business', enabling Irishmen 'to sell, at a much higher price, their honor, their integrity, and the interests of their country'. Given the extent of government influence and the exclusion of three-quarters of the nation from the franchise, reform had little chance of passing through the Irish Parliament. The Volunteers' attempt at reform had failed because it 'was built on too narrow a foundation...they failed because they did not deserve to succeed... they were disgraced, because they were illiberal, and degraded, because they were unjust'. The lesson: 'no reform can ever be obtained which shall not comprehensively embrace Irishmen of all denominations'. Oppressors, after all, can hardly complain at being themselves oppressed. Irishmen were now faced with two choices, they could remain oppressed, unknown in Europe, 'the prey to England'; or they could exert their power to secure 'a complete and radical emancipation of our country'. The former Tone refuses to countenance. Rather they must 'put away childish fears, look our situation in the face like men [and]...speak to this ghostly spectre of our distempered imagination, the genius of Irish Catholicity!'.

That 'spectre' he examines under two headings: danger to church establishment and danger to property. The latter he counters with arguments similar to those used by Russell in his preparatory jottings for his Catholic essays: the decay of the old Catholic families, who had posed the threat, and safety in the self-interest of those Catholics who had invested in land themselves after thr repeal of the relevant penal statutes. Tone then confronts that common argument against the immediate emancipation of the Catholics, their assumed ignorance, the idea that Catholics were 'incapable of liberty' and the need for a lengthy period of re-education before civil and political liberties could be restored to them. That they might be ignorant, Tone accepts, but since it was the Protestants who had excluded them from education and driven their clergy to seek it abroad, they could hardly be blamed for the consequences of the 'cruel injustice of Protestant bigotry'. 'We plunge them by law, and continue them by statute, in gross ignorance, and then we make the incapacity we have created an argument for their exclusion from the common rights of man! We plead our crime in justification of itself'. As for the idea that they are not prepared for liberty, were the Polish? Were the French? Peasantries were the same the world over, but the French Catholic gentry were as enlightened as any gentry. Catholic emancipation is not a disease that we prepare for by inoculation. 'Liberty is the vital principle of man: he that is prepared to live is prepared for freedom'.

Tone then arrives at the most common objection: their popery, their attachment to a foreign power and to tenets rendering them naturally disloyal and intolerant. These he demolishes by pointing to the disappearance of the Stuart threat, the widely publicised verdicts of the European universities, elicited by the English Catholics in their recent campaign, and the 'stupendous' revolution in France where the Pope was burnt in effigy and Catholics and Protestants sit together in the Legislative Assembly. Such critics were living in the past. Popery was dead. 'The emancipated and liberal Irishman, like the emancipated Frenchman, may go to mass, may tell his beads, or sprinkle his mistress with holy water; but neither the one nor the other will attend to the rusty and extinguished thunderbolts of the Vatican...which, indeed, his Holiness is now-a-days too prudent and cautious to issue'. It was persecution which bound papist to priest, priest to Pope; remove it and the binding would be undone. It is wrong to assume that what once was true always remains so.

As to their numbers, and Protestant fears that once Catholics were admitted to Parliament they would take over, Tone points to the existing Protestant Parliament and concludes that they had little to boast about. The Catholics could not be more corrupt. Nor were the fears of a Catholic majority realistic, given the disproportionate ownership of property by Protestants. As a further precaution, they could simply restrict the franchise to £10 freeholders and at a stroke also rid the constitution of that 'wretched tribe of forty shilling freeholders, whom we see driven to their octennial market, by their landlords, as much their property as the sheep or the bullocks'. This would have the dual virtue of purifying the Protestant interest and restoring the natural weight to 'the sound and respectable part of the Catholic community'.

But this was to confine his case to expediency. What about those natural rights of man of which they spoke so frequently? Could they exclude the Catholics from the natural right to freedom, or hope to carry reform against government influence without increasing that of the people? The Catholics held the balance between the Protestants and government. Government recognised this and courted the Catholics. If it succeeded it would then be invincible. The Catholics would be alienated from the Protestants 'by repeated suspicion, and unremitting ill usage' and attached to the government by gratitude. The choice was stark: 'reform and the Catholics, justice and liberty' or 'unconditional submission to the present, and every future Administration'. The Protestants could not have it both ways. If we continue to resist Catholic emancipation, he comments, 'at least be consistent, and cease to murmur at the oppression of the Government which grinds us'. Let government continue 'to play upon the terrors of the Protestants, the hopes of the Catholics, and balancing the one party by the other, plunder and laugh at, and defy both', let England continue to check our rising commerce and our country remain obscure, wretched, barbarous, 'so long as we can prevent the Catholics from rising to equality with ourselves', and 'in the spirit of the envious man in the fable, bear to lose one of our eyes, so that our neighbor may lose both'.[22]

It is a clever pamphlet, which adopts a conversational tone and establishes an immediate bond of identity with its author's intended audience by the assertion of his own Protestantism and the association of himself with their fears. It takes a secular line, suggesting that religion holds little sway in these enlightened times and by implication that the Protestants were terrifying themselves with obsolete horrors. Like all Tone's writings, the *Argument* says nothing new and owed much to ideas then in general circulation. But it speaks to the moment in plain, practical terms, and reproduces those ideas in immediately recognisable form. There are no frills, no deviations and the prose is carried along by a hard-hitting and co-herent argument which presents Protestant readers with a stark and urgent decision. Accept the Catholics as allies and emancipation as part of the overall reform programme, or abandon reform altogether.

Tone's total lack of understanding of the Catholic peasantry was to cause problems for later generations of Catholic nationalists. Tone was no democrat and it is unrealistic to expect him to have been so. He spoke for his own class, the urban middle class, Catholic and Protestant alike, and few on the Catholic Committee showed any more understanding than he of the general mass of Catholic peasantry. But his assumption of their ignorance was very Protestant, and typical of the time. It is not generally borne out by modern research.[23]

The pamphlet was an immediate success. Total sales of 6,000 by early 1792 put it in the best-seller league and a further 10,000 were printed that year by the United Irish Society. It was held at the time and since to have been largely responsible for that change in Presbyterian attitudes which permitted their unlikely merger with the Catholics in the United Irish Society. Such a union had been mooted at the time of the reform conventions in the 1780s, although its prospect had been greatly exaggerated by government fears. Tone did not write his pamphlet in an isolated garret. It was part of a determined onslaught by the advanced reformers on the divisive religious prejudices which helped government resist reform, and it was seen as such by the Belfast Dissenters.

But Tone's success in breaking down Presbyterian prejudice should not be exaggerated. It never was entirely removed. Far more important was the impact of the work on the Catholics. It was only when *they* dropped their reservations about the reformers that the radical Protestants and Dissenters shelved their suspicions. Tone and his friends in Dublin were rather more aware of Catholic caution than the Belfast men, and a secondary theme in the *Argument* urges Catholics likewise to join with their Protestant friends. Tone was highly critical of the Catholic clergy, although he removed the criticism from the second edition, by which time the Catholics had indeed come round.[24] Keogh and other Catholic leaders had been spoken to earlier that summer, but Drennan felt they would join with the reformers only if it could be demonstrated that a large proportion of the northern Protestants supported their cause. 'At present the Catholics are cautious', he wrote to Sam McTier on 31 August. 'They think you are squibbing only in the paper without any serious intention of doing them service...they therefore naturally lean to government who promises fair, rather than to old enemies who put on a face of friendship'. Government had strong allies in what Drennan called 'the aristocratical part' of the Catholics. The Papal Nuncio himself had issued a strong rebuke to the Catholics of Elphin for publicly thanking the Belfast Volunteers for their declaration of the summer, and firmly instructed their clergy to oppose any union between Catholics and Presbyterians.[25]

Tone's pamphlet had the intended impact on leading Catholics. Charles O'Conor, son of the founder of the Catholic Committee, referred to 'our friend Mr Tone'. 'A better pamphlet than Tone's I have never read', wrote O'Conor's nephew, Hugh McDermot. 'It is from the beginning to end a chain of close argument linked together by strong facts and forcible deductions. It speaks to the heart as well as to the head. . .it certainly ought to become the manual of every person who is worthy of being called an Irishman.'[26]

At last the Catholics were dropping their shield. Keogh had enlisted the services of Edmund Burke's son Richard as Catholic agent in England, and in October, Braughall, McKenna, and about 40 other reforming Catholics set up a new Catholic Society in Dublin, designed to counter the pro-government element in the Catholic Committee. On 21 October, McKenna, as secretary, issued a declaration of the new society's aims. The document marked a notable departure from existing Catholic tactics and represented quite a challenge to Protestant claims to be more enlightened than their Catholic fellow countrymen.

It opened with a call to Catholics to throw off all traces of slavishness. 'In the present enlightened and improving period of society, it is not for the Irish Roman Catholics alone to continue silent'. The Catholics should use every 'legal and constitutional' means to secure their emancipation. But repeal of all penal statutes against Catholics would achieve little unless the 'jealousies' which separated them from their 'Protestant brethren' were likewise re-moved. 'It is time we should cease to be distinct nations, forcibly enclosed within the limits of one island.' It was their enemies who kept them divided. 'Countrymen! Too long have we suffered our-selves to be opposed in rival factions to each other, the sport of those who felt no tenderness for either.' The objects which divided their ancestors had ceased to exist. 'It is time we should cease to be distinct nations, forcibly enclosed within the limits of one island. It shall be a capital object of our institution to encourage the spirit of harmony and sentiments of affection.'[27]

McKenna's pamphlet and the new direction taken by the Dublin Catholics reflected a general impatience on the part of reformers that summer. The feeling produced Tone's pamphlet and there are signs that the different religious groupings in Dublin were already coming together before the United Irish Society was formally established in October. The similarities between Tone's and McKenna's pamphlets suggest as much. Westmorland took the rapid circulation of Tone's *Argument* as a sign that the dreaded alliance between Catholics and Dissenters was imminent, and Hobart tried unsuccessfully to persuade the Catholic Committee to repudiate McKenna's *Declaration*. Whitehall at first thought Westmorland was exaggerating. But by the end of the year the changed mood in Ireland and above all the prospect of an alliance between Catholics and Dissenters were producing a positive response to Catholic demands.[28]

III

The race was on for the Catholic soul. Would they throw their weight behind the radical reformers or would they be won over by government concessions? Drennan would later accuse the Catholics of playing government and reformers off against one another, of having two strings to their bow. The accusation was true enough. But Drennan's irritation was naïve and his biographer detects some personal pique in it.[29] England had always proved a better friend to the Catholics than had their fellow countrymen. They had little reason to trust the Protestants, even less the Dissenters. Independence from England held no advantage for the Catholics. Tone's reaction was rather more pragmatic. In time he too came to suspect that the Catholics were not really committed to reform and would abandon it on emancipation. Nevertheless he continued to campaign for emancipation because he considered their cause just, and in the United Irish Society would often be found swimming against the general tide in his claims for the interdependence of reform and Catholic emancipation.[30]

Events now began to move very fast. On 4 October the three Belfast Volunteer corps gathered at the White Linen Hall to propose an answer to the Catholic addresses of thanks for Belfast's July resolutions. The meeting was chaired by Sinclair and its reply pledged their joint efforts 'to restore to *Irishmen*—their long lost rights'. Their main object was 'an adequate representation of the People in Parliament', and they hoped to lay all differences 'with the bones of our ancestors'. 'Differing in our religion...but resembling each other in the great features of humanity; let us unite to vindicate the rights of our common nature; let the decisive and unanimous voice of the society at large, of the body of the People, the mighty and irresistible whole—be heard,—it will—it must be obeyed.'[31]

Immediately after the meeting Sinclair wrote excitedly to Russell: 'our three corps met this day at the White Linen Hall when I had the honour to preside as Chairman and the paper I now enclose you was unanimously agreed to; indeed I may say more, for it was agreed to with *acclamations according to the French mode*. After the business was settled a committee was appointed consisting of three from each corps for the purpose of corresponding with such Catholics or others as may be disposed to communicate with us'. He feared that a new outbreak of sectarian troubles in places like Armagh might thwart their campaign to win over the Catholics. But Russell now felt 'coalition' inevitable and urged his friends to 'work tooth and nail' to break down opposition.[32]

The establishment of two new newspapers in Dublin and Belfast was to be part of that process. In Dublin a thrice-weekly evening paper, to be called the *National Journal*, was mooted. Russell—who had resigned his commission in the army and was then in Dublin without paid employment[33]—was to be editor and Tone wrote the prospectus. This appeared in a handbill on 4 October. The object of the new paper would be 'to unite and emancipate ALL THE PEOPLE OF IRELAND' and to encourage mutual understanding between 'the GREAT SECTS'. It would eschew all existing parties for 'THE PARTY OF THE PEOPLE', 'remove all distinction between Irishmen' and 'secure to the people their due weight, by purifying, *completely*, their representation in Parliament'. Donations of £550 had been raised and publication would start in January 1792.[34]

Plans for a second Belfast newspaper to be run on 'independent principles' also took shape in September 1791. A meeting of sub-scribers to what became the *Northern Star* met at the house of the veteran reformer Tom McCabe in North Street on Friday, 23 September, and balloted for an editorial committee. The group also included the founding United Irishmen William Tennent, the ship-brokers William and Henry Haslett, Sam Neilson, William Simms, who with his brother Robert ran a tannery business, another tanner, William McCleery, and the linen draper Gilbert McIlveen. Neilson topped the poll in the vote for editor. The thirty-year-old son of a Presbyterian minister, Neilson had already made a fortune from his woollen drapery business in Bridge Street. He was an advanced radical, nicknamed 'the Jacobin' in Tone's journals, and was the guiding hand behind the *Northern Star* until its suppression in 1797. He was also one of the chief architects of the United Irishmen and became a particular friend of Tone.[35]

With a starting capital of £1,000, the *Northern Star* printed its prospectus on 18 November. Its aims were to be the promotion of parliamentary reform, 'the union of Irishmen' and the abolition of 'those distinctions which neither reason nor religion can at this day justify'. Impediments to Irish commerce and manufacture would be highlighted and full reports appear of events in America and France.[36] The first issue appeared on Monday, 2 January 1792, and for the next five years it was Ireland's most independent and popular provincial newspaper, an effective mouthpiece for the United Irish-men and a powerful moulder of opinion. The Dublin sister paper petered out after a few issues. A replacement editor could not be found after Russell had returned north to take up a magistracy in Tyrone, arranged by the Knox family.[37]

Tone's *Argument* was already causing a sensation in Ulster before it was taken up by the Belfast Society of United Irishmen and circulated in a special twopenny edition. Tone was made an honorary member of the First Volunteer Company and invited to Belfast to assist in the formation of the Society of United Irishmen.[38] 'You have no doubt read with attention Tone's "Argument on behalf of the Catholics of Ireland"', wrote Dr Haliday to Charlemont on 5 November. 'It is calculated to make, and has actually made here, a general impression in their [the Catholics'] favour.' Although Haliday did not agree with its conclusions, he thought the tide of support for Tone's *Argument* 'too strong at present to be directly resisted', and those who adhered to their 'old horrors and dread of popery' were looked upon as 'men of little mind'.[39] The pamphlet had brought Tone instant fame and the correspondence of reformers generally in these months breathes a buoyancy and optimism unknown even at the height of Volunteering.

9

Belfast and the Society of United Irishmen

Tone and Russell travelled to Belfast on 10 October. The recently established mail coach from Dublin left from the Belfast Hotel in Capel Street at 10.30 three mornings a week. At £1.16s. 3d. for an inside seat (five times the average weekly wage for a weaver), the fare was expensive and the journey long, taking until the following evening.[1] Tone had cavilled at the expenditure involved when Russell invited him to attend the July celebrations, and throughout his two-week stay in October his journals reveal that characteristic consciousness of the cost of things.[2] They arrived in Belfast on the evening of Tuesday, 11 October.[3]

I

Belfast in 1791, with its population of 18,320, was small and intimate. Whig Club members, Volunteers and United Irishmen shared the same membership, mixed socially and attended the same Presbyterian meeting houses. This was the middle-class capital of Ireland, and like many other towns in Ulster Belfast had a very Protestant aspect, which made English travellers feel at home. It was, according to Arthur Young, 'a very well-built town of brick, The streets are broad and strait...lively and busy'.[4] The town was dominated by its entrepreneurial business class and Tone found its members as animated about the loss of a new power loom to the town as about radical politics.[5] Indeed all too often their enthusiasms were dictated by economic issues and their opposition to the American war owed as much to that war's closure of markets as to patriotism.

In 1791 Belfast was thriving. Its mill owners were passionate innovators, particularly in the field of new technology. The auction of John Haslett's Waring Street cotton factory in 1798 listed carding machines, spinning jennies and 'a horizontal wheel for turning the machinery' among its contents. In 1791 there were 695 looms operating in the town and by 1800 11 factories gave employment to 27,000 people within a ten-mile radius. Although cotton still dominated Belfast's economy, the damp climate and abundant streams tumbling from the Antrim plateau made it perfect for linen production and its hills were dotted with bleaching greens.[6]

Tone was fascinated by what he saw. 'Rode out with P.P. [Russell] and Sinclair to see his bleach-green', he wrote in his journal for 24 October. 'A noble concern; extensive machinery'. Sinclair, he noted, had been the first to introduce American potash, and he applauded the extensive use of machinery in the interests of progress, despite the massive loss of employment and resistance from the work force. 'Great command of water, which is omnipotent in the linen, etc. Three falls of 21 feet each in 10 acres, and ten more in the glen if necessary. A most romantic and beautiful country'.[7]

By the 1790s Belfast had replaced Dublin as the main centre for Irish linen exports, with maritime developments to match. Much of the surrounding countryside served the needs of the town's industrial growth and was extensively populated by weavers occupying tiny farms. Business revolved round the old Brown Linen Hall in Donegall Street and a new White Linen Hall. Built through public subscription in the 1780s, it stood on the site of the present-day City Hall and dominated the up-and-coming fashionable Linenhall Street (Donegall Place). The list of subscribers in 1782–3 is revealing. Of the future United Irish leaders, Thomas McCabe and Gilbert McIlveen donated £100 each, the apothecary John Campbell £200. Neilson, the Hasletts, the Simmses and Russell's particular friends, the McCracken and Templeton families, also contributed.[8] This was a tightly knit, often intermarried business world, its centre within yards of High Street, the main thoroughfare.

Like the White Linen Hall, the poorhouse and infirmary to the north-west of the town (still standing in Clifton Street) was also something of a monument to the Presbyterian mercantile community which dominated the town's civic life. It was another project paid for by public subscription, organised by those same men who had been involved in the White Linen Hall. Designed by Robert Joy, Henry's brother, it was one of those exercises in pragmatic philanthropy which marked much of late eighteenth-century thinking. The problems of poverty were answered by the philosophy of work, and Joy, McCabe and John McCracken rounded off their enterprise by introducing cotton spinning as employment for the young inmates.[9]

However rapid its industrialisation, Belfast was still very much a market town. In 1791 it was congested and dirty, with dunghills a constant nuisance in the streets and pigs wandering at will. The streets were unpaved and unlit and peopled by a complete cross-section of society. A famous painting of High Street in 1786 shows the masts of ships docked at the end of the street, and in the left foreground the Donegall Arms, where Tone and Russell often dined and socialised. Rebuilt in 1786 by Thomas Sheridan, its distinctive roofline was one of Belfast's landmarks until it finally succumbed to urban planners in the 1980s.

Bridge Street, which linked High Street to Waring Street, opened on to the elegant new Exchange Building and Assembly Rooms (today the Northern Bank), built in 1769 and designed by the distinguished Palladian architect Sir Robert Taylor. It stood at the juncture of Bridge, Rosemary, North and Waring Streets, the so-called 'Four Corners', a large open public space, where the main open-air public meetings took place and where publishers advertised the latest books and pamphlets. This central network of streets was linked by innumerable entries and lanes lined with small shops and inns, and peopled by ships' chandlers, rope-makers and carpenters. It was in one of these, Sugarhouse Entry—destroyed in the blitz of 1941—that the United Irish Society was founded.

Belfast was a closed borough. Its members were returned by the sovereign and twelve burgesses, many of whom were absentees. Lacking a parliament—indeed lacking even a sizeable political class, since none of these rich Belfast merchants could vote for their MPs— Belfast had few ostentatious town houses like those of the southern aristocrats. Linenhall Street, running between the White Linen Hall and High Street, was beginning to be laid out as a fashionable area for the rich. There the Marquis of Donegall—sovereign of Belfast— and a number of its magistrates were investing in handsome terraces. It was Belfast's only really fashionable area, but by the end of the 1790s it was setting new standards of cleanliness, which were beginning to radiate out to the rest of the town.[10]

It was an introspective town. Drennan, a native son, found it stifling, though it was much to the taste of Tone who revelled in intimate friendship. The other side of Belfast's internationalist think-ing and industrialising economy was a provincialism which isolated it from the rest of the country and bred in its citizens an instinctive distrust and very often an intellectual disdain for their fellow countrymen. Certainly Tone and Russell found a remarkable igno-rance of Catholicism among these northerners. It bred extremes of unrealistic fear and—when countered—equally unrealistic optimism about the nature of popery and the ease with which obstacles to religious co-operation might be overcome. The town was physically cut off from the rest of the country. A daily postal service with Dublin had only been established in 1789. Transport was erratic and rudimentary. There was still no means of transport to the west of Ireland, and even within the province communications were difficult.[11]

The town was predominently Presbyterian, as were the neighbouring counties of Antrim and Down. There were five Presbyterian
meeting houses, three in Rosemary Lane alone (and two of them of
the New Light persuasion). The number of Catholics was insignificant, if on the increase. Only 7 were recorded in 1708, 556 by 1779,
and Belfast acquired its first mass house in 1784. By the 1790s rapid
industrialisation was bringing more and more Catholics into the
town, and suburbs of mud cabins sprang up to the north and west to
accommodate them. Even then, they accounted for only 8 per cent of
the population. With such insignificant numbers, active sectarianism
was negligible. But growing industrialisation brought in rural out-
workers and with them that sectarian strife already rampant in
neighbouring counties. The bitter sectarian rioting that had gone
on in Armagh since the 1780s between Catholic Defenders and
Protestant Peep-of-Day Boys was already sweeping through other
counties by the early '90s.[12]

II

But Belfast had yet to experience it, and in 1791 Tone found
'blend[ing] of the sects' fashionable—one hairdresser even boasting
of having his two children christened by a priest, though he himself
was a Dissenter. Among those of the so-called 'secret committee' of
Volunteers responsible for inviting him to Belfast, Tone likewise
found a general willingness to co-operate with and learn more about
the Catholics. Russell assumed the role of spokesman for the Catholics. He had communicated with members of the Catholic Committee that summer and gave the Belfast committee a full history of
its proceedings.

With the Northern Whig Club, however, it was quite another
matter, and Tone recounts 'a furious battle' on the Catholic issue,
just after he had taken up his membership, paid his fees and signed
their declaration. Bruce assumed the leadership of the anti-papists,
presenting an emotional case one day at the McTiers' house in
Cunningham Row, which took the reformers nearly two hours
to disentangle. 'His ideas', Tone noted, 'are, 1st. Danger to true
religion, inasmuch as the Roman Catholics would, if emancipated,
establish an *inquisition*. 2nd. Danger to property by reviving the
Court of Claims, and admitting any evidence to substantiate Catholic titles. 3rd. Danger, generally, of throwing the power into their
hands, which would make this a Catholic government, incapable of
enjoying or extending liberty'. These were the same arguments
which had been used against Catholic reform for much of the
century. But Tone still found the majority of the Northern Whig
Club, apart from himself, Russell, McTier and the timber merchant

and Volunteer, Robert Getty, supporting them, while at the same time protesting their liberality and good will towards Catholics generally.[13]

Tone was angry and depressed by such initial opposition and tried to brush it aside by dismissing it as wine talk. But he did recognise the need to tread carefully in Belfast. The ground would first have to be prepared by a writing campaign. Indeed the heady optimism of much of Tone's journal may present a rather different image of the man than that perceived by contemporaries. He met and liked Haliday and the respect was mutual, despite Tone's rabid emancipationism. 'The gentleman himself', Haliday wrote to Charlemont on 5 November, 'passed a good many days among us lately, and proselyted [sic] not a few. I thought myself so unlucky in seeing so little of him; professional and other engagements deprived me of the pleasure of meeting him except for one day, when his good sense and modest unassuming courage were truly engaging. I believe it was under his auspices that the society of "United Irishmen" at Belfast was formed'.[14]

This had been the main reason for Tone's journey north, and correspondence over the previous few months reveals a rather different lead-in to the formation of the famous movement than is commonly presented. It was not entirely a Belfast initiative. Rather members of Tone's old political club at Trinity, Catholics such as McCormick, the Dublin printer John Chambers, seasoned radicals like Tandy and Rowan, and Belfast men like McTier, Sinclair and McCabe had been in frequent communication over the summer. The name of the society and its prospectus had already been decided. Tone's July resolutions were to be remodelled—which he did on his first day in Belfast—printed and widely distributed, and a special United Irish Society edition of his *Argument* was already being printed by Chambers before Tone and Russell set off for Belfast. Its appearance was to coincide with the inauguration of the new society, and Tone wrote impatiently on 13 October urging Chambers to make haste. Chambers was also printing the prospectus for the *National Journal*, and Tone and Russell returned to their inn on the night of the 16th to find 2,000 of these sent instead of the pamphlet. Tone was beside himself with frustration, and writes of storming and cursing while Russell teased him by quoting Seneca and Boethius *De Consolatione*. The commissioned re-edition of the *Argument* did finally arrive during his stay in Belfast—the first batch of a printing of 10,000 ordered by the United Irish Society—and was advertised in the *News Letter* at threepence on 25 October.[15]

There was another reason for Tone's frustration. Preparations for the launching of the new society were proceeding far too leisurely.

'We journalize everything here,' he complained to Chambers two days after his arrival, 'but nothing more than eating and drinking has yet gone forward'. On the previous day, the 12th, he, Russell, McTier and McCabe had made arrangements for a dinner at which his resolutions would be discussed. Tone marvelled at the changed opinion in Belfast which had rejected them as 'too hazardous' in July, but now required him to remodel them as 'too tame'. It was not till Friday, 14 October, that a full meeting of the 'secret committee' was convened and the Society of United Irishmen established. The committee was composed of Sinclair, McTier, Neilson, McCleery, McCabe, the Simmses, Henry Haslett, John Campbell, McIlveen and William Tennent. The thirty-two-year-old Tennent was the eldest son of a Presbyterian minister and one of the most progressive of the Belfast merchants. He went on to found Belfast's first bank, was considered by the government 'a person of the first abilities' and one of the more dangerous United Irish leaders.[16] Tone and Russell were sworn in as members and the United Irish Society held its inaugural meeting on Tuesday, 18 October. Twenty-eight members were present and Tone's resolutions were accepted unanimously. A copy was sent to Tandy, McKenna and McCormick in Dublin, with a request for cooperation, and plans were laid for a wider distribution elsewhere in the country.

DECLARATION AND RESOLUTIONS
OF THE SOCIETY OF UNITED IRISHMEN OF BELFAST

In the present great era of reform, when unjust governments are falling in every quarter of Europe; when religious persecution is compelled to abjure her tyranny over conscience; when the rights of man are ascertained in theory, and that theory substantiated by practice; when antiquity can no longer defend absurd and oppressive forms, against the common sense and common interests of mankind; when all government is acknowledged to originate from the people, and to be so far only obligatory as it protects their rights and promotes their welfare: We think it our duty, as Irishmen, to come forward, and state what we feel to be our heavy grievance, and what we know to be its effectual remedy. WE HAVE NO NATIONAL GOVERNMENT; we are ruled by Englishmen, and the servants of Englishmen, whose object is the interest of another country, whose instrument is corruption, and whose strength is the weakness of Ireland; and these men have the whole of the power and patronage of the country, as means to seduce and to subdue the honesty and the spirit of her representatives in the legislature. Such an extrinsic power, acting with uniform force in a direction too frequently opposite to the true line of our obvious interests, can be resisted with effect solely by *unanimity, decision, and spirit in the people*; qualities which may be exerted most legally, constitutionally, and efficaciously, by that great measure essential to the prosperity and freedom of Ireland. AN EQUAL RE-PRESENTATION OF ALL THE PEOPLE IN PARLIA-MENT. We do not here mention as grievances, the rejection of a place-bill, of a pension-bill, of a responsibility-bill, the sale of Peerages in one House, the corruption publicly avowed in the other, nor the notorious infamy of borough traffic between both; not that we are insensible of their enormity, but that we consider them as but symptoms of that mortal disease which corrodes the vitals of our Constitution, and leaves to the people, in their own Government, but the shadow of a name.

Impressed with these sentiments, we have agreed to form an association, to be called 'THE SOCIETY OF UNITED IRISHMEN:' And we do pledge ourselves to our country, and mutually to each other, that we will steadily support, and endeavor, by all due means, to carry into effect, the following resolutions:

First, Resolved, That the weight of English influence in the Government of this country is so great, as to require a cordial union among ALL THE PEOPLE OF IRELAND, to maintain that balance which is essential to the preservation of our liberties, and the ex-tension of our commerce.

Second, That the sole constitutional mode by which this influence can be opposed, is by a complete and radical reform of the re-presentation of the people in Parliament.

Third, That no reform is practicable, efficacious, or just, which shall not include Irishmen of every *religious* persuasion.

Satisfied, as we are, that the intestine divisions among Irishmen have too often given encouragement and impunity to profligate, audacious, and corrupt Administrations, in measures which, but for these divisions, they durst not have attempted; we submit our resolutions to the nation, as the basis of our political faith.

We have now gone to what we conceive to be the remedy. With a Parliament thus reformed, every thing is easy; without it, nothing can be done: and we do call on and most earnestly exhort our countrymen in general to follow our example, and to form similar societies in every quarter of the kingdom, for the pro-motion of constitutional knowledge, the abolition of bigotry in religion and politics, and the equal distribution of the rights of man through all sects and denominations of Irishmen. The people, when thus collected, will feel their own weight, and secure that power which theory has already admitted as their portion, and to which, if they be not aroused by their present provocations to vindicate it, they deserve to forfeit their pretensions FOR EVER.

The final document differed in a number of respects from the July original. The October version is a much more determined and radical document. The call for radical reform and religious co-operation and the attack on government for sustaining divisions are both more forceful and, significantly, the earlier favourable references to the Whigs have been dropped.[17]

Tone later claimed that by this stage his mind was 'quite made up' on the viability of an independent Ireland existing separately from England. He, Russell, McTier, Sinclair and Digges spoke of such an eventuality while he was in Belfast. Digges thought France would assist, and painted a glowing picture of an independent Ireland, unencumbered by debt and surpassing England in arts, commerce and manufacture. Sinclair expressed the same opinion over dinner one evening. He thought trade would suffer a temporary interruption but would recover quickly, and Russell felt the English army would be annihilated in the event of a revolution.[18] These were private opinions, however, and should not be attributed to the United Irish Society generally. Armed revolt was never a serious proposition at this stage, however much they complained of the British connection. Even Tone was not an active separatist until 1795, whatever his views on the viability of an independent Ireland.

III

Tone's visit to Belfast marked the start of his regular journals. It is through them that Tone has become one of the most popular of Irish historical figures. Their tenor is fast, perceptive and amusing, though their flippancy has given rise to serious misunderstandings about Tone's character. The idea originated in his special friendship with Russell, and much of the tongue-in-cheek posturing is directed at his friend. 'I did not tell you my news', he wrote to Matilda from Belfast on 20 October, 'as I journalize everything, and promise myself great pleasure from reading over my papers with you. I have christened Russell by the name of P.P. Clerk of this Parish, and he makes a very conspicuous figure in my memoirs.' There follow competing postscripts from the two friends. Russell: 'Dear Matty— As to anything your wise husband may have said of me, I neither desire to know, nor do I care..."*I had a friend*"'. Tone had spent much of the previous day chastising Russell for his drinking and late nights and the latter had risen particularly early that morning to disprove the accusations. 'I am at present composing a pretty moral treatise on temperance, and will dedicate it to myself, for I don't know who is likely to profit so much by it.' Tone: 'P.P. has been scribbling his bit of nonsense. He is a great fool, and I have much trouble to manage him. I assure you that you will be much amused by his exploits in my journal, which is a thousand times wittier than Swift's...P.P. calls me "his friend Mr John Hutton"....He is writing a journal, but mine is worth fifty of it'.[19] It was, alas, too true. Russell did not write with facility.

Russell had commenced his journal earlier[20] and it may well have been his idea to exchange in writing the lengthy conversational observations which were such a part of their friendship. Certainly Tone's daily account of his two weeks in Belfast tells us rather more of their friendship than of the United Irishmen. Russell was the constant object of Tone's teasing. On his first Sunday in Belfast, Tone accompanied Russell to church and listened to 'a vile sermon' denouncing smuggling as disloyal. Tone thought it nonsense, but Russell took it to heart and was greatly distressed by it. After church they joined the Belfast Sunday strollers on the Mall, which ran along the Blackstaff River south of Belfast, from the White Linen Hall to Joy's Paper Mill. Russell's sense of guilt at his own moral failings intensified as Tone remarked on how all the women were flirting with him.

In Belfast at that time a large number of card clubs, dances, balls and coteries were held and the two friends were on the receiving end of some lavish private hospitality. At his home in Bridge Street Dr James McDonnell, one of the town's outstanding intellectual figures at the time, though unusual in his Gaelic-Irish background, was one of their more frequent hosts. 'I find the people here extremely civil', Tone wrote to Matilda, 'I have dined out every day since I came here, and have now more engagements than I can possibly fulfil'. He disliked the card clubs, accompanied Russell twice to coteries at the Donegall Arms, but did not enjoy them.[21] He found the women ugly, disapproved of their heavy make-up and had a dispute with Russell about the teeth of one unfortunate young lady.[22] These were a particular obsession with him and suggest worries about his own. On the second occasion, when much against his better inclinations Tone had agreed to accompany his friend, Russell lost his nerve in the lobby and they returned home. There Russell again changed his mind and wanted to return. It was after midnight and Tone was angry with him.

It was just the kind of indecision in Russell which Tone mocked when in good humour, but criticised when not. Every journal entry carries references to Russell's hang-ups: 'in the blue devils—thinks he is losing his faculties' and 'P.P. at home in the horrors; thinks himself sick generally'. Tone blamed these rather on Russell's drinking, smoking and late nights and constantly nagged him about his bad habits. 15 October: 'I had been lecturing P.P. on the state of his nerves, and the necessity of early hours; to which he agreed, and as the first fruits of my advice and his reformation, sat up with Digges until three o'clock in the morning, being four hours after I had gone to bed'. Tone looked upon his friend as something of a wayward 'youth' and frequently assumed an elder-brother role.[23] Russell wore his mental anguish openly and tended to invite such chiding from his friends.[24]

Russell took the criticism in good part, and seems to have been rather more tolerant of Tone's failings than Tone of his. On Sunday the 23rd Alexander Stewart had them to dinner 'with a parcel of squires of County Down'. The conversation was dominated by 'Fox hunting, hare hunting, buck hunting' and the superiority of the northern potatoes. They then went on to the Washington Club, where in Tone's opinion another silly argument was in progress. It had been a tiring day which ended with Tone getting drunk in the Donegall Arms. The next morning he was sick and felt guilty about his rudeness to Russell, who took it all with patience.

No stay in a new town would have been complete without a visit to the theatre and Tone and Russell took in the *Carmelite*, playing in Rosemary Lane. It was not, however, one of the theatre's better seasons. It had been neglected by actor-manager Atkins because of his plans to build a second theatre in Belfast and another in Derry. A promising season with the celebrated Thomas Ryder was cut short by illness on 10 October and Tone and Russell were not impressed by the remaining actors. Instead they spent their time searching the audience for a pretty face. Russell fell asleep and they left early.[25]

The conventional image of Tone is of a heavy-drinking, fast-living adventurer. Certainly he had, by his own admission, 'a strong attachment to pleasures and amusements',[26] and, like his contemporaries drank large quantities of wine. But it did not agree with him. He was not in robust health and was invariably ill after long journeys and late nights. On one stormy night in Belfast he got wet and caught a violent cold. He suffered from sleeplessness, though clearly needing a lot of sleep, and even in Belfast, where he threw himself into a round of socialising, he was in bed early most nights. Though remembered for his nervous energy, his reserves of strength were low and he tired easily. As for the racy image, Tone was indeed flirtatious, but this was combined with considerable prudishness in sexual matters and even the London liaisons were not one-night stands. There was also a meticulousness bordering on the punctilious in Tone, which made him such a contrast to Russell and so impatient of sloppiness in others.

Much of the misunderstanding of Tone's character lies in the very nature of the journals. Unlike those of Russell, which are very obviously dashed off in the nature of a diary, there is a surety and flow in Tone's journals, a gaiety which sometimes appears flippant. This is not to deny that the edited version does somewhat alter the character of the original notebooks. Nor did it become common knowledge that they were so edited until the 1930s, long after Tone had already become part of historical legend.[27] Large chunks were omitted by his widow and son, references to his early affairs and to women generally, criticisms of Matilda's family, of America (where she then resided) and of friends still living in 1826 being the most notable examples. Tone and his family had indeed suffered considerably because of his political activities, and by 1826 Matilda would have liked to present Tone as the pure republican hero of her own perceptions. That said, the pruning exercise was far more restrained than it might have been. The character of the journals was altered more by his son's painstaking and otherwise commendable arrangement and editing.

The original journals were written in small brown leather notebooks which would have fitted into a side pocket. They do not reveal the clear sense of direction to be found in the edited version, although this does emerge after 1796. Rather each notebook might contain a diary entry, a draft letter or article, quotations from other works, accounts, lists, personal reminders, doodles and passable sketches of things and people Tone found ridiculous—judges' wigs, jackboots, ludicrous ladies' headdresses.[28] An early essay later entitled 'On the English Connection' in fact bears no such title and gives a misleading idea of a steady progression to republican revolutionary.[29]

The journals have given rise to accusations that Tone was creating his own myth for posterity. But until 1796 there is little reason to doubt his assertion that they were kept primarily for the amusement of the two people who mattered most in his life, Matilda and Russell. No journals were kept during periods when he and Matilda were together. The listing of his own achievements was part of that friendly rivalry with Russell, already evident in their correspondence, and Russell's self-torture was played up for Matty's amusement, as was Tone's constant swearing which so offended nineteenth-century readers. 'I have been wrong in not mentioning in a note that all these exclamatory oaths are *quoted not sworn*'—as indeed they are in the manuscript journals—Matilda explained to her friend Eliza Fletcher;

'they were constant exclamations of my grandfather a very old clergyman and used to amaze and amuse Tone'.[30] The aggressive self-confidence of parts of the journals did not exist in reality. Tone desperately needed Russell, more than Russell needed him, and his anguished loneliness in Paris in 1796 was to produce hundreds of pages of self-analysis and less of the clever raciness of those written in Ireland.

Much of the pace and tone of the journals comes from Tone's tendency to speak through witty and often ludicrous quotations. It was a trait common in eighteenth-century journals, though it figures to an unusual degree in Tone. It was also part of the 'in' language the trio had created for themselves and the friendly rivalry persisted in attempts to outdo one another in their choice of apt phrases. In this respect, Tone admitted Russell's superiority. From exile in America he recalled nostalgically 'that particular style of conversation which we had framed for ourselves...those strained quotations, absurd phrases and extravagant sallies which people in the unreserve of affectionate intercourse indulge themselves in'.[31]

Many of the quotations are from Shakespeare—the most popular dramatist throughout the eighteenth century—and even in his schooldays Tone was known for the facility with which he could quote the Bard. Falstaff, with his 'wit and alacrity of mind' and contempt for 'sober reputation' was clearly the favourite character.[32] Other favourite texts include Gay's *Beggar's Opera*, Sheridan's *School for Scandal* and *The Rivals* and the plays of O'Keefe and Farquhar all of which played regularly in Dublin. Otherwise the journals read like the Top Twenty of the eighteenth-century educated man's reading list, Pope, Swift, Defoe, Richardson, Goldsmith, Sterne, Smollett, Fielding and the occasional if predictable foreign work such as Voltaire or Laclos. One will search in vain for Montesquieu or Rousseau. These journals were never intended to be a political treatise.

IV

The Belfast trip had been an overwhelming success and Tone and Russell were seen off on the 27th by the many new friends they had made. Back in Dublin they acted as ambassadors from the north and helped found the Dublin Society of United Irishmen on the same model. A preliminary meeting at Doyle's tavern brought together Tandy, Todd Jones, Drennan, Pollock, Tone, Russell and Catholic representatives such as McKenna, MacNeven and McCormick. There was some initial disagreement on whether to campaign first for emancipation or for reform. Tone argued for a compact between Protestants and Catholics. They should come forward on the basis of 'common interests' and base their demands on union, and he arranged to breakfast with MacNeven to overcome the latter's doubts. The Dublin Society was duly inaugurated on 9 November and Tone's resolutions adopted.[33]

Tone had helped convince the future United Irishmen, Protestant and Catholic alike, that reform and emancipation went hand in hand. A dramatic change had occurred in Belfast's attitude on the Catholic issue and Haliday attributed it largely to Tone's *Argument*. Even he had been influenced. The Whigs ought to recognise that emancipation was coming, he told Charlemont, and proclaim their support before the Catholics were entirely bought off by the government. The Catholics were now up for aucton, with government and Protestant reformers bidding against each other.[34] Haliday's analysis was correct. In a very short time opinion on the Catholic issue had changed dramatically, even in British governing circles. The Catholics no longer needed to grovel for redress and they too recognised their new strength.

The role of Tone's *Argument* in the change of climate is unmistakable. He returned to Dublin to find it 'running like wildfire' and admitted that he was 'somewhat vain' about its achievements, particularly in the north.[35] A Belfast town meeting was called in January 1792 to debate the Catholic issue and prepare a petition to Parliament. Such a meeting would have been inconceivable six months earlier. A motion by Bruce and Haliday for gradual emancipation, on a 'time to time' basis, was overwhelmingly defeated and, given the altered climate, even the minority felt compelled to issue a statement declaring their only objection was whether emancipation should be immediate or progressive. Belfast's Catholic petition, carrying over 600 signatures, duly went up to Parliament on 8 February.[36]

But the influence was not all one way. Tone was enraptured by Belfast and the new friends he had met there.[37] The Belfast Dissenters came to represent his ideal of middle-class virtue and their anti-aristocratic and anti-English views deeply influenced his own. 'The Dissenters of the north, and more especially of the town of Belfast, are, from the genius of their religion, and from the superior diffusion of political information among them, sincere and enlightened Republicans', he would write in 1796. 'They have among them but few great landed proprietors. . . they have ever, in a degree, opposed the usurpations of England, whose protection, as well from their numbers and spirit as the nature of their property, they did not, like the Protestant aristocracy, feel necessary for their existence.'[38] Tone himself never entirely abandoned that instinctive deference to rank so ingrained in the stratified society of the south, so absent in the northern Dissenters. And just as it was from Dissenting circles in England that a middle-class identity and political philosophy emerged far in advance of the times, so it was among his Belfast friends that Tone's anti-aristocratic views developed—a far more potent force in his outlook than his anti-Englishness.

Sectarian identity is such a part of modern Irish history that it is all too easy to see Protestants and Catholics as mutually hostile homogenous groupings. Religion was indeed fundamental to eighteenth-century thought throughout Europe, but not always in denominationally stratified form. Class identity cut across religious divides. Tone and the advanced reformers had identified a middle-class dislike of aristocratic monopoly on both sides of the religious divide. It was the same force which was causing radical change throughout the western world and in 1791–2 was set fair to do likewise in Ireland.

IV

AGENT TO
THE CATHOLICS
(1792–1793)

10
Uniting the Sects

ıe and Russell returned to Dublin in October 1791 as agents
ı the north. They brought with them the prospect of an alliance
veen the Catholics and the Dissenters, a prospect which was to
ıten the government into concession. The authorities had good
ın for anxiety, for it was this alliance of advanced Catholics
adical Presbyterians which was to produce Irish republicanism.
such an alliance was long in coming and even Tone quickly
loned the United Irishmen to concentrate on the more pressing
of Catholic emancipation. It was the most electric issue of the
and was to dominate the remainder of his political career in
nd.

I

Dublin Tone found himself courted by the leading Catholics. The
mation of the Dublin Society of United Irishmen came at a critical
ıe. There was a new-found Catholic confidence in the justice of
eir cause and the number of advanced Catholics who joined the
Jnited Irishmen is significant.[1] McKenna's *Declaration*, published
n November 1791, captured their mood. 'Within a few months',
wrote the American consul in Dublin, 'the Catholics, as if by elec-
trical impulse, have met in large bodies and passed resolutions to
remain no longer in this excluded state.' He predicted general ferment if their petitions were rejected and thought the government
was taking a short view of the situation in trying to divide and
conquer.[2] Dublin Castle miscalculated badly in continuing to
demand the conventional submissiveness from this new Catholic
movement. In doing so it became embroiled in a policy conflict with
Whitehall which prefigured the Fitzwilliam crisis of 1795.

Already anxious at developments in France, and faced with growing radicalism at home, England saw the real threat in Ireland as
the prospective alliance between the Francophile Dissenters and the
Catholics. Pitt's cabinet recognised the natural conservatism of the
Catholics and sought to anchor their loyalty by timely concession.
They could not reasonably be denied the recent concessions made to
the English Catholics, and London was prepared also to offer a

limited restoration of the elective franchise. Westmorland argued that the Irish Protestants would not accept the concessions of Mitford's Act, let alone the extras, though his claim seems to have been based almost entirely on advice from that handful of key office-holders, notably Fitzgibbon, Foster and Beresford, known collectively as the 'Irish cabinet'.[3]

English ignorance of things Irish was at the bottom of such impolitic leniency, they said. She should be told 'that the private fortune of every man, as well as the establishment here were at stake ... and that ... every concession gave the Catholics additional strength to attack and overpower the constitution both in church and state'. There was a heated exchange of letters to convince the British government that the maintenance of Protestant Ascendancy was essential to the connection. It was a suggestion which found little sympathy in London. The British public and Parliament would not see fit to support the Irish government, wrote Home Secretary Dundas tetchily, if it was 'a mere question of whether one description of Irishmen or another are to enjoy a monopoly of pre-eminence ... there cannot be a permanency in the frame of the Government and constitution of Ireland, unless the Protestants will lay aside their prejudices, forgo their exclusive preeminence and gradually open their arms to the Roman Catholics'.[4]

It was this kind of attack on the *raison d'être* of Protestant Ascendancy which would force the Irish politicians to close ranks over the next few years in an increasingly sectarian definition of their power base. Westmorland thought Pitt was punishing the Irish for the regency crisis.[5] Others felt he was listening to the evil counsel of their ex-viceroy, the Marquis of Buckingham. Buckingham was indeed feeding his brother Grenville with his own distrust of Irish politicians. They could not reasonably expect Britain to support the Protestant interests on the same lines as established at the time of Elizabeth I. His conviction that a limited Catholic franchise would fortify the existing constitution against republicanism and a 'French system' was widely shared in Whitehall. Grenville expressed his fears that the Irish government would dig its heels in too soon, be forced to give way too late, and thereby lose the advantage of liberality which might attach the majority of the populace to government. He felt that Dublin Castle was underestimating the danger from the rising spirit in the north and sought some means of gaining independent information on opinion there.[6]

Against London's better judgement, however, the opinions of the Irish cabinet prevailed. The Mitford bill's concessions, less, however, the right to carry arms or to sit on a grand jury, were reluctantly accepted. But the limited admission of Catholics to the county franchise was totally rejected, although central to their demands. No mention of concessions was to be made in the King's speech opening the new parliamentary session in January 1792 (which Dundas found alarming, given the rise in Catholic expectations), and Dublin sought to introduce a clause firmly closing the door to further concessions. This Whitehall rejected out of hand as an incitement which would destroy any Catholic gratitude for the proposed relief act.[7] More alarmingly, Dublin embarked on a policy destined to bring the feared alliance between the Catholics and Dissenters closer.

This involved wooing the leaders of both religious groups on to the side of government and declaring the remainder 'violent agitators'. The Presbyterian clergy were enticed with an increase in the *regium donum*—a state payment to Dissenting clergy.[8] Four members of the Catholic Committee were summoned to an audience with the Chief Secretary on 26 November 1791 and asked to disavow McKenna's pamphlet under the implied threat of receiving no concession if they refused. Byrne tried to distance the Catholics from McKenna's work, but his fellow delegates sympathised with its sentiments and were irritated at Hobart's attempt to impugn the loyalty of the Catholic body in general.[9] Hobart was insisting on the same kind of deferential waiting on the government's good intentions which had characterised relations between the Catholic Committee and the Castle since the mid-century. He persuaded the leading Catholic gentry and hierarchy to present an address along these lines, independently of the general body of the Catholics, and to promote a series of Catholic addresses of loyalty. Much as Westmorland exulted in having 'effected the separation we wished',[10] the divide-and-rule tactic backfired badly, producing the expulsion from the Committee of the 68 'Kenmarites' who had signed the address and destroying Catholic faith in the good will of the Irish government.

A formal declaration of the Catholic Committee's new decisiveness was drawn up at a meeting on 14 January 1792 and released to the Irish and London press. It condemned the Catholic nobles and gentry for accommodating 'the spirit of domineering' and 'tardiness of attention' which characterised the government's approach to the Catholic issue, and was particularly critical of 'the injudicious interference of some of our Prelates'. It accused the Castle of trying to hide the strength of Catholic feeling from the King, while Hobart's imperious treatment of their leaders at the November meeting still rankled. McKenna's pamphlet had been used by Hobart and the Kenmarites 'as a pretext for insinuating that the tranquillity of the country was endangered'. Yet the offending pamphlet, declared the Committee, 'contains only a statement of melanchoy facts, and we defy our adversaries to prove, that it contains one word inconsis-

tent with the strictest principles of religion and of loyalty'. A resolution was passed to apply to Parliament for a further repeal of the penal laws, and a proposal to leave the nature of that concession to 'the wisdom and benevolence of the legislature' was withheld.[11]

II

There was another reason for growing Catholic assertiveness and Protestant entrenchment. The secret was out that England supported the Catholic cause. On 3 January 1792 John Keogh arrived from England with the Catholics' new English agent Richard Burke. The appointment seemed a stroke of genius. Young Burke was sufficiently conservative for government to concede Catholic demands without appearing to give way to threats. His father's passionate support of the Catholic cause was well known, he carried considerable weight with Irish MPs, and—at a time when he was breaking away from his Foxite companions in England—he had opened up important communication ties with Pitt's cabinet, notably through Dundas.

Although he later denied it when challenged by Westmorland, Dundas had been rather too open with young Burke, who intimated to everyone in Ireland that London was instructing Dublin to concede Catholic demands.[12] Hints of English interference in the Irish legislative process hit a raw nerve with Irish politicians. 'If the suspicion shall be confirmed (a suspicion too much strengthened by your dispatch and the questionable language and situation of Mr R. Burke)', wrote Westmorland, 'that the British Government means to take up the Catholics and to play what is called a Catholic game, the Protestants would turn against Government and no administration would be able to conduct His Majesty's business.'[13]

In fact Richard Burke was an all-round disaster. He meant well and was a good friend to the Irish Catholics. But his desperation to succeed in a cause so dear to the father he idolised lent to all he did a peremptory impatience which was compounded by major defects of character. Everyone expected rather too much of Richard, his father included, and when he meekly thanked those attending a dinner in his honour in Cork and sat down without delivering the expected Burkean oratory, his audience looked on in stunned disbelief.[14] Moreover he had a natural hauteur which may well have come across as the common enough English superciliousness towards the Irish, and which irritated friends and foes alike. Drennan disliked him, suspecting (correctly) that he sought to divide the Catholics from the Presbyterians. His peremptory letters to Dublin Castle reinforced its intransigence. His threat of dire consequences if Catholic demands went unheard was so indiscreet that Hobart warned of the damage to his cause of such a suggestion, were it to get abroad. His long, complaining letters in Dundas damaged the Catholic cause even in that quarter, and ministers came to dread the arrival of 'so much writing in so bad a hand'.[15] But it was his disastrous mishandling of the Catholic petition to the Irish Parliament in January 1792 which convinced the Catholic Committee that he had to go.

Much of the petition which Richard Burke drew up for the Committee had been dictated by his father and the son's tendency to personalise the petition dogged its turbulent progress. The Committee had asked John Egan, the Opposition MP and friend of Grattan, to present it. But Burke refused to make the alterations required by the two politicians and asked an old friend of his father (Charles O'Hara, MP for Sligo) to present it instead. Tension was rising in both the House and in Dublin city over the Catholic issue. On 20 January 1792 the Dublin Corporation had voted resolutions supporting the Protestant Ascendancy and instructing the Dublin members to vote against Catholic concessions. Government supporters were in a mutinous mood, despite Westmorland's successful exclusion of any mention of the Catholic business from the King's speech and an eleventh-hour attempt to call them to order with assurances that the government had no intention of granting either the franchise or the right to carry arms.

Burke learnt of the decision not to grant the franchise on 23 January and a note of desperation coloured his already rash progress. When the embarrassed O'Hara stood up in the House of Commons on the 25th to present the petition he muffed things badly. So anxious was he to dissociate himself from it, that he claimed he was presenting it as a favour to an individual, thereby undermining its force as a Catholic Committee petition.[16] When he got into further difficulty, Burke took the hazardous step of coming down from the public gallery almost on to the floor of the House to advise him, causing an uproar and demands for his arrest on breach of privilege. The petition was abandoned, and a revised version finally presented by Egan on 18 February. The problem now was how to get rid of Burke without offending his father, a feat which the combined talents of Keogh and Tone pulled off so well that young Burke never realised he had been ditched.

III

In the parliamentary session which opened on 19 January, the worst fears of Pitt and Dundas were realised. The Catholic relief bill was introduced on the 25th. On the first reading abuse was showered on the Catholic Committee and the rejected Catholic nobles praised for their moderation. The bill was denounced as giving in to 'the

clamorous demands of discontented men, who forgot the decorum
of solicitation in the impetuosity of their ambition'.

Over the next month the hostility of members vented itself in
attacks on the Belfast Presbyterians, the United Irishmen and the
personnel of the Catholic Committee. In thus associating the three
groups as public enemies, government supporters were promoting
the alliance so dreaded by Dublin Castle and Whitehall alike. A petition
from Belfast on behalf of the Catholics, and signed by more than 600
people, was presented to the House on 8 February.[17] It occasioned
a vindictive attack by government supporters on the Belfast Presbyterians, Sir Boyle Roche denouncing them as 'a turbulent, disorderly
set of people, whom no King can govern, or no God can please'. He
dismissed the almost beatified Dungannon Convention of 1783 as
'disgraceful to this country', and accused the Catholic leaders of
being 'turbulent men, shop-keepers and shop-lifters'. None were
members of Ireland's ancient nobility or gentry. They were rather
'obscure' men, Byrne 'a sugar-baker, a seller of wines and other
commodities', Keogh 'a retailer of poplins in Dame Street', all of
them men who 'met over their porter to consider of commanding
the Government'. The same personal attack was extended to the
United Irishmen, Tandy's singularly ugly appearance offering a
ready target for innuendo. Westmorland wrote triumphantly to
Dundas on 28 January of having undermined the levellers and republicans and of his hopes of soon returning the Catholic Committee
to the leadership of 'the respectable part of their communion'.[18]

But it was the debate on the Catholic petition, finally presented
on 18 February, and calling for a limited restoration of the franchise,
which fixed the lines of contest. Member after member stood up to
define that Protestant cultural superiority and Catholic dependency
which was assumed by the term 'Protestant Ascendancy'. The term
was novel, coined in response to the progressive repeal of the penal
laws.[19] The Whigs—with a few notable exceptions—revealed themselves part of the same enclosed élite and no friends to the Catholics,
with Ponsonby prominent among the anti's and delivering a stiff
rebuke to Tone for his pro-Catholic stance.[20] The debates showed
conclusively that the Protestant Ascendancy would never accept
sharing power with Catholics, and despite warnings by some MPs
of the danger of treating a loyal people with indignity, the Catholic
petition was rejected by a huge majority of 208 to 25. The Belfast
petition shared the same fate.

It was almost unheard of to treat a petition thus, and even Hobart
was unhappy at the 'insulting triumph' of its opponents. The bill
which eventually passed through the House of Commons on 23
February was robbed of its conciliatory intent. Its concessions—

Catholics were to be admitted to the bar, have the right to inter-
marry with Protestants, teach school and take on apprentices—were
nullified by the rejection of a limited admission to the county franchise (which would have opened less than one fifth of the seats to
Catholic votes), and the retention of a number of clauses denying
equality to Catholics, even in those areas where the act sought to
be conciliatory.[21]

Although the Catholics continued to consult with Grattan and
other opposition members, and for a while flirted with the pro-
Catholic Abercorn group, the parliamentary session of January–
March 1792 marked the beginning of Catholic alienation from
parliamentary politics altogether. Fundamental to this was the
disarray of the Whig Club.[22] The performance of the Whigs in
Parliament on the Catholic issue was symptomatic of their disintegration. Grattan, Curran, Egan, Browne and Hutchinson had
taken up the Catholic cause and were ostracised from Whig society
in consequence. Charlemont had been prominent among the opponents of the Catholic bill. Ponsonby verged on moderation, but was
prepared to play the Protestant card to embarrass the government.
Leinster alone of the great borough owners was sympathetic, but
then got cold feet. The campaign on 'patriot' issues, more or less
orchestrated since the regency episode, suffered, and the opposition
Whigs entered the war crisis divided and bereft of their traditional
supporters.[23]

Yet Hobart and Westmorland were delighted with the outcome
of the session. All along they had been far more anxious about the
reaction of their Protestant friends than those of either the Catholics
or the Presbyterians, and in the event felt they had escaped lightly.[24]
Certainly the Catholic issue fell out of ministerial correspondence
for many months, and Westmorland did not share England's fears
that France might capitalise on Irish discontent.[25] It was typical of
the Castle's short-sightedness in these years. Its handling of the
Catholic issue in preceding months had totally altered the balance of
extra-parliamentary politics. Significant sections of the politically
aware, of all religions, had been re-educated. The debates in Parliament had aroused unusual levels of interest. The avenues leading to
the House were thronged, as people clamoured to get seats in the
public gallery, and Tone was among the crowd which packed the
gallery at each session.[26]

At the opening of the session the United Irishmen had published
A Digest of the Popery Laws, which stripped the statutes of their legal
jargon and listed in plain English the disabilities under which the
Catholics still suffered. Many were shocked at what they read and
the pamphlet went immediately into a second edition. It was part of

an explosion of pamphlet and press reports on the Catholic issue. 'We are now getting ready 60,000 pamphlets to inform the nation', wrote Keogh in March.[27] Among them was a reissue of Tone's *Argument*. He wrote a new introduction for the 1792 edition, confidently proclaiming that his opinion in 'that same great cause' had been confirmed by recent events. 'Already I behold a revolution commencing in the public mind—the day is broke, and every hour brings success nearer—to us investigation is victory—the cause of the Catholics is the cause of truth, justice, and liberty, and under that conviction, it would be almost impious to doubt the event.'[28]

The intemperate ultra-Protestantism of many politicians and public figures provoked an immediate Catholic reaction. The Catholic Committee had issued a statement on 4 February denying that they had any desire 'to endanger the security of the Protestant ascendancy'. On 17 March they issued a further statement emphatically rejecting the many accusations that the Catholic Church condoned the dethronment of heretic princes and the murder of Protestants. They proclaimed their loyalty to George III, and denied that the Pope was infallible or had any right to absolve Catholics from civil oaths, contracts and their allegiance to civil powers. It was, said Bishop Delaney, like the maidservant declaring for the twelfth time that she had not taken her mistress's spoon, for the Catholic Committee had been issuing such denials since the mid-century.[29] At the heart of Protestant resistance were traditional fears for their property. The Catholic Committee went to great lengths to disavow any desire to overturn the landed settlement.[30]

The new aggressive secularism of the Catholic Committee seemed to confirm the lesson being taken from events in France by the advanced radicals in Dublin and Belfast. The Committee's dramatic rejection of the Kenmarites suggested that this most aristocratic, most hierarchical of religions was breaking its chains. Even among those who supported the Catholic cause a sense of the superiority of Protestantism comes through in the assertion that Catholicism has changed its colour, the papacy lost its force and the Catholics become more like others. 'The spirit of the Catholic religion is softened and refined', claimed one of the ablest speakers on the Catholic side in the debate on the relief bill, 'the influence of the pope, feeble...his power overthrown in France, tottering in Germany, resisted in Italy, and formidable no where.' It was an argument for changed times which the press took up enthusiastically, one writer in the *Freeman's Journal* congratulating the Catholics on the disappearance of 'the narrow prejudices...interwoven with their faith' and pointing to France as visible refutation of 'the vulgar idea, that despotism and the Roman Catholic religion are inseparable in a state'.[31]

Such lingering suspicions and Catholic fears of weakening their campaign by association with the northern republicans continued to bedevil a full alliance on a joint Catholic emancipation-reform platform. In 1792, however, Ascendancy triumphalism had produced an aggressiveness among the Catholics which temporarily overcame the mutual distrust. Writing the history of the times over a decade later, Emmet recalled the impact on the United Irishmen of these developments. Government treatment of the Catholics was bringing about a 'formidable union of the sects', and the Catholic issue came to dominate the early meetings of the Dublin Society of United Irishmen.[32]

Catholic Agent

The most significant outcome of these months was to strengthen the alliance between the Catholics and Dissenters, 'binding the[m] . . . together by a community of insult', as Emmet recalled.[1] The attempt of the government to separate Catholics from radicals was public knowledge by early 1792, and the United Irishmen and Catholic Committee sought to guard against any rift. Informal contacts between the two organisations increased through the winter and spring months as key positions in both came to be dominated by the same men. The increasing involvement of Tone in their activities was indicative of the progressive radicalisation of the Catholics. For, contrary to his disclaimer of influence in the United Irishmen, Tone's prominent role in the early activities of the Dublin Society soon had him in open conflict with the authorities.

I

Tone's correspondence at this time reflects his excessive, almost romantic admiration for the spirit of Belfast, prompting Sam McTier to comment: 'He mistakes the situation of this town and country around, they are still full of prejudice, which time only can remove'.[2] Tone continued to view the Dublin United Irish Society as a poor reflection of that in Belfast and he reported on its activities to his northern friends as if to a parent society.[3] In particular he complained of the admission test adopted for the Dublin Society at the end of 1791, claiming that it would deter new members and that its language was complicated, 'superfluous' and 'commanding'. It was a criticism of the laboured style of Drennan, who drafted the test, and Tone was not alone in this view.[4] Indeed he may have been irked at the choice of Drennan rather than himself as the Dublin Society's main scribe. But most of all he had heard of a split in the Belfast United Irishmen, when a group opposed to the test broke away and formed another society.

It was possibly Russell's influence which made Tone so combative at the turn of the year, and he regained his prominence in the Dublin Society after Russell's departure for Dungannon in January 1792. He eventually took the test when his fears of Belfast's disapproval were calmed. The test was popular with the Catholics as proof of United Irish commitment to emancipation—on which the government had been casting some doubt—and this may well have been an additional consideration in Tone's submission. Tone, however, was right in his prediction that the test would be divisive. Any hint of secrecy made moderates nervous and provided their enemies with a tool against them. In Belfast it provoked a heated correspondence in the press. In Dublin it discouraged new members and its retention was urged by a government spy for that very reason.[5]

The United Irish Society met on alternate Friday evenings in the Music Hall, Fishamble Street, a short walk towards the river from Christ Church, and, before it fell on hard times in the 1780s, the venue for some of Dublin's most lavish social occasions, including the first performance of Handel's *Messiah*.[6] By the end of January the Society was attracting an average attendance of 60, including the government spy—Thomas Collins, a bankrupt Dublin businessman—to whom we owe the very full account of the proceedings of these months. Some 400 members paid subscriptions during the Society's two and a half years of existence, though attendance rarely exceeded double figures. Its early development was very different from that of the Belfast Society, which quickly spawned other small and informally run societies, some attracting an almost exclusively artisanal membership. In contrast the Dublin Society was monolithic. It had an elaborate set of committees, which met privately, reported quarterly and conducted most of the Society's important business. Its membership was largely professional or mercantile, with a sprinkling of gentry. Although textile merchants and manufacturers made up the bulk of the membership, Society affairs were dominated by the legal profession—a dominance reflected in its procedural formality and the dramatic decline in attendance during assizes.[7]

In a vitriolic attack an ex-member, the Catholic printer William Paulet Carey, lashed out at the '*aristocracy* of the learned professions' which controlled the Society. Carey had personal reasons for such bitterness. But he was right in his picture of the Dublin Society as dominated by a small clique.[8] Although Tone receives rather better treatment from Carey's pen—as one of those 'literary patriots' who had written for the Catholics—he was nevertheless part of that clique and was regularly appointed to its committees. The group included almost all those who went on to lead the movement's republican phase, among them Tone's particular friends, Rowan, Emmet, John Sweetman, Richard McCormick and, when in town, Russell.[9]

Nor could one be poor and be an active member. Some of the most prosperous Dublin merchants were members at one time or another, notably Henry Jackson (iron founder), Oliver Bond (whole-sale woollen draper), Richard McCormick (poplin manufacturer). Simon Butler and Beauchamp Bagenal Harvey were successful bar-risters and landed gentry, while the 1798 auction of paintings be-longing to John Sweetman (porter brewer) revealed a stunning collection which included works by Vermeer, Murillo, Rubens, Hans Holbein, Caracci and Teniers.[10] Members paid a half-yearly admission fee of one guinea, and were expected to subscribe to the legal expenses of those involved in disputes with the authorities. Moreover, one was made to feel an outcast for nonpayment.[11]

The Dublin Society was soon absorbed into the damagoguery of Dublin city politics, of which Tandy was the uncrowned king. It was as part of this ongoing clash between the government and the Dublin radicals that the Society first became embroiled with the authorities. The occasion was the attack on Tandy by the Attorney-General, John Toler, during the debate on the 1792 Catholic bill. The identi-fication of the Society with Tandy placed it in an invidious situation from the outset. But it had received worse insults than the throw-away comment on its secretary's physiognomy, and there would have been no confrontation had not Tandy demanded a written explanation. Toler responded by a veiled challenge, which Tandy declined to take up, thereby, some thought, bringing dishonour on the Society. This was further compounded by Tandy's undig-nified escape through the parlour window when the sergeant-at-arms arrived to arrest him for breach of parliamentary privilege.

The Society—Tone included—was annoyed that Tandy had embroiled it in such a personal matter and indeed in his own dis-honourable handling of it. The affair was discussed at its 25 February session. Butler stood down from the chair, since he too was in dis-pute with Toler, and Rowan and Tone took over as provisional chairman and secretary respectively. The Catholic members were angry that their campaign should have been compromised at such a time and refused to sign their names to Tandy's defence. But the Society had to make some response, and the meeting passed a series of resolutions, signed by Tone as pro-secretary, and subsequently printed in all the leading papers.

The resolutions were a declaration of war between the Society and the Castle. They contrasted the United Irish aim of promoting such 'great national objects' as 'union among Irishmen of all religious persuasions', with the threat to liberty posed by Parliament's 'ex-ercise of undefined privilege...[and]unlimited prerogative', and contemptuously dismissed *the scorn of official station*, or the scoff of *unprincipled venality*'.[12]

The wording is unquestionably Tone's and he plays a prominent role in this defiant attempt to wrest honour from an otherwise pitiful situation.[13] Only his growing anti-parliamentarianism can explain Tone's stand in this otherwise farcical dispute. As signatories of the resolutions, Tone and Rowan were in breach of parliamentary privilege. They were ordered to attend the bar of the House on Monday, 27 February and provokingly appeared in the gallery dressed in their Whig Club uniforms. They were waiting to be called when a fire broke out in the House and within two hours the great dome crashed amidst dreadful confusion.[14]

Society business continued to be dominated by the Tandy affair throughout that spring and summer. On Sunday, 4 March, Butler was summoned by Fitzgibbon and told that his association with the United Irishmen was a disgrace to his profession as a lawyer and his status as a gentleman. But the Lord Chancellor's main attack was directed at Tone, of whom he spoke in 'the harshest and most contemptuous terms of disapprobation'. Butler threatened to publish their conversation in the press, at which Fitzgibbon quickly climbed down, claiming that he meant no disrespect to either man and that 'on the contrary he entertained a very high opinion' of Tone.[15] Fitzgibbon's extraordinary outburst was a sign of the peculiar vigilance directed on Tone's new career by his wife's powerful kinsman, for he was not seen as a particular threat at the time.

Tandy paraded his victory after his release on 17 April, and subsequent acquittal on 11 June, and Society statements on the affair baited leading government supporters.[16] It was a foolish move, more reminiscent of the demagoguery of city politics than the novelty of radical reformism, and it was to draw the wrath of the authorities upon the Society the following year. But Tone was increasingly diverted from the United Irish Society by the Catholic issue. He neglected to send out notices for the Society's meetings on 2 March and 13 April, and relinquished the pro-secretaryship on 25 April, having again delayed circulating a Society letter which was to have complimented Tandy.[17]

II

Even if developing friendships and natural instincts kept Tone at the centre of the new movement in these months, he still had a family and a living to make and we should not be misled by his journals into getting things out of proportion. The journals are incomplete for the period: none at all for November 1791 to July 1792, precious few for 1793 and a virtual blank for 1794–5. It is all too easy to blame the hapless Reynolds. There may well have been little to lose anyway from these years. The bustle of life was such as to allow little time for journalising.

The family were living in the barony of North Naas, County Kildare, on a 'small strip or piece of ground with the dwelling house and out offices...known by the name of Chateau Bowe'. It figures in Tone's journals as 'Chateau Boue', a typical Tone pun on its real name, and was part of the family property lost by Peter Tone to his brother in 1790. Jonathan Tone allowed his nephew to live there and bequeathed it to him in 1793. It consisted of almost two acres of land laid out in flowers and vegetables. It fired Tone's interest in botany, and though he professed never to understand it, he was a tolerable gardener. He was also a keen sportsman and went fishing and part-ridge shooting in the lush Kildare countryside when Russell came to visit.[18]

A second child, William, had been born to the Tones on 29 April 1791. Matilda recalled the event many years later. 'I see, feel and hear all that was around me 36 years ago, my little room and every thing in it, my bed, my babe in arms, and above all he that came every instant with a heart glowing with love and joy and tenderness to look if we were well, and to caress and bless us, and my little Maria then 5 years old standing at the bedside...how I was loved and cherished then!' William's christening is one of the last occasions on which a gathering of Tone's old friends from Trinity and Middle Temple days is recorded. Plunket's brother attended, the newly ordained Magee officiated (his first ceremony as a minister), and George Knox and Thomas Russell's father were godfathers.[19] But from the summer on the friends who would become part of Tone's future political development increasingly replaced those of his youth.

In November 1791 Tone had lingered in Dublin after his return from Belfast, caught up in the swell of the new politics. Letters to Matilda were dashed off and full of excuses for not rejoining his family in the country. Matilda was having difficulty coping with the children. Young William was a handful. She was suffering from persistent headaches and urged him to return home. 'I learn, and am sorry, that you have got a return of the pain in your head', he replied. 'Willy is growing too strong for you, and, therefore, I beg you wean him immediately. He is old enough now, and you must not injure your health for that little monkey, especially when you know how precious your health is to me.' But the excitement of developments in Dublin, and his key role in the talks leading up to the foundation of the Dublin Society of United Irishmen made him reluctant to leave. 'My stay in town is of such infinite consequence, that I am sure you would not wish me to quit, whilst things are in their present train. If you can get Mary down, I shall be very happy; I leave it to you, as I am with my head, hands and heart, so full of business, that I have scarcely time to subscribe myself, yours very sincerely, MIRABEAU'.[20]

That winter Tone found new lodgings in town in Queen Street, just north of the river. Though these were but a twenty-minute walk from College Green, and a pleasant one along the quays— Tone was an avid walker—he had never lived so far from the centre of things. Moreover, the new location was an insalubrious part of town, backing on to the great wholesale market of Smithfield. The narrow passages and streets were choked with animals. The stench from accumulated offal and ordure was often intolerable, and the area was the scene of frequent rioting, bull-baiting and other violent pastimes.[21] The lodgings were unfurnished and Tone spent much of January and February 1792 making them habitable.[22] By 23 February Matilda had packed his belongings—which he had listed— for a lengthier stay in Dublin.

There is a punctiliousness and sense of order about Tone's habit of listing things. Even the papers which survive contain detailed lists of expenditures, provisions purchased, household needs (down to curtains and cutlery). From these we know that he took snuff and had a sweet tooth (which may explain his dental fixation, noted earlier). From two lists of clothing purchased or packed (one of which is that of February 1792) we can reconstruct something of how Tone was turned out at the height of his political career in Ireland. A wig was an essential part of male dress until the very last years of the century. An earlier list records the purchase of a 'Powder bag', and from Barrington's description and an early portrait of about 1791, it seems that Tone wore the kind of half-wig or toupee fashionable at the time, in which one's own hair, swept back at the front, merged into a wig with a roll-curl covering each ear and tied back behind.[23] But a decline in the fashion for wigs after the French Revolution was accelerated by the tax imposed on hair power in 1795, and Tone too abandoned their use.

He had a taste for current fashions in dress. As waistcoats became shorter and breeches tighter, in the closing decades of the century, it was *de rigueur* for the fashionable man to display a fine leg. So we have Tone with his blue coat over white waistcoat, white breeches and white silk stockings, or green over buff accessories—with an array of other waistcoats from ribbed cotton to striped or patterned silk for special occasions. Large quantities of shirts and cravats were likewise packed for him in 1792, while the inclusion of boots, flannel under-waistcoats, and a number of pairs of leather and old 'thickset' (stout twilled cotton) breeches betrays the many hours he spent on horseback that year. It was every inch the wardrobe of a gentleman and the February list is rounded off by '9 Books—razors + Comb 1 silver medal 1 Flute 1 Towel 1 nightcap—pamphlets—1 pr gloves.' He probably then set out for town with his brother Matthew, who left for England—*en route* for America—the following day. He and William had tried unsuccessfully to mount a cotton business in Prosperous, County Kildare, and William had left for India a week earlier. Tone never saw him again.[24]

He was still panning around for a career. The old nagging worries about finance were haunting him in the form of 'an increasing family totally unprovided for'. He continued to attend court and appears still to have had some legal commitments. But his incidental writings of the period reflect his growing belief in natural rights and individual liberty, and an irritation with the irrationality of the law, which effectively banished any desire to learn its intricacies.[25] More immediately, he needed a steadier source of income than that offered by the vagaries of the bar.

Tone hoped that Lieutenant-Colonel Henry Barry, whom he had befriended through Russell in 1791, might help find Russell another commission and rescue him from his position as a magistrate in Tyrone, which was becoming increasingly distasteful to him.[26] Tone also asked Barry to use his friendship with the Rawdon family to seek employment for himself. Francis Rawdon was typical of the kind of politico-military figure with whom Tone frequently identified. He had fought with distinction in the American war and, as a close friend of the Prince of Wales, was prominent among the English opposition Whigs. He was Irish-born and his family had considerable property in Ireland—notably in the north—which he was to inherit, with the Moira title, in 1793. He was a major spokesman for Ireland in the British Parliament, where he was already an advocate of Catholic emancipation.[27] As Westmorland's star declined in Ireland through 1792, Rawdon's was one of the names rumoured as his successor. Tone wrote to him on several occasions about the state of Ireland, possibly seeking to extend the career of political writer which he was already pursuing with the Catholics.[28] John Russell was critical of his brother's association with Barry, 'that orator of Debretts—and lick-spillane of great men'.[29] In the hierarchical system of political patronage, however, such courtship of the great was a necessary evil and Tone was as guilty of it as Barry.

In the event the overtures produced nothing. But Tone had been given an entrée to the Moira family. He became a regular visitor at the magnificent Moira House on Ussher's Island in Dublin. It was one of the Whigs' social landmarks and Wesley thought it surpassed in elegance any house he had seen in England. Tone became ac-

quainted with Rawdon's mother, Lady Moira, Countess of Hunt-
ingdon, and though she proclaimed herself 'a firm *aristocrat*', immune
to any attempted conversion to democracy, she found Tone 'sensible
and pleasant' and admitted a delight in 'good sense in whatever
drapery it presents itself'.[30] It is yet another insight into the public
image of Tone which ill accords with the rakishness of the
autobiography.

III

Tone's lengthy flirtation with the Whig aristocracy occurred at a
time when he was openly attacking privilege and the landed classes
generally. Yet even in later years Tone retained a natural deference
towards Irish noble families who espoused the popular cause. This
was the old concept of the noble as patriarch and protector. By the
end of the eighteenth century, however, the term 'aristocracy' had
acquired another meaning, that of a jealously narrow, often mean,
monopoly of power. It was privilege as unjust monopoly which
dominated the writings of Tone in the early months of 1792.

In a squib of January, signed 'Liberty Boy', he attacked the Castle's
tactic of splitting the Catholic leadership by wooing their gentry.
'They have got some men among you of very high rank, and very
low principles, to go about begging your names...to slavish and
shabby addresses to the Castle', upon which he launched into a
virulent attack on those Catholic nobles who toadied to the Castle
in hopes of securing a reversal of the seventeenth-century attainders
against their titles.[31] Is it worth condemning your children to eternal
slavery, he asks, to satisfy the corrupt ambitions of such selfish
men, who would sell their brethren to be 'called my Lord at the
Castle' or to wear 'a big wig and a black gown in the Four Courts'?
Have faith in your Committee, he urges, those wise men and gallant
patriots...who have cordially shaken hands with your Protestant
countrymen'.[32]

Some weeks later the squires of County Down were the object of
attack. Tone was called upon by his Belfast friends in their dispute
with the Down Hunt. They were under attack for bailing out a small
farmer imprisoned for selling a hare, which was prohibited under the
game laws. In two articles which appeared in the *Northern Star* on 28
January and 15 February 1792, Tone contrasted the basic humanity
of the Belfast people with the pretentious privilege of the huffing,
intoxicated aristocrats who picked upon the small man. 'It is something more than ridiculous to see a set of country squires, hot from
the chase, flushed with wine, and still more intoxicated with an idle
and imaginary idea of their own consequence, presuming...to
condemn the conduct of men, actuated...by a much nobler motive.'

The same men who arrogate to themselves this exclusive privilege were alike both makers and executors of the laws: 'they are legislators, judges and parties; a degree of unjust confusion to be found, perhaps, in no other part of our very extensive and complicated code. Many were members of the Northern Whig Club, whose declaration and principles denounced oppressive laws. 'I cannot bear to see or hear a set of men get together and rail at the profligacy of government. . . and yet, themselves, deliberately sending a man. . . to the common jail, for the atrocious offence of appropriating that to himself, which God and nature admit to be his property, equally with that of the most Aristocratic country justice, that ever in the pomp, and pride, and plenitude, and privilege of his office thought proper to commit him.' It would not be the last time that Tone lashed out at biased authority, 'the judge as a party', and 'that execrable and contemptible corps, the country gentlemen of Ireland'.[33]

By April he was denying that titles carried any automatic right to respect, and in a long critique of a contemporary pamphlet, *The Protestant Interest in Ireland Ascertained*. Tone launched into a discussion on the location of authority in civil society. *The Protestant Interest* had attacked the Catholic campaigners' use of current arguments about liberty and equality and the 'speculative doctrine' that no man could be bound by laws to which he did not consent. Tone was to claim that he had no consciously worked-out political philosophy in these years. His ideas were the product of direct experience and that Newtonian rational empiricism which Trinity instilled in its undergraduates. He had a particular facility for stripping political claims of their acceptable gloss, and his answer to *The Protestant Interest* reveals him not as a sophisticated political thinker, but as a politicised individual frustrated by political rhetoric which was frequently at odds with everyday reality.

He loses patience with the pamphlet's 'silly ostentation of scholastic knowledge', this attempt to philosophise away Catholic grievances by 'syllogisms' and 'sophistry'. Forget about man in his natural state, he says; look at him instead 'as we find him in Ireland'. The idea of 'tacit consent'—which the writer of the pamphlet had argued from Locke—Tone attacks as nonsense, as any Catholic asked if he tacitly consented to the penal laws which made him a slave would confirm, while the assertion that Paine denied the validity of fixed government in his claim that no generation could bind future ones by its acts, Tone dismisses as illogical. The power of parliaments to legislate is delegated power; they can only make laws, not 'unmake the power from which themselves were but an emanation'—else parliaments could act as they liked. Acts are binding on future generations, not on the authority of our ancestors 'but by our acquiescence, which gives them a sanction'. 'Paine's meaning is so obvious, that it must be something worse than dullness which can misunderstand it.' The claim that a constitution is immutable makes nonsense of every constitutional landmark from Magna Carta to Ireland's 1782. Liberty rests in the right to consent to the laws by which one is governed, argues Tone, and the removal of that right from the Catholics was such an invasion of privilege as to amount to a breach of the original contract and a dissolution of government.[34] Although there is little that is novel in this work, it does show that by 1792 Tone had turned his back on the Lockean tradition at the heart of his own education and had accepted popular sovereignty as the basis of political power.[35]

In his rejection of 'faction', 'party' and 'aristocratical government', his acceptance of popular sovereignty and his anti-clericalism and deism, Tone was in the mainstream of contemporary European thinking.[36] But he arrived at his conclusions by a different route. Rousseau's epoch-making *Social Contract*—with its doctrine of the inalienability of sovereignty, arising from the people and re-maining with the people—was first published in 1762 and was well known in Ireland.[37] But Tone's adoption of the theory of popular sovereignty came from a pragmatic assessment of the Irish situation and a recognition of the nonsense of the contract theory when the majority Catholic population was excluded and victimised by the very government to whom it was supposed to have entrusted power. Having made that discovery, he would then cite Molyneux, Hume, and above all Paine (interestingly, not Rousseau) in support of his case.[38] But it was a 'theory' home-produced by the situation in Ireland.

IV

Given Tone's high profile in confrontation politics that spring of 1792, his increasing favour with the leading Catholics was a token of the change which was taking place in their Committee. He was already a regular guest at their dinners and was present at the farewell dinner for Richard Burke on 2 April. The reissue of his *Argument* reaffirmed his standing as the leading Catholic pleader and he was thanked by a meeting of the Belfast Catholics on 6 April. The fol-lowing day the chairman wrote personally to Tone, transmitting their resolutions and thanking him for his 'exertions in the cause of emancipating the Catholics of this kingdom from their degraded situation'. Once again Belfast had afforded Tone the recognition he so craved, and he was delighted. The Catholic issue was now assuming the proportions of a major achievement, an area in which his reputation was already made.[39]

Shortly after Burke's departure, Keogh and Sweetman intimated to Tone the Catholic Committee's intention of appointing him agent in Burke's place, with the face-saving title of Assistant Secretary. The appointment was formally confirmed in July.[40] The £200 salary came as a godsend. But it would not have lasted long and scarcely compensated for the incessant travelling, letter-writing and mundane paper work into which Tone was launched for the next ten months and which increasingly took him away from home. Signs are that continuing financial worries might have forced him into routine employment had not Matilda's support confirmed him in his desire to follow through the Catholic business.

Richard Burke had been bombarding Dundas with his usual long-winded complaints. Although Dundas sympathised with many of them, the agreement not to go over the heads of the Irish government— a concession painfully won by the Castle in the lead-up to the 1792 parliamentary session—still applied,[41] and Burke told the Catholics as much on 17 June. But Keogh's dislike for Burke was unabated and he communicated it to Tone in their travels that summer. The result was that, when Tone was instructed by the Committee on 24 July to prepare an answer to Burke's letter, it became the channel for dispensing with his services altogether. 'Wrote the letter to Burke, giving him his congé,' he wrote in his diary for 24 July, 'regretting that ministry in England had, by adopting a determined neutrality, rendered further application to them useless, and of course deprived the Catholics of the powerful aid of his talents, and giving him a remote prospect that he might again be employed on some future emergency. All very civil and indefinite.' But the sub-committee thought it 'too pointed a dismissal' and its tone was softened accordingly. Burke never read it as a dismissal and continued to complicate the work of the Catholic Committee by importuning Dundas in its name and insisting on returning to Ireland as its agent.[42]

Tone is sometimes represented as having manipulated the Catholic Committee for his revolutionary designs.[43] This is a common assumption in retrospective history, which sees Tone primarily as a United Irishman and revolutionary rather than a campaigner for Catholic emancipation. In fact the reality was quite the reverse, and when disagreements did arise between the Catholic Committee and the Society of United Irishmen, Tone's loyalty remained with the Catholics. His many writings of the period were almost entirely in the service of the Catholic Committee and contain little of the personal hobby-horsing of his earlier works. Conscious of his admitted vanity about his writing ability, Tone describes at length how he decided to conduct this 'the literary part of the [Catholics'] warfare'. He had sufficient example before him of the loss of reputation of some who had written on behalf of the Committee 'but who did not stand criticism as I did without wincing', and after the shambles of Burke's intervention Tone felt he had to conduct himself with circumspection.

> In reviewing the conduct of my predecessor, Richard Burke, I saw that the rock on which he split was an overweening opinion of his own talents and judgement, and a desire, which he had not art enough to conceal, of guiding at his pleasure the measures of the committee. I therefore determined to model my conduct with the greatest caution in that respect. I seldom or never offered my opinion unless it was called for in the sub-committee...Another rule which I adopted for my conduct was, in all the papers I had occasion to write, to remember I was not speaking for myself, but for the Catholic body,...to be never wedded to my own compositions,...and to change without reluctance whatever the committee thought fit to alter, even in cases where perhaps my own judgement was otherwise.[44]

Certainly Tone's writings of the period show him as an effective service writer. His appointment as assistant secretary and agent to the Catholic Committee in July 1792 inaugurated the most hectic and most productive year of his life. Yet Tone's public role in these months was very different from that depicted in his journal, which, in the nature of private diaries, whisks us at Voltairean pace through an exciting world, with Tone himself at its centre. The journals, however, are not the public Tone. He was no public leader, rarely initiated policy and spent much of his political career in Ireland writing service documents. Though widely recognised as the Catholics' chief publicist, his name all but disappears from government documentation for this period. He was content to fold circulars, readily assumed the role of stage-hand and, while the Catholic issue hung in the balance, shelved his reform sympathies. The long, often frustrating campaigning of the years 1792–4, the stumping up and down the country, the repetition of jaded arguments, make for boring reading and writing, and it is all too tempting to take a short-cut through it by concentrating on the romantic revolutionary image. Yet the former was the natural Tone and his preferred role had he had any choice in the matter. Most of the Catholic activists were also United Irishmen and frequently the most militant at Society meetings. The idea that Tone somehow led the Catholics towards revolution is groundless.

12

Mission to the North

Tone was immediately involved in a dramatic new Catholic initiative. In the recent parliamentary debates the Catholic Committee had been dismissed as an unrepresentative group of factious Dublin tradesmen. Its members responded with a plan to remodel the Committee on such a representative basis that opponents could never again use such an excuse to resist Catholic demands. As a preliminary a reconciliation was effected with the seceders of December. In May 1792 instructions went out to the country to elect delegates to a Catholic Convention, and Keogh set off for Munster on the first leg of a national tour to win over the provincial gentry and clergy. His subsequent journey north with Tone was part of the reason for Tone's appointment, and highlights the new brand of aggressiveness brought by Keogh to the Committee in the aftermath of the challenge thrown down by the Protestant Ascendancy. Tone was a bridge to the Ulster Dissenters, so disliked by both English and Irish governments. In 1792 Keogh was quite prepared to play upon government fears of republicanism and French influence, however much he tried to distance himself from both after war erupted in 1793.[1]

I

Tone's attendance at Belfast's Bastille Day celebrations in the summer of 1792 was to be the occasion for a show of unity among the reformers and the Catholics. Tone and Drennan had been invited to prepare addresses for the occasion. Drennan's address to the French National Assembly – enthusiastically supporting its war effort—posed no problem. But Tone's address to the people of Ireland was another matter, and he expected opposition. To prepare the ground he left Dublin several days before the Catholic delegates; he was accompanied by Whitley Stokes, who was on his way to Scotland. They arrived in Belfast on Tuesday, 10 July.

By contrast with his first visit to Belfast, Tone was in melancholy mood. The shuffling, erudite Stokes had not been good company in the coach, and Tone avoided him over the next few days. He missed Russell greatly. There was no reason to stay sober without the satisfaction of parading it before his inebriate friend. 'Generally sulky', he commented. 'Want P.P. in order to advise him; just in a humour to give advice.' He compounded the extreme fatigue he always experienced after travel by sitting up late. He dined frequently with the 'old set'—Sinclair, Simms, McDonnell and McCabe. But he admitted that it was not as much fun as the last time. The memory he took away from an evening at Sinclair's was of bashing his knee against a chair 'like a jackanapes', while playing blindman's buff, and getting 'drowned in the rain coming home at one in the morning'.

The ready and casual social entry Russell's companionship had provided was not there. Instead of the busy round of social engagements of the previous October, time hung heavy on Tone's hands. He whiled it away by attending the harpers' festival in the Assembly Rooms, where everyone else seemed to be going anyway. But he did not share Belfast's sudden reawakening to its Gaelic past.[2] He found the music tiresome and repetitive. None of it was new. Seven of the ten performers were 'execrable', though the one he singled out did eventually win the competition. Indeed the romantic Ossianic revival, sweeping Europe in the latter decades of the century and spawning something of a Gaelic revival among the Irish intelligentsia, seems entirely to have bypassed Tone. His knowledge of Irish history was sketchy and did not start much before the seventeenth century. He had little antiquarian interest in the distant past, and like Swift and Molyneux selected episodes from that past to reach the pre-conceived conclusion of English aggression. There is also in Tone a tendency to compensate for his own Protestantism by attacking the Protestant record in Ireland and assuming that the Catholics were the only true Irish.[3]

Given his very modest reputation in Dublin, Tone was surprised to find himself a man of some repute in Belfast. But it was the unflattering reputation of a dangerous manipulator, bringing untold dangers from the south, notably in the form of Catholics, and he was warned that opponents were spreading malicious rumours about him. 'The time to time people say with great gravity that Mr Hutton [Russell's nickname for Tone] is come down to force seditious papers down their throats. Mr Hutton a man of great consequence, as it seems. . . . Mr Hutton almost angry at all this nonsense and very sorry that any man, woman, or child in Belfast should listen to such trash.' He makes light of the terrors caused by the arrival of the Catholic delegates, Keogh, McCormick, McKenna and a number of others. But Tone knew that the two main rumour-mongers—the Volunteer captain, Waddell Cunningham, and the *News Letter* proprietor, Henry Joy—were no fools and the whole experience shook his idealised view of the advanced opinions of the north.

The bone of contention was his address. Though commissioned

by his Belfast friends, it was Tone's first public exercise as Catholic agent and was studiously moderate. It traced an identity of interest between the Irish Catholics and the people of Belfast 'trained from our infancy in a love of freedom, and an abhorrence of tyranny', and combating the same 'infamous conspiracy of slaves and despots'. It declared the war not of France's making, dismissed her internal up-heavals as 'accidental [if regrettable] irregularities', and applauded her renunciation of wars of conquest and her proclamation of univer-sal brotherhood and peace. As to the Irish constitution, Catholics had no need, like the French, to pull it up by the roots:

> Ours is an easier and less unpleasing task; to remove with a steady and temperate resolution, the abuses which the lapse of many years, inattention and supineness in the great body of the people, and unremitting vigilance in the rulers to invade and plunder them of their rights, have suffered to overgrow and to deform that beautiful system of government, so admirably suited to our situation, our habits, and our wishes. We have not to innovate, but to restore. The just prerogatives of our monarch we respect and will maintain.

It is a call for a return to an original contract which is quite out of tune with Tone's adulation of Paine and his philosophy of breaking with the past, and is a token of his sublimation of more radical ideas for the greater good of Catholic reforms during his period as Catholic agent.

Tone had set out to dissociate both reform and Catholic emanci-pation from republicanism.[4] It is only in his suggested remedy for correcting abuses that we get a taste of his Paineite views: 'by re-storing to us THE PEOPLE, what we, for ourselves, demand as our right, our due weight and influence in that estate, which is our pro-perty, the REPRESENTATION OF THE PEOPLE IN PARLIAMENT'. On the whole, however, the address is a good example of how Tone could trim his sails to the wind and take on board the criticisms of others, for it had been considerably modified after his arrival in Belfast. The sequel to his remarks about the people was to have been a demand for Catholic equality. But Tone was persuaded by his Belfast friends to modify this paragraph. The final version referred to the Catholics only obliquely, denying the value of any reform which did not in-clude all denominations and denouncing political inequality based on religious opinions.

Neilson had discovered Cunningham trying to turn the country corps of Volunteers against the Catholics, and woke Tone in the middle of the night to warn of trouble the next day. The Dublin representatives too began to fear a possible confrontation over the

Catholic issue. Tandy—who had arrived with an entire retinue—and McKenna urged dropping the Catholic clause altogether. But McKenna's influence was fading. He proved a disruptive influence in Belfast, and though Tone saw personal spite in Keogh's efforts to influence him against the former Catholic tribune, he needed little persuading. Keogh thought this the time to test the Presbyterians' professed unity of purpose with the Catholics and—with Sinclair— is most favourably represented in Tone's account of the Belfast trip. By contrast Tone figures only obliquely in Keogh's lengthy account. Although he speaks of 'a friend of mine who is very justly high in their [the Dissenters] confidence', Tone is never mentioned by name, and Keogh himself assumed full credit for bringing these dangerous Dissenters to express their aims so moderately and so constitution- ally. He repeatedly dangled before Whitehall the prospect of the Catholics as a moderating force and was no great friend to the Pres- byterians.[5] It took Tone almost a year to recognise this.

But the coming together for the first time of these Dublin Catholics and Belfast radicals makes salutary reading. The Dubliners seemed to think the Belfast men less sincere in their pro-Catholic statements and more militant than they actually were, and Tone had to step in more than once to bridge the gulf of understanding. Sinclair, shocked at the imputation that they might resort to armed force, dismissed out of hand recommendations of 'stronger measures'. This McKenna interpreted as northern unwillingness to support their cause and urged his colleagues not to bring the matter forward at all. Rumours of French arms being landed in the north were rife, and Sinclair was perhaps oversensitive about the image being put about of the Belfast Presbyterians as revolutionaries. But many Catholics shared such suspicions, and the incident revealed the fragility of the Catholic–Dissenter 'alliance'. Moreover, Tone's second trip to Ulster showed the emancipationist stand of Belfast radicalism to be unre- presentative of the province generally. Such was the anti-popery of many of the Volunteer corps pouring into the town from the adjacent countryside for the 14 July celebrations that Tone thought many 'no better than Peep-of-Day boys'.

Little wonder that he was apprehensive when roused by Neilson early on Saturday the 14th to prepare for the fateful day. Preparations had been making for some weeks, and the excitement on the day recalled the heyday of the Volunteers. At 9 a.m. the different corps paraded down High Street, 'Drums beating, colours flying, and all the honours of war'. Tone, in 'regimentals', rode out of town with the 790 Volunteers to the review ground in the Falls, where some 20,000 spectators were gathered. There he spent most of the time in 'a council of war', in an adjacent potato field, with representatives from the different groupings. All save Tone and Sinclair felt it would damage the Catholic cause to risk rejection at this stage and proposed withholding the address. Tone felt such action would simply endorse the malicious rumours being spread and that at the very worst a rejection would stop the Catholics deluding themselves into expecting support where none existed. It was scarcely wise advice when the threat of alliance with the Dissenters was their most effective weapon, but typical of Tone's impatience with subterfuge.

In the event Sinclair agreed to go ahead with the presentation, Tone at the last minute having substituted 'Irishmen of every religious denomination' for the word 'Catholic'. At three o'clock they marched back into town and were joined by hundreds of people sporting green ribands and laurel leaves in their hats. The parade was preceded by boys in national uniform carrying banners representing Ireland, America, France, Poland, Great Britain and Ireland—the last bearing the motto 'Unite and be free'. The green 'flag borne by a group of 180 from the parishes of Carnmoney and Templepatrick, bearing the motto 'Superstitious jealousy, the curse of the Irish Bastille; let us unite and destroy it!', must have given heart to Tone—who certainly came away from the day thinking the Antrim people better democrats than those from Down. The parade wound its way through the main streets to the White Linen Hall, fired three *feux de joie* and assembled inside. Sinclair rose to propose the two addresses. Drennan's was accepted unanimously and with 'energetic bursts of applause'.

But Tone's address produced a debate which went on till seven that evening. A number of the country corps withdrew before the end of the debate—a withdrawal interpreted by some as a sign of their disgust at the sentiments expressed in the address, by others as necessitated by their long march home.[6] Whichever way there can be no doubt that opposition to the address would have been greater had the County Down Volunteers remained. As it was, the document had no easy passage. Several opponents had heard rumours of 'an intemperate address' and came with speeches prepared. Joy proposed expunging the offending paragraph on the grounds that the Catholics were not yet prepared for emancipation. He hoped to see the day come when it could be granted with safety and moved that the word 'gradual' be introduced. But Joy found himself in a minority. He had made his speech without having fully listened to the reading of the address. On being challenged, he insisted on reading the offending paragraph for himself and was thrown when the words did not match up to his exaggerated fears.[7]

Tone was surprised and relieved at the overwhelming majority in favour of Catholic emancipation when the question was put, and was particularly impressed by the favourable speeches of the Dissenting clergymen. The gloom of the preceding days disappeared from his journal and at the banquet which followed in the Donegall Arms, he was in celebratory mood. 'Dinner at the Donegal[1] Arms: Every body as happy as a King...Huzza! God bless every body!...who would have thought it this morning? Huzza!—generally drunk: broke my glass thumping the table: Home, God knows how, or when. Huzza!' Toasts were drunk to France, Poland, America, the union of Irishmen, the sovereignty of the people and a host more, specially prepared by the committee on to which Tone had been drafted on his arrival in Belfast. Songs were likewise composed for the occasion, sung at the banquet and published in a commemoration booklet shortly afterwards. Most applauded the French Revolution. But Tone's 'New Song Addressed to Irishmen' looked inward to Ireland and was particularly suited to the occasion:

When Rome, by dividing had conquered the world,
And land after land into slavery hurl'd,
Hibernia escap'd, for t'was Heaven's decree,
That Ierne united, should ever be free,

Her harp then delighted the nations around,
By its music entranced, their own suff'rings were drown'd,
In arts and in Learning, the foremost were we,
And Ireland united was happy and free

But soon—ah! too soon, did fell discord begin;
Our domestic contentions, let foreigners in.
Too well they improved the advantage we gave,
When they came to assist, they remained to enslave.

From that fatal hour, our freedom was lost,
Peace, Virtue, and Learning, were fled from our coast
And the Island of Saints, might more fitly be named
The Land of Tormentors, the place of the damn'd.

Then let us remember our madness no more,
What we lost by division, let union restore,
Let us firmly unite, and our covenant be,
Together to fall, or together be free.[8]

It is a rollicking popular verse, which captures nicely his most consistent argument: for unity read freedom, for division, enslavement.

II

Tone was in holiday mood after the success of the 14th. The morning headaches which were a feature of his journal entries until then—though he had been much more abstemious than usual—disappeared, and he determined to set off for Dungannon to see Russell.[9] But his new responsibilities to the Catholic Committee impinged. A letter signed 'AB' had appeared in the *News Letter* for 13 July urging the Catholic Committee to condemn the Defenders. The letter was prompted by a resurgence of sectarian conflict in south Down, caused by that old irritant to Protestants—Catholics carrying arms. 'The Papists, or rather (as it is the fashion to stile them the Roman Catholicks of Ireland)', complained one local magistrate to Lord Bayhem, 'are arming and have as regular meetings as our Volunteers formerly had...the defenders...are in regular companies'.[10] A new upsurge in Protestant Volunteering was the outcome. The United Irishmen applauded the rapid spread of Volunteering that summer as a sign of a new reforming spirit in the north. But as Tone recognised, Volunteers could equally be raised on anti-Catholic principles in counties like Down, Armagh, Louth and Monaghan, which experienced escalating Defender troubles that summer and autumn.[11]

Rumours spread of the Catholics importing arms from abroad, which incensed Tone, who considered it an excuse by the authorities to arouse opposition to reform. But the French minister in London complained that large-scale arms purchases by the Irish had tripled prices and though Whitehall found insufficient evidence to endorse the rumours, Dublin Castle was genuinely alarmed.[12] Whatever the origin of the rumours, a general arming by both sides in the disturbed counties was indisputable.

But there was little sympathy elsewhere in Ireland for the northern Protestants. Even opponents of Catholic emancipation expressed their horror at such sectarianism,[13] and Westmorland was to tell Pitt that 'these republicans' were far from agreed on Catholic reform: 'more bigoted...Protestants do not exist [than the County Down Volunteers], and their arming is solely against the Papists'. Westmorland blamed the local gentry, notably Lord Annesley, and considered their calls for military assistance alarmist.[14] Annesley was a noted anti-papist and member of the Beresford clan, and Keogh saw the troubles as part of the anti-Catholic campaign by the 'monopolists' in the Castle.[15] The local gentry in turn blamed the government: 'I very much wish that no further extension of privilege may be granted to our Irish Papists,' wrote Bayhem's correspondent; 'we live in a Protestant part of the Kingdom, and even there I see they are not to be trusted'.

Tone's 'XY' in response to 'AB'—the first in a long series of exchanges that summer—was published in the *Northern Star* on 14 July. He revealed that the Catholic Committee had approached some Belfast people a year earlier and offered to mediate in the sectarian conflict in the north, but were advised that tempers then were too heated. He again tendered the offer to meet with the respectable gentlemen from any disturbed county, pointing out that the Catholic Committee was as anxious as anyone to put an end to the disturbances. 'However, a few of the misguided and ignorant rabble of that persuasion have been misled into acts of violence, in which they have...been at least equalled by their adversaries'.[16]

In view of Tone's recommendations, Neilson suggested that some of the Catholic delegates travel to Rathfriland, the centre of the disturbances. They prevailed on Tone to accompany them and in dismay he shelved his plans for a visit to Dungannon. Within half an hour of the decision he, Neilson and Neilson's wife Anne set out for south Down, spent the night with a local family of radical sympathies, the Lowrys, and were escorted to Rathfriland the following morning by young Alexander Lowry. Keogh joined them from Downpatrick.

Built on the summit of a steep hill, on the site of the former Magennis castle, Rathfriland was one of those neatly laid-out Protestant towns in which John Wesley had felt so at home. At the centre was a market square, whose inn and houses had been partly built from the stones of the castle dismantled by its first Protestant proprietor in the aftermath of the 1641 rebellion.[17]

The Catholic delegation met with a number of local dignitaries, clergy of all denominations, gentry, magistrates and Volunteer officers. Although there was much recrimination on both sides, the general consensus was that the Protestants were the aggressors, offence having been taken 'at the Catholics marching about in military array, and firing shots at unseasonable times'. The Catholic Committee members agreed that such assemblies should be stopped. But while Tone was more prepared than Keogh to see wrong on both sides, he protested against the Catholics' arms being confiscated altogether—which he thought would be impossible in any event. The Catholics would be discouraged from parading. A pastoral letter from the Catholic bishop and a circular letter from the Catholic Committee to this effect would be read from all the pulpits, and the Protestants for their part agreed to maintain peace against all transgressors, regardless of religion. They all parted on excellent terms and Tone thought of heading off to see Russell, only to be thwarted once more by the recognition that Russell himself would be away from Dungannon by the time he reached there. Reluctantly he set off for Dublin in Keogh's company.

Three days after his return to Dublin Tone wrote another 'XY' letter reporting the success of their Rathfriland meeting and informing the *News Letter* correspondent that the Catholic Committee address to the Defenders was going forward. The address was composed the day following his return, submitted to Grattan for approval on the 21st, to the sub-committee the next day, and 1,000 copies ordered from Byrne on the 24th. It called upon the Catholics to desist from 'arraying' in arms. The Committee had been assured by the Volunteers and 'respectable Protestants' in the Rathfriland area that every man would be protected regardless of religion. Tone's address promised that any 'peaceable' Catholic who had been attacked would be defended and pointed to the Committee's aim of securing equal treatment for Catholics before the laws.[18] Signs were that the lower-class Catholics were now looking to the Catholic Committee rather than the priests for social leadership, and its leaders might well have acted as an agency of social control had they been able to deliver on such promises.

III

On 7 August Tone, Keogh and Neilson again left Dublin to take the address back to the troubled areas of Down. They stopped at Drogheda, then a small town, enclosing four broad streets and a collection of 'miserable cottages' within ancient walls.[19] Tone was unwell for much of his stay there, recording unusually early nights and only one light moment when he spent an evening with 'a parcel of girls' at the home of James Bird, one of the town's leading merchants and chairman of its Catholic Committee. His new position, following in the wake of Keogh's whirlwind tour, was exhausting. They had stopped to meet with the northern bishops. The meeting was a tribute to Keogh's pursuit of Catholic unity. The episcopacy generally preferred to avoid politics for fear of alienating the government, and the Ulster bishops were the most aloof of all. Yet even the anti-clerical Tone was much impressed by them, particularly by Dr Plunket, Bishop of Meath. This is not surprising, for it was Plunket who had criticised the support by Archbishop Troy of Dublin of the seceders earlier in the year. Moreover, he had spent 27 years in Paris, and was deemed the leader of the 'Gallican' party within the Irish Church.[20]

But although things had gone well in Drogheda, news came through that a second visit to Rathfriland would not be welcomed. The three men were warned that their lives might even be in danger, and accordingly set off with 'four cases of pistols'. On arrival they encountered considerble hostility. The town's only inn refused them accommodation. The local gentry, with whom they had met on the previous occasion, all found excuses to stay away, and they had to be escorted out of the town. In contrast the hospitality of the local Catholic gentry came as a relief. A tour to Rostrevor with its breathtaking scenery, three days with friends in Belfast, and assurances that

1. Mrs Margaret Tone with her sons Theobald and Matthew (Madden, *United Irishmen*)

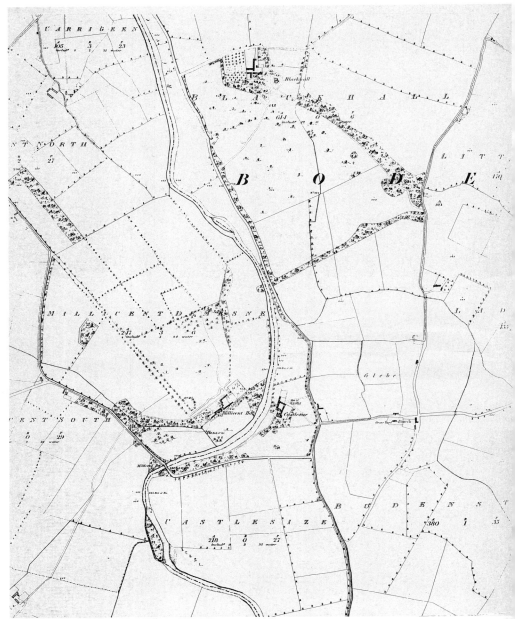

2. Bodenstown parish, showing the Tone house opposite the church, Millicent House and Chateau Boue—reputedly among the buildings at Blackhall (1839 Ordnance Survey map)

Wheatley, The Volunteers in College Green (courtesy National Gallery of Ireland)

The Library, Trinity College (James Malton, *A Picturesque and Descriptive View of the City of blin . . . in 1791*)

5. Provost's House, Dublin, showing part of Grafton Street (Malton, *View of Dublin*)

6. Parliament House, College Green, Dublin (Malton, *View of Dublin*)

The Irish House of Commons in 1790, from a painting by Henry Barraud and John Hayter. (courtesy Ulster Museum)

Stephen's Green, Dublin (courtesy of the National Library of Ireland)

9. Capel Street, Dublin, leading to Dublin Castle and opening to the right and left into Ormond Quay (Malton, *View of Dublin*)

10. Tholsel, Dublin (Malton, *View of Dublin*)

1. Theobald Wolfe Tone in Volunteer Uniform (Madden, *United Irishmen*)

12. Thomas Russell (Madden, *United Irishmen*)

13. John Fitzgibbon, Earl of Clare (Maxwell, *Rebellion*)

14. John Keogh (Gwynne, *Keog*

15. Archibald Hamilton Rowan (courtesy National Library of Ireland)

16. William James MacNeven (Madden, *United Irishmen*)

17. William Drennan (courtesy Ulster Museum)

18. Samuel Neilson (courtesy Ulster Museum)

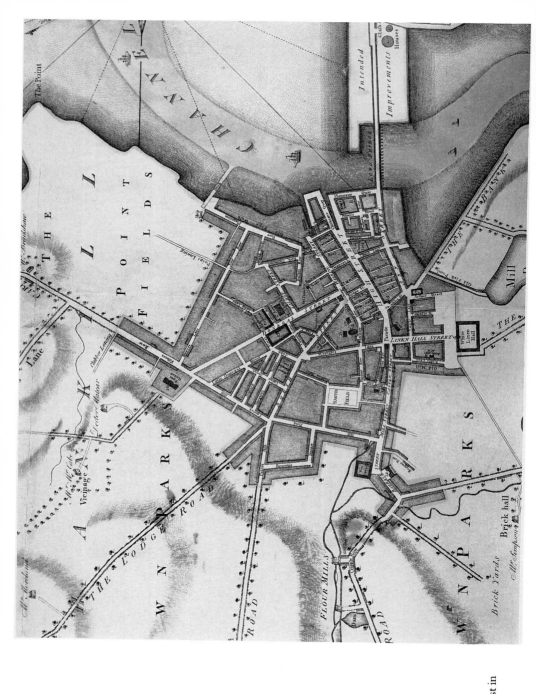

19. Williamson, Belfast in 1791 (courtesy Ulster Museum)

20. Nixon, High Street, Belfast, in 1786 (courtesy Ulster Museum)

21. Thompson, Belfast from Cromac Water Mill, showing the Mall and Cave Hill (courtesy Ulster Museum)

22. Bastille day celebrations, Belfast 1792 (courtesy National Library of Ireland)

23. Thomas Addis Emmet (Madden, *United Irishmen*)

24. Revd William Jackson (*Walker's Hibernian Magazine*, 1795)

25. Newgate Prison, Dublin (courtesy National Library of Ireland)

26. Nicholl, McArt's Fort, Belfast (courtesy Ulster Museum)

all the Dissenting clergy were well disposed to Catholic emancipation, caused Tone to dismiss the Rathfriland episode as an inconvenience, which would not stop 'the growing liberty of Ireland'. It
was typical of Tone's romantic attachment to his belief that the
future for a more liberal Ireland lay with the advanced thinkers in the
north, and a return visit to Rathfriland on 16 August, *en route* back to
Dublin, suggested that once again the trouble could be traced back to
the Protestant gentry.

At a meeting with Lord Downshire (governor of County Down,
and the most powerful magnate in Ulster) and his son Lord
Hillsborough, the younger man did nothing to disguise his dislike
of the Catholics. He drew no distinction between the Catholic Committee and the Defenders, was angry at the Committee's interference,
and proclaimed that force was the only way of putting down the
disturbances. During a courtesy call on Lord Moira at Montalto, just
outside Ballinahinch, Tone introduced Keogh and was told of
Annesley's bigotry and reputed mistreatment of the Catholics. It
fuelled Tone's anger with the local aristocracy, evident even through
the studied moderation of his 'XY' account of the visit, which appeared in the *Northern Star* and *News Letter* on 23 August. At this
point the exchange of correspondence through the press came to an
abrupt end, 'AB' taking sides on the sectarian divide and criticising
the Catholic Committee for its interference.

The second Down venture, however—whilst a chastening reminder of the strength of religious discord—was a major success in
the continuing drive to unite the Catholics. A reconciliation of contending parties of Catholics at Newry was effected and the Defenders
from Dundalk looked to Tone to represent them at the next assizes.
Tone declined—almost certainly because of his full-time commitment to the Catholic Committee, for he was to take up their brief
two years later—and recommended instead his old friend Jebb. The
Newry reconciliation came after news of the conversion of some
Peep-of-Day Boys at Ballinahinch, and Tone—unusually, with his
new circumspection, and as he admits '*entre deux vins*'—proposed the
establishment of a Society of United Irishmen. He was pleasantly
surprised at the welcome the proposal received: 'wonderful to see
how rapidly the Catholic mind is rising', he wrote—a telling reminder that, however just he felt the Catholic cause, he shared a
belief with many other less friendly Protestants that the Catholics
still needed educating into liberty.

Tone was well pleased with the trip and plans were mounted to
distribute the address—even to the offending aristocrats—as a public
display of the Catholic Committee's conciliatory role. But his two
journeys north that summer considerably altered his perception of

Presbyterian liberality. He recognised that Belfast alone supported the Catholic cause and blamed the Dissenters for alienating the Catholics from the reform issue. 'Oh why are not those *fellows in the North* sufficiently enlightened to join heartily with us!', he wrote. 'Then indeed something might be done—reform! liberty and equality! The XX [Catholics] would I think join them.'[21] He admitted that he too had once thought the Catholics 'incurable Tories'. But he was now prepared to put reform on the back burner, in the expectation that the Catholics, having experienced liberty, would in time become friends to liberty and enemies to bad government. Many wondered at his studious refusal to discuss internal Catholic matters. Drennan pitied such 'an excellent man' being 'harnessed...with others and other opinions'. Butler thought Tone had been bought off.[22]

The about-turn of Tone's *News Letter* correspondent 'AB' was symptomatic of deeper difficulties. By all means deal with your own kind, 'AB' had argued, but to assume a role as mediator was to attack the power of the Protestant establishment. The Committee was genuinely embarrassed by the Defender troubles which swept through south Ulster and north Leinster that year, but the Ascendancy had already made the troubles a stalking-ground to assert its power.[23] In the role the Catholic Committee adopted that summer as an afterthought to its Belfast mission, it touched a raw nerve and ultimately supplied the Ascendancy with its most effective argument against Catholic emancipation, the threat of popular rebellion.[24]

13

Ascendancy on the Attack

The journey north had been gruelling, involving much late-night travel on horseback along dreadful roads.[1] Tone was tired and so the summer was to continue. The reason was the new plan to re-form the Catholic Committee on a truly representative basis, with delegates elected by primary assemblies from every county and town. It was a plan so revolutionary in scope that even United Irish critics of the Catholics looked on with awed admiration. The outcome was the celebrated Catholic Convention of December 1792. Its delegates were effectively elected by universal (if indirect) Catholic suffrage, and the extensive paper work and correspondence involved were largely handled by Tone. Catholic anger at their treatment in the recent parliamentary session produced an uncharacteristic, almost militant confidence which the establishment found unnerving. The elections and propaganda of the summer and autumn months of 1792 spread that new militancy into the countryside and to social levels not normally conversant with politics. It was the consequent erosion of deference and feared breakdown of traditional modes of social control over a Catholic populace long deemed inferior which produced the ensuing Protestant backlash.

I

Instructions for the election of delegates were circulated that summer and became the object of a concerted attack by the grand juries and the landlord interests they represented. The Catholic Committee, in seeking a popular mandate to convene nationally, was bypassing the source of Protestant authority in the Dublin Parliament. The projected Covention was denounced as a 'Popish congress', modelled on the French Revolutionary example and threatening to 'overawe' the 'Protestant Parliament'. The assumed disloyalty, slavishness and general inferiority of the Catholics were again put forward to justify the maintenance of Protestant ascendancy.

But once again it was the loss of control, implied in the Catholics' defiant shift from traditionally submissive tactics, which produced most stridency. The *Freeman's Journal* contrasted 'the too forward interference of a few traders' to Kenmare's moderation. It accused the Catholic Committee of ingratitude in not thanking Parliament for the recent concessions, and warned that 'to contend for *equality* is to endeavour for the overthrow of *subordination*'. The Fermanagh grand jury urged 'submissive gratitude' on the Catholics as the only way 'to merit the extension of future favours'.[2] In the absence of parliamentary news, during an unusually long recess, such attacks dominated press reports till the end of the year.

Initially stunned by the virulence of the attack, the sub-committee soon returned the fire, and the knowledge that a number of the 'Irish Cabinet' were behind the grand jury resolutions reinforced Catholic determination to bypass the Irish administration altogether. Tone was commissioned to seek advice on the legality of the proposed convention, and armed with the necessary assurances, the Catholics mounted a counter-attack in the press. The prototype and earliest protest had come from the Londonderry grand jury and was engineered by John Beresford. It declared the activities of the Catholics as unconstitutional and destructive to Protestant Ascendancy and the constitution as established in 1688. These last the jurors vowed to defend with their 'lives and fortunes' and urged the Catholics to seek further favour through 'the same well-regulated conduct, which has already excited the attention of the legislature on their behalf'.[3]

Tone read the resolutions on the morning of 8 August in Drogheda's coffee-house, and sat down 'in a horrible rage' to reply. The outcome was a long letter signed 'Vindex', which appeared in the *Northern Star* on 11 August and the *Dublin Evening Post* three days later. 'Vindex' links the Catholic demands with those made by the Volunteers a decade earlier. Though they eventually resulted in the 1782 constitution, they too were dismissed at the time as unconstitutional and with better cause. For they were an armed association dictating to the legislature, whereas the Catholics sought 'dutifully, humbly, and *constitutionally* to petition their Sovereign and the Legislature, to be restored to the rank of men, and to the common protection which the law should hold out to all peaceable citizens'. Despite the nation-wide outburst by the grand juries, there was a growing recognition among politicians that constitutional liberties based on the rights of property could not be withheld from the growing number of propertied Catholics. 'Vindex' captures the new mood. 'You will not allow them any share in the framing of the laws, by which their lives and properties are to be influenced; you would put them out of the pale of the constitution, and make them outlaws in their native land.' Aggrieved subjects, his letter asserts, have the right to petition.[4]

The grand jury resolutions were a clumsy literary effort and the message of 'Vindex' is weakened by an almost adolescent parade of erudition to show the grand jurors up as country bumpkins. It gave the government press the excuse it needed, and Vindex's 'insipid and offensive pedantry' and 'flimsy puerility' was used to dismiss the whole exercise as 'unworthy of notice'—'the quibbling of an un-briefed lawyer'.[5] Tone had been carried away by his anger that morning and the real message of his long grammatical critique only becomes clear in several further pieces published some weeks later.

Here the literary inadequacies of the grand jurors form part of a more measured attack on the hypocrisy of those who argued the sup-posed illiteracy of the Catholics in justification of their exclusion from political rights. With every opponent rallying to define this concept of Protestant Ascendancy, Tone assumed the character of the ordinary man, the 'poor Protestant', the 'petty juror', the 'Derry farmer', and stripped the concept of 'Protestant Ascendancy' down to size. Properly explained, it was no more than 'slavery to Irish Pro-testants, under an English ascendancy, another degree of slavery to Presbyterians, under an Irish Episcopacy' and a much greater degree of slavery for Catholics. 'In a word, it is Irish slavery, continued by means of internal divisions, while England looks on...and beholds the blessed effects of her maxim *Divide et Impera*.'[6]

But it was the Dublin Corporation's more lengthy definition and defence of the Protestant Ascendancy on 11 September which drew Tone's most withering attack. The Corporation dismissed as vain Catholic hopes of sharing power with Protestants. God had given victory to Protestant liberty over popish tyranny a hundred years earlier. 'The Protestants of Ireland would not be compelled by any authority whatever to abandon the political situation which their forefathers had won with their swords and which is therefore their birthright, or to surrender their religion at the footstool of Popery.' It criticised the Catholics for their lack of gratitude when every con-cession was made short of the exercise of political power, and this the Corporation declared incompatible with the Protestant Ascendancy. This it defined as 'A Protestant King of Ireland, A Protestant Parlia-ment, A Protestant hierarchy, Protestant elections and Government, Benches of Justice and Army through all their branches Protestant, and the system supported by a connection with the Protestant realm of Britain'.[7]

Tone poured scorn on such lofty language and stripped it down to its base in political jobbery. The Protestant Ascendancy was nothing more than a 'chain of monopoly', extending from the throne to the tide-waiter; 'it is an infamous system of corruption, which exhausts the vital juices of seven-eighths of this country...it is the pillar of a rotten Government; it is plundering the poor by tithes and by taxes; it is a long pension list, rotten boroughs, and no popular representation...it is inexhaustible pillage to a dozen men, and hopeless poverty to millions. The exasperated exaggeration aside, Tone was voicing a widely held view that the Protestant Ascendancy notion was a screen for a baser monopoly of jobs and power.[8] He adopts an ironic tone in referring to the ingratitude of these Catholics in possession of 'such vast immunities', and in one of his characteristic pieces in which he assumes the guise of the ordinary man, he shows the reality of the situation, even for the wealthy Catholic: compelled to live 'in a state of inferiority to every little Protestant Squire', the channels for advancement closed to his offspring. There was always the bar for his younger son, 'but he dislikes the profession wherein his ambition (of which he already has a great deal) is circumscribed'. Tone was arguing a middle-class case. Indeed the Catholic campaign of these years was part of a wider movement to open up politics to the middle classes.

Tone's output of articles on the Catholic issue increased dramatically in these weeks. They are well-written and punchy in style, even if their content—the French Revolution's destruction of popery, the injustice of taxation without representation—is unexceptional. Tone warns the Ascendancy that protection and allegiance are reciprocal. But in the long term it was a contest for power, as the Ascendancy realised, and Tone was disingenuous in depicting the Catholic campaign as nothing more than a demand for basic justice.[9]

II

The virulence of the Ascendancy addresses and the blatant involvement of the Castle caused the campaign to backfire. Catholics throughout the country and their friends (not least in parts of the north) responded with confident and reasoned refutations. The overall result was an upsurge of Catholic awareness, confidence and determination, while many who had opposed the Catholic franchise only months earlier became more conciliatory.[10] On 23 September Tone re-read his unpublished reply to *The Protestant Interest* and marvelled at the pains he had taken then to prove points now accepted as axioms. Even the Ponsonbys had come over by the end of the year. The long-standing Volunteer tradition of parading before William of Orange's statue in College Green, on the anniversary of his birthday, was abandoned as a mark of respect to the Catholics, prompting Haliday's bitter observation: 'I suppose we shall have no more meetings on 4 November...lest we should give offence to the tender consciences of those soi-disant Catholic and ci-devant Papists. I think, with old 'Shandy', that there is an infinite deal in a name.'[11] A brisk business developed in key Catholic pamphlets and Tone's

Argument was among those which went on sale in Belfast at the sub-
sidised price of a penny.[12]

Richard Burke had returned to Ireland amidst the uproar caused
by the elections and wrote angrily to his political friends in England
that the Castle set were 'playing a game of their own—in which they
have made Lord Westmorland an accomplice. The real object is to
make an ostentation of difficulties—to bring forth and exhibit in
every possible manner, the prejudices of *the country gentlemen*, in
order to convince the English Government that measures of
conciliation cannot be carried'.[13] Certainly Westmorland played
down London's alarms about Irish discontent, urging instead the
need to placate the Protestants. It was well known that Westmorland
was in the pocket of his Irish ministers. Rumours of a change of
administration and talks of a possible coalition in England with the
Portland Whigs, in which the Irish viceroyalty would be on offer,
further weakened his authority.

It was against this background that the Catholic leaders proposed
securing the services of a sympathetic new Lord Lieutenant. Keogh
asked Tone to explore with his friend George Knox the possibility of
a reforming Abercorn administration. Knox and his older brother
Thomas were part of the small group of talented and ambitious
young MPs who made up the independent, though pro-government,
Abercorn connection. Abercorn had Irish ambitions and, as one of
Pitt's friends at Cambridge, he made no secret of his belief that he
had Pitt's ear on Irish issues. At breakfast with Tone on Saturday, 29
September, Keogh suggested a scheme whereby Abercorn would be
persuaded to assume the Lord Lieutenancy, take up the Catholic
cause and dump Beresford and Fitzgibbon. Tone was deeply
troubled by the suggestion, and rightly so, for it was a similar plan
two years later which was to cause the Fitzwilliam crisis. Moreover,
although George Knox had consistently shown himself a friend to
the Catholics, Abercorn had not used his supposed friendship with
Pitt to support their case in London. And, perhaps most importantly,
Pitt did not like Abercorn. He complained of his 'intolerable pride',
thought he would be 'troublesome' in Ireland, and determined never
to send him there.[14]

But Tone was disturbed by Keogh's suggestion, and his mental
debate reflects considerable confusion about the country's political
future. In the first place he thought a change of administration would
mean sacrificing reform and with it that Catholic-Dissenter alliance
which he had spent the past year forging. If this happened he felt the
Dissenters of the north would have only themselves to blame for not
coming forward to support Catholic emancipation, and he was ir-

ritated at their failure to do so. Secondly, however much he disliked the present administration, at least it was successful in stemming excessive English interference. Keogh's plan, by throwing Catholic support behind an Abercorn administration, would considerably strengthen English influence: 'the Crown, as it is improperly said, but more truly the Oligarchy has already much too great a portion of power in our system, which power I have never hitherto known them to exercise for any good purpose'.[15] And yet, Tone consoled himself, the emancipation of three million Catholics justified the means, and having enjoyed freedom and the accompanying prosperity, Catholics in time would 'come to think like other people' and recognise the evils of bad government. It was a measure of how far Tone was prepared to compromise his convictions for the Catholic cause, though he would have preferred emancipation to come about through internal unity, through a Catholic–Dissenter alliance, without the need to run to England.

He raised the Abercorn plan with Knox during a morning stroll in St Stephen's Green on 25 October and they continued their discussions over breakfast on the 31st. He spoke of growing Catholic expectations and the danger of violence if disappointed, particuarly in the event of war. He did not relish the prospect of upheaval, but declared himself 'decidedly of opinion that the Government of Ireland must either alter their whole system, or be subverted by force, of which God knows the event'. Although from quite different social backgrounds, Knox and Tone shared a contempt for existing politicians. They complained of the wickedness of the present government and talked flippantly of bringing each other into power. But Knox was anxious not to be seen as working against the government, which he normally supported. Keogh was proceeding with a haste which might hurt Knox's interests and Tone tried to protect his friend from the consequences. In the event the scheme came to nothing, for the full Catholic Committee preferred to work through Westmorland, rather than commit their cause to any 'junto'. Moreover, Abercorn's response to the overture was a demand that the Catholics renounce their present plans and rely entirely on him, whereupon Keogh despaired of the scheme and Knox sailed for England.[16]

It was a measure of a certain desperation creeping into Catholic affairs.[17] The growing militancy of the Catholics was indisputable. Keogh was keeping many options open. At the United Irish Society Collins thought the Catholics (particularly Keogh and McCormick) militant separatists, and even allowing for Collins's marked antipopery, Keogh had a tendency to tailor his language to his audience.[18] Tone prided himself on having convinced the Catholics to base their demand for the franchise on the Paineite principle of the people's right to vote for the laws by which it was governed. But the leading Catholics needed little education in 'democratic principles'. In September Keogh published anonymously a squib—*Common Sense to the Presbyterians of the Province of Ulster*—which evoked the doctrine of no taxation without representation in support of reform and emancipation. In the process he made an attack on the reputations of the leading Castle politicians and their dependants so personal that Drennan thought the document put men's lives at risk.[19]

It was Tone's association with the Catholic campaign rather than the United Irishmen which was gaining him the nickname 'Marat' among his legal acquaintances, and caused his old college friend Miller to wonder that he could still frequent such an aristocratic institution as Trinity.[20] Yet although he angered Grattan by remarks dismissive of the Irish Parliament, and was growing weary of those Whig preoccupations which had still dominated his thinking only months earlier, he was happy enough to utilise conventional politics to achieve his ends. He spent much of that summer in the country and town houses of the Whig gentry, and was even gratified when the Ponsonbys were won over. His Protestantism, though it rankled with some of the rural Catholic delegates, gave him a certain neutrality and both Grattan and Knox preferred to communicate through him rather than directly with the sub-committee.[21]

14

Catholic Convention

The Catholic electoral arrangements which gave rise to such protests involved attaching two members from every county and major town in the country to the existing Dublin-based Committee. The meeting of these delegates became the celebrated Catholic Convention of December 1792. Arrangements were master-minded by the handful of men composing the sub-committee in Dublin, but more often than not by Tone and Keogh alone. Each parish was to nominate two electors to attend county meetings, where delegates to the national convention would be chosen. Unlike the landed gentry of the earlier Committee, who acted as individuals and were responsible only to themselves, delegates chosen in 1792 were to 'hold themselves accountable to those from whom they derive their trust', and were liable to removal by those same 'constituents' if they acted 'in opposition to the general will, and the public good'. The authorities denounced the plan as French in inspiration.[1] The Catholics denied the charge, claimed that it was thoroughly English, and cited Hume's *Essay on a Perfect Commonwealth* as the model.[2] Although the original plan of maintaining constant communication with the mass of the people was dropped as 'too hardy', the stridency of the Protestant response should be seen in the light of this phenomenon of a national body of lay Catholics meeting for the first time that century, utterly convinced of the justice of their cause, and using methods of political organisation which were nothing short of revolutionary.[3]

I

By 1 October 18 counties had returned members, and a further 9 were expected to do so. However, several areas continued to present difficulties. Kenmare's influence in Kerry worked against the campaign. But Mayo presented the main problem. Here the moderately reformist MP, Denis Browne, was trying to boost his own electoral interests by persuading the Catholics to break away from the national movement and present a separate petition. The delay in Mayo was also affecting Galway. The national effort could not afford to lose these, the country's two main Catholic counties and heartland of the original Catholic Committee.[4]

A mission to the Catholic leaders of both counties as they assembled at Ballinasloe fair was suggested. Tone and Braughall were chosen to conduct it, the first time, Tone remarks in his journal, that he had been entrusted by Keogh with a separate mission. Keogh himself declined to go, intimating a dislike for that hazard of eighteenth-century travel, wet sheets. Tone was sceptical, but that was unfair. Keogh had a chest complaint which would have been aggravated by the unusual wetness of the season, and had already spent a considerable amount of time travelling on Catholic business. As it was, Tone himself would soon become a victim of the unusually inclement weather.[5] These traditionalist Catholic gentry had complained to Keogh about the involvement of a Protestant in their business and it is symptomatic of his mood at the time that he should have chosen to send Tone to them.[6] Braughall had been a spirited member of the Catholic Committee since 1786. He was something of an intellectual. Tone liked him and was a frequent dinner guest at his house in Eccles Street on the northern perimeter of Dublin city.[7]

The two men left Dublin on the evening of 8 October, Tone having been compelled to abandon a sociable weekend with Matilda and his United Irish friends at Rowan's residence, at Rathcoffey in County Kildare. It was a token of the seriousness with which he took the Catholic business, for he always found the United Irishmen better company. At the gates of the Phoenix Park—whose rutted roads had long been a source of complaint and a scene of frequent accidents and robberies—their coach was stopped by footpads. Tone wanted to get out and fight them, reflecting only after the event on the folly of such a move. But the threat was enough and the robbers moved on. At 3 a.m., they are again forced to stop at Kinnegad in Westmeath to change a wheel, and Tone had to descend amidst the mud and squelch of several weeks of rain to help hold up the carriage. The lame, sixty-three-year-old Braughall was past such feats.

Tone's comments on his four-day visit to the west reflects the narrowness of his eastern, urbanised experience. Though Ballinasloe was said to be host to the greatest cattle fair in Europe, he found it a dreary, noisy and vulgar town. Accommodation was difficult to find, expensive and overcrowded, and despite the fatigue of the journey and unusually early nights, the singing, snoring and music-making of the other inmates robbed Tone of the sleep he badly needed. The wine he found 'poisonous' and the food bad, consisting largely of fried steak and great quantities of onions—a fare he admitted 'not to my taste', quoting from Pope's *Autumn Pastoral* '"Go gentle gales"—fragrant and pretty!' on the physical consequences. The Catholic gentry were 'intolerably dull', their conversation dominated by 'handicapping, wagers, horse-racing, swapping' (it was the eve of the Castlebar races in County Galway). He liked James Plunket, however, a future United Irish leader in Mayo, and Sir Thomas French, who was to form part of the Catholic delegation to London in December and who on this occasion chaired the meeting called of the Galway and Mayo Catholics.

Their reluctance to send delegates to the Convention was based on rumours that the Catholic aristocrats disapproved. Now that Keogh had engineered a reconciliation, the two emissaries managed to dispose of this and other misconceptions. Nevertheless, Tone felt they had given a rather poor account of themselves—Braughall making 'a very long, rambling, diffuse, bad statement', followed by an equally poor performance by himself. 'Mr Hutton...no great orator at a set speech, tho he converses well enough...he is in fact not only modest but sheepish which is a shame! Mr Hutton had probably better talents and to a moral certainty, better education, and beyond all question more knowledge of the subject than any of his hearers yet after all he made but a poor exhibition.'[8] He lamented that even Keogh, 'in his digressive, rambling style, would have beat Mr Hutton all to nothing', and determined to 'get rid of that vicious modesty which obscures the great splendour and brilliancy of his natural talents'. However the object of the meeting was attained and the Connacht gentry agreed to return French and Christopher Bellew as delegates.

Browne continued to be a disruptive influence, however, and Tone spent his last night in Ballinasloe reflecting on the evils of aristocracy, both locally and in the form of the published letters of Ireland's former Lord Lieutenant, Lord Chesterfield—his reading material for the trip. He was startled to find a real-life representation of the 'monstrous' fictional character of Valmont in *Les Liaisons dangereuses* (who had set about and succeeded in disrupting a happy marriage for the whim of another), just the advice which Chesterfield gave to his son. Tone was deeply shocked at such a 'base... unnatural' recommendation and was recalled momentarily to his duties towards his own son.[9]

II

He had been particularly neglectful of his family during 1792. With Russell still in the north, there was little shared friendship for Matilda, and only fleetingly was she exposed to the new friends Tone was making. She spent some time in town with him, leaving the children in the country. She disliked the social gatherings to which he was increasingly invited, and as often as not did not accompany him. 'I am to dine today at Mr Dixon's at Kilmainham[10] with a horrible large company', she wrote to Margaret Russell on 5 September; 'I have been invited frequently and always sent an apology, but today it was impossible. I never saw one of the family, and I am frightened out of my wits. I am to be as fine as a jay.' She recalled the happy days spent with Russell at Irishtown. 'We have no such friends now.'[11]

The spirit of the letter is not so much that of anger as of head-shaking at her husband's incorrigibility. For weeks she had been trying to persuade him to spend a Sunday in Kildare. 'Tone has constantly disappointed me, and though he has promised to come with me next Sunday certainly, I shall wait no longer. . . . If all men knew how to treat women as Tom [Russell] does, we should be much better than we are.' It was not the first time she had teased Tone by such unfavourable comparisons with his friend. The letter was meant for his eyes as much as for her friend's, for she passed it over to him for completion. 'Mrs Tone has been writing some of her stuff', adds Tone, 'and I must finish it, she says, while she is dressing.'

But Matilda's scolding had reached its mark. He did make the journey to Kildare the following Sunday, having given up his lodgings to move back to the country. It was some time since he had seen young William and he was pleasantly surprised at how big he had grown. But even in Kildare the round of business quickly took him away again. He dined and slept elsewhere on that first night at home (8 September), as he did frequently in the weeks prior to his departure for Connacht. Thereafter his family disappears almost entirely from his journal, and visits home are so infrequent as to merit special mention. 'Spend evening at home with my innocent family —very pleasant—after all Home is Home', he enters for 17 November, then moves immediately to other matters only to pull himself up short with the critical reminder, 'I had like to forget!' The edited version of his remark disguises the implied dullness of family life, in contrast to the rush of business in town which the original conveys.[12]

For the rest of the year he lived an errant existence between Chateau Boue, various inns, and friends' houses, using Trinity as his mailing address. The three weeks prior to his Connacht venture saw a host of trips into the surrounding countryside to meet with Catholic Committee members, Whig politicians and eminent lawyers, and he slept in his clothes at an inn near the canal one night to be off early in the morning. He lamented the heavy drinking and sickness the following day, which invariably resulted from such meetings. 'It is downright scandalous to see in this, and other journals, how often that occurrence takes place, yet I call myself a sober man!'[13]

In September Tone's uncle Jonathan and his sister Fanny both died of tuberculosis, within a week of each other, and were buried in the family plot at Bodenstown.[14] Amidst the bustle of the Catholic business, Tone helped sort out Jonathan's affairs. With his aunt Mary Dunbavin and his uncle Matthew, he was one of the beneficiaries of his uncle's will.[15] Russell's affairs too had reached another crisis. He had resigned his magistracy, proposed going to France, possibly to enter the Revolutionary armies, and asked Tone to procure letters of recommendation to Paris. It was a wild scheme in those frantic first weeks of the Terror after the September massacres. Tone's views on the Revolution mirrored those of his Belfast friends. Though he flinched at the bloodshed, he remained unswerving in his admiration for France, despite such 'accidental irregularities'.[16] News of the French victory at Valmy over the invading Prussians reached Ireland in the first days of October and Tone mused on how, if single, he too would choose to go to France and 'supersede Kellerman', one of the generals victorious at Valmy.[17]

Tone spoke of Russell's plans to his friend's father, of his 'flattering prospects of advancement' in France, and of the recommendations he would carry to 'the first characters in the National Assembly'. The Tone family had been close to Captain Russell since they first befriended his son, and in the hectic weeks leading up to the Catholic Convention Tone had the additional worry of the old man's rapidly declining health. With Thomas Russell not expected in town until 3 December, Tone visited the father frequently as he lay ill at the Royal Hospital, taking the whole family there on 1 December, and returning again on Sunday, 2nd, the eve of the Catholic Convention. Three days later the Captain died, confiding Margaret Russell to the care of her brother and effectively terminating Thomas's French plans. His father was buried on the 8th. Russell contained his emotion, but Tone wept copiously.[18]

III

Tone continued to play a prominent role in the United Irish Society in these months, attending fortnightly sessions, sitting on key committees and communicating frequently with the Belfast Society.[19] There was nothing incompatible in the two roles, as United Irishman and Catholic agent, since Keogh, McCormick, Sweetman and several other sub-committee members were also active United Irishmen. But by now parliamentary reform and support of the French—though he was unhappy at the lack of attachment to both on the part of many Catholics—were taking a back seat to his Catholic work. He thought the United Irish call for Dublin to illuminate in celebration of French victories was unwise; and although he approved of a new Volunteer company being raised by Rowan and Tandy, he wondered at the wisdom of copying its uniform directly from the French National Guard.

Tone's most immediate duty on his return from Mayo was to organise a mass meeting of the Dublin Catholics in response to the attack by the Dublin Corporation. It met on Wednesday, 31 October. Tone reported 640 summonses taken at the door, and many more attending without them. The meeting was a reiteration of the Catholics' determination to hold the December Convention and the speeches were proclaimed by Drennan and Edmund Burke alike as better than anything to be heard in Parliament. Tone thought the speech of Dr Ryan (a member of the sub-committee) the best— which says much for his own preferences, for Ryan's had the 'classic and cultivated elegance' of a university graduate, while he found that of the self-made Keogh 'rambling and confused, but full of matter'.[20]

The description captures accurately enough the contrast in the two speeches. On paper Ryan's is the more eloquent and forceful, while Keogh covers old ground. It is, however, less than fair to Keogh, whose 'artful and argumentative' style, as Emmet described it, seemed perfectly adapted to the occasion.[21] It was typical of the intellectual contempt which Tone frequently displayed towards those with inflated views of their own talent. Often it was justified, and he rarely stinted on merited praise. But it highlights his own sense of frustration at being bred as part of an intellectual élite, though forced by social and political constraints to watch others less talented hold the limelight.

Tone was happy enough to act as Keogh's subordinate, provided Keogh recognised his abilities. But Keogh's own insecurities frequently prevented him from doing so. Mount Jerome became a second home to Tone, and he and Keogh were constantly in each other's company during these months. The journal's racy shorthand contains many criticisms of Keogh's vanity and 'popery' (in the sense of the kind of conservative attachment to Rome which the reformers claimed was a thing of the past). Both criticisms were justified and Keogh's vanity is well documented. But in Tone's Paris diary he places Keogh on the same plane with Russell among those he most admires, and during his term as secretary and agent there is a constant search for Keogh's approval. This craving for the admiration of those he respected is characteristic of Tone, and may well explain a certain secretiveness in his behaviour and a tendency to want to do things himself in order to win their applause for his achievements. Tone was theoretically an employee rather than a spokesman of the sub-committee. There is no record of his speaking at major meetings. But he had been taken on because of his reputation as a Catholic campaigner, he was not paid regularly and the time was not far off when he would rebel against being treated by Keogh as some kind of minion.

Over the next four weeks Tone's timetable was dominated by preparations for the Convention. He wrote the proposed petitions to the King and to Parliament, an address to the nation and a *Vindication* of the Committee in response to the grand jury resolutions. It was a trying and testing time. Would their efforts to ensure a united Catholic front prove successful? Although every county had returned delegates, there were still worrying signs of attempts by the Castle to influence the more timid, and there was a repeat of the old tactic of frightening the Catholic prelates into opposition. But the sub-committee had handled the Catholic bishops with great skill. Archbishop Troy now recognised the widespread Catholic support for the Committee, and was convinced that the clergy had to stand with its people.[22] Ultimately Troy and Bishop Moylan of Cork attended one of the Convention's sessions and headed the list of signatories to the petition.

But Tone's and Keogh's anxiety persisted well into the Convention's five-day meeting and work continued behind the scenes to reconcile differences and instil confidence into the country delegates. Tone felt no expense should be spared in fitting out the venue for the meeting, to 'give the country delegates a high idea of their own consequence, and the importance of the business'. He suggested hiring the Rotunda for the occasion—a significant gesture, in view of the failure of the last Volunteer convention there because of its split on the Catholic issue. But this was refused by the board of governors after Charlemont had objected, and only days before the delegates were to arrive in Dublin the Tailors' Hall in Back Lane was secured. It had recently become the regular venue for the United Irish Society, and the hundred members who attended its Friday meeting on 7 December must have brushed shoulders with the Catholics.

This would explain Tone's strained relations with his United Irish colleagues at the time. Nothing could be allowed to jeopardise the fragile Catholic unity. A delegation of United Irishmen was not admitted to the Catholic meeting, and despite Neilson's appeals from Belfast that Tone keep them fully informed of proceedings, Tone sent nothing. Such silence on the part of the Catholics raised suspicions that they might act timidly and undermine the general reform campaign, and a meeting of 'select' United Irishmen in Belfast wrote to 'their brother Tone', saying as much. Mrs McTier told Drennan of the letter, thereby fuelling his suspicions when Tone kept it from his United Irish colleagues in Dublin.[23]

The Convention opened on 3 December—233 delegates packing the 200-capacity hall—and declared itself 'the only power competent to speak the sense of the Catholics of Ireland'. It then went into committee to discuss the petition to the King. Each paragraph was approved unanimously until the last, spelling out their demands. Luke Teeling, a linen merchant from Lisburn in County Antrim, proposed that nothing short of complete emancipation should be asked for. He did so at the request of the Belfast Presbyterians, whom he had consulted prior to his departure, and Robert Simms thought it only right to alert Tone, whom the Belfast men still considered their representative in Dublin. The effect was electric, even the cautious expressing their support. Tone slipped Keogh a note saying that they should push it. But Keogh warned them to consider the lateness of the hour and the risk of incurring the accusation that they had taken such a decision 'in a fit of enthusiasm', and he counselled delay until the next day.

That evening convivial gatherings in the homes of the Dublin members further cemented the growing sense of unity and dispelled doubts. In the course of the following day's debate on Teeling's motion, issues were aired and supported which twelve months previously would have terrified the country Catholics. Teeling further urged the demand for total emancipation as coinciding with the wishes of their friends in Belfast, whose support had already been of such benefit. The Catholics should use the occasion to show their unity with the Dissenters. There was much talk of taking the sense of the people in the event of refusal, though they dismissed all rumours of violence and republicanism. But McKenna's eulogy of the existing constitution drew the riposte: 'time enough to praise when we come to enjoy it'.

The amendment having been approved, the debate then proceeded to the manner of the petition's presentation and it must have been gratifying to Tone to find that it was the very counties of Galway and Mayo which had proved so difficult to convert that summer which grasped the nettle and proposed bypassing the detested Irish administration altogether and presenting the petition directly to the King. Some of the country delegates were reluctant to administer such a public snub to the Lord Lieutenant, and on the 5th received an assurance from Richard Hely-Hutchinson, Lord Donoughmore—son of Trinity's Provost and a proven friend to the Catholics—that if the petition was submitted through the Castle it would be instantly dispatched to London. Keogh persuaded the Convention to postpone a decision while Donoughmore secured the necessary assurances. Tone's comment on this surprising turn of events captures the change which had occurred in the Catholic body over the preceding months. 'There can hardly be imagined a revolution more curious and unexpected than that which was occurring in the General Committee. The very men who a few months before could not obtain an answer at the Castle, sat with their watches in their hands, *minuting* that Government which had repelled them with disdain.' In two hours Donoughmore returned to inform the Convention of Hobart's refusal to give such an undertaking.

The news hardened the determination of the delegates. The total contempt of the Convention for the Irish government was manifest, even the moderate McKenna condemning its duplicity. The sub-committee told George Knox 'that they had been so deceived, cajoled and finally insulted in that quarter that they were determined never to appear before the Secretary [Hobart] again', and fears that the Donoughmore incident might swing the Convention behind another approach to the Castle led to further frantic discussions with Knox to effect a total change of administration.[24] Most of the speeches to the Convention reflected the growing hostility to Westmorland's administration. 'The present Govenment have not the confidence of the people', declared Devereux of Wexford. 'Will you trust your petition with such men?' cried Keogh and was greeted 'with an unanimous repeated, and indignant—"No!"'. Five delegates—Keogh, Devereux, Byrne, Bellew and Sir Thomas French (an enlightened choice representing new capital and old gentry)—were then chosen to take the petition directly to London, and the last day of the Convention was occupied discussing Tone's *Vindication of the Conduct and Principles of the Catholics of Ireland*.[25]

The *Vindication*—published as a pamphlet early in 1793—is one of Tone's service documents. It contrasts the humble and reasonable petitions of the Catholics with the exaggeration and cavil of the grand juries' resolutions. Most of the signatories of these resolutions were men 'either high in the Government of this country, or enjoying very lucrative places under that Government'. Tone singles out Foster's role in the Louth resolutions, and Fitzgibbon's in Limerick. Though the involvement of both figures was notorious and already much attacked elsewhere, the Convention spent its final day debating the wisdom of such a personal attack. This in itself is a telling reflection on the personal nature of Irish politics of all hues, for the pamphlet also contains a Paineite analysis of the Catholics' situation which went unnoticed. But those who had led the advance guard from the outset (notably Sweetman and Devereux) upheld Tone's attack and went further in their condemnation of Fitzgibbon. There should be 'no weakness, shuffling, or indecision', warned Devereux. The enemies of the Catholics should be openly identified as such. The passages in question were let stand and cannot have endeared Tone to his kinsman, let alone left him any future scope for legal preferment.

But Tone also discusses the Catholic issue in terms of the constitutional status of Ireland. He decries those critics who denounce Catholic reform as a danger to the connection with Britain. The Catholics are 'good and loyal subjects'. The real enemies of the connection are those who claim that Catholic liberty is incompatible with loyalty, and who reduce the question 'to the dreadful alternative of slavery or resistance'.

Tone lists the laws under which the Catholics still suffer, the worst of which is their exclusion from the elective franchise. Nor is this a theoretical grievance, as he shows by pointing to their expulsion from tenancies to create Protestant freeholders at election time.[26] Society cannot exist without the security of property and personal liberty denied to the Catholics. Tone's personal attachment to the idea of a united nation, free of religious division—the starting-point for his Catholic campaign—is again aired. Otherwise we cannot expect to find much original thinking in this or his other service documents for the Catholic Committee. Their power lies rather in their representation of the righting of wrongs as basic common sense, and Tone thought the Castle guilty of lack of vision in its refusal to do so. 'Early and moderate concessions to the just demands of the nation may prevent mischief, but that is a degree of wisdom which Fitzgibbon never will be able to reach.'[27]

Dublin Castle viewed the Catholic Convention, and in particular its decision to go over the government's head directly to London, as a direct challenge to its authority, and proposed the introduction of new legislation to prevent such meetings in future. This is what comes of your delaying my knighthood, Westmorland wrote petulantly to Pitt. Pitt confirmed the knighthood by return, adding that he hoped Westmorland would not be forced to put his chivalry to the proof. The ridiculousness of the exchange aside, Pitt by this stage had accepted Westmorland's claims that Catholic emancipation could not be granted under the present system without destroying the Protestant interest and endangering the connection, and he hoped that both parties would come to see a union of the two Parliaments as the only answer. For the moment, with war on the horizon, and conceiving the northern 'levellers' as the real threat, Whitehall felt that some concession had to be made to the Catholics, and appealed to Dublin to send over advisers so that the two governments could present a united front. But the feeling remained strong in Dublin that England was responsible for raising such expectations among the Catholics, and no one was sent to London until long after the Catholic delegates had returned from there.[28]

The Convention was a triumph for the sub-committee's work through the summer. Tone adopted it as his model for representative government, and as such it would appear in his 1796 recommendations for a future Irish republic. But in his euphoria he misjudged the hard-won unity of December 1792 for an advance in political radicalism. Rather the unity came from 'a sense of sectional outrage',[29] and those like Teeling, Sweetman and Devereux, who dominated proceedings, gave an unreal gloss of radicalism which was not representative of the body as a whole. Teeling may have secured a vote of thanks to the citizens of Belfast, but there was no official acknowledgement of the Belfast United Irishmen's declaration of support and in the flurry of Castle-running during the Convention, one member of the sub-committee, Dr Ryan, assured Under-Secretary Cooke that they had no intention of joining with the Dissenters. The desire to win the Catholics from such an alliance became increasingly imperative that winter, and explains the Castle's sudden conversion to limited conciliation as the new parliamentary session approached.[30]

15
Hopes Dashed

The Catholic delegates, with Tone as secretary, left for London four days after the Convention broke up. Contrary winds prevented them sailing from Dublin to Liverpool; so they crossed instead to Scotland travelling—some thought unwisely—via Belfast. Arriving at 9 a.m. on 12 December, they breakfasted at the Donegall Arms with a number of prominent citizens and reformers. A great crowd outside chanted: 'Success attend you! Union! Equal Laws, and Down with the Ascendancy', and insisted on drawing their carriage across the Long Bridge on the road to Donaghadee. Though Tone scarcely figures in other reports of the mission, he was singled out for particular attention by the Belfast press, signifying his special prominence in the town.[1]

As a token of their new dignity and firmness, the Catholic delegates had been instructed to adopt a determined tone with the London government and 'to take an hotel, and make a superb appearance'. They accordingly took up residence in Grevier's Hotel, Jermyn Street, on their arrival in London and conducted their business 'in great state, making a splendid appearance'. Keogh in particular looked 'very grand and very vain' in his silk stockings and curled and powdered wig. They were entertained lavishly by Lord Rawdon and assisted by a number of Irish reforming MPs then in London.[2]

Through Knox they sought an audience with Abercorn, but were anxious not to give offence to ministers by openly visiting 'other persons of consequence'. Knox therefore proposed a meeting at his own lodgings. But Abercorn objected to 'anything which (however unjustly) might carry with it the appearance of clandestine proceeding on my part', and insisted 'that it must be perfectly understood that it is their desire to see me, not mine to see them'. The delegates accordingly called at his London residence on the 21st. What passed threatened to reduce the Catholics to the position of servile supplicants which they had spent the entire year surmounting. Abercorn represented them as having eagerly sought him out both in Ireland and England, attributed to them certain principles which they rejected, criticised them for not applying to the government in Ireland, and sent them away without any promise of support. Tone went immediately to Knox to complain of their treatment. Knox was annoyed, blamed Abercorn and resented the implied criticism of his own handling of the negotiations. The incident did little harm to Knox's relations with Abercorn, and did not alter Abercorn's support for Catholic emancipation. But the dignity which the delegates were so anxious to maintain had been hurt and the contact was not renewed.[3]

Nor were they received at Whitehall in the manner which their new strength had led them to expect. Dundas hoped to defer formal discussions until Dublin responded to his appeal for advisers. But the delegates grew restive and he agreed to set 2 January 1793 as the date for an official audience with the King. He went as far as he could, without committing either government, to assure the delegates that measures would be taken for their further relief. In return he asked for assurances that they would divest themselves of 'dangerous associations'. It was not the answer the delegates might have wished. But Tone admitted that in the circumstances it was probably all they could expect, and both Dundas's general demeanour and their 'most gracious reception' by the King convinced him that full emancipation would be forthcoming. Certainly the word went out publicly that the British government would urge relief upon the Castle.[4]

I

The delegates had guessed correctly the real state of Dundas's feelings. In contrast to 1792, the King's speech to the Irish Parliament was altered in London that year to include mention of a Catholic relief bill. To Dublin it looked like the Castle was being sent another dictate from London and, Westmorland complained, had all the appearance of ministers having given way to intimidation. The complaint elicited a stern response from Dundas, some 31 pages in length. It would have been improper for the monarch not to receive a petition from a body of his loyal subjects. Dublin was perfectly aware of the British government's desire to grant further concessions, yet had declined London's appeal for advisers on the specious excuse of not wanting to alienate Protestants by supporting, or Catholics by opposing, the Convention's petition. London's unilateral action, Dundas remarked caustically 'would relieve them of their difficulty'. While perfectly willing to assert their support for the Protestant form of government, ministers in London differed from Dublin on the best means of upholding it. And to Westmorland's fears that Dublin would be called upon year after year to make concessions, Dundas replied by pointing to his dispatches of 1791, in which he had expressed his belief that the franchise would quieten Catholic agitation. He feared now it would not be enough.[5]

The King's speech opening the new Irish parliamentary session on

10 January 1793 committed the government to further Catholic relief and cast its supporters into considerable disarray. The speech made the proposed bill a public or government measure which they were expected to support, and most were given little more than twenty-four hours' notice of the changed status of a measure they had come prepared to oppose. Even leading members of government like Fitzgibbon had not been consulted, and the handling of the affair sparked off a parliamentary crisis. The English minister it seemed was forcing his will upon the Irish Parliament and making nonsense of the 1782 settlement. What is more, although Pitt had been in favour of granting the Catholic franchise before the Catholic Convention met, the timing suggested that he was giving way to extra-parliamentary pressure. This robbed the Irish Parliament of the authority on which the Protestant Ascendancy relied and forced members to vent their insecurities in bigoted outpourings. The Catholics were accused of deceiving the King, of being in thrall to 'the bishop of Rome, a foreign prince' and in a perpetual state of rebellion against the Protestant state, and the granting of political rights to the Catholics was declared incompatible with 'a free Protestant Government'.[6] Fitzgibbon was among the most vociferous in his attack. Tone wanted to confront him publicly, but was outvoted on the sub-committee.[7]

Given this novel inability of the government to manage its own supporters, the introduction of the bill was delayed until Monday, 8 February, while the Castle sought to stem the parliamentary revolt. Hobart had a series of interviews with the Catholic negotiators, led by Keogh, and wrung from them an admission that they might accept concessions short of total emancipation. In the circumstances it is hard to blame Keogh for his 'bird in the hand' approach, particularly since he did appear to speak for the changed spirit in the Catholic body.[8] By now London too had set its face against granting the Catholics the right to sit in Parliament.[9]

Such horse-trading allowed Hobart to introduce a bill which would give the Catholics the franchise on the same basis as Protestants, qualify them to sit on grand and petty juries, become magistrates, hold military commissions and most civil offices, endow colleges and schools, take degrees at Dublin University, and carry arms—subject to a property qualification. These were indeed substantial concessions and would have been inconceivable a year before. Although they fell short of total Catholic demands—and many in Parliament, supporters and opponents alike, saw the absurdity of granting the vote without representation—Keogh was probably right in recognising that it was as much as they could hope for that session, given the atmosphere of an impending crisis in which the bill was introduced. A proposal for full emancipation, introduced in an able speech by George Knox, commanded some parliamentary support, and even those most keenly disappointed by the partial relief of 1793 confidently expected the rest to follow.[10] The tone of the ensuing debate, however, suggested otherwise.

Hobart tried to explain away the *volte-face* of the Castle, arguing that the old spirit of popery was dead. Foster, Fitzgibbon and many others were unconvinced. Old fears about the deposing power of the Pope and Catholics' refusal to keep faith with heretics were revived, with the implication that the Catholics were inherently hostile to the constitution and incapable of loyalty. Foster gutted the Catholic petition, taking up every loosely made point to suggest their disloyalty, and producing his trump argument against emancipation: that the King's coronation oath debarred the full admission of Catholics to the constitution.[11]

The accusations prompted a lengthy pastoral letter from Troy, which quickly went into a second edition. In his *Duties of Christian Citizens*, the Archbishop explained in detail the teachings of the Catholic Church on the relationship between Catholic subjects and their English Protestant King. He dismissed accusations of Catholic disloyalty by showing the very nature of the faith as royalist, and declared that the deposing power of the Pope and the breaking of faith with heretics were never an article of Catholic faith. The Catholic Committee was furious at the publication of the pastoral letter at such a sensitive time. Fitzgibbon used it to prove that the religious tenets of the Catholics debarred them from the the constitution and Hobart thought it essential that such tenets be openly disavowed. The upshot was the insertion into the 1793 bill of an additional clause requiring Catholic voters to deny papal infallibility and the power of the confessional to absolve all sins, to vow recognition of the country's landed establishment and do nothing to weaken its Protestant religion and government.[12]

The requirement of this new oath was a token of the continuing distrust of Catholics. Nor was that distrust confined to traditional supporters of the government. Indeed the Whigs' introduction of a motion for parliamentary reform in the middle of the debate—when they had yet to work out details and did not do so for another five months—was considered by many a ploy to deflect attention from the Catholic issue. The issue had brought turmoil into the traditional alliances on which Irish government was based and in a remarkable act of retaliation on England for forcing the Catholic franchise on them, government supporters passed almost all the Opposition measures designed to reduce English influence which they had spent the last decade rejecting.[13]

Ironically the radicals in the Catholic Committee and the United Irishmen found themselves at one with some of the Ascendancy in proclaiming the need to link Catholic enfranchisement with a measure of parliamentary reform—the one to increase the popular vote, the other to fortify the Protestant vote as a counter-weight to the influx of new Catholic voters. Neither group was to be satisfied and the radicals viewed with dismay the fortification of landlord and indeed government influence by the accession of some 30,000 newly-enfranchised 40 s. freeholders.[14]

II

The excitement and anticipation of the period after the Catholic Convention had kept many country delegates in Dublin, and sub-committee meetings drew large attendances. But in the aftermath of the partial relief of the 1793 act, when they had come to expect total emancipation, the Catholic Committee tore itself apart in mutual recrimination. There is no indication that London had ever contemplated including the right to sit in Parliament among the concessions. But given the clear conviction among so many, including Tone and several of the delegates to London, that this was fundamental to their demands, one cannot escape the conclusion of divided counsel. 'The demand of [the] Catholics was *total*', claimed Edward Sweetman in a stormy *post mortem*, 'Why is their relief *partial*?' There were suspicions that the delegates had not done their duty and a fuller report was demanded of them. They had held out in London for full emancipation, Devereux asserted, and he demanded an account from Keogh of what had passed in a private interview he had with Dundas's Under-Secretary, Evan Nepean. This Keogh wriggled out of by reporting simply on their joint meetings with Dundas. But there are major discrepancies between Keogh's and the official Whitehall account of what was agreed with the delegates.[15] Keogh was generally suspected of having bargained with the ministers in England and his reputation plummeted in consequence.[16]

The 'sneaking spirit of compromise', as Tone called it, continued to whittle away the Catholic determination of December. 'And so Gog's [Keogh's] puffing is come to this! I always thought when the crisis arrived, that he would be shy.'[17] The tensions posed by his own efforts to avoid disunity prior to Christmas erupted in an open breach with Keogh. 'Tone and Keogh have quarrelled', wrote Knox to Abercorn. 'Keogh says he thwarted him, and wanted to push the Catholics into a union with Belfast. Tone says Keogh tyrannised over him, and wanted to make him dependent.'[18] Tone organised a 'council of war' among the malcontents. Keogh accused him of holding conversations 'in corners', which was true. Tone countered that he had never said anything on Catholic affairs which he could not repeat to anyone in the room, which was also true. But the conflict was peevish and Knox was irritated at its pettiness.[19] Sweetman calmed tempers by eulogising Tone's contribution to the campaign— but the precarious united front was no more, and Tone's bitter frustration at having come within sight of total success, only to lose it, is unmistakable.[20] In the event, the troubled parliamentary session intensified Tone's contempt for the Irish Parliament. It is an interesting comment on his future republicanism that throughout this episode, England, and most notably George III, were seen by him as the better friends to Ireland.

The last days of the Committee's existence confirmed critics' fears that the Catholics would abandon reform once they had achieved their own ends. Those of the Committee who were also United Irishmen warned against deserting their Protestant friends and reminded their co-religionists of the services rendered their cause by Belfast. Ryan pronounced himself 'No friend to a mere Catholic interest, nor desirous to see Catholic Ascendancy succeed Protestant Ascendancy. Let us lay down the character of a sect, and take up the character of a people.' But the partial if substantial relief measure of 1793 effectively distanced most propertied Catholics from the radicals. The act opened up the county constituencies, but left the boroughs—the real bone of contention with reformers— unchanged.[21] The Committee voted itself out of existence in the last week of April 1793, disgusting the handful of radical members by also thanking their old enemy, Hobart. Remaining funds were disposed of, and if £1,500 was voted in thanks to Tone for his services, the £2,000 voted for a statue of the King spoke volumes for the satisfied moderation in which the most effective Catholic organ of the century dissolved itself.[22]

The 1793 Relief Act placed the Irish Catholics on a more favourable footing than their English counterparts. It was a measure of how attrition and popular mobilisation could in time erode the opposition of those in power. But the act had been robbed of its conciliatory effect by the manner in which it had been passed. Many of those obliged to vote for it had made no secret of their revulsion. Nor were any of the government supporters who had so manifestly gone against government policy rebuked or removed. Indeed the appointment of Fitzgibbon to head a committee of enquiry into the cause of recent Defender troubles, at the most sensitive point in the debates, was provocative. The report he produced implicated the Catholic Committee directly in the disturbances and left Tone— directed to draw up the Committee's defence—still speechless with anger when he came to record these events two years later.

Nor was Tone alone in his bitter disappointment at the failure to achieve total emancipation. He thought the radical defect of the 1793 bill was the exclusion of the Catholic leaders from the constitution. 'If the Catholics deserved what has been granted, they deserved what has been withheld. They receive a benefit with one hand, and a blow with the other, and their rising gratitude is checked by their just resentment.'[23] Since people like Teeling, Lewins, MacNeven, McCormick and other members of the Catholic Committee would soon become some of the most active leaders of the republicanised United Irishmen, one cannot deny that their continued exclusion from Parliament helped cement the republican alliance.

The parliamentary crisis of 1793 was indeed a watershed in Irish history, but in terms of its contribution to early Irish republicanism this was not immediately apparent. More important was its effect on the Protestant politicians. Catholic Committee disclaimers of any desire to overturn the landed establishment and take revenge on the Protestants were accurate enough. But they spoke for the Catholic gentry and middle class, not for a largely Catholic populace, elements of which were beginning to call for just such a programme. The Protestant fears were genuine and not entirely groundless. England, with her own Protestantism dominant, dismissed them as pure bigotry and her unsympathetic handling of the situation intensified Protestant insecurity. Yet having encouraged the Catholics to look to London, thereby contributing to their growing loss of confidence in the Irish political system, Pitt's government by 1793 had adopted the same anti-emancipation, anti-reform stance, and left in place those same politicians with a mandate to suppress the very campaign it had once encouraged.[24] The confusion caused within the Ascendancy by what was given, and among moderates and radicals by what was withheld, caused a major reshuffling on the Irish political scene and with it that polarisation from which the crisis of the 1790s developed.

V

WAR CRISIS
(1793)

16
Witch Hunt

In the event Tone and his fellow protesters on the Catholic Committee were right. Keogh himself came to recognise as much, when even the concessions of the 1793 Relief Act continued to be blocked by the Ascendancy. The year following the passage of the act was to be the decisive turning-point in Ireland's drift towards revolution. The heightened expectations in which 1793 opened were dashed within a matter of months, leaving United Irishmen and Catholic leaders alike in disarray. Tone's journals for these months do not survive, but he appears to have been left as directionless by the turn of events as his friends.

I

The war which broke out between Britain and France in February 1793 had been threatening for many months. The Catholic Convention of December 1792 met to the sound of recruiting drums beating through the city; trade was interrupted and there was mounting economic distress. The impending war was likewise the occasion for the government to implement plans for a militia, designed to curb the Volunteers once and for all.[1] But the Volunteering ideal was sacrosanct in Ireland, and initially the government was inhibited by fears of offending the old Volunteers. The United Irishmen obligingly supplied the excuse.[2]

The United Irish-inspired Volunteer revival peaked in December 1792 with plans for a national battalion. Its motto was 'liberty and equality', its emblem a harp without the crown, its uniform modelled on the French National Guard, and so it was nicknamed and attacked by its detractors. The Dublin Society of United Irishmen was conducting 1780s politics in changed times. It was a gesture typical of the bluster of its Tandy phase, and many members thought the move unwise.[3] Uniforms were displayed in the Dublin shops and cannon ordered from Henry Jackson's foundry. On 10 December the government issued a proclamation threatening to disperse the new force if it assembled.

Even then the United Irish Society took little account of the new mood. On the 16th it issued an address to the Volunteers calling on them to take up arms once again in defence of Ireland. It attacked government as 'that faction which misrepresents the King to the People, and the People to the King', proclaimed the attainment of public happiness the end of all government, called for full Catholic emancipation and radical parliamentary reform, and recommended another Dungannon convention like the famous Volunteer ones of 1782–3.[4] Rowan and Tandy then set out to call the government's bluff by distributing the address to some 150 Volunteers meeting in Pardon's fencing school in Cope Street. Several government agents, attracted by the crowds, attended the meeting.[5] The government was advised that the paper was not treasonable, but by the time the culprits were taken up and tried, a year later, changed times had defined sedition more narrowly. Plans were made meanwhile to march older Volunteer corps out of Dublin for a review to test government resolve. As they assembled in Ship Street they were ordered by the Police Commissioner to disperse.[6]

The incident worried Tone, and with good reason. The reputation of the Volunteers had allowed bodies like the United Irishmen to grow up under their wing and still provided the bridge across which radicals, moderates and conservatives could meet. But although the Castle did not yet consider the United Irishmen a particular threat, it found in them 'a very popular justification for our exertions', notably the suppression of the Volunteers.[7] The 'National Guard' experiment alienated many old Volunteers and with their collusion the government was able to suppress Volunteering completely over the next few months, even in its stronghold of Ulster.

Although Tone was involved in the committee setting up the new Volunteers and had suggested the motto and emblem which caused so much trouble, he and the Catholic members of the Dublin Society thought it unwise to have followed the French model, or to have met publicly at such a time.[8] Tone attended the United Irish Society intermittently throughout his period as Catholic agent and regularly for several months after his return from London. But his role was that of Catholic spokesman or 'popish agent', as Collins preferred to call him. While the Catholic relief bill was going through Parliament, he tended, with his friends Russell, Sweetman and McCormick, to be a moderating force in the Society, and thought its call for the Catholics to pronounce in favour of reform 'mischievous'.[9]

At a time when the heightened expectation of major reforms was drawing the largest attendance ever at the United Irish Society—200 at the meeting of 21 December 1792, and Collins reported soaring membership[10]—the 'backwardness' of its Catholic members led to major divisions. Tone was playing a fence-sitting role whose difficulty revealed itself in his irritability with Drennan and his infrequent correspondence with Neilson. Accused by Drennan of being in the Catholics' pocket, by Keogh of wanting to push the Catholics into a union with Belfast, his frustration erupted in the quarrels with Keogh at the Catholic Committee, and for the first time in over a year he returned to play a prominent role in the United Irishmen's reform campaign. The reason for his quarrel with Keogh was that instinctive dislike of being talked down to.[11] He had been 'muzzled' too long. His pay as Catholic agent was raised by subscription. He almost certainly had to ask for it, which would have aggravated his sensitivity in such matters, and loans from Keogh were quickly called in. Indeed in 1795 Tone was still owed much of the money voted him two years earlier—a ploy by the Catholics, thought Drennan, to keep their agent in tow.[12]

But as the Catholics held their breath in fear of disrupting the passage of the Catholic bill, the threat to the government from the advanced reformers was effectively removed and much of the machinery which had facilitated the progress of the Catholic cause was dismantled. The same parliamentary session saw a stringent Gunpowder (arms) Act,[13] A Militia Act, a proclamation effectively suppressing the Volunteers, a military purge of Belfast, and a Convention Act, which made it impossible for a body like the Catholic Convention to meet again. Russell claimed that he and Tone had foreseen this and tried to warn the Catholics, but were not listened to.[14]

Certainly the mood at the opening of the parliamentary session in January 1793 was very different from that at its close in August. Just before Christmas 1792 warrants went out against Rowan, Tandy, the printers of the Volunteers' address, and the proprietors of the *Northern Star*, and measures were taken to check the more outspoken of the provincial press. The arrival of troops in Belfast fuelled rumours of a government purge.[15] The Castle's dislike of Belfast had communicated itself to the troops and from the outset they acted towards the inhabitants with a provocation born of the conviction that it would be applauded by their superiors. Suspected United men were beaten up and the prank by some youths of getting a fiddler to play the *Ça ira* was the signal for the dragoons to spill out of the taverns on Saturday, 15 March, and attack the houses of known radicals.

Many townsmen were injured as the soldiers ran amok, and a town meeting held the troops entirely responsible. But none were prosecuted, and General White wrote proudly to Dublin about 'the charming boys' of the 17th Light Dragoons who had succeeded in quietening the town and humbling the great men of sedition. Westmorland had been urged by his advisers to suppress illegal associations in Belfast, but had thought it would be 'a very ticklish business'.

He was delighted with the opportunity the military riot afforded of doing so. White spoke melodramatically of his role in Belfast as akin to that of General Gage in Boston before the American war. But he had encountered little opposition and the government was pleasantly surprised at the ease with which the northern Volunteers were disarmed.[16]

It was a token of the exaggerated vision of the town's republicanism that it could be subdued so easily. In fact the tide had already turned against the United Irishmen there, and Belfast was quiet that summer as the rest of the country was torn by anti-militia disturbances. Many blamed the United Irishmen for bringing such ill repute on the town and for the military vengeance which continued through the summer. The soldiers seemed to have been given *carte blanche* and their presence expelled all the former fun from the coteries and coffee-houses. The *Northern Star* very nearly sold out to the government.[17] Belfast's image of itself as having led the Catholics and the country in the campaign for their rights contributed to its sense of abandonment and the belated Catholic declaration for reform came too late for a reconciliation to be easily attained.[18]

II

On 11 January 1793 the Dublin Society of United Irishmen appointed a committee of 21 to draw up a plan of reform. Tone, Russell, Butler, Drennan, Tandy, Chambers, Rowan, Bond and McCormick were among its members. The committee worked quickly and had a number of plans ready for private circulation by mid-January. The discussion documents reveal a far less dangerous organisation than either its public pronouncements or government fears suggest. The final document, to be released almost reluctantly a year later, did contain many of the demands already central to the British radical programme, notably universal manhood suffrage, annual parliaments and payment of MPs. But it had been pushed through with difficulty, the abandonment of property qualifications having passed by a majority of only 2. All were agreed on the necessity of curtailing opportunities for government corruption, and government pensioners would be disfranchised. But borough patrons were to be compensated for their losses, the secret ballot was rejected, and there was considerable scepticism about the ability of the people to make sound judgements in their choice of candidates. There was no desire to undermine the existing monarchical constitution, and nervousness about charges of republicanism deterred publication when the plan was finally completed in April 1793.[19]

Yet even their very social conservatism was part of eighteenth-century classical republicanism. Rousseau had rejected the secret ballot as destructive of republican virtue in classical Rome. Those who raised the strongest objections in the United Irish Society were products of a classical education, and there is little need to look beyond this as a source for many of their ideas. But a mistrust of the masses, and the moral corruption involved in secret voting, is a particular feature of Godwin's *Enquiry Concerning Political Justice* (1793), which was very popular in some United Irish circles.[20]

The United Irishmen's attempt to put together proposals on parliamentary reform, their main platform, was overdue, and largely a reaction to events which rapidly overtook it. The parliamentary opposition had already espoused reform and, despite mutual suspicions, the United Irish Society was prepared to support this Whig initiative.[21] On 14 January 1793 William Ponsonby announced his intention of introducing a bill for the 'more equal representation of the people in parliament.' But the sight of such an aristocratic grouping adopting reform was greeted with cynicism by fellow MPs, and as the session progressed it became clear that many were supporting it as a diversion from the Catholic business.[22] Certainly their reform plan was scarcely pushed with conviction. Specific proposals were introduced only at the very end of the session, they involved little more than a limited extension of the franchise and county representation, and were promoted with such obvious lack of commitment that Hobart was confident about deferring discussion till the following year. By then the deteriorating internal and international situation ensured the overwhelming rejection of what even moderate reformers felt was a derisory bill.[23]

In drawing up their own reform proposals, a number of United Irishmen preferred to await the outcome of another Ulster reform convention planned for February 1793. The convention which met at Dungannon, however, was something of an anachronism, a symbolic throwback to the time when Ulster had led the nation, a role which Tone and others still accorded it. Tone followed the proceedings closely, attempting at the last minute to brief Sinclair, who was the delegate for Antrim. In the event he and many others were disappointed. Three counties sent no representatives. Representatives did include a number of leading United Irishmen—Dr James Reynolds, a physician from Tyrone, and the Revd William Steele Dickson, besides Sinclair. But its complexion was overwhelmingly conservative, even aristocratic.[24] A short sitting produced a series of generalised resolutions, calling for complete Catholic emancipation and a radical reform of Parliament. The Volunteers were applauded and the project of a militia attacked.[25]

But other resolutions were far more conciliatory of their critics than the United Irishmen would have wanted. The opening resolutions were fulsome in their declaration of attachment to the existing constitution and rejected 'with abhorrence' republican forms of government. These Tone and Drennan criticised as sanctioning the charges of republicanism frequently made against the reformers. There was no condemnation of the war, and although Reynolds and Sinclair argued at length for such a declaration, the mood of the meeting was against the French. The Dungannon convention reflected the moderate reaction against the United Irishmen, even in the north. It nevertheless fuelled the government campaign to outlaw such extra-parliamentary bodies altogether.[26]

III

The failure of the convention to censure the war came as a particular shock to the United Irishmen. Dublin's dependence on the textile trades made it especially vulnerable to the immediate economic crisis. The collapse of several major cotton and silk businesses had put thousands out of work during an extremely severe winter and early spring. The quays were crowded with people begging, and by May the women were attacking the baker's shops.[27]

The United Irishmen had predicted that the authorities would use the war as an excuse 'to persecute principles',[28] and the entire year has the atmosphere of a witch hunt. A secret committee of the House of Lords sat from February to March examining witnesses. Butler and Bond challenged its authority in a paper circulated in Dublin and affixed by some wag to the very door of the Lords' chamber on the night of 1 March. The two were instantly imprisoned without trial for six months and fined £500. Reynolds was jailed as well when he too refused to recognise the Lords' authority to summon witnesses.[29]

Tone learnt that his letter to Russell of July 1791 had become an object of particular attention and in dismay wondered how it could have fallen into the hands of government. Burrowes and Pollock—to whom he had shown it at the time—denied any responsibility when questioned about it. Tone forgave Burrowes after the circumstances were explained, but Pollock—already in government employ—was marked out for literary vengeance. Russell blamed Digges, though could not believe him 'such a villain'.[30] Why Tone himself was not questioned, when a special messenger was sent to Ulster to fetch Russell, is baffling, particularly since the letter soon became the Chancellor's main proof that the United Irish Society was treasonable. It is another indication that few, besides Fitzgibbon thought Tone dangerous. He had, after all, little public visibility at the time. He rarely spoke at either the Catholic Committee or the United Irishmen and his publications were usually signed by others.

The Lords' report was rushed through and appeared on 7 March.

It pointed to the Defender disturbances which had raged in a number of counties throughout the autumn and winter, and by a juxtaposition of facts managed to link them to seditious clubs in Belfast and Dublin, and to the Catholic Committee and its convention. The Lords also accused the Catholics of levying money for improper purposes and cited a letter of Sweetman's to a friend in Dundalk, in reply to a legal query about Defender offences, to imply Catholic collusion. The report endorsed the belief that the Catholic relief bill was being passed with ill grace by officials who would avail themselves of every opportunity to thwart its application.[31] Tone was called upon by the Catholics' sub-committee to write its defence. He pointed to its role the previous year in calming the disturbances, revealed that Sweetman had declined the request for legal help, and explained in detail now the Committee's finances had been expended. Such angry rectitude was typical of Tone when his exaggerated sense of honour was offended.[32]

At the United Irish Society, Beauchamp Bagenal Harvey and Russell took over the places vacated by their imprisoned chairman and secretary. A sense of crisis hit the Society. Attendance plummeted and there was increasing unwillingness to subscribe to the mounting legal costs of fellow members. The profligacy of the prisoners in Newgate caused a rebellion against such constant requests for money, and an attempt to set up a United Irish relief fund for the city's starving manufacturers drew the protest that the Society should pay its own debts first. The expense of maintaining Butler and Bond in prison was getting out of hand. At the outset their lavish dinners had been a gesture of defiance towards the government. Men summoned from the farthest parts of the country by the House of Lords committee would call at Newgate first for instructions.[33] But Butler had carried the festivities to extremes and many were scandalised at the enormous bills for wine and fruit which the Society had to pay. Mrs McTier—then in Dublin—reported that Butler's mistress had taken away large baskets of fruit from Newgate, and mused on the corruption by association of Bond's Presbyterian morals.[34]

Catholic members made no secret of their fears that the charges of sedition increasingly levelled against the Society were harming their cause.[35] Tone was commissioned to write the Society's defence. In contrast to the normally provocative United Irish publications of the period, it is a muted document. Drennan, who thought it otherwise a good address, felt it lacked passion.[36] What it did do was to set out starkly and somewhat chillingly the new situation. It detailed the Society's achievements and the expectations of attaining their ends that year. 'At the opening of this session every man thought that the unanimous wish of the nation on two great questions must be gratified:—that the Catholics must be completely emancipated, and a radical reform in parliament effectuated; but this delusion was soon removed. It was suddenly discovered, that it was necessary to have a *strong Government* in Ireland'. War was declared, Ireland's rising prosperity ruined, 20,000 regular troops and 16,000 militia legislated for, a secret committee acted as judge and jury, a gunpowder bill was passed, the Volunteers insulted and the only body capable of opposition attacked.

With this Tone juxtaposed what had not been done: the complete emancipation of the Catholics (the relief bill then going through Parliament, he dismissed as *'partial and illusory'*), and a reform of Parliament. He called on the people to make their will known in a national convention. But there is also in this defence an air of resigned defeatism, already reflected in correspondence with Neilson. Did the people, Tone wondered, actually want reform: 'If a nation wills a bad government, it ought to have that government. We have no power, and we have no right to force men to be free'.[37] It is a conviction which crops up several times in Tone's writings. He was no doctrinaire. It was only the belief—pushed upon him, it must be said, by his friends—that the Irish populace wanted revolution, which two years later led him to assume the mantle of revolutionary agent. Throughout his life the actions which propelled him into confrontation politics were at the instigation of others. He rarely initiated events and was just as likely to walk away from them. So it was in the course of 1793 as signs of political failure mounted.

IV

There is an air of genuinely shocked innocence about United Irish reaction to the official clamp-down. But from the authorities' viewpoint things looked quite different, and the reaction took place against a background of disturbances such as the country had not seen in a century. That winter a war was waged by the Defenders, once confined to pockets of south-east Ulster, now spreading rapidly along the eastern seaboard and into the Irish midlands. Although traditional grievances such as tithes, high rents, hearth tax, county taxes and church dues figured in their demands, these Defenders were quite different from previous popular movements. They were militantly Catholic, and their sectarian identity was fuelled by the Protestant bias of the landlords and magistrates at the assizes of 1792, and most of all by their fanatical campaign against the Catholic Relief Act. Pitt was particularly alarmed at landlords arming their Protestant tenants against the Catholics, since London's policy on the eve of war was to attach the Catholics to the constitution rather than alienate them from it.[38]

There was an element of self-defence in Defender efforts to arm themselves. But the co-ordinated arms raids on Protestant houses, the nocturnal drilling under elected captains, the extensive swearing in, the sheer absence of subordination among formerly peaceable Catholics shook the confidence of the Protestant gentry, and rightly so. For the Defenders confidently expected the overthrow of the existing system, possibly with the assistance of France.[39] Although the down-swing in the textile industry was to send large numbers of those involved in domestic industry into the Defenders, their campaign cannot convincingly be explained in economic terms. Rather they are part of that tradition of popular rebellion in pre-industrial Europe sparked off by heightened, often millenarian, expectations of Utopian change. The government saw the Catholic Committee and the United Irishmen as behind Defenderism. But their role was indirect and there was little justification for the government's pursuit of individuals.

The propaganda of both movements had created unreal expectations of revolutionary change. The Catholic campaign of 1792 had been so orchestrated as to reach the level of every parish in the country. It was conducted in a glare of publicity, through a nation-wide network of delegates, and its printers' bills are a token of the outpouring of literature which so raised the consciousness of the Catholic populace.[40] It was no accident that the peak of Defender activity coincided with the sitting of the Catholic Convention in Dublin.

It was the Defenders' knowledge of and admiration for events in France, however, which gave their actions and utterances revolutionary overtones. Russell was to find widespread support for the French a year later in those very areas where Defenderism had been most active the previous winter.[41] The newspapers of the day carried lengthy reports from France and there was sufficient literacy in the villages for information to reach a wider audience than is apparent from sales figures.

But it was the outpourings of propaganda by the United Irishmen which, in terms accessible to the common men, illustrated the benefits to be expected from emancipation, reform and events in France. By attributing every wrong to biased privilege, the Society also contributed to that general sense of alienation from their rulers so apparent among the populace in these years. The United Irishmen whipped up discontent with squibs, handbills, popular ballads, broadsheets, printed on one side only for easy display, issuing from the *Northern Star* office, from Chambers's, Byrne's or McAllister's presses, sometimes from Rowan's private printing press at Rath-coffey, left in bundles on the table of the United Irish Society, circulated far afield particularly by the legal men on circuit, used as wrappers for commercial goods, distributed by pedlars and hawkers and pushed gratis through people's doors.[42] The question the United Irishmen would have to answer over the next two years was whether they were prepared to lead that public opinion which they had educated to the idea of resistance.

Typical of these broadsides was Tone's *A Liberty Weaver to the Manufacturers of Dublin*. Like his *Liberty Boy* the previous year, it adopts a conversational, down-to-earth style, shows a familiarity with the living conditions and daily problems of the Dublin poor, and breathes the same dislike for great men. Posing as 'a poor weaver in the Liberty', he recalls the miseries of the American war, when crowds were sent begging into the streets and he barely preserved his family from starving. 'The great people who go to war never think of these things'. What is it to us if the French choose to cut off their King's head? What right have we to meddle in their disputes? Whoever wins the battle it will be the poor who suffer and no great talk of 'balance of power' or 'glory to the British flag' will put clothes on our backs or food in our mouths. 'God forgive the great people, whoever they are, that advised our good King to this war,—there is not one of them will lose an hour's sleep or a meal's meat by it. . . . I wish before they were so brave in declaring this war, that they had taken a walk through the Liberty and other places that I could bring them to—but God help the poor; for they are able to help nobody and therefore nobody cares for them'.[43] Many of the ideas in this piece are typical of classical republicanism. Notable is the dislike of war as a device of the ruling classes to increase taxation and patronage. It was an argument likewise put forward by Paine.[44] It is, however, important to recognise that eighteenth-century republicanism was not incompatible with monarchy or necessarily attached to the principle of violent revolution, and Tone was not yet a rebel.

The United Irishmen were acutely media-conscious. They regarded the dissemination of populist literature as a primary function, and when curtailed by the clamp-down of 1793–4 many felt they should simply close up shop. Tone was considered one of the Society's most talented writers, in terms of his ability to write 'plain stuff. . .more popularly' than Drennan, the scribe of the '80s, and Drennan's recognition that his 'political quiver is spent' coincides with his deepening dislike of Tone.[45]

The anti-militia riots of the summer of 1793 were to reveal how far advanced was this educative process. The authorities had decided to make 'an awful example' at the spring assizes. Large numbers of Defenders were executed—some immediately upon sentencing—and others transported. In the same climate of fear which was sending hundreds fleeing to the hills to avoid arrest, Tandy was warned by McCormick not to answer a charge at Dundalk of distributing Keogh's *Common sense*, since plans were afoot to turn the charge into one of Defenderism. This had enough truth in it to convince Tandy to flee the country. One of the greatest thorns to the government for over a decade had finally gone, and the *Freeman's Journal* crowed over this particular victory for the rest of the year.[46]

The militia bill which passed through the Irish Parliament in March and April 1793 provided for a force of 16,000, to be raised by compulsory ballot. Lists of those eligible would be displayed outside parish churches and quotas set for each county. The militia was intended to remove the excuse for the Volunteers by providing a force for home defence. More immediately it would permit the release of regulars which England needed for the war with France. The inadequacy of existing forces to quell internal disorder had been made painfully clear the previous winter, recognition of which helped dictate the severity of the landed classes' response to the riots that summer.

Militia raised for home duties during the American war had been sent overseas and there were enough reminders like Tone's broadside around that summer to push home the precedent.[47] It was fears of being posted abroad and the compulsory nature of the levy which were the main causes of the riots. But the discontent which spread through every province that summer ran deeper. At Dingle in County Kerry the resisters were heard to say that 'liberty and equality should only govern in future,' that they would 'put to death all the gentlemen of landed property' and that they expected foreign aid.[48] In Sligo, Mayo and Roscommon rioters expected an equal distribution of property and made victims swear to be loyal to the Catholic cause.[49]

The recent Catholic Relief Act figured prominently in rioters' statements, and though full Catholic emancipation would have meant little to those resisting the militia, the sentiment that 'something still remained undone', of expectations unfulfilled, had conveyed itself to the Catholic populace generally.[50] One land agent in Sligo thought the real cause of the disturbances 'the late Popery Act, from the violent opposition given to it by the Protestants, and the great exertions made by the Papists, and the infinite benefits the people of that persuasion were taught to think would arise from that law to everyone.'[51]

More than anything, the riots revealed popular alienation from authority and a breakdown of the forces of social control. The Catholic gentry had proved an important force for control in the past. By refusing to grant them political power, claimed George

Knox, the government had divided them from the lower orders, breaking 'the chain of obedience and protection which formed civil society.'[52] When the Catholic gentry in Sligo were called upon to help quell the disturbances, they eagerly assumed the responsibility.[53] Yet commissions in the militia (to which the law now entitled them) were largely withheld. The Militia Act itself had been proposed by one of the Catholics' greatest enemies, Lord Hillsborough, and Keogh later complained 'that the names of the officers were nearly a list of the Grand Juries who voted for our perpetual slavery.' As a result local Catholics held back.[54] The government, Keogh argued, had been within easy reach of gaining the support of the Catholic leaders and with them their considerable powers of control over the lower orders. Instead they were unable to deliver on promises and their influence disintegrated.[55]

The breakdown in the existing social order was likewise reflected in the readiness of crowds to take on the fire power of the soldiers and of the Protestant gentry to use military force as first resort. Five times as many casualties were sustained during the militia riots as in disturbances over the past thirty years.[56] By July 1793 Dublin was appealing to England for urgent military supplies because of increased calls upon those in Ireland.[57]

By August the troubles had been suppressed sufficiently for Westmorland to release the required troops to England. But the polity which had sustained relative peace for much of the century was shattered irretrievably. The destruction of Protestant confidence was an important factor in the crisis, dictating the intensified and increasingly sectarian coercion. Defenderism had now spread to hitherto untouched and traditionally law-abiding counties in the west, and henceforth peace was maintained by force alone. For a while the Catholic leaders retained a hope that England would again force its will on the Irish Parliament. But England likewise saw full emancipation as unattainable unless accompanied by a union, and the gradual recognition of this sent many Catholics into the United Irishmen. The militia rioters already viewed people like the imprisoned Butler and Bond as popular heroes and increasingly over the next years the United Irishmen came to supply that social leadership abandoned by the gentry.

The United Irish Society in Disarray

The United Irish Society continued to disintegrate through the spring and summer of 1793.[1] It took almost two months of meetings to get through two addresses, one to the Catholics, one to the nation. Drennan had drawn up both. Part of the problem was Drennan's literary style, which had developed many idiosyncrasies. But it was the principle of addressing the Catholics separately which caused most complaint. Drennan's paper urged them not to abandon reform, and he was annoyed at Tone who seemed to be compromising on the issue. Tone could be sharp, even with those he liked, and his penchant for mockery would have wounded the morbidly sensitive Drennan. Drennan was bitter that the Catholics never employed him professionally and irritated at the influence Tone wielded over opinion in Belfast.[2] But the main reason for the disputes of these months was the fear of publishing anything, and the address which eventually emerged on 7 June was so trimmed and sanitised that even Collins found it anodyne.[3]

I

After the dissolution of the Catholic Committee, Tone seems to have gone into semi-retirement in Kildare, and when in town, he confined his socialising to a few friends. On 9 May Russell arrived in Dublin, summoned to appear before the Lords' committee. He was urged by friends to testify. Reynolds' refusal had simply landed him in prison and few wished to see further martyrs created. Tone came up to town on the morning of Russell's examination (10 May) to advise his friend, but in the event the Lords did not ask Russell about Tone's 1791 letter.[4]

That night they attended the United Irish Society. Since December it had been meeting in the Tailors' Hall, Back Lane. Built in 1706 on the site of a former Jesuit college, it was one of the largest public rooms in Dublin and was used for all manner of meetings, from the grand lodge of freemasons to the Catholic Convention of 1792. Situated in the run-down part of Dublin near Christ Church, its access was through the dimly lit, narrow and foulsmelling area of Skinner-row, High Street and Nicholas Street. 'The very aspect of the place seemed to render it adapted for cherishing a conspiracy', reflected a former Trinity College student who attended the United Irish Society early in 1793. The entrance was through a dusky hall, whose broad, low stairs were lighted by a tallow candle. By its rays one glimpsed the unfurnished room occupied by the old woman who looked after the place. The stairs led to an upper committee room, equally cheerless, giving on to a small gallery, from which the main meeting room could be observed. This was 'a spacious and lofty apartment', measuring some 21 feet by 45. It was decorated with portraits of Charles I and II, William of Orange and Swift. The United Irish Society met with all the ceremonial of a debating club. Its officers sat in the middle of the room, the president, who exercised total control over procedural matters, occupying an elevated ceremonial chair at the head of the table.

The former student went on to describe Tone as 'a slight, effeminate-looking man, with a hatchet face, a long aquiline nose, rather handsome and genteel looking, with lank, straight hair, combed down on his sickly red cheek.' His manner of speaking was 'polite and gentlemanly, but totally devoid of anything like energy or vigour. I set him down as a worthy, good-natured, flimsy man, in whom there was no harm, and as the least likely person in the world to do mischief to the state.' Tandy this observer proclaimed 'the ugliest man I have ever gazed on', with his 'dark, yellow, truculent-looking countenance...long-drooping nose...remarkable hanging-down look, and an occasional twitching or convulsive motion of his nose and mouth.' But Rowan's appearance filled him with admiration, as it did everyone who met him. 'I thought him not only the most handsome, but the largest man I had ever seen. Tone and Tandy looked like pigmies beside him...with such an external to make him feared, he had a courtesy of manner that excited love and confidence.'[5]

On that evening of 10 May, when Tone and Russell went to the Society, there were only 40 members present—a remarkable decline from attendances averaging over 100 during the excitement of the Catholic Convention—and the whole night was spent debating Drennan's address. The collapse of the United Irishmen when confronted had surprised the Castle, for the demagoguery of its latest officers seemed to confirm government fears that it was in league with France. Lord Edward Fitzgerald, the Duke of Leinster's younger brother and one of the leading forces in the Society after 1795, was not yet a member. But he was already closely associated with its leaders, and in France, from which he had recently returned, he had raised the possibility of a French-backed rising in Ireland and had left his friend Thomas Paine to conduct negotiations with the French ministers.

John and Henry Sheares, barristers, ex-Trinity men and members of a prosperous Cork banking family, had likewise just returned from France. Like Lord Edward, they had been members of the Jacobin Club and associated with a group of British and Irish resident in Paris and committed to the idea of international revolution. Henry Sheares was promoted to the presidency of the United Irish Society in May 1793, almost certainly thanks to the low attendance, and he introduced an inflammatory note ill attuned to the Society's newly cautious mood.[6] Tone was one of those who withdrew entirely from the Society for the rest of the year 'because of his opposition to violent speeches and writings which would give a handle to government to attack them', as Matilda later claimed. 'Lord Edward Fitzgerald and the Sheares who had just come from Paris were *playing revolution* and did mischief.'[7] Mrs McTier was astonished at how extreme the political talk was in Dublin, by comparison with Belfast,[8] and the appointment of Sheares allowed Fitzgibbon to attack the United Irishmen as agents of the French Jacobins.[9]

Yet if these firebrands planned rebellion, Hobart wrote in July, they were not playing their cards well in allowing themselves to be defeated by the government crack-down.[10] The United Irishmen had no plans beyond Catholic emancipation and parliamentary reform. Indeed they had given little thought to the kind of state which would emerge if such concessions were made. They had set out to raise public consciousness through an unprecedented outpouring of propaganda, with little thought of how that consciousness would be used or of how they would cope with failure—hence the directionless nature of the response of 1793. When the government acted, they collapsed through their own constitutionalism.

II

The few insights which we have into Tone's private thoughts at this time reveal an overriding belief that reform no longer had any support in the country and that the populace by its apathy had left its champions to suffer the consequences of their reform efforts. He and Russell talked seriously of emigrating to America.[11] They were not alone in their belief that the campaign had failed. Yet few seriously contemplated French-backed revolution, even if such a threat had surfaced in their writings. Indeed when the Fitzgerald–Paine plans produced a secret French mission to Dublin in May 1793, the offer of military aid was rejected by those introduced to the scheme, Butler, Bond, Rowan and Reynolds.[12]

Tone's name appears neither among the group of putative conspirators, nor in the correspondence of government agents during a summer which witnessed a sustained attack on the United Irish

Society. Only in Fitzgibbon's personal campaign was he singled out as dangerous, and the 1791 letter was produced at regular intervals as proof of this. Fitzgibbon had swallowed the pill of the 1793 Relief Act with obvious distaste and the secret committee report was part of his crusade to link the Catholics with sedition. On 14 May he sent a copy of Tone's letter to Pitt in support of his claim. Tone, the Catholics' 'cabinet minister and adviser, who first proposed an alliance between the Puritans and Catholics', he explained, 'is the son of a bankrupt tradesman, and has the merit of being the founder of the Society of United Irishmen. He was also the original projector of the Catholic Convention, drew up the Circular letter issued in the course of last summer . . . and composes most of he seditious and treasonable libels which are put forth by the Society of United Irishmen.' The 1791 letter and the payment to Tone of 'very large sums' were cited as proof that the Catholics' 'great object' was to separate Ireland from England. The fact that Tone was a member of the bar was an aggravation of guilt, and Fitzgibbon concluded with a side-swipe at George Knox whose connections should have guarded him against the friendship of such a man.[13]

In the House of Lords on Monday, 8 July, Fitzgibbon launched a virulent attack on the Dublin United Irish Society. Two days later he narrowed down the charge of 'so many self-created congresses . . . the seditious clubs and meetings, and a convention recently held in this city' to 'the advice of a worthy professional gentleman in this city, who had been rewarded by a handsome present from one of them, for his useful opinions'. He attributed the revival of such congresses to 'some gentlemen, who I am very sorry to say belong to my profession' and the Catholic one to 'the worthy gentleman alluded to', and in support he produced Tone's letter. 'It is a confidential dispatch from a gentleman who wears a bar-gown, one of the leading members of the worthy Society of United Irishmen.' He then read the entire letter, showing Tone to be the author of the original resolutions and attributing to the United Irish Society as a whole Tone's private views on separation. 'These are the sentiments of this father of the Society of United Irishmen', Fitzgibbon continued, 'who has been voted upwards of two thousand pounds by the Catholic Convention, who struck out for them that plan of election which he received from his friends and associates in France.' The Catholic elections, he claimed, were designed to establish contact with the lower orders and engage them in an insurrection which was to have taken place when France repulsed the allied armies the previous year.[14]

Some Catholic and United Irish leaders did become active revolutionaries after 1795. But in 1793 Fitzgibbon's speech and the secret committee report, for which he was largely responsible, involved

such a stringing together of facts, perhaps accurate enough individually, as to amount to a total falsehood. Two years later Tone wrote
that the Chancellor's substitution of 'we' and 'our' for the first
person in his 1791 letter was an attempt to convey the idea of a
conspiracy, and that until 1794–5 he was innocent of such charges.[15]
It is a claim borne out by his actions over the next year.

Everyone involved, Tone included, was shocked at the public
revelation of the 1791 letter. Tone claims to have considered it so
unimportant at the time that he did not retain a copy. The original
is now in the Burrowes papers in the Royal Irish Academy, though
Burrowes himself could not remember having seen it. Indeed he
protested in 1793 at Tone's 'unjustifiable' use of his name as one of
those who had approved it. But Burrowes was notoriously forgetful.
Tone denied associating Burrowes's name with the sentiments of the
private letter (which was true, for he claimed only to have sought his
friends' advice on the resolutions, not the attached statement). He told
Burrowes that he had read the declaration to him before sending it to
Belfast and 'that he thought he was warranted, by my reception of
it, to state that I approved of it', as Burrowes later explained. 'He
disavowed in the strongest manner having had any intention of
insinuating that I concurred with him in any of the sentiments
contained in his letter, which he said he had stated as his own
exclusively'—an explanation which Burrowes accepted, 'such is my
opinion of Tone's veracity.'[16]

Tone's rebuttal of the Chancellor's speech, identifying himself as
its object and showing that, despite the current clamp-down, he felt
safe in the knowledge of his own innocence, was written immediately
on reading the newspaper version of Fitzgibbon's speech. It does not
accurately convey the fury Tone felt at what he considered a peculiarly dishonourable usage of a private letter. It was to become something of an obsession with him, as his own betrayal of the legal élite
had become with Fitzgibbon, and set the two on a lifelong collision
course.

The response of 11 July is shot through with this sense of offended
honour. Tone claims that the letter voiced a private opinion which he
had had no intention of making public. He rejects the charge of
'rebelling against Great Britain' on the grounds that his allegiance
was to the 'King of Ireland' and that to attempt to reduce the influence of England upon Ireland's government was not treason. He
thought there were many irregularities in the connection between the
two countries, and cites in particular the royal residence in England,
trade restrictions and discrimination against Irish manufactures. But
he is sure no one in Ireland would look to separation except 'upon
great provocation' and 'in the last extremity.'

British influence, however, could also be exerted to the benefit of

Ireland, and Tone cites with approval the influence of the King and Pitt in forcing the recent Catholic Relief Act upon the reluctant Irish politicians, 'even the grave and steady sage, the deep lawyer, and profound politician...[who] made wry faces, and gulped hard; however, he did swallow the pill'. He thinks it foolish of Fitzgibbon publicly to parade such talk of separation: 'it would have been more wise, as well as more honorable, if the private correspondence of so obscure an individual as myself had been suffered to pass unobserved.' He is dismissive of the idea that he has a 'theory of politics'. But such public attention forced him to declare his beliefs.

> What is the evil of this country? British influence. What is the remedy? A reform in Parliament. How is that attainable? By a union of all the people....But of this creed, separation makes no part. If it were, *res integra*, God forbid but I should prefer independence; but Ireland being connected as she is, I for one do not wish to break that connection, provided it can be, as I'm sure it can, preserved consistently with the honor, the interests, and the happiness of Ireland. If I were, on the other hand, satisfied that it could not be so preserved, I would hold it a sacred duty to endeavour, by all possible means, to break it, even though for so doing, a great lawyer were to tell me *'that I was rebelling against Great Britain'*.

Tone's stand on offended honour was disingenuous. He was separatist in thinking, even if not actively so. But private beliefs which had caused little panic in 1791 were semi-treasonable when publicised in 1793, for Britain was now at war with revolutionary France and Fitzgibbon also accused Tone of being in league with his country's enemies. Such an accusation worried Tone, but in his confident reassertion of his 1791 'discovery' he was certain that his stance was not treasonable. Certainly in his proclaimed loyalty to the King of Ireland rather than England (a dual-monarchy concept which by 1793 he certainly recognised as a fiction), and his attack on excessive English influence in the government of Ireland he was on Whig ground. At the opening of the war the term 'independence', harking back to the 1782 constitution, did not hold the treasonable associations it was later to do. But it was Tone as campaigner for Catholic emancipation rather than Tone as republican who was being pursued. He was accused of encouraging the Catholics to set up their own Convention as a rival to the Irish Parliament. This was the real reason for Fitzgibbon's attack. It was after all as one of the 'alarming Catholic papers' that the famous 1791 letter first drew the attention of the authorities,[17] and Tone thought his uniting in himself the three objects of opprobrium—the Catholic Committee, Belfast and the

Society of United Irishmen—was the probable reason for govern-ment vengeance.[18]

III

The prominent role of Beresford, Foster and Fitzgibbon in whipping up anti-Catholic fervour, and latterly Fitzgibbon's personal witch hunt, convinced Tone that the root cancer in Ireland was the faction in power at the Castle. Fitzgibbon he began to consider the evil genius of Ireland's troubles and he let as many as he thought had influence know about it.[19] He had few complaints about the London government, which puts into perspective his comments about the connection in his July protest, and still sought constitutional remedies to Ireland's ills, notably through a change of administration.[20]

In August Tone sent Rawdon (now the 2nd Earl of Moira) a memorandum on the situation in Ireland, asking him to bring it to the attention of his political friends in London. In it he depicts Fitz-gibbon as responsible for the continuing discontent in Ireland. He argues that the Catholic relief bill had been robbed of its conciliatory effect by the virulence of the Chancellor's language in Parliament and the misstatements of the secret report. The Convention Act and the influence used to prevent Catholics benefiting from the recent con-cessions was 'an effort of posthumous malice' by those who had been forced to pass the act against their will. How different could things be were 'this imperious persecuting spirit abandoned.' Instead of Britain being required to keep a force of 30,000 in the country, dis-turbances would be tranquillised and the people join with the government in common cause.[21]

There was indeed a real possibility in 1793 of a radical alteration in Ireland's ministerial arrangements. For most of the year Pitt had been wooing the Portland Whigs into a wartime coalition. The departure of Hobart at the end of the year, and his replacement by a Whig, Sylvester Douglas, was a good omen.[22] Lord Loughborough had been the first to come over and was acting as go-between for Pitt with the other Whigs. It was to him that Moira read Tone's state-ment in September, but he was discouraged by the response. 'The statement was treated by him as very unimportant, and I could get nothing from him beyond an admission that the Irish chancellor had not been judicious in his behavior [sic].' In fact Loughborough and the rest of the Whigs were all too well aware of Fitzgibbon's 'pre-judices', particularly against the Catholics, and some weeks later Loughborough complained of him in terms reflecting the case put by Tone and Moira. If the Irish viceroyalty was on offer to the Whigs— and Pitt had made noises to that effect—major changes at the Castle would follow. The clamp-down in Ireland was not altogether approved of by London. The Irish cabinet had few friends there during 1792–3, and Fitzgibbon's intemperance was particularly disliked.[23]

Such correspondence suggests friendly relations between Tone and Moira, and a third child born to the Tones on 23 June 1793 was christened Francis Rawdon, after Moira, who stood as godfather. Moira also asked Tone to use his influence with his friends to secure recruits for his friend Major Doyle's regiment of militia. Doyle was a pro-emancipationist and popular with the Catholics. Recruiting for his regiment scarcely required the intercession of the former Catholic agent.[24] But it is ironic to find Tone involved with that patronage aspect of the new militia so criticised by its opponents, and his correspondence with Moira is a significant reminder that he still thought of solutions in terms of Whiggish palace revolutions.

Moira was flattered by the attention he received in Ireland and for a while seems positively to have encouraged rumours that he might become Lord Lieutenant. On 20 August the late Catholic Committee organised a dinner for him at Daly's in Anglesea Street, Dublin. No expense was spared, and members of the opposition Whigs and other figures of fashion were invited. But the toasts, which took note of every parliamentary member who had supported the Catholic cause, mentioned neither the United Irishmen nor the Dungannon convention. Such a snub reacted upon the already heightened northern sense of having been abandoned and produced a stinging attack by Neilson on the Catholics. The refusal to recognise their contribution 'when ransacking the very dregs of royalty, aristocracy, and pseudo-patriotism for toasts' was an insult to Ulster and to the United Irishmen. McCormick thought Neilson's accusations exaggerated, but in general well founded, and he planned to travel to Belfast to patch things up.[25]

Tone's part in the controversial dinner is difficult to trace. He and Keogh were responsible for drawing up the toasts. Prompted by Keogh's claim that if Tone had drafted any toasts for Belfast they would have been accepted, Drennan accused Tone of duplicity, complaining about Keogh one minute, working with him the next, and not being genuine about union between the United Irishmen and the Catholics. Tone's failure to refer to Belfast in the toasts is indeed unusual, if true, though Drennan of late had been ready to attack Tone on any pretext. Moira offered real hope, and pragmatism may have dictated the silence of 20 August. The United Irish Society was in bad odour that summer and Tone's own fading commitment was registered in his non-attendance. It is less easy to dismiss the accusation of back-room bitching about Keogh, of which Tone, McCormick and several others were guilty.

Tone still considered the Catholic business unfinished. Many

Catholic leaders were likewise becoming disillusioned at the partial nature of their emancipation after the 1793 Relief Act, and by the end of the year were returning to the United Irish Society. Very quickly the limits of what they had gained became clear. With a parliamentary election far off, the concession of the franchise brought little immediate satisfaction. Far more important would have been their admission to those municipal, legal and trade bodies to which their mercantile and financial standing entitled them. But obstacles were put in the way of Catholics taking degrees at Dublin University, while the admission of Catholic merchants to guilds and corporations was still opposed as endangering the Protestant establishment and introducing the despotic tendencies of popery. There was an instinctive revulsion at these pushy Catholics no longer 'respectfully soliciting but arrogantly demanding a participation' in such bodies, and the government press reflected Protestant distaste at their sudden appearance in circles from which they were formerly excluded.[26] Several dubious prosecutions of leading Catholic figures and the general tenor of the parliamentary language of government supporters augured ill.[27]

IV

The United Irish Society limped along through the autumn, the scanty attendance throwing the Sheares's excessive parade of French principles into greater relief.[28] But there was little else happening. Tone had ceased attendance entirely, until he and Russell were called in by Rowan to help in a rescue operation in December. Four societies were still meeting in Belfast, and Rowan had been given cause to think the spirit higher there than in Dublin. Rowan wrote to his two friends suggesting the formation of a club 'to bring up the south to reform by writing and distribution'. The names mentioned as possible members were McCormick, Reynolds, Emmet, John Sweetman, Rowan, Tone and Russell. McCormick refused to include Keogh and called him a traitor. Tone was rather more conciliatory. He and Russell acted as mediators with Keogh, who 'offers to do anything', seeing 'his popularity gone'. Another dinner was suggested. Tone was doubtful, Russell positively opposed. McCormick declared the suggested date of 2 January as the anniversary of the day when 'the cause of Ireland was lost in England by the delegates', and the attempted reconciliation collapsed.[29]

Tone and Russell were therefore in very low spirits at the end of the year. Perhaps the gloom was relieved by visits to the theatre where Mrs Siddons was playing Isabella and Mrs Randolph. But even here the low ebb of reforming fortunes was displayed when Rowan was booed from the gods.[30] 'In this kingdom the popular

party are behaving as badly as the others', wrote Russell. 'No con-
cert. No plan. Every day sinking. . . . Fright, pride and jealously have
laid us asleep.' Tone told him as they kept Christmas at Chateau
Boue that he had decided to return to the bar, hateful though he
found it. He criticised Russell for abandoning his position at Dungannon, overcame his reluctance to accept an offer of the librarianship
of the Belfast Society for Promoting Knowledge, and recommended
marriage. Tone had a healthier respect for the practicalities of life
than his friend, and seemed resigned to a more mundane existence as
he moved the entire family back to Dublin. He had received little of
the money owed him by the Catholics, for the country delegates
neglected their subscription once the Committee was dissolved, and
he was supporting his younger siblings as well as his own family.[31]

Russell mused despairingly on how he had ruined himself working for the good of the country. His resignation from his magistracy
had left him in a financial situation more parlous than ever, and Tone
was just one of many from whom he borrowed. But it was the
leaders he blamed for the present situation. More and more he was
becoming convinced that the people themselves would find their
own salvation and that within four to five years there would be a
revolution. His conviction that the people generally were in favour
of the French became his main topic of conversation at the dinners
attended by himself and Tone at the turn of the year.

However, Tone's disillusionment at the internal situation of the
country was deeper. He even considered the northerners as 'cowards
and braggadocios' and thought 'nothing [was] to be expected from
this country except from the sans culottes who are too ignorant for
any thinking man to wish to see in power'. Tone's radicalism did not
go beyond the middling sort and he never lost his dislike of popular
tumult. But Russell tested his convictions by conducting his own
survey of popular thinking. His influence upon Tone had always
been profound and over the next two years his communications
helped produce a dramatic change in his friend's thinking.[32]

In the first few months of 1794 the *coup de grâce* was applied to the
United Irish movement. On 21 December 1793 Rowan had finally
been arrested for distributing the address to the Volunteers the
previous year. At first Drennan assumed it would be 'a lawyer's
business'. In the weeks before the trial on 29 January, however,
his opinion changed. Three respectable Catholic merchants from
Drogheda—leading lights in the Catholic Convention—were arrested on charges of tendering unlawful oaths, and brought by
soldiers to Newgate prison in Dublin. The *Northern Star* proprietors
were likewise arrested and in Dublin awaiting trial, and it was rumoured there had been attempts to bribe witnesses into claiming that

Tandy, Rowan and the Catholic leaders alike were associated with the Defenders.

Rowan's trial on 29 January 1794 was considered by all sides as a showdown with government. Huge crowds gathered in the snow outside the court and Rowan's defence counsel were chaired home by torchlight that evening. Soldiers were drawn up in the very hall of the Four Courts and detachments of horse guards lined the surrounding streets and lanes. The court was packed with United Irishmen, and Tone was almost certainly among them. The Attorney-General made out a case for a connection between the United Irish Society and the French. Two soldiers had been bribed with offers of promotion to implicate Rowan.[33] The jury had clearly been interfered with and took only ten minutes to return a verdict of guilty. Rowan was smuggled out the back door to Newgate to avoid a riot. A week later he was sentenced to two years' imprisonment, £500 fine, a bail of £2,000 personally and two sureties each of £1,000 to keep the peace for seven years after his release.[34]

Rowan's standing as a major landowner, barrister and prominent radical campaigner since the 1780s had attracted considerable public attention to his trial and the shock at his sentence was correspondingly great. The Dublin United Irish Society was stricken by fear of spies and imminent prosecution. Collins reported that all important proceedings would in future be conducted in secret, and dissolution of the Society seemed imminent.[35] The Castle was delighted at the good effects of the trial, and with the Opposition proving so co-operative on security measures, it looked forward to a quiet parliamentary session.[36]

Thomas Addis Emmet, looking back on these events, remembered the sense that Ireland was somehow sitting on a volcano, but a total lack of direction among those who had led the reform campaign. 'The press had been overawed and subdued: numberless prosecutions had been commenced....The expectations of the reformers had been blasted, their plans had been defeated, and decisive means had been taken by government to prevent their being resumed. It became therefore necessary to wait for new events, from which might be formed new plans.' The events of which he spoke came from two sources: from France, and from those Irish 'sans culottes' whose virtues Russell had impressed upon Tone.[37]

VI

REVOLUTIONARY
(1794–1795)

18
Treason

On the day Russell set off for Ulster, Saturday, 18 January 1794, he and Tone walked the length of the Phoenix Park in Dublin. Tone spoke of his growing disillusionment with politics.[1] His long association with the Catholics opened up a new line of legal patronage, and a commission as junior defence counsel in the key case against three leading Drogheda Catholics augured well for his otherwise unenthusiastic return to his profession. Within three months, however, his fate had been decided by other events and he was launched into that career as revolutionary republican for which he is best known.

I

Though now living in Dublin, Tone continued to shun the United Irish Society, which, as its rump membership readily admitted, was only rescued 'from that state of insignificance into which it had lately fallen' by a parliamentary attack on its reform plan. The plan was distributed as a broadsheet which also carried an address to 'the poorer classes of the community'. But like the accompanying account of the Society's proceedings, it seemed something of a swansong. Rumours circulated of spies within the organisation, and its imminent suppression. Collins hinted to his employers that rich pickings could be had from the seizure of the Society's books, still left openly on its table each Friday.[2] The government crack-down finally occurred on Friday, 23 May, after the arrest of a French agent implicated the Society in treason.

On Thursday, 3 April, two men arrived from England and took rooms at Hyde's Coffee House in Dame Street. It was bitterly cold for the time of year. Snow still covered the surrounding mountains[3] and the men complained of the discomfort of Irish lodgings by comparison with those they had left behind in England. One of the travellers, the Revd William Jackson, though Irish, had spent most of his life in England and had few acquaintances in Ireland. Oxford educated, one-time curate of St. Mary-le-Strand in London and later chaplain to the Duchess of Kingston, he had developed a passion for radical politics at the time of the American war, and had lately lived in Paris as part of the same group of English-speaking Francophiles to which Lord Edward Fitzgerald, Paine, and the Sheares brothers had gravitated. In the new Anglophobic turn of French politics he was now the most unlikely of secret agents on a fact-finding mission to England and Ireland. He had already spent two months in England, mixing with his many radical acquaintances. But he had come away with the unsatisfactory finding that a French landing would be repulsed by the bulk of the English populace. At first he met with the same response in Ireland.

His companion, an English attorney, John Cockayne, effected an introduction to the United Irish Society through Leonard McNally, whom he had known as a barrister in London. Although there had been much talk of a French invasion attempt on Ireland, Butler brushed such suggestions aside. From the outset there was considerable suspicion of the involvement of Cockayne.[4] But Lewins—increasingly emerging as one of the extremists of the Society—thought Jackson should discuss the issue with Rowan.

Newgate prison, where Rowan was imprisoned, was situated in the Little Green near Tone's childhood home in Stafford Street. It was a forbidding building, a model of the eighteenth-century criminal code's deterrence by terror. It was a black building, with a central edifice of granite dominated by a hanging stake and hangman's gallery. Rowan was a privileged inmate. His confinement was as informal as that of Butler and Bond. He was treated with deference by the gaolers, had total freedom of movement within Newgate itself, and so unrestricted were the visiting arrangements that his wife and family dined there every evening.[5] Imprisonment had made Rowan something of a national hero. He held court in his prison apartments and addresses flowed in from all parts of the country. Tone was among the many regular visitors. But the other inmates were kept in quite desperate conditions and Rowan's visitors would have passed the tiny holes which were the only source of light in the cells, and from which alms bags were suspended by prisoners begging for coins to pay the expenses of their own imprisonment.

Tone shared Rowan's eagerness to hear fresh news from France, and was made privy to his talks with Jackson. On Saturday, 12 April, he had mingled with old college friends at a large meeting in the William Street Exhibition Rooms, convened in support of the Historical Society, which had been expelled from college premises.[6] The next morning, Sunday, he called on Jackson in Dame Street. They met again the following day at Newgate. The conversation turned on the state of the country. Rowan and Tone agreed that the people were near to open resistance. It was exactly what Jackson had come to hear and he wrote to his contacts in London that 'he had found warmer persons in Ireland than he had expected'.[7] If such facts were known in France, he told Tone and Rowan, the Irish would

receive certain assistance. Rowan showed Tone a statement of the
anticipated reaction of England to a French invasion, which Jackson
had secured from the English Opposition MP, Benjamin Vaughan.
It claimed that such an attempt would be resisted by almost every
sector of the population. Tone considered the statement 'admirably
drawn up', asserted that Ireland's situation was very different, and
thought that this could likewise be demonstrated on paper.

Rowan had quickly entered into the real reason for Jackson's Irish
visit, and was even providing a cover for the correspondence with
France through his family relationship with one of Jackson's continental associates.[8] But at this stage Tone may not have known the
real destination of the proposed statement. Underemployed, with
time on his hands, and, whatever his abhorrence of aristocracy generally, ever deferential to men of rank with reformist sympathies,[9]
Tone acceded to Rowan's request that he compose such a statement.

It was dashed off on the evening of the 14th, and was partially
reworked by Rowan. It combines all Tone's shibboleths—England,
the aristocracy and privilege—into his first real exercise in revolutionary propaganda. Little wonder that Jackson was pleased. Vaughan's English statement stressed the general attachment of the people
to the government and the isolation of the friends of liberty. In contrast, Tone portrays Ireland as a conquered country, its government
'a government of force', operated by a Protestant aristocracy in the
interests of England and lacking a base in the affections of the people.
'In Ireland, a conquered and oppressed and insulted country, the
name of England and her power is universally odious, save with
those who have an interest in maintaining it.' The Dissenters and
Catholics Tone depicts as universally hostile to England; they 'would
probably throw off the yoke, if they saw any force in the country
sufficiently strong to resort to for defence.'

But he was unwilling to support a French invasion at any cost.
The French must disclaim any idea of conquest at the outset, announce their intention of helping the people 'establish on a permanent basis the independence of their country', and promise
protection for the persons and property of those who offered no
resistance. He envisaged a co-ordinated landing at multiple points,
which would maximise support and minimise resistance. The document reiterates Tone's faith in the republicanism of the Ulster
Dissenters, whom he thought would lead the revolt.

Much of this simply echoes what Tone was saying as early as
1791, and he believed that the document did not constitute treason.
But he now considered England rather than the Dublin government
the source of Ireland's troubles, 'the hatred of the English name
resulting from the tyranny of nearly seven centuries'. Was this

simply the characteristic Tone device of telling an audience what it wanted to hear? Certainly his actions over the next year do not indicate that he was ready to promote revolt against English rule. The document does, however, reflect another significant change in opinion which helps explain Tone's commitment, a year later, to the idea of national revolution. Three years earlier he had been sceptical about the political understanding of the ordinary Catholic. By 1794 Russell's arguments to the contrary had made their mark. Tone's preparation for the Drogheda trials would have involved an analysis of Defenderism—illustrating as it did the people's ability to organise in their own cause without the interference of leaders of higher social status—and he was impressed. 'The Catholics... have, within these two years, received a great degree of information.... there seems to be a spirit rising amongst the people which never appeared before, but which is spreading most rapidly, as will appear by the Defenders and other insurgents.'[10]

All of this would become the staple of Tone's later statements in France. But it is not a polished document. It does not represent an ideal plan of action. Rather it suggests some attempt to rationalise what had been happening in Ireland over the past two years. Tone had been a voice of restraint in the United Irish Society before he ceased attending. He still shied away from the idea of revolution and very soon regretted this statement, particularly since Jackson and Rowan were so delighted with it that they now considered him the perfect candidate to put Ireland's case before the French.

On Tuesday, 15 April, Tone was called to Drogheda to prepare for the forthcoming trials and wrote to Jackson breaking a dinner engagement for the Wednesday. Rowan alerted Jackson that Tone would be calling at Newgate the following morning. It was then that Tone first learnt of the project of sending an Irish agent to France, and the full import of what he had become involved in. He retrieved his paper from Jackson, consented to Rowan taking a copy of it, but asked him to burn the original immediately afterwards. Rowan it seems returned the paper, but not before he took several copies and embroidered it into a much more positive invitation to the French to invade.[11] Tone did not reject the commission outright—indeed he almost certainly said 'yes' at some stage—but was so thrown by the suggestion that neither he nor Cockayne, who was present, could state positively what his answer had been. He protested his domestic responsibilities, the need to support a wife and children, the loss of professional opportunity and the forfeit of the still-unpaid fee from the Catholics in the event of his departure—anxieties which Jackson's vague references to the generosity of the French nation were insufficient to allay.

After Tone had left for Drogheda, Rowan looked around for someone else to perform such a mission and suggested Reynolds. But Jackson was much impressed with Tone and had set his heart on him or no one. He delayed his departure from Ireland to await Tone's answer.[12] Rowan wrote urgently to Tone to return to Dublin, which he did immediately on receipt of the letter, on Saturday morning, 19 April. Given his own dislike of travelling and the commencement of the Drogheda trials the following Monday, the action suggests that Tone had not entirely dismissed Jackson's proposal and might have responded differently had positive inducements been offered to remove his domestic worries. The prospect of a French invasion and possible separation from England was a common topic of conversation at this time. Tone's son claims that his father and Curran spoke during the Drogheda trials of the need to break the connection with England, and the belief that such men might be called upon for support may well have contributed to Tone's dilemma.[13] The resort to French arms was by no means a foregone conclusion at this stage.

Tone was considerably irritated at being rushed up to town when Rowan had nothing new to say. It was Easter Saturday and on that religious occasion the Drogheda trials were seen as an important showpiece in the contest between the Catholic Committee and the government. Tone placated Rowan with a promise to call on Jackson on Sunday morning, but instead took himself back to Drogheda by the evening coach. Jackson was prepared to wait, and both he and Rowan still considered Tone persuadable.

On his return to town on Thursday, 24th, however, Tone finally rejected the suggested mission—sustained perhaps by some relief afforded his recent despair about the state of the country by the triumphant acquittal of the Drogheda Catholics. Jackson appended this intelligence to a letter to France, 'the person' having told him that morning 'that his private affairs will not permit him' to undertake the mission. Instead he sent copies Rowan had made of Tone's memorial, with a number of other letters, by the open post, via merchant houses in Hamburg and the French minister to Holland. These were intercepted and Jackson was arrested at his hotel on the morning of Monday the 28th. There the arresting officers found papers scattered carelessly around the room, including Tone's letter breaking their dinner engagement and others from Rowan.[14]

II

Dublin Castle had been following Jackson's movements since his arrival in Ireland, for Cockayne, already a government informant of some years' standing,[15] had alerted Whitehall to Jackson's intentions even before they left England. In view of Jackson's associations not only with leading radicals in London but with a number of opposition politicians, Pitt took a particular interest. In a personal interview he encouraged Cockayne to accompany Jackson to Ireland in exchange for assurances that he would not be called as a witness. Jackson's natural conviviality—one of his many flaws as a secret agent—accounts for the ready involvement of an old friend in the venture and the ex-curate's smothering companionship and late-night drinking sessions at Hyde's seriously affected Cockayne's capacity for espionage. Hurried visits to Lord Clonmell's house in Grafton Street, frantic letters to Pitt, written early in the morning as Jackson slept off the effects of their late nights, tell their own story. His Irish interlocutors were evidently out of sympathy with Pitt's offer of immunity, and Cockayne avoided occasions for intelligence-gathering in the anticipation—accurate, in the event—that the undertaking would not be honoured. In the discussions with Rowan he took himself off to the other end of the room and proved a lamentable witness, refusing even to sign his affidavit unless Pitt sent through a formal pardon.

Tone, having acquired some eleventh-hour discretion, assumed the same policy, and in Newgate the reluctant conspirator and the reluctant informer made small talk out of earshot while Jackson and Rowan plotted. Given Cockayne's reluctance to testify, Tone's paper was the only real evidence of treason. The day after his departure for Drogheda Westmorland told Pitt that the paper 'goes little short of proving treasonable designs on Tone and Hamilton Rowan.'[16]

Tone had no illusions about the danger in which he now found himself. The night of Jackson's committal (28 April), a distraught Cockayne returned from an all-day interrogation by the Privy Council and gained access to Jackson and Rowan. He told of his refusal to sign a deposition, claimed that he had implicated no one by name and assured the two men that in any event the evidence of one witness was insufficient to convict in a case of treason—which may have been true for England, but was certainly not for Ireland.

Tone also came to Newgate that night and they agreed that if questioned, they would speak the truth 'consistent with our own personal safety; for that all attempts at fabrication would add infamy to peril'. But fear led to mutual recrimination. Rowan accused Tone of misleading him. Tone was dismayed at Rowan's incaution and at the involvement of Cockayne, and that old sense of having been used partially explains his readiness to compromise with the government.[17] But he admitted later to being afraid, and the daily expectation of being 'seized and hanged' hardened him. He and Rowan agreed to take measures to save themselves each consistent with the other's safety. Rowan announced his plan to escape, which he effected on 1 May. Tone sought help from Peter Burrowes, now a King's Counsel, urging him to contact the government through Marcus Beresford, and to tell him what had happened. Cockayne had already told the government everything anyway. Tone offered to leave Ireland entirely and hoped that the government would permit Rowan to do likewise. In this they would have commanded considerable public support, for after Rowan's rigged trial it was generally assumed that the Jackson episode was yet another scheme to entrap him.

To the government Tone was small fry. Moreover Westmorland admitted not having 'a tittle of evidence' against him.[18] All the copies of his statement were, after all, in Rowan's hand. It was Rowan they wanted to make an example of, and, with the continued signs of Cockayne's reluctance, Marcus Beresford was urged to contact Tone and offer immunity in return for evidence. Beresford spent all of Monday April 28, trying to locate Tone's lodgings and returning to the Castle at frequent intervals for instructions, since a deal with Tone would only be useful if Cockayne persisted in his reluctance to testify. It was a reflection of Tone's withdrawal from active radicalism in the preceding months, and indeed of his lack of importance in government eyes, that so few knew where he lived.

In the event Rowan's flight on 1 May, and that of Reynolds shortly afterwards, removed some of the pressure, and in return for a full statement of his own involvement, Tone was granted immunity from prosecution. He had friends in high places, and his neighbours and long-time patrons in Kildare stepped in, in the person of the Attorney-General, Arthur Wolfe. But even Fitzgibbon seems to have fallen in with what the Castle generally considered a good bargain to be rid of Tone. He was thought a nuisance rather than a threat, a talented tool in the hands of the Catholics rather than a major conspirator. Beresford, having failed to persuade Tone to testify against Jackson, and given the strong probability that the government would be unable to convict him if prosecuted, wrote to his father, John Beresford, on 7 May: 'it would not be a bad bargain for Government to get rid of him; and more especially so as the Roman Catholics are now hatching mischief, and he has already approved himself so dangerous a tool in their hands—as undoubtedly he was the person who planned and carried into effect their Convention, and who contrived to unite the Presbyterians with them in the furtherance of their object.' He pointed to renewed Catholic plans to petition the King. 'To get rid of Tone I consider an object worth attaining.' Beresford had accordingly settled for a detailed statement by Tone of his conversations with Jackson and an undertaking to quit the country on the understanding that his narrative would be used to secure his conviction should he return.[19] Tone's 'narrative', written and signed on 3 May 1794, is—apart from some inaccuracies in dates—a fair account of his involvement in the Jackson affair. Beresford kept the bargain faithfully. However, the statement did amount to 'a confession of his own treason', as Tone's friends were told in 1798, and 'would and was intended to hang him in case of his ever returning.'[20]

With another Catholic emancipation conflict pending, the haste and alacrity of the Irish government to make such a deal with Tone can best be explained in terms of its opposition to further Catholic reform. This was certainly Grattan's opinion; the remarkable immunity from prosecution Tone had been granted, he interpreted as a government ploy to implicate the Catholics in sedition, and he sought—unsuccessfully, as it turned out—to convince the Catholic Committee to dump Tone.[21] At Marcus Beresford's insistence, Tone withdrew to Chateau Boue—'to avoid the importuning of the Catholics, who wish him to write for them, and the attendance on the trial of the printers of the Northern Star, which he was to have attended'—and spent that summer compiling a history of Ireland.[22]

London, however, did not share Dublin's views. Jackson's entanglements in Ireland were crucial to the picture developing at Whitehall of a spreading web of English sedition, and ministers needed to expose Jackson in order to convict their own 'conspirators', rounded up in a swoop that May. Beresford's father, then in London, wrote of Whitehall's anger at Rowan's escape. They had heard nothing of any bargain with Tone and the new Irish Chief Secretary, Sylvester Douglas, thought he should hang. Indeed London was thinking of netting jointly a catch of Irish and English conspirators by getting Jackson to inform, and Westmorland was ordered not to make any bargain with Tone. Westmorland argued that they had insufficient evidence against him and Reynolds to make a case. He thought them 'hardly worth punishing' and would leave Tone 'on parole' till further instructed. He was more disturbed at London's plans to persuade Jackson to turn King's evidence. It would confirm the rumours that he was a British spy sent to trap the reformers. He did attempt to prevent any bargain being made with Tone, only to find that Marcus Beresford had already concluded one.[23] Tone had indeed got off lightly and recognised all too well how very imprudent he had been.

III

The events sent panic through the remnants of the United Irish Society. On Friday, May 2, several members arrived at the Tailors'

Hall to find it in darkness, the caretaker having been told that there would be no meeting. Gradually, however, enough members trickled in to hold one and they defiantly distanced themselves from the actions of Rowan, Tone and Reynolds. But on 23 May the Society was raided, its papers seized and its formal existence terminated. On 11 May Drennan was arrested for his Volunteer address of 1792. The *Northern Star* proprietors were in Dublin awaiting trial, and the worst was feared for the verdict. Thomas Addis Emmet, another regular visitor to the imprisoned Rowan, was panic-stricken and hourly expected arrest. With rumours that some 40 warrants were out against the reformers, Tone must have worried about how his own immunity would appear to others. He made a point of walking openly in the streets to show that he had nothing to hide. On the night of Drennan's release on bail (Tuesday, 12 May) he called at Drennan's Dame Street home, with Sampson, but waited below, 'as he said the messengers might have a warrant for him also'.[24]

When Tone's compromise was agreed is unclear, though he later claimed to have received written confirmation of it from one of the Under-Secretaries. Its existence is mentioned in Drennan's correspondence for mid-July and it is a remarkable testimony to Tone's reputation as a man of honour that even bitter critics like Drennan found nothing dishonourable in it. 'T[one] has, I believe, entered into some honourable compromise with Government. He will not give evidence against any man, which saves his own honour. He will not be prosecuted, and will probably get good recommendations for India, for to get him out of the Kingdom is, I believe, an object they think worth absolving for what is past.' Indeed Drennan was critical of Rowan for implicating so many by his incaution, and thought they were well rid of him.[25] But Tone having been named in the June indictment of Jackson, whose trial was persistently postponed, the cloud remained for the rest of the year.

Emergence of a Revolutionary

Jackson's trial was continually postponed and by the turn of the year there were hopes that he might be treated leniently. The not-guilty verdicts returned in the trials of Drennan, the *Northern Star* proprietors, and similar trials in England restored some temporary calm to reformism. With the downfall of Robespierre in France the reformers' criticism of the war and admiration for the French Revoluion—so noticeably muted during the Terror—returned. The Catholic campaign and the United Irishmen alike revived in a low-key fashion. But on the whole Tone appears to have maintained his bargain with Beresford until formally invited back as agent by the Catholics in December 1794. By then the climate had changed so dramatically as to suggest that in his case bygones might be put aside.

I

The main reason was the possibility of a total change in Irish politics favourable to Catholic claims. Rumours of a coalition between the Pitt government and the Portland Whigs had been current since 1792 and it was generally assumed that the Irish viceroyalty would go to the Whigs. The formal accession of the Whigs to the coalition took place in July 1794. Within weeks the Whig candidate for the Irish post, Earl Fitzwilliam, was canvassing the Irish opposition, and a change in the system of governing Ireland was confidently expected.[1] Grattan was invited to London for negotiations and on his return told the Dublin Catholics to recommence their campaign. By October they were being courted on all sides and once again the populace was brought into the fray by a vigorous publicity campaign. Rumour had it that even Rowan and Tandy might be allowed to return under the new regime.[2] On 23 December the Dublin Catholics met to celebrate the second anniversary of their Convention and resolved to petition the incoming administration for a total repeal of the remaining penal laws. Grattan was approached to present the petition and Tone was called back as agent.

But if Tone expected to be rehabilitated he was rudely disabused. Fitzwilliam's sweep of offices to bring in the Ponsonby clan displaced the leading persons responsible for the compromise with

Tone. Understandable pique against someone he had once sponsored strengthened Ponsonby's conviction that Tone should have hanged, and he warned Tone that he would not find the new Attorney-General (the office Ponsonby was promised) as accommodating as the old. Grattan added his voice to Ponsonby's in suggesting that Tone must have made some dishonourable deal with the government to have escaped so lightly. This from someone whom Tone admired came as a particular shock.[3]

His retention by the Catholics in the face of such pressures some, including Drennan, thought unwise. Tone's gratitude to them for not abandoning him was effusive and his earlier doubts about Keogh vanished. It shows how far many of the Catholic leaders had progressed in their readiness to espouse more extreme measures. McCormick, Lewins and Sweetman were central figures in the regrouping of the United Irishmen, and Drennan noted with satisfaction the disappearance of the Catholics' long-standing reluctance to throw in their lot with the Protestant radicals.[4]

Most of all, however, their more relaxed attitude towards the radicals was symptomatic of the overwhelming confidence with which Catholic Ireland viewed the prospect of a new administration.[5] The recognition that the 1793 Catholic Relief Act had altered little on the ground united them as never before, and Fitzwilliam learned quickly that the old tactic of detaching the landed Catholics from the Dublin Committee was no longer viable. Even before then, indeed within three days of his arrival, he had written urgently to London announcing his conviction that the Catholic question could not be put off, although Whitehall had urged delay. Before he received an answer, Fitzwilliam had given Grattan leave to introduce a relief bill. London was horrified and on 23 February 1795 Fitzwilliam was abruptly recalled.[6]

Apportioning blame for the Fitzwilliam fiasco has long occupied historians. It was one of those affairs in which with hindsight everyone could have done better, and its tragicomic character only heightens its sadness. At the time it was Fitzwilliam's ministerial changes rather than the Catholic issue which were held responsible for his abrupt recall, and the mob fury which greeted the arrival of his successor, Lord Camden, was directed against the same old hate figures, Foster, Beresford, and above all Fitzgibbon. The regency episode of 1789 clouded discussions, as ousted officials played upon London's reluctance to see loyal servants like John Beresford and Fitzgibbon replaced by the very set which had deserted to the Prince of Wales.

Fitzwilliam had handled the dismissals with a considerable lack of sensitivity. They were such public knowledge even before he landed in Dublin that the confident expectation of a clean sweep of all their enemies was a factor in Catholic confidence and Whig triumphalism at the turn of the year. Fitzwilliam's preference for the advice and company of the Ponsonbys (to whom he was related by marriage) was manifest from the moment of his arrival and he snubbed many of those in office.[7] At the Castle he insisted on a rigorous and foppish ceremonial alien to these Irish country squires, and Fitzgibbon was sent away for appearing in boots and breeches. The new Lord Lieutenant barely put in an appearance at the admittedly endless round of dinners in Irish political circles, and even Drennan was critical, wondering 'whether this piety and pomposity will do with the Irish.'[8]

Pitt's policy after 1793 was to prevent further agitation on the Catholic issue for the duration of the war, and his resolve hardened through the autumn and winter of 1794 as the war on the Continent turned decidedly in France's favour.[9] Fitzwilliam's instructions, however, had been confused, the only clear one being a directive to act with caution, which he decidedly did not do. But his Burkean sense of mission towards Ireland was well-known and much of the fault must lie with his immediate masters, Pitt and Portland. Certainly his frantic letters asking for instructions, commencing only two days after his arrival, were left unanswered until 14 February. Two days after Grattan was given leave to introduce the Catholic measure, Fitzwilliam was urged to postpone it. He erupted in an angry refusal to do so and was recalled the following week.[10]

The news hit the Irish press on 26 February. Even the *Freeman's Journal* was incredulous. The *Northern Star* declared it 'a misfortune so sudden and unexpected' as to cause 'general alarm and despondency.'[11] The town of Belfast sent a delegation to Dublin to express its dismay to the outgoing Lord Lieutenant.[12] Similar addresses came from all parts of the country, and on the day of Fitzwilliam's departure Belfast and Dublin went into public mourning. In defiant mood the Dublin Catholics met at Francis Street chapel on 27 February. An address to the King was approved. It would be taken to London by Keogh, Byrne and John Hussey (Baron Galtrim), with Tone again as secretary. Drennan wondered at the wisdom of involving Tone so publicly, concluding that he was being sent to keep a watch on Keogh, 'confiding, and I believe justly, more in Tone's steadiness than in that of the other.'[13] In fact Tone had never lost his popularity with the Catholics, besides which they were in no mood to trim sails with the London ministers. The crisis had destroyed for good the old sense that Pitt was their friend, and the thanks voted by the meeting to the people of Belfast was a public declaration of the change of mood which had occurred since 1793.[14]

The delegation arrived in London on Monday, March 9, took up residence at the Bath Hotel, Arlington Street, and called on Portland the following day.[15] They told him of their despair of getting justice in Ireland while their enemies (notably Fitzgibbon) were in power, pointed to the trials of the leading Drogheda Catholics and the threats made against Byrne and Keogh as examples of how they were being punished for the 1793 bill, and cited the precedent of their reception by Dundas to persuade the Home Secretary to give them an answer in London rather than channelling it through those same enemies in Dublin.[16] On 13 March they were permitted to deliver their petition to the King, but at a public levee rather than a private audience, at which they felt they were made an object of ridicule.[17] They received no intimation of government intentions and repeated appeals to Portland were firmly declined by references to the Lord Lieutenant as the proper channel for such requests. They were 'disgusted by the hauteur with which they were received in England' and back in Ireland rumours about their dissatisfaction produced reports that they had actually been arrested and imprisoned.[18]

The full extent of their discontent was revealed in a massive meeting of Catholics called at Francis Street chapel on 9 April. Over 4,000 were said to have attended and the atmosphere was excited. Keogh, in a heated speech, laid to earth the notion that England was their friend. 'He trusted...that the Catholics of Ireland, refused this time, would never again seek the favour of the British Cabinet.' MacNeven and Lewins expressed real hostility towards England. 'The people of Ireland are never more to look up to the Cabinet of England for protection or relief.' There was no advantage in remaining loyal and peaceable. Fitzwilliam had recently published a vindication which claimed that Pitt planned a union of the two countries as the price of emancipation. The speakers at the Francis Street meeting declared that the independence of their country would not be traded for their own liberty. Nothing would make them abandon their Protestant brethren. 'The present', Keogh declared, 'was the last time the Catholics would ever assemble in a distinct body—their cause being no longer a distinct cause, but adopted by their Protestant brethren as the common cause of Ireland.' Thanks were offered to 'our Protestant brethren of Belfast and Dublin', and, in a pointed snub of the authorities on the eve of Jackson's trial, to their secretary, T.W. Tone, 'for the readiness with which he accompanied our deputies to England, and the many other important services he has rendered to the Catholic body in their pursuit of Emancipation; services which no gratitude can over-rate, and no remuneration can overpay.'

For many present these proceedings announced the long-awaited merger of the Catholics with the United Irishmen.[19] The new mood was a significant break with Catholic Committee practice since 1791.

It also made the hierarchy more receptive to the concept of an Irish seminary, which London held out to soften the rejection of emancipation.[20] But it was too great a price to pay for what was being withheld in 1795 and the reforming Catholics' lack of interest in the proposal was yet another token of their abandonment of sectional issues. The hope of securing emancipation, which had led the Catholics to distance their cause from that of the reformers, was no more. Camden, Fitzwilliam's successor, arrived on 31 March with strict instructions to resist further Catholic claims and win back Protestant support for the government.[21] The elevation of Fitzgibbon to an earldom in June was one of the more immediate and public affirmations of the new policy.

The Fitzwilliam crisis is considered one of the crucial turning-points in Ireland's drift towards rebellion.[22] The formation of an underground separatist movement was already under way in the north. But the national basis which would transform it from a nest of conspirators into a national liberation movement was lacking until 1795. Popular alienation from the government had already occurred. Fitzwilliam commented with some relief that such discontent lacked leaders of influence because of the loyalty of the leading Catholics. Two months later, however, the new Chief Secretary, Thomas Pelham, expressed his alarm at the widespread mistrust of England and the way the connection was being represented as the source of Ireland's troubles.[23] The Fitzwilliam crisis was seen by many as a national insult.[24] The combination of forces which was to turn the United Irishmen from an urban intellectual élite into a mass popular movement took place as a direct result. Tone became part of that transformation.

II

The trial of Jackson finally took place on 23 April 1795. By now, however, there was considerable public sympathy for him, and with Cockayne's continued prevarication a 'guilty' verdict was not a foregone conclusion.[25] Many thought a 'not guilty' verdict would pave the way for the return of Rowan, Tandy and Reynolds, and such an expectation may well account for Tone's continued residence in Ireland, despite the voluntary exile agreement. In the event Jackson was found guilty of treason, despite a savage character assassination of Cockayne by the defence counsel, Curran and Ponsonby. Jackson was brought up for sentence on Tuesday, 28 April, but died in the dock from a self-administered dose of poison.

The trial and its aftermath became a *cause célèbre* in Ireland. It was reported in great detail in the press, and accounts serialised in the magazines and rushed into print by competing pamphleteers. Few would have been ignorant thereafter of Tone's central role. Defence and prosecution counsel alike were incensed that Tone had not been called to testify, and in effect he was tried *in absentia*. Significant too was the protest by the Solicitor-General, testifying to the absence of full ministerial support for the compromise made with Tone the previous year. If Tone needed any further reminder of the threat to his immunity should he remain in Ireland, this was it. When called upon to explain his absence from court, Jackson's counsel answered that the crown might have had him as a witness 'but I have heard there was a compromise with Mr Tone by government that he was not to be prosecuted.'[26]

Tone read the statement in the newspapers and instantly penned an answer. The style of the reply is agitated. He gives a fair rendering of what had been agreed with Marcus Beresford, accepts that any action the government chose to take against him would be justified, but reveals that on two separate occasions he had been assured that he would not be called as a witness. There is a full admission of involvement with Jackson, but no repentance and a prickly self-righteous insistence that he had acted honourably. 'Whether this . . . be a compromise or not, I hope, at least, it is no dishonorable one. I have betrayed no friend; I have revealed no secret; I have abused no confidence. For what I had done, I was ready to suffer; I would, if necessary, submit, I hope, to death, but I would not to what I consider disgrace. As to the part of my conduct which was introductory to this unfortunate business, I leave it, without anxiety, to the censure of all inclined to condemn it.'[27]

The tetchiness of the piece derived from a belief, not so much that he had done nothing wrong as that he had done nothing dishonourable. This he followed up with the same public parade of his rectitude as in 1794. 'Tone walks the streets I find', wrote Drennan to his brother-in-law, 'and therefore I suppose has secured himself by some negotiation . . . which I doubt not is honourable on his part, for I believe he would have suffered himself rather than be evidence against any poor unfortunate man, and as he stays here, notwithstanding, he has certainly triumphed.'[28] On the day of Jackson's trial Tone had pointedly entered the most crowded coffee-houses and bookshops and paraded in the most public streets. That he was still at large caused an outcry among certain powerful persons, and to avoid implicating his friends Tone refrained from calling on them.[29]

The following week, on the night of 4–5 May, Grattan's Catholic bill was defeated by 84 votes to 155 after a 19-hour sitting in which the flirtation of the Catholics' agent with treason was used as one of the main arguments against concession.[30] Tone was advised 'if he consulted his safety, to withdraw from Ireland', and Pelham told

the House on the 8th that Tone had resigned his position with the
Catholic Committee and struck his name from the roll of the bar.
'He is said to have obtained a conditional *nolle prosequi*, for those
implications of a treasonable nature alledged against him on the trial
of Jackson, on provision that he is never more to appear in this
country.'[31] There can be little doubt that some action would have
been taken against Tone had he not made an immediate move to
leave the country.

Tone had now attained public notoriety. He was being depicted as
a dangerous revolutionary. That he shortly stepped into the role
should not disguise the fact that it was being created for him, and
that he assumed it in an atmosphere of unreality, turbulence and total
personal upheaval. Until the spring of 1795 Tone would not have felt
himself part of some kind of conspiracy. Rather, in the build-up to
the Fitzwilliam episode and the overwhelming public support for the
removal of Fitzgibbon and his colleagues, he would have felt that he
was participating in a wider movement which included many prominent gentry and MPs. Indeed on the night of 4 May, in a speech
much admired by Tone, Arthur O'Connor, member for Philips-
town, accused ministers of being traitors to the people and of
driving them into the arms of any foreign power willing to help
them 'break the chains of bondage.'[32] The outcome of Jackson's trial
came as a rude shock.

Within two weeks of Pelham's statement Tone had disposed of his
property in Kildare and made arrangements to travel to America.
The speed with which the Catholic Committee produced the money
owed to him is a token of its own change of mood, and indeed its
sense of real danger. In the belief that the parliamentary attack was
a preliminary to one upon its members, the Committee advised
Lewins to return immediately from England, where he might have
fallen foul of the Suspension of Habeas Corpus Act, and rallied to
help Tone. The Committee had never been quite as parsimonious as
Drennan suggested. Its members recognised the professional losses
sustained by Butler, Tone and Todd Jones in the Catholic cause.
They had stepped in to prevent the compulsory sale of Butler's
library, and advanced some temporary relief to Tone from their
personal funds: 'for the resentment of our enemies opposes his professional pursuits, and if abandoned will force him to quit the kingdom. . . already our enemies trumpet forth our want of gratitude. . . .
if we fail in discharging the obligation we have undertaken, a spirit of
resentment may turn against our future interests the literary talents
that was so useful to our cause'. The country delegates subscribed
little more than £200 of the £1,500 voted in April 1793. Ultimately, it
seems, the Dublin members had to foot the entire bill.[33]

The turmoil of the sudden upheaval is apparent in Tone's terse description of the events. The Tones had had a fourth child, Richard, sometime in 1794—when, we do not know. But he died about this time, adding to the family's affliction. Tone sold everything, save his books, 'a very good selection of about six hundred volumes', which he cared enough about to transport to America. Chateau Boue he made over to Matthew Donnellan—a member of the Catholic Committee, whose family in Kildare were sub-tenants of the Tones—for rent of 'one peppercorn (if demanded)', and the deeds were signed in Dublin on the day of Tone's departure, 20 May.[34] McCormick and Keogh secured an additional £300 of the arrears owing to him. Tone settled his debts and was left with £796 to re-start life in America.[35] Todd Jones supplied contacts in Philadelphia, and a remarkable array of friends rallied round, including even lost ones like Plunket, to whom Tone almost certainly wrote just before leaving Dublin. It was a token of his troubled emotions upon leaving, perhaps with personal debts unfulfilled. Plunket replied in some sadness:

Dear Tone,
I embrace with great pleasure the idea and opportunity of renewing our old habits of intimacy and friendship. Long as they have been interrupted, I can assure you that no hostile sentiment towards you ever found admittance into my mind. Regret, allow me the expression, on your account, apprehension for the public, and great pain at being deprived of the social, happy, and unrestrained intercourse which had for so many years subsisted between us, were the sum of my feelings. Some of them, perhaps, were mistaken, but there can be no use now in any retrospect of that kind. It is not without a degree of melancholy I reflect that your present destination makes it probable that we may never meet again, and talk and laugh together as we used to do, though it is difficult to determine whether these jumbling times may not again bring us together. In all events, I shall be most happy to hear from you, and write to you, often and fully....If I had known your departure was to have been so very immediate, I would not have suffered you to slip away without a personal meeting. [Here Plunket offered to write on Tone's behalf to connections in America]...I beg, you will give my best regards to Mrs Tone, and believe me, dear Tone, with great truth, your friend, W. PLUNKET, May 29th, 1795.[36]

Tone also wrote to George Knox. But the letter only reached him after Tone had already left Dublin. He too was taken aback at the suddenness of Tone's departure and asked for an address in America to which things could be forwarded, since any letters through the post office would surely be opened. 'It gives me great pleasure to find you are so well reconciled to emigration. It is your lot to-day, it may be mine to-morrow; these are times when every man of steady principles, must expect to have them put to the trial, and if your *Paineism* has sunk you, my *Montesquieuism*[37] may not long keep me afloat.' Five days later Knox wrote again, sending a packet of books and other things for the Tones' voyage, and announcing that he had been turned out of his position for supporting the Catholic bill.[38]

The letters of Plunket and Knox—both committed emancipationists—hint at the turmoil in opinion caused by the Fitzwilliam episode and its sequel. There is a sense of Tone as the victim of principles which they alike shared. Soon his old schoolmate, Charles Kendal Bushe, now a rising young barrister and MP, was voicing the same sentiments publicly. Most believed that Tone was a reckless, if talented, idealist, whose punishment had exceeded the crime.

III

Tone prevailed on his father to allow his brother Arthur to accompany them to America, and since they were also taking his sister Mary, and William and Matthew Tone were already overseas, the distress of his parents was considerable.[39] As an eldest son Tone took his responsibilities towards his younger siblings seriously. For over a year the antics of young Arthur had been a worry. He had the restlessness of all the Tones to an exaggerated degree—'a singular boy, irregular and incorrect', as Matilda remembered him, 'but bold and generous'—and though but twelve at the time, he had set his heart on the sea. His father wanted to give him a classical education, but he constantly ran away from school. At least Tone had learnt from his own experience 'that it is foolish to struggle against a propensity of that kind'. He thought 'a voyage or two may cool him', and proposed placing him in the American navy.[40]

Although Tone joked about becoming an American farmer, his departure from Ireland was no simple emigration. A year after his rejection of Jackson's suggestion of an Irish embassy to Paris, he sailed from Ireland with just such a commission, turning near-flight into glorious mission. Fundamental to the transformation was the influence of his friend, Thomas Russell. Russell's personal melancholia had been reactivated by the depressing political situation. News in March 1794 of his favourite brother's death in India sent him into a spiral of despair which was completed by word that Eliza Goddard was to marry another. Tone had heard of Ambrose Russell's death in January 1794, but delayed informing his friend for fear that he would abandon an offer of paid employment in Belfast.[41] It was a strange act of friendship, but the state of Russell's mind in these months receives corroboration in Mrs McTier's letters to her brother. Russell's poverty became legendary in Belfast. Mrs McTier agonised over his sufferings when he could not even afford a black coat to mourn his brother. He lived in a 'melancholy lodging...in a dark and gloomy entry', scarcely ate and mixed with company socially far beneath him. She impressed on Drennan Russell's contribution to the Catholic and reform campaigns, suggested all kinds of literary ventures which might bring him an income, and ultimately appealed to Keogh.[42]

The United Irish Society in the north had retained a cell-like existence very different from the public pirouetting of the over-sized Dublin body. It had, moreover, made significant headway among the skilled trades, whereas the élitism of the Dublin Society bothered some of its socially inferior members and in part explains its sometimes reckless outspokenness.[43] Russell was unusual in belonging to both worlds. He had espoused the idea of armed revolution much earlier than Tone, whose distrust of the Irish 'sans culottes' never left him. Russell was likewise convinced of the desire of the French to invade Ireland, and he considered revolution inevitable.[44] Given such feelings and his willingness to mix with them socially, Russell was popular with 'the young men' of Belfast, who were 'far more violent than the others'. They were suspicious of those leaders involved with the *Northern Star*, considered them 'not ready enough for the field', but accepted Russell as someone who 'would be ready to act'.[45]

Over the next few months the United Irish movement in Antrim and Down was reorganised from 'the base of society', as Emmet described the process, 'the obscurity of its members' acting as a form of protection with government attention concentrated on the celebrities.[46] Russell seems to have been the crucial bridge between these men and the original United Irish leaders.[47] He also spent much time with Tone during these months and would have influenced the latter's growing belief that the Irish were perhaps more ready for action than he had supposed. News reaching Drennan and the Castle alike in April 1795 was that something new was afoot. After his brush with prison the previous year, a more cautious Drennan urged his sister to hint to all her United Irish friends not to make him their confidant.[48] Following the Jackson episode, Tone would have been more easily persuaded.

The continuing military clamp-down had already brought lower-class Catholics and Presbyterians into the United Irishmen in the Belfast area. It took the Fitzwilliam episode, however, and the subsequent rejection of both Catholic and reform bills, to add the southern Catholics to the movement. In Dublin efforts at regrouping the United Irishmen had been in motion since the previous summer.

Emmet was the moving force. Leading Catholics like McCormick, Lewins, Sweetman, MacNeven and Keogh were more amenable to an alliance than a year previously. But until the spring of 1795 Tone took a back seat. Decisions and plans were effectively suspended for the duration of Fitzwilliam's viceroyalty. His recall and the delegates' treatment in London, however, tipped the balance, and by early April the Catholic leaders were pushing for negotiations with the northerners.[49] The Catholic Committee was finally dissolved the following month, a major row between Byrne and Keogh symbolising the rupture of many of its most active members with constitutional politics.[50]

That April plans were adopted to send an agent to France. It was the one point on which all parties had come to agree, and so it would remain for the rest of the decade. How and when the choice fell on Tone is unclear. His name does not appear in accounts reaching the Castle of the regrouping. But once his intended departure was known, his association with those involved, particularly with the Catholics, would have made him a natural choice. The idea of a secret embassy to France should the Catholic bill fail was already being contemplated by the leading Dublin Catholics, and by Tone as their associate, before the end of March.[51]

Tone's own account tells of an afternoon spent with Emmet and Russell in late April or early May. They were walking back to town from Emmet's country villa at Rathfarnham when Tone explained his scheme of using his American exile as a stepping-stone to France. There he would apply for French assistance in a bid for Irish independence. 'I told them that I considered my compromise with government to extend no further than the banks of the Delaware...that, undoubtedly, I was guilty of a great offence against the existing government; that, in consequence, I was going into exile; and that I considered that exile as a full expiation for the offence.' He also told McCormick and Keogh of his plans and likewise received their endorsement. Russell would have informed the Belfast people of Tone's offer when he returned to the town in late April or early May and Tone's 'appointment' was ratified both in Dublin and Belfast, or as Lewins later told Bonaparte, by 'the leading Patriots, Catholic and Presbyterian alike.'[52]

However, it would be wrong to view these developments as the emergence of a movement for national independence, and the later confusion of the United Irish leaders themselves over precise datings tells its own story. It is significant that it was to Russell they looked for enlightenment.[53] The movement had not yet spread beyond Antrim and Down and it was representatives from these two counties alone who met in Belfast on 10 May to ratify the constitution of the new oathbound United Irish movement. Tone took the oath on 10 June.[54] Yet although this group declared its aims to be a republican government and separation from England, the new constitution and oath mentioned neither. Rather members swore 'to obtain an equal, full and adequate representation of *all* the people of Ireland', and the words 'in parliament' were omitted to permit republicans and reformers to work together.[55] A republic, assisted by the French, was by no means the agreed programme of the disparate collection of people now forming under the rejuvenated United Irish banner, and it remained a contentious issue among the Dublin leaders for years to come.

Most of Tone's retrospective account reveals his anxieties that such a plan might be viewed as dishonourable. He was surprised that the government had not extracted from him an undertaking to desist from such activities in exile; 'so it was, however, that either despising my efforts, or looking upon themselves as too firmly established to dread anything from France [and there were elements of both], they suffered me to depart, without demanding any satisfaction whatsoever on that topic'. But he admitted that he would have had problems had such an undertaking been required.[56]

IV

The new organisation was in its very early stages when Tone and his family reached Belfast on 21 May. But one thing is certain, it now involved formal contact with the Defenders, justifying Tone's later claims to speak for them as well as for the Catholic and Presbyterian leaders. Yet Tone himself spent little time talking of such things in his final weeks in Ireland. Rather Belfast—which had launched his political career amidst festivities in 1791— saw him out in like fashion. His friends entertained him in style. A marquee was hired for a dinner in the Deer Park, and a long trip arranged to Ram's Island on Lough Neagh. 'Lord John Tones having been here these last 3 weeks', wrote Russell to his brother on the day of their departure, there had been 'no lack of whiskey, claret and burgundy'.[57]

In the atmosphere of danger and tension in which Tone left Dublin, the Belfast trip cast a glow over an otherwise distasteful experience—and so indeed Tone remembered it: 'certainly the whole of our deportment and reception at Belfast very little resembled those of a man who escaped with his life only by miracle, and who was driven into exile to avoid a more disgraceful fate'. Though not normally given to effusiveness, Tone continued to describe his debt to Belfast in terms which convey something of his gratitude. 'You know I do not deal in professions', he wrote to Russell from America three months later, 'but the kindness I have ever received in Belfast, and most especially during my last stay there, when I so much needed it, I shall remember while I have life with sentiments of the warmest gratitude. . . . Call. . . on all my friends and thank them for their kindness to me. You will not say more for me than I feel.'[58] Tone's Belfast friends also raised a subscription for him—reported to have reached £1,500—which, in line with his constant embarrassment about financial affairs, he does not mention in his memoirs.[59]

The experience had the effect of solemnising an informal engagement, and when the practicalities of everyday life in America dimmed the sense of obligation, a reminder from those same friends sufficed to send Tone instantly to France. One incident in particular stood out in Tone's memory and has become part of the Tone legend. Tone, Russell, Neilson, Simms, McCracken and a few others ascended the highest point of the Cave Hill at McArt's Fort. It afforded spectacular views over Belfast, its Lough, and, on a clear day over much of Ulster. There they made, 'a most solemn obligation. . . never to desist in our efforts until we had subverted the authority of England over our country, and asserted our independence.'

The McCrackens organised a farewell party on Saturday, 12 June, with games for the children and musical entertainment arranged by Bunting, one of the earliest collectors of traditional Irish airs, then living with the McCrackens. It was an emotional evening and Matilda was particularly affected. The following day they wrote their farewell to John Russell, Mary and Matilda revealing their distress at the prospect of exile, Tone in contrast displaying his ability to turn his back on the past once the break had been made:

> I write this from Belfast on my way to America. I have been fighting my way here a long time, and at last finding all further contest on my part unprofitable and indeed impossible I yield to what I cannot any longer oppose. Under this emigration I find complete support in the testimony of my own conscience, the spirit of my family, and the kindness and affection of my friends; especially those of this town. . .indeed I am overpowered with their kindness. . . . We go on board this evening—Adieu Dear John, God Bless you.[60]

The Tones boarded the *Cincinnatus* that evening, accompanied to the last by their friends and showered with all manner of gifts for their journey.[61]

Tone's involvement with Jackson was to become part of his accreditation with the French. But his exile and new career as republican diplomat were not the outcome of free choice. Rather he was making a virtue of necessity, the influence and encouragement of friends alone endowing his move with a retrospective sense of national mission. Until 1795 the conception of Tone as gifted, likeable, honourable, a tool in the hands of others rather than a danger in himself, had both retained for him the protection of people like Beresford and Wolfe and gained that surprising immunity which would certainly not have been accorded Keogh or Drennan. Dublin Castle had received information early in June that Tone's American exile was but a feint for a mission to France. It is a token of how the Castle viewed Tone that no attempt was made to stop his departure.[62] This belief that Tone had been little more than a talented medium likewise provided a screen for the new and, one might say, uncharacteristic career on which he now embarked so successfully. Tone's achievements in France are surprising. They do not invalidate the above reading of his earlier years. He would never have starred in a traditional career which required deference to others and a public presence. Given a sense of mission and total control over its exercise, however, he was to prove a secret diplomat of remarkable ability.

20
Exile in America

When Tone left Ireland his French plans were as ill formulated as his political philosophy. A year later in Paris he was acting out the role of a fully fledged revolutionary. Fundamental to the process was his American experience. To the Irish reformers America was the original land of liberty, and Tone and Russell had talked of emigrating there.[1] But in August 1795 Tone arrived in the new American capital at the height of a vicious partisan contest which was to determine the future structure of American politics. What he saw was an apparent life-and-death struggle between 'aristocracy' and 'democracy', in which the former had aligned itself with Britain against France. The experience soured his view of Americans, sharpened his sense of Irishness and anti-Englishness, and helped define his republicanism.

I

The *Cincinnatus* sailed with some 300 passengers on board. Many would have been emigrants, Presbyterians and skilled artisans for the most part.[2] Tone, as a gentleman, was in a minority and adopted a suitably paternalistic stance towards his fellow passengers. Conditions were cramped, and though the Tones had hired a 'state cabin', it measured little more than eight feet by six. Supplies donated by their Belfast friends were shared with the other passengers, and the instructions accompanying Dr MrDonnell's medicine chest allowed Tone to act as ship's doctor. He tried, with some success, to introduce a sense of order and hygiene among the passengers, and the overcrowding and shortage of fresh water notwithstanding, prided himself on landing his 'patients' safely, with the loss of but one, after the six-week voyage.[3]

The crossing was calm, uneventful and at times even exhilarating when the Tones sighted a shoal of porpoises, a dolphin, or now and again a shark or whale. After five weeks at sea, however, the vessel was stopped by three English frigates and boarded by a recruiting party. For two days the party remained on board, harassing passengers and crew alike, then pressed all the deckhands save one, and 48 of the passengers, into the British navy. Tone was wearing trousers rather than the breeches normal for a gentleman, and he too would have been pressed but for the screams of Mary and Matilda. Such incidents were frequent and had recently provoked an official complaint from the American government.[4] Tone reflected on the tragic irony of those who may have fled from 'the tyranny of a bad government at home' only to fall under a more severe tyranny on the seas. 'So much for this just and necessary war', he commented in Voltairean strain to Russell.[5] He discovered that 210 of the 220 men on board one of the frigates were Irish, which added weight to his inflated view of English naval dependence on Irish manpower.[6]

On 1 August they sailed up the Delaware River, past well-tended fields and orchards and busy trading and milling centres.[7] They landed at Wilmington, where the Tones put up at one of the town's more famous inns, at Third and Market Streets. It was kept by Captain Patrick O'Flynn, an Irishman and friend of George Washington. O'Flynn was something of a character and his tavern was a popular meeting place for those active in politics. Here Tone would have heard of the bitter controversy dividing the nation over the proposed Jay treaty with England; Wilmington citizens voted overwhelmingly against it at a town meeting on 5 August.[8] At Wilmington the Tones were befriended by an elderly Yorkshireman, General Humpton, who had fought on the American side during the Revolution and who helped them get settled in Philadelphia.

Philadelphia—the American capital since 1790—was an elegant if crowded, expensive and overconfident city. The dominant merchant class, with its country estates and elegant town houses, had a lavish life-style more akin to that of Ireland's aristocracy than Tone's merchant friends in Belfast and Dublin.[9] In 1795 the eastern United States was experiencing an unusually hot summer. The low, flat position of the city, surrounded by marshes as yet undrained, made the air peculiarly unhealthy. The threat of yellow fever was ever present, not helped by the refuse which blocked the streets in the bustling commercial centre around the port and market on Second Street.[10] Outbreaks of the disease occurred every summer, but that of 1793–4, which had carried off a tenth of Philadelphia's population, had been well publicised in Ireland. Tone worried about such things, and the heat and implicit threat must have added to the discomfiture so evident in his writings of these months. He complains frequently of headaches caused by the intense heat and of inability to work. It added to his unfavourable opinion of the nation's capital city, which he voiced in a letter to Russell on 7 August. The countryside was indeed beautiful, but in a picture-book way, devoid of character; 'like a beautiful scene in a theatre, the effect at proper distance is admirable but it will not bear a minute inspection'. The

people he thought 'not to be amiable; they seem selfish and interested, and they do fleece us émigrés, at a most unmerciful rate'.[11]

He sought out Reynolds, who was now well established in Philadelphia and able to practise his profession, and through him learnt
of Rowan's arrival from France some weeks earlier. Rowan had suffered imprisonment under the Terror. He had been liberated and
helped by Irish sympathisers within the French Ministry of Foreign
Affairs (notably by the Kerryman Nicholas Madgett), only to be
caught up in the confusion and recrimination of the Thermidorean
period. But he had good contacts in both French and American political circles, and it was through him that Tone was befriended by the
governor of Pennsylvania, Thomas Mifflin, and, more immediately,
was introduced to the French minister in Philadelphia, Pierre Adet.[12]

II

It was not the best of times for a recently arrived British subject to
call on the French minister to the United States. The war between
France and England had polarised American politics. Though the
United States was neutral in the conflict, France expected her moral
support under an existing treaty. But if the Democratic Republicans
and public opinion generally favoured the French, the dominant
Federalist Party was pro-British, and the Federalist John Jay had
been sent to London in the autumn of 1794 with extensive powers to
negotiate a treaty. Theoretically President Washington was above
partisan politics, and the pro-French Republican from Virginia,
James Monroe, was sent as the new American minister to France to
assuage French displeasure at the negotiations.

Monroe at first acted indiscreetly, with an emotional speech in
favour of the French Revolution. Nevertheless, at a time of deteriorating relations between America and France, he was probably
the only minister acceptable to Paris, and he scored some notable
diplomatic victories despite the growing tension. By late 1795, however, his position was becoming untenable. He was not kept informed of Jay's progress, and the secrecy with which Jay and his
fellow Federalists conducted their negotiations aggravated Monroe's
sense of isolation, fanned French suspicions, and brought Monroe to
the verge of siding with the French against his Federalist masters
in Philadelphia. Although the terms of Jay's treaty were known in
government circles by March 1795, Monroe only learnt of them in
the following November.[13]

The terms of the treaty were leaked by a furious Adet to the
fiercely Republican Philadelphia paper the Aurora, abstracted in the
issue for 29 June, and published in full in a pamphlet four days later.[14]
They were even worse than opponents had expected. There was

no mention of Britain's many infractions of the 1783 peace treaty; American ports were not to be used by the ships or privateers of Britain's enemies, thereby contravening the treaty with France; the clause permitting goods bound for French ports to be taken off American ships effectively sanctioned continued British naval attacks on American shipping, while the running sore of impressment was not addressed. There were some commercial gains; but they seemed trivial by comparison and there was an immediate outcry against this, possibly America's most unpopular treaty. Anti-treaty meetings were convened in all the major cities and Jay claimed with much justification that he found his way home by the light of the many effigies of him burnt by protesters.[15]

But the *Aurora* leak was quickly followed by a major political scandal engineered by Britain and discreditable to France and the Republicans alike. In one of its many raids on American ships in 1794, Britain had captured the correspondence of Adet's predecessor, Joseph Fauchet, suggesting that he had had some shady financial dealings with the anti-treaty US Secretary of State, Edmund Randolph. The letters, however, were only released in July 1795 at the height of the Jay treaty controversy. The treaty had been passed by the required two-thirds majority in the Federalist-dominated Senate in late June. But President Washington wavered until the Randolph–Fauchet scandal removed lingering doubts, and he formally ratified the treaty in August.[16] Adet, unlike his predecessors, had little faith in American friendship.[17] At first he demanded to be recalled by Paris when news broke of the treaty's ratification, then settled down to undermine the Federalists, with the assistance of the Republicans.[18] Adet's changing attitude to Tone must be seen against this background.

Their first meeting on the morning of 10 August was polite but strained. Tone presented a letter of introduction from Rowan and his certificates from the Catholic Committee, the United Irishmen and the Belfast Volunteers. Though the two men were exactly the same age, thirty-two, Tone was a novice compared with this former French colonial secretary and envoy to Geneva. Tone explained his work with the Catholics and the reasons for his flight. He had been 'instructed by his fellow citizens to inform the French minister in the United States about the situation in Ireland and the opinions of its people'. He told Adet of their desire to break their chains, and declare their independence from England, and represented the advantages which would result for the French republic. Adet asked him to draw up a memoir to this effect.

But Tone was dissatisfied with their meeting. He returned to the inn at which he and his family were staying and worked through the hottest time of the day[19] to produce a lengthy report elucidating points he had made that morning. The document is yet another sign that Tone was more effective on paper than in speech. Attaching a printed report of Jackson's trial, he drew Adet's attention to Vaughan's statement that a French invasion would find little support in England and contrasted this with his own claims for Ireland. Clearly Adet had expressed scepticism. Tone's letter betrays some irritability at this perceived blindness and he makes a powerful, if somewhat overstated, case to the contrary. 'I beg leave to mention to you that I presume England is the enemy the most formidable to France of the whole confederacy against her, as well by her money as by her navy.' Yet France seemed unaware of the fact that two-thirds of that navy was manned by Irishmen. Since 1793 Ireland had supplied 180,000 men to England's armed forces and much of her provisions. If Ireland withheld her support, England could scarcely continue the war. Were Ireland to join with France, England would be destroyed and 'the Liberty of Mankind' assured. To invade England would be folly, since its populace would oppose any such attempt, whereas an invasion of Ireland would be supported by seven-eighths of its people, 'the Aristocracy' alone opposing. The British forces in Ireland, Tone claimed, were largely composed of Irish militia (17,500 of a total 30,000), the remainder 'of the ruins of the British army from Flanders, new levies and several regiments of Scotch fencibles...in a most wretched state as to appearance and discipline.' If France sent a large supply of arms, ammunition and artillery, of which there was a great shortage in Ireland, 'some money until the Irish can make arrangements for themselves' and not less than 20,000 troops, France would be sure of detaching Ireland from England.

Tone was right about the weakness of England's military position in Ireland. Militia and fencibles were increasingly replacing regulars removed for war service overseas.[20] His letter also contains a detailed programme for subverting Britain's armed forces and the clearest statement he was to make of the anticipated political outcome in Ireland. Written in haste, and within days of his arrival in America, the letter contrasts sharply with the half-baked statement to Jackson and testifies to the impact of the discussions Tone had with the United Irishmen, notably those in Belfast, prior to his departure. The militiamen were to be won over by a mixture of material reward (not least by promotion of the more intelligent to commissions in an Irish army) and emotional appeals 'addressing proper proclamations to them on the enormity of fighting against their own country and relations to which Irishmen are very much attached'.

Similar proclamations would be issued to the Irish in the British navy, urging them to capture their ships and return with them to

Ireland, and offering increased pay, the right to choose their own officers, and a fair division of prize money in an Irish navy. Even if such proclamations failed, 'it would raise such a spirit of suspicion and distrust and such a foundation for mutiny and desertion in the British navy, as must very materially embarrass her operations at sea'. Tone's claim that two-thirds of the British navy was composed of Irishmen was certainly exaggerated. But it was a common exaggeration at the time and no government official was able to put a precise figure to the numbers of Irish in the fleet.[21] It was indeed the large Irish element in the British navy which was attracting attention in Paris,[22] and the series of mutinies which erupted in 1797–8 were to show the accuracy of much of what Tone claimed.

But such a propaganda campaign was to be conducted by a provisional Irish government, with France's role confined to that of military assistance. The French should publish a proclamation immediately upon arrival, Tone wrote, assuring the Irish that they came as allies, 'to subvert the ancient tyranny of their oppressors', establish freedom of religion, abolish all unjust distinctions and 'oppressive establishments', assure protection of person and property to all who acted as good citizens, and announce 'the severest penalties' for those who adhered to the enemy. The proclamation should call on the Irish people to choose 'provisional deputies to frame a form of Government, and it should pledge the faith of the French Republic to guarantee that form, subject only to this condition, that it should be totally separated and independent of England'. There is a sense of urgency: if anything was to be done this was the critical moment. The people of Ireland are 'for the first time in six hundred years united among themselves and all sects and parties save the aristocracy and the rich join in the utmost hatred and abhorrence of England and an affectionate regard for the French Republic'. Having apologised for the haste of the document—'I find the intense heat of the climate so different from that I have been used to [that it] affects my head extremely'—Tone returned with it to Adet's residence.[23] Three days later he completed and delivered the fuller memoir requested by Adet at their meeting.

The new document reiterated many of the points already made in that drawn up for Jackson sixteen months previously[24] and in the letter of 10 August. Once again, however, it bore the imprint of Belfast. There was now a Scottish dimension to Tone's plans for revolution in Ireland, and he told of Scottish agents having been recently in Ireland to this end.[25] He represented the willingness of a Belfast merchant house to send provisions to France and fit out corsairs against England, and made enquiries on behalf of another manufacturer about establishing a cotton business in France. Tone likewise outlined the plight of his brother Matthew, who had been in prison in France since he left to join the French army in 1794.[26] It was that mixture of the public and private which characterised Tone's political career, and may well have clouded any sense of urgency, for Adet was unenthusiastic about Tone's suggestion that he should travel to France. But although Adet waited till October to send Tone's memoir to Paris, his covering letter was supportive. August and September were bad months for him. He had frequently complained of overwork and infrequent instructions from Paris, and the Randolph–Fauchet crisis was not the only one to break around the time of Tone's communications.[27] By the end of November, when Tone returned to see him, Adet's fury at England assured him a readier hearing.

III

Tone's letter of 10 August is the first evidence of a developing nationalism sharpened by exile. In the little group of Irish exiles gathered in Philadelphia (soon also to include Tandy), Tone was alone in his unwavering desire to return to Ireland.[28] It was a desire fashioned by his dislike for the American people. Tone's initial fears about the Americans were amply confirmed after several weeks' residence in Philadelphia. By September he had developed 'a most unqualified dislike' for its people. He thought them 'a selfish, churlish, unsocial race, totally absorbed in making money...half English, half Dutch, with the worst qualities of both countries'. They were 'the most disgusting race, eaten up with all the vice of commerce and that vilest of all pride, the pride of the purse'.[29] It was typical of Tone's black-and-white approach to things, though much of what he says of the nation's new capital is endorsed by contemporary commentators and subsequent historians.[30]

When he moved his family 25 miles west of Philadelphia, however, he thought the farmers (the ideal of the Democratic Republicans) equally objectionable. His main complaint against the Americans was that they were cultureless, but with their lack of deference and overweening confidence they were too insensitive to recognise it. 'In the country parts of Pennsylvania the farmers are extremely ignorant and boorish, particularly the Germans and their descendants who abound. There is something too in the Quaker manners extremely unfavourable to anything like polished society.' However sympathetic he was to the plight of the poor, Tone was part of an educated élite, a culture snob in many ways, and he was offended by those who did not know their place in the cultural hierarchy. The swaggering confidence of American youths disgusted him only marginally less than the lower-class Irish in America who seemed to have

acquired the bad attitudes of the natives. 'They are as boorish and
ignorant as the Germans, as uncivil and uncouth as the Quakers, and
as they have ten times more animal spirits than both they are much
more actively troublesome.'[31] Both Tone and Matilda were concerned at the thought of bringing up children 'in the boorish ignorance of the peasants about us', of giving them an education which
would only make them discontented in a society 'wherein learning
and talents were useless'.[32]

Other British visitors reacted similarly. Edward Thornton,
British vice-consul in Philadelphia, was struck by the degree of
national vanity among 'the common people', which displayed itself
in 'vulgarity and a perfect absence on all occasions of ceremony and
respect'. Philadelphia, lacking a theatre until 1794—and even then
acquiring one which resembled Dublin's Astley's Circus more than
the Crow Street theatre—Thornton found 'more barren of amusement or novelty' than anywhere he had ever visited, an observation
borne out by the city's newspapers.[33] From a different political
perspective, Thomas Cooper, the Manchester reformer, found a
'literary class' as yet undeveloped in America, but in more charitable
vein, discovered much good sense, if little learning 'in the European
sense of the word'.[34] For Tone, who had felt so ill at ease in Ballinasloe, whose diaries and correspondence contain as much literary
and theatrical commentary as political, America must indeed have
seemed a cultural desert. The rarefied atmosphere in which this man
of letters had developed and operated is nowhere better illustrated
than by its loss in America.

But it was for his little daughter, Maria, that Tone fretted most.
The idea of a young women of 'sensibility and tenderness' married to
'a clown without delicacy or refinement...tormented me beyond
enduring; and I am sure no unfortunate lover, in the paroxysm of
jealousy ever looked forward with greater horror to the union of his
Mistress with his rival'. Death itself he thought preferable. A father's
understandable worries aside, Tone's agitation on this matter is as
revealing of his attitude towards women as the total omission from
his journals of references to politicised women like Mary Ann
McCracken, though he was a frequent visitor at her home. It was
Eliza Martin all over again, beatified yet role-imprisoned.[35]

America was seared into Tone's memory. In France he could not
recollect or speak of the country without making almost fanatical
criticisms. It became the sort of hell on earth to which he and his
family might be consigned if his French mission failed, and that
feeling undoubtedly dictated his equally exaggerated bias in favour
of France. There was clearly great unhappiness in America, which
Matilda likewise felt, and in the 1820s her clinical precision in

excising Tone's many unfavourable references to the country suggests a deeper motive than the fact of her own residence in America
at the time. In 1795 Tone pined for his friends in Ireland and romanticised the homeland he had left. He vowed never to take American
citizenship or to become involved in American politics, although
Reynolds was in the process of doing both. Tone's long letters to
Russell, detailing his disillusionment, had such an effect on his friend
that in 1802, alone of the Irish state prisoners, Russell refused to
contemplate America as the place to which they might be liberated.[36]

IV

Tone was a man given to instant impressions and delayed reassess-
ments. His reactions to America owed not a little to inflated expectations and might have mellowed in time, as Rowan's did. But his
response to the political and consitutional system is more complicated. With its plethora of coffee-houses, incestuous political gossip
and fiercely partisan press, Philadelphia was not so unlike the world
he had left behind in Dublin. Yet Tone had not liked the Dublin
coffee-houses, and he found distasteful the air of intrigue, conspiracy
and sheer vitriol which characterised these teething years of America's
party system. What may have been acceptable in the old corrupt
monarchies was objectionable in the first working democratic republic, and once again we see that purism in Tone which preferred the
openness of attacks by the Parisian mob to the shuffling pettiness of
the Dublin rioters, and outright confrontation to Keogh's curtain
compromise.

Tone arrived in France in 1796 a confirmed republican in the sense
that the term was understood in Ireland thereafter. His American
experience was fundamental to the crystallisation of ideas only half
formulated before he left Ireland. At the height of the conflict with
the grand juries in 1792, Tone had published an analysis of the
American Constitution in the *Northern Star*. He set out clearly and
accurately its main clauses, with little commentary other than to
highlight those elements which placed it apart from Britain's so-
called 'Glorious Constitution in Church and State.' These were
chiefly the debarment of office-holders from seeking election to
Congress, legislative controls over the executive, the opening up of
the franchise to owners of property other than land, freedom of
religion and speech and the right of assembly and petitioning.[37] The
contrast with the system he was fighting then was so blatant as to
arouse unreal expectations of what he would find in America and
proportionate disillusionment when the reality proved otherwise.
However perfect its written Constitution appeared, in America he
found a manipulation of power similar to that in Ireland. The virtues

of freedom of religion and speech, which had appeared so laudable in 1792 and which he would have seen in action in 1795, no longer seemed important in the face of the struggle he perceived between aristocracy and democracy. In this reduction of the issues at stake, Tone was fast becoming a zealot.[38]

Although Tone's company in Philadelphia was largely that of the exiled Irish, the Irish-Americans were an important force among the Democratic Republicans and were particularly disliked by the Federalists. The Republicans saw a natural affinity between Ireland's struggle against British 'tyranny' and their own against the Anglo-phile Federalists.[39] Tone devoured the newspapers (notably the highly partisan *Aurora*), haunted the bookshops and quickly acquired a good knowledge of American political rhetoric. Friendship networks and natural inclination brought him quickly into the Republican fold.

American historians have become polarised in a long-running debate about the political philosophy of this, the formative period of the American party system. The argument centres on the respective contributions of Lockean liberalism (the idea of responsible self-interest leading to social good) and classical republicanism (with its ethos of civic virtue, the good of the commonweal, restraint on private interests, and representative government).[40] The niceties of the debate need not concern us here. But in 1795 the Democratic Republicans held the high moral ground as self-proclaimed prophets of pure republicanism, and in the conflict between them and the Federalists Tone encountered the rhetoric of classical republicanism applied to a situation which mirrored the one he had left behind, and delineated it far more clearly.

To the Republicans, the Federalists, with their undisguised attachment to titles and executive power, were tories, neo-monarchists and aristocrats. In their programme for taxation and commerce, they were the party of big money against the small man and the farmer in particular, and hostile to the rights of individual states. In foreign policy they were pro-British and anti-French. They were, in the Republicans' most effective rhetoric, a faction working against the general good, a commercial aristocracy operating through corruption and influence. Whereas the Republicans claimed to believe in the right of informed public will to dictate the governing process, the Federalists distrusted the people, saw democracy as the route to demagoguery and license, and supported strong government and executive power. With Federalists dominating the executive and the Senate, Republican rhetoric struck home.[41] It touched on sensitivities left over from before the Revolutionary War, and given the widespread public opposition to Federalist policies, even an observer more impartial than Tone might have been forgiven for viewing the crisis of that year as a contest between democracy and executive tyranny.[42]

Republican rhetoric utilised a language that was immediately recognisable to Tone. In America he saw unfolding that same struggle between aristocracy (by which he meant those who monopolised power against the interests of the people) and democracy, which he now considered was in progress in Ireland. And that aristocracy was as corrupt, anti-French and pro-British as the one in Ireland. Tone wrote of his feelings to Russell on 1 September. The conflict over the Jay treaty (though he thought it a dishonourable betrayal of the Americans' French ally) was not the real issue. It was rather whether aristocracy as a governing principle would prevail over democracy. 'What is it to me whether it is an Aristocracy of merchants or of peers, elected or hereditary? It is still an Aristocracy incompatible with the existence of genuine liberty.' In pursuit of wealth this 'Mercantile Peerage' had sacrificed the interests of the nation, abandoned the friend (France) to whom she owed her existence and adhered to her 'ancient Tyrant' (England).[43] 'I see more clearly than ever, or more properly the theory is now supported by the fact, that Liberty must destroy Aristocracy under every possible modification, or surrender her existence.' The American Constitution, and the form of government erected under it, should have neutralised 'the poison from Royalty and Aristocracy'. And yet the aristocratic part of that Constitution (in the President and Senate) had undermined its democratic element. Washington Tone still admired as the father of American independence, but he subscribed to the increasingly bitter attack by the Democratic Republicans on his Presidency. 'Power long exercised would corrupt an Angel. I do believe from my very soul that Washington is a very honest man. . . . But he is a high-flying aristocrat. . . . When people once desert principles and attach themselves to men, adieu to all public virtue.' Tone saw in Washington the principle of royalty sustaining aristocracy, and in a particularly notable incident of the Philadelphia plutocracy influencing the outcome of the campaign for the Jay treaty, he saw a corruption operating 'that would do honour to the Old Countries'.[44]

The language is unmistakably that of the Democratic Republicans, much of it taken directly from the *Aurora*. Indeed Tone's passion for political information is reflected in his purchase of Randolph's lengthy and controversial *Vindication* even though it had been extracted by many of the newspapers. The American political debate had brought into sharper focus the situation in Ireland: 'if I wanted anything to confirm me in my political creed, [what he saw in America] would completely furnish it.' If he was already beginning to see in Ireland an aristocratic faction, operating against the interests of the people, and the whole orchestrated by England, the Republican press in America, with its daily dose of Anglophobia, crystallised and simplified his vision.[45] Commenting on the differences between the visible affluence of the Americans, their cheap government and apparently light taxation, Tone loses his temper at the thought of the financial burdens imposed by the monarchical system at home: 'I have not the temper to go on. These are the things that make men Republicans...and this will be yet, with God's help, the system of Ireland and of Europe.'[46]

At some stage Tone was taken up by that most irrepressible (and intriguing) of the Republicans, John Beckley. As Clerk of the House of Representatives, Beckley was privy to information which he consistently leaked to a circle of key Republican leaders, notably Jefferson, Madison, and, more immediately important for Tone, James Monroe. Beckley was something of a scandalmonger, and his incessant correspondence fuelled Republican mistrust of the Federalist administration. He was intensely anti-British, referred disparagingly to the Federalists as the 'British party', fed the newspapers with much of their anti-British propaganda and contributed to Monroe's growing sense of bitterness that the Federalists' Anglophilia was making his position in France untenable. As the only Republican left in office by the end of 1795, Monroe's days were indeed numbered. It is against this background that Beckley's espousal of Tone should be seen and it was via his coded correspondence with Monroe that Tone effected his entry to France in 1796.[47]

V

After the discouraging interview with Adet in August, Tone turned his attention to settling his family. The expense of lodging in Philadelphia was crippling. By the third week in August they had moved 25 miles west of Philadelphia, first to the small town of Westchester —a town of some fifty houses, a court-houe, gaol and Roman Catholic church—then to Downingstown, some 8 miles further to the east of Brandywine Creek.[48]

Tone was assisted in his search for a home by General Humpton, and almost certainly by another new friend, General Thomas Mifflin, the popular governor of Pennsylvania. Former Quartermaster of the Continental army, Mifflin was one of those military figures with whom Tone so frequently identified, a larger-than-life man, who lived far beyond his means and was noted for his lavish hospitality. Tone would have been a frequent caller at his offices in the State House in Chestnut Street (now Independence Hall), his town residence at 248 High Street, and his country house at the Falls of the

Schuylkill. Rowan too had been adopted by the genial general. A moderate Republican, though as violently pro-French as any, Mifflin was successfully re-elected as governor in October 1795. Through him Tone was able to retain his respect for the American Constitution generally, even if he had lost it for its people.[49]

On 31 August he returned to Philadelphia to draw his bill of exchange on Messrs William Smith & Co, and to begin the search for a more permanent home. Smith dissuaded him from his initial plan of becoming a frontiersman in the West. Land was cheap. But relations with the Indians remained bad, and such areas were prey to continuous attack. 'As I have no great talent for the tomahawk', Tone wrote to Russell, 'I have therefore given up going into the woods.'[50] Rowan was critical of American attitudes to Indians and slaves.[51] If Tone felt the same, he did not say so in any of his letters that reached their destination. The Republican press was filled with stories that Britain was inciting the Indians against the settlers. Can Tone's tendency always to believe the worst of England account for his silence?

The original American colonies in the East were expensive to live in. Tone had not anticipated having to make such an outlay, and contemplated returning to the law for livelihood. He had after all a personal recommendation from Todd Jones to Dr Edwards, Chief Justice of the Court of Common Pleas at Philadelphia and a Republican sympathiser. It may well have been Edwards's absence in Europe which quickly closed the law option.[52] Tone thought of settling in Rhode Island, then at Winchester in Virginia, and also looked into the Carolinas and Georgia. Travelling in America was notoriously difficult; even the roads between New York and Philadelphia—by far the best in the country—were bad, and the taverns little better. They were infested by bugs, and most were run by military officers, whose insatiable curiosity added further to the inconvenience by an intensive cross-examination of the traveller.[53]

After 'diverse excursions, on foot and in the stage-wagons', Tone finally settled on Princeton, New Jersey, as a desirable area, the attraction of 'a college and some good society'[54] swaying his decision as much as the price of property. Princeton was a handsome town of some eighty dwellings and a Presbyterian church. It was overlooked by the stone-built and much-acclaimed Nassau Hall College, which still had a good library, despite extensive destruction during the Revolutionary War. The town was set in picturesque wooded surroundings, with large black-walnut trees and plantations of Italian mulberries for the culture of silkworms. The area was also noted for its abundance of partridge and wood pigeon, and for its cider presses. The farmers were mainly Dutch and German, 'being very industrious and intent on making money', and it was undoubtedly here that Tone developed his dislike of Dutch farming people. New Jersey was also one of the few northern states to have retained slavery.[55]

At first Tone agreed to purchase a plantation of 100 acres.[56] But the Dutch owner raised the asking price of £750, and Tone 'broke off the treaty in rage'. Eventually he agreed with a Captain Leonard on a plantation of 180 acres, 'beautifully situated within two miles of Princeton, and half of it under timber'. Tone thought it good value at £1,180—and correctly so, with land in the state selling for £8 to £10 an acre.[57] The soil was light and sandy, and though he thought the buildings 'mean', he proposed building 'a mansion' the following year. Ninety acres were already cleared, which he thought as much as he would be able to manage. On 8 October he wrote to Russell with an agricultural shopping list: '20 lbs Lucerne seed, 30 lbs sainfoin, 5 lbs common furze seed, 2–3 quarts haw stones'. Tone was about to remedy Thomas Cooper's main complaint of American farming habits: the absence of proper enclosures and hedging.[58] 'Take care that the seeds are fresh and do get them packed up carefully in the sheet lead which comes round the tea [which Robert Getty would supply]. . . and have the whole enclosed in a small deal box, pitched in all the seams and watertight', which last Henry Joy McCracken would see to. In the same box Russell was to send the transactions of the Bath Society, the linen given Tone by McDonnell but which he had forgotten to bring, and Miller's gardening dictionary. He returned to Princeton two weeks later to sign the deeds and hired a small house for the winter, furnishing it 'frugally and decently' and moving his family there from Pennsylvania. 'I fitted up my study and began to think my lot was cast to be an American farmer.'

But his mind began to flit to future plans. He chafed at the thought of enforced idleness that winter, and proposed forming a farmers' club in the spring. A small annual subscription would go on purchasing an agricultural library, importing seeds from Europe for experiment, introducing produce from other states and trying them in New Jersey, and perhaps awarding honorary premiums. But not for Tone anything quite so restricted. He also proposed introducing 'fairs and markets on the Irish system', for he was surprised to find that none existed in America. The thought of Russell's reaction, however, interrupted his flight of fancy. 'I daresay you are amused at the idea of my being the father of a farming club after assisting in framing societies of so very different a nature, but I see no way of being useful here.'

Initial overtures proved discouraging. He therefore switched to another project, first outlined in his 1 September letter: that of writing the 'Memoirs of the Catholic Committee' and sending them to Chambers for publication. Though, as he said, 'men are very soon forgot when out of sight, perhaps a work with my name may call the public attention a little. I shall be very moderate, and I suppose I need not say to you, strictly and rigorously adhesive to truth.' He hoped 'with a copious appendix' it would make a large octavo volume, and if printed by subscription at half a guinea, that his friends in Belfast would exert themselves on his behalf and 'my old Catholic noble and approved good masters would not neglect me. I hope I may, if I succeed, get some character and some money, both of which will be very acceptable to me, for I am entirely too poor for America'.[59]

It was symptomatic of his apathy about American affairs, which had set in very soon after his arrival. His politics did not travel well and he admits 'the irresistible affection by which man is drawn to his native soil and how flat and uninteresting the parties and the politics of other countries appear'. Loss of friendship becomes linked with loss of homeland. In exile all the emotionalism and chauvinism of modern nationalism comes to the fore. He reads about escalating Defender troubles, and while he gives little thought to America's unfortunates, he agonises over the misery of these Irishmen driven thus to sacrifice their lives. He never reconciled himself to permanent residence in America. 'I cannot look on this as my country,' he had written as early as 1 September, 'nor believe that some prosperous event may not yet recall us. . . . You have a country worth struggling for, whose value I never knew until I lost it.' Even the better experience of New Jersey, whose people he found 'lively and disengaged', had not reconciled him to exile. By the end of October he was speaking of his Irishness as 'inflexible'. 'My regret for the loss of my country is so mixed with opposite passions, with indignation, and with hope', that he is clearly only marking time till he can return.

Tone was experiencing that inability to accept exile which was to characterise the history of Irish emigration. He had not anticipated such a root attachment to the Irish soil, though there are signs of it in his early political writings. The man who had consciously avoided emotionalism now devotes page after page to laments for the loss of Irish friendship and society. The letters betray an unhappiness which is not evident before 1795, and there is perhaps more to his American interlude than we are told. The playful cynicism and sheer resilience of 'John Hutton' is gone and he now verges on the maudlin.

Loneliness, frustration, indignation and the new political clarity of an outsider imposes a retrospective pattern on his own past. He sees himself as the 'convenient scape-goat' of a contemptuous gentry,[60] condemned to 'a painful exile' for a cause, the 'emancipation' of his country, in which cause 'I may now say I was ready to devote my life'.[61] The unhappiness he has experienced in America is rationalised as part of that process of victimisation, of might defeating right.

I have not escaped so many dangers and subdued so many difficulties to get swamped at last here. One way or the other I shall make it out, and in the worst event I shall console myself with the reflection that I am suffering in consequence of an endeavour to serve my country to the very best of my ability, my judgement and my conscience. . . . I doubt not at all that the truth will finally prevail, but I am not like King Hezekiah, for I wish that this great thing *should* happen in my day: at all events I have the consolation to think that in my humble station I have, to *this hour*, left *no one measure untried* which was likely to forward what I consider was the cause of truth, justice and liberty.[62]

The unhappiness in America intensified Tone's emotional attachment to his friends in Belfast and Dublin, and it was in this frame of mind that he received letters from Russell, Keogh and the Simmses urging him to new efforts to negotiate with France. Apart from a handful of letters, Tone did not shower his friends with news, as did Reynolds and Tandy. It was Tandy's letters which first alerted the Irish authorities to the possibility of a 'seditious convention' forming in America. Even then Tone was not considered a danger. 'Tone keeps quite retired', McNally told the government. 'Study is his object and he is preparing a work for the press.' It was under cover of such assumptions that Tone was to carry out quite devastating secret diplomacy in France before the authorities were aware of his presence there.[63]

VI

The background to the letters of September 1795—received by Tone in late November—were the worst Defender troubles since 1793. Tone was surprised to read that they had even extended into his home county of Kildare, hitherto so peaceful. He read of these Defenders swearing to join the French and although he thought the troubles a senseless waste of life, he considered the Defenders 'fellow-sufferers' and wrote asking Russell for information on the outcome of their trials.[64] The letters from Russell and from William and Robert Simms expressed anxiety that the troubles would simply fill the country with military and destroy the nascent revolutionary movement. The United Irish Society was spreading rapidly through parts of Ulster, and hope now centred on French assistance. Even the Catholics thought further petitioning fruitless. But the time was not yet ripe for a French invasion, and considerable disquiet was expressed at a letter received from Reynolds, telling of his and Rowan's talks with the French, claiming that they were about to send a force and urging immediate action in Ireland. 'A wilder scheme was never thought of', wrote Tone's friends from Belfast, 'it would be the certain means of overrunning us with *Bulls* [i.e., British], which would prevent any idea of exertion. Despotism in the extreme, misery of every kind, and the banishment or death of all our best friends, would be the result.' But since they were sure Tone had spoken with the French more recently, they hoped all such ideas would be dropped until they could guarantee internal support for an invasion.[65]

Mrs Rowan disliked most of her husband's United Irish colleagues, and after the Jackson episode she considered Tone the 'archdeceiver...[whose] wicked principles and artful manners have destroyed us'. She was not at all pleased to find him and Rowan together again in Philadelphia. But in Ireland it was Rowan who was considered to have acted irresponsibly, and the September letters from Belfast were not the only sign that Tone was considered the more level-headed.[66]

It was, however, Keogh's letter which determined Tone to seek another audience with Adet. Keogh assured Tone that he lived in the memory of those who had been 'worthy of your friendship' and wondered if America recognised 'genius when it flies to her shores'. He asked why Tone had not answered an earlier letter (Tone had not received it), and assured him that his friends the Catholics had turned their backs on the politicians and would no longer settle for halfmeasures. He spoke a great deal of 'friendship', reminded Tone of their last conversation and hoped like Washington he would quit the plough when his country called.

> How often have we anticipated *your return* to your friends—to your country?...*I am sanguine in my expectations* to see you and your family live in the country you love, suitable to your genius and your patriotism. I am growing old...do not wonder then, if I should wish ardently that you may arrange your affairs, so as to *return to us, and if not soon, it may be too late for me*, perhaps even for yourself....Your old companions of the Sub-committee, are as you left them. I saw MacCormick this day, for some time. His wishes for your return fully *coincide* with *mine*, and he thinks that it will not be your fault, and that you will omit nothing, consistent with principles, for so fair and honorable an object. And I own that I have such an opinion, let me say experience of you, that I think you cannot fail to succeed in any attempt in the line of your profession.... *Once more*, Tone, *remember*, and *execute* your *garden* conversation.[67]

Given Tone's state of mind, his longing for friends and home, and the beginnings of a sense of destiny, Keogh's letter was a powerful mix, even without the heavily emphasised instructions. Financial worries had continued to dog his life in America, and if he needed any further encouragement to leave for France, William Simms offered it in the form of a substantial loan. When Tone returned to see Adet, he was therefore able to reject the Frenchman's offer of financial assistance, and with it the obligations it might entail.[68] There was little doubt what course of action Tone would take. Once again friendship was launching him down a road which, left to himself, he might not have pursued. He admitted as much in France some months later. 'I had very little expectation of success the day I left Sandy Hook, and in fact I came merely to discharge a duty.'[69]

If Tone suffered in America, Matilda's lot was worse. In a revealing letter to Russell some months later, she told of her unhappiness, ill health and lack of comfort there. Travel was difficult and tiring enough, but worse with the children, and her sadness after Tone finally left for France was only relieved by visits from Reynolds and Tandy. We rarely hear her speak except at turning-points for Tone, when her firmness and ability to endure hardship always allowed him to abandon family commitments in pursuit of his unconventional career. Matilda though still young was tough. We know that from family evidence and from her few surviving letters. She did not hold much with letter-writing, thought it 'idle' if not strictly necessary, and was sometimes almost hurtfully blunt. But she shared Tone's political opinions and in moments of possible weakness her views pushed him on.[70] So it was in November 1795. Having read the letters from Ireland, she and Mary strengthened his resolve to leave for France, and the next morning he set off from Princeton for Philadelphia.

He showed Adet the letters and was surprised to find his reception quite different from that of August. Rowan had written to Madgett in August and Madgett had been urging on his employers the usefulness of the Irish exiles in America. From the dates of Madgett's communications, however, it is clear that they had little to do with Adet's change of opinion. Nor can the government in Paris have had time to reply to his October dispatch. Rather Tone owed his warm reception to Adet's own belief that the pro-British party in America had to be subverted. In an angry and bitter dispatch of 2 December Adet outlined his new thinking to the French government. Public protest against the Jay treaty was subsiding. Why, he asks in exasperation, is the French government allowing itself to be cajoled by America while it negotiates away French rights with the British? Why has he been left without instructions for eight months when the situation has changed so dramatically? Why wait on events? Why not make them happen? Over the next year this is precisely what he did, joining forces with Beckley to undermine the Federalists in the forthcoming Presidential elections.

But it was his frustrated anger against Britain (so obvious in this December dispatch) which caused Adet to see Tone as something of a gift from heaven, and he approved his mission to the French government. Beckley, already in on the secret, wrote in code to Monroe, explaining that Tone was 'an agent from Ireland in whom you may confide. His object is to obtain of France aid in favor of his distressed country...his name is Theobald Wolfe Tone. He is the friend of Hamilton Rowan and a person in whom his countrymen fully confide'.[71] Benjamin Franklin Bache, editor of the *Aurora*, was likewise involved and Tone would later use him as a channel for correspondence from France.[72]

There had been problems in communicating with Ireland. Tone therefore sent to Princeton for his brother Arthur, gave him instructions to inform Neilson, Simms, Russell, Keogh and McCormick of his intended voyage to France, and to tell everyone else (especially his parents) that he had settled in Princeton. Arthur was then embarked on 10 December on board the *Susannah*, bound for Belfast, where he arrived the following January.[73] Tone converted his property into bank stock, gave a general power of attorney to his wife, had a final interview with Adet, and spent his last day in Philadelphia with his friends and fellow exiles, Reynolds, Rowan and Tandy. He and Rowan then set off for Princeton, arriving on 13 December. Tone, Matilda and Mary sat up late talking, and he left for New York at four the next morning, astonished by the steadiness of the two women. On the 16th he arrived in New York and booked a passage to France on board the *Jersey*. The following day his career as republican agent commenced. He reopened his journal—dormant since 1793—signing himself. 'James Smith', the new identity he was to retain until the last weeks of his life.[74] The unadventurous *nom de guerre* was not his personal choice, but imposed by the immediate availability of a passport in that name.[75] He sailed on 1 January. The previous day he received a letter from Matilda telling him she was pregnant. She had deliberately kept the information from him in order not to sway his decision.[76]

VII

MISSION TO FRANCE
(1796–1797)

21
Republican 'Ambassador' in Paris

Tone arrived at Le Havre on 2 February 1796 after a stormy winter passage. He carried coded introductions from Beckley and Adet but no formal instructions or accreditation from the United Irishmen. He was therefore given total freedom to conduct his mission according to his own guidelines, and proved an effective negotiator. Tone's negotiations in Paris helped shape France's Irish policy for many years to come, and played a crucial role in securing French backing for a major invasion attempt at the end of 1796. Yet his methods were singular. They could easily have backfired had they not accommodated so well the character of the Directory—the regime which governed France from September 1795 to October 1799. Tone's natural single-mindedness and impatience of red tape brought him almost inevitably to the notice of the main policy-makers, and events took over thereafter.

I

After the bloodshed and turmoil of the Terror and the Thermidorean period, France in 1796 had acquired a moderate, but constitutionally weak, regime in the Directory. National fatigue expressed itself in widespread public apathy. The very constitution inaugurating the Directory encapsulated its weakness. The five members were elected by the two legislative councils which maintained control of finances. A restricted franchise and the annual replacement of a third of their members brought into the legislative councils royalist or Jacobin elements who were hostile to the very existence of the regime. Deprived of legislative and financial teeth, the Directory in time became the prisoner of the military, on which it depended for the many coups designed to restore the political balance. The Directory inherited an empty treasury, valueless paper money, a collapse in the social services, national divisions and an all-engrossing war.

Of the five Directors, La Réveillière-Lépeaux, the well-intentioned and virtuous disciple of Rousseau, and Letourneur, the former civil servant and cipher of Carnot, were nonentities. The three 'matadors of the Directory' were Carnot, former member of the Committee of Public Safety, Reubell, the Germanic lawyer from Alsace and a fierce anti-Jacobin, and Barras, the dissolute aristocrat from Provence, whose debauchery and corruption lent to the regime an air of sexual licence which repelled Tone. Reubell and Carnot controlled foreign affairs and war respectively, and had wider powers over the conduct of these matters than any regime since 1789. But the two men disliked each other intensely. Reubell, arthritic, irritable, brusque and sarcastic, never forgot that Carnot had been one of those responsible for his disgrace under the Terror. Carnot, sharp-tongued, irascible and vindictive, likewise remembered that Reubell and Barras had voted against him in that May 1795 session of the Convention when he had been saved by the famous cry of one deputy: 'He organised victory!' Yet both men were work-horses, with an enormous grasp of the detail of administration, and each had enough respect for the other to be able to co-operate on important issues.

The weaknesses of the Directory are often exaggerated. In France Tone found a nation bent on living normally, with theatres full, food cheap and little of the fear which had greeted Rowan only a year earlier. He also noted high church attendance and non-observance of the *décadi*, with general abstention from work on Sundays. Can he have been so besotted with the regime which adopted him as to be blind to its faults? There is indeed an element of this, and Tone found admirable that very bourgeois ethos so criticised by historians.[2] But what struck him most was the sheer normality of life in France under the Directory, when even such a determined Francophile as himself had been led to expect otherwise. This indeed is the period's greatest claim to respect. It witnessed an effort to return to normality after the excesses of the previous four years. If the people were apathetic, it was a token of that very normality. No one was executed for *incivisme* under the Directory.[3]

Apart from the good roads and the apparently abundant crops he saw in the fields of Normandy as he travelled from Le Havre to Paris, Tone was impressed by the deference and sentimentality of the French, when he had read so much of their insubordinate and sanguinary nature. Instead he found servants 'remarkably civil, attentive, and humble' and the behaviour of the young men 'extremely decorous and proper'. He appreciated such things after America. At the theatre—which in Paris became his major diversion he was struck by the audiences' preference for the most banal and sentimental 'fable' to the stirring propaganda of revolutionary set pieces. They insisted on happy endings to Shakespeare's great tragedies, which Tone considered barbaric.

MARCH 21ST. Went to see '*Othello*', not translated, but only '*taken from the English*'. Poor Shakespear! I felt for him. The French

Tragedy is a pitiful performance, filled with false sentiment; the Moor whines most abominably, and Iago is a person of a very pretty morality. The author apologizes for softening the villainy of the latter character, as well as for saving the life of Desdemona, and substituting a happy termination in place of the sublime and terrible conclusion of the English Tragedy, by saying that the *Humanity* of the French Nation, and their *morality* would be shocked by such exhibitions. '*Marry come up indeed!—people's ears are sometimes the nicest part about them.*' I admire a Nation that will guillotine sixty people a day for months, men, women, and children, and cannot bear the catastrophe of a dramatic exhibition!...the French are more struck with any little incident of tenderness on the stage, a thousand times than the English, which is strange!—in short the French *are* a humane people, when they are not mad.[4]

The Directory had made efforts to use the theatre as a means of disseminating patriotic propaganda. Tone was witnessing its failure to do so, though he himself was entirely taken in by the revolutionary set pieces, devoting page after page to descriptions of the stage celebrations of revolutionary events and battles, and admitting to being reduced to tears by the spectacle.[5]

It is in his Paris journal that the picture of Tone as cultured man comes out most forcibly. He was a competent critic of theatre, ballet and opera, and his views on the strengths and weaknesses of the French stage would have found endorsement in contemporary reviews. The French he found incomparable in dance and costume, but less talented as actors and singers than the English. He admitted, however, that his standards were high, for he had seen Mrs Siddons perform, and this father of Irish republicanism could still long for a time when he might again see Sheridan's *School for Scandal* on an English stage. Opera he attended more often in Paris than the theatre, largely, he claimed, because the music was easier to follow than the French. Yet the operas he attended were all familiar pieces. Salieri's *Tarrari* he had seen twenty times before, even though he thought him very inferior to Gluck. He also spent time at the growing Parisian art collections 'ransacked' from recent military campaigns and was mesmerised by Le Brun's *Magdalen*, 'a production of consummate genius'.[6]

Reports of famine in France Tone now dismissed as propaganda. There was indeed a great shortage of white bread, but the coffee-houses were full, the coffee excellent and the wine copious, at times perhaps too copious. His carefully accounted lists of fare are so long and elaborate that Matilda and William Tone omit from the published *Life* as much as they leave in.[7] In truth Tone spent so much time alone in Paris that his meals were newsworthy. He pursued his mission with an ascetic singleness of purpose. Celebrations such as that in a Champs-Elysées cabaret on 20 April, after which he returned home 'in a state of considerable elevation', with 'near [three] bottles of Burgundy in my head', were rare.[8] But such journal entries did not quite measure up to Matilda's picture of someone who had sacrificed everything for his country. More small, and otherwise insignificant, detail is omitted from Tone's published Paris journal than elsewhere.

Nowhere is this more apparent than in his many references to French women. The puritanism of the Terror had confined women to traditional roles. Both prostitution and the political organisation of women were suppressed. But new legislation on divorce and a relaxation of sexual and social conventions gave women a new prominence under the Directory. In Paris the famous society hostesses, Madame Tallien, Joséphine de Beauharnais and Madame Récamier, were the models for a host of courtesans who revolved around the *nouveaux riches* and the political and military leaders of Directorial society. *Filles de joie* abounded, notably in the Palais Égalité (Palais Royal), the recognised centre of prostitution in the capital, near which Tone lived in his first months in Paris. The deputies and military who frequented the area were their particular clientèle. Tone's moral puritanism and his republican idealism were offended by it all, particularly at the blatant use of their position by the Republic's politicians to obtain sexual favours. 'I do not like to see the Republic pimp for Legendre', he noted of the liaison between Louis Legendre, member of the Convention and former Terrorist, with the beautiful actress Louise Contat, 'but people here mind these things much less than I do, for on this topic I have perhaps extravagant notions of delicacy and refinement, and their manners are horribly dissolute.'[9] Tone seems to have kept his virtue in Paris, though he admitted on one notable occasion, when his landlady made advances, that there was no great boast in it. Although he admired their quick wit and liveliness, he found French women generally ugly, any natural beauty being hidden by current fashions, particularly the general use of wigs.[10] Tone's Paris journal is an accurate reflection of life in this, Europe's most populous city. After Dublin, he was less disturbed than other foreign visitors by the noise, the overcrowding and the dirt, and the huge crowds in the streets and public gardens were very often his only company.[11]

All the Irish newspapers carried reports of French affairs. Tone had a remarkably good memory for detail and his Paris journal reveals a sound knowledge of French events, policies and people since

1789. His attitude to France was typical of the United Irishmen. He considered the French to be fighting for liberty everywhere and was prepared to overlook internal troubles as temporary irregularities. But the United Irishmen frowned silently upon the Terror and Tone disliked its excesses and bloodshed. Much of his anger at Legendre was provoked by the knowledge that he had been a member of the Terror's great police Committee of General Security. He considered the Revolutionary Tribunal 'that consummation of all iniquities and horror' and he was impressed to find trial by jury and the rule of law operating under the Directory.[12] He was distressed at the sight of the Temple prison, where Louis XVI had been held, even though at the time he had considered the King's execution *'necessary'* if regrettable.[13] On a visit to the Panthéon he admired the concept behind such a cenotaph, 'sacred to everything that is sublime, illustrious, and patriotic.' But he thought the French had 'overshot the mark,' having already jettisoned figures like Marat and Mirabeau. 'If we have a republic in Ireland, we must build a Pantheon, but we must not, like the French, be in too great a hurry to people it.'[14] His request that the French send a large force to Ireland was determined by his dislike of bloodshed. He wanted 'a war, not an insurrection', and hoped that even the aristocrats who opposed them might be spared and permitted to emigrate to England: 'for I am like Parson Adams in Fielding's *Joseph Andrews, "I do not desire to have the blood even of the wicked upon me"'*.[15]

He even felt some compassion for the French aristocracy. The lavish splendour of former aristocratic residences was like nothing he had seen before and he applauded the fact that they were either shut up or generally open to 'the slaves of the feudal system' who had once built and decorated them. Even the English gentry come in for some praise, by contrast. His Enlightenment affinity for the natural is repelled by the formal sterility of Versailles; 'all in the old school, straight alleys, clipt hedges, round basins, marble statues, and systems of terraces. It is a detestable style.' In contrast he found the Petit Trianon and its 'English style' enchanting. It would be beautiful in England, he reflected, 'but in France it is like a fairy ground. There have been some pretty frolics executed here by the late queen and her favourites.'[16] But the reflection on Marie Antoinette's fate made him melancholy.

He had befriended some returning *émigrés* on the ship over from America, former naval officers and minor nobles, Dupetit Thouars and Roussillon.

It is a pity they should be Aristocrats, yet I can hardly be angry with them, Aristocracy has been most terribly humbled in France, and this reverse of fortune is too much for them. It is not only their own downfall but the exaltation of others, whom they were accustomed to despise, which mortifies them; and in fact, when I come to analyse their complaints, there is so much fanciful grievance mixed with severe actual suffering, that it abates a good deal of the compassion I should otherwise feel for them; and I must add that much of what they regret, they are deprived of most meritoriously, and many of the pleasures they have lost, were the pleasures of the most depraved luxury, splendid indeed but most abominably vicious—it is not fair however to judge too hardly of them, now they are down, but I confess I should be most sincerely sorry to be a witness to their resurrection.[17]

Yet it is instructive that the friendship arose. Whatever his republicanism, Tone was no democrat. At the theatre he sat in a box rather than on the benches. He applauded the persistence of social deference. He was shocked at the disorderliness and apparent absence of procedural rules in the French legislature. He thought the Council of Five Hundred 'looked more like their countrymen who broke into the Roman Senate, than like the Senators assembled in their ivory chairs to receive them'. If the room reminded him of meetings of the Catholic Committee in Back Lane, he thought 'the General Committee looked more like gentlemen, and were ten times more regular and orderly, or, in a word, like a legislative body'.[18] He likewise was shocked at the slovenly appearance and lack of discipline of the French soldiery. He admits to being a great martinet in such matters. But his opinion softened in time. He recognised that discipline was no substitute for enthusiasm, as the continuing French victories proved. He disliked extremes, and his basic human compassion sets him apart from many other modern revolutionaries. In France he opposed the extreme right and left with equal passion and applauded the collapse of the Babeuf conspiracy in April 1796. His support for the moderate regime of the Directory was unwavering, and if he thought it at times too mild, it was because he felt its tolerance of criticism encouraged those very forces which sought its destruction.

II

Tone arrived in Paris on 12 February and took lodgings at the Hôtel des Étrangers, rue Vivienne, behind the Palais Égalité. Three days later he visited Monroe in the rue Clichy on the northern outskirts of Paris. It was Monroe who provided his entrée to the Minister of Foreign Affairs, Charles Delacroix. For a long time Tone was unsure of his French and preferred to negotiate with English-speaking officials. In consequence Monroe became one of his main supports in Paris, though much of their conversation was taken up with

Monroe's difficulties rather than Tone's.[19] And indeed Monroe's were many. His embarrassment with his home government had been intensified by Tom Paine. Rescued from prison by Monroe under the Thermidoreans, Paine remained an increasingly unwelcome (and expensive) guest in Monroe's house, from which he launched a series of attacks on the Washington government and on Jay's treaty. The issuing of American passports to British subjects, many of them suspected spies, was increasing tension. The main culprit was the blatantly pro-British American consul in Hamburg.[20] But Monroe came in for much of the fire and Delacroix was unhappy that Tone had told the American so much about his mission to France.[21] In fact Monroe's support was essential to Tone. His line to America was the only contact he had with Ireland, and Monroe remained a good friend to the mission.

Tone made a number of such diplomatic errors at the outset, largely because his sources of information on recent French affairs had dried up. The American papers carried little French news. In Le Havre he was dismayed to find no newspapers in the coffee-houses, and his access to French papers remained patchy. In consequence he was still proposing Pichegru or Moreau to lead an Irish expedition when their royalist sympathies were already known. But he learnt quickly, and within a matter of weeks had sensed the workings and weaknesses of the Directory sufficiently to cut through the red tape and get to those who made the decisions.

The division of power at the centre of the Directory encouraged a divisive unilateralism. A powerful Director commanded a personal following, and bitter rivalries ensued. Although the Directory is credited with starting something like a modern civil service, there was little *exprit de corps* among its ministers. They never met collectively, indeed were prevented by the constitution from taking collective decisions.[22] Foreign affairs in 1796 were the specific concern of Reubell, an Alsatian committed to a natural frontiers policy and to a concentration of military effort against Austria. Delacroix was his man, chosen for his very facelessness. Undistinguished he may have been, but his industry matched that of his masters.[23] Beneath Delacroix operated a range of specialist bureaus, including the Bureau de Traduction, recently transferred from the Marine Ministry, and with it that maker of so many past Irish missions, Nicholas Madgett. Madgett had been tireless in keeping the Irish issue before succeeding French regimes, and most recently his report on the Irish in Philadelphia had resulted in a ministerial recommendation to invite Tone to Paris.[24] It was natural that Delacroix should have brought him into the negotiations with Tone.

But ministers had little power in Directorial France, let alone their underlings, and Madgett was very unimportant in the decision-making process. He was also living in an earlier age. Subversion was his business. He talked of sending arms and agents to Ireland, of organising an Irish *chouannerie*[25] and mutinies in the British fleet, when Tone looked to substantial military assistance, a regulated campaign rather than cloak-and-dagger diversions. In this Tone's instincts were correct. Foreigners were suspected of involvement in France's internal conspiracies and were closely watched in Paris. The Italians in particular were denounced and expelled from the city some months later.[26] Although he thought Madgett honest, everything about him irritated Tone. He was inefficient, something of an intriguer, and prey to petty vanities which made him claim powers he did not have. His scheme for recruiting Irish prisoners of war Tone thought an unnecessary security risk, and he was right.[27]

Madgett was typical of many of the employees in Foreign Affairs. The ministry was notorious for its slackness and inefficiency. There were too many underpaid clerks and insufficient security to handle matters as important as a proposed Irish invasion, and Tone's ill-ease was well founded.[28] Certainly the Ministry was living up to its reputation for getting bogged down in detail. Although Tone repeated his claim that Ireland was ripe for revolt, he insisted that nothing would happen unless the French arrived with a force of 15,000 to 20,000 men under a well-known general. But Delacroix and Madgett envisaged help on such a small scale that its outcome would be doubtful. Madgett pursued his Chouan and naval schemes throughout March, failed to get Tone's memorials through the system quickly, and seemed determined to keep Tone to himself. This was only personal vanity, for a good many of Tone's arguments were getting through the system, even if presented as Madgett's own rather than Tone's.[29]

Tone became suspicious that the Directory was listening to others, without telling him. Waiting in Delacroix's antechamber one day, he was joined by a small, suspicious-looking man, who proceeded to read an English newspaper. He was William Duckett, a former seminary student from Kerry, and one of Madgett's pool of Irish agents under the Committee of Public Safety. He was well informed on Ireland, having conducted several missions there, one as recently as 1795, and his many memorials in the early months of 1796 endorsed much of what Tone was saying. Tone, ever prone to instant judgements, considered him a spy, and, plagued by Delacroix's and Madgett's claims that he was an Irish patriot, effectively destroyed Duckett's credibility with the Directory.[30]

In many respects Tone was less than fair to Duckett, but in the context of his mission his instincts were right. Duckett was a subversive, and an effective one, with a particular skill for stirring up trouble in the British navy. His style and policy were totally contrary to what Tone was trying to achieve for Ireland. In France Duckett had a reputation as an intriguer and something of a trouble-maker and was well known to the British authorities. Tone's tactic from the outset had been one of remaining almost totally isolated to preserve secrecy. His success was so complete that the British and Irish authorities did not learn of his presence in Paris until 1797 and never discovered the details of his early mission.

Yet he did not relish such isolation. For days on end he was forced to be a tourist. But in the heavy snows of March Paris looked melancholy. He would pick up bargain books on bookstalls and sit for hours in the cafés reading them. The theatre became his main recourse, but plays he used to see in Dublin with Matilda or Russell made him sad. Discussion with (and admiration by) like minds had been a key element in his success as a political writer in Ireland. In France he spent weeks writing memorials and proclamations which would have been dashed off in a matter of hours in Ireland, and he began to feel that his talent as a writer had gone. Certainly the flair for discovery had. His journal entries became longer as sleeplessness kept him writing into the early hours of the morning. 'Am I not to be sincerely pitied here?', he wrote on 29 March. 'I do not know a soul! I speak the language but with great difficulty! I live in Taverns, which I detest! I cannot be always reading; and I find by experience that when one reads *perforce*, there is not much of either profit or pleasure to be derived from it...I return to my apartment, which is notwithstanding, a very neat one, as if I was returning to gaol, and finally I go to bed at night as if I was mounting the guillotine—I do lead a dog's life of it here that is the truth of it.'[31]

It was, however, the slow progress of his mission which lay behind such ill-ease. He unburdened himself on 23 February to Monroe, who advised him to abandon this 'subaltern way of doing business' and go straight to the Directory. It was good advice. The Directors jealously guarded policy-making, frequently even from their ministers, and in his choice of Carnot, whose name was known and admired in Ireland, Tone carried his negotiations on to an entirely different plane.

Carnot brought to the Directory that same single-minded concentration of goals with which he had turned the tide of the European war in France's favour in the Year II (1793–4). He owed his survival after the fall of Robespierre to a pragmatic ability to move with the tide. In 1796–7 the political complexion of France seemed increasingly conservative, and it is ironic that in the coup of Fructidor 1797 this former Terrorist was jettisoned for suspected royalism. It was, however, a settling of old scores as much as anything else. The five Directors had all brought past dissensions with them, and by the spring of 1796 their short-lived attempt at teamwork was already falling apart. Carnot's unilateralism and tendency to invade the other Directors' departments was a particularly sore point. In the Directory, where he had responsibility for war, his goal of peace at all costs conflicted with Reubell's natural-frontier policy, and Carnot constantly invaded Reubell's particular preserve of foreign affairs.[32] The inefficiency of the ministry gave him ample material for criticism and Tone's complaints fed his campaign for Delacroix's removal. During his term as president of the Directory (June–August 1796) Carnot bypassed Foreign Affairs entirely, and the quite remarkable success of the Irish negotiations were due in no small measure to their incorporation into France's war machine.[33]

Such a takeover by Carnot might well have jeopardised the Irish business had the Directors not found a common aim in their shared Anglophobia and their desire to avenge the British-backed civil war in western France. General Hoche was drawing to a close his campaign in Brittany just as Tone began his negotiations in Paris. Soon a huge unoccupied army would be available there. Prussia was already out of the war. An armistice had been signed with Austria in December. Bonaparte's victories in Italy were yet to come. England remained France's chief antagonist. Tone's proposals were taken up, because, for the moment, they accorded well with France's war strategy.

Tone acted immediately on Monroe's advice. On 24 February he walked to the Directory's seat in the former Palais de Luxembourg 'in a fright...conning speeches in execrable French all the way.' On arrival he entered the first office he came to and 'demanded at once to see Carnot...with a courage truly heroic.'[34] This was a typical piece of Tone self-mockery, for it was Carnot's day to hold a public audience. There was no problem in seeing him, even in obtaining a private audience, which Tone did. The Directory, for all its faults, was an accessible regime. Most of its actions were public and its decisions printed in the press. The most characteristic example of its open-door policy were the daily public audiences, through which Tone first gained entry to Carnot. With the Directory, the Revolution was settling down, and the new sense of permanency was underlined by an exaggerated display of protocol and attention to externals. The Luxembourg was splendidly furnished from the former royal court, though the Directors had been hard put to find a chair when they first assumed office. They, their ministers, diplomats and the deputies all wore the elaborate classically-inspired costumes created by David. Strange that Tone, who had objected so violently to the legal dress of the Irish courts, should have found nothing to criticise in the richly embroidered draperies of the French republican officials.

Tone told Carnot of his background and mission, outlined the internal situation in Ireland, asserted the desire of the vast majority of its people to break with England, and asked for French assistance. He explained his reluctance to leave such important business in the hands of 'a mere *Commis*' such as Madgett, and told Carnot that his organisation of France's military victories was much admired in Ireland. Carnot expressed scepticism at several points. Tone assured him that he was putting everything on paper for Delacroix, 'which would explain to him in detail all I knew on the subject, better than I could in conversation'.[35]

He spoke but the truth. Tone's conduct of his mission, haunting the Luxembourg, nagging ministers and officials, his sheer zeal and enthusiasm, gave rise to suspicions that he was overstating his case. It was 'an unfortunate circle', Tone admitted; 'the more earnestness I show to convince...the more enthusiasm I manifest'.[36] No such reservations were entertained about his written submissions, which in time won lasting approval.

Tone's two memorials, drawn up in February 1796, and making their way rapidly through the French ministries by April, were much admired in France, both at the time and later.[37] They contained little that was new. Indeed Tone had said it all so often before that personal boredom may explain the difficulty he had in writing them. But there is a precision and lack of emotionalism which conveyed his message more effectively than his verbal representations. Starting from the premise that England was France's worst enemy, he outlined why it was through Ireland that she could best be defeated. He explained how the historical animosities between Catholics and Presbyterians had been eroded over the past years, urging on the French government the novelty and importance of this 'national union' of Catholics and Dissenters, ready to act against 'the common enemy'. He detailed the rapid spread of the new United Irish organisation and of Defenderism, representing both movements as pro-French (which was true), and as organised to liberate their country from England (which was only partially so).

But the landing of a large French force was an essential prerequisite to a war of independence. This would prevent civil war, turn it into a revolution rather than an insurrection, facilitate the immediate establishment of a revolutionary government and, given the proper guarantees, win over hesitant militiamen and property owners. Tone opposed any general attack on property, and throughout the negotiations dismissed any idea of restoring land confiscated from the Catholics. The French general must issue a manifesto immediately upon landing disavowing all idea of conquest, offering security and protection to religion and property and inviting the people to form a national convention which in turn would establish a government. The nucleus of such a government was already in place in the Catholic Committee, joined by the leaders of the Ulster Presbyterians. Together they would form a provisional convention which would issue a series of proclamations: one, to the people, would announce their independence and declare adherence to Britain as treasonable; others, to the militia, to Irishmen serving in the British navy and to those living in British dominions, would recall them to allegiance to their country. A final proclamation to the people of England and Scotland would explain that the Irish sought only independence, not bloodshed, and urge those people not to support their government in a war against Ireland. Only if this failed would the threat of confiscation of English property in Ireland be held out, which Tone calculated would cause not a few absentees to hesitate. He outlined in detail the forces, artillery, and financial backing required by the Irish. Ulster would act as the military spearhead and the landing take place either at Carrickfergus or Galway.[38]

Tone's tendency to gloss over Ireland's religious divisions is manifest in these documents, though conscious exaggeration is less easy to detect. The communications he had received from Ireland prior to his departure from America had represented 'the magnitude and universality of popular discontent in Ireland', as did the press reports (notably of Irish parliamentary debates) reaching the Directory in these early months of Tone's mission.[39] It was a matter of convincing France that Ireland was revolutionary enough to merit help, but not so revolutionised as not to need it, and on the whole Tone did not overstep these bounds. But he was compelled to play down the religious elements in Defenderism to counteract France's persistent impression of the Defenders as some kind of Irish Chouans. *Chouannerie* was in essence a revolt by the Breton peasantry against the incursive centralisation of the Revolution, notably its religious reforms. It became part of the counter-revolution and as such was fed by England. The civil war was conducted with a primeval ferocity and at times deteriorated into outright banditry. Tone was correct in denying priestly influence in Defenderism. The Irish Catholic hierarchy did likewise.[40] The kind of alliance of nobles, clergy and peasantry, on which the counter-revolution in France—and *chouannerie* in particular—was based, did not exist in Ireland. Indeed it would have been impossible, given the religious gulf between a largely Catholic peasantry and a largely Protestant landed class. The French were more likely to be opposed by a cross-class Protestant alliance, infinitely smaller than that behind *chouannerie* in France.

General Hoche, commander of the army of the west and France's most fêted general after his successful termination of the civil war there, had already suggested taking revenge on England for the horrors of that war by promoting Chouan-like guerrilla warfare in Britain. General Humbert, one of Hoche's officers with a particular aptitude for such wrecking ventures, offered to lead an expedition. His offer was accepted and in April 1796 Hoche was instructed to prepare a force of 1,000 to 1,500 men which Humbert would take to Cornwall and Wales.[41]

Tone did not blame France for wanting to avenge the havoc caused by England's promotion of civil war, but a reverse *chouannerie* he thought was not the way. In England, he argued, the peasantry bore no relationship to that in Brittany and he refused a request to write a proclamation for an English *chouannerie*. Few things caused him more irritation at the Directory's apparent lack of vision than its plans for an Irish *chouannerie*. Such a scheme, he argued in a stiffly worded protest of 3 April, would simply provoke partial and easily suppressed insurrections. Ireland, not England, would be the sufferer. The propertied would take fright, the reform campaign would be put back fifteen years, the authorities would use the excuse for a security clamp-down, and altogether the hand of the government would be considerably strengthened. Most of all it would be ruinous to any full-scale expedition. Madgett's excursions to recruit Irish prisoners of war for such a venture he thought an irritating diversion, entirely typical of Madgett's way of 'making revolutions'.[42] Plans for an Irish *chouannerie* were eventually dropped, even if those for England continued.

III

On 14 March Carnot brought General Henry Clarke, head of the War Ministry's Bureau Topographique et Historique Militaire, into the business. Clarke's Irish forebears had followed James II to France after his defeat in Ireland. Both the General and his father had served in France's Irish regiments before the Revolution, and the family benefited from the patronage of the Duke of Orléans. Clarke spoke English fluently, and had been in Ireland during his posting to the French embassy in London in the years 1789–91. But Tone found his knowledge of the country antiquated, and as he walked with this 'handsome, smooth-faced young man' (Clarke was thirty at the time) to his offices in the Hôtel de la Trémouille, in the rue de Vaugirard opposite the Luxembourg, he thought he was once again being handed over to a mere *commis*. In fact he had been introduced into Carnot's own particular enclave. Clarke's bureau had been created by Carnot under the Committee of Public Safety. It coordinated plans for military operations directly with the generals and was the most powerful of the nine specialist bureaus operating under the Directory. Its personnel was permanent and it was in this bureau rather than in the ministries that campaign strategy was decided. The involvement of Clarke was indeed a sign that Carnot was taking the Irish affair seriously.[43]

Clarke had not yet seen Tone's memorials, but he had ordered up boxes of documents on Ireland going back to the *ancien régime* and seemed to Tone very ill informed of the changes which had occurred in Ireland in recent years. He thought the establishment of an Irish republic allied to France unlikely, given Ireland's attachment to monarchy and the influence of the priests, and seemed to think the aristocracy (even Fitzgibbon) would participate in an independence movement. Tone's irritation was mingled with baffled amusement at this suggestion. 'Any one who knows Ireland will readily believe that I did not find it easy to make a serious answer to this question. Yes, Fitzgibbon would be very likely, from his situation, his principles, his hopes, and his fears, his property, and the general tenor of his conduct, to begin a revolution in Ireland!'[44]

The ignorance in the Bureau Topographique et Historique, when Tone had so often explained things at Foreign Affairs, was typical of the personalisation of affairs under the Directory. A month had elapsed since he delivered his memorials on Ireland to Madgett, and still they had not got through to Carnot. On the morning of 22 March he took matters into his own hands, called on Madgett, and told him Carnot wanted his memorials. 'He boggled a good deal, and I got almost angry', wrote Tone. 'It would be a most extraordinary thing indeed if one of the Executive Directory could not command a paper of that kind out of the pocket of Citizen Madgett. . . . I do not understand people being idle and giving themselves airs, and wanting to make revolutions while they are grumbling at the trouble of writing a few sheets of paper.' Instead Madgett was preoccupied with his prisoner-of-war scheme, which Tone thought 'damned nonsense' and very probably 'a small matter of Job à l'Irlandaise and that there is some cash to be touched. . . . He is always hunting for maps, and then he thinks he is making revolutions. I believe he is very sincere in the business, but he does, to be sure, at times, pester me most confoundedly.' In the end Tone simply made copies of his memorials himself.[45]

Tone was anxious about the apparent duplicity of his meetings with Carnot and Clarke. Monroe had brushed aside his fears, but when Delacroix and Madgett learnt of the meetings, he was considerably embarrassed. Such deception was not his style. He vowed not to repeat the mistake and seems to have taken pains to smooth Foreign Affairs's ruffled feathers.[46] But it was just the kind of action which most piqued Delacroix, particularly at a time when Carnot was trying to put him out of office. Indeed his suggestion that Tone use his line to the Directory to suggest the employment in Ireland of Prieur de la Marne reeks of revenge. Carnot, in his growing conservatism, can hardly have been expected to welcome the promotion of this ex-Terrorist, arrested after the Paris 'rising' of April 1795. Delacroix, whatever his mediocrity, was perfectly capable of sabotaging secret negotiations and did so three months later in the case of one of Carnot's secret agents.[47] That he did not do so in Tone's case suggests that Reubell too was supporting a possible Irish venture.

Clarke was impressed by Tone's memorials and reported favourably on them to Carnot. The grilling Tone received at their first two meetings had given way by early April to lengthy, relaxed conversations. On 8 April Carnot ordered copies of the memorials sent to the Minister of Marine, Truguet, and to General Hoche. In May, however, Tone's relations with Carnot and Clarke seemed to deteriorate. He was constantly assured by Foreign Affairs that preparations for an Irish expedition were proceeding. Yet Clarke seemed determined to keep him in the dark. He should have known better than to have credited anything coming out of Foreign Affairs. But Clarke's pedigree, his service in those very Irish regiments which had transferred to British service after the Revolution, his apparent obsession with royalism and priestcraft, aroused fears of betrayal in Tone. His haughtiness of manner reacted on Tone's sensitivities and the feeling that he was being talked down to introduced a frosty note into their May correspondence.[48] That month, however, the Directory was preoccupied with the Babeuf conspiracy and the ensuing financial crisis. Moreover, with Austria's rupture of the armistice, Clarke was heavily involved in plans for a renewed military campaign. His irritation at Tone's persistence was entirely justified.

Even a rather foolish attempt by Tone to draw Clarke by engaging his private interests with promises of glory and wealth in Ireland, was treated more kindly than it deserved. If he did not give Tone more information, Clarke explained, it was because, for the moment, he was not allowed to.[49] Indeed the reason for such reticence was a greater seriousness of purpose, and before the end of May plans were already under way to send help to the Irish. Tone's claims were fully endorsed by newspaper reports and the need for more immediate information on Ireland became increasingly apparent.

Tone had not been in touch with Ireland since Arthur was sent there, and although word had got through of his safe arrival in Paris, he was eager to alert his friends to developments.[50] Finding a suitable candidate for such a mission, however, proved difficult. Given the language requirement it was perhaps inevitable that leftovers from

Madgett's pool and Irish living in France since the *ancien régime* should suggest themselves. Tone rebelled at first. The suggestion of a former Capuchin friar so raised his anti-clerical hackles that Matilda felt compelled to censor his words in the published journals. He told Delacroix that he had 'a strong objection to letting priests into the business at all; that I had the very worst opinion of them, and that in Ireland especially they were very bigoted and ignorant, slaves to Rome and of course enemies to the French Revolution'.[51] Indeed with Bonaparte's capture of the Papal States that summer he even suggested compelling the Pope to urge greater compliance on the Irish clergy. The suggestion was not as far-fetched as it seems, for this is precisely what the Directory was attempting to do with its own refractory clergy and may well have been the inspiration for Tone's suggestion.

Tone was happier with Delacroix's next choice of agent, Eugene Aherne, a thirty-year-old former medical student from County Kerry, recently returned from a lengthy mission to Scotland.[52] Indeed he ended up sharing lodgings with Aherne at no. 7 Petite rue Roch Poissonnière, in Montmartre. However, their over-amorous landlady, Mlle Boivet, soon proved a problem in more ways than one. Tone came to dread encountering her, though with his money fast running out, more through debt than threatened virtue. Aherne too, then locked in a battle with the various ministries for reimbursement of his Scottish expenses, had been compelled to lodge his clothes and watch with the lady as surety for unpaid rent.[53]

Clarke had drawn up Aherne's instructions in mid-April and briefed him over Delacroix's head. Delacroix in reaction took a cavalier approach to the mission, handed over the instructions to Tone for alteration and told Aherne to disregard those which seemed irrelevant. The instructions in fact were carefully and tightly worded and were typical of Clarke's attention to detail. Tone recognised Clarke's hand in the questions about the role of the priests and the Catholics' monarchical leanings. He thought they contained 'a great deal of trash mixed with some good sense' and in a sharply worded reply he said as much.[54]

But the instructions also revealed how much of Tone's advice had been accepted and the depth of Clarke's own investigations since their first meeting in March. They contained the first positive offer of French assistance (the Irish leaders, whom Tone was to indicate, were to be offered 10,000 troops and arms for 20,000 more), and detailed instructions for organising the northern counties, where the landing was to take place. Moreover all question of the Irish rising unaided was abandoned. Not only was an insurrection prior to a French landing no longer expected, it was positively discouraged.[55]

But Aherne was always a Foreign Affairs man. He had after all been working with Madgett for some years, and even Tone—though at the time displeased with Clarke—distanced himself from the two men's malicious gossip against the General.[56] On 27 May Clarke had Aherne replaced by his own cousin, Richard O'Shee, in a knuckle-rapping directive to Delacroix. Tone, he claimed, had already been told too much by Foreign Affairs, and though he was thought 'a very spirited Irishmen, whom the Directory hoped to employ', he and Aherne were now too close for the latter to secure information independently. O'Shee did set out on his Irish mission, stopping with the French minister in Hamburg on 17 June. But he never actually arrived in Ireland and the strange exchange of letters between Clarke and Delacroix suggests that his mission was simply part of the process whereby Irish matters were taken away from Foreign Affairs entirely after May 1796.[57]

By then the Directory had already decided on an Irish invasion and wrote to Hoche on 19 June,

'We intend, Citizen General, to restore to a people ripe for revolution the independence and liberty for which it clamours. Ireland has groaned under the hateful yoke of England for centuries. The Defenders...are already secretly armed...and the very hope of help from the French Republic has persuaded them to defer insurrection until their arrival....Detach Ireland from England, and she will be reduced to a second-rate power and deprived of most of her superiority over the seas. The advantages to France of an independent Ireland are so manifold that they need not be listed.'

Sixteen thousand troops would be landed in Connacht in three different stages. The fleet already destined for India, and due to leave by 1 August, was to land 5,000 soldiers at Galway, 10,000 guns and enough artillery to maintain themselves until reinforcements arrived. A second force of 6,000 would follow, composed of 'corps francs' (irregulars) 'to purge France of many dangerous individuals', even former Chouans who wanted to re-enter French service—but commanded by officers known for their zeal and discipline. A third force of 5,000, composed largely of foreign deserters, and clothed in the uniforms landed by England at Quiberon, would sail simultaneously from Holland. Meanwhile a Chouan diversion would be staged in Wales and Cornwall.[58] An ill-thought-out scheme which doubled up on existing naval arrangements, it was to undergo considerable modification in the course of the summer.

Although the order was signed by the three leading Directors, the Irish expedition had to all intents and purposes become Carnot's particular concern, and had been treated as such from the earliest days of Tone's audiences with him. Carnot wrote privately to Hoche on 22 June airing his views on Ireland as England's Vendée: 'As for myself, I see in the success of this operation the downfall of the most dangerous of our enemies. I see in it the safety of France for centuries to come'. But would Hoche accept such a command, leave the huge army of some 140,000 he then commanded for such a piecemeal expeditionary force? The tone Carnot takes is instructive, for Hoche was no ordinary general.

The son of a royal groom, Lazare Hoche was a man of brilliance and had been a general by the age of twenty-five. As commander of the combined armies in the west, he had been vested with more power than any of the Republic's other generals and had used it with considerable vigour, deploying his army in flying columns to defeat *chouannerie* at its own game.[59] His political acumen was as great. Correspondence from Paris was deferential in tone. Carnot, who would always take the side of the generals against the politicians, implies a deep personal interest in promoting Hoche's career, holds out the prospect of further glory in thus defeating England and flatters him about his particular qualification for such an expedition.

> No one can instil such fear into the English or deal the fatal blow better than the man who crushed the cancer of the Vendée and the Chouans; I am convinced that your name alone will double our strength in enemy eyes, intensify their terror and increase the confidence of the Irish who want to break the yoke of their oppressors. It is a task worthy of you. I have decided to propose that the Directory place you at the head of this expedition; but I wanted to find out first if this would be agreeable to you. . . . let me know and start thinking right away about how we would execute it.[60]

He was likewise sent a manifesto to the Irish people commissioned from Tone and told that its author, 'an Irishman deputed to France by the Irish Defenders', would be sent to him as *chef de brigade*. 'He has much ability and will be extremely useful. He knows the country, the mind of the people and the character of the leading figures in Ireland. He can contribute much to the success of the expedition which has been assigned to you'.[61]

It was an accolade which hardly squared with Tone's feelings about the way he had been handled. The truth was that there had never been any doubt about his credentials, but he had succeeded so well in subduing his natural optimism that he scarcely recognised it. He had in fact helped to create a different mental climate about Ireland, a climate in which its people could now be viewed as a friendly nation, with whose assistance England might be defeated. It was a new climate which turned the Directory's plans for a wrecking diversion into a full-scale campaign for Irish liberation. However piecemeal the initial proposals of 19 June, the choice of Hoche told a different story. If he accepted, he was unlikely to sail except with an expedition guaranteed the success and glory to which he had become accustomed. Tone was finally told of the new plan on 23 June. After months of frustration, his mission, it seemed, had been entirely successful.

22

Irish Invasion Plans

As the Directory set out its plans for Ireland, Tone's mission received powerful reinforcement from an unexpected source. Lord Edward Fitzgerald and Arthur O'Connor had defected from Ireland's ruling élite and joined forces with the United Irishmen. By early June they had arrived on the Continent with instructions to open communication with the Directory and with Tone. The United Irishmen believed that uncontrolled and piecemeal popular insurgency in Ireland was drawing such a reaction from the authorities that if French help did not arrive soon organised resistance would be entirely suppressed. The nature of the disturbances which raged through Ulster, Leinster and Connacht differed from region to region, becoming more agrarian as one moved inland from the urban centres. But three things were common to all: support for the French, a growing politicisation, and alienation from the state.[1] All three were intensified by the nature of the disturbances which flared out from Armagh and south Down from the late summer of 1796.

The ritualised sectarian conflict in these areas took on a new character with the upgrading of the Peep-of-Day Boys to the Orange Order in September 1795. The result was an orchestrated campaign of intimidation and expulsion of Catholics from Armagh, to which many magistrates turned a blind eye.[2] The Castle was disturbed at such blatant association of the law with sectarianism, fearing, correctly, that it would send hordes of Catholics into the United Irishmen.[3] But it was difficult for most of the populace to credit the Irish and English governments' commitment to due process of the law when the irregularities themselves were legitimised by statute in the 1796 parliamentary session.

In 1795 the response of the military commander Carhampton to the troubles in the west had been to clear the jails and send many untried prisoners into the navy. Magistrates elsewhere emulated this efficient remedy, and many of them faced prosecution by the turn of the year.[4] The government's answer was the passage in February 1796 of an Indemnity Act, granting magistrates immunity from prosecution for actions taken to quell the recent disturbances. It was followed by an Insurrection Act legalising such actions, making the administering of oaths a capital offence and the taking of them punishable by transportation. Magistrates could proclaim an area as disturbed, and thereby assume wide-ranging powers to search and declare a curfew.[5] Camden had bowed to pressure from the country gentlemen, whose unanimity on the issue was registered in the passage of the act without a division, despite Lord Edward's attempt to secure one. There was by now no effective Irish parliamentary opposition.

These events were a mixed blessing for the new United Irish organisation. On the one hand they did present it with the potential for a popular base. An agreement was reached between United leaders in Belfast and the Defenders in Dublin at the end of 1795, whereby an adherent to either became a member of both organisations.[6] But the show trials of the autumn and spring assizes, the many executions, and the new legislation turned the intelligence tide in the government's favour. Information of such authenticity began to flow so rapidly into the Castle that it was just a matter of time before the leaders were arrested, and they knew it. Consequently McCormick, Lewins and two of the Belfast leaders, Robert Simms and George Tennent, accepted Lord Edward's suggestion of a second mission to France to alert the Directory to the urgency of the new situation in Ireland.[7] The accession of Fitzgerald and O'Connor to the United Irish movement never represented a split in the landed gentry significant enough to ensure the kind of success such a development brought to the American Revolution. But the stature of the two men and their recognised position as social leaders raised the nascent and still very fragmented Irish revolutionary movement on to a new plane.

Lord Edward arrived in Hamburg with his wife on 14 May and immediately contacted Reinhard, the French minister there and an old acquaintance. Reinhard thought him energetic and honourable, but rather young and inexperienced and his French wife's family connections with the Orléanist émigrés aroused predictable suspicions. Nevertheless, Fitzgerald did succeed in conveying the urgency of the situation in Ireland, and the need for help to arrive soon, if at all. He offered to contact Tone to bring him up to date on developments in Ireland. Delacroix had Reinhard's letter reporting this deciphered and laid before the Directory. He responded officially on 31 May: 'The Directory...is already informed of the present situation in Ireland. The person you mention as coming from America has in reality been here for several months. It [the Directory] recognises the importance of the proposed operation and is about to put it into execution'.[8] In fact the Directors had already decided on an Irish invasion before the new plea was placed before

them. But it both strengthened Tone's position and helped transform
the unsatisfactory French naval plans of June into ones for a full-scale
invasion force by the end of the summer.

It was O'Connor, who arrived in Hamburg on 5 June, who
pushed the message home. He was a talented negotiator and despite
extremely poor French impressed the French officials with his arguments. These differed little from Tone's, and the two emissaries
expected to see him had their request to travel to Paris been granted.
But once the decision had been taken on the Irish expedition,
Carnot's natural penchant for secrecy took over. The French papers
were already picking up rumours about the Directory's Irish plans.
Lord Edward was well known in Paris, O'Connor not so, though his
name was, and any hint of Irish missionaries there was to be avoided.
They were even kept apart from O'Shee—who arrived in Hamburg
on 18 June—and Tone was told about the mission only obliquely.

At his meeting with Clarke on 28 June Tone expressed doubts
about Madgett's suggestion that he write to his friends in Ireland. If
he could say nothing about the plans in hand he thought it better not
to write at all, since all he could say was that he was alive and well in
Paris. 'As to that,' replied Clarke, 'your friends know it already', and
he responded, to Tone's evident surprise, by intimating that some
separate communication had been opened with Ireland. He then
showed him a paper sent by Lord Edward and O'Connor from
Basle—whence they had journeyed to avoid the curiosity of the
alerted Hamburg émigrés. Clarke wondered if Tone knew the handwriting, which he did not, and proceeded to read it to him. It
outlined in terms similar to Tone's the internal situation in Ireland,
asserting that the Protestant aristocracy alone was against revolution,
and that large numbers of militiamen had been sworn in to the
United Irishmen. The 14 northernmost counties had been organised,
and they were rapidly gaining members in the other 18. But the
United Irishmen were in severe need of arms and artillery, the
operation of the Gunpowder and Insurrection Acts made it impossible for them to act without French assistance, and Lord Edward
and O'Connor had been deputed 'to ask the French government for
help in effecting their separation from England'.[9]

Tone's response is illuminating. Clarke had stopped at the point
stating that two deputies had been sent to negotiate terms. He
laughed as he told Tone that he would guess the source if he went on,
and asked if Tone knew of this organisation. In contrast to his
irritation at having Duckett pushed upon him, Tone was not at
all upset at finding others in the business. He admitted his own
information to be twelve months old, was privately delighted that
everything he heard agreed with what he had already stated, and that
his own credit was thereby established beyond all doubt.[10]

I

On 12 July Tone was called urgently to the Luxembourg.[11] After waiting two hours, 'a very handsome, well made young fellow in a brown coat and nankin pantaloons' entered, asked if he was Citoyen Smith, otherwise Wolfe Tone, and introduced himself as General Hoche.[12] Hoche had greeted the Irish proposals of the Directory with enthusiasm, but had detected the flaws in the June plan. He disliked the idea of splitting preparations between Brest and Holland. Better send 16,000 to 20,000 from his own army, for they were 'troops accustomed to that kind of warfare, and would greatly facilitate...the insurrection'. If the Directory decided otherwise, Hoche feared that desertion and pillage might cause the expedition to fail. 'You can dispose of your riff-raff to England', he added, and requested permission to come to Paris.[13] From his experiences in the Vendée and in Brittany Hoche was well used to the kind of problem Ireland would present. In the west he had recognised that a military solution was not the long-term answer and in a 'hearts-and-minds' operation had insisted on religious tolerance and an end to military pillaging.[14] Significantly, in his talks in Paris, Hoche was most concerned about ensuring regular supplies for his troops, internal support and long-term political solutions.

Hoche had studied Tone's two memoranda and on 12 July questioned him closely on the supplies he could expect for his troops in Ireland, and the likelihood of opposition from the priests or support from the military. Supplies Tone thought not a problem, nor the strength of opposition from the priests, as their influence over the people had greatly diminished. Nevertheless he urged 'leaning to the side of caution, and refraining from shocking their prejudices unnecessarily', since they might then 'secure their neutrality, if not their support'. As for the army, he thought most were 'wretched bad troops', and he hoped the militia would come over. But he warned not to count on it and the French should make their plans accordingly. All would depend on the numbers sent by the French, and Tone tried to draw Hoche on this point. 'Undoubtedly, replied he; men will not sacrifice themselves when they do not see a reasonable prospect of support; but if I go, you may be sure I will go in sufficient force.' He would make his arrangements to leave nothing to chance and 'for his own reputation, see that all the arrangements were made on a proper scale'.[15] Hoche, however, was most concerned about the form of government to be established in Ireland after a successful invasion and the glory that would accrue to the maker of a new nation. He accepted Tone's claim that the Catholic Committee should form the basis of a provisional government, but only after questioning him intensively about Ireland's assumed preference for a monarchy.

On 16 July Hoche sought instructions from the Directory on how he should act in Ireland: should he place himself at the head of an Irish insurrection, should be supply an Irish candidate if the people remained attached to a monarchical system of government, should Ireland be treated as a conquest if England preserved sufficient force to keep it in submission?[16] If Ireland formed a government like that in France, replied Carnot, the chances of an alliance between the two countries would be increased, and it was Hoche himself who should play the major role in forming a government. As long as the French troops remained in Ireland, they should hold the reins of government, not to undermine Irish independence, but to prevent English intrigues until a general peace could be declared. The Irish must recognise that they owed their independence to France, and repay the debt by an alliance against England and a grant of favoured-nation status in commerce. Hoche should assume direction of any insurrection and avoid being treated as the commander of an auxiliary corps. Tone's recommendations for a provisional government were accepted, but although France would prefer an elected convention she was prepared to entertain an Irish monarchy, if that was what the population desired. Ireland was to be treated as a friendly nation and disruption kept to a minimum. A liberated Ireland would be expected to assist in an invasion of England, whose defeat was the ultimate object of Hoche's expedition.[17]

Apart from the continuing belief in Ireland's attachment to monarchy, there was little in the correspondence between Hoche and Carnot that Tone would have found objectionable. He supported the idea of military government until victory was achieved, but he was anxious about excessive French interference in an Irish government. He told Clarke as much on 18 July, and returned to the topic some days later. French influence in an independent Ireland, he conceded, would be great; 'but the surest way to keep it would be not to assume it', and the French must expect no say in government. Ireland stood in the same situation as America, which France had helped to independence, not as Holland (where Clarke had indicated continuing French influence in government), which was a conquest, and Tone hoped the French would take great care in their choice of chargés d'affaires.[18]

Clarke had suggested that Tone himself might act as French representative in Ireland, indeed serve as the native chief who might satisfy Irish monarchical leanings. Tone was taken aback by the former suggestion and rightly dismissive of the latter, claiming he 'had neither the desire nor the talents to aspire so high'. Whatever sociability and wit he had displayed in the past, Tone's seriousness of purpose in Paris seems to have expelled both from his French negotiations. Although Clarke thought highly of Tone, there is very often a jovial mocking of his seriousness, which Tone frequently misinterprets. Hoche took the gentler approach. But it is unlikely that Hoche would have been so much predisposed towards Tone had Clarke not already laid the ground, and from their first meeting Tone found himself intimately involved in the preparations for an Irish expedition.

On the evening of Hoche's arrival, Tone dined at the Luxembourg with Carnot, Clarke, Hoche, Truguet, the Minister of Marine, Lagarde, Secretary-General of the Directory, and a number of others responsible for orchestrating the Irish invasion plans. For hours they discussed their plans for Ireland unreservedly before going into a private session. Tone walked in the Luxembourg gardens with Lagarde, listening to the symphony being performed in La Réveillière's apartments while on the floor below his fellow Director was planning the defeat of England. Clarke emerged from the closed session and assured Tone that 'every thing was now settled'.[19]

Over the next two weeks details of a major Irish expedition were finalised. At secret sessions on 16 and 20 July the Directory appointed Hoche commander-in-chief of an army of 15,000 'destined to effect the revolution in Ireland'. He was given full powers to hasten preparations, to make naval as well as military requisitions, and to dispatch secret agents where necessary. The various corps destined for England under Generals Humbert and Quantin were likewise placed under his orders. Fifty thousand guns, large supplies of mortar shells, and shoes for the troops were ordered immediately for Brest, and the War Minister was warned that he would be held personally responsible for any unjustified delay.[20] On the 23rd Hoche showed Tone his own proclamation, now printed, signed by Hoche and ready for distribution upon landing in Ireland. He was meeting with Tone in regular morning sessions, the 7 a.m. appointments forcing Tone to rise a good deal earlier than was his custom.

As part of the preparations Hoche's aide-de-camp was dispatched to Switzerland on the 22nd to escort O'Connor to the General's headquarters in Brittany, and Hoche left Paris on 12 August to keep the appointment.[21] Hoche had checked on Tone's views of O'Connor and Fitzgerald and the complimentary answers he received were as much a fortification of their mission as theirs had been of Tone's own. The refrain about an independent Ireland being run by a native chief, heard more often in Paris at this very time, clearly had the two men in mind.

In March Tone had asked Clarke if he could have a commission in any Irish expedition the French sent: 'I was willing to encounter danger, as a soldier, but...I had a violent objection to being hanged as a traitor;...as to rank it was indifferent to me, my only object being a certainty of being treated as a soldier, in case the fortune of war should throw me into the hands of the enemy, who I knew would otherwise show me no mercy'.[22] In July Tone was appointed *chef de brigade* (colonel) in Hoche's army. Initially he was to have commanded a regiment of some 250 to 260 dragoons, taken from the former *Légion de Police à Cheval*. But the complement could not be made up and instead he was attached to the infantry and deprived, he noted in some disappointment, of the chance of entering Ireland 'at the head of a regiment of horse'.[23] Yet as Clarke saluted him as 'a brother officer' Tone was overcome with emotion. It was, after all, the fulfilment of a lifelong ambition. As he donned his regimentals he admitted to being 'as pleased as a little boy in his first breeches', and walked around Paris to show himself off much as he had done all those years ago in his Volunteer uniform.[24]

But he soon pulled himself down to earth with reflections on his own penury. 'I cannot help this morning thinking of *Gil Blas*, when he was secretary to the *Duke of Lerma*', he wrote on 13 July. 'Yesterday I dined with *Carnot*, and to-day I should be puzzled to raise a guinea.'[25] His pay was nothing—35 francs in cash, 600 in *mandats* (which he calculated worth about sixpence), altogether about £3. 2s. 6d per month—and even that would be a long time in coming through. In addition he would have an allowance of rations amounting to one and a half pounds of meat per month, four and a half of bread, and quantities of haricot beans, salt and wood. What he was to do with these he had no idea. His most pressing need was cash to pay for his lodgings, 'for I dread my little *bossue* of a landlady more than the enemy a thousand times', and the anxiety disguised for some time any sense of triumph at what had been achieved.[26]

On 18 July he wrote 'a threatening letter to *Citizen Carnot*, telling him "*if he did not put five pounds in a sartin place!!*"' In fact it was a respectful but firm letter, typical of Tone's official correspondence and written in stilted, if grammatically correct, French. After six months of defraying all his own expenses 'on business of the utmost importance', he was now '*absolutely without money*' and appealed to Carnot to apply for assistance 'conformable to the services rendered, to the sacrifices I have already made and will make in the future'. Money was the very commodity in shortest supply under the Directory. Clarke was sure there would be none forthcoming, and had to move heaven and earth to procure Tone three months' pay in advance. In the end Tone had to borrow from Monroe. He hated filling his pages with such matters: 'damn the money....It degrades the dignity of my history'.[27]

As Tone awaited orders to leave for the west, a letter arrived from

America, the first since he had sailed from New York. It was from Rowan, dated 30 March, not, as he had hoped, from his wife. Rowan calmed his fears about his family. Matthew Tone had arrived in America the previous December and was acting as their protector. It somehow brought Tone back to reality and made him recognise the strangeness of the position in which he found himself. Hoche had been remarkably attentive to him, even to the point of offering a place in his own carriage for the journey west, and was applying for Tone's promotion to adjutant-general and admission to the General Staff. 'I believe I am not sufficiently sensible of it', Tone wrote on 27 July. 'The fact is, I am surprised, myself, at the *sangfroid* with which I regard the progress of my business here, so infinitely beyond my expectations; I had very little expectation of success the day I left Sandy Hook...things have turned out miraculously, to be sure.... It is like a romance absolutely.'[28] He reflected on the many frustrations he had felt 'dancing attendance on others', and vowed never to give himself airs if he ever reached such a station of importance himself.

II

Nowhere is the complexity of Tone's character better illustrated than in the comparison between the reality of his work in Paris and his own perceptions of it. If he presented his case to the Directory and its officials with a confidence which carried conviction, his private journal reveals anything but confidence. An early letter to Delacroix describing his background is almost diffident. He lays no claim to having been the founder of the United Irish Society and depicts his mission as that of a delegate from others, 'men who would lead public opinion in Ireland in the event of a revolution'.[29] He even sought a written statement from the Directory 'that I might have on my return a testimonial to show my country men that I had to the best of my power executed their instructions'.[30] He is surprised at the contrast between his own obscurity and the magnitude of what he was doing, finds it laughable that Delacroix should be using him to recommend Prieur to the Directory and treats the suggestion as not quite serious— displaying a modesty which spared him the effects of this particular act of sabotage.

Most of all he frets about jeopardising his mission by any weakness or indiscretion. He is worried about how his actions will be viewed by his friends in Ireland, and at each success admits how much he longs for their admiration.[31] Those harrowing months of 1795 before his exile loom large in his memory, and those involved on both sides are offstage actors in his Paris mission. He reflects on the difference between his new situation and that of a year ago, 'hunted from my own country as a traitor, living obscurely in America as an exile, and received in France, by the Executive Directory *almost* as an Ambassador'. He thought of his friends who would not speak to him because he was a republican, and saw their attitude as a self-fulfilling prophesy. He felt, however, they had been premature in their judgement, and, reflecting on Fitzgibbon's attack, was prompted to repeat Shylock's words ' "He called me dog before he had a cause" '.[32]

However prominent his name was to become in Irish historiography, Tone never thought of himself as a political leader. Nor does he ever make any claim to be 'the father' of Irish republicanism. After Irish independence he hoped rather to continue in his pre-1795 role as conciliator and bridge between the Catholics and the Presbyterians.[33] Indeed he speaks frequently of his mission as fulfilling a personal debt to his friends on the Catholic Committee. 'I owe unspeakable obligations . . . to my masters of the General Committee: I have in consequence not lost sight of their honor or their interests here, as will appear from my memorials delivered to the Executive Directory, in which I have endeavoured to make them the basis of the National Legislature. . . . I have, I think, done my duty by them, and in part at least acquitted the debt of gratitude I owe them.'[34]

This is not to say that Tone was the totally selfless and virtuous paragon of republican mythology. He craved reputation and admiration. 'Have I no selfish motives?' he asks on 27 March. 'Yes, I have!—If I succeed here, I feel I shall have strong claims on the gratitude of my Country . . . I shall certainly hope for some honorable station that will reward me for the sacrifices I have already made and the dangers I have incurred.'[35] Later, as the months of negotiating begin to bear fruit, he recalls how Russell was always 'foretelling great things' for him. 'He said that I would make a greater figure, and that I had more talents than Plunket or Burrowes; for the talents, *negatur*, but for the figure, the Devil puts it into my head sometimes that he was right. . . . My name may be spoken of yet.'[36]

Tone never considered himself some kind of secret ambassador until Madgett referred to him as such on 20 February. For a while he was rather taken by the vision of himself as a future Irish ambassador to France, living with his wife and family in Paris, inviting Russell to 'l'hôtel d'Irlande' to negotiate over several bottles of 'diplomatic burgundy'. But he soon brushed the suggestion aside: 'when a government was formed in Ireland it would be time enough to talk of embassies'.[37]

However, as Tone is told less and less of what is happening through April and May he begins to use the notion of being a secret Irish envoy to insist on being kept informed. The tendency intensifies

27. Second Street, Philadelphia (Scharf and Westcott, *History of Philadelphia*)

28. Thomas Mifflin (Armor, *Lives of the Governors of Pennsylvania*)

29. James Monroe (Hamilton ed., *Writings of James Monroe*)

Translation of our Bill at the Restauration
in the Palais Royal. Feb.ʳ 12. 1796 —

Two loaves (excellent) —— Livres	70 —
Soup ——————	70 —
Burgundy ——————	200 —
Fowl ——————	270 —
Salad ——————	200 —
Colliflowers ——————	110 —
Carp fried ——————	150. —
Apricots, in Brandy, ——	100 —
Coffee ——————	160 —
Liqueurs ——————	160 —
Livres	1490

What would I have given to have had
P:P: with me! — Indeed we would have discussed another Bottle of the Burgundy, or by
our Lady, some two or three — "The rogue
has given me medicines to make me love him; yes,
I have drank medicines". How he would enjoy
France, not excepting even her wines! —

30. Entry in Tone's Paris Journal, 12 Feb 1796, dinner at D'Aucourt's restaurant in the Palais
Royale (courtesy the Board of Trinity College, Dublin)

1. Public audience with the Directory (Mansell Collection)

2. Vazsic, Gallery of the Palais Royale (courtesy Bibliothèque Nationale)

33. The Opéra, Paris (courtesy
Musée Carnavalet, Paris)

34. Louise Contat as Suzannah in
the *Marriage of Figaro* (courtesy
Bibliothèque Nationale)

a

b

5. The Directors: a. Carnot b. Reubell c. La Réveillière–Lépeaux d. Barras (courtesy Bibliothèque Nationale)

c

d

36. General Clarke (courtesy Bibliothèque Nationale)

37. General Hoche (courtesy Bibliothèque Nationale)

38. Hue, The port of Brest in 1794 (courtesy Musée de la Marine, Paris)

39. Truguet, Minister of Marine (courtesy Bibliothèque Nationale)

40. General Chérin (courtesy Bibliothèque Nationale)

41. Thomas Paine (courtesy Bibliothèque Nationale)

42. General Kilmaine (courtesy Bibliothèque Nationale)

3. General Daendels (courtesy Bibliothèque Nationale)

44. Lord Edward Fitzgerald (Madden, *United Irishmen*)

45. Napper Tandy (Madden, *United Irishmen*)

46. Talleyrand (courtesy Bibliothèque Nationale)

47. Crepin, The combat of the frigate 'La Loire', off Lough Swilly, Oct. 1798 (courtesy Musée de Brest)

48. Capture of the French Fleet off Lough Swilly, October 1798, after a painting by Capt. M. Oates (courtesy National Maritime Museum, Greenwich)

Within the image: *The Hoche in tow of the Doris* after Warn's action. 12 Oct 1798

49. The *Hoche* in tow of the *Doris*, Oct. 1798, after a painting by N. Pocock (courtesy National Maritime Museum, Greenwich)

50. Theobald Wolfe Tone, after his capture in October 1798 (*Walker's Hibernian Magazine*)

The Unfortunate
THEOBALD WOLFE TONE, ESQ.

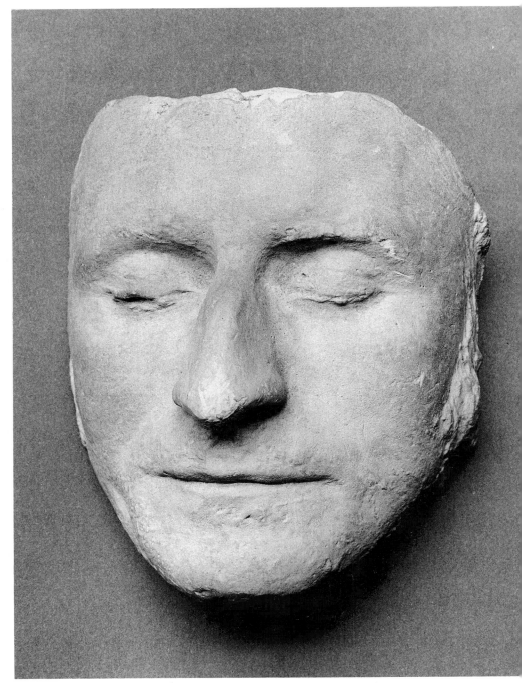

51. Death-mask of Tone (courtesy The Board of Trinity College, Dublin)

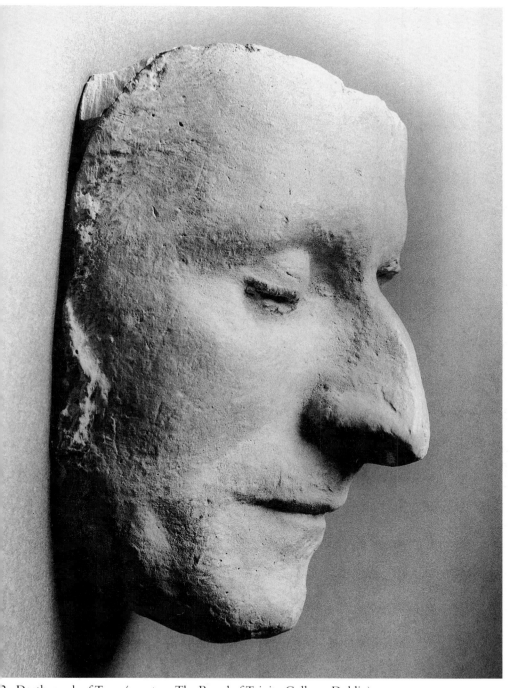

2. Death-mask of Tone (courtesy The Board of Trinity College, Dublin)

53. William Theobald Wolfe Tone (Madden, *United Irishmen*)

in June and July as his money runs out and he stands on his dignity as an official of the Irish 'nation' as a reflexive cover for his own embarrassment. 'I have written a short letter to Carnot', he wrote to Clarke on 18 July, '... mentioning the expence I have been at, and praying the Directory to accord me such assistance as he may think reasonable. I hope you will see that it will not be for the dignity of the republic to leave me in any difficulties, especially when my request is moderate. You must see that some money is indispensably necessary for my equipment etc. and as I am here a kind of ambassador *incognito*, I consider any sum advanced to me, as given on account of my country and as such to be repaid.'[38] But such pomposity was out of character and privately he recognised the ridiculousness of the situation. 'So here I am, with exactly two louis in my exchequer, negotiating with the French Government, and planning revolutions —I must say it is truly original.... I reckon I am the poorest ambassador today in Paris.'[39] Indeed what strikes one most about these journals and the documentation of Tone's Paris mission is the infrequency of any mention of those concepts of nationhood, the armed struggle or English tyranny with which his name is so often associated. And when they do appear the terms are invoked rather to assert his own purity of motive and indeed to instil some Dutch courage in him for a very lonely and otherwise daunting task. All of which makes the autobiography (written in Paris) the more surprising, as it is sometimes interpreted as Tone creating his own myth for posterity.

These 'Memorandums, relative to my Life and Opinions', or autobiography, were written in Paris between 7 August and 8 September 1796. They were edited by Tone's widow and son and form the basis of the published *Life*, with the 17 surviving notebooks of his day-to-day journal broken into supportive appendices. The editorial process thereby endowed two quite separate works with a consistency which in reality they did not possess. Certainly the printed version ensured a greater prominence to the 'Memorandums' than to the more accurate portrayal of his own character in the journals. There is an apparent clarity of interpretation which has raised them to the level of gospel. But the writing of the 'Memorandums' came on the heels of a long period of clarifying, synthesising and, inevitably, propagandising, as Tone argued the Irish case with the Directory, and their polemic is quite out of character with the general style of the daily journals. They were also written during that hiatus in Paris between completing his mission and leaving to take up his posting with the Irish expedition. Tone is genuinely surprised at what has been achieved. Throughout his months in Paris he tends to knock any emergent sense of destiny on the head as wishful thinking.

Success, when it came in July and August, did so suddenly, and following upon so many months of frustration left Tone in something of a daze. It was, he admitted, like a 'romance', and in this frame of mind he set out to explain how he had arrived at such a point. The sense of destiny, which is evident in the autobiography, was a feeling of the moment. It does not re-emerge in the continuing journals. The timing of the composition of the autobiography is therefore essential to its understanding.

Tone was a faithful recorder of the events through which he lived. But his knowledge of Irish history was poor. In this he was typical of his time. Eighteenth-century Ireland did not produce a Hume or a Robertson, and what passed for Irish history was little more than propaganda, or, more charitably, committed history dictated by sectarian leanings.[40] In the liberal ethos of Trinity College in the 1780s it was fashionable to take the Catholic side in debates on the 1641 rising. Tone was present at such debates, and if his friend Thomas Addis Emmet traced his own radicalism to the reading of Curry's *Civil Wars*, with its Catholic viewpoint, he cannot have been alone in that.[41] Tone may have been writing some kind of political testimonial for posterity, in Paris in 1796, but it is not always clear that this was his intention. He was simply writing history as it was written at the time. Yet in doing so he produced the first nationalist reading of Irish history, a reading that was to become the gospel of Irish republicanism. The elements of that gospel, stripped of its American and French terminology, are that the Catholics are the Irish nation proper; Protestant power is based on 'massacre and plunder' and penalisation of the Catholics, reducing them to the slavishness which the Catholic Committee finally broke in 1792.

In this reading Protestant nationalism does not figure: the Catholic 'patriot parliament' of 1689 (misdated in Tone's account as 1688) he sees as fighting for 'national supremacy', because it denied the right of England to legislate for Ireland. But the narrow Protestantism of future Parliaments negates the validity of their similar stand. Nor does he recognise that the men of the 'patriot parliament' were Old English, rather than Gaelic Irish, or that they never sought to assert their independence from England. The northern Presbyterians are spared such blanket condemnation by virtue of their anti-Englishness, anti-Episcopalianism, and what Tone sees as their natural republicanism. In all he rather glamorises the Presbyterians and never comes to terms with their anti-popery.

In his journals Tone spoke of those who had snubbed him for his political opinions and of how his current station placed him 'on as high a ground' as any of them.[42] In August 1796 he had greater cause to feel satisfied, and his youthful rejection by Pitt, his irritation with the Ponsonbys who treated him as a hack, and the haughtiness of the English and their agents in Ireland all become conflated. His hatred of an aristocratic faction is subsumed by his recognition of England as the evil genius. In looking back on his own political development he admits that he did not actively seek a republic, that the pinnacle of his ambition for a while was a seat in the Irish Parliament and that his anti-Englishness was an instinct rather than a principle. Yet although his journal shows a more contained dislike of England, similar to that felt by the Protestant Ascendancy itself, the process of exile—in particular his writings for the Directory—had funnelled all his own and Ireland's troubles to one source: English rule. The atmosphere in France in 1796 would in itself have crystallised such feelings, for Anglophobia was all-pervasive, and France's attribution of every problem to her evil neighbour provided a ready model.

Tone's application of the model to Ireland began late in March. He was asked to write two manifestos, one for dissemination by the commander of the proposed Chouan-like expedition to England, the second by the general landing in Ireland. Tone was irritated. He had not yet recognised that part of his mission in France was to write French propaganda. Eventually he refused to compose the English manifesto and took nearly six weeks to write the Irish one. Since he did not want to do it anyway, he adopted a mischievous approach, ending up, as he often did, convincing himself by his own writing. 'At work this morning at my manifesto', he wrote on 25 March. 'I find a strong disposition to be scurrilous against the English Government, which I will not check.' The outcome was the rambling and emotional 'Address to the People of Ireland'. It was more a personal testament than the required propaganda and he was asked to make a number of changes before it was sent to Hoche.[43]

In this the aristocratic faction—so often the butt of Tone's criticism—appears only as the 'renegade Irishman'. The main attack is directed at England's 'tyrannical dominion' and 'flagrant despotism' in Ireland, 'a haughty conqueror' who 'for seven centuries' had plundered Ireland of its men and natural wealth, reduced its peasantry to a state of misery (the description of which is a caricature of the peasant's lot such as appears nowhere else in Tone's works) and kept the country in thrall by exciting religious divisions and bribing its governors.

By September the emotional propaganda of the invasion manifesto had been refined and accepted as his 'theory', a theory which in retrospect Tone saw as having dictated his actions since 1791: 'that the influence of England was the radical vice of our Government, . . . that Ireland would never be free, prosperous, or

happy, until she was independent, and that independence was unattainable whilst the connection with England existed'. It was a
'theory' discovered only at the end of his first 'volume', which
had started out as an unpretentious affair. Volume II in contrast is
entitled 'Memorandum, relative to my Life and Opinions 1796'. it
has become a personal manifesto, and the elements in his 'theory'
re-sorted accordingly. 'To subvert the tyranny of our execrable Government, to break the connection with England, the never-failing
source of all our political evils, and to assert the independence of my
country—these were my objects. To unite the whole people of
Ireland, to abolish the memory of all past dissensions, and to substitute the common name of Irishman in the place of the denominations of Protestant, Catholic and Dissenter—these were my means.'
In thus reversing the order of things, that union of sects which he
more than anyone else had stood for when in Ireland was taking a
secondary place to independence and the way being prepared for
others to jettison it altogether.[44]

23

Adjutant-General

Tone left Paris for Rennes on the afternoon of 17 September 1796, having taken his farewell of Madgett and Aherne and written formal letters of thanks to Carnot and Delacroix.[1] For three days and nights they travelled without stopping to avoid attack in Chouan country. The journey took its toll. Illness caused Tone to miss a grand ball given by Hoche in the Hotel de Ville at Rennes. Not that he thought the ladies of the town attractive; on the contrary he considered them 'villainous ugly'. But he was robbed of his first chance to show off that uniform which had been the object of his youthful ambition.[2]

Indeed Tone's career as a French officer is an indication of how very different things might have been had his father accommodated his military leanings. The ease with which he settled into military life is remarkable, considering his lack of previous experience. His natural sensitivity would have picked up any criticism of his in-experience and rapid promotion to adjutant-general. Yet he was readily accepted as one of the General Staff and lodged with Hoche and the other officers at headquarters in the former Bishop's Palace. It was 'a superb mansion', notes Tone, 'but not much the better of the Revolution', with its chapel now serving as military stables. The veteran Colonel Henry Shee, uncle and guardian to Clarke, was to become a particular friend. Tone worked closely with him planning troop dispositions and routes for the forthcoming landing.

He loved the camaraderie, indeed the very carelessness, of military life. He even accepted the need sometimes to go without a bed and without sleep—a great sacrifice for Tone—as one of the conditions of military life. The comradeship more than compensated for it, and he recounts with obvious pleasure how he and Hoche's aide-de-camp, Privat, 'lay awake half the night laughing and making execrable puns', though sleeping rough on a floor in Montauban. 'I like this life of all things'. Tone admitted. 'There is a gaiety and a carelessness about military men, which interests me infinitely.'[3] Since the French army now looked after his material needs, there was none of the nagging financial worry which had infused his Paris journal with its ill-ease.

A sense of insecurity continued for some weeks, however, as he noticed an apparent coolness on the part of Hoche. Hoche set his mind at rest. Indeed the General's assurances of friendship astonished and at times embarrassed Tone. Hoche displayed it straight away by sending Duckett, of whom Tone had complained, back to Paris.[4] Tone's constant need to be accepted by those he admired had greatly exacerbated his situation in Paris, separated from his Irish friends and colleagues and with no new set yet established. Relations with Clarke had never been warm. His acceptance by Hoche and the other French officers restored his confidence. His flair for writing revived, and although he acted as propagandist at military headquarters in Rennes, composing all the handbills and addresses to be distributed when the expedition arrived in Ireland, he never complained at being used as a service writer, as he had done in Paris.

It is not surprising that Tone found Hoche so captivating. To all the command and presence of a general were attached an enormous charm and sympathy. The two men shared many characteristics. Hoche worried about his health, loved praise more than power, was as suspicious of others as was Tone himself. Hoche's motives in promoting the Irish expedition combined republican zeal with the quest for military glory, and not a little pique at the attention being showered upon Bonaparte. Austria's rupture of the armistice in July switched military attention back to the Rhine and southern Europe, and the unexpected importance of the Italian campaign altered the nature of the French war effort in the closing months of 1796. As mounting difficulties prevented the departure of the Irish expedition, Hoche wondered if he had miscalculated in accepting his present command.[5] But his Bonaparte fixation should not be overemphasised in Hoche's motivation. There was considerable rivalry among all the French generals. Hoche was the most sincere republican among them, and in his correspondence of these months a genuine republican idealism, the pursuit of glory and an intense hatred of England are intertwined.

In time Tone's feelings for Hoche amounted to near-adulation. He was not the only one to see the expedition's fate vested in the young general, and he was sometimes critical of the chances Hoche took with his own life. Only days before they sailed he disappeared, to spend two days and nights with 'a charming little aristocrat', all of whose relations were Chouans, without telling his staff where he had gone. It would not have been the first time in these weeks that an attempt was made on his life: 'if anything happened Hoche, there is an end of our business—it was damned indiscreet in him, but God forbid I should be the man to accuse him, for I have been buffeted myself so often by the foul fiend that it would be rather indecent in me to censure him—(sings) "*'Tis woman that seduces all mankind*".

I do not think, however (but God knows) that, under the present circumstances, I would have gone catterwauling for two days among the Chouans....I was very angry with him, which, as I never did a foolish thing myself in my life, for the sake of a woman, was but reasonable'.[6]

I

In the course of that summer French plans for Ireland had been radically altered. They now believed that they were invading a friendly country, and so the troops were ordered to behave. Plans for Chouan-like landings were switched entirely to England.[7] There would be two landings in England, one under General Quantin in the north-east near Newcastle, the other under Humbert in the south-west near Bristol. The object was to create havoc and panic; Bristol was to be razed and Liverpool threatened with a similar fate to extort compensation. Neither French general was noted for his intelligence. But Humbert was known to be recklessly courageous, and their recent experience suppressing *chouannerie* recommended them for such *coups de main*.[8] The two forces became receptacles for deserters, convicts released on Hoche's orders, trouble-makers sent by their commanding officers and, symbolically, ex-Chouans who had been persuaded to turn on their former ally. It was out-and-out piracy, and Hoche's reputation, and with it the Irish plans, were to suffer when the plans for England became public. Tone watched Humbert's Légion Noire at Brest and thought them 'desperadoes', not dissimilar 'either in appearance or morality' from the faction-fighters of Dublin's Ormond Quay.[9] The scene around Dunkirk, where Quantin's rag-tag force was gathering, became one of considerable confusion. The men arriving at the depots were half starved and inadequately clothed. The regulars refused to serve with them and huge numbers deserted, taking their baggage and arms with them. By late November, when he was removed from the command, Quantin was a nervous wreck.[10]

He was replaced by the seventy-year-old American, Colonel William Tate, who had raised men for France in America and recently offered to lead a buccaneering expedition to Bermuda.[11] Hoche asked Tone to translate and copy the new instructions. He did so with obvious concern, and worked himself into a passion about England in justification: 'it is these considerations which steel me against horrors which I should otherwise shudder to think of. Yet I cannot but remark what misery the execution of the orders which I have transcribed, and assisted in framing, may produce.' He was particularly concerned by the instructions to burn Bristol:

the third city of the British dominions in which there is perhaps property to the amount of five millions...it is no slight affair; thousands and thousands of families, if the attempt succeeds, will be reduced to beggary—I cannot help it!—If it must be, it must, and I will never blame the French for any degree of misery which they may inflict on the people of England—I do not think my morality, or feeling, is much improved by my promotion to the rank of Adjutant-General—The truth is I hate the very name of England; I hated her before my exile; I hate her since, and I will hate her always![12]

Hoche pursued the invasion plans with a new sense of mission after his meetings with Tone and O'Connor. He had been assured by O'Connor that the Defenders were well organised and that 15,000 men and 5,000 horses would be ready when the French arrived.[13] On his return to Brest on 26 September, Hoche found the Irish plans in abeyance as the naval commander Villaret continued preparations for the already agreed Indian expedition. Warning letters from Bruix, director of the port of Brest, and from Hoche's aide-de-camp Simon, fed his naturally suspicious nature. In a series of letters to Clarke and the Directory in the first week of October he denounced the naval commanders, claimed the Irish expedition the only way to force England to make peace, and urged the abandonment of the Indian expedition. Hoche was right in his accusations of bad faith in the naval command. The case of Tone's returned émigré friends re-enlisting in the navy was not unusual. The naval command was suspected of royalism and in Villaret's case the accusation was all too true.[14]

But the blame for the delays cannot be laid entirely at the navy's door. The Indian expedition was part of the Directory's obligations to its Dutch ally, who had already paid a subsidy of 3,000,000 guilders, and Truguet was reluctant to abandon it.[15] Villaret did not receive clear instructions about the Irish plans until the Indian expedition was cancelled on 13 October.[16] Moreover the problems of paying the men and equipping the expedition would have defied the efforts of the most committed. In July Hoche had forced through approval of 250,000 francs in specie for the Irish expedition. But the Directory could not impose its will on the Treasury, and three months later the money still had not arrived.[17] Contractors, port workers and troops were unpaid. All down the line Hoche was having to assume personal control. It was taking its toll of his patience. Time was slipping away and he cast anxious side-glances at the achievements of rival generals elsewhere. Early in October he seized the initiative and distributed shoes, shirts and jackets to the workers who had been unpaid for five months. By December he was recommending melting down the copper and bronze in Brest and making money on the spot, and he still had to find 7,000 sailors before the expedition could sail.[18]

But Villaret did not abandon the Indian plans and ignored Truguet's instruction of October to concentrate efforts on Ireland. Tone attended a dinner of the military and naval command on 4 November. 'This dinner is to manifest to the public that there is a perfect harmony between the land and sea service, which I am sorry to see is far from being the case.'[19] Villaret was raising all manner of objections to sending his ships to sea. Relations between the army and navy were already so soured that Hoche issued a statement to his troops denying the slanderous rumours being put about and attempting to put a stop to the conflicts and duels which had already begun.[20] Why were the naval officers he had recommended not appointed?, Hoche wrote in exasperation to the Directory on 6 November. 'Because he [Villaret] thought it would be difficult to command men more intelligent than he....Give me a naval commander and we will sail.'[21] The Directory had been pushing the Irish preparations with renewed vigour, to strengthen its hand in forthcoming peace negotiations with England, and Villaret's complaints were not well received. On 17 November he was removed and replaced by Morard de Galles.[22]

The victory was but partial. Morard was another aristocrat, a veteran of the American war, and in Hoche's eyes at fifty-five too old. More to the point. Morard was a reluctant commander. He pleaded ill health and poor eyesight and tendered his resignation, but to no avail.[23] Moreover his instructions took no account of previous naval objections, although Hoche's overall control was reaffirmed.[24]

II

Hoche's impatience and frustration reached a new peak with news brought by sailors on 3 November of a rising in Ireland. From their different perspectives both Truguet and Tone dismissed the report as sailors' exaggeration.[25] But it reinforced Hoche's complaints about the delays and his own sense of urgency was now entirely shared by Paris. After months of inadequate instructions and indecision, from late October the Directory shared Hoche's view that Ireland held the key to England's defeat and to lasting peace.[26] On 23 October Lord Malmesbury arrived in Paris as England's negotiator in tentative peace discussions. Few in France thought England sincere, and so confident had the Directory become about success in Ireland that it used the negotiations to intensify French Anglophobia.[27] Time enough to discuss peace, wrote Truguet in optimistic mood on 13 October, with 10,000 French troops in Ireland.[28]

The secrecy surrounding the preparations was now almost total. The Paris newspapers had given up trying to discover the destination of the Brest preparations and Malmesbury was likewise confused.[29] Hoche had false documentation printed to mislead the British into thinking Portugal the French destination. The destination was handwritten at the last moment into pre-printed instructions, which were sealed in packages to be opened at sea.[30] Hoche's secrecy was becoming obsessive, and ultimately tied the fate of the expedition to his person.

On 13 November Tone was sent among the British prisoners of war at Pontanezen to recruit for the coming expedition. He was struck by the character differences between the Irish and English there. Tone had supplied them with wine. The Irish, though half naked and starved, forgot their cares. Most enlisted without hesitation, and wanted to flog the English who did not do so. In contrast the English balanced the pros and cons and asked what reward they would get if they joined up. The Irish prisoners reminded Tone of the warring gangs on Dublin's quays. But he preferred their emotionalism to the calculation of the others, even if he admired the English soldiers' sense of honour in refusing to fight against their country. On several other occasions he had reason to pay tribute to the honour of the English, a worthy foe much as he thought Fitzgibbon, though he rarely had a good word to say for the English government. Among the prisoners he discovered a little English boy, William White, a foundling from Dorset, whom he took as his servant. 'He is so young that he will not be of much use to me', remarked Tone, 'but he was an orphan and half naked.'[31]

News of the supposed Irish rising intensified Hoche's anxiety that the French had not arrived at the time indicated to O'Connor. Tone likewise was anxious. On 29 October he had read a newspaper report taken from the *Northern Star* of 16 September telling of the arrest of many of his Belfast friends. Dublin Castle thought Ireland in a state of 'smothered rebellion' by the end of the summer. Defenders and United Irishmen were being urged to conserve their strength in expectation of imminent French help, and envoys were reputed to have been in Paris making arrangements for the landing. Reports came in of widespread disaffection among the militia, and of arms having been landed from France. Tone was sceptical about the latter. Shee assured him that they were true. Certainly an American cutter, the *Olive Branch*, was captured out of France in November, carrying 20,000 stand of arms and a train of artillery, destined, it was thought for Ireland.[32] Camden held out little hope of defending

Ireland in the event of a French landing, however small, and when the Ulster United movement was successfully infiltrated by spies, the information obtained was used to issue warrants for high treason against the Ulster leaders, including Russell, Neilson, Charles Teeling and McCracken.[33] Parliament was recalled early to rush through the suspension of habeas corpus, and by November the Insurrection Act was in force through much of the north. Yet Camden recognised that the effects of the new clamp-down would not be felt for some time, and he predicted a major rising in the north if the French landed.[34]

Tone was *en route* from Rennes to Brest when he read the news of his friends' arrest, and was distracted almost beyond expression. He had already read of Edward Sweetman's death in a duel in March, and he now reflected on how desolate would be his future on losing such friends. He regretted in particular the levity with which he had always spoken of Russell. The desire to save them spurred his impatience to sail.[35] However much he doubted reports coming through of an Irish rising, he agreed with Hoche that someone should be sent immediately to secure up-to-date information on the current situation in Ireland.

Bernard MacSheehy, a twenty-two-year-old ex-student of the Irish College, one of Madgett's protégés, was chosen. Tone, who was pestered by MacSheehy at Rennes, thought him a fool, and worse still a fool who gave himself airs and graces.[36] Tone did not suffer fools gladly and though he often jumped to conclusions rather too quickly about a person's character, in MacSheehy's case his judgement appears to have been sound. The younger man was prone to exaggeration, self-aggrandisement and intrigue, and was at the centre of a divisive conflict among the exiled Irish some years later.[37]

Yet *faute de mieux* Tone recommended him that November for the fact-finding mission. Hoche had arranged for an American ship to leave that very evening, 7 November. MacSheehy was to secure information on the state of Ireland, the temper of the people, the disposition of the troops, whether the French were expected and in what place. Tone was concerned that no information on the French preparations was to be given in return, and as he equipped MacSheehy with Irish-style clothes he added a number of instructions of his own. He was to call on Bond and McCormick and as credentials was to relate certain facts which could only have come from Tone himself. He was to tell them that Tone was at Brest, 'that I had the rank of adjutant general in the army of the republic, and that I was in good repute with the general and the government', that an expedition was 'in great forwardness at Brest' and that they should do all in their power to postpone the trials of their arrested friends, as 'in a short time we should be there to rescue them'. Tone then walked with him down to the quay and MacSheehy sailed that night.[38]

Although MacSheehy's reports exaggerated his own firmness (which at the last moment Tone found wanting) and the dangers he had encountered, he conducted his mission well. He arrived in Dublin on 26 November, and with some difficulty established contact and overcame the doubts of Bond and McCormick. He also spoke with MacNeven and Lewins and sent someone to bring back information from Ulster. He was assured that many militiamen and yeomen had been won over and that the United Irish movement had begun to spread from the north through the south and west, that if the French could carry on their campaign in Ireland for two months without making any levy on the Irish people, success would be guaranteed. The Irish asked for large supplies of arms and artillery, and thought 18,000 to 20,000 French (the main force to land near Galway, a second landing at Lough Swilly) would be enough to expel the English entirely. Crown forces in Ireland then stood at 45,000, 25,000 of whom were militia and many of them Defenders. But apart from 10,000 near Dublin and 5,000 at Belfast, the rest of the force was scattered over the island.[39] MacSheehy was assured that in the north 50,000 would join the French and that measures had already been taken to ensure the necessary horses and equipages in the designated ports.[40] He returned to Brest on 18 December, two days after the expedition had finally sailed, but in time to infuse a new sense of urgency and purpose into a follow-up expedition organising under General Hédouville.[41]

III

On 30 November Tone was ordered to prepare for embarkation. Accordingly, he packed his trunk and wrote to Matilda. He had written on 26 May telling her to come to France, only to discover that the ship which carried the letter had been captured by the English. He repeated his instructions in another of 28 July and Matilda had left Princeton on 10 October.[42] He had heard some months previously of a tragic case of a mother and her children perishing within sight of France, and the thought of his family now at sea and all 'the perils of a winter passage' caused him to fear that his distress on going aboard would be misinterpreted.

Yet in his letter to his wife he had to address the possibility of his own death: 'should that event happen, I hope you will have the courage to support the loss as may become you, as well for your own sake as that of our dear children. . . .I need not add any cold arguments on the folly of grieving for what is not to be retrieved. . . . should the worst happen, remember you will be their only parent—I

need not, indeed I cannot say more'. If he was killed and the
expedition succeeded, she was to go to Ireland. 'I do not think so ill
of my country or my friends as to doubt that in that case provision
will be made for you and my children.' If it failed she was to address
herself to Carnot, Clarke, Colonel Shee 'who is my particular friend'
and Hoche. 'God knows whether all this will produce anything, for
the government here is, I know, in the last distress for money.'
If her application failed he trusted Matthew would stay with her
and it would be her choice whether to remain in France or return
to America.

Yet he was optimistic of success, if they did not meet up with the
English fleet—and orders were to avoid a sea battle at all costs.
'When the country is once emancipated, there will be I think no
situation that I will, in reason, demand which will be refused me',
and if they succeeded he thought he would have earned it. Once
again, however, it was not political leadership to which he aspired,
but a commission in the new Irish army, and he presumed he would
not be offered a rank lower than that he already held. Then Mary
would at last see him in what she used to call his *Etat Militaire*,
trading his blue and scarlet French uniform for one 'as green as a
leek, which I think will be *more becoming*'.

The third possibility was that the expedition would be forced back
to France, in which case he promised to settle down 'and devote
the remainder of my life to making you happy and educating our
children'. He was weary of their perpetual separation. Yet this was a
gloomy prospect, for then their friends in prison would fall and he
relives his 'unspeakable distress' at Sweetman's death and the arrests.
It is a long, cramped letter, written over the two days while he
awaited orders to embark and *more rambling than was normal for Tone*.
Having started out steadily enough, the two days waiting for final
orders take their toll and his anxieties come out towards the end.
'This letter is dreadfully unconnected, but the fact is, I write in a state
of the utmost anxiety and incertitude...uncertain of your fate and
that of our children, uncertain of my own...I think it is hardly
possible to conceive a more painful and anxious situation; add to this,
that I am obliged to devour my uneasiness, from the fear of appearing
disheartened at the moment of embarkation.' At that moment he was
told to be ready to embark in half an hour. He signed the letter with
his own name, as if this expedition would be the final arbiter of his
fate.[43]

The *Indomptable* in which Tone was to sail was a fast-sailing ship
of the line of 80 guns, the largest of the expeditionary force. It was
commanded by Captain Bedout, a Canadian who spoke English and
whom Tone considered one of the few sincere officers of the navy. It

was a sound judgement. Bedout was one of those officers Hoche had campaigned to have included in the naval command.[44] The officers on board included, besides Tone, the military commander General Chérin, Hoche's particular friend, Chasseloup, Vaudré, artillery commander, and Simon, who with Tone was to command the main deck and who also spoke English. A woman in boy's clothes—the wife of one of the *commissaires*—had joined them, and although Tone thought her 'not very handsome', possessed of 'no talents, and (between friends) she was originally a Fille de joie at Paris', he approved of the civilising influence a woman's presence had on them. The ceiling of the officers' mess was lined with firelocks for the expedition, the weather was calm and the sight of the ships at anchor and the strains of military music delighted Tone. Yet he was not so enamoured of the French as not to have reservations about how they would act in Ireland. Corruption in military supply was rife and he wondered how they would control 'the little army of commissaires, ready to eat up the country, who would sacrifice the liberty of Ireland, the interests of the Republic, and the honor of the General, for half a crown'.[45]

Another two weeks was to elapse before the expedition finally sailed. Although the spirit of the troops remained excellent, opposition from the naval command continued. Supplies were running low and even Truguet was growing weary of his officers' vacillation.[46] Hoche believed that they must either leave immediately or abandon the expedition. In an angry letter to the War Minister Petiet on 8 December he decided on the latter. 'After trying everything I am now forced to give up my enterprise, our detestable navy can and will do nothing: I now offer to the Government the 16,000 troops I have reserved for this expedition.'[47] The minister was staggered by the dispatch and contacted Carnot for advice. The Directory now began to take seriously naval arguments that such an expedition would damage their already inferior fleet. On the 17th the Irish expedition was cancelled and Hoche ordered to take his troops to Italy.[48]

However, the long-awaited arrival on 12 December of Vice-Admiral Richery with five ships and three frigates altered the mental climate in Brest. The fact that he had come through the English blockade was a major achievement, even if most of his ships required repairs and only two ships and two frigates proved sufficiently seaworthy to sail with the expedition. Hoche wrote to the Directory, apologising for the despondency of his previous dispatch and proposing to work night and day to overcome the obstacles put in his way by the naval commanders.[49] Things were not ready to the navy's satisfaction; inadequately prepared signals and a continuing shortage of sailors hounded the enterprise from the outset. Yet on the morning of the 15th the expedition finally sailed. Hoche had joined Morard de Galles on the frigate *La Fraternité*. His reason for going on board a frigate rather than the flagship baffled others besides Tone. It was not so much that Hoche distrusted Morard. Rather, it was to stop the scandalous insubordination of the navy.[50]

News of the sailing revived the Directory's enthusiasm. Hédouville was to sail with another 17,000 troops as soon as possible. Truguet was sent personally to Brest to help remove obstacles to the departure and on the 19th Malmesbury was ordered out of Paris.[51] Forty-three vessels, 17 of which were ships of the line, and 14,450 troops had left with Hoche and more artillery, arms and ammunition for the Irish than Tone could ever have hoped for. Weather conditions were perfect. The British fleet was ill prepared. Few expeditions sailing from French shores under the Directory had a better chance of success. Few were to be so ill-fated.

Bantry Bay

Tone's roughly written and cramped journal of the voyage is the most vivid account of the French expedition to have survived, and its accuracy is confirmed by the accounts of the other officers.[1] Aside from the continuing disagreements and a remarkable run of bad weather, what emerges most forcibly from these accounts is France's naval ineptitude by contrast with her astounding military record. 'We set sail like children getting out of school', wrote one officer, and within sight of port a number of ships, including the *Fraternité*, collided. Disaster struck before they had even reached the open sea. To avoid the blockading British fleet, a decision was made to sail south, at night-time, via the Pointe du Raz with its treacherous reefs and turbulent seas. Tone learnt from Bedout that the *Indomptable* had almost struck a rock, in which case 'we should have gone to pieces in a quarter of an hour', and Bedout admitted he would rather endure three sea engagements than pass through the Raz again at night.

Others had not been so fortunate. The *Séduisant* (a 74-gun ship of the line) had foundered near the same spot, with the loss of all but 45 of the 1,300 men on board. Fog and poor visibility the following morning scattered the fleet. Only 17 ships remained together of the original 43, and worst of all the *Fraternité* was missing, Morard de Galles's signals for a change of course having become confused with the distress signals of the *Séduisant*. On the night of the 19th they separated again, and in moderate weather, which augured ill for their fate when bad weather set in on the 20th. Tone by this stage was too upset to partake of the military company he so enjoyed, choosing instead to walk alone in the gallery.[2] By then the *Fraternité* had been blown out into the Atlantic.

The loss of Hoche was irreparable, particularly since he had kept his intentions so secret that many officers did not learn of the expedition's destination until they opened their sealed packets on the 20th. With the loss of the *Fraternité*, Bouvet and Grouchy assumed command and opened the packet containing the secret instructions. Bantry Bay was their destination, and failing that the mouth of the Shannon. Bantry had replaced Galway because of the lateness of the season, its proximity to France, and rumours that the defending forces had learnt of their Galway plans.[3] But the instructions of

Morard de Galles should the fleet become separated were to cruise five days off Mizen Head, a further three off the mouth of the Shannon, and if no frigate arrived with further instructions, to return to Brest. The orders were designed only for individual ships, but conflicted sufficiently with those of Hoche to be used by the reluctant naval commanders in justification of their action in not entering Bantry Bay.[4]

At dawn on the 21st they sighted the Irish coast. By midday they were approaching Bantry Bay. The mountains were covered with snow and some of the officers became dispirited at no sign of welcome from the Irish people.[5] They seemed near enough to Ireland to toss a biscuit on land. Then to Tone's consternation they sailed away to begin their cruise off Cape Clear, which they mistook for Mizen Head. They had regrouped to 36 ships, and here they were wasting time and losing the advantage of surprise. Moreover, apart from Simon and Bedout, Tone found most of the officers speaking as if the expedition had already failed. 'I do not at all like the countenance of the État Major in this crisis; when they speak of the expedition, it is in a style of despondence. . . . I see nothing of that spirit of enterprise, combined with a steady resolution, which our present situation demands.'[6] He was not alone in criticising the defeatism of the second-in-command and their failure to adapt their instructions to the new situation.

They were told by several Irish pilots that no other French ships had been sighted off the Irish coast. With the weather deteriorating fast, Grouchy decided on the 22nd to anchor in Bantry Bay. Sixteen ships, including the *Indomptable*, entered the Bay. Bouvet remained with 19 outside. All the printed papers, including Tone's addresses, had been lost on the *Fraternité* and as they anchored off Bere Island on the evening of the 22nd he and Chérin set to preparing new addresses.

Tone had to compose them anew, and given the circumstances his three addresses to the Irish peasantry, militia, and to Irishmen serving in the British navy are good examples of his gifts as a propagandist. Like all good propaganda, they are totally one-sided. The lot of the Irish peasant is equated with that of his French counterpart before the Revolution, fleeced by the landlords and clergy. But the Revolution abolished unjust distinctions, taxes and tithes, expelled the peasant's enemies and allowed him for the first time to enjoy the fruits of his labour. Did Tone believe all this? Almost certainly—he never recognised that *chouannerie* was a symptom of more widespread peasant discontent with revolutionary change. But he had no illusions about popular motivation, and the address was firmly directed at the Irish peasantry's self-interest, as were the other two to the militia and the sailors. To the one he holds out the promise of commissions open to talent in an Irish army, just as they were in France; to the others an equal share in prize money for bringing their vessels to Irish ports. The papers play upon Irish attachment to family by claiming that now Ireland was independent they would simply be turning their arms against their own kin. They likewise pick up on the Irishman's historic grievance of being treated as inferior by Englishmen.[7]

That night a driving gale separated the ships in the Bay and scattered those outside. By the morning of the 23rd only 6,400 men remained. Hoche, had they but known, was only two leagues away, kept back by the adverse winds.[8] Tone, in a moment of desperation, offered to lead the ill-famed Légion des Francs to Sligo Bay, supposing none of the French generals would wish to risk his reputation on 'such a desperate exercise' and knowing how expendable was the Légion. He was astonished to find his fellow officers in agreement that a landing should be attempted.

As the storm continued to rage, a boat was lowered and Chérin, Vaudré and Tone rowed to the *Immortalité* to convince Grouchy. Surprised by his readiness to risk all, their desperation gave way to a nervous gaiety at the ridiculousness of their situation. None had ever commanded so few men, and here they were about to invade Ireland, with no money, no tents, no horses, and but four pieces of artillery. The landing was to take place the next day, Christmas. They would march on Cork, then on Dublin. If they met significant resistance in either place, they would turn towards the Shannon and head north. Grouchy wrote to the Directory requesting reinforcements, and the dispatch of some fast-sailing vessels with arms to their supporters in Ulster. But the determination which had so pleasantly surprised Tone and his fellow officers that morning was only apparent. Grouchy's letters announcing the new strategy to the Directory and the Minister of War reveal his characteristic hesitancy and defeatism, for which he was to be damned at Waterloo. Whatever happened, he disclaimed responsibility in advance, blaming Hoche for failing to share details of his overall plan with his officers.[9]

Grouchy prepared a new proclamation to the soldiers, instructing them to treat the Irish as friends. Property and persons were to be respected and pillage would be punishable by death. Yet, with the Légion des Francs in the advance guard—contrary to Hoche's original orders—it is unlikely that such instructions could have been obeyed. Another address to the Irish people was likewise prepared, which Tone translated and copied that evening, along wth various other documents. The French, the address assured them, had come as allies to help in their long struggle against 'proud England'. For too long had she treated Ireland as a conquered province, importing her soldiers and sailors, subordinating Ireland's commerce and Parliament to her own. Join with France against our common enemy, said the address, and expel the evils of this military presence for good.[10]

The soldiers were already growing restless, and the news that they would soon touch land was greeted enthusiastically.[11] An eerie jollity prevailed that night on the *Indomptable*. Tone could not sleep in the storm. He paced the gallery, wrapped in his greatcoat, and 'devoured by the most gloomy reflections'. They were making no progress towards their landing spot because of the raging winds, and Tone recognised that those same winds would soon carry the British fleet to lock them in the Bay. The reflection brought to mind the fate which now almost certainly awaited him. The choice was bleak; he would either be killed in battle or hanged and disembowelled as a traitor. He reflected on the trail of accident and error which had befallen the French forces since they left Brest, and concluded that human error had destroyed their chance of success. For by now he had little hope of it. 'I see nothing before me, unless a miracle be wrought in our favor, but the ruin of the expedition, the slavery of my country and my own destruction. . . . I have a merry Christmas of it today'.[12]

That night the storm grew worse, and through the driving snow and hail they heard shouts from a frigate, which they assumed to be Bouvet's, telling them to cut their cables and sail for France. They had received no previous signal and waited for daylight, thinking it perhaps an enemy ruse. But it was true. At daylight they saw that the *Immortalité*, carrying both naval and military commanders, had gone, and over the next few days the continuing storm forced others to cut their cables and make for home. By the 27th only 10 sail and 4,000 men remained. That night, wrote Tone in his journal, 'it blew a perfect hurricane'. The *Indomptable* ran foul of the frigate *Résolue*, dismasted her and sprung a leak in her own bowsprit.[13] Tone was sea-sick. Water poured into the quarter-gallery, destroying 30 cases of biscuit when their supply situation was already desperate. Water filled the officers' cabin and Tone resigned himself to death. They managed, however, to sail to the second rendezvous, at the mouth of the Shannon, cruised for two days, then steered for France. At daylight on New Year's Day they sighted Ushant. 'The weather was beautiful, the sea calm', commented Vaudré ironically, and that afternoon the little flotilla of eight vessels sailed into Brest. There they found the *Immortalité* and two other ships. Four more returned some hours later. Altogether only 15 of the original 43 ships which had sailed in December had returned to port. 'England has not had such an escape since the Spanish Armada', commented Tone. He doubted if the French would ever make another attempt and accepted that he must now regard himself as a Frenchman and arrange his affairs accordingly.

I

The French ships had sailed to Ireland and back without encountering a single English ship. Britain's mastery of the seas in the 1790s was often more apparent than real, and at the end of 1796 the French could also count on aid from the Dutch and Spanish fleets. England's strategy of open blockade was particularly ineffective. This involved junior commanders cruising off Brest and alerting stations at Cork, Lisbon, and the Channel Fleet at Spithead, if the French sailed. In December 1796 Sir Edward Pellew was cruising within sight of Brest, while the main British squadron under Vice-Admiral Colpoys stood well out to sea and the Channel Fleet under Bridport was 200 miles away wintering at Spithead. Pellew saw the French leave on the 16th and dispatched frigates to alert both commanders. Hoche's deception tactics and the ruse of sailing south round the Pointe du Raz fooled the British commanders into thinking Portugal, rather than Ireland, was Hoche's destination. The bad weather prevented Colpoys and Pellew from meeting up, and Colpoys returned to Spithead on 31 December, his ships buffeted and damaged by the adverse winds.

That day intelligence was received at the Admiralty that the French were in Bantry Bay. The defending forces were totally unprepared. Since they had known for months of the French preparations, the complacency and lack of imagination of Britain's naval and political leaders alike is staggering. Reporting to Dublin on the 21st the first news of Hoche's departure, the Admiralty declared its certainty that he had gone to Spain or Portugal. No fleet, it thought, would risk the voyage to Ireland in winter.[14] High winds not only interrupted communications from Ireland, but also pinned British ships in port until 3 January, by which time most of the French fleet had been and gone.[15]

Throughout the later months of 1796 expectations of an attempt on Ireland ran high in Dublin Castle. Ireland's defence forces were not geared to combating an invading enemy and Camden was irritated by London's condescending assurances that Ireland was safe in the wrap of British naval supremacy.[16] Crown forces in Ireland at the end of 1796 totalled 11,555 infantry, 4,157 cavalry, 21,000 militia.[17] But most were scattered in garrisons intended to deal with domestic disaffection, or the gentry's perceptions of such, and the conflicting needs of concentration for defence and splinterisation for policing duties could only have been resolved by the creation of two entirely different forces.[18] The militia was part of the answer. But in 1796 it was deeply suspect, and Dublin was only just organising a largely Protestant yeomanry force when the French arrived.[19] There were never enough regulars and so concerned was the government at mounting subversion in the north that a series of defence reports indicating Cork and Bantry Bay as the country's most vulnerable points were ignored.[20] There were already 1,600 French prisoners-of-war in the area, 200 of them on parole, and less than 2,000 troops between Bantry and Cork when the French arrived. It would have taken two weeks to collect a force equal to that of the French. In quality, there would have been no comparison, and even Fitzgibbon dismissed the British regulars as 'scabby, beggar fencible regiments, which had more the appearance of Falstaff's recruits than of soldiers to whom the defence of the country was to be entrusted'. Commanders in the Cork region were pessimistic about their ability to defend the area, and Fitzgibbon admitted that if the French had succeeded in landing they would have made it to Dublin with ease.[21]

The scenes in the main towns on news of the French arrival were chaotic. Reports of the French ships in Bantry Bay reached Dublin on Saturday, 24 December.[22] A flurry of military preparations kept the city's inhabitants awake that night, and troops marched out early the next morning, leaving Dublin to the defence of irregulars. Camden feared a financial crisis. Cash payments were suspended in Cork, and a similar crisis was narrowly prevented in Dublin. Military were rushed to the threatened area, leaving other parts of the country—notably the north, where most expected the main French attempt still to be made—at risk in their rear. When French ships were sighted off the west, the orders were countermanded and they were ordered back to the north and west. The terrible weather conditions and rutted roads added to the chaos, and the experience of the two fencible regiments marched to Bandon then back to Cork, and given an hour's rest before setting off again for the Shannon, was typical.[23] Britain experienced a serious shortage of infantry throughout the war and Home Secretary Portland admitted after the event that they could not have spared more than a thousand men to help Ireland had the French landed.[24] However, although a number of militia regiments in the north had been successfully infiltrated by the United Irishmen, there was little sign of open disaffection during the invasion crisis, and much would have depended upon the French attaining some notable victories.

More important in the scale of incalculables was the reaction of the Irish populace. The French troops had been taught to see the venture as a war of liberation and they overestimated the spontaneity of Irish support. 'They think they have nothing to do but to land', reported an Irish merchant captain captured by the French ships, 'that the people of Ireland will embrace them with open arms, and that they will take possession in a very short time'. It was a comment reiterated by other Irish seamen who encountered French ships and endorses French descriptions of the troops' eagerness to land and their high spirits, despite the deprivations.[25] They were baffled at receiving 'no sign of recognition and fraternity from the Irish people', as they lay off the coast, and doubts about the friendly disposition of the Irish destroyed public support for any follow-up in the early months of 1797.[26]

French perceptions of Irish willingness to revolt were indeed inflated, and most of the warnings by Tone, O'Connor and others, that the response of the Irish would depend on the strength of the French forces and their initial actions upon landing, were conveniently forgotten. Outside Ulster the United Irishmen were not well organised. But in anticipation of a French attempt in the spring of 1797, rather than the winter, preparations had already commenced to extend the new organisation into the other provinces, and orders had gone out to the Defenders to keep their powder dry. If the authorities pointed to the quiet of the country as proof of its loyalty, it could with equal plausibility be used to prove the success of United Irish organisation, and privately the Castle admitted as much. The United Irishmen had remained inactive, their representatives later told the Directory, because the French did not land and arrived both in an unexpected place and at an unexpected time. MacSheehy had said nothing about the time of landing, which is why the French were not expected till the following spring.[27] Indeed all accounts agree that the United Irish leaders redoubled their efforts to prevent a premature rising in the belief that the contradictory reports reaching them about the French off Munster were either an attempt by the Castle to provoke premature action, or a decoy for the real French landing which they still expected to take place either in Galway or the north.[28]

After the immediate panic had passed, recriminations began. Neither the London or Dublin government was permitted any triumph in the expedition's failure. They even lost the propaganda battle. Both opposition MPs and United Irishmen argued that if the largely Catholic populace was as loyal as the government claimed, it deserved the political rights which were still withheld. At the height of the panic the Belfast United Irish leaders were able to carry a town meeting on this very point.[29]

The confidence of the government was badly shaken. Camden and his Irish ministers had publicly to defend England while privately fuming at the neglect which had placed them in such a position.[30] That last resort of defence, British naval supremacy—so often used by Dublin to parry attacks by its critics—was now a subject for lampoon.[31] In both parliaments public enquiries were demanded, and Spencer, First Lord of the Admiralty—already under pressure from problems which would lead to full-scale naval mutiny some months later—almost resigned over the attack on his role in the fiasco.[32] But it was a political rather than a naval problem, and the navy was left to bear, unfairly, the brunt of the blame. It was the same old problem of England expecting Ireland to look after herself. Camden had not even been kept regularly informed of intelligence reports from France, most of which suggested that Ireland was the object of Hoche's preparations. It was a lesson which the Irish loyalists took to heart in security measures implemented the following year.

II

France should have taken comfort from her enemy tearing itself apart in the recriminations which followed the expedition. But she was too busy doing the same herself. The *Indomptable* and the other ships which had made Brest on 1 January, and the ships which straggled back over the next week, were all damaged in one way or another, and although efforts continued to get the second expedition out, the navy protested that repairs would take three months to complete.[33] The Paris press, belatedly favourable to the project after news of the successful sailing in December, changed its tune dramatically in the second week of January. With elections in the offing and the royalist campaign growing apace, the failed expedition offered ready ammunition to the Directory's detractors. It was criticised for risking the fleet in winter and depleting already strained financial resources. Expectations of popular support in Ireland were dismissed as a fable and public opinion was generally against a second attempt.[34] 'It is very easy to find fault, *after* the event,' Tone wrote gloomily, 'and so easy to demonstrate that an expedition which had actually failed, could not possibly have succeeded!'[35]

The officers who had participated fed press attacks with their mutual recriminations. The naval command was very generally attacked. There were calls for Truguet's removal and Bouvet was imprisoned, then relieved of his command.[36] Grouchy, bent on self-justification, prevented others, notably Chérin, from putting their case directly to the government. Instead he sent Tone and Simon to Paris with letters for the Minister of War and the Directory. They arrived on 13 January and their audience with the full Directory was a token of how seriously it was taking the affair. It knew that a successful landing by Hoche would tip the scales overnight, and for a time every effort was made to get Hédouville's force out. The return of the *Fraternité* on 13 January and the reports of the losses sustained made this impossible, and national attention switched again to Italy and the campaign against Austria.

After repeated attempts, the *Fraternité* had finally neared the Irish coast on 30 December. Three French ships came into view, all badly damaged, one already sinking, another dismasted. By 5 January, still kept from the coast by adverse winds and with only five days' supplies left, the *Fraternité* turned for home. Throughout the vessel's troubled voyage, illness had confined Hoche to his cabin. Persistently snapped at by British vessels, the ship changed course for La Rochelle to avoid an enemy fleet of 37 sail outside the entrance to Brest. On the 11th they sighted the Raz, but with bad weather threatening to blow them out to sea again, Hoche took to a rowboat, which ran aground on a sand bank. Wet, tired and angry, Hoche reached La Rochelle on 12 January.[37] Barras recalled him 'quivering with rage and broken with grief' as he recounted details of the expedition to the Directory. He was in no mood for the excuses and recriminations being aired publicly by his officers, and was furious at Grouchy's claims that he had never received firm instructions for landing at Bantry Bay. Ultimately Hoche was content to have Grouchy sent off to Italy, for the offence of this 'inconsequential paper-pusher' was one of cupidity rather than malevolence.[38] Tone stood by Grouchy, even against Hoche's justified attacks, largely because of the cabals mounted against the former after their return. Tone detested intrigue and in the circumstances thought Grouchy had done his best.[39]

Carnot, Letourneur and Truguet wanted to mount another Irish expedition, but they were opposed by the other Directors, and Truguet was disciplined for failing to produce an accurate statement of French losses. Eleven vessels and some 5,000 men had been lost, as well as all the returned ships being damaged. The sufferings of the men had been considerable, and near-mutiny reigned as they were kept on board the returned ships in anticipation of a second attempt.[40] In fact Hoche had already decided to abandon the Irish expedition and transfer back to his old command on the Rhine, recognising, correctly, that the nation's laurels would go to that general who could push Austria to peace. The Directory could not have afforded to maintain so many troops in idleness at Brest awaiting naval repairs, and Hoche understood as much.

It was less easy to redeploy the 1,400 prisoners of war, released convicts, ex-Chouans and disruptive regulars who comprised Tate's force, and, two months late, it finally sailed on 13 February. Since the original object of creating a diversion from Hoche's expedition no longer applied, it may well be that a desire simply to dispose of such an unsavoury force played a larger role than Anglophobia in the orders which reached Hédouville from the Minister of Marine in the last days of January.[41] Having landed successfully in Pembrokeshire, Wales, on the night of 22–23 February, the force proved totally uncontrollable, and Tate surrendered within twenty-four hours. England's first concern was to get rid of the invaders by sending them back to France, and the ports of northern and western France were put on alert to intercept the prisoners before they vanished into civilian society. Hédouville's argument, that the successful landing revealed the continuing ineffectiveness of Britain's blockade, carried little weight in the howl of protest which greeted news of a venture which would have gone unnoticed had Hoche's expedition succeeded.[42] The whole incident fed the Directory's critics at home with further ammunition and set it on a collision course with the councils which culminated in the coup attempts of the summer.

Several of the officers returned from the Bantry Bay expedition had sailed with Tate. Tone's frame of mind in the weeks after his return was such that he even contemplated participating in a piratical venture which would have ended almost certainly in his capture. He wrote to Tate on 19 January offering his services in terms suggesting friendly relations. 'My mind is in a situation which I cannot describe,' he admitted. He had no money—the officers had not been paid before they left—and he had just received a letter from his wife, announcing the family's arrival in Hamburg after a stormy passage in the same weather which had destroyed the expedition, and which had left her dreadfully ill. 'In short I am at present in a situation where I would recommend to my enemies, if I have any, to come and indulge themselves with the prospect.'[43] For the whole of January Tone wrote nothing in his journal. All the old insecurities about his position returned. Could he remain in the French army now that the Irish plans had been dropped, or continue negotiations when there was little immediate likelihood of the venture being renewed?[44] From such a state of aimlessness and despondency he was rescued by Hoche's return to Paris. His own fate and that of the Irish business became intertwined with that of Hoche himself.

Roving Mission in Northern Europe

It was not in Tone's nature to despair for long. Hoche's appointment on 24 January 1797 to command the Sambre and Meuse army effectively terminated any immediate plans for Ireland. But Hoche assured Tone that those plans were merely suspended. He had greeted Tone like a long-lost friend, dispelled his worries about how his own conduct would be viewed in the aftermath of the Bantry Bay failure, and invited him to join his staff on the Rhine. Tone had not expected to be retained in the French army and was delighted by Hoche's trust and the resolution of worries about his personal and financial future. 'I feel this moment like a man who is just awakened from a long terrible dream', he wrote on the last day of January.[1]

Hoche was genuine in his assurances. He had not abandoned his dream of attacking England at the source, and for the next eight months his headquarters on the Rhine were the nerve centre for France's Irish plans. But these did not amount to much. Events had moved on since 1796. Tone in Germany, then in Holland, was too far removed from the centre to recognise this. In 1796 his natural acuteness had sensed the prevailing political winds. In contrast the 1797 diary reveals an ignorance produced by distance. Bantry Bay was not a defeat for either France or Hoche. But it might as well have been. France had no money of her own with which to maintain her armies. Success depended on maintaining them on conquered territory. In contrast to Bonaparte, Hoche had a reputation for treating such territories with fairness, and he was respected in the occupied Rhineland. But he was still imposing monthly levies of 3,000,000 to 12,000,000 *livres* on the left bank of the Rhine alone, and retained tithes and many seigneurial dues to satisfy the Directory's financial expectations.[2]

How Ireland would have fared had the French landed is speculation, but financial terms were apparently settled with Hoche (undoubtedly by O'Connor) and the United Irishmen were not such hopeless romantics as to expect to receive French services gratis.[3] France had not foreseen that she would emerge with a fleet so crippled and no return on a significant investment of money and manpower. Hoche's star was down. Only by the kind of victories which commanded public support could a French general dictate to the politicians, as Hoche once had done and Bonaparte now did with much more ruthlessness. The former's move to the Rhine was partly to regain the reputation lost to Bonaparte, and Tone was sometimes critical of Hoche's obsessive jealousy of the other general.[4]

With Pichegru discredited and Moreau's reputation declining thanks to indecisive leadership and suspected royalism, Hoche was Bonaparte's most formidable rival. The nation's gratitude would fall to the general who forced Austria to make peace. But Bonaparte quickly stole the scene by signing peace preliminaries at Leoben on 18 April. He had been given no diplomatic powers to do so. Moreover, in failing to hold out for France's natural boundaries he had abandoned her most consistent aim in the continental war. He had done so on the very day that Hoche crossed the Rhine and defeated the Austrians, thereby all but guaranteeing the Rhine boundary which Bonaparte had just thrown away. Only Carnot accepted Bonaparte's move unequivocally. Barras acquiesced through fear of disclosure of his own shady dealings with the Republic of Venice. The other Directors were furious but helpless in the face of public euphoria.[5] For the remainder of 1797 Ireland was an option which surfaced intermittently. But on the whole the Directory was preoccupied by difficult peace negotiations with Austria and by an internal political crisis.

I

Tone did not join Hoche on the Rhine until 7 April, only days before the campaign opened. The intervening months in Paris were a strange hiatus. An uncomfortable aimlessness entered his life, aggravated by his lack of residential roots or the anchor of his few material possessions. By the end of February his trunk, containing his 'two gold watches and chains and my flute, and my papers, and all that makes life dear to me', still had not arrived from Brest.[6] He had accepted the suspension of invasion plans and the cessation of negotiations. With Clarke gone—sent to Italy in November—his dealings with the Directory would have been difficult in any event, and Tone found Clarke's successor Dupont far less willing to provide access to Carnot. Little wonder that he came to vest the future in Hoche. He could not see any conflict between being a full-time French soldier and the purpose for which he had come to France, for Hoche had invited him into his army for the specific purpose of keeping the lines to Ireland open.[7]

He called frequently on Monroe, who was just then being recalled to America, and it was undoubtedly through Monroe that he met Thomas Paine. Tone liked him instantly: 'he is vain beyond all belief, but he has reason to be vain and for my part I forgive him. He has done wonders for the cause of liberty, both in America and Europe, and I believe him to be conscientiously an honest man. He converses extremely well, and I find him wittier in discourse than in his writings, where his humour is clumsy enough'. It was the kind of intelligent conversation for which Tone had longed since his arrival in France. 'My mind is overgrown with docks and thistles for want of cultivation', he complained. The few Irishmen in Paris he found 'sad vulgar wretches, and I have been used to rather better company in all respects'.

Paine was writing his reply to the Bishop of Llandaff and seemed prouder of this than of his political writings. The attack on Anglicanism's stranglehold over the nation's political and economic life was part and parcel of Rational Dissent. Tone's stance, in contrast, was areligious—some thought, quite wrongly, irreligious—and though otherwise a great admirer of Paine, he disliked his *Age of Reason* and attacked him for priding himself 'more on his theology than his politics'. They also talked of Burke, whom Tone had known in England, and of the 'shattered state of his mind'. Paine attributed it to the impact of his *Rights of Man*, Tone, correctly, to the premature death of Burke's only son Richard. 'I have seen, myself, the workings of a father's grief on his spirit', he added in his only reference to the death in infancy of his fourth born. He had heard Paine drank like a fish, 'a misfortune which I have known to befall other justly celebrated patriots', Tone mused, and that the best time to catch him was late at night with a bottle of brandy and water before him.[8]

On his transfer to the Rhine, Tone instructed his family to remain in Hamburg. In the correspondence which ensued he caught up on the news which he had missed during his isolation of 1796. Russell's fate was first in his thoughts, after that of his family. When Tone was in Bantry Bay, Russell had published an angry rebuttal of charges that he was about to turn King's evidence, and had used the occasion to reassert the original aims of the United Irishmen.[9]

Tone had wondered at hearing nothing from Arthur since he sailed for Ireland. Arthur had conveyed his message to the United Irishmen in Belfast and Dublin, then became quite a problem to Tone's friends and family. His parents were trying to settle him to a trade, but the apprenticeship fees were beyond their means. Margaret Tone was unhappy that her eldest son had taken Arthur to America 'against our consent', and wrote to Russell asking if 'his brother' had mentioned advancing any money for Arthur. 'We are very loathe to call upon The [Tone] who has a family of his own but our circumstances are such that we cannot help it.' She appealed to

Russell for a speedy answer, 'as the boy is losing his time at present lounging about Dublin which is a thing we do not like'.

Arthur was taken in hand by Tone's Belfast friends, the Simmses, the McCrackens, and above all by Russell. But he appears to have let them down, abandoned whatever trade he had been apprenticed to and returned to Dublin. In a barely literate letter to Russell, revealing all too well the signs of his disrupted schooling, he appealed to be allowed to return to Belfast. He had fought with his father, confessed his conduct was not all it should have been, asked Russell to tell Simms what a miserable life he was living in Dublin, and promised to reform. With arrests mounting, however, Tone's Dublin friends feared for Arthur's safety and towards the end of 1796 fitted him out again for America, where he arrived after all the family but Matthew had already left for Europe.[10]

But it was immediate family concerns which dominated Tone's correspondence of January to March 1797. Reynolds had not fulfilled his instructions. Tone had asked him to send all his papers with Matilda and to convert her stock into specie. He did neither, and Matilda was experiencing difficulty converting her bills of exchange. 'That carelessness is so like him', wrote Tone of Reynolds on receipt of an undated letter from him; yet 'with all his enthusiasm, [he] is so sincerely honest!' It was a compliment Matilda was unwilling to accept for Reynolds two decades later, with the memory of his inexplicable loss of Tone's papers still fresh.[11]

Matilda's health caused particular concern. She appears to have lost the baby which she had been expecting when Tone left America, and was in poor health when she reached Hamburg. There she succumbed to a nervous ailment after reading of the Bantry Bay failure, many weeks before learning of Tone's safe return. He tried to cheer her up with schemes for buying a cottage in France and living on his half-pay. But at one time he feared for her life. His letters contain detailed advice and remedies which tell as much of his own fears as those for Matilda. At least, he consoled himself, she had no cough, and no sign of 'that horrible disorder which, above all others, I most dreaded'. The medical history of his own family gave him good reason to fear tuberculosis. It would eventually kill all his children and would probably have brought him to an early death from natural causes. For Matilda he prescribed fresh milk, seltzer water, and veal broth, listing their beneficial properties and methods of preparation. She was not to attempt to travel to France in the winter, but to take lodgings in a village near Hamburg, she was to avoid getting her feet wet and wear a flannel vest.

Maria had sent him her first letters and he enlisted her help in controlling Frank, who seems to have been a difficult infant. 'I suppose he and I will have fifty battles when we meet', wrote Tone. William was to commence his education, if he had not already done so, and 'to cultivate his understanding'. It was the start of a long correspondence in France in which we see Tone the doting father, the 'fadoff' of his baby talk with Maria. The letters are emotional, almost gushing. But he was embarrassed by his own emotions and had difficulty paying compliments except in worn phrases quite out of tune with his own command of written English.[12]

Tone was again short of ready cash. By mid–February he was having difficulty with his old landlady, probably for this very reason. He moved out temporarily to the Hôtel des États–Unis, rue de Tournon, near the Luxembourg, then back to his old district in the rue de Clery two weeks later. Hoche and Shee wondered what detained him in Paris.[13] The simple answer was money, or lack of it. On 10 March he finally received the advance pay customary for soldiers entering a campaign and his travel expenses on the 24th. His travel plans were made the following day.

On one of his last nights in Paris he sent out for punch and reflected on his year in France. What he remembered most was the loneliness. 'Of all the privations I have ever suffered, that which I most sensibly feel is the want of a friend since my arrival in France, to whom I could open my heart.' He had read much, but with little profit, for there was no one to discuss it with. 'If I had my dear and unfortunate friend Russell beside me, to consult on every occasion, I should no doubt have conducted myself infinitely better, and at all events I should have had infinitely more enjoyment'. His intoxication shows in the increasingly unsteady handwriting in the journal for that night, as he admitted frankly on re–reading the entry a month later.[14]

II

Tone arrived at Hoche's Cologne headquarters on 7 April. He was pleased with his situation in the Sambre and Meuse army and his good standing with the other officers, many of whom were old colleagues from the Bantry Bay expedition. He was particularly proud of Vaudré's comment on hearing they were to be colleagues: '"*Eh bien*," said he, "*C'est un brave homme de plus*".' Tone was not so well pleased at being saddled with MacSheehy as adjoint.[15]

Matilda's illness had made him determined to seek immediate leave. The campaign was about to commence. At Bonn he saw the advance posts of the enemy on the other side of the Rhine. He felt thwarted at being deprived of his first taste of active service and anxious for fear his departure might be construed as dishonourable. In fact Hoche was more than happy for Tone to visit his family. It was Tone's continuing embarrassment that persuaded Hoche to make out his permit in terms of a mission, though in fact the general had no specific mission in mind for Tone, beyond assuring the United Irishmen that Hoche and the French government were determined on emancipating Ireland, that preparations were making for another attempt, and would be concluded as soon as affairs on the Continent permitted. Hoche was particularly concerned that this message should be made known through the newspapers, to assure the Irish people that the French had not abandoned them; all of this Tone conveyed in a letter to McCormick.[16]

At 5 a.m. on 20 April Tone left Cologne to rejoin his family. By 2 May, when he reached Groningen in Holland, he had spent all but eleven days of the past five weeks on the road, with the attendant ravages of night travel and disrupted sleep. Throughout he kept a detailed travel journal. Tone the revolutionary was always tempered by Tone the aesthete. The journals convey a breadth of knowledge about foreign countries and their histories, a thirst for further information which he sought from local inhabitants and other travellers, and he resorted instinctively to the coffee houses where newspapers were to be had. In almost every way he found continential taste inferior to that of England. He was dismayed by the ravages the French had caused to such magnificent buildings as the palace of the Elector of Cologne or the splendid Benedictine abbey at Liège. He purchased sheet music at Hammel's in Amsterdam to be able to say that he had been in the world's best music store. The musical abilities of ballad singers and the cleanliness of Holland caused him to blush at the slovenliness of the Irish. But he attributed that to poverty, and was struck by the prosperity of industrialised peoples in Germany and Holland. He had brought from his observation of the City of London 'a very high notion of the spirit of commerce' and it was strengthend by what he saw in Holland. It was certainly not from Tone that later republican nationalism derived its ambivalence towards economic progress and romanticisation of the peasant.

It is, however, his views on the religious and governing systems of the various countries which are most revealing. On religion his views were stereotypes of Enlightenment thinking. He was fascinated by the depths of 'superstition' of the people of Cologne and the many processions of Holy Week, but surprised to find high mass on Easter Sunday less elaborate than he had expected. He attended two different masses that day. But it is the regular clergy, the friars and monks, who emerge as the real villains, and Tone sees them as the same fat, licentious bullies portrayed by Voltaire or Hogarth. He witnessed a pretty nun being put to flight from a Cologne church by 'a villainous overgrown friar' and fumed at the evils of convent life.

'Poor soul, I pitied her from the very bottom of my heart, and laying aside all grosser considerations, should have rejoiced to have battered down the gates of the convent, and rescued her from her prison. They are most infernal institutions, these convents.'[17] He was happier with the service in a Dutch Protestant church and praised the civic veneration which sited the tombs of great military heroes like De Ruyter and Van Galen in place of an altar.

He travelled specially to The Hague to see the Batavian Convention, thought its members 'very plain and respectable', like his 'old and much and ever respected masters of the General Committee', and was prompted to a comparison with other 'deliberative bodies' of which he had direct experience. Of those in England, America, France and Ireland (including the Catholic Committee and 'our shabby Volunteer Convention of 1783'), he found the Irish legislature 'the most shamelessly profligate and abandoned by all sense of virtue, principle, or even common decency'. He thought all public officials should be liberally paid to ensure efficiency and honesty, and attributed the inefficiency of the French bureaucracy to the inability of the government to pay its functionaries.

Tone was an advocate of strong government. He could find only French royalist papers in the coffee houses of The Hague, and was scandalised by their attacks on the Directory. He thought French liberality in this respect was actually endangering the existence of the government. He would not destroy liberty of the press, 'but I would most certainly restrain it within just and reasonable limits'. Indeed at times Tone comes very near to condoning the tyranny of democracy:

...the Government of a Republic properly organized and freely and frequently chosen by the people should be *a strong Government*; it is the interest and the security of the people themselves, and the truest and best support of their liberty, that the Government which they have chosen, should not be insulted with impunity; it is the people themselves who are degraded and insulted in the persons of their Government—I would, therefore, have strong and severe laws against libels and calumny, and I do not apprehend the least danger to the just and reasonable liberty of the press from the execution of those laws, where the magistrates, the judges, and the jury are freely named by the people; the very same laws which, under the English constitution I regard as tyrannical and unjust, I would in a free Republic preserve, and even strengthen. . . . I do not see why tyrants alone should be protected by the laws, and liberty left unprotected and defenceless. . . . It is less dangerous for a Government to be feared, or even hated, than despised.[18]

There is indeed a toughness in Tone's nature, often disguised by the soul-searching and insecurities of the journals. It reveals itself in several incidents during his spring journey through northern Europe. He had set off from Utrecht for Amsterdam in a barge so 'villainous' that it made the Irish canal boats appear luxurious. He failed to get a cabin and was squashed among 'the common lumber', some thirty passengers, half of them Jews and all the men smoking pipes. He was suffocated and in ill humour. The skipper refused to accept his French money. A young Jew who offered to help but short-changed him was quickly compelled to submit when Tone made it clear he would stand for no nonsense. Another altercation followed with an admittedly troublesome passenger, in which Tone again was the victor, despite the language difficulties. He then mischievously talked his way into the good graces of a pretty Dutch girl and fell asleep on her lap. Tone was offended by the sight of her lover, a fat older man, with such a young and pretty mistress.

He was impressed by Holland, by its neatness and cleanliness, and the apparent honesty and good nature of its people. The neat Dutch gardens and well-kept German farms played upon the intermittent conflict he felt between domesticity and a life of adventure.[19] But it was friends and family rather than the style of life for which he longed. Books, papers and one or two cherished items apart, Tone had a singular lack of attachment to material possessions. His restless nature made him well-equipped for the life he had drifted into.

On the evening of 7 May Matilda and the children finally arrived at Groningen. They were accompanied by Mary and her new fiancé, Jean Frédéric Giauque, a young Swiss merchant living in Hamburg. Theirs had been a short but intense courtship on board ship from America, which Tone thought 'perfectly in the style of the romantic adventures of our family'. Matilda thought so too and excised the comment.[20] For two weeks the family travelled together through Holland and Belgium, at the end of which time Tone returned to Germany and his family went on to Paris, where Shee had offered a welcome in his home at Nanterre until they could find suitable lodging.[21]

III

Tone had had no direct communication from Ireland since he left America and most of his information about internal developments there came from English newspapers. The anti-government *Courier*, for which many United Irish sympathisers were writing, was responding to the continental interest in Irish affairs after Bantry Bay by increased coverage.[22] In February Tone read of Fitzgibbon's attack on himself in the Irish Parliament. The attempted French invasion had occasioned bitter criticism of both governments. Fitz-gibbon countered with yet another reading of Tone's 1791 letter to prove the reality of a republican conspiracy and made it the centrepiece of another secret committee report two months later. He 'did me the favour to abuse me twice by name as the father of the United Irishmen', commented Tone. 'I thought *he* had forgotten *me*'.[23] Well might he have been surprised. There was no reason at the time for Fitzgibbon's attack, for everyone else believed Tone to be still in America.[24]

He also read of more arrests at home. 'There is now scarcely any one of my friends in Ireland but is in prison and most of them in peril of their lives, for the system of Terror is carried as far there as ever it was in France in the time of Robespierre.'[25] The situation in Ireland was indeed deteriorating. By June some 103 of the Ulster leaders would be in prison and the province under martial law. Tone felt the time had come for a properly appointed representative to be sent from Ireland. On 24 February he called on Monroe with an eight-page letter for Robert Simms and his friends in Ireland. He gave an account of the late expedition, assured them of the determination of the French to send help, urged them to refrain from any premature rising, and asked them to send 'a proper person' to confer with the Directory.[26] The nature of his own mission had changed. With his transfer to the Rhine he was in no position to keep Irish affairs constantly in the view of the Directory, even if he had had any new information to convey.

In a rapidly developing crisis Tone's communication route via America was no longer viable. Mary's and Giauque's residence in Hamburg opened up new possibilities. After Leoben Hoche was attempting to reactivate dormant plans for a strike against England, and at Groningen Tone instructed Giauque to have Reinhard send any messengers from Ireland to Hoche's headquarters.[27] But in Ireland nothing had been heard of French plans since Bantry Bay, and events were moving far too rapidly to wait on France's pleasure.

The United Irish Society had begun to organise itself on a military footing only in the last few months of 1796. Its numbers increased dramatically after Bantry Bay, particularly in the north. By February 1797 the authorities were speaking of Ulster as in a state of rebellion and responded accordingly. With the rank and file questioning their leaders' policy of holding back till the French arrived, it became a matter of urgency to discover France's intentions. The national committee of the United Irishmen held an extraordinary meeting in Dublin early in February. It formed a secret committee of Lord Edward Fitzgerald, McCormick and T.A. Emmet to appoint an envoy to France. The choice fell on Tone's old Catholic Committee colleague, the attorney Edward Lewins. He spoke fluent French and was already well acquainted with France, having been a student at the Irish College in Paris.[28] He was briefed intensively on United Irish strength and needs, and arrived in Hamburg towards the end of March, where he was introduced to Reinhard through Lady Fitzgerald's relatives.

In Lewins the United Irish leaders had anticipated Tone's February letter and appointed an official plenipotentiary to negotiate with France. Tone's mission had never had such sanction, for no revolutionary organisation existed in 1795. Where Tone had been arbiter of his own conduct in France, Lewins was issued detailed instructions. He was to thank the Directory for the Bantry Bay attempt, ask for another expedition of 20,000 to 25,000 men and 100,000 guns, and for a commitment from France to insist on Irish independence in any peace negotiated with England. In return 30,000 to 40,000 Irishmen would join the expedition, Ireland would not lay down arms until her independence was assured and England defeated, and France would be reimbursed all costs. Lewins was also to approach France's Dutch and Spanish allies, and since he would carry no documents, he was to contact Tone who would vouch for his mission.

Despite his credentials, there was something in Lewins's character which the French did not like, and he was constantly having to invoke Tone's recommendation to allay French suspicions. Reinhard could not say why he felt so ill at ease about him. Everything Lewins said seemed authentic, and Reinhard sought and received an assurance of the validity of his mission from Lord Edward and McCormick. Lewins's manner of negotiation, which McNally described as 'scholastic, pedantic and sophistical', may not have helped. And his physical appearance—he is described as being smallish and thick-set, with sunken eyes, prominent eyebrows and protuberant chin—reads like the popular eighteenth-century caricature of an attorney.[29] Reinhard's suspicions, and the delays while he checked, angered and alienated Lewins. News of the proclamation of martial law in the north and the growing demand of the Ulstermen for an immediate rising, even without the French, was relayed to him by McCormick early in May. They now required a force of only 5,000 to 10,000 French, but immediately. Lewins thought Ireland could liberate herself without any foreign aid, and though he denied having said any such thing when challenged by Reinhard, he spoke for a growing number of United Irish leaders who now suspected France's motives.[30]

Lewins was finally permitted to join Hoche at a secret destination in Hesse-Cassel on 29 May. Armed with the new information received from McCormick, he told Hoche that France might now render Ireland independent with the minimum of help. Hoche presented the case skilfully in his report to the Directory the following day, playing upon the Directory's jealousy of its allies to push it to action. He told how the Spanish minister in Hamburg had rushed through approval of financial support for the Irish after meeting Lewins, insinuated that he was unable to tell Lewins anything because he did not know the Directory's intentions, and was dispatching Simon to Paris for consultation.[31]

Tone arrived at Hoche's Friedberg headquarters on 1 June. He read the Irish parliamentary secret committee report in the press and was surprised at the progress the United Irish organisation had made since he left the country. But he also learnt of its progressive suppression, and of the final destruction of the *Northern Star* presses, after the paper had survived two previous attacks. He wrote to Shee of his fears that the movement was about to be put down, and all this at a time when the English fleet was locked up in home ports by a mutiny which had been raging since April.[32]

On 12 June Tone was dispatched by Hoche to bring Lewins to Coblenz. Tone had spoken highly of Lewins's abilities and patriotism and was much impressed to discover that he had been sent as the official representative by 'the Executive Committee of the United People of Ireland'. Had Tone been superseded? Tone did not see things in such a light, although there were some initial worries that he and Lewins might differ on the best means of pursuing the mission, and a desire that his own sacrifices and achievements be fully recognised. In a statement to the United Irish executive, drawn up by Lewins (though clearly with Tone's collaboration), Tone is described as 'the man whom of all others you could most wish to see' returning with an invasion force.

> He who has been perhaps the very first to broach openly and in public the idea of the independance [sic] of Ireland, and who has since sacrified everything which is dear to man for the attainment of this great object, whose conduct has been such as to obtain for him, while in his own country, the confidence of every honest Irishman, and since he has quit it, to insure him that of the two governments who co-operate in our delivery, and to obtain for him a distinguished rank in their armies, in a word, our ancient colleague and indefatiguable agent, Theobald Wolfe Tone...your confidence in his integrity, patriotism and talents, cannot be too great.[33]

Lewins recognised Tone's already established reputation and his connections in France and was anxious that his full approval of his, Lewins's, mission should be known to the French authorities. Their roles became complementary, Tone working with any expeditionary force to be sent, Lewins pursuing negotiations in Paris.

The Directory had not abandoned the idea of another attempt on Ireland. The divisions Hoche had created for the follow-up to Bantry Bay were retained at Brest. Reports of the escalating crisis in Ireland flowed into the Luxembourg during May, and the relevant ministries displayed a keen interest in Lewins's communications.[34] But when Simon arrived in Paris on 5 June, he found a political crisis brewing there too and had difficulty gaining access to the Directors. The spring elections had produced a royalist landslide. Letourneur, Carnot's only ally in the Directory, was replaced by the royalist candidate and ex-ambassador to Switzerland, Barthélemy. Carnot, whom London considered the only Director with enough vision to organise a direct attack on the British Isles, became increasingly isolated, as he too was suspected of leanings towards the moderate royalists.[35] The Directory was acting at odds with itself. Ministerial changes were rumoured in those very departments most closely associated with Irish operations. Everyone seemed to support Hoche's plan for another attempt on Ireland, but in the long term. With Malmesbury poised to return to France for renewed peace negotiations, signs that Prussia might break the armistice, the need to retain forces on the Continent pending a final treaty with Austria, and most of all the likelihood of an internal political crisis, everyone in Paris had reason to prevaricate.

Yet Simon's letter to Hoche of 7 June, relating the initial response of the Directory, was not discouraging, and Hoche added his own optimistic gloss when showing it to Tone and Lewins on the 21st. They were told that the government had not abandoned its projects against England and was always willing to send help to the Irish, though it could not spare the necessary ships or troops at that moment. But it was that part of Simon's letter stating that France would not make peace with England without stipulating terms for Ireland which most impressed Tone and satisfied one of Lewins's main demands.[36]

Simon, however, was relating a private conversation with Carnot, and although much of what he said was Directory policy, the formal document which went out four days later was much less encouraging and marked a real deterioration in Ireland's role in France's war strategy. It agreed with Hoche that the present ferment in Ireland offered the best opportunity of defeating England. But the fate of the Continent had to be resolved before any expedition could be organised, and in the meantime the French would sustain the Irish by arms shipments, much as England had done the Chouans. Yes, the independence of Ireland would serve France's interests. But that

independence could not be guaranteed by France, for fear of jeopardising peace negotiations with Austria. The Irish in other words
could not expect to be represented in peace talks with England, as
Carnot had wanted.[37]

Repeated offers of the navy of the Batavian Republic, however,
were taken up, and plans mounted in June to send 15,000 Dutch and
6,000 French soldiers to Ireland with Hoche as overall commander.[38]
The Dutch commander-in-chief, General Daendels, had written to
Hoche asking to see him and 'the deputy of the people of Ireland'.
Tone and Lewins accordingly joined Hoche in The Hague on 27
June. They had a rendezvous that night at the theatre, and back
at his lodgings in the Hotel Lion d'Or, Hoche briefed them for
their meeting with the Batavian Committee of Foreign Affairs the
following morning. The Dutch had some 24 to 26 vessels ready at
the Texel. But they wanted the opportunity to prove their mettle
independently and were unhappy about overall French control.
Hoche offered to withdraw his own command in response to their
evident dislike of the existing plan—a magnanimous gesture, Tone
thought, knowing Hoche's 'devouring passion for fame' and particular ambition to destroy the power of England.[39]

But Hoche had not renounced his ambition of confronting
England directly. He was confident of his ability to manipulate Paris.
He told the two Irishmen that Truguet's vanity would be so offended
at the thought of the Dutch capturing such laurels, that he would
move heaven and earth to have a French expedition leave shortly
after them. He was right, and when Tone rejoined Hoche at Cologne
on 1 July, Hoche had just received instructions to take command of
an Irish expedition from Brest. It would consist of 6,000 to 8,000
men and be ready to sail at the same time as that from the Texel.
But Hoche should try to raise the necessary finance in the conquered territories, for there was no money available in the Marine
Ministry.[40] Lewins was to liaise with Hoche in Paris. Tone would
accompany the Dutch expedition from the Texel, and he returned
immediately to The Hague for that purpose. 'He will be most useful
to you', Hoche wrote to Daendels, 'for it is from him that I have
partly drawn the information which I have used to organise the
expedition.'[41]

'Since the 13th of last month I have scarcely been two days in one
place,' Tone wrote to Matilda on 1 July, the eve of his departure for
Holland, 'and I am fatigued to death.' But he had not been in such
good spirits for months. 'You have doubtless read a great part, at
least, of my journals. Well the last fortnight has been more curious
and more in the extravagant line of our history than all you have
read.' He dared not tell her why in this letter, though it contained so

much of their own personal nonsense and favourite quotations that any spy would have been hard put to decipher it. But the following day he wrote from The Hague via Lewins, who was about to leave for Paris. 'I am now adjutant general in the service of the French and Batavian republics, which you will allow is droll; I expect to set off for the Texel in three days and probably before ten, I shall be ploughing the raging main. Our affairs never wore so favorable an appearance as now; you know I am not too sanguine; every thing human is uncertain, but I do think we have every rational ground to expect success.' He was sending MacSheehy to Paris to collect his trunk, and she was to cut up his clothes for the children. MacSheehy would bring her his pay. 'He is a blockhead, but be civil to him', he added. He made final preparations in The Hague, including the ordering of a green uniform to wear in Ireland, and on 9 July he set off for the Texel.[42]

Tone had good reason to be optimistic. Over 20,000 troops, in two expeditions, were destined for Lough Swilly, in the north of Ireland,[43] and despite recent reverses, United Irish strength was incomparably greater than at the time of Bantry Bay. At the Texel Tone found the Dutch fleet superior, supplies in greater abundance, and relations between the military and navy infinitely better than at Brest. He was delighted with Daendels and the naval commander De Winter, both of whom possessed that frankness he had admired in the Dutch people generally. Once he had cleared with Daendels the issue of non-interference in Ireland's domestic concerns, he seemed far more content with his new Dutch allies than with the French a year earlier. 'There never was, and there never will be such an expedition as ours if it succeeds.' Its object was not dynastic or territorial, as in the past, but rather 'to change the destiny of Europe, to emancipate one, perhaps three nations; to open the sea to the commerce of the world; to found a new empire, to demolish an ancient one; to subvert a tyranny of six hundred years.'[44] It was a French world vision of the destruction of Albion, and was characteristic of Tone's tendency to raise Irish independence from a domestic squabble to a key role in a new international order.

26

Demise of Hoche

The Texel fleet was due to sail with 13,544 men for Ireland on 16 July. Hoche was on his way to Paris, Lewins already there, and the detachments from Hoche's army destined for Brest were on the move. But on 18 July news reached Paris of Hoche's troops spilling over the constitutional boundaries of the capital, beyond which troops were debarred. Hoche had been enlisted in a prospective coup against the royalist councils, and was to be the new War Minister in the ministerial purge which would follow. At their inn in The Hague Hoche had spoken to Tone and Lewins of his fears that the royalists were trying to destroy the government and his determination to march his army against Paris rather than let them succeed. He had assumed the role of protector of the republic in good faith and was startled at the dressing-down he received before a full meeting of the Directory, unprotected by Barras who had enlisted his services. Hoche became the scapegoat of the thwarted coup. He was vilified by the press and councils, who demanded his arrest. For a general to whom reputation was everything, such an attack on his patriotism was devastating and Hoche went into immediate and permanent decline.[1]

Lewins had expected to co-operate with Hoche in preparing the forthcoming expedition. Instead Hoche told him they had been betrayed, and warned him to speak to no one.[2] Hoche did urge the Directory to proceed with the Irish plans and was ordered on 26 July to continue his march to Brest. But he considered this a move of his enemies to get rid of him, refused himself to embark and returned abruptly to Germany. In any event the Irish venture had been revealed in the councils and England alerted, and the troops were in no mood for another long march to shifting destinations.[3] No one seemed to know what was happening. Lord Malmesbury, recently arrived at Lille to carry on peace negotiations, thought the Irish expedition a ruse to bring the troops to Paris.[4] But the Marine and War Ministers had issued orders for the expedition in all sincerity, and were dismayed that the public protests of the councils and the press necessitated its abandonment.[5]

I

Tone did not learn of these events until much later and wondered at Lewins's lack of communication. For almost two months he remained trapped in the Texel by adverse winds, less able to communicate than usual because he could speak no Dutch. He consoled himself that he had been through worse times. But every line of his journals and letters reveals his mounting frustration and sense of helplessness. Sheer boredom set in. He passed his time reading Voltaire, deciphering the Dutch newspapers with the aid of a dictionary, playing flute duets with De Winter and compiling a list of the ships in Duncan's blockading force from Steel's list of the British navy. But this was a dispiriting exercise, as it made clear Duncan's increasing superiority. 'We divert ourselves as well we can', he told Matilda on 21 July, 'but you will judge that I pass my time very badly'. Things had been bad enough on the Brest fleet, 'but at least we had some conversation. But here—well'.

On 9 August he went on shore and walked over the greater part of the island of Texel. Consisting largely of land reclaimed from the sea, it was flat and barren. Yet it supported five attractive towns, innumerable neat farms and a population of well-fed and well-clothed peasants. Such, thought Tone, 'are the inconceivable efforts of liberty and good government'. The recognition hardly cheered him. 'I thought of Ireland a thousand times, with her admirable soil and climate, and the vast advantages which nature has showered down upon her, and which are all blasted by the malignant influence of her execrable government, till my blood boiled within me with rage and vexation.'[6]

By the second week of August Tone could see reinforcements arriving for Duncan's fleet after the suppression of the mutinies.[7] The news from Brest was even worse, with the port heavily blockaded and no French ships in a fit condition to put to sea. Tone recognised that their original plan was no longer viable. Daendels talked of sending the Dutch forces to Yarmouth in England. In the absence of public support Tone felt that they would simply lose an army, and instead suggested a spectacular push for London with a Tate-like venture to create panic. He also supported De Winter's suggestion of publicly cancelling the expedition, then taking advantage of the enemy's relaxation of vigilance to rush 2,500 to 3,000 élite troops, artillery and arms to the north of Ireland. It was better than nothing, and the Irish would have to act like the French in the Vendée—a *chouannerie*, in other words, something Tone had violently opposed in the past. It was a mark of his growing desperation as he saw yet another expedition foundering. 'I do not know but there is something in the expedition proposed more analogous to my disposition and habits of thinking, which is a confession on my part more honest than wise, for I feel very sensibly there is no common sense in it, but after all, it is my disposition, and I cannot help it—I am growing utterly desperate'.[8]

He had written frequently to Hoche, most recently on 31 July, urging him to push the Brest preparations with his government. They had now lost a month at the Texel and given the enemy time to reinforce his strength. A small force immediately would be of infinitely greater value than a large one in the long term; 'time may be of the essence, for you know that public spirit cannot remain raised for ever.... Who's to say whether the unfortunate Irish, hopeless of help, may not surrender'.[9]

Tone's fears were confirmed five days later when he was joined on board the *Vrijheid* by two of the Ulster leaders. They were Alexander Lowry from the County Down Catholic family which had befriended Tone in 1792, and the Belfast Presbyterian, John Tennent, younger brother to William, one of the founders of the United Irishmen in 1791.[10] They told of growing repression in Ireland and of the military purge of the north. The people had watched the mutinies in the British fleet subside without the arrival of the French help long promised them, and had lost confidence in their leaders whom they almost suspected of deceiving them. The committees in the north had repeatedly urged a rising before their new strength was eroded.[11] But the Dublin executive adhered to its established policy of holding back until the French arrived, and a major north–south split had taken place in the United Irish command.

It had come to a head at a meeting in Dublin in the first week of June. Lowry, Tennent and three others (Bartholomew Teeling, Joseph Orr and Samuel Turner) presented Ulster's case for a rising, but were overruled. Keogh, McCormick and Braughall objected so violently to a rising that they did not even attend. Something of a generation gap was developing in the Society between the founding members (including all of Tone's friends and all the ex-Catholic Committee members) and the younger militants. As the Ulster delegates returned home from the meeting they learnt that warrants were out for their arrests. They fled to England, and from there to France, and were followed by others holding very different views from Lewins about the conduct of his mission.[12]

The northerners' outlook was more in tune with French policy after Bantry Bay, which wanted Irish hopes sustained by frequent communication and a rising prior to committing French troops. Reinhard was particularly impressed with Turner, who arrived in Hamburg on 10 June. He was followed by Tennent, Lowry and Teeling, all alike asking for French assistance, but without Lewins's evident mistrust. Teeling was sent back with information about the Texel fleet and Tone's participation, information which partially calmed the developing rift in Ireland.[13] But the expectation of an Irish rising occurring before the French would help was a change in French policy since 1796 which was not fully communicated to either Tone or Lewins, and Hoche's constant assurances gave them little cause to change tack.

Unaware of recent developments, Tone had continued to caution delay in his February letter home. It arrived in May. It was the first communication about French intentions received by the United Irishmen since Bantry Bay and was instrumental in holding back Ulster's impatience.[14] But Tone would almost certainly have supported the call for an immediate rising had he been in Ireland. He thought there had been 'a great want of spirit in the leaders in Dublin' and was particularly upset that many militiamen had been won over and then left to face the consequences. 'It is hard to judge at this distance, but it seems to me to have been an unpardonable weakness, if not downright cowardice to have let such a great occasion slip.' He was loath to admit the criticisms of many who were his friends, though from past experience he thought the charges all too true. 'Keogh I know is not fit for a coup de main; he has got, as Lewins tells me, McCormick latterly into his hands, and besides Dick is now past the age of adventure. I am surprised that Emmet did not show more energy, because I know he is as brave as Cesar [sic], of his person—it seems to me to have been such an occasion missed as we can hardly expect to see return.'[15]

Lack of information about French intentions was crippling the home movement. The secrecy of 1796 and the policy of withholding information about the French negotiations from lower committees was no longer viable in the conditions of 1797. Even Lowry, a member of the Ulster executive, had not been told of Tone's or Lewins's missions, and Dublin's vague assurances of French help irritated and ultimately alienated those on the receiving end of the military clamp-down. But the national executive itself was as much in the dark about French intentions after Bantry Bay as were their followers. The whole movement was hanging on every snippet of news from France.[16] Tone was not fully aware of the changed circumstances which made frequent communication so essential. Lewins should have been, and his continued silence in these crucial months led to fears that he was not carrying out instructions and a call for his removal. Many of Tone's personal loyalties were coloured by the 1795 crisis in his life. Lewins was one of those who had stood by him, and the recognition muted any doubts Tone had of Lewins's conduct in France.[17]

The criticisms of Lewins were not entirely justified. He had been compelled to kick his heels in Hamburg for nearly two months, his many communications to Paris unanswered while the French checked on his credentials. He was then sworn to silence on the naval preparations, first by the Batavian government, then by Hoche. Nevertheless there was some truth in the accusation that he was too leisurely in the conduct of his mission. He was more aware of Tone's shadow than he should have been, far too deferential to the French and less willing than Tone to dispense with convention. Despite Clarke's momentary doubts about Tone's methods, the French liked his spirited approach and were more impressed by the stream of impatient northerners arriving that summer than by the official representatives sent from Dublin.[18]

With no word of Lewins, mounting anxieties about the onset of peace talks between England and France and the deteriorating situation in Ireland, the United Irish executive responded to Tone's letter by sending Dr MacNeven. He arrived in Hamburg on 21 June. Reinhard, having already heard the northern delegates' reports, was irritated by MacNeven's reserve, his insistence on French guarantees and his preference for a smaller force which would remain under Irish control. These were cautions which Tone was still urging on the Batavians and Hoche alike, and the northerners' infatuation with the French blinded them to France's unholy treatment of occupied countries.

The documentation for MacNeven's mission is impressive and was admitted as such when it fell into the hands of the British authorities. It detailed the exact strength of the United Irishmen and the relative merits of various landing places in Ireland, reiterated Lewins's request for the inclusion of Irish independence as a condition in the Lille peace negotiations and fully endorsed the latter's position as United Irish plenipotentiary. MacNeven travelled to Paris and was presented by Lewins to Barras and the Ministers of Marine and Foreign Affairs. But it was from Hoche that he received assurances of 10,000 troops, to be landed before the end of October. The new endorsement of his mission seemed to shake Lewins out of his torpor and from September the Paris negotiations again assumed something of their former importance.[19]

II

Tone, Lowry and Tennent had accompanied Daendels to The Hague to present the changed circumstances at the Texel to the Batavian government. Given the lateness of the season, Daendels proposed sending the troops to Scotland, taking the major towns and by feigned attacks over the border, creating the impression that England herself was under attack, while the bulk of the army sailed for Ireland from the western ports. The four men returned to the Texel on the 30th to find no change in the weather and the blockading fleet reinforced to 21 sail of the line. It was 54 days since Tone had first boarded the *Vrijheid*, and the chances of getting to Ireland before the winter were slight. In the circumstances he had accepted Daendels's Scottish plan. But after this, the second, failed enterprise, and the real possibility that peace would be concluded between France and England, Tone reviewed his future options. The resulting eight-page letter, written to Matilda on 31 August, is something of a personal manifesto.

Tone had never thought of his activities in France as those of a single individual. Even now it was the plight of himself and his friends as a group, in the event of peace and a reinforcement of English rule over Ireland, which he addressed. In that event 'it is no country for us'. Men who had hazarded all 'to throw off the yoke' could hardly submit when that yoke was tightened. 'If the patriots of Ireland have acted really upon principle, I cannot suppose that a vast number of them will not emigrate, *en masse*....if they are not capable of that exertion, they have deceived themselves exceedingly in the idea that they have the energy to make revolutions'.

Positive action not grudging submission should mark the true revolutionary. He looked to the Dutch planning to flood their country against Louis XIV and sail for India, to Cromwell and Hampden choosing exile in America rather than submit to oppression. 'I love my country; I would hazard my life with pleasure for her independence, so long as I saw a shadow of a possibility of success; it is only in the case of utter desperation, such as for example a peace between France and England, leaving us at the mercy of the latter, that I would think of voluntary exile.' That exile in Tone's eyes would be no desertion of principle:

> if we cannot obtain the permission to breathe in our own country, but by an indecent prostitution at the feet of our oppressor, surely it is time for us to think of quitting a soil, no longer fit for us nor we for it.—But more; exile is terrible, I feel it well; it is however to be borne by men who have acted and suffered together, who know and respect each other's principles...who have hazarded so much for their country, and who yield at last only to an inevitable necessity; and I still think there is among us enough of virtue and of resolution to embrace even banishment rather than slavery; we have at least the energy of despair.

Matilda was to show the letter to their friends in Paris; 'and you, the dearest of my friends...where is the country that with the society of those we love and esteem we could not be happy in?'.

But where should they go? After direct experience he found America—at least the former British colonies—'of all the places I have yet seen, by far the most disagreeable to live in'. Recent French acquisitions like Louisiana, or Corfu, suggested themselves, and he had spoken to Daendels and De Winter about certain Dutch colonies. They might set up a republic in the Sandwich Islands, the preferred, though 'the wildest of all' his schemes. He tried to dismiss the thought that his friends in Ireland might, after all, submit; 'surely there is yet such a thing as principle to which a man will sacrifice everything. . . . I do not think so ill of my countrymen as to suppose I am singular in the determination.' He feared Matilda might think he was romanticising: 'if you think I am a wrongheaded enthusiast, do not scruple to tell me so, for I in some degree suspect it myself.'[20]

Tone's letters to Matilda are full of assurances that whatever might pass, she could be sure of his doing the honourable thing. He speaks to her as someone who shares his ideals, has the strength to endure the same sacrifices, and the ability to anchor an enthusiasm in his character which frequently made him oblivious to realities. In his 31 August letter he treats the possibility of his own death in a matter-of-fact way arising partly out of his own embarrassment at displays of emotion, partly out of his recognition of Matilda's strength. 'Dear love, we know one another now; I do not make a parade of commonplace topics to support you in my absence; I am going in a just and honorable cause. . .and if the worst should happen, I know my countrymen will take care of you, and that my children will find a father in every honest Irishman. . . .I offer you no consolation for you require none; we will both do our duty.'[21]

III

On 3 September Tone was dispatched by Daendels to Hoche's headquarters at Wetzlar to seek his opinion on the new Scottish scheme. It had now grown to grandiose proportions, with proposals to follow up the first landing with another of 15,000 men taken from the French troops in Dutch pay, an invasion of England from Scotland to force her to make peace, and the dispatch of 5,000 of the French to Ireland after England had withdrawn troops from there for home defence. In such an event Daendels expressed his willingness to serve under Hoche as commander of the combined forces. If Hoche agreed Tone was to urge the need for better relations between Paris and the Batavians, who were discontented with France's lack of communication and refusal to involve them in the Lille peace negotiations.[22]

Tone travelled via Brussels to see Lowry and Tennent off to Paris, and arrived at Hoche's headquarters on 13 September. Hoche did not like the plan. The English would cut off the Irish Sea before troops from the second landing could sail for Ireland. Tone agreed that the second landing was impracticable, but thought the plan to move against England good. If it succeeded her discomfiture would be great. If it failed, France would not lose, since the full costs would be borne by the Dutch. Hoche promised to give an answer in three to four days, and to send Tone to Paris with the decision.

But Tone was less worried about the outcome than the dreadful physical change which had occurred in Hoche since their last meeting. The attacks by the French press had taken their toll. Tone saw the signs of galloping consumption, with which he was all too familiar, and was distressed that no one, not even Hoche's physicians, seemed to recognise it. By the 17th the General could no longer walk, and had to be carried by four grenadiers from room to room. 'It is terrible to see a fine handsome fellow, in the very flower of youth and strength, so reduced', wrote Tone in his journal that day. 'My heart bleeds for him.' Two days later Hoche was dead. He was twenty-nine. Clearly in distress, Tone wrote with the news to Matilda:

> Dearest Love, it is with the most inexpressible concern that I have to acquaint you that we have lost our brave general, Hoche; he died this morning at four o'clock, I think of what we call a galloping decay—judge of the distress and confusion we are all in, especially at this important period—No later than yesterday I had a message from him relating to our affair—send this letter to Giauque [Lewins had assumed Tone's brother-in-law's name as pseudonym] instantly, and let him take his measures accordingly— I know not what I may do, myself, on this occasion, nor shall I for a few days—adieu, dearest Life; I am in very sincere affliction.[23]

His ties with the Sambre and Meuse army now broken, Tone set off for Paris, stopping at Bonn with his friend Colonel Shee. It was the anniversary of the establishment of the French Republic. At a civic dinner he promised 'a very pretty woman' that he would meet her that evening at a ball given by the municipality; 'but I will deceive her like a false traitor, and go to my innocent bed'. He had probably been flirting as usual, and exaggerated the incident to show his love for Matilda, whose letter he had just received, 'which has put me out of conceit with all women but herself'.[24]

In truth he had no spirit for enjoyment that night. He drank little at dinner, a fact in itself worthy of comment in his journal. Tone had been close to Hoche and was among those intimates of his whom Chérin contacted some months later,[25] asking them to contribute to an official biography. But the loss of the General was more than personal, and his death stunned those Irish whose communication with France had been almost entirely through him. Writers with views as divergent as those of the nationalist historian P.S. O'Hegarty and John Stuart Mill came to see Bantry Bay and the loss of Hoche as a major disaster in Irish history.[26] It is debatable whether Hoche could have protected Ireland from France's increasingly exploitative foreign policy. In his time, however, he never relinquished his ambition of defeating Britain, and he could always be relied upon to push Irish interests. He left behind a coterie of devoted generals who would remain good friends to Tone and his successors. But no one of Hoche's stature or power emerged to fill the void left by his death, and the Irish mission to France went into terminal decline after his death.

VIII

FINAL DAYS
(1797–1798)

Mission in Decline

After Hoche's death, the Irish mission to France began to fall apart. The successful *coup d'état* of 18 Fructidor (4 September) against the royalists ushered in a more cynical Directorial regime. Gone were those remnants of idealism and internationalism which had assisted Tone's negotiations in 1796. Established communication channels had been ruptured by Hoche's death and by the extensive changes in personnel in the political upheavals of 1797. The Irish played their part by exporting their domestic disagreements.

I

Barras assured Lewins that Hoche's death changed nothing. But the Irish would have to wait until the spring before France could send help. Nor could he undertake to include Irish independence as a condition in any peace treaty, even though he promised that they would have their independence.[1] Those assurances became the basis for a disastrous United Irish strategy, permitting the Irish authorities to demolish the movement's strength while it continued to hold back in expectation of a French force which never materialised. Although the French assurances were not entirely groundless, Lewins and his compatriots were ill advised in placing so much store by them. Barras was not to be trusted. His deviousness, cynicism and corruption have come to be associated generally with the second Directory, which was inaugurated in September 1797.

But neither Tone nor Lewins were to know that. They must have been relieved to receive any communication from the Directory at a time when Tone felt he was having to start all over again. Almost everyone with whom he had worked since 1796 was gone. Clarke's old bureau, Carnot's particular enclave, had become a source of serious security leaks. It was in ill odour with the generals and possessed little of its former power. Clarke too was one of the casualties of Fructidor. His Orléanist past and attachment to Carnot rendered him suspect. Only Bonaparte's intervention saved him from prison, and he remained under a cloud for the next two years.[2] Most of the familiar ministers had been removed. An old enemy of Hoche, Schérer, was at the War Ministry, and Lewins could get nowhere with Truguet's replacement at the Ministry of Marine, Pléville le Peley.

Tone read of the coup on 14 September. He rejoiced that the Republic had been saved, but could not believe Carnot a royalist, an opinion shared by so many others that he was allowed to escape. At Bonn Tone spoke to Shee of his dismay at having to start again from scratch. Simon shared Shee's anxiety about Tone's 'want of acquaintances and friends of principle' to introduce him to the right people. He wrote on 28 September telling Tone that Chérin and Debelle (Hoche's brother-in-law) were then in Paris and where he could find them.[3] Debelle, Tone found, knew nothing. He and Lewins were able to present Barras with details of Daendels's Scottish proposals, and were heard 'very attentively'. But Barras had been far more interested in Madame Tallien, the celebrated Parisian hostess, with whom, Tone commented drily, 'he retired into an inner room, where they continued, I have no doubt, very seriously employed for about half an hour'.[4]

Rescue came in the form of Tone's one-time colleague at Rennes, General Hédouville. He welcomed Tone as an old friend, undertook to secure permission from the military authorities for him to remain in Paris and to apply for his arrears in pay. He also spoke to Barras on his behalf and introduced him to the Director La Réveillière-Lépaux, and to Talleyrand and Schérer, new Ministers of Foreign Affairs and of War. But there was no easy entrée to any of them and in December Tone was still lamenting the need 'to solicit and crave' permission to contribute anything to the Directory's plans. Towards the end of October he learnt from the press of the formation of an Armée d'Angleterre. Formerly he would have been briefed privately.[5] It was not that Tone had lost standing with the French. Far from it. He was now used regularly to vouch for any Irish arriving on the Continent. It was, however, the routine task of a permanent exile rather than the pressurised role of a negotiator, and at times Tone himself lost patience.[6] It was quite a come-down from the position he had occupied on the eve of the Bantry Bay expedition or at Hoche's German headquarters.

In such circumstances Tone welcomed the friendship and patronage of Daendels. They corresponded regularly and in time Daendels and his wife became family friends of the Tones. Tone shopped for Mme Daendels in Paris, undertaking commissions for porcelain cups, hats, shoes and silk stockings in the latest fashions and colours. In return Daendels provided information on the composition, uniforms and methods of promotion of the Batavian army. Tone was thinking of writing a history of his campaigns, and made a start in May 1798.[7]

Daendels was typical of the powerful men to whom Tone gravitated in these years. As with Hoche, he would have recognised many of his own character traits in Daendels. Something of a romantic, Daendels's warmth and charisma are evident in their correspondence. He was also an adventurer. Like Hoche he craved glory and reputation, was ready to take chances, and preferred the daring, the exemplary, the frontal attack (both in politics and war) to the devious. He hated weakness and delays, and had that energy and spirit which Tone considered so essential in the revolutionary patriot. Daendels was just what the Irish venture needed. But he was no Hoche. His daring was sometimes rash. He had a history of making foolhardy moves and minimising difficulties. His Yarmouth scheme, which even Tone thought unrealistic, was entirely in character. Tone never balked at risking a small force in a daring strike, but not an entire army in a hopeless venture.

Daendels, a year older than Tone, had been among the youngest and most radical of the Dutch patriots of 1786–7. Exiled in France with his compatriots for the next eight years, he was well used to the kind of bickering and disunity which Tone was now reporting among the Irish exiles. He was no lover of the English, who had backed the Stadtholder against the patriots, and had been one of the more Francophile among the Dutch exiles. He remained so even though many Dutch were disillusioned at the harsh terms of their 'liberation' by the French army in 1795. Thereafter he shared France's growing irritation at the political weakness and disunity of the Batavian Republic, and, after years of wrangling, at the Batavian Assembly's rejection of a new constitution in August 1797. That was the prelude to a Fructidor-type coup the following January, in which Daendels assumed the leading role. At a time when he could not always trust the Dutch appointee to Paris, Daendels used Tone as something of a personal envoy in the run-up to the January coup, and many of his complaints to the Directory about internal Batavian politics were channelled through him. Tone was a willing recruit in the campaign to remedy the political frailty of the Batavian Republic. He fully accepted French complaints that it was weakening the war effort, and supported Daendels's call for a Dutch Fructidor against internal enemies.[8]

It was the recognition of Holland's poor showing in the war which had forced a reluctant De Winter out of the Texel on 7 October. The sailing was senseless; even Tone thought so. The fleet had sailed, it seemed, for no purpose other than to prove Dutch mettle in direct combat with the English. On 11 October it duly met Duncan's greatly superior force and was severely defeated within sight of the Dutch coast at the battle of Camperdown. The Dutch fleet was

decimated. Only 13 ships returned of the 27 which had sailed; 9 of
the original ships of the line were lost or captured, among them the
Vrijheid, taken with the green flag Tone was to have hoisted in
Ireland.[9]

News of Camperdown, and the recognition that the French had
no intention of mounting a winter expedition, produced one of the
schemes characteristic of Tone when cornered. It explains why,
perhaps surprisingly, he had supported Tate's expedition. The scheme
involved taking advantage of England's complacency after Camperdown to rush 5,000 élite troops under Daendels to the north of
Ireland. It was just the kind of venture suited to Daendels's temperament. 'I recognise that this enterprise is daring in the extreme,
if not downright reckless', wrote Tone. But 'I think I understand
you well enough to know what decision you will take in difficult
circumstances'. Tone tended to minimise the naval difficulties, but
he had taken advice from the Irish exiles in Paris and was assured that
even a small landing would trigger off a rising. Such a landing at the
end of 1797 might indeed have rescued the disintegrating United
Irish movement, and a rising prompted France to new efforts, as it
would do the following year.

Daendels replied that such an expedition would be impossible in
the atmosphere of recrimination after Camperdown, even if they
could maintain the necessary secrecy. But he was itching for a direct
strike at England, and knew that France could easily tighten the
screws on the Dutch to restore their fleet. He wrote to the Minister
of Marine and to General Desaix, interim commander of the Armée
d'Angleterre in Bonaparte's absence, offering Dutch participation
in France's naval plans. The Dutch navy was duly included in an
order of 14 December, and Daendels asked Tone to send an English,
Irish and Scottish representative to Holland. Tone sent Aherne, for
Daendels had become quite mesmerised by the Scottish plan.[10]

II

Daendels was never a total substitute for Hoche. But his friendship
for Tone was genuine, his commitment to a direct attack on Britain
greater than that of any French general, and he afforded Tone and
Lewins many of the openings they needed, even permitting them
to deliver his letters personally to Desaix. It was Desaix who introduced them to Bonaparte on 21 December, and several further
meetings followed. Tone did not know quite what to make of
Bonaparte. He was somewhat in awe of his military reputation and
was clearly delighted that the great general seemed to think well of
him. Tone accorded precedence to Lewins as 'our Ambassador'. But
it was to Tone that Bonaparte addressed his military queries. Tone

disclaimed having any great military experience. '"*Mais vous êtes brave*," Bonaparte replied. *"Eh bien . . . cela suffit"*'.[11]

Yet after a series of meetings with 'the greatest man in Europe', Tone was astonished at how little he had to say of him. Bonaparte had been characteristically inscrutable, listening attentively but saying little. He lived in the greatest simplicity; his house in the rue Chantereine, near the Opéra, was small, neat and furnished in the classical mode. 'He is about five feet six inches high, slender, and well made, but stoops considerably', Tone observed; 'he looks at least ten years older than he is. . . . His face is that of a profound thinker, but bears no marks of that great enthusiasm and unceasing activity by which he has been so much distinguished. It is rather to my mind the countenance of a mathematician than of a General.' Bonaparte's manner was cold, if civil, and they could elicit no information from him on French plans for Ireland, or for that matter on the projected expedition to England. Lewins presented him with nearly all the documentation of the Irish mission, including copies of Tone's 1795 and 1796 memorials. Tone in particular was always referred to in documents of this period as having the confidence of General Hoche, and it seems unlikely that Bonaparte ever contemplated taking up the pet scheme of his arch-rival. Indeed, despite the orders issuing from the War Ministry for a massive movement of troops to the northern and western coasts, Desaix and Bonaparte found preparations in the ports little advanced by February 1798, and Bonaparte decided then on his ill-fated expedition to Egypt. The English expedition was suspended and the Irish-born General Kilmaine put in command of the remnants of the army dotted about the northern and western coasts of France.[12]

Throughout these months Tone received no further information about the Directory's plans for Ireland. Indeed he knew less of what was happening than in the first months after his arrival in France, and he admitted as much to Daendels on 3 February 1798. This was only his third letter since October, despite Daendels's request for frequent information, and it contained scarcely any news, for Tone had none to give.[13] He had become far too trusting of France's good intentions and was accepting groundless assurances from Barras, Talleyrand and Desaix, with none of the old scepticism or demands for guarantees on how the French would act in Ireland. Had he lost his touch? Had he gone too far in ceding the ground to Lewins? Had he perhaps been out of Ireland too long and become far too Francophile?

Certainly he looked upon the French expulsion of the Pope from Rome in February 1798 as an 'event . . . of a magnitude scarce, if at all, inferior in importance, to that of the French revolution'. The event is described in the propagandist terminology of the French press as justified retaliation for the murder in Rome of the French General Duphot. There were indeed signs that the Pope, Naples and Austria alike had been behind the murder. But France had been seeking an excuse to provoke a rupture with the Pope. Tone might hail the establishment of a Roman Republic as a demonstration of popular will or a revival of the spirit of ancient Rome. In fact it was the result of Bonapartist machinations, and was proclaimed by a tiny group of puppet republicans to a crowd of bemused spectators.[14]

A typical product of the Enlightenment, Tone was anti-clerical, though a believer in a deity. There is also a sense of the papacy as the incarnation of evil. In the dethronement of the Pope he saw the workings of 'a special Providence guiding the affairs of Europe... and turning everything to the great end of the emancipation of mankind from the yoke of religious and political superstitition, under which they have so long groaned'.[15]

More surprisingly, Tone thoroughly approved of the second Directory's more aggressive and interventionist foreign policy, scarcely giving a thought to the implications if Ireland won independence through French assistance. In almost every case he was accepting one-sided reports in French newspapers. He welcomed the 'fructi-dorisation' of Holland, with its message of increasing French interference in the domestic affairs of sister republics. He had even played a minor role in the preliminaries to the coup, having participated in the discussions between Daendels's emissary and General Desaix, and was forewarned of it by Meyer, the Dutch minister in Paris. Tone thought the French had acted with remarkable restraint, having 'conquered' Holland, but left it free to organise its own government and constitution, only to find no progress whatsoever after three years. He fully accepted the charge that such political weakness damaged the war effort, and in his capacity to see the will of the majority thus overruled in the interests of a perceived ultimate good, he showed just how far his French experience had developed the hard-liner revolutionary in him. 'Individually, I wish most heartily it were otherwise, for I am sorry to see a people incapable to profit of such a great occasion as the Dutch have had in their hands, but if unfortunately the fact be against them, I must once more acquit the French for their interposition, and I think I should do so, even in the case of my own country, if she were to show similar incapacity in like circumstances, which however I am far from apprehending would be the case.'[16] Since Tone, like his fellow United Irishmen, lived under the illusion that everyone in Ireland except members of the Established Church was fundamentally republican, there would be no question there of forcing its people to be free.

III

There was probably very little Tone or Lewins could have done to arrest the disintegration of their mission. It was largely due to outside causes: Hoche's death, the alteration in Directorial strategy and outlook after Fructidor, England's recovery, new threats of war on the Continent, and—not least—competition from other foreign revolutionaries, who were returning to Paris in numbers not seen since the early 1790s. The intensity and secrecy of Tone's mission in 1796 had paid dividends. But it was directed at securing success in the short term and could not—indeed should not—have been maintained indefinitely. Against a background of escalating crisis in Ireland in 1797–8, the failure of the original United Irish leaders to communicate details of the French mission had split the movement irrevocably by the beginning of 1798. Sometimes, indeed, there was little to tell. The pace of the Irish mission decelerated during 1797. There were fewer meetings with ministers and none with the Directors themselves between October 1797 and April 1798, by which time Tone and Lewins had left Paris altogether.[17] United Irish expectations of their agents in France had increased just as changed circumstances there made it more difficult to repeat Tone's earlier success. Lewins came in for heavy criticism and Tone was invariably, if reluctantly, drawn into the controversy.

It started with Napper Tandy's arrival from America in June 1797, amidst the same kind of public display for which he was so noted in Ireland. His journey across the Atlantic, through Cuxhaven and Hamburg, was tracked by English agents because of the attention he drew to himself.[18] Arriving in Paris before Lewins, he tried to take charge of Irish matters, and intrigued against Lewins when his own seniority was not recognised. His stream of letters to his son in Dublin opened the United Irishmen's secret diplomacy to Castle scrutiny. It was Dublin's first news of Tone's activities in France, and with it the secrecy which he had maintained so effectively was destroyed. The letters spun quite a yarn. Tandy claimed to have assumed command of Irish affairs in France and depicted himself as the Irish republican generalissimo who would lead the French forces to Ireland.[19] It was the role he coveted for himself in his communications with the French ministers, and the grant of a commission in the French army to Tone was the source of considerable jealousy and complaint.

Tone was not at all pleased at Tandy's arrival in France. Tandy joined forces with Madgett and together they wrote to Tone in June 1797. But, knowing Tandy of old, Tone was anxious to conceal his presence at the Texel and complimented Matilda for feigning ignorance when asked his whereabouts. Tandy complained that Tone and Lewins were keeping information from him. In this their instincts were right and other United Irishmen in France thought likewise.[20] Tone considered himself above party and tried to act as mediator on his arrival in Paris that October.[21] But the lines of division had been drawn in his absence, and his name was already associated with that of Lewins. Tandy's inflated claims and ego would have alienated Tone in any event, and should have isolated Tandy as similar behaviour had done in 1792. But events in Ireland were flooding France with a new breed of Irishman. Fed on repeated assurances of French help and expecting French support as their right, they were critical of the apparent exclusiveness of Tone and Lewins and gravitated towards the opposition set up by Tandy.

Tandy and his group went public and enlisted the press in their campaign. The worst offender was the Scottish patriot, Thomas Muir, recently escaped from his exile in Botany Bay. Though he was still a young man, Muir's mental and physical state had deteriorated considerably since he was transported in 1794. He too was claiming to speak for Ireland, as well as for Scotland and England, and he bombarded the Directory with memorials to that effect. The United Irishmen then in Paris—with the exception of Tandy—delegated Tone, Lewins, Orr and Lowry to caution Muir. They were staggered by his vanity and obstinacy. 'I could scarcely conceive such a degree of self-sufficiency to exist', wrote Tone; 'he told us roundly that he knew as much of our country as we did, and . . . had as much of the confidence of the United Irishmen as we had . . . that he seldom acted without due reflection, and that when once he had taken his party, it was impossible to change him and that as to what he had written relative to the United Irishmen, he had the sanction of . . . *the most respectable individual of that body*', by whom they presumed he meant Tandy. For nearly three hours they tried to dissuade him from making such declarations and parted 'very drily'. Muir and Tandy were well matched, and although Tone's tendency to assume an attitude of unassailable purity probably aggravated relations, there was much truth in his claim that 'Tandy and Muir are puffing one another here for their private advancement'.[22]

The two had established a particular relationship with Nicholas de Bonneville, an old associate of the British and Irish in Paris, now editor of the influential daily the *Bien Informé*. After nearly a year of seeing the Irish business and Tandy's claims paraded in print by Bonneville, Tone exploded in September 1798, upon reading an account of Tandy leading some kind of 'Army of Avengers' to Ireland. 'I never will believe that any cause can be served by forgery and falsehood', wrote Tone, 'especially when it is wrapped up in such impenetrable nonsense: is there no way of reducing that idiot Bonneville to reason?...and not by his egregious trash and lies to throw at once a burlesque and a discredit on our business?'[23] The issue was Tandy's address to the Irish people, melodramatically entitled 'Northern Army of Avengers', and calling for 'a war of extermination' against their enemies.[24]

At first the Tandy faction was composed largely of figures from an earlier generation, claiming primacy on past, often faded, reputations. Many were not even Irishmen. The group included Bonneville, Muir, Thomas Paine (although he remained on good terms with the Tones[25]), the fifty-eight-year-old Madgett, now out of office altogether, John Hurford Stone, and William Duckett, who after 1796 had little reason to like Tone. To these were added a number of recent exiles from the split which had occurred in the United Irish movement at home. Notable among them were the northerners James Coigley (a Catholic priest) and Arthur MacMahon (a Presbyterian minister). All fed home discontent about Lewins, and Coigley, of whom Tone complained in particular,[26] returned to Ireland at the end of 1797 to secure a replacement. Muir was claiming that France would be better advised to send her forces to Scotland, since the United Irishmen did not want her help, and the exaggerated claims of English rebelliousness put forward by this group were a further element disrupting Irish talks in Paris.[27]

All of Tandy's party were living in straitened circumstances, and Tone and Lewins were comfortably off by comparison, which became another running sore.[28] Some were seeking relief from the French government long before such help became common among the Irish generally, and although the French did not complain of Tandy's application, they thought some others mere adventurers.[29] In the records of the Police and Foreign Affairs ministries of the period only Tone and Lewins are recognised as official Irish representatives, in France at the Republic's invitation. All the rest, Tandy included, are classified as 'refugees'.[30] The standing of Tone and Lewins with the French authorities was not noticeably damaged by the in-fighting. The disputes only served to increase French trust in the established negotiators who had already proved themselves.[31] There was considerable sympathy for Tandy, because of his great age and undoubted reputation.[32] But the standing of the Irish generally suffered, and in December 1797 Reinhard was warned not to issue any further passports to Irishmen seeking entry to France.[33]

Tone was automatically consulted about Irish applications for passports and residence and travel permits. The power this placed in his hands must have rankled with some. But power was not something in which he was interested, and he conducted the business efficiently and fairly, always involving other United Irishmen in cases where he did not himself know the candidate. In due course he was asked about many of those involved in the intrigues against him, and in the circumstances his comments were even-handed. Coigley and MacMahon he described as zealous patriots persecuted by England. Tandy too he supported, and whilst this was in October 1797, before the rift had become unbridgeable, his comments on Muir in March 1798 were more generous than the Scot deserved: 'Not being well-acquainted with this person, all I can tell you is that I believe him to be an honest man,...a warm patriot in his native country...deported for it by the English government'. As for Ireland, however, 'he knows scarcely anything, having, as a stranger, no connections in that country, and all the important events having taken place after his transportation'.[34] Tone's system of validation operated well provided he or his colleagues in Paris recognised the names of the new arrivals. But this was becoming increasingly difficult, and his suggestion that some kind of quarantine way-station be set up at Liège was accepted as future French policy.[35]

IV

If continental divisions among the United Irishmen only marginally damaged the mission in France, their impact on the domestic movement was more serious. Suspicion of the Catholic leaders, which had dogged the United Irish Society from the outset, had deepened after the Bantry Bay attempt. They had always been suspected of limited commitment to revolution and with former Catholic Committee members and their supporters leading the anti-rising party in 1797, the disagreements with the northerners inevitably acquired religious overtones. Lewins was not trusted, and the religious factor was decisive in providing the British authorities with their most important information source of the decade. This was Samuel Turner, who had so impressed Reinhard and coloured his attitudes to the Irish on the Continent.

A native of Newry in Ulster, son of a magistrate, Trinity graduate and barrister, Turner joined the United Irishmen only in 1797 and had a reputation as a hothead. With so many northern leaders in prison, he was quickly elevated to the United Irish executive and to a military command in his home county. In June 1797 he had travelled to France, one of a number of younger Ulster leaders who were beginning to act independently of the Dublin executive. In October 1797 he arrived in London and called at the London house of his County Down neighbour, Tone's old adversary, Lord Downshire. He claimed to have discovered that 'the object of the Papists was the ruin and destruction of the country and the establishment of a tyranny far worse than what was complained of by the reformers'. He also wrote some months later to Talleyrand, claiming to speak for a large body of respectable Protestants and asking the Directory to guarantee their property against the historic pretensions of the Catholics.[36] Turner gave Downshire an account of developments within the United Irish Society over the past year, including what he knew of the French negotiations. The Irish government hoped to use Turner's evidence against the United Irish prisoners, whom it had been unable to bring to trial, for want of such evidence. But Whitehall was unwilling to reveal in open court the source of its evidence. Turner remained immune until he 'retired' in 1803, and his flow of information continued uninterrupted until then.[37]

Turner was as critical of Tandy's antics as was Tone. 'Napper Tandy is looked upon as a madman', he told Downshire, 'and struts about in the streets in national uniform calling himself a major.'[38] In Paris Turner shared lodgings in the rue de Fromentin, Clichy, with Tennent, Lowry, Teeling and Orr. His reports did not criticise Tone, even though they gave a very full account of his activities in France, past and present. But Lewins was savaged and his reputation systematically undermined in regular communications with Lord Edward Fitzgerald. Turner's correspondence fed militant discontent and helped produce a campaign for Lewins's removal by the end of the year. His information enabled the Irish authorities to intercept a number of letters from France, including one from Teeling which would have calmed growing doubts about Lewins.[39]

Turner seems to have played a significant, if background, role in the disputes within the United leadership. Not only did he whip up the United Irish militants' dissatisfaction with Lewins, but in France he expanded Lord Edward's comments into a report of Lewins's imminent replacement, and generally created the illusion that the militants on the United Irish executive possessed more power than they had in reality.[40] In fact they were consistently outvoted and Lewins retained the confidence of the majority.

It was Turner likewise who provided Tone's critics with a weapon which he found particularly wounding. We do not know the full details, but it involved other members of the Tone family, notably Mary and her husband. Since the spring of 1797, Tone, Lewins, Teeling, Tennent and Lowry had used the Hamburg-based Giauque as a medium of correspondence. It should have been a perfect arrangement, Giauque having mercantile contacts and Mary, having lived with the Tones, knowing many of those active in the early years of the United Irish movement. It was perhaps the couple's over-involvement which came to rankle with the disgruntled, for in regular communications to Reinhard the Giauques were also vetting new arrivals. Turner claimed that Giauque had revealed to a fellow Swiss the presence of the United Irishmen in Hamburg, and the credulous Reinhard, completely under Turner's influence, was later to deflect criticism on to Giauque when reprimanded for his incaution in granting passports to the Irish.[41] Turner's information was usually reliable, and there is a hint in a letter of Matilda's that Giauque may not always have acted properly.[42] Tone learnt of the attack in April 1798. But he thought any public quarrel would simply disgrace the Irish in France and harm Mary's name, and recommended 'letting the matter die in silence'.[43]

The Giauques, with their new son, had just moved to Paris. Matthew Tone had arrived in Paris in January 1798 and Arthur too was expected to travel from Hamburg, where he had arrived from America in April 1798. Tone contacted his old comrades in arms, De Winter and Bruix, the latter now French Minister of Marine, and succeeded in placing Arthur in the Dutch navy. In May they also heard from William after a silence of six years. He had done well in India, and with rumours afloat of French plans to attack English interests there, Tone recommended him to the French.[44] It must have appeared as if Tone had recruited his entire family into the business. He had spoken before of providing for all his family and friends—'who, luckily, are not many'—should they succeed in liberating Ireland, never recognising in this the very jobbery he so criticised in the existing Irish establishment.[45]

Tone disdained intrigue. If he could not confront and expose it, he tended to walk away from it. A meeting of Irish in Paris was called by Tandy and Coigley against himself and Lewins. Lewins refused to attend. Tone did so, 'and when I appeared, there was no one found to bring forward a charge against me, though I called three times to know'. He gives few details in his journals of 'these dirty little intrigues...which I scorn to commit to paper', and he warned Matilda to take the same line and to welcome all Irish in Paris regardless of party. But he ceased to communicate with Tandy, and was glad to have the excuse of military service away from Paris to turn his back on the dispute altogether.[46]

Tone was far too sensitive, however, not to be upset by 'their singular meanness'. He was deeply hurt personally, worried about the impact it had on the French and even more so on his future reputation in Ireland. He was accused of sacrificing the interest of his country to his own. For someone who made such a stand on purity and who increasingly saw his personal sacrifices as part of his revolutionary credentials, such an accusation had a particular sting. Recognising that 'there was no one so mean, who does not have the power to do harm', he sought written testimonials to use against his detractors 'in the event of a return to my own country'.[47] 'No one knows better than I', he wrote to Talleyrand, 'how little I have to boast of in terms of merit, service, or sacrifice; but for integrity and disinterestedness I can say I have never been wanting;...if you believe my conduct here has been that of an honest man, who has tried to the best of his ability to serve the cause of liberty and his country, without ever stooping so low as to derive any personal advantage, I beg of you in all earnestness to reply to this letter...a favorable reply from you will overcome all calumny.' Talleyrand assured him that he had heard nothing said against himself or Lewins, 'but even if he had', Tone writes, 'he should pay it no attention, the opinion of government being made up in our favour'.[48]

Tone also appealed to those who had been witness to his mission at its height, and was gratified by a glowing testimonial from Clarke on 11 April:

> My dear Smith,...I should be more than happy to testify on every occasion that you not only pleaded the cause of the Irish republicans with eloquence, but that you sought to push their cause with a devotion and an assiduous zeal of which I have long been a witness. Indeed, in a position which might so easily have exposed you to suggestions of intrigue, you knew how to avoid such dangers, and in my eyes you behaved with a dignity and disinterestedness fully becoming the role you had assumed, the cause of free men you were championing, and the esteem which such conduct won for you among those who knew you particularly.[49]

This was praise indeed from his one-time sparring partner, of little use in France because of Clarke's exile from public life, and clearly intended for a future in Ireland.

Tone wrote too to Delacroix, then French ambassador to the Batavian Republic, asking him in particular to state if he had ever pursued his own personal interests. The request was enclosed in a letter to Daendels which shows just how much the attacks had upset him. Daendels delivered the letter immediately and was promised the required testimonial in the near future. There is no sign that it was ever sent. Relations between Daendels and Delacroix were bad. The General had been playing upon the Directory's doubts about its ambassador to secure his removal, and this task was effected in another coup led by Daendels on 12 June.[50]

Tone thought Lewins was making a good job of his mission and the petty-mindedness of some of the attacks served to fasten his loyalty.[51] But over the next two years, after Tone and Tandy were gone, much of the criticism of Lewins proved justified. When all the United Irishmen in Paris—including those whom Tone had befriended—joined forces in one body, Lewins remained aloof and intransigent, continuing to conduct his mission according to his original brief when changed times required more flexibility. He was particularly unsympathetic about relief payments for the Irish, even though the Directory had already accepted such payments as policy. This later inflexibility may be the key to the dissatisfaction of 1797–8.

Tone was becoming more critical of Lewins in his final months in France. He sympathised with the plight of the 'young men' in Paris and did raise with the French the prospect of long-term assistance.[52] One wonders if in later years he might indeed have acted as the mediator which Tandy's and Muir's posturings prevented in 1798. Possibly; but ultimately it seems more likely that Tone would have turned his back completely on the bickering which was to convulse the Irish in France over the next decade, and possibly on the Irish cause entirely. For even with Tandy's influence removed, there would be other prima donnas who thrived on faction. Tone admits in April 1798 that the 'determination' and 'the pleasure I formerly felt in pursuing this great object, is considerably diminished by recent experience'.[53]

It is a revealing statement. Tone had made considerable personal sacrifices and his critics chose their ground badly in accusing him of personal gain and intrigue. The 'pleasure' in such sacrifice came from the conviction of total purity, total rectitude, the very suffering sanctifying cause and proponent. The reward Tone expected was in reputation and the gratitude of his countrymen, and his detractors seemed determined to deprive him even of those. Having always assumed that national gratitude would be forthcoming, he had good cause to feel hurt and disappointed. It gave a certain Olympian quality to his final months, the purist revolutionary courting fate as proof of principle.

The secrecy and intimacy of the early days of the mission to France, and indeed of the nascent republican movement in Ireland, had suited Tone's own natural inclinations. His intimate circle in Ireland had been small. But things had changed in both countries. The extension of the movement, its growing militancy and restiveness, the influx of Irish into France and soon the growing signs that England knew everything anyway, demanded a greater openness than in the past. The squabbles in Paris were not peculiar to the Irish. They were experienced by almost every other exiled group of the period and were part of the inevitable war-weariness, the frustration of waiting and the attacks by a new generation on those perceived as the old guard. All of this would not have been apparent to Tone at the time. The genuine concerns of many who gravitated to Tandy were swamped by his destructive vanity and intriguing nature. Given the success of Tone's methods in 1796 and France's preference for secrecy, there seemed little immediate reason to alter the tactics. It is nevertheless hard to escape the conclusion that Tone and Lewins were rapidly becoming men of the past.

28

Crisis

On 25 March 1798 Tone received orders to join the Armée d'Angleterre at Rouen where he arrived on 5 April. For the next three months he kicked his heels in frustrated inactivity, his bafflement increasing daily about France's reported plans for an attack on England. Although the English expedition had been abandoned early in March, and Bonaparte had embarked on his Egyptian campaign, there was no public announcement.[1] Tone, without access to the Paris papers or communications from Lewins, was desperate for news. He was bored and frustrated. No staff headquarters had been set up. There was nothing to do at Rouen, except read, write, paint and go to the theatre.[2]

I

Letters to Matilda were more frequent than on previous separations. There are signs of increasing domesticity after six months of as normal marital life as they had ever had, and Tone showed a desire to return to Paris as frequently as possible. For nearly a month before leaving Paris in April, he had hunted unsuccessfully for new lodgings for his family. They were having problems with the landlady at 9 cul de sac Notre-Dame-des-Champs. With hindsight he recognised his mistake in not bringing over his family in 1796 and realising his assets by purchasing property in the French countryside. But he had not then envisaged such an extended residence in France. Matilda and Matthew found new lodgings some weeks later at 29 rue des Batailles, Chaillot, on the outskirts of Paris and presumably cheaper. Tone had secured a captaincy in the French army for his brother, and while he awaited orders Matthew lodged with Matilda: 'the difference of expense to her will be but trifling', wrote Tone from Rouen, 'and everything here is dearer than at Paris'. But he hoped that Mary and Giauque might be able to accommodate Arthur when he arrived.[3]

The children's education was a matter of much concern to him, and there are echoes of his father's complaints about himself: 'make the boys mind their books...if ever I come to be any thing it will be all along of my learning'.[4] Music figures prominently; sheet music was ordered from Holland, and Matilda was instructed to keep the piano in tune, employ a tutor and make the children practise regularly.[5] Maria, now twelve, was an eager pupil, and the seven-year-old William was already showing some literary talent. But the five-year-old Frank had inherited much of the Tone waywardness: 'he bids fair to attain the reputation of his uncle William, of being *"an amorous young man"*...I guess we shall have divers escapades to overlook on his account, and I hope we may have the good sense to do so'. Frank, indeed, sounds a good deal like his father and had already developed Tone's fastidiousness in dress. 'I do not think he promises to show as much in the literary world, as Will, but in return...he will tye his cravat a great deal better, and we cannot have all the good things of this life together.'[6]

Many of the instructions and commands carry denials that Tone intends them as such. Matilda was perfectly capable of managing things herself and seems at times to have told him so. Comments by Tone about the dutiful wife and mother are made tongue in cheek. He himself is rather more reserved on such issues, and he warned her never to enter any of the government bureaus without Lewins, 'seeing that there is nothing I more dislike than to see women alone in such places'.[7]

Financial concerns are never far from his mind, even if the humiliating anxieties of 1796 are no longer present. His military pay was increased in May and he was able to send Matilda 300 francs (about £15) a month. He carefully accounts outstanding loans, discreetly reminding Daendels about the 400 Dutch florins he had advanced to Aherne for his journey to Holland, and the costs of Mme Daendels's commissions.[8] He wants Maria to have music and dancing lessons. But although his recommendation for Matilda to attend these lessons owes something to his strict sense of propriety about leaving Maria alone with a dancing master, the desire to ensure value for money was uppermost. Matilda was expected to strike a hard bargain over payment. She took on a helper, Marianne Gaudel, a big and it seems a somewhat slatternly woman. Against Matilda's complaints Tone defended her: 'I have a better opinion of the poor unchaste than many people entertain'. But, again for reasons of economy, Matilda was not to let her buy provisions for the family.[9]

For two weeks he had leave in Paris and returned on 17 May even more dissatisfied with the stagnant life at Rouen.[10] He had travelled back through a raging storm. 'Dear Love,' he wrote next day to Matilda,

> I arrived here yesterday, twelve o'clock, as tired as a horse, and in all my travels I do not think I ever spent a day so ill; I bear every separation worse than the last; after wandering about this town,

without well knowing where I was going, at last the hour of dinner arrived, where, as the sublimest grief, you know, will at last condescend to eat, and I will add from my own experience, to *drink* also, I made to my inn, and, remembering Voltaire's advice, '*Ou bien buvez, c'est un parti fort sage!*' I sat down to a mutton chop, and a choice little *vin de Beaune*, which I never quit while there was a drop of the comfort remaining;—I do not wonder that grief drives people to drink, for I found yesterday, experimentally, that wine is a sovereign remedy against despair.[11]

He was contemplating applying again for leave when ordered to Le Havre on 28 May as adjutant to the commanding general. In the move he finally got rid of MacSheehy, much to his relief, 'for if ever there was a rascal in the world, devoid of all principle, he is one'. Le Havre and the other northern ports were being heavily shelled by the British, and though Tone complained of having little to do but walk round the ramparts in his general's uniform, he was highly commended for his service in the port.[12]

During this time, however, the growing crisis in Ireland was never far from Tone's mind and explains his frustration at being entrammelled by routine military duties. News continued to come through of the intrigues in Paris. As Tone and Lewins—gone to Holland on private affairs—were no longer in the city, there was no established channel for communication with the French ministers. A general free-for-all resulted, with Muir, Turner and others independently representing Irish interests to Talleyrand, and Muir's advisory role increasing.[13] For a while Tone and Matilda even had doubts about Bartholomew Teeling and Orr, and watched to see which way new arrivals such as Russell's nephew, William Hamilton, would behave. Orr had been unsuccessfully petitioning the Police Ministry for a passport and had written to ask Tone to intercede. Tone was angry at Orr's having taken independent action, after the efforts he and Lewins had made on his behalf some months earlier. 'I presume he sees now that it is more than *ask and have*, in the bureaus of the police, and that should teach him to judge more charitably of Lewins....I had a good mind to write him a lecture thereupon.' Tone did write to the Police Minister as requested. But he told Orr, he doubted the application would succeed, 'considerable pains having been taken to diminish my credit; if any I might be supposed to have'. 'Let him chew upon that', he wrote to Matilda.[14]

By the end of May 1798 Tone thought there was about as much chance of an attempt on England as on the moon. The Directory was preoccupied with the Jacobin resurgence at the spring elections.[15] French military strength had now been diverted to the Rhine and the

Mediterranean. The ships to convey the original Armée d'Angleterre had never existed and on the eve of the 1798 rebellion in Ireland France had no plans whatsoever to send the help on which United Irish plans had hung for the last two years. Tone heard of the appointment of his old *émigré* friend, Dupetit Thouars, to a command on the Toulon expedition. He wrote on 24 May congratulating him and offering to join him, in terms of such exaggerated deference and enthusiasm that the old Tone is scarcely recognisable.[16] Two days later he also wrote to Kilmaine offering to go to India, since that seemed to be Bonaparte's ultimate destination and there was little chance now of an Irish expedition.[17]

The arrival of Grouchy at Rouen caused Tone to reflect back on better times. Both recognised the opportunity they had lost at Bantry Bay: 'poor Hoche! It is now that we feel the loss of his friendship and influence! If he were alive he would be in Ireland in a month, if he went only with his *état major*, in a fishing boat; I fear, we shall not after all, easily meet with his fellow'.[18] Tone could contemplate going to fight the English in India because he had entirely abandoned hope of an Irish expedition and he still did not think the Irish capable of rising without French help. He was soon proved wrong.

II

Since January, Ireland had been moving rapidly towards a crisis. The military purge of Ulster was progressively extended to other counties. The United Irish ranks filled with new recruits who enlisted out of sheer panic. The old policy of waiting on the French seemed no longer sound. The Leinster leaders met at Oliver Bond's house in Dublin on 12 March to decide the issue of an immediate rising. The meeting was raided and all except a handful of latecomers, which included Lord Edward Fitzgerald, were arrested. The authorities had been told of the meeting by Thomas Reynolds, husband of Matilda's sister Harriet. It simply added to Tone's contempt for the Witheringtons, for he thought Reynolds too spineless to have taken such a step without Harriet's prompting. Plans for a May rising went ahead amidst some confusion after further arrests including that of Lord Edward himself on 19 May.

Tone's distress increased apace as he read of these events, and there are signs that desperation was temporarily unhinging his mind. At nearly thirty-five he was conscious of the gap opening up between himself and the second generation of United Irishmen. The time for achievement was already past. 'Today is my birth day', he wrote on 20 June. 'I am thirty-five years of age; more than half the career of my life is finished, and how little have I yet been able to do!'[19] On 26

March, just before leaving Paris for Rouen, he had read of the arrests at Bond's. Nearly all his old friends still at liberty were among those arrested, including Emmet, Bond, John Sweetman, MacNeven and Henry Jackson. 'I have not received such a shock from all that has passed since I left Ireland...what a triumph at this moment for Fitzgibbon!' He learnt of Russell's deteriorating health in prison and brooded on the fate of the two men he most esteemed, Emmet and Russell, both now in danger of 'a violent and ignominious death'. He admitted to being so 'completely deranged' at the thought that 'I can scarce write connectedly,' a comment which his distressed letters of these weeks bear out.[20]

A long, impassioned plea to Talleyrand to help his country savoured of desperation. He scoured the papers, read of Fitzgibbon's purge of Trinity and the suspension of Whitley Stokes, an attack by the military on the house of an old friend of his father, and the arrest and death in prison of Lord Edward Fitzgerald. He ran through the litany of all his friends in prison or in exile and expressed some surprise that Keogh alone had escaped. 'Judge what I feel at this moment,' he wrote to Matilda from Le Havre on 12 June, 'when I reflect on the helpless situation I am in here, with my blood boiling within me and absolutely unable to make the smallest effort....I was ill all day yesterday with sheer rage and vexation.'[21]

Such thoughts produced a sudden shift in outlook. Revenge, not hitherto part of Tone's republicanism, began to dominate his thinking. 'Well, if our unfortunate country is doomed to sustain the unspeakable loss of so many brave and virtuous citizens, woe to their tyrants if ever we reach our destination. I feel my mind growing every hour more and more savage. Measures appear to me now justified by necessity, which six months ago I would have regarded with horror. There is now no medium'. When he left Ireland in 1795 the United Irishmen had had no desire to attack or distribute property. Now he felt such an eventuality justified and the Irish gentry had but themselves to blame. Had they acted as proper patriots, as natural leaders to the people, instead of such 'miserable slaves' of England, caring only for their rent-rolls, their places and their pensions, 'our Revolution would have been accomplished without a shock, or perhaps one drop of blood spilled'. Instead the gentry had been condemned by 'public sentiment' and in the words of the Bible he predicted their destruction: '"*They shall perish like their own dung; they that have seen them shall say, where are they?*"' He thought of the contrast with Lord Edward: 'If the blood of this brave young man be shed by the hand of his enemies, it will be no ordinary vengeance that will content the People, whenever the day of retribution arrives'. He was particularly upset at reports of old friends and reformers like Griffith and Parsons leading the militia and yeomen against their fellow countrymen.[22]

Tone had missed the polarisation of the Irish populace which had occurred since 1796 and still thought in terms of an English faction confronting the people. Yet his vengefulness was out of character, and tells us much of the disturbed state of his mind in these final months. There is a new fatalism and in it glimmers of one of the hallmarks of future republican nationalism: the belief in the sanctity of the blood sacrifice, of victory in defeat. On 17 June he learnt that a rising had finally erupted in Ireland, and prepared to set off for Paris. Would the French now help? Kilmaine was doubtful, for he had seen the state of the navy. No matter, reflected Tone. Even if 'the rebellion, as they call it' were crushed, repression could not win; 'the 18,000 victims sacrificed by Alva in the low countries... did not prevent the establishment of the liberty of Holland; from the blood of every one of the martyrs of the liberty of Ireland will spring, I hope, thousands to revenge their fall'.[23]

III

News of the Irish revolt took everyone, Tone included, by surprise. He had been given no reason to think that the old policy of waiting for the French had been abandoned and only two months previously had dismissed rumours of a rising. But there was no doubt about the news coming through to France that June. On 24–25 May Dublin and the adjacent counties had risen. The rising spread through the south-east and finally to Ulster on 7 June. In France the news produced such a frenzied rush to get help to Ireland that basic caution was thrown to the winds. Although Lewins was closely questioned by the Directory on the situation, the other Irishmen in Paris did not use him as a medium. Lowry, Orr, Hamilton and Teeling presented a separate petition on 16 June. With the apparent confidence of desperation they asked for only 1,000 troops and 5,000 stand of arms, to be landed in the north or north-west. At least Lewins had asked for 5,000 troops and 30,000 stand of arms, even if he likewise exaggerated the support the French might expect.[24] Tandy and his supporters dropped all pretence of secrecy with the formal creation of a Parisian United Irish Society and a delegation to the Council of Five Hundred. On 14 July they were fêted by the Council in terms reminiscent of France's early internationalism before the outbreak of European war.[25] There is no record of approaches from Tone, recalled to Paris by the Minister of Marine—he alone of the Irish exiles accepted Lewins as their official spokesman.

On 25 June the Directory initiated plans for a new Irish expedition, and with Chérin placed in overall military command and Bruix in charge of preparations at the centre, something of Hoche's old commitment pervaded the preparations. But there was no one of Hoche's stature to whip Directors, ministers and contractors into action. The Directory's instructions were not followed up and its attention was soon distracted by events on the Continent. The piece-meal Irish expeditions of 1798 may have owed something to the exaggerated claims of the United Irishmen in Paris, but they were equally a product of the Directory's expectations of getting something for nothing. Semi-piratical ventures, such as those rejected by Hoche and Tone in 1796, became a substitute for proper military planning, and the composition of the small forces which finally sailed during August and September 1798 tell their own story.

The immediate object was to send arms and leaders to the Irish. The focus was on Ulster, where, according to early reports, the revolt had not yet erupted. Tone was baffled at the failure of the Ulstermen to lead the way, as he had always expected: 'are they afraid?—have they changed their opinions?—What can be the cause of their passive submission, at this moment, so little suited to their former zeal and activity?' He recalled Digges, 'a rascal', but never-theless 'a man of great sense', asserting that a southerner, once roused, was worth twenty northerners and wondered if, after all, he had been right. 'If it should prove so, what a mortification for me, who have so long looked up with admiration to the North, and especially to Belfast!'[26] In fact the successful disarming of Ulster in 1797 had broken the United Irish movement there, and the Ulster rising when it did erupt was a shadow of what it would have been a year earlier.

Theoretically weather conditions should have favoured a summer expedition by the French. But the prevailing winds and extended daylight acted in Britain's favour. It was an argument used success-fully by the Batavians to counter France's suggestion that they should supply the main expedition. Instead France had to settle for the immediate dispatch of two Dutch ships to the north of Ireland. They would carry 280 French and Batavian soldiers, 20 officers, and substantial supplies of artillery and arms, and assure the United Irish executive of more substantial help in the autumn. Duckett, who knew little about Ulster, would advise on places of landing. He had been supplied with the sizeable budget of 24,000 francs to spend in support of the Irish rising (largely it seems on his pet venture of stirring up the Irish in the British navy). It was a side-show typical of the adventurism of the 1798 preparations, and required the kind of time to implement which, with the Irish insurgents already suc-cumbing to government forces, was no longer available.[27] All Tone's arguments of 1796 might as well never have been made.

He would have been even more disturbed by plans for an advance force to be dispatched from Dunkirk: for Tandy, with most of the Irishmen recently arrived on the Continent, regardless of their background, was being sent from there to lead the Ulster rebels. The principles of those accompanying him were doubtful. Some simply regarded the venture as a free passage home and several turned informers. The whole troupe acted with such incaution at Dunkirk that England was immediately alerted. The town was filling with Irish and Anglo-Americans, wrote the Directory's *commissaire* on 9 August, 'for a destination so secret that I have not been told of it', yet which seemed to be a matter of public knowledge. A fast-sailing corsair, the *Anacréon*, was to take them north. But they spent two weeks idling in the town's hotels before the vessel could be got ready, and, by all accounts, spoke freely of their plans. Nor were the handful of French on board any more impressive. 'How the Irish will laugh at you when they see them arrive', mocked the owner of the *Anacréon*.[28] Tandy refused to take those who had acted against him in Paris, and the French officers on board wondered what had possessed the Directory to appoint to such a command someone so obviously incapable.[29]

If Bruix was committed to helping the Irish, the situation was quite the reverse with Schérer, the War Minister. He was an old enemy of Hoche, and Tone had wondered whether the Irish cause would suffer by his appointment. Schérer was certainly not well disposed towards the 1798 schemes and he and Chérin clashed on a number of occasions, the latter's natural irritability aggravated by illness. 'The Minister Schérer', he wrote in frustration to Bruix on 26 July, 'continues for some unknown reason to publicly give this important expedition the aspect of a force of filibusters and vagabonds', sending everyone and anyone regardless of suitability.[30]

The main expedition was to consist of 8,000 men, and smaller expeditions would sail from Brest under General Hardy and from Rochefort under the irrepressible Humbert. They were to make for Donegal and, failing that, for Killala in the north-west, and Hardy was to assume overall command of their combined forces. Tone, Hamilton and several other Irishmen were sent to Brest, Matthew Tone and Bartholomew Teeling to Rochefort.

Tone was sent by Bruix to calm troubles which had broken out between the Irish and English prisoners of war at news of the rebellion, and to recruit for the expedition.[31] He finally arrived at Brest on 1 August. Tone liked Hardy—who had been with Hoche on the Rhine—and the naval commander, Bompard, 'a smart little man', who put him in mind of Griffith of Millicent. He also found the army and navy at Brest working together more harmoniously than in 1796.[32] The various addresses prepared for Bantry Bay were sent for and revised by Tone. Two new ones were prepared for distribution to the Irish people and the United Irishmen and were run off as posters and handbills. 'We are at work on divers proclamations and other "*inflamatory branches of learning*"', he wrote flippantly to Matilda on 7 August; 'we have likewise overhauled some ancient mischief, intended to be made use of eighteen months ago, which we find still serviceable; so that it seems treason, like Anderson's pills will "*keep good for years in any climate*"'. He would send her copies, he said, 'when God sends time'.

The new addresses invoked the memory of Hoche and Bantry Bay, and told the Irish that the French had come to assist them 'to break the barbarous yoke under which you groan'. But the new elements of vengeance and glorification in the blood sacrifice are dominant. 'Rest in peace, gallant, and unspotted spirits of Fitzgerald, of Crosbie, of Coigley, of Orr, of Harvey![33] Your blood shed for the sacred cause of Liberty, shall cement the independence of Ireland; it circulates in the veins of all your countrymen, and the United Republicans swear to punish your assassins.' Tone had changed his opinion of Coigley after his conduct at his recent trial and execution in England, but the draft proclamation still shows some hesitation to include him in such a pantheon.[34]

The enthusiastic rush of instructions for the expedition had not been translated into supplies and men. The Treasury had not released the assigned money. The soldiers and sailors had not been paid and near-mutiny erupted at sea on both expeditions. The officers did not fare any better. 'Touching money matters', Tone wrote to Matilda on 14 August, 'I have not yet received a *sous* and last night I was obliged to give my *last* five guineas to our countrymen here. I can shift better than they can; I hope to receive a month's pay today, but it will not be possible to remit you any part of it; you must therefore carry on the war as you can....I am mortified at not being able to send you a remittance but you know it is not my fault.'[35]

Helped by a zealous local divisional commander, and with his characteristic tendency to ignore difficulties, Humbert had sailed on 6 August with 1,019 men. 'The little expedition to Ireland is on the seas', wrote Barras, 'in the hands of sailors who so far have not had much experience'.[36] It was hardly designed to strike terror into the defending forces in Ireland, and government supporters breathed a sigh of relief (too soon as it turned out) when the reported French preparations appeared to have produced such a mouse.[37]

'This has totally upset my plan of campaign', wrote Hardy to Bruix, 'and will impede my operatons. I know Humbert and I fear everything may be turned upside down before I arrive'. Humbert's courage was indisputable, but courage in the present circumstances was not enough, and the tiny force faced almost certain defeat if reinforcements did not follow immediately.[38] As the sailing from Brest continued to be delayed, however, the attention of the Directory was diverted to other trouble spots and when Chérin himself was ordered to Italy in the last week of August, he took it as a personal reprimand and resigned his commission. Tone, always slow to change an opinion once formed, doubted that Chérin had ever had any intention of coming to Brest. But aside from the difficulties created in Paris, and his own personal hang-ups, Chérin's commitment to Hoche's legacy was total. He warned the Directory that the Irish had risen because of hopes generated by France herself. A personal interview with the Directory on 6 July had secured a promise of 8,000 men, but neither they nor their arms had been forthcoming. Now he was reproached for not leaving with a smaller force, when Hoche had failed with an infinitely superior one and the advantage of surprise.[39] With ships lying unrepaired all round the French coasts, however, and such a shortage of trained sailors that appeals went out even to exiled *émigrés* to return, Chérin's demands would have been difficult to implement.

News of early successes by Humbert and of large numbers of Irish rallying to the French standard reached Paris on 12 September, and suddenly the Irish plans were infused with an urgency which might have paid dividends two months earlier.[40] Although still short on supplies and men, Hardy had finally embarked his force on 14 August. Tone accompanied him on board the 74-gun flagship, the *Hoche*, carrying 640 men and 24 officers. Like all the ships to sail for Ireland that summer, it was grossly overcrowded.[41] Altogether 2,291 men, 26 servants, 17 women and 7 children embarked, on board 1 ship of the line, 8 frigates (including the ill-fated *Fraternité*) and a schooner. But as they waited a favourable wind, the British blockade was steadily tightened. They tried sailing on a light breeze on the 21st, but a collison between two of the frigates forced a return to port and brought about a further intensified blockade.[42]

V

Throughout these weeks Tone seemed uncharacteristically detached. In his letters he scarcely commented on the preparations, and admitted to being so little interested in what was happening around him that he wrote nothing in his journal. There is little of the frustration at delays which had characterised the weeks before Bantry Bay and latterly at Le Havre and Rouen. He hears without apparent emotion of the collapse of the rebellion. The north had hung back awaiting a lead from Dublin which never came, then risen in two counties only. Robert Simms, one of Ulster's adjutant-generals, had refused to countenance such a partial rising and resigned on its eve. It is typical of Tone's almost uncritical loyalty to his friends that Simms was spared any reproof. 'I am sorry to say the North appears to have done a *cochonnerie* in the business [made a mess of things], which I am pretty clear they have; it is however some comfort that our friend Simms is out of the scrape'.

Tone welcomed a proposed agreement between his friends in prison in return for their self-banishment. 'Is poor Russell at last out of the scrape. . . . Would he were in Holstein, with all my soul: I am afraid he would break parole and come to Paris, if it were only to see you and Maria. If that should happen take care of him and let him *imbibe*'. His renewed dream of some kind of colony of friends in exile was short-lived, however, for Matilda's next letter brought news of an American destination for the exiles. 'I am truly sorry they are obliged to go to that abominable climate, country, and people'. In fact America refused to have them and they remained in prison until the Peace of Amiens in 1802. Tone would not have known the precise terms made by the state prisoners in what came to be known as the Kilmainham Treaty. Those involved gave full information about the French negotiations, and were bitterly criticised by the French who landed with Humbert.[43]

There is a light-hearted bravado about Tone's letters of these months which contrasts sharply with the almost certain recognition of failure. In part it was an effort to brush aside Matilda's fears. She was fretting more than usual about the chance of losing him. 'I am sorry to see by the style of your letter', he wrote on 29 August, 'that it was written in great agitation. I am not a man to despise danger more than another, but I do assure you I see very little in our expedition; our only difficulty is the passage. . . . I therefore expect to have the pleasure of sharing with you the task of educating and providing for the Babs, at the same time that, if any thing were to happen to me, I assure you I rely with the most implicit confidence both on your courage and conduct; but all this between us is quite unnecessary', and the topic is consciously trivialised. The issue of his possible death he again brushes aside in a matter-of-fact farewell letter on 9 September. The letter is almost abrupt, and is in telling contrast to the long and uncharacteristically emotional farewell letters preceding the Bantry Bay and Texel expeditions.[44]

The entire correspondence breathes a resignation to the inevitable. He reads without any of his previous anger the *Bien Informé*'s detailed reports of the Brest expedition and of his own presence on it. Before leaving Paris he had applied to have his own name reinstated on his commission, and was taking the altered military documents with him to Ireland. The elaborately printed notepaper he used for his correspondence carried the heading 'Liberté, Erin Go Brah!, Egalité', surmounting a logo of Hibernia and, also in print, 'Adjutant General T. Wolfe Tone'. Secrecy, always so vital to Tone in previous projects, no longer seemed important. 'At the period of this expedition he was hopeless of its success', writes his son. 'He had all along deprecated the idea of those attempts on a small scale. But he had also declared repeatedly that if the Government sent only a corporal's guard, he felt it his duty to go along with them'.[45]

What Tone dreaded most was death at sea and the chance that his family would be supported by no country. If he fell in Ireland at least he felt sure his countrymen would adopt them. But he had no illusions about the fate which awaited him if he were captured there. He had spoken of it frequently in the past, notably while anchored in Bantry Bay: 'if we are taken, my fate will not be a mild one; the best I can expect is to be shot as an *émigré rentré*, unless I have the good fortune to be killed in the action....Perhaps I may be reserved for a trial, for the sake of striking terror into others, in which case I shall be hanged as a traitor, and embowelled, etc. As to the embowelling, *"je m'en fiche"*; if ever they hang me, they are welcome to embowell me if they please.'[46]

In 1796 Tone had flattered himself as to his reputation. Then he was still considered an unfortunate visionary who had more than paid his debt by exile in America, where he was thought still to be. In 1798, however, the role he had played over the past two years was public knowledge. His fate seemed inevitable and he had decided to take control. He had already made the decision 'never to suffer the indignity of a public execution' before he left Paris, and had discussed it with Matilda. The decision helps explain the strange nature of their correspondence over the next few weeks. It also accommodates the new developments in Tone's thought about the dignity of sacrifice. 'In setting off for that last unfortunate expedition,' Matilda later wrote, 'he told me he knew his life was gone, but that executed he never would be, and urged the care of our darling babies to me.'[47] And so he acted in these last weeks. Just before he embarked on the expedition, he went before two public notaries in Brest and signed over to Matilda full power of attorney.[48] Tone embarked for Ireland that summer in the knowledge that defeat and death were inevitable.

Trial and Death

The Brest fleet finally sailed on 6 September. But lack of wind, the mutinous disposition of the crews and the poor state of repair of the ships caused further delays. Bompard was forced to put in at Camaret, just out from Brest, only finally emerging on 16 September.[1] London had been receiving precise details of the Brest preparations from the outset.[2] Humbert had already surrendered, the Dutch vessels were blocked in port, and Tandy's tiny force was on the point of sailing away from Ireland, having learnt of the collapse of resistance there. So much time had elapsed since Humbert's departure, over a month before, that Hardy's and Bompard's venture was suicidal. Fully alerted and prepared, the British fleet simply chose its moment. The French were spotted by two English frigates, which alerted the main blockading fleet and tracked Bompard's flotilla until it arrived off the Irish coast, despite a massive and time-consuming detour by the French out into the Atlantic. Lough Swilly, their destination, had been the object of intensive naval screening since a defence report of April had confirmed Turner's intelligence that it was the most likely place for a French landing.[3]

A severe storm broke just as the French neared the northern Irish coast. Too heavily laden for easy manoeuvrability and already damaged by the voyage, they were chased by Sir John Borlase Warren and forced to join battle at dawn on 12 October. The *Hoche* put up a stubborn defence and the battle raged until the afternoon. Casualties on board were high; some 200 men were killed or wounded, and by mid-morning medical stations were reporting their inability to cope. Tone commanded one of the batteries and would have been in the thick of the battle.[4] In howling seas, its main topmast gone, its sails in tatters, the *Hoche* struck and was sinking with five feet of water in its hold, when it was finally surrounded and captured. Most of the accompanying frigates were chased and taken in separate engagements. Only three of the ten ships which had sailed with Bompard a month earlier made it back to France.[5]

The officers were transferred to the British ship the *Robuste*, which was to sail for Portsmouth with the *Hoche* in tow. But for over a fortnight they were battered and blown far off course by the continuing storm. Rations had been reduced to a quarter when they finally entered Lough Swilly on 31 October, and Hardy saw with surprise and regret the excellent facilities it offered. But for the storm, Tone would have ended up in an English prisoner-of-war depot with the other French officers, all of whom were taken directly to England and eventually exchanged back to France. Arthur Tone too was a prisoner of war in England awaiting exchange, having been captured on board one of the Dutch frigates.[6]

<h1 style="text-align:center">I</h1>

Tone was among the first batch of prisoners brought on shore at Buncrana. He had been on board ship for some six weeks, much of that time in stormy seas. Prone to seasickness, extreme fatigue and of a nervous disposition, he had always feared that his external appearance would be misinterpreted as showing weakness. The physical and mental strain he was under became apparent after his arrival in Dublin, but if he felt any in Donegal, it did not show. It has been said that Tone might have escaped had he not been recognised by his old college fellow and contemporary at the bar, Sir George Hill. Hill was MP for Londonderry, a magistrate, a colonel, in the militia, a yeomanry captain, son-in-law to John Beresford and an arch-loyalist—the very epitome of the Ascendancy. But Tone's presence on board the *Hoche* was known in any case. He had no intention of escaping and so he acted.[7]

He was the first to step out of the boat filled with prisoners as it pulled into Buncrana on the morning of 3 November and he made a point of addressing the waiting Hill. 'This morning some hundreds of the prisoners are just landed', reported Hill to Edward Cooke at the Castle; 'the first man who stepped out of the boat habited as an officer was T.W. Tone; he recognised and addressed me instantly with as much sang-froid as you might expect from his character.'[8]

Simon, who with Tone had been summoned on shore by the area commander, Lord Cavan, remained twenty-four hours with Cavan and Hill, and was treated with much respect by his hosts. He told them of Hoche's negotiations with the Irish in 1796 and of Tone's part in the expedition that year.[9] As a warm friend of Tone's, it is inconceivable that Simon would have been so open had he not felt Tone would have wanted it that way. There were others besides Hill who would have known Tone in Dublin. The area was defended, not by English regulars, but by Irish militia officered by that same Irish landed Ascendancy with whom Tone had once associated, then rejected so publicly. This was no dignified military surrender to a wartime enemy, as Tone had envisaged it. Rather he had plummeted from the heights of international politics back into the incestuous little world which he had left behind, a world in which he was a traitor and a renegade. In the view of his captors, for Tone to stand on his dignity and insist on receiving the respect due to his rank in the French army was arrogant, and an aggravation of his offence, and unlike the other officers he was sent off to Derry and chained in prison.

Death Tone had accepted as inevitable, but the indignity of being treated like a common criminal he had not anticipated. He wrote in some surprise to Cavan assuming that such orders had been given in ignorance of the rank he held in the French army. He had shown his commissions to the officer who had implemented Cavan's orders and General Hardy could verify them. 'Under these circumstances I address myself to your Lordship as a man of honour and a soldier; and I do protest in the most precise and strongest manner against the indignity intended against the honour of the French army in my person; and I claim the rights of privilege as a prisoner of war.' Cavan thought it 'an impudent letter for a man in his situation' and replied: 'I looked on you (and you have proved yourself) a traitor and rebel to your sovereign and native country, and as such you shall be treated by me....I lament as a man, the fate that awaits you.'[10]

Tone's indignation at the treatment he received in no way invalidates his acceptance of the fact that his own life was forfeit. His letters to the Castle, to the Directory and to Niou (French *commissaire* for the exchange of prisoners of war) reflected his attachment to the French army and a mental outlook which had become that of a French officer. 'The Honour of the French nation is pledged to support me as a citizen and an officer', he wrote to the Chief Secretary, Castlereagh. 'I trust therefore his Excellency, the Lord Lieutenant, will be pleased to give the necessary orders that I may be treated as a prisoner of war, with such attention as is due to the rank I have the honour to hold in the armies of the French Republic....I mention this with the more confidence, from the generous manner in which our government has behaved to such British officers as the fortune of war has thrown into our hands.'[11]

Hardy too—alerted by a letter from Tone—was surprised at the treatment accorded him and wrote instantly to Lord Cornwallis, the Lord Lieutenant: 'I will not touch on the question of grievances you may have against this officer; but he is a French citizen, member of the French army, prisoner of war, and for each of these reasons he should be treated with consideration and respect....Adjutant General Wolfe Tone is a good citizen; his courage and spirited behaviour have gained for him the confidence of the French Government and the esteem of all honorable soldiers....I was astonished to learn that you were treating him like a criminal'. Cornwallis's secretary, Captain Herbert Taylor, replied on his behalf: 'Theobald

Wolfe Tone is known only to his Excellency as a traitor, who sought to return to Ireland in order to attempt by armed force what he failed to achieve by intrigue, who has never ceased to promote rebellion and discord, and who at last is about to receive the punishment due to the crimes he has been guilty of committing against his King and his country.'[12] The response would have heartened many critics of Cornwallis, then under bitter attack for his leniency towards the rebels.

In the circumstances Tone's expectations of being treated as a noble adversary were quite unrealistic. He had returned to Ireland in the wake of a bloody rebellion in which over 20,000 had been killed and enormous barbarities committed by both sides and for which many in authority held him personally responsible. His career since 1795 had been laid before the public by Fitzgibbon in the course of the last parliamentiary session and in a secret report published in the press in August.[13] He was also mentioned by name in a recent Banishment Act, under which a return to Ireland was liable to the death penalty. Yet although Tone had frequently used the word 'traitor' flippantly, he had always seen his own role in the light of his exaggerated notions of honour. In France he had become increasingly detached, a pure, uncompromising conscience rising above the often unpleasant realities of republicanism in operation. The same notions of honour and dignity he brought to his role as French officer, and he could compartmentalise his life sufficiently to see that role as separate (and increasingly so) from that of a United Irishman. When confronted with the word 'traitorously' at his trial some weeks later, he was taken aback, and while pleading guilty to the charge of being in arms against the King, he did not accept the implication of treason.

The only documentation produced at Tone's trial were his commission and passport. Where were the thousands of addresses and proclamations loaded on to the *Hoche* at Brest? Most surprising of all, where was Tone's journal of these last weeks? As to the former, Warren reported that 'large quantities of papers were torn and thrown overboard' before the *Hoche* was taken.[14] Local magistrates who boarded the ship had helped themselves to souvenirs. Tone's trunk was rifled, John Boyd of Letterkenny, colonel of the Donegal militia, magistrate and deputy governor of the county, taking his personal copies of the *Address to the People of Ireland*, printed in 1796 and re-issued in 1798, and of *Belmont Castle*, and possibly others. Under-Secretary Cooke was known to have a private museum of the rebellion. To this Hill and Cavan sent a green flag taken on board the *Hoche*, and from Tone's trunk his cap and uniform.[15] If a journal had existed, it would have been found. That Tone had kept none is further testimony to his acceptance of the likelihood that he would not be returning from this voyage.

II

Tone was sent to Dublin still in irons and under heavy military escort. Captain Elias Thackeray of the Cambridgeshire militia later recalled the journey, commenting that 'Tone was the most delightful companion he ever travelled with'. On the last morning they breakfasted at an inn thirteen miles from Dublin. Despite Thackeray's protest, Tone insisted on changing into full-dress uniform for the last stage of the journey.[16] On entering Dublin they passed the magnificant new Four Courts on the Liffey as the lawyers were coming out, and Tone is said to have commented on old acquaintances he saw looking out of windows. 'It is said he looked well and unembarrassed', wrote Drennan to his sister.[17] Tone was brought to the Castle and committed to the Provost prison in the Royal Barracks, the scene of his boyhood expeditions to watch the military parades. Located on the insalubrious north-west side of town, just off the quays, it was 'a filthy, close, dank, and pestilential place of confinement, with a small court yard, and some ill-constructed sheds, set up to afford increased accommodation to the multitude of persons daily sent to the depôt'.[18] From here Matthew Tone and Bartholomew Teeling had been led to execution only weeks earlier, after the defeat of Humbert's forces in September.

Tone's old friends were prisoners elsewhere, the principal state prisoners who had negotiated the recent agreement with the government, Emmet and MacNeven among them, in Kilmainham. The Newgate inmates, notably Russell, were annoyed that the others were not using their direct line to the Castle to do something for Tone. 'It is impossible for anyone to be more concerned or more anxious than we all are about the fate of Tone', wrote Emmet to Russell. 'There is not a thing that would appear to us to have any chance of succeeding in saving his life that we would not gladly do. But it is owing to that very feeling that your letter has embarrassed us most exceedingly, because it seems to imply that you and your fellow prisoners imagine some such thing could be done.' They had nothing left to bargain with, since they had already given their information and agreed to voluntary banishment in return for Bond's life. Moreover, the day they were at the Castle 'the Chancellor mentioned that Tone had before he left the kingdom signed such a confession of his own treason, as would and was intended to hang him in case of his ever returning'. In such circumstances their interference would only aggravate Tone's plight.[19]

Russell also wrote to Burrowes, who likewise held out little hope of saving Tone's life.

> I shall not hesitate to give our friend every assistance in my power. Much as I condemn his late proceedings, I cannot forget how estimable a man he was and how much he was my friend. I must however fairly tell you that I think his case totally hopeless and that postponement untill a tryal by jury can be had is the utmost to be hoped. In a letter to Lord Cornwallis he has announced himself a French officer, and the nature of the expedition in which he was engaged cannot be doubtful. The nature of his departure from this country will not furnish any legal advantages. . . . It is the most testing terrain I ever engaged in but I shall not disdain it and if I learn anything consolatary (of which I despair) will put you in poss[essi]on of it.[20]

Burrowes engaged Curran, and they asked Tone's former colleagues on the Catholic Committee for help with his legal expenses. None came forward and the finger of accusation has long been pointed at Keogh for his apparently treacherous behaviour. The truth of this story is debatable, as is much surrounding Tone's last days. Matilda did not totally reject Keogh, even though she heard that he had also refused to contribute to a subscription mounted by Tone's friends for his family.[21] Keogh's role in the rebellion year is indeed baffling. Having until early 1798 been one of the foremost members of the United Irish executive, he was left strangely immune as everyone around him was arrested. That he had withdrawn before plans were finally made for the rebellion is undeniable, and despite suspicions at the time there is no evidence in government records that he turned informer.

As for the other Catholic Committee members, most of those who had been close to Tone were either dead, in prison, or in exile. The Catholic Committee had been an essentially conservative body, even if its sub-committee was not, and Tone's career after 1795 would have been seen as a startling instance of treachery.[22] Foremost among those to experience such feelings was Dr McDonnell of Belfast. In McDonnell's account of these events Tone emerges in a Machiavellian light, using the Catholics as pawns in his revolutionary plans. McDonnell was criticised for his rejection of his old friends. But he was a generous man. His feelings cannot be lightly dismissed and were undoubtedly shared by others. Tone's personality had captivated many and they felt betrayed by revelations of his treason.[23]

III

Tone was tried in the Royal Barracks by a military court of seven officers and a judge advocate on Saturday, 10 November. The court was exceedingly crowded and the Dublin press followed the events with obsessive interest. But the provincial press, even the *Belfast News Letter*, took only a passing interest. The infamy of Tone's name among the loyalist élite was not yet matched by a counter-reputation among the general populace. It was loyalists who packed the court that morning. Although Sinclair was there, there would have been few others who sympathised with Tone's views. That same Dublin establishment which had helped make him a republican now provided the elements for a future republican martyrology.

Commentators said he looked flushed and at first greatly agitated. He asked for a glass of water and thereafter 'he behaved with great firmness'.[24] He was dressed in full ceremonial French uniform: 'a large and fiercely cocked hat, with broad gold lace, and the tricoloured cockade, a blue uniform coat, with gold and embroidered collar, and two large gold epaulets, blue pantaloons with gold laced garters at the knees, and short boots bound at the tops with gold lace'.[25] The *Freeman's Journal* thought him not so thin and pale as when he had left Ireland in 1795.[26] Charges of treason were read out. Tone was reluctant to accept the word 'traitorously' but pleaded guilty to the charges made against him and asked the court's permission to explain his actions. After the court expressed some reservations, and cautioned him that it might operate to his prejudice, he was allowed to read from the paper he carried.

> Mr President and Gentlemen of the Court Martial. It is not my intention to give the Court any trouble; I admit the charge against me in the fullest extent; what I have done, I have done, and I am prepared to stand the consequences.
>
> The great object of my life has been the independence of my country; for that I have sacrificed every thing that is most dear to man; placed in an honorable poverty I have more than once rejected offers considerable to a man in my circumstances, where the condition expected was in opposition to my principles; for them I have braved difficulty and danger: I have submitted to exile and to bondage; I have exposed myself to the rage of the Ocean and the fire of the enemy; after an honorable combat that should have interested the feelings of a generous foe, I have been marched through the country in Irons to the disgrace alone of whoever gave the order; I have devoted even my wife and my children; after that last effort it is little to say that I am ready to lay down my life.

Whatever I have said, written, or thought on the subject of Ireland I now reiterate: looking upon the connexion with England to have been her bane I have endeavoured by every means in my power to break that connexion; I have laboured in consequence to create a people in Ireland by raising three Millions of my Countrymen to the rank of Citizens.

At this point the court intervened. One member thought Tone deliberately inflammatory, which he denied. The judge accepted his denial, but commented that it would only act to his prejudice. Tone agreed to strike out the offending passages, though he said nothing 'that has not been already uttered, with respect to me, in both houses of parliament, where my name has been so often quoted'. He was then allowed to proceed.

Having considered the resources of this Country and satisfied that she was too weak to assert her liberty by her own proper means, I sought assistance where I thought assistance was to be found; I have been in consequence in France where without patron or protector, without art or intrigue I have had the honor to be adopted as a Citizen and advanced to a superior rank in the armies of the Republic; I have in consequence faithfully discharged my duty as a soldier; I have had the confidence of the French Government, the approbation of my Generals and the esteem of my brave comrades; it is not the sentence of any Court however I may personally respect the members who compose it that can destroy the consolation I feel from these considerations.

Such are my principles such has been my conduct; if in consequence of the measures in which I have been engaged misfortunes have been brought upon this country, I heartily lament it, but let it be remembered that it is now nearly four years since I have quitted Ireland and consequently I have been personally concerned in none of them; if I am rightly informed very great atrocities have been committed on both sides, but that does not at all diminish my regret; for a fair and open war I was prepared; if that has degenerated into a system of assassination, massacre, and plunder I do again most sincerely lament it, and those few who know me personally will give me I am sure credit for the assertion.

I will not detain you longer; in this world success is every thing; I have attempted to follow the same line in which Washington succeeded and Kosciusko failed; I have attempted to establish the independence of my country; I have failed in the attempt; my life is in consequence forfeited and I submit; the Court will do their duty and I shall endeavour to do mine.

Asked if there was anything more he had to say, Tone requested the death of a soldier by firing squad. It was a privilege France had accorded even to the Chouan leaders and he trusted he would not be refused by men 'susceptible of the nice feelings of a soldier's honour....It is not from any personal feeling that I make this request, but from a respect to the uniform which I wear, and to the brave army in which I have fought'. He offered again his military papers in proof of his commission in the French army and repeated his desire for an honourable death. Told that it would be the Lord Lieutenant who would make the final decision, Tone bowed and thanked the court for the indulgence extended to him and retired, surrounded by the guard which had escorted him there.

The full text of Tone's speech was not published at the time. 'It has not been circulated,' wrote Cornwallis's secretary, transmitting a copy of the speech to London; 'treat it as a private communication.' The enclosed paper contained the passage which Tone had been obliged to strike out. It seems innocuous enough at this distance in time. But it raked over the coals of the heated Catholic campaign of 1792–5 at a time when the emancipation issue was jeopardising British hopes for a union of the two legislatures.

> I have laboured to abolish the infernal spirit of religious persecution by uniting the Catholics and the Dissenters; to the former I owe more than can ever be repaid; the services I was so fortunate to render them, they rewarded munificently but they did more; when the public cry was raised against me, when the friends of my youth swarmed off and left me alone, the Catholics did not desert me; they had the virtue even to sacrifice their own interests to a rigid principle of honor; they refused though strongly urged to disgrace a man who whatever his conduct towards the Government might have been, had faithfully and conscientiously discharged his duty towards them, and in so doing though it was in my own case, I will say they showed an instance of public virtue and honor of which I know not whether there exists another example.[27]

This passage was eventually printed in the 1849 *Cornwallis Correspondence*. The original of Tone's speech is not extant. But the copies made of it by Dublin Castle have survived, although they have never been published. Most works use the version which appears in the Howells' *State Trials* (1809–28), taken largely from a contemporary pamphlet.[28] Versions taken down in shorthand at the trial differ considerably from the copies of the original. Most offend by elaborations which rob the original of that simplicity of style which was Tone's hallmark. Later versions go further. In the one which appears in his son's edition of his journals, the calm dignity and resignation, which contemporaries noted particularly in Tone's demeanour, is replaced by a more confrontational, more crusading style, and the members of the court depicted as far more tyrannical than would appear to have been the case.[29] Tone's courtroom speech was no oration from the dock, such as those which were to become a part of Irish nationalist tradition, no appeal to posterity or glorification in his own martyrdom. Indeed he welcomed a trial by military officers and his respectful attitude towards them appears to have been genuine.[30]

Tone's trial was a brief affair. His admission of the charges ensured that, and one commentator lamented the lack of opportunity for any display of eloquence. Tone would have been incapable of that. His speech was read out from a written text. It was an acceptance of failure rather than a Pearse-like glorying in it and continued that note of fatalism so evident during his final days in France. If he gloried in anything, it was not that he had successfully negotiated military assistance, but that he had been accepted as a good soldier and had done so without intrigue or material gain. After the catastrophe of 1798 it is almost anachronistic, a speech still dominated by Enlightenment ideals. There is much about honour, duty, faithfulness and friendship, and another reference to the wound inflicted by the desertion of those he had thought his friends. The attempt to break the connection with England and to heal the religious divisions in Ireland are briefly mentioned, not as visions to be fulfilled in the future, but as explanations of his own motivation. His speech was a personal statement, not a political manifesto. It is a sad document, an admission of how badly wrong things had gone and an acceptance of death as the price of failure.

IV

Tone knew he would be condemned to death, the mode of execution alone remaining in doubt. He refused to see either friends or family, knowing all too well the emotion and weakening of resolution which would result. On the afternoon of his trial he wrote to Emmet, MacNeven, O'Connor and John Sweetman. 'My dear friends, The fortune of war has thrown me into the hands of government, and I am utterly ignorant of what fate may attend me; but in the worst event, I hope I shall bear it like a man, and that my death will not disgrace my life.' He had heard they were to go to America and asked them to take care of his wife and children, left destitute by his death. 'As Irishmen, as men of honour, I rely you will, according to your means, do for them what I as your friend would do for your families in similar circumstances'. . . Adopt my boys, give them that education which I had promised myself to bestow on them. But especially, protect my wife and daughter, whose sex and whose weakness give them a double claim on your humanity.'[31]

He likewise wrote in farewell to his father and hoped that he had not been hurt by his refusal to see him. 'I had not the courage to support a meeting, which could lead to nothing, and would put us both to insufferable pain. . . . I beg my sincerest and most respectable duty to my mother, Your affectionate son, T.W. TONE, Adjutant General.'[32] He wrote to Kilmaine, to Shee, to Bruix and to the Directory asking them to help his wife and family. Bruix, he told Shee, 'as an excellent husband and a fond father, can appreciate what I feel in writing this letter', and he asked him to communicate his letter to 'my friend Clarke, who I am sure will interest himself warmly in the fate of my family, as no man in France better knows my conduct and principles'.[33] He asked for his money, £50, and possessions to be divided between his wife and father,[34] left a ring containing Hoche's hair to Emmet,[35] and his pocket-book to Sweet-man. The red leather pocket-book, with its green silk lining, is today in the National Museum of Ireland. It is badly water-stained, a reflection possibly of the dreadful conditions on board the *Hoche*. Tone has written his name clearly on the inside, the date, 11 November 1798, and from Virgil the quotation '*Te nunc habit ista secundum*'. The poet has been given a flute by the dying Damaetus, with the words: 'Now for its second master, it has thee'. Inside is an unfinished note from Peter Tone: 'Dear Sir, The enclosed has been ordered by my son to be delivered to you in Remembrance of him. The night that—'.[36]

To Matilda, Tone wrote a final letter:

Dearest Love,

The hour is at last come, when we must part; as no words can express what I feel for you and our children, I shall not attempt it; complaint of any kind would be beneath your courage or mine; be assured I will die as I have lived, and that you will have no reason to blush for me.—

I have written on your behalf to the French government, to the Minister of Marine, to General Kilmaine, and to Mr Shee; with the latter I wish you especially to advise; in Ireland I have written to your brother Harry, and to those of my friends who are about to go into exile, and whom I am sure will not abandon you.

Adieu, dearest Love, I find it impossible to finish this letter; give my love to Mary and above all things remember that you are now the only parent of our dearest children, and that the best proof you can give of your affection for me, will be to preserve yourself for their education—God Almighty bless you, all

> Your's ever
> T W TONE

I think you have a friend in Wilkins who will not desert you; remember me to Lewins affectionately.[37]

Later that day he wrote again to say he had received assurances from her brother Edward and sister Harriet that they would assist his family. But he refused Harriet's desire to see him, 'having determined to speak to no one of my friends, not even my father, from motives of humanity to them and myself—it is a very great consolation to me that your family are determined to assist you; as to the manner of that assistance, I leave it to their affection for you, and your own excellent good sense.... Adieu, Dearest Love; keep your courage, as I have kept mine; my mind is as tranquil this moment as at any period of my life; cherish my memory, and especially preserve your health and spirits for the sake of our dearest children. Your ever affectionate, T W TONE'. The firm hardwriting of these last letters bears out his assurances about his state of mind.[38]

Tone learnt finally of his fate on the evening of Sunday, 11 November. He was to be hanged, not at the adjacent Arbour Hill like Matthew, but publicly at Newgate at 1 p.m. the following day, seemingly at the request of his old opponents on the Dublin Corporation. But Cornwallis had remitted that part of the sentence requiring that 'his head be struck off, fixed on a pike and placed in the most conspicuous part of the city.'[39] A final letter was written to Sandys, Brigadier-Major of the Dublin garrison, with responsibility for the Provost prison. Sandys has an evil reputation in Irish nationalist tradition, but Tone claimed on several occasions that he had acted well towards him. 'You have acted towards me like a brave man and an officer', he wrote in this final letter. 'My death clears all, and I hope I shall have died like a man.'[40] He was also said to have left a note explaining 'that if they had sentenced him to be shot, he would not have shrunk from his fate'.[41] That night Tone cut his throat, some said with his own penknife, others with a razor left in the cell by his brother. The sentinel found him in a pool of blood at 4 a.m., his windpipe almost severed. He alerted Sandys who summoned Dr Benjamin Lentaigne, a Frenchman and assistant surgeon to the 5th Dragoons. Three other surgeons were called in. Tone's wound was sewn up, pronounced extremely serious but not fatal, and orders for the execution were not yet countermanded.[42]

But when the court of King's Bench opened the following morning at eleven, Curran, on an affidavit from Tone's father, challenged the conviction by military court when the civil courts were still sitting and moved for a writ of habeas corpus. An accident of timing—the court of King's Bench not sitting till that day—had prevented an earlier applicaton. Legal opinion suppported Curran's contention that martial and civil law were incompatible. Although civil law had not been suspended during the rebellion, martial law operated in much of the country and many rebels had been tried and convicted by military tribunals. As peace was restored their continued use to try civilians came under increasing criticism, not least from Cornwallis himself. It is unlikely that the appeal to civil law would have produced a different verdict or left sufficient time for the French government to intervene,[43] but it created a legal crisis which was only resolved by legislation the following year.

The court was even more packed than on the day of the trial, the crowd spilling out into the entrance hall, assured of the oratory which had been denied them the preceding Friday.[44] The presiding judge that morning was the Attorney-General, Tone's old neigbour in Kildare and mentor, Arthur Wolfe, recently created Baron Kilwarden. He instantly ordered a writ prepared, and on Curran's plea that the execution might go ahead in the meantime, sent a sheriff to the prison to alert the provost-marshal to the court's decision and to ensure suspension of the execution. Thousands had been gathering since morning to witness the execution and every window opposite Newgate was rented out. The order caused obvious embarrassment at the barracks. The sheriff returned shortly to the court to report that General Craig, Dublin district commander, claimed that he had to obey Major Sandys, Major Sandys claiming in turn that he must obey the Lord Lieutenant.

Meanwhile Peter Tone had returned to report that Craig would not obey the writ and the sheriff was ordered back to take Tone, Major Sandys and the provost-marshal into custody. The sheriff was unable to gain admittance to the barracks, but was told of Tone's attempted suicide and returned to court, accompanied by Dr Lentaigne. He told of how he had been called in at 4 a.m. and had closed the wound. But they would not know for four days whether the wound would prove mortal. 'His head is now kept in one position. *A sentinel is over him, to prevent his speaking.* His removal would kill him.' The newspapers also reported that Tone had been put in a straitjacket to prevent any further attempt at suicide. Curran applied to the court for further medical aid and the admission of Tone's friends to him, but was refused.[45]

Tone's condition deteriorated towards the end of the week. His wound became infected and his lungs inflamed. There had been signs that he was unwell even before the suicide attempt, and he had had to leave the court supported by Sandys. By Sunday he was in extreme pain and delirious. An incoherent note written by him that evening suggests that either someone was taking advantage of his delirium or that he was hallucinating. Whichever way he begged Sandys to 'come and take charge'.[46] He died the following morning, Monday, 19 November.

A coroner's inquest was held that same day and Lord Castlereagh gave permission for the body to be delivered to Tone's friends, 'but on the express condition that no assemblage of people shall be permitted and that it be interred in the most private manner'.[47] The body was taken on the 20th to the house of relatives, the Dunbavins, at 52 High Street, where Tone's parents were living in straitened circumstances. He was laid out on the second floor and a plaster cast taken of his face. Matilda was never able to secure one of the busts produced from it, although two of them have survived.[48] For two days mourners in great numbers called to pay their respects. Tone's hair was cut and divided among the family, some being sent to Matilda in Paris by her sister Catherine Heavyside.[49] Tone was buried quietly in the family plot at Bodenstown. His remains left Dublin on the morning of the 21st in the midst of a storm and accompanied by William Dunbavin and James Ebbs, a fellow yeoman and brazier from Bride Street.[50] Peter Tone's distress at the loss of his favourite son was such that he was unable to attend the funeral.

Tone's possessions—117 crowns and his trunk of clothes—were handed over to his father. A further 116 crowns and a gold watch were given to Edward Witherington for Matilda. She asked Edward to give them to Tone's father. Many years passed and Peter Tone was dead before Edward fulfilled the undertaking. Harriet did nothing. Despite Tone's hopes, only Catherine Heavyside remained close to his widow. The rift with the Witheringtons was never healed. Sandys, whatever Tone's good opinion of him, retained the most valuable items from Tone's trunk as forfeited property.[51]

For well over a century nationalist opinion in Ireland could not accept Tone's suicide, and the fact that no acquaintance gained access to him in that last week of his life gave rise to all kinds of rumours. The suicide, however, is indisputable. Even his son accepts it, and in the circumstances he was treated well by the authorities. Contrary to myth, a regular coroner's inquest was held on Tone's body on the morning of his death and the opinions of three other surgeons taken. It returned a verdict of death by inflammation of the lungs due to 'self-murder'. The body was then given up immediately at his mother's request.[52] Madden's history of these times is fiercely anti-government. He would have been the first to countenance accusations of foul play, had they been true. But Madden came to know Dr Lentaigne in later life and from first-hand evidence accepts that Tone died by his own hand.[53] Fitzgibbon, ironically, played no part in the fate of the man he had hounded for so many years. He was in England discussing the prospective union with ministers and did not return until the evening of 12 November, after Tone had already made the attempt on his life.

In the event his death spared the authorities considerable embarrassment. Legal opinion at the time thought Curran's case against the operation of martial law unanswerable. Large numbers had been convicted under martial law that summer and it was feared Tone's case would provide the model for similar appeals. The issue of conflicting jurisdictions was a subject of major contention at the time, for, whatever the many barbarities in the field, once prisoners reached the courts the legal fraternity and the English in Ireland were keen to apply strict rules of law. Only weeks before Tone's trial Cornwallis had overturned the verdict of a court martial and debarred its members from sitting on future trials. The last thing the Castle needed was the very public contest which Curran was preparing to launch in the courts. London thought the Irish authorities had botched the entire business.[54] Tone's suicide was a godsend. 'We had got into a little scrape by bringing up Mr Tone for trial to Dublin by a court-martial, sitting by the side of the Court of King's Bench', wrote Fitzgibbon to Lord Auckland on 15 November. 'We shall probably get out of it by the death of Mr Tone who was suffered to cut his throat on the day appointed for his execution'.[55] It is a telling letter on the passive role of the authorities in Tone's death. But the hand was his own.

Tone's trial and the manner of his death aroused conflicting emotions in Ireland. Many felt with Hill that the original sentence should have been carried out: 'I would have sewed up his neck and finished the business', he commented to Cooke, a view shared by Fitzgibbon, irritated by Kilwarden's judgement.[56] But most of the accounts which have survived were written by ex-Trinity men and those who still remembered Tone as the sparkling conversationalist and rising talent of the late '80s and early '90s. Many who opposed his principles were impressed by his conduct at his trial. 'Never was the public mind here so occupied as by this gentleman's fate', wrote a Dublin correspondent to the *Courier*; 'such was the estimation in which he was held, from his brilliant talents and his many virtues, that he had the rare facility of calling forth the regret of all ranks of men, even of those who most differed from him in political principles'.[57] There is a sense of bafflement, almost of betrayal, that such a man could have turned out to be a villain. Tone's betrayal of those who had helped him escape the consequences of the Jackson affair was invoked almost as a greater crime than his against his country.[58]

Tone's suicide was much criticised at the time and seemed the final proof of his irreligion, to which ultimately his wayward development, so ill attuned to his early promise, was attributed. 'I think it very remarkable that this man was highly esteemed also for *his moral qualities*', wrote Thomas Prior, future Vice-Provost of Trinity and an admirer of Tone when a young student: 'a melancholy instance of our inability to judge aright of moral worth—but perhaps moral qualities unconnected with religious sentiment can never be relied on'.[59] 'The unfortunate Tone, by attempting his own life', wrote a Dublin correspondent of Lord Moira's chaplain. '. . . did not display that fortitude and magnanimity which his conduct at his trial promised. When a man dares a crime of such magnitude as his, he ought to be prepared to abide its consequences—he loses the merit of that martyrdom which he seemed to glory in'.[60]

In his final letter to Sandys, Tone had written: 'I trust my old acquaintance, *Marsden*, will not suffer my memory to be unnecessarily insulted.' It was symptomatic of the situation facing many of Tone's United Irish colleagues, confronting a political and legal establishment manned by those of whom they had once been friends and colleagues. Marsden's and Tone's early careers had been intertwined, first as students together at Trinity and active members of the Historical Society, then in London at the Inns of Court, finally in Dublin as members of the outer bar. Their social backgrounds were much the same. Now Marsden was one of the Assistant Secretaries at the Castle, though regarded as a sympathetic influence by others as well as Tone.[61] The relationship was representative of the intensity of the emotional and personal involvement by the authorities in the events of '98. In those few square miles of Dublin city members of the Ascendancy and future republicans had once rubbed shoulders. In the small world of Irish politics, Tone and his friends had turned on their own.

But they were uncomfortable with the concept of popular revolution and repelled by its manifestations in 1798. America rather than France was their preferred model, a military campaign rather than a rebellion their preferred means. After the bloodshed of 1798, however, it was an impossible position to defend and Tone knew it. Since 1795 Tone had actively supported the idea of armed resistance. But he had believed, naïvely, that civilian bloodshed would be minimal. His capacity for self-deception is nowhere better illustrated, and his attempt to distance himself from the turn of events in 1798 has the aspect of a rude awakening. He had followed through a concept as far as he could take it, and was already closing the door on his recent past before he left France. Reputation and national gratitute he craved. Both eventually came, but with a twist which he would not much have relished, for more than anyone else Tone was to become to symbol of physical-force republicanism.

30
Aftermath

News of Bompard's defeat reached Paris at the end of October.[1] Matilda appealed in person to Talleyrand, La Révellière-Lépeaux (then president of the Directory), Bruix and the Dutch ambassador to claim Tone as a prisoner of war. She was received with particular kindness by Talleyrand, who was to remain a good friend to the family through successive regimes. Talleyrand and La Révellière assured her that France would intervene on Tone's behalf and that English officers who were prisoners in France would be held to account for his safety. Matilda also enlisted the help of Kilmaine and De Winter, both of whom responded in terms showing their esteem for Tone. She herself was preparing to travel to Ireland when news came through at the end of November of Tone's death.[2]

France would almost certainly have made some representation on behalf of Tone. There were many precedents, and Niou was a particularly effective official. Aware of the danger to the Irish if they were discovered among the French prisoners of war in England, he worked quickly and successfully to ensure their exchange.[3] It is doubtful, however, whether such intercession would have made any difference in Tone's case. His French uniform was as much an aggravation of his offence as a British one had been to the royalists at Quiberon.

Tone had been accepted in France almost as an honorary Frenchman. The French newspapers devoted an unusual amount of attention to his court-martial and death. It was of course good propaganda, this soldier of liberty martyred by the English. But the newspaper coverage represented a cross-section of opinion, much of it anti-government. Tone was recognised both by the press and his former military colleagues as a distinguished French officer.[4] He had settled well into military life and become increasingly removed from the Irish mission in consequence. His indignation at the dishonour shown the French uniform by his treatment was quite genuine, even if the authorities in Ireland considered it a startling piece of impudence.

Matilda at twenty-nine was left destitute by Tone's death. His last plea to the Directory to help his family produced immediate relief of 1,200 francs and assurances of a pension.[5] But her fight for pension rights was prolonged and was disrupted by the political crisis which destroyed the Directory in 1799. It was the personal intervention of the Bonaparte family—first by Lucien as president of the Council of Five Hundred, then by Napoleon himself—which finally secured pension rights for Matilda in May 1804. The pension continued to be paid by successive French regimes until her death in America in 1849.[6]

Tone's old friends Shee and Simon pushed her case. But on the whole she acted for herself. Matilda was no shrinking violet. She was fearless in promoting the interests of her children and disagreed violently with Clarke—restored to favour as War Minister after 1807—about her son's military career. In many other ways she was in total contrast to her husband. She was fretful and pessimistic, and most of all she was proud. In April 1803 she returned a relief payment being made to all Irish 'refugees', on the grounds that Tone was a French officer, not a refugee, and that it was a life pension she had been taught to expect from the French nation.[7] In 1812, she rejected a bursary for William at the military academy, when his course there had only another year to run and when an earlier application by her had been ignored, on the grounds that: 'it was now too late to be a favour'.[8]

She had good reason for the bitterness and self-pity in her correspondence, for the promises made to Tone by her family were never kept. Nor did any of the Tones survive to help. Mary Tone and Giauque left for Santo Domingo in 1799 and died there of yellow fever shortly afterwards. William Tone, on hearing of his brother's death, immediately assumed the responsibilities of the eldest son. From India he sent Matilda £233 and undertook to provide for her needs and the children's education. But he died in action before he could fulfill his undertaking.[9] Arthur let her down badly, leaving Europe for America around 1804–5, neglecting to keep in touch until she had given him up for dead. In 1812 she learnt that he was serving in the American navy. 'I must say it was very cruel of him to conceal his existence from his few remaining relations', she wrote bitterly, and declared that she had no desire to see him again.[10]

Matilda lived a relatively solitary life in Paris. She did not forget the disagreements of 1797–8 and met only with those Irish exiles who had been Tone's friends. At the end of 1802 the family was joined briefly by Russell, Thomas Emmet and MacNeven, who had been released from prison when peace was concluded between Britain and France. Russell returned to Ireland to lead the Ulster side of the ill-fated rising of July 1803—led by Thomas Emmet's younger brother, Robert—and was hanged at Downpatrick in October 1803. Thomas Emmet and MacNeven had left France for America by

1805, both to pursue highly successful careers in their respective professions.

After 1803 the United Irishmen in France had disintegrated into warring factions. They were shunned by Matilda, angry at their efforts to harness the Tone name to their tarnished cause. She blamed them for enticing Arthur away from the Dutch navy with promises of another French expedition to Ireland which never materialised. An Irish Legion had been formed by Napoleon in 1804, but its history was blighted by internal quarrels. It gradually lost its Irish character and name, became the receptacle for any and every foreigner in France, and gained a reputation for indiscipline.[11] Yet one can sympathise with the irritation and bafflement of some of the Irish at being dismissed by Tone's family, when his name still counted for something with French officialdom.[12]

But it was the Irish criticism of Matilda's protectiveness of her son William which drew her most bitter attack. All the Tone children fell victim to the family scourge of tuberculosis. Maria died in 1803, aged sixteen, Francis in 1806, aged thirteen. Shortly afterwards William too fell ill, though he recovered after a spell in warmer climes.[13] Thereafter Matilda watched over him with a suffocating vigilance, even during his military training at the Imperial Cavalry School at St. Germain. William, always more placid than his father, never rebelled against such protectiveness. Adversity had created a relationship of considerable intensity between mother and son,[14] and William's well-being and education became for Matilda a mission in memory of Tone. She was not about to squander the fruits of that care on the French-based remnants of the United Irish movement, whom she considered 'a disreputable set of Irish', and her attachment to France, like Tone's, at times overwhelmed her Irishness.[15]

When she entered William at St. Germain in 1810 the United Irish exiles asked why he had not been enlisted in the Irish Legion. She answered that his weak health was unsuited to infantry life and she feared for his safety if captured by the English. They appealed over her head to Clarke, arguing that they had supported her since Tone's death, which was untrue—though Matilda had received the proceeds of a subscription raised in Ireland[16]—and was just the kind of 'indelicacy' certain to arouse Matilda's ire. In a heated exchange with Clarke, who likewise thought her son should enter the Irish Legion, she argued that William had some claim upon the French nation 'purchased' by his father's blood. To enter the Irish Legion would be to renounce all prospect of a military career, 'to retrograde, and declare himself a foreigner; any uneducated lad from the wildest part of Ireland, would have an equal right to enter it'. She never would consent to him serving as an 'emigrant' in 'that little corps of foreigners', but wanted him to be a 'Frenchman'.[17]

> I had undertaken (as I may say) a great enterprize, that of restoring my boy to health and establishing him honorably in the world [she wrote to a friend in March 1813]; if I had failed you might perhaps have heard that Tone's family was quite extinguished...but I have succeeded to my utmost wish and now my task in life is finished....his Father's friends thought differently and I was extremely harassed and perplexed by advice to send him into the world and even with reproaches that I kept him tied to my apron string and sacrificed him to the satisfaction of keeping him to look at....Oh how ungenerous they have been to me, Good God! How did the Irish ever get the character of a generous nation? But indeed it is only themselves who say it....Good God! do the Irish think that because Tone volunteered in their service and shed his best blood in their cause and left his family destitute in a foreign country that his posterity are to be their slaves.[18]

William fulfilled his father's military ambitions. He fought in Napoleon's campaigns of 1813–14 and was awarded the Légion d'Honneur after the battle of Leipzig. Throughout he received assistance from his father's military colleagues, notably Alexander Dalton—a nephew of Colonel Shee—who had accompanied Tone to Bantry Bay and whose brother acted as Tone's aide-de-camp in 1798.[19] William continued to serve under the first Restoration in 1814, but supported Napoleon during the Hundred Days. At the second Restoration of the monarchy in 1815, he resigned his commission and he and his mother decided to leave France.[20] With peace re-established in 1815, Matilda applied for permission to return to Ireland. Dublin Castle successfully opposed the application, although London might have been prepared to take a softer line.[21]

They eventually settled in America, at Georgetown near Washington, D.C. Tone's living nightmare had materialised without him, although it was in a different America that his family settled and in more comfortable circumstances. The Scottish radical, Thomas Wilson, whom they had first met on the passage from America in 1796, had remained their friend and benefactor throughout the years. In 1816 he and Matilda were married—ironically, at the British Embassy in Paris—and they spent a year in Edinburgh before they left for America.[22] Tone had come to know and respect Wilson and would have thought him a worthy protector of his family. But Matilda, her son, and later Irish nationalists were at pains to depict it as a marriage of friendship, and Matilda never ceased to think of herself as the widow of Tone.[23] William studied law in America and followed a career in the American War Office.[24] He married Catherine Sampson, daughter of their old Dublin acquaintance, William Sampson, by whom he had a daughter, Grace Georgiana. He died of tuberculosis in 1828, aged thirty-eight, Matilda in 1849, at the age of eighty.

Contrary to her stance in Paris, in America Matilda was happy for the Tone name to become the mascot of developing American-Irish nationalism. She became custodian of Tone's memory, and with the *Life* and frequent articles in the press, the principal promoter of the Tone cult.[25] Her very funeral was a tribute to her success, and representatives from the American Irish societies, American and French generals and the French ambassador to the United States gathered in the pouring rain to pay tribute through Tone's widow to that cult which she and her son had bequeathed to posterity.[26]

CONCLUSION

The Cult of Tone

Of the many heroes of Irish nationalist tradition Wolfe Tone must surely enjoy the widest appeal. The reason for such appeal is Tone's *Life*. Its style and intimacy are ageless and it has been packaged over the years to reach the widest audience. The severe editing of successive editions, giving prominence to the retrospective autobiography while omitting the bulk of the journals and writings, has allowed Tone to be presented as an unflinching republican.[1] In the twentieth century his name has been increasingly attached to the armed-force, anti-English and exclusively Catholic brand of Irish republicanism, and the *Life* itself condensed into his famous declaration penned in Mlle Boivet's lodgings in August 1796:

> To subvert the tyranny of our execrable government, to break the connection with England, the never failing source of all our political evils, and to assert the independence of my country— these were my objects. To unite the whole people of Ireland, to abolish the memory of all past dissentions, and to substitute the common name of Irishman, in the place of the denominations of Protestant, Catholic and Dissenter—these were my means.

It has become the most quoted passage of Irish history.

I

The Tone cult only came to maturity a century after his death. It was not created by the publication of the *Life* in 1826, but it would not have developed as it did without it. Matilda's reluctance to have the journals published evaporated after Wilson's death in 1824 and more immediately after the appearance in the *New Monthly Magazine* of two articles containing detailed extracts from them and highly inaccurate passages about her own life after Tone's death.[2] The *Life* appeared at the height of the campaign for Catholic emancipation in 1826, and was used by one of the leading campaigners, Richard Lalor Sheil, as an object-lesson to England and to Irish Protestant landlords of the consequences of again refusing Catholic rights.[3] Reviews were generally favourable, if sometimes critical of the direction of Tone's career after 1795, and Matilda was urged to order a second printing.[4] But in Ireland the 1798 rebellion had terrified Protestant and Catholic alike. Catholics sought assimilation into the existing constitution and were reluctant to recall past rebelliousness. With O'Connell's dominance of Irish politics and his disapproval of the United Irishmen and their methods, the *Life's* potential remained dormant until the 1840s. Matilda, a keen observer of events in Ireland, frowned upon O'Connell and by 1837 was complaining that Tone had been overshadowed.[5]

But if organised republicanism was non-existent in the O'Connell era, its threat was a live force in determining the reaction of the authorities. Sheil was prosecuted for his Tone speech. John Keogh's public praise of Tone over a decade earlier was interpreted as proof of the Catholic emancipation movement's 'thorough contempt for the legitimate government, [and] for the British connection'.[6] Moreover, long before interest in Tone revived in the 1840s, a strong grass-roots tradition had developed of anti-Englishness and admiration for the men of '98 which was intensified by O'Connell's political mobilisation of the Catholic populace.[7]

At first Tone did not figure prominently in this developing popular nationalism, which concentrated largely on local events and figures like Robert Emmet. The same was true of the romantic nationalism of the intellectuals, nourished by the writings of Thomas Moore. Only Lady Morgan, of the numerous Irish fiction writers in the first half of the century, mentioned Tone.[8] Matilda held Moore partly responsible for this neglect and thought he had 'behaved shabbily to us'.[9] Others pointed to the poverty of Tone's mother, who lived in cheap lodgings in Monck Place, Phibsborough, until her death in 1818.[10] Worries about Mrs Tone's financial plight almost led Matilda to publish Tone's journals in 1814, much against her better judgement, until she learnt that Peter Burrowes was paying a small annuity to the mother of his old friend.[11]

In Kildare, however, the Tone cult had already started. Peter Tone's funeral in 1805 drew huge crowds.[12] By 1843, when Thomas Davis and the editor of the *Freeman's Journal,* Dr John Gray, visited Bodenstown, they found Tone's grave, though unmarked, the object of local veneration. 'No one walks on that grave', a local blacksmith told them; 'and even the children are taught by the grey-haired men not to harm it'.[13] Dr Gray wrote to Tone's widow, telling of their pilgrimage. She responded with an impassioned plea for a headstone to be erected at Bodenstown. The letter, signed 'MATILDA WOLFE TONE', is representative of Matilda's mission to win for Tone his rightful place in the nation's gratitude. She spoke of his having 'laid down his life a self-devoted martyr for his country' at 'the hands of Ruthless Power', of 'his family . . . destroyed, his race extinct' and his body mouldering 'in an obscure grave'.[14] The stone was duly laid in

1844 by the Young Irelanders, the first nationalist grouping to look to Tone as their model.

II

It was Thomas Davis and his circle of Young Irelanders in the *Nation* newspaper which launched the Tone cult in the 1840s and popularised details of his life. Thereafter Tone's *Life* became standard reading for generations of nationalist leaders. A young Dublin Protestant, graduate of Trinity, member of the Irish bar and skilful journalist, Davis saw himself as inheriting Tone's mantle.[15] At a time when romantic nationalism was sweeping Europe, Davis had a mission. It was to educate the populace about its patriotic past. The *Nation* newspaper, which he co-founded, was consciously directed at a popular audience, and ballads and poems from it were reproduced in the frequently reprinted booklet, *The Spirit of the Nation*, first published in 1843.[16] Yeats claimed that in 1895 it was 'on the counter of every country stationer', by which time its ballads—including Davis's 'Tone's Grave'— had been thoroughly absorbed into popular tradition.[17] A life of Tone, to be written by Davis, was to have been the centrepiece of the Young Irelanders' shilling 'Library of Ireland' history series. Davis died in September 1845 before completing it, leaving behind a plan, notes, a first chapter and a dedication to Matilda Tone. These reveal Davis's total adulation of Tone and that sense of being his heir which characterises Young Ireland's writings generally.[18] Davis and the Young Irelanders both moulded popular Irish nationalism and elevated Tone as its central inspiration.

Young Ireland's investiture of Tone as the founder of Irish republican nationalism coincided with the issue of R.R. Madden's *United Irishmen*. Matilda thought it 'feeble but honest, slovenly written and printed', and was angry that Madden had not talked with her when he was in America researching the work. Yet for all that she proclaimed it 'a good Book', whose treatment of Tone measured up to her desire for recognition of him, and a later volume of 1846 dealt in detail with Tone.[19] 'I think this little revival [of writing] is good for us of 98', she wrote to her daughter-in-law, 'for we were slipping a little into the background'.[20]

The Young Irelanders, like the United Irishmen, were not doctrinaire on the issue of armed resistance. But a second generation was led into hopeless revolt in 1848. They were to take with them into Fenianism—the most enduring militant Irish republican movement until the rise of the IRA—both Young Ireland's adulation of Tone and its later lurch towards armed resistance. John Mitchel, the Ulster Presbyterian descendant of Tone's old Belfast colleagues, the Hasletts, and most doctrinaire of the Young Irelanders, led the way with his new weekly *The United Irishman*. Taking as its motto Tone's words—'Our independence must be had at all hazards. If the men of property will not support us, they must fall: we can support ourselves by the aid of that numerous and respectable class of the community, the Men of no property'—it breathed that hatred of English rule and commitment to arms which became the hallmark of republican nationalism thereafter.[21] The tradition of the unfinished, centuries-old struggle against England was skilfully conveyed in the simplistic message of Mitchel's intransigent republicanism, and his interpretation of Tone inspired a succession of young intellectuals from the Fenians onward. Not least influential was his promotion of the Tone cult with the developing Irish-American nationalism[22]

Republicanism remained weak when constitutional and parliamentary campaigns were in the ascendant. But with the demise of the Independent Irish Party at Westminster, militant republicanism revived in the late 1860s and '70s. It was assisted, not so much by the hopeless Fenian rising of 1867 and the bombing campaign in England, as by the executions and prison sentences which followed. The theme of the martyred dead was already strong in popular balladry and literature before Davis.[23] But it was Fenianism's promotion of the memory of Ireland's dead that made Bodenstown a spot which pilgrims visited regularly, and by 1873 Davis's stone had been chipped away by souvenir hunters.[24]

The theme of martyrdom was given a new handbook in the 1867 twopenny pamphlet *Speeches from the Dock*. With Tone's picture as frontispiece, it included short biographies and details of the trials of Tone and most of the leading rebels, from Robert Emmet to the Fenians. It was edited by the moderate nationalists T.D. and A.M. Sullivan, and was scarcely a manifesto of physical force. However, the rhetoric of revolution and admiration for Tone is common to nationalism of all hues, and *Speeches from the Dock* represents Tone as the defiant victim of an unjust oppressor and already firmly installed in traditions of the noble failure and republican martyrdom.[25] The book was continually updated and added to as it was reprinted, reaching a 39th edition by 1887 and going through another as recently as 1968. The editorial changes reflect the growing refinement of the Tone story. Most noticeable is the gradation from Sullivan's critical acceptance of his suicide to the assertion, in the 1945 and 1968 editions, that he was 'murdered' by an 'agent of England'.[26]

Tone's trial speech, even in edited versions, never had the making of a romantic myth, as did that of Robert Emmet, or Patrick Pearse's graveside orations. It contained none of that glorification of martyrdom at the hands of British tyranny which has made the trial speech such a feature of Irish nationalist tradition. But it was through such publications that details of his life became widely known. Yeats, for all his criticism of the literary efforts of Davis and Young Ireland, considered Davis and Tone among 'the patron saints of nationality', and included Tone's *Life* on his lists of best Irish books.[27]

III

By the 1890s and early 1900s, when the Tone cult emerged fully fledged, the groundwork was already laid and familiarity with the details of his life was generally assumed. The 1898 centenary celebrations united all shades of nationalist opinion. Tone's message of the unity of Irishmen was the watchword, and he became the central figure in the centenary celebrations. These reached a climax in Bodenstown churchyard on Sunday, 19 June, in a gathering which demonstrated the common allegiance of all nationalists to Tone.[28] The following day a great convention was called in Dublin to inaugurate a Wolfe Tone memorial fund. The theme again was unity, and the date for the national commemoration of '98 was switched from July to August to coincide with the planned laying of the Wolfe Tone memorial stone at the north-west corner of St. Stephen's Green. The stone, hewn from McArt's fort on the Cave Hill overlooking Belfast, was laid in a great public demonstration on 15 August with a trowel sent from America by Grace Maxwell, Tone's granddaughter.[29]

But if the celebrations of 1898 were a public demonstration of the prominent position Tone had already acquired in nationalist tradition, they also highlighted his rejection by the Ulster Protestants. Protestant nationalists like Davis laid greater emphasis on Tone's union of creeds than on his separatism.[30] McArt's fort in Belfast promised to become another Bodenstown for northern nationalists, linking them to Tone, to '98 and beyond to an ancient Gaelic past, for it was held to be the spot where clan chieftains had been sworn.[31] But '98 parades in Belfast were stoned, monuments destroyed and the *Belfast News Letter* attacked the Bodenstown and Stephen's Green ceremonies. It did not condemn the United Irishmen out of hand, and claimed some affinity with those from the north, like Neilson, McCracken and Drennan. A certain Presbyterian pride in their ancestors who were 'out' in '98 sometimes manifests itself, though it derives from that continuing sense of Ulster having been more advanced than the rest of the country.[32] But O'Connell's militant Catholicism and attack on English rule in Ireland deepened northern Protestant perceptions of the independence tradition as 'popish', and with his absorption into nationalist mythology, Tone is seen as tainted by southern 'popery'. The *News Letter* located the United Irish Society's 'capital' in the Vatican, and Tone was denounced as an 'adventurer', who became a 'patriot' only when thwarted as a place-hunter and snubbed by Pitt. He was a 'degraded character' whose autobiography was evidence to his 'sordid motives' and whose admitted literary talents were misdirected.[33]

But it was not until the twentieth century that Tone became firmly identified with militant Irish republicanism. The celebrations of 1898, and those for the centenary of Robert Emmet's rebellion in 1903, gave rise to Sinn Féin, the republican Dungannon Clubs and most of all the revival of the Fenian IRB, which in time came to absorb them all. Within a few years the Wolfe Tone Memorial Committee had become a front for the IRB and Bodenstown the symbol of militant republicanism. The Tone cult, the romantic nationalism of Davis and the Young Irelanders, the Irish-Irelandism of the Gaelic League, the mysticism of the literary revival and the commitment of Fenianism to armed struggle were merged in the years before 1916 into a new religion. It was through Pearse's enunciation of this republican faith that the Tone cult was transmitted to militant republicanism. In his rendering the theme of the noble failure was given a messianic element in the purifying quality of the blood sacrifice, and Pearse became mesmerised by the idea of martyrdom and bloodshed, whatever the odds, as an element in ultimate victory.

His first public expression of this new republican gospel was at the Bodenstown celebrations of 22 June 1913. 'We have come to the holiest place in Ireland; holier to us even than the place where Patrick sleeps in Down. Patrick brought us life, but this man died for us... the greatest of all that have died for Ireland'. It was Tone, Pearse claimed, who first formulated 'the gospel of Irish Nationalism' and 'armed his generation in defence of it'. To join with Tone 'is to come unto a new baptism, unto a new regeneration and cleansing'. He identified himself and his audience with Tone the man, with his friendships, his family, his death and his work 'still unaccomplished'. 'And let us make no mistake as to what Tone sought to do, and what remains for us to do. We need not re-state our programme. Tone has stated it for us', and he repeated Tone's 'theory' of 1796. 'I find here all the philosophy of Irish Nationalism'... We pledge ourselves to follow in the steps of Tone, never to rest...until his work be accomplished.' And that 'fight for freedom' should proceed even if at first doomed to failure. The outcome was the 1916 rising. For Pearse, Tone was Irish nationalism's towering genius, his published *Life* the first 'gospel of the New Testament of Irish Nationality.'[34]

In the twentieth century the Bodenstown ceremony has become a permanent fixture in the republican calendar. Here IRA followers become 're-dedicated' to their republican faith and to 'the armed struggle to break the English connection and set up a secular Republic. . . the dream of our founding father, Wolfe Tone'.[35] While constitutional nationalists go to Bodenstown to re-state their commitment to Irish reunification, preferring to single out the 'common name of Irishman' theme in Tone's writings, in the hope of some day reconciling the Ulster Protestants to their ultimate aim of a united Ireland.[36]

IV

Tone's reputation as the 'father' of Irish republican nationalism is accepted by every political grouping in Ireland. But each takes from the Tone tradition only what it needs to sustain its own stance. Nowhere is this better illustrated than by the annual pilgrimages of different groups of nationalists to Bodenstown on different days, the constitutionalists disassociating themselves from the IRA's ceremony and from the physical-force element in Tone's legacy. The divided occasion symbolises that ambivalence towards armed resistance which lies at the heart of Irish nationalism. It is not necessarily a violent, nor even a separatist tradition. But it readily adopts the rhetoric of revolution and Anglophobia and looks to the same heroes as the militant republicans.

Tone has likewise been subsumed by the mystical Gaelic reading of Irish nationality. But his anti-popery and dismissal of things Gaelic, indeed his very Protestantism, has caused some embarrassment and led to the absurd claim that his attacks on the papacy were due to ignorance of the 'true church'.[37] Indeed in the 1930s there was some debate as to whether Tone could be accepted as the founder of a nationalism which had become almost exclusively Catholic. The outspoken Bishop O'Doherty of Galway denounced Tone and the United Irishmen as 'exemplars of conduct unfitting for Catholics, young or old, to imitate'. The attack became hysterical in the clerical student, Leo McCabe's, *Wolfe Tone and the United Irishmen: For or Against Christ?* (1937). McCabe denounced 'That murderous and poisonous growth in Catholic Ireland's system. . .her amazing cult. . .of the leadership and ideals of Wolfe Tone and the other anti-Catholic United Irishmen'. He considered as heresy Davis's elevation of Tone to sainthood and of nationalism to the status of a religion. Such attacks were the products of the triumphal Catholicism of the new Irish state and the perceived threat from communism. But they were unusual in the history of the Tone cult and they sparked off quite a controversy. The clergy were attacked as 'slaves of English imperialism' and defenders sought to depict Tone as a Catholic champion.[38] Most Catholic readings ignore Tone's anti-clericalism and anti-popery, making him out to be some Catholic saviour in the same mould as O'Connell.[39] Tone's suicide has likewise caused difficulty, and popular tradition still attributes it to 'British murder'. There is even the unlikely suggestion that the wound was inflicted in a brawl between the guards.[40]

Critics of Tone get short shrift from Irish Catholics. Even in the 1930s, when physical-force methods were out of fashion, Frank MacDermot's balanced life of Tone was attacked as showing 'a complete lack of any philosophy of Irish history', of a permanent 'underground nation...the spirit of Ireland' working through such instruments as Tone.[41] In the 1980s such views are denounced as 'snobbish', 'toney' Hibernian, 'shoneen',[42] and 'revisionist'—this last, a term normally applied to scholars using scientific standards of research to re-interpret the myths and long-held truths of the past, now used more frequently as a term of abuse to describe those who attack romantic nationalist historiography. 'There are today, politicians, historians and intellectuals (and newspaper editors)', Danny Morrison of Sinn Féin told the Bodenstown gathering in June 1981, 'men of property, who spend hours swivelling in their leather chairs, their judgement tempered and choked by their own affluence, concocting distortions of republican history to berate us...[and] to support their contention about just how different the Republican Movement today is supposedly from the Republican Movement of the past'.[43]

Tone was passionately Irish. But he was part of an élite and had a very Protestant perception of the Irish masses. He thought them vulgar, lacking in spirit and prone to graft and deceit. He had little sympathy with the romantic cultural nationalism which was beginning to develop in his own day, and would have decried the additional barrier erected between Irishmen by the new Irish state's emphasis on Gaelic culture and language.

Nor was he the democrat of tradition, a reputation largely based on his much misunderstood reference to 'the men of no property'.[44] Its use by those seeking to find an element in Tone to which all religions can subscribe is on the increase. Tone had considerable compassion for the poor. But his opinion of their judgement and political capacities was low and he had no intention whatsoever of involving them directly in politics. Property in the eighteenth century meant first and foremost landed property. His 'respectable' men of no property were the middle classes who composed the Catholic and United Irish leadership alike. Irish republican separatism started out as a campaign to secure political power for the middle classes.

But let's not be pious. The Ulster Protestants who claim Tone's hatred of England and his takeover by Catholic republicans as reasons for their rejection of him,[45] or the IRA, who point to his support for 'armed revolt' in justification of their claim to be 'the followers of Tone', are both correct in their different ways. Tone did seek Irish independence, he did dislike England, he did resort to arms to achieve his aims. And whatever the impact of Presbyterianism on his thinking, he did link the cause of Irish nationalism to Catholicism. Constitutional nationalists sanitise the Tone tradition, taking the safe elements, whitewashing the rest.

Tone's thought processes were simplistic, and one of his greatest failings was his inability to see the many gradations of opinion between the ultra-loyalist and the separatist. He also suffered from the common human tendency to conflate sacrifice with rectitude. Yet both traits were part of that single-mindedness which made him such an effective revolutionary. Once a decision had been taken, he pursued it with a stubborn sense of conviction which was often rash, but rarely unconvincing. Not having been a revolutionary before 1795, when pushed into becoming one he responded with all the zeal of a convert. But it was a single-mindedness which could just as easily propel Tone in one direction as another, and one may query his having emerged as a revolutionary had it not been for the exceptional nature of the times in which he lived. His story is not that of Ireland and Irish republicanism alone, but of the impact of the French Revolution generally. The story was repeated in almost every other European country, even if few of them are still living through the after-effects in quite the same way as Ireland is today. However, the movement which Tone helped found had already, before he died, acquired aspects quite alien to his own ideals. His ideals were of an age which had already passed, and one suspects that his own militant republicanism might not have outlived that recognition. For his reputation as nationalist hero, his death was perhaps timely.

Yet Tone's autobiography will continue to be the centrepiece of popular Irish nationalism. Everything about his life—his intense loyalty to friends, his capacity for sacrifice, his inflated sense of honour, his rakish youth and dramatic death—is the very stuff of romantic legend. It has proved a potent mix. Tone may not have been an original thinker, or the kind of powerful charismatic figure one might expect of someone with his revolutionary reputation. But he voiced a hitherto confused aspiration for independence with a clarity and conviction which was his hallmark. He endowed that aspiration with the nobility of personal sacrifice and with a sincerity for which even his opponents gave him credit. If Fitzgibbon's claim that Tone was the 'father' of Ireland's first republican movement had little foundation in 1793, Tone has for a century and a half been recognised as the originator of an ideology which continues to dictate the shape of Irish politics.[46]

NOTES
SELECT BIBLIOGRAPHY
INDEX

Notes

List of Abbreviations and Short Forms

MANUSCRIPT SOURCES

AAE	Archives des Affaires Étrangères, Paris
ADSM	Archives Départmentales de la Seine-Maritime, Rouen
AHG	Archives Historiques de la Guerre, Paris
AN	Archives Nationales, Paris
BL	British Library, London
Bodl.	Bodleian Library, Oxford
DDA	Dublin Diocesan Archives
GSA	Algemeen Rijksarchief (General State Archives), The Hague, Netherlands
Kent AO	Kent Archives Office, Maidstone
LC	Library of Congress, Washington, D.C.
NLI	National Library of Ireland, Dublin
NYPL	New York Public Library, New York
PRO	Public Record Office, London
PROI	Public Record Office of Ireland, Dublin
PRONI	Public Record Office of Northern Ireland, Belfast
RIA	Royal Irish Academy, Dublin
SPOI	State Paper Office of Ireland, Dublin
TCD	Trinity College, Dublin

A full list of MS sources will be found in the Select Bibliography.

PUBLISHED SOURCES

AHR	American Historical Review
AhRf	Annales historiques de la Révolution française
BNL	Belfast News Letter
DEP	Dublin Evening Post
FJ	Freeman's Journal
IHS	Irish Historical Studies
Life	Life of Theobald Wolfe Tone, ed. by his son William Theobald Wolfe Tone, 2 vols. (Washington, 1826)
NS	Northern Star
UJA	Ulster Journal of Archaeology
WMQ	William and Mary Quarterly

All other published sources are given in full at the first citation, and cited thereafter by author and short title only; for a full list of the principal published sources see the Select Bibliography.

Introduction

[1] See Ruth Dudley Edwards, *Patrick Pearse, the Triumph of Failure* (London, 1977), 341, on the instructions for teaching history in Irish schools, 1922.

[2] Many of Tone's pre-1796 papers and books were left in America, in the custody of the Ulster United Irishman, Dr James Reynolds, who subsequently lost them. Some were retrieved by Tone's son and widow and a number of the books were bequeathed by his great-granddaughter to the American Irish Historical Society. See Vincent O'Reilly, 'Books from the Libraries of Theobald Wolfe Tone and William Sampson', *Bull. Amer. Irish Hist. Soc.*, II (1924), 5–15. These now appear to have been lost. The staff of the Society's library claimed no knowledge of this collection when I visited its New York premises in 1987, and subsequent communications have produced no further evidence of their whereabouts. Other items were said to have been destroyed in New York early in this century—see *Irish Independent*, 11 Feb 1924.

[3] *Memoirs of William Sampson* (NY, 1807), 262.

[4] See, however, Tom Dunne's lively essay, *Theobald Wolfe Tone, Colonial Outsider: An Analysis of his Political Philosophy* (Cork, 1982). Though considerably one-sided, in the modern revisionist mould, it nevertheless contains some fresh insights which depart from the unhelpful and unquestioning reverence of most of the works on Tone.

[5] The name derived from Henry Grattan (1746–1820), the brilliant orator and reformist MP, whose name has come to be associated with the reform campaigns of the last two decades of the Irish Parliament.

Chapter 1

[1] *History of the Tone Family*, comp. Frank Jerome Tone (Niagara Falls, NY, 1944), 35.

[2] Maurice Craig, *Dublin 1660–1860* (London 1952; repr. Dublin, 1969), 178; J. J. McGregor, *New Picture of Dublin* (Dublin, 1821), 35; Ruth Lavelle and Paul Huggard, 'The Parish Poor of St. Mark's', in David Dickson, ed., *The Gorgeous Mask: Dublin 1700–1850* (Dublin, 1987), 86–7.

[3] William Tone's father Hugh Tone was Dublin-born. His wife's family were French. See *History of the Tone Family*, 33–5.

[4] See unsigned review of the *Life* in *Quarterly Rev.* XXXVI (1827), 78.

[5] Reg. Deeds Ire., 236/228/154381, 337/17/22480, 341/388/228952, deeds relating to the Stafford Street property, 315/399/213902, Drumcondra, and *Life*, I. 29–30, for Summerhill. See also J. F. Fuller, 'The Tones: Father and Son', *Jnl Cork Hist. and Arch. Soc.*, XXIX (1929), 96–8.

[6] David Dickson, *New Foundations: Ireland 1660–1800* (Dublin, 1987), 120–4.

[7] *Life*, I. 203, recounts voting for members of the City's Common Council in 1792, by virtue of his membership of the Saddlers, which he would have acquired through his father. See also Mel Doyle, 'The Dublin Guilds and Journeymen's Clubs', *Saothar*, III (1977), 6–14; John J. Webb, *The Guilds of Dublin* (Dublin, 1929), 246–50.

[8] *History of the Tone Family*, 3–32; and see ch. 4, sec. III.

[9] PRO, Betham Abstracts: Prerogative Wills, Bet. 1/42/317, John Lamport, Dublin Mariner, 1747; Sir Arthur Vicars, ed., *Index to Prerogative Wills of Ireland 1536–1810* (Dublin, 1897), 276.

[10] Eileen O'Byrne, ed., *The Convert Rolls* (Ir. Mss. Comm., Dublin, 1981), 269.

[11] TCD, MS 873/32, account of Tone given to R. R. Madden by his cousin, Mrs Bull; *Faulkner's Dublin Jnl*, 20 Nov 1798; King's Inns, Tone's 'Memorial to be admitted to the degree of barrister', 4 May 1789, claims both father and mother as 'Protestants of the Church of Ireland as by law established'. See *Life*, I. 17, for signs that the Established Church played a significant part in the family's life.

[12] Tone does not mention Fanny by name and her existence has been ignored by historians. But his widow gives details, Tone (Dickason) MSS, Matilda Tone to Catherine Anne Tone, 22 Dec 1829; also his son in *Life*, II. 561

[13] *Life*, I. 12–16.

[14] See, e.g., TCD, MS 868/2/139–42, 176, 181, 202–3, Margaret Tone's 1796 letters on

Arthur and Theobald; MS 873/35, copy Matilda Tone to Margaret Tone, 11 May 1810; RIA, MS 23 K. 53, Matilda to Peter Burrowes, 27 Dec 1816.

[15] TCD, MS 2046/6v, omitted from the published *Life*; Tone (Dickason) MSS, Tone to Matilda, 2 Sept 1798, on his mother's sufferings.

[16] George Wolfe, 'The Wolfe Family of Co. Kildare', *Jnl Co. Kildare Arch. Soc.*, III (1899–1902), 361–7; Revd William Sherlock, 'Further notes on the History and Antiquities of the Parish of Clane', ibid., IV (1903–5), 35–46.

[17] Tone (Dickason) MSS, Matilda Tone to Catherine Anne Tone, 22 Dec 1829; Reg. Deeds Ire., 297/347/195310, 302/262/20020, 374/532/250721, for the sublettings, and 419/287/273989, deed making over all the lands to Jonathan Tone, 30 Jan 1790. The deeds only provide the acreage of Cassumsize, 124, and Sallins, just over 43. We do not know that of the lands at Whitechurch and Bodenstown.

[18] *FJ*, 24 Nov 1798.

[19] *Life*, I. 17.

[20] *Remains of the Revd Samuel O'Sullivan DD*, ed. Revd J. C. Martin, DD, and Revd Mortimer O'Sullivan, DD, 3 vols. (Dublin, 1853), II. 261. Thomas Sheridan, *View of the State of School-Education in Ireland* (Dublin, 1787); W. B. Stanford, *Ireland and the Classical Tradition* (Dublin, 1976), 34, 38; *Dublin Mag. and Irish Monthly Reg.* (Nov 1798), 327, for Craig's school.

[21] Constantia Maxwell, *A History of Trinity College, Dublin, 1591–1821* (Dublin, 1946), 153–4; Stanford, *Ireland and the Classical Tradition*, 30–2; T. W. Stubbs, *The History of the University of Dublin* (Dublin, 1889), 204–5.

[22] *Life*, I. 18–19.

[23] *Remains of Revd Samuel O'Sullivan*, II. 261–2.

[24] *Life*, I. 19.

[25] Lady Morgan, *The O'Briens and the O'Flahertys*, 4 vols. (Paris, 1828), I. 182, II. 16–17; TCD, MS Mun V/462 and V/91; Stubbs, *History of the University of Dublin*, 318; Maxwell, *History of Trinity College, Dublin*, 44–5.

[26] Oliver Goldsmith, *Enquiry into the Present State of Polite Learning in Europe*, in *Collected Works*, ed. A. Friedman, 5 vols. (Oxford, 1966), I. 335–6.

[27] Constantia Maxwell, *Dublin under the Georges* (Dublin, 1946), 52–3; W. MacNeille Dixon, *Trinity College, Dublin* (London, 1902), 168–9; *Walker's Hib. Mag.* (Dec 1793), 524; TCD, MS Mun V/3; NLI, MS 772(1)/2–16, Extracts from the Diary of Austin Cooper, 1782–1815.

[28] *Belmont Castle; or, Suffering Sensibility, containing the genuine and interesting correspondence of several persons of fashion* (Dublin, 1790), 201.

[29] Morgan, *O'Briens and O'Flahertys*, III. 81–6; *Walker's Hib. Mag.* (1781), 111; Dickson, *The Gorgeous Mask*, vii–ix, and 1–16.

[30] Cited in Dixon, *Trinity College, Dublin*, 171; J. E. Walsh, *Sketches of Ireland Sixty Years Ago* (Dublin, 1847), 5–9, 14–15; Sir Jonah Barrington, *Personal Sketches of his own Times*, 3rd edn., 2 vols. (London, 1832), I. 367–9.

[31] L. M. Cullen, *The Emergence of Modern Ireland* (London, 1981), 242–3; *Walker's Hib. Mag.* (Dec 1793), 524; Stubbs, *History of the University of Dublin*, 331; R. F. Foster, *Modern Ireland 1600–1972* (London, 1988), 176–7; Elizabeth Malcolm, *'Ireland Sober, Ireland Free': Drink and Temperance in Nineteenth-Century Ireland* (Dublin, 1986), 21–9.

[32] See Jacqueline R. Hill, 'National Festivals, the State and "Protestant ascendancy" in Ireland, 1790–1829', *IHS*, XXIV (May 1984), 30–51.

[33] *Walker's Hib. Mag.* (Nov 1781), 616; Morgan, *O'Briens and O'Flahertys*, 105–41.

[34] James Gandon, 1743–1820, architect of some of the finest public buildings of the period, notably the Customs House and the Four Courts.

[35] Reg. Deeds Ire., 346/109/230775, Peter Tone's surrender of a lease on houses in Lower Ormond Quay, 6 Feb 1782; BL, Add. MS 34419(ii)/338, Under-Secretary Cooke's description, 1783; Walsh, *Ireland Sixty Years Ago*, 54, 73–5, 80; McGregor, *New Picture of Dublin*, 313–14; J. L. De Lactocnaye, *A Frenchman's Walk through Ireland, 1796–7*, 2nd edn., ed. J. A. Gamble (Belfast, 1984), 17–18; *FJ*, 14 Apr 1791.

[36] *Alumni Dublinenses: a Register of the Students, Graduates, Professors, and Provosts of Trinity College, in the University of Dublin*, ed. G. D. Burtchaell and T. U. Sadleir (London, 1924), 576; Stubbs, *History of the University of Dublin*, 282–5.

[37] J. R. O'Flanagan, *The Lives of the Lord Chancellors and Keepers of the Great Seal of Ireland*, 2 vols. (London, 1870), II. 409–13; *The Life, Letters, and Speeches of Lord Plunket*, ed. the Hon. David Plunket, 2 vols. (London, 1867), I. 39; *Speeches at the Bar and in the Senate by the Rt. Hon. W. Conyngham Plunket*, ed. J. C. Hoey (Dublin, 1865), viii.

[38] *The Parliamentary Register: or, History of. . . House of Commons of Ireland*, 17 vols. (Dublin, 1782–1801), XVII. 196–7; *Life*, II. 30, and see ch. 29 for Tone's trial speech; Revd A. H. Kenney, *The Works of the Most Revd. William Magee DD*, 2 vols. (London, 1842), I. xxii.

[39] *Memoirs, Journal, and Correspondence of Thomas Moore*, ed. the Rt. Hon. Lord John Russell, MP, 6 vols. (London, 1853–4), I. 36; Stubbs, *History of the University of Dublin*, 254–5, 279–80; TCD, MS Mun. V/4, Register of Censures.

[40] TCD, MS Mun. V/53. 466–8; R. B. McDowell and D. A. Webb, *Trinity College Dublin 1592–1952: An Academic History* (Cambridge, 1982), 106–7.

[41] McDowell and Webb. *Trinity College Dublin*, 30–71; TCD, MS 2245, Michael Wycherley's notebook, 1781–2. Richard Ashcraft, *Revolutionary Politics and Locke's 'Two Treatises of Government'* (Princeton, N.J., 1986); Isaac Kramnick, 'Republican Revisionism Revisited', *AHR*, LXXXVII, no. 3 (June 1982), 629–50.

[42] TCD, MS 2046/8.

[43] TCD, MS Mun. V/5.27.2, Attendance at lectures 1750–92.

[44] McDowell and Webb, *Trinity College Dublin*, 104.

[45] TCD, MS 2046/8v; MS Mun. V/27.3, Examination results, 1781–5; Stubbs, *History of the University of Dublin*, 249, 257–60.

[46] TCD, MS 2046/9; *Life*, I. 19–21; *FJ*, 24 Nov 1798; Barrington, *Personal Sketches*, I, 270–300; Walsh, *Ireland Sixty Years Ago*, 22–3.

Chapter 2

[1] *Post-Chaise Companion: or Traveller's Directory Through Ireland* (London, 1784), 59.

[2] *Freeman's Journal*, 24 Nov 1798, claimed that Griffith paid for Tone's education at the Middle Temple after the robbery at his father's house. I have found no corroboration for this, though it is almost certainly true.

[3] Shevawn Lynam, *Humanity Dick: A Biography of Richard Martin, MP, 1754–1834* (London, 1975), 44–55; De Lactocnaye, *A Frenchman's Walk through Ireland*, 156–7, 161–3.

[4] *FJ*, 17–22 Dec 1791; *Ten Thousand Pounds!!! Trial between Richard Martin, Esq. (of Dangan) and John Petrie Esq. (of Essex) for Criminal Conversation with the Plaintiff's Wife* (Dublin, 1792).

[5] *Walker's Hib. Mag.* (May 1781), 568; Maxwell, *Dublin under the Georges*, 202–10.

[6] TCD, MS Mun. Soc. Hist. 4, minutes for 23 June 1784 meeting; Mun. V/5, Registers of the Board, vol. 3, fos. 466–8; W. S. Clarke, *The Irish Stage in the County Towns 1720–1800* (Oxford, 1965), 122, 256.

[7] *FJ*, 11 May 1786; Nicholas Rowe *The Fair Penitent, as performed at the Theatre Royal* (London, 1791).

[8] Clarke, *Irish Stage in the County Towns*, 11–14; James Hardiman, *The History of the Town and County of Galway* (Galway, 1926), 195; Lynam, *Humanity Dick*, 49–50.

[9] John Home, *Douglas: A Tragedy* (London, 1777).

[10] Morgan, *O'Briens and O'Flahertys*, III. 29.

[11] There was a particularly virulent outbreak of smallpox in Dublin in 1776, in which many children died; see NLI, MS 4481/2v.

[12] TCD, MS 873/38, Sir Philip Crampton to Dr Madden, 3 May 1843.

[13] TCD, MS 873/38, op. cit. The physical description is based on observation of Tone's death mask in Trinity College, Dublin (there is another in the American-Irish Historical Library, New York); *FJ*, 13 Nov 1798; Tone (Dickason) MSS, his Volunteer certificate, 10 June 1795; Mary McNeill, *The Life and Times of Mary Ann McCracken, 1770–1886: A Belfast Panorama* (Dublin, 1960), 127; Barrington, *Personal Sketches*, I. 278–82.

[14] Rowe, *The Fair Penitent*, 12; *Belmont Castle*, 195–6.

[15] TCD, MS 2046/67.

[16] Lynam, *Humanity Dick*, 82–3.

[17] *FJ*, 17–22 Dec 1791.

[18] TCD, MS 2046/9v–11, gives a complete account of the affair; it has also been printed, *The Autobiography of Theobald Wolfe Tone*, ed. S. O'Faolain (London, 1937), 9–13.

[19] TCD, MS Mun. V/27(3), Examination Returns, 1784; Maxwell, *History of Trinity College, Dublin* 132–3; Stubbs, *History of the University of Dublin*, 206.

[20] TCD, MS Mun. Soc. Hist. 40–1, Abstracts of Journals: 1770–93.

[21] TCD, MS Mun. Soc. Hist. 6 fos. 51–4.

[22] Hist. Soc. Pa., Edward Carey Gardiner Papers, Thomas Addis Emmet to Matthew Carey, 22 Apr 1819.

[23] TCD, MS Mun. Soc. Hist. 5 fos. 2–10.

[24] *FJ*, 24 Nov 1798. TCD, MS Mun. Soc. Hist. 4–6, Journals 1782–9; Plunket, *Life, Letters and Speeches*, I. 31–3; George D. Burtchaell, 'Theobald Wolfe Tone and the College Historical Society', *Jnl Roy. Soc. Antiqs. Ire.*, XVIII (1887–8), 391–9; T. S. C. Dagg, *The College Historical Society: A History (1770–1920)* (Dublin, 1969).

[25] R. R. Madden, *The United Irishmen, their Lives and Times*, 3 ser. 7 vols. (London, 1842–5), 2nd ser. vol. II. 1–17.

[26] *Life*, I. 40–1; *Select Speeches of the late Peter Burrowes, Esq. K.C., at the Bar and in Parliament*, ed Waldron O. Burrowes (Dublin, 1850), 66–9, 32–3; Plunket, *Life, Letters and Speeches*, I. 36; W. H. Curran, *Sketches of the Irish Bar*, 2 vols. (London, 1855), I. 390–4.

[27] *Life*, II. 489; Stubbs, *History of the University of Dublin*, 295–301.

[28] See TCD, MS Mun. V/5, Registers of the Board, vol. 4, fo. 32, and Burtchaell and Sadleir, *Alumni Dublinenses*, 890, for Witherington.

[29] Craig, *Dublin*, 105; Dickson, *The Gorgeous Mask*, vii–ix.

[30] *The Gentleman's and Citizen's Almanach*, comp. Samuel Wilson (Dublin, 1776), 82.

[31] *Marriage Entries from the Registers of the Parishes of St. Andrew, St. Anne, St. Audoen and St. Bride, 1632–1800*, ed. D. A. Chart (London, 1913), 70; *Life*, I. 21.

[32] TCD, MS 2046/25–6.

[33] The position of auditor was equivalent to the presidency of the Oxford or Cambridge Union; see Dixon, *Trinity College, Dublin*, 136.

[34] TCD, MS Mun. V/27(3), Examination returns, 1771–97; Mun. Soc. Hist. 5/141–71, 188, 236.

[35] TCD, MS Mun. Soc. Hist. 5/264.

[36] TCD, MS 2046/12v–14; the criticism of Matilda's family is omitted from *Life*, I. 24.

[37] TCD, MS Mun. Soc. Hist. 5/301 and 6/38 and 48.

[38] TCD, MS 3805/25–37, draft of the speech; MS Mun. Soc. Hist. 6/118, 131; see also *Art and Oratory: Bicentenary of the College History Society, 1770–1920* (Dublin, 1970), 32–5.

[39] TCD, MS Mun. Soc. Hist. 6/147, 157, 168, 171, 293.

[40] *Life*, I. 22.

Chapter 3

[1] Daniel Duman, *The Judicial Bench in England 1727–1875: The Reshaping of an Élite* (London, 1982); also his 'The English Bar in the Georgian Era', in *Lawyers in Early Modern Europe and America*, ed. Wilfrid Prest (London, 1981), 86–107; Paul Lucas, 'A Collective Biography of Students and Barristers of Lincoln's Inn, 1680–1804: A Study in the "Aristocratic Resurgence" of the Eighteenth Century', *Jnl Mod. Hist.*, XLVI (1974), 227–61.

[2] *Life*, I. 24; J. A. Picton, *Memorials of Liverpool*, 2 vols. (London, 1893), I. 223, 237, 252–3; J. J. Bagley, *Lancashire Diarists* (London, 1975), 163. I am grateful to Jenny Kermode of Liverpool University for help on these points. See also *Personal Recollections of the Life and Times . . . of Valentine Lord Cloncurry* (Dublin, 1849), 40, for travel between Dublin and London.

[3] W. H. Curran, *The Life of the Rt. Hon. John Philpot Curran, late Master of the Rolls in Ireland*, 2 vols. (London, 1819), I. 35.

[4] *Morning Post*, 25 May 1788; John Campbell, *The Lives of the Lord Chancellors and Keepers of the Great Seals of England*, 7 vols. (London, 1845–7), V. 392–3; VII. 51; M. D. George, *London Life in the Eighteenth Century*, 2nd edn. (London, 1965), 74–108; *European Mag.* XI (Jan–June 1787), 118–19.

[5] William Makepeace Thackeray, *The History of Pendennis: His Fortunes and Misfortunes, his Friends and Greatest Enemy*, 2 vols. (London, 1849–50), I. 309–10.

[6] TCD, MS 2046/17–18; *Life*, I. 75, 367; *The Autobiography of Francis Place*, ed. Mary Thrale (Cambridge, 1972), 27, 34–91; George, *London Life in the Eighteenth Century*, 271–2.

[7] Middle Temple Lib., Rentals, 1776–96; W. T. Loftie, *The Inns of Court and Chancery* (London, 1895), 122–65.

[8] Thackeray, *Pendennis*, I. 288–90.

[9] George Godwin, *The Middle Temple: The Society and Fellowship* (London, 1954), 115.

[10] H. A. C. Sturgess, ed., *Register of Admissions to the Hon. Society of the Middle Temple*, 3 vols. (London, 1949), II. 398; Middle Temple Lib., Barristers' Ledger, 227, and Students' Ledger, 252; Burtchaell and Sadleir, *Alumni Dublinenses*, 435, 744.

[11] See good description in Thackeray, *Pendennis*, I. 301.

[12] TCD, MS 2046/15; *The Records of the Hon. Society of Lincoln's Inn: Admissions and Chapel Registers*, 2 vols. (Lincoln's Inn [London], 1896), I. 502; Joseph Foster, *Alumni Oxonienses, 1500–1886*, 4 vols. (Oxford, 1891), II. 806; A. P. W. Malcomson, *John Foster: The Politics of the Anglo-Irish Ascendancy* (Oxford, 1978), 206–7, 416–17.

[13] *Belmont Castle*, 7–8, 'a portrait of J.W. B–l' is pencilled in Tone's personal copy, now in the National Library of Ireland; Middle Temple Lib., Students' Ledger, 469.

[14] NLI, MS 3212/4–6; Middle Temple Lib., Index to Minutes of Parliament, 1787, 63; Students' Ledger, 1787, 252; Burtchaell and Sadleir, *Alumni Dublinenses*, 474.

[15] *The House of Commons 1790–1820*, ed. R. G. Thorne, 5 vols. (London, 1986), V. 522–4. I am indebted to Dr Eveline Cruikshanks for making this information available to me prior to its publication. Nat. Reg. Arch., list Wharton, Beverley Park, York; *Records, Lincoln's Inn*, vol. I: *Admissions, 1420–1799*, 510; Lucas, 'Collective Biography of...Lincoln's Inn', 235n. and Table A1. See *Life*, II. 5, for evidence that Tone had been to Yorkshire.

[16] TCD, MS 2046/15; *Life*, I. 25–6.

[17] NLI, MS 3212/4–6.

[18] *DNB*, XXXV. 313; Charles Phillips, *Curran and His Contemporaries* (London, 1850), 45–6.

[19] TCD, MS 2046/1v–2.

[20] Chambers in the Inns were normally let for life, and Tone would have sublet from one Charles Renshaw. The annual rent for the first floor of no. 4 is listed in 1770 as £14; see R. A. Roberts, ed., *A Calendar of the Inner Temple Records*, 5 vols. (London, 1936), vol. V: *1751–1800*, 250, 422, 499.

[21] *Life*, I. 12, 24–6, 40, and II. 75, 120, 130, 135; TCD, MS 2046/15v.

[22] *Belmont Castle*, vi.

[23] TCD, MS 2046/17–18; *Belmont Castle*, v.

[24] NLI, MS 3212/4–6.

[25] *Life*, I. 25.

[26] *European Mag.*, XI (1787), 51, XIII (1788), 275; *Morning Post*, 15, 19 Jan, and 2 Feb 1788.

[27] Plunket, *Life, Letters and Speeches*, I. 60–1.

[28] See, p. 284.

[29] RIA, MS 12. P. 13, Journal kept by D. O'Connell, 1795–9, fos. 8–9, 19, 23; see also description of Erskine's legal education in Campbell, *Lives of the Lord Chancellors*, VII. 385–8.

[30] *Life*, I. 297–8; Thackeray, *Pendennis*, II. 298.

[31] NLI, MS 3212/4–6.

[32] TCD, MS 2046/15; *Life*, I. 25; Middle Temple Lib. Treasurer's Accounts, 1787, 60.

[33] NLI, MS 3212/4–6.

[34] *European Mag.*, XIV (Nov 1788), 348 and 352.

[35] TCD, MS 2046/14v.

[36] M. J. MacManus, 'Bibliography of Theobald Wolfe Tone', *Dublin Mag.*, XV, no.3 (July–Sept 1940), 6, 12; also his 'The Man who Stole Wolfe Tone's Books', *Irish Press*, 1 July 1942.

[37] See T. C. Mitchell, ed., *Captain Cook and the South Pacific* (Canberra, 1979), esp. 81–136; also Robin Fisher and Hugh Johnston, eds., *Captain Cook and His Times* (London, 1979), 6–7, 161.

[38] See, e.g., discussion of Anson in his *A Voyage Round the World*, ed. G. Williams (London, 1974), ix–x—it had gone through 15 editions by 1780; *Voyages of Capt. Dampier with the Buccaneers of America* (London, 1785); George Anson, *A Voyage to the South Seas* (London, 1745); see Tone's notes in *Life*, I. 538–9, taken from *A Voyage to the Pacific Ocean*, 2nd edn., 3

vols. (London, 1785), III. 20, 28, 50, 86, 102–3, 115, 118. D. Mitchell, *Pirates* (London, 1976), 19–20, 55–79.

[39] *Life*, II. 113, also 104.

[40] *Life*, I. 26–7, 37; Tone (Dickason) MSS, Tone to Matilda, 31 Aug 1798. The original memoirs of 10 and 23 Aug 1788 are in PRO, PRO 30/8/330/227–33.

[41] TCD, MS 2046/14, also 17v; Westminster Hall was home of the common law courts, where a spectators' gallery was reserved for the law students.

[42] See, e.g., Madden, *United Irishmen*, 3rd ser, I. 126–7; Henry Boylan, *Wolfe Tone* (Dublin, 1981), 8–9; and the hostile reviewer of the *Life*, in *Quarterly Rev.* XXXVI (June–Oct. 1827), 63, 78.

[43] Phillips, *Curran and his Contemporaries*, 28; *Life of Curran*, I. 27–79; *Memoirs of the Life and Times of the Rt. Hon. Henry Grattan*, ed. Henry Grattan Junior, 5 vols. (London, 1839–46), I. 114; RIA, MS 12. P. 13, O'Connell's journal, fos. 3–13.

[44] William Holdsworth, *A History of English Law*, 12 vols. (London, 1938), XII. 15, also 16–17, 77, 89–91; Duman, *Judicial Bench*, 9; T. Ruggles, *The Barrister; or, Strictures on the Education Proper for the Bar*, 2 vols. (London, 1792), I. 23, 36–7, 52–3; Brian Abel-Smith and Robert Stevens, *Lawyers and the Courts: A Sociological Study of the English Legal System 1750–1965* (London, 1967), 25.

[45] *The Works of Henry Fielding Esq.*, ed. A. Murphy, 10 vols. (London, 1821), I. 204.

[46] See, e.g., Horace Twiss, Esq., *The Public and Private Life of Lord Chancellor Eldon*, 3 vols. (London, 1844), I. 85.

[47] TCD, MS 2046/16v–17; see *Life*, II. 560–1, for William's aversion to East India Company service.

[48] Plunket, *Life, Letters and Speeches*, I. 60–1.

[49] Middle Temple Lib., Students' Ledger, 469.

Chapter 4

[1] Curran, *Sketches of the Irish Bar*, I. 118; *Sketches, Legal and Political of the late Rt. Hon, Richard Lalor Sheil*, ed. M. W. Savage, Esq., 2 vols. (London, 1855), I. 220; E. M. Johnston, *Great Britain and Ireland, 1760–1800* (Edinburgh, 1963), 235–6.

[2] See, e.g., NLI, MS 873/35, Matilda to Margaret Tone, 11 May 1810.

[3] James W. Phillips, ' Bibliographical Inquiry into Printing and Bookselling in Dublin from 1670–1800' (University of Dublin, Ph.D. thesis, 1952), 138–9; Maxwell, *Dublin under the Georges*, 63–4; *Life*, I. 28; J. T. Gilbert, *A History of the City of Dublin*, 3 vols. (Dublin, 1859), II. 278, III. 196–243.

[4] *Universal Mag. and Rev.*, I–VII (1789–92), listing Tone among the subscribers, and his initialled review of a work on Falstaff, II. 122–6; possibly also that of *Belmont Castle*, IV. 489: see ch. 6, n. 25.

[5] Gilbert, *History of Dublin*, I. 278, III. 211–16.

[6] *FJ*, 28 Feb, 29 Dec 1789, 8 June 1790.

[7] TCD, MS Mun. Soc. Hist. 6, fos. 38, 48, 51.

[8] TCD, MS Mun. Soc. Hist. 6 fo. 92.

[9] See e.g., TCD, MS Mun. Soc. Hist. 6, fos. 114, 118, 126, 142, 168, 171, for some of Tone's interventions June–Dec 1789; *FJ*, 7, 11 Feb 1789; Thomas J. Westropp, 'A Glimpse of Trinity College, Dublin under Provost Hely-Hutchinson (from original letters)', *Jnl Roy. Soc. Antiqs. of Ire.*, XVIII (1887–8), 400–3. The Society was eventually expelled from college premises in 1794 and met instead at the Exhibition Rooms in William Street—see Dagg, *College Historical Society*, 71–3.

[10] *Universal Mag.*, I. 559; *FJ*, 11 June 1789.

[11] TCD, MS Mun. Soc. Hist. 6 fo. 293, also 147, 166, 168; Dagg, *College Historical Society*, 60–72.

[12] Tone (Dickason) MSS, Tone's degree certificate dated Feb 1789.

[13] Colum Kenny, 'The Exclusion of Catholics from the Legal Profession in Ireland, 1537–1829', *IHS*, XXV (1987), 327–57.

[14] King's Inns, Dublin, Admission Papers, T. W. Tone, Middle Temple certificate, oath and Memorial; Edward Keane, Beryl P. Phair, and Thomas U. Sadleir, *King's Inns Admission*

Papers 1607–1867 (Dublin, 1982), viii–x; and King's Inns, Benchers' Minute Book 3–5, for admission requirements. Catholics were not admitted to the Irish bar till 1793 and continued to be frowned upon thereafter.

[15] Gilbert, *History of Dublin*, I. 136–7, 144–5, 182–3; Maxwell, *Dublin under the Georges*, 72.

[16] See, e.g., E. B. Mitford, *The Life of Lord Redesdale* (London, 1939), 59.

[17] Curran, *Sketches of the Irish Bar*, I. 100–11, 279–93; Phillips, *Curran and his Contemporaries*, 333.

[18] Phillips, *Curran and his Contemporaries*, 359–61; Sheil, *Sketches, Legal and Political*, I. 7, also 92–8, 212.

[19] Curran, *Sketches of the Irish Bar*, I. 80, 118.

[20] Sheil, *Sketches, Legal and Political*, I. 200; F. Elrington Ball, *The Judges in Ireland, 1221–1921*, 2 vols. (London, 1926), II. 163–9, 177; O'Flanagan, *Lives of the Lord Chancellors of Ireland*, II. 325; *FJ*, 2 July 1789: R. B. McDowell, *Ireland in the Age of Imperialism and Revolution* (Oxford, 1979), 64.

[21] F. MacDermot, *Theobald Wolfe Tone and His Times*, rev. edn. (Tralee, 1969), 24–5.

[22] PRONI, T. 2541/IB1/4/26, Geo. Knox to Abercorn, 20 July 1793.

[23] Sheil, *Sketches, Legal and Political*, I. 200n.

[24] *Life*, I. 138–9 and II. 373; Ball, *Judges in Ireland*, II. 171–7, 180; Curran, *Sketches of the Irish Bar*, I. 80; W. J. Fitzpatrick, *Irish Wits and Worthies* (Dublin, 1873), 13; Plunket, *Life, Letters and Speeches*, I. 46–7.

[25] *Life*, II. 309 and 468; O'Flanagan, *Lives of the Lord Chancellors*, II. 156–283; *FJ*, 28 Apr, 19 and 23 June 1789; *Poems by the late Edward Lysaght Esq.* (Dublin, 1811), 4; C. Litton Falkiner, *Studies in Irish History and Biography* (London, 1902), 101–54.

[26] TCD, MS 3805/11v; *Life*, I. 138.

[27] *Life of Curran*, I. 196–201, 281–95; Phillips, *Curran and His Contemporaries*, 144–50.

[28] Curran, *Sketches of the Irish Bar*, I. 112–13.

[29] *Saunders's News Letter*, 27 Apr 1793; Curran, *Sketches of the Irish Bar*, I. 109–12.

[30] Curran, *Sketches of the Irish Bar*, I. 216–17; *FJ*, 30 July and 8 Aug 1789; SPOI, 620/20/33/4, journal entry of Thomas Russell on the expense of an assize town.

[31] *Life*, I. 29; Campbell, *Lives of the Lord Chancellors*, V. 232–4; Sheil, *Sketches, Legal and Political*, II. 116–17.

[32] Curran, *Sketches of the Irish Bar*, I. 276; Tone (Dickason) MSS, Tone to Dick Sharkey, undated (containing also remnants of rough pencilled accounts); TCD, MS 3805/8–9, 15–16, Tone's accounts for this first circuit.

[33] Duman, *Judicial Bench*, 55–6.

[34] Barrington, *Personal Sketches*, I. 279; TCD, MS 3365/66v.

[35] *Quarterly Rev.*, XXXVI (1827), 77. Grattan suffered similar gibes; see, e.g., *FJ*, 11 Feb 1789, also 14 Oct 1789, general attack on unsuccessful barristers.

[36] *Life*, I. 138; Sheil, *Sketches, Legal and Political*, I. 41; H. MacDougall, *Sketches of Irish Political Characters of the Present Day* (London, 1799), 139, 249; Campbell, *Lives of the Lord Chancellors*, V. 233–4.

[37] TCD, MS 2046/6v.

[38] Fuller, 'The Tones: Father and Son', 93–101; see also *FJ*, 3 June 1790, on conditions in debtors' prison.

[39] PROI, Betham Abstracts: Prerogative Wills, Bet. 1/69/89, Jonathan Tone of Cassumsize, Co. Kildare, abstract of will dated 20 Sept 1792, naming Tone, his uncle Matthew and aunt Mary Dunbavin as beneficiaries— the original was destroyed in 1921. *Life*, I. 182.

[40] TCD, MS 2046/18v.

[41] Tone (Dickason) MSS. Tone to Sharkey, undated. 'Master Brooke' is possibly a reference to Brooks's club in London.

[42] See *FJ*, 15 June 1789, on the costs of a Chancery suit; Sheil, *Sketches, Legal and Political*, I. 149.

[43] *FJ*, 23 June, 22 Oct, 7 Nov 1789.

[44] TCD, MS, 2046/19, 3806/5–6; Reg. Deeds, 341/388/228952 and 236/228/154381, for the value of the properties in 1781 and 1765 respectively.

[45] TCD, MS 2046/19, omitted from *Life*, I. 30. Reg. Deeds, 419/287/273989, deed making over the lands to Jonathan Tone, 30 Jan 1790.

⁴⁶ TCD, MS 2046/12, omitted from *Life*, I. 22.
⁴⁷ TCD, MS 2046/25–6; RIA, MS 24. K. 53, Matilda to Burrowes, 27 Dec 1816.

Chapter 5

¹ Falkiner, *Studies in Irish History and Biography*, 108. In 1789 110 of the 300 Irish MPs were placemen; see Denis Kennedy, 'The Irish Whigs 1789–1795' (Univ. of Toronto Ph.D. thesis, 1971), 10–12. See also A. P. W. Malcomson, 'The Parliamentary Traffic of This Country', in *Penal Era and Golden Age: Essays in Irish History, 1690–1800*, ed. Thomas Bartlett and D. W. Hayton (Belfast, 1979), 137–61. But see David Large, 'The Irish House of Commons in 1769', *IHS*, XI (1958), 25–7, for the important role of the independents.
² Malcomson, *John Foster*, xix.
³ M. G. R. O'Brien, 'The Exercise of Legislative Power in Ireland, 1782–1800' (Cambridge Univ. Ph.D. thesis, 1983), 100–86.
⁴ Grattan, *Life and Times*, III. 362, also 343–6; *FJ*, 5–17 Feb 1789.
⁵ *FJ*, 12 Feb 1789.
⁶ *Life*, I. 138; Nicholas Robinson, 'Caricature and Regency Crisis: An Irish perspective', *Eighteenth-Century Ireland*, I (1986), 157–76.
⁷ *FJ*, 19 and 28 Feb, 5 Mar 1789; *Lord Shannon's Letters to His Son: A calendar of letters written by the 2nd Earl of Shannon to his son, Viscount Boyle, 1790–1802*, ed. Esther Hewitt (PRONI, 1982), xliii–xliv.
⁸ Grattan, *Life and Times*, III. 434–7.
⁹ *FJ*, 14, 28 Apr 1789, 15 May 1790; McDowell, *Ireland in the Age of Imperialism and Revolution*, 345–6.
¹⁰ With a few exceptions the Whig Club was dominated by the nobility and gentry and had no popular base; see Kennedy, 'Irish Whigs', 76–88.
¹¹ TCD, MS 2041/30–31, jottings on the Dublin police.
¹² Francis Plowden, *An Historical Review of the State of Ireland*, 5 vols. (Philadelphia, 1806), [hereinafter *History of Ireland*] III. 275–6; *FJ*, 24, 30 July 1789, 19–26 Nov 1790.
¹³ It was he and Jebb who had proposed the vote of thanks to the author of a composition signed 'Whig', read to the Historical Society on the evening of 24 June; see TCD, MS Mun. Soc. Hist., 6. 126.
¹⁴ TCD, MS 2046/19v.
¹⁵ Gilbert, *History of Dublin*, III. 134–5.
¹⁶ TCD, MS 2046/21v; *Life*, I. 32.
¹⁷ *Parl. Reg.*, X. 77–80, 240–60; *FJ*, 18 Feb 1790; N.D. Atkinson, 'Sir Laurence Parsons, Second Earl of Rosse, 1758–1841' (Dublin Univ. Ph.D. thesis, 1962), 110–18; PRONI, A calendar of the papers of the Earl of Rosse Birr Castle County Offaly, 13–20, F/13.
¹⁸ W. E. H. Lecky, *A History of Ireland in the Eighteenth Century*, new edn., 5 vols. (London, 1892), III. 5–7, 8n.
¹⁹ Cited in Atkinson, 'Sir Laurence Parsons', 119.
²⁰ TCD, MS 2046/19v.
²¹ *A Review of the Conduct of Administration During the Seventh Session of Parliament Addressed to the Constitutional Electors and Free People of Ireland...By an Independent Irish Whig* (Dublin, 1790). A shortened version appears in *Life*, I. 299–323. See also TCD, MS 2041/18, his exaggerated reverence for the 1782 'constitution'.
²² *FJ*, 10 Apr 1790.
²³ *Life*, I. 30.
²⁴ [Peter Burrowes], *Plain Arguments in Defence of the People's Absolute Dominion over the Constitution in which the Question of Roman Catholic Emancipation is Fully Considered* (Dublin, 1784).
²⁵ John Dunn, *Political Obligation in its Historical Context: Essays in political theory* (Cambridge, 1980), 53–77; Caroline Robbins, *The Eighteenth-Century Commonwealthman* (Cambridge, Mass., 1959), 137–43; David Berman, 'Enlightenment and Counter-Enlightenment in Irish Philosophy', *Archiv für Geschichte der philosophie*, LXIV, no. 2 (1982), 148–9; J. C. D. Clark, *Revolution and Rebellion: State and Society in England in the Seventeenth and Eighteenth Centuries* (Cambridge, 1986), 46–50, 323; Ashcraft, *Revolutionary Politics and Locke's 'Two Treatises'*, particularly ch. 8 and pp. 183–4.

[26] *Life*, I. 394–5.

[27] See J. W. Gough, *John Locke's Political Philosophy*, 2nd edn. (Oxford, 1973), 154–92.

[28] *Life*, I. 152; Colin Bonwick, 'Joseph Priestley: Emigrant and Jeffersonian', *Enlightenment and Dissent*, II (1983), 3–22; Marc Philp, 'Rational Religion and Political Radicalism', ibid., IV (1985), 35–46; John Seed, 'Gentlemen Dissenters: The Social and Political Meanings of Rational Dissent in the 1770s and 1780s', *Hist. Jnl*, XXVIII, no. 2 (1985), 299–325; also Clark, *Revolution and Rebellion*, 323–5—though see Joanna Innes, 'Jonathan Clark, Social History and England's "Ancien Régime"', *Past and Present*, no. 115 (May 1987), esp. 186–94. For Tone's admiration of Cromwell, see Tone (Dickason) MSS, Tone to Matilda, 31 Aug 1797.

[29] See Michael Durey, 'Thomas Paine's Apostles: Radical Émigrés and the Triumph of Jeffersonian Republicanism', *WMQ*, XLIV (1987), 681–8, particularly 675–8; J. G. A. Pocock, *The Machiavellian Moment: Florentine Political Thought and the Atlantic Republican Tradition* (Princeton, N.J. 1975), chs. xiv–xv.

[30] SPOI, 620/15/6/10, Thomas Russell's journal, 9 Apr [1791]; *Charlemont MSS. The Manuscripts and Correspondence of James, first Earl of Charlemont*, HMC, 13th report, app. pt. viii, vol II (London, 1894), 125.

[31] *Charlemont MSS*, II. 114–21; *FJ*, 3 June 1790; *The Autobiography of Archibald Hamilton Rowan*, ed. William H. Drummond (IUP repr., Shannon, 1972), 149–52; 'Forbes Letters', ed. T. J. Kiernan, *Anal. Hib.*, no. 8 (Mar 1938), 361–2.

[32] TCD, MS 3805/20v; *Life*, I. 31; for the hearing of the case see *FJ*, 3 June, 3 July 1790, 10 and 19 Feb 1791. See also McDowell, *Ireland in the Age of Imperialism and Revolution*, 118–19.

[33] *Life*, I. 37.

[34] TCD, MS 2041/1v.

[35] TCD, MS 2041/8v.

[36] *FJ*, 8–15 May 1790; *Universal Mag.*, III (May 1790), 496; Grattan, *Life and Times*, III. 460–3.

[37] *Life of Curran*, I. 287–95; Grattan, *Life and Times*, IV. 1–25; O'Flanagan, *Lives of the Lord Chancellors*, II. 204–8; *FJ*, 19 May, 17 June, 24 July 1790; *Charlemont MSS*, II. 127–9.

[38] *Life*, I. 138–40; *FJ*, 16 Oct 1790.

[39] *FJ*, 17 May, 1 and 22 June 1790.

[40] TCD, MS 2046/22; *Life*, I. 33.

[41] *FJ*, 1–6 July 1790. The policy of entering a war at England's command was unpopular; see *DEP*, 7 and 12 Apr 1790.

[42] Though the Whig Club was not unanimous in supporting the war; see *FJ*, 12 Oct 1790.

[43] Two particular sore spots were the monopoly of the East India Company and Ireland's inability to re-export colonial goods to England. Both were partly remedied in 1793—see *A New History of Ireland*, vol. IV: *Eighteenth-Century Ireland 1691–1800*, ed. T. W. Moody and W. E. Vaughan (Oxford, 1986), 192–3 and 334–5.

[44] *Spanish War: An Enquiry How Far Ireland is Bound of Right to Embark in the Impending Contest on the Side of Great Britain* (Dublin, 1790); *Life*, I. 325–40. The pamphlet is signed 'Hibernicus', possibly in response to a letter to the *FJ* (11 May), supporting the war and signed 'Merus Hibernicus'.

[45] TCD, MS 2046/22.

[46] *Life*, I. 560–3. I have not been able to find this letter published in the newspapers of the day.

[47] Tone's son claims the entire printing was bought up by the government; *Life*, I. iv.

Chapter 6

[1] Cited in Gilbert, *History of Dublin*, II. 30.

[2] McNeill, *Mary Ann McCracken*, 72–3.

[3] SPOI 620/50/2, Memoir of a conversation between Revd F. Archer and Thomas Russell at Kilmainham, 3 Oct 1803; Séamus N. MacGiolla Easpaig, *Tomás Ruiséil* (Dublin, 1957), 17–18. Dr C. J. Woods kindly made available to me a translation of this work.

[4] TCD, MS 873/654, 668–70, 676, notes and correspondence of Russell's nephew, J. A. Russell, in 1843.

[5] TCD, MS 868/2/124, [John Russell] to Thomas Russell, 3 May 1795; see also Matilda's very critical letter of 11 Sept 1796 in SPOI, 620/25/136.

[6] TCD, MS 868/1/184; Russell's journals are scattered through TCD, Sirr MS 868/1, and SPOI, Rebellion Papers 620/15, 20, 21, with various other writings in 620/53–4, all in his almost illegible scrawl. Dr C. J. Woods is preparing an edition of the journals for publication.

[7] PRO, H.O. 100/114/123, information on a conversation with Russell, enclosed in Wickham to John King, 24 Oct 1803; TCD, MS 868/1/21–3, 52–3 and SPOI, 620/21/23/102–12 on the Moravians.

[8] PRONI, D. 591/449, Mrs McTier to Drennan, 16 Nov 1793.

[9] See, e.g., SPOI, 620/20/33/68, entry for [July 1793].

[10] *The Works of Jonathan Swift, DD*, 9 vols. (London, 1755), vol. II, pt. ii, 156–65. One of the *Martin Scriblerus* series, the *Memoir* has also been attributed to Pope and Arbuthnot, with help—according to G.A. Aitken, *The Life and Works of John Arbuthnot* (Oxford, 1892), 59—from John Gay.

[11] *Life*, II. 223.

[12] MacGiolla Easpaig, *Tomás Ruiséil*, 19–25; Fuller, 'The Tones: Father and Son', 96.

[13] SPOI, 620/16/3, Tone to Russell, 1 Sept 1795. This letter has been published in the *Irish Press*, 4 Oct 1955.

[14] TCD, MS 2046/26–26v; *Life*, I. 34–5.

[15] *FJ*, 27 July, 10 Aug and 2 Sept 1790; Maxwell, *Dublin under the Georges*, 263.

[16] TCD, MS 2046/28, also 3085/11v–12 for furnishing details of the cottage.

[17] Tone (Dickason) MSS, 'Fugitive Pieces by William Tone (and others), 1790'.

[18] TCD, MS 2046/27v–30; *Life*, I. 35–6.

[19] Tone (Dickason) MSS, Tone to Matilda, 20 July 1797; *The Letters of Wolfe Tone*, ed. Bulmer Hobson (Dublin, [1921]), 19.

[20] TCD, MS 3085/12–15.

[21] PRO, H.O. 100/32/10–11 and 100/33/143–4, the Lord Lieutenant's letters on the crisis, 3 Jan and 17 Oct 1791; *FJ*, 22 July and 10 Aug 1790, comments on the fate of the Spanish-American colonies.

[22] *The Journals of Captain James Cook on his Voyages of Discovery*, ed. J. G. Beaglehole, 5 vols. (Hakluyt Society, London, 1955–7), III. 264–7, 473–91, 571–632, and Tone's notes from this in TCD, MS 28v–30 and *Life*, I. 538–9.

[23] John Lynch, 'British Policy and Spanish America, 1783–88', *Jnl Latin American Studies*, I (1969), 1–30. On Digges see *The John Carroll Papers*, ed. Thomas O'Brien, 3 vols. (Notre Dame, Ind., 1976), II. 25–6. For Russell's and Tone's friendship with Digges see SPOI, 620/15/6/3/7–8, 107 and *Life*, I. 141, 143–52, and II. 510.

[24] TCD, MS 3086/28 and 10, 17–30, the project, correspondence and notes, carefully transcribed by Tone into a notebook; Tone (Dickason) MSS, originals of Richmond's, Scrope Bernard's and Grenville's letters; all the foregoing reproduced in *Life*, I. 519–42; see also 36–8.

[25] *Universal Mag.*, IV (July–Dec 1790), 489; *FJ*, 13 Nov, also 6 Nov and 28 Oct 1790. See M. J. MacManus, 'When Wolfe Tone Wrote a Novel', *Irish Press*, Christmas No., 1934, also Francis O'Kelly, 'Wolfe Tone's Novel', *Irish Book Lover* (Mar–Apr 1935), 47–8.

[26] *FJ*, 18 Nov 1790, also 10 Feb 1791.

[27] TCD, MS 2046/50.

[28] *Life*, I. 58–9.

[29] Tone (Dickason) MSS, Tone to Matilda, undated letter from Dublin, and the edited version in *Life*, I. 153.

[30] TCD, MS Mun. Soc. Hist. 6 fos. 286 and 293.

[31] SPOI, 620/15/6/104, 107–8.

[32] Morgan, *O'Briens and O'Flahertys*, III. 75; Rowan, *Autobiography*, 139; Colin P. Hill, 'William Drennan and the Radical Movement for Irish Reform 1779–1794', 2 vols. (Univ. of Dublin, M. Litt thesis, 1967).

[33] *Life*, I. 546–7.

[34] Hill, 'William Drennan', I. 74 and 79.

[35] Burrowes, in *Plain Arguments* had made the point in 1784.

[36] See Russell's notes on the Catholic issue in SPOI, 620/15/6/3/9, 24, 101–6. Tone's essays and jottings concerning the club are in TCD, MS 2041/2–20v and *Life*, I. 38–9, 545–59.

[37] See ch. 8, sec. I.

[38] RIA, MS 23. K. 53, Tone to Russell, 9 [July] 1791.

[39] Kennedy, 'Irish Whigs', 226–9. Such an opening of the political system was fundamental to Rational Dissent.

[40] See, e.g., *Charlemont MSS*, II. 119–21; and see ch. 7 n. 15.

[41] SPOI, 620/20/33/3–4, Russell's journal entry Mar 1793; *The Drennan Letters, 1776–1819*, ed. D. A. Chart (Belfast, 1931), 168.

[42] PRO, H.O. 100/33/81–2, Westmorland to [Dundas], 11 July 1791, enclosing, 91–3, copy of Tone's resolutions and letter.

[43] Falkiner, *Studies in Irish History and Biography*, 131, suggests as much.

Chapter 7

[1] See PRONI, D. 456/6 [Revd William Bruce] to Drennan, 19 Nov 1791, for a good e.g. of this. Also Marianne Elliott, *Watchmen in Sion: The Protestant Idea of Liberty* (Belfast, 1985).

[2] *A New History of Ireland*, vol. III: *Early Modern Ireland, 1534–1691*, ed. T. W. Moody, F. X. Martin and F. J. Byrne (Oxford, 1976), 13, citing Arthur Young's figures. By a 1704 act a Catholic could not buy land or lease it for longer than 31 years, and on his death it was divided among the heirs. This act, however, was generally evaded.

[3] Thomas Wyse, *Historical Sketches of the Late Catholic Association*, 2 vols. (London, 1829), I. 89–90, and Sheil, *Sketches, Legal and Political*, I. 153–4.

[4] S. J. Connolly, 'Religion and History', *Irish Econ. and Soc. Hist.*, X (1883), 66–80, and his 'The Penal Laws', unpub. paper delivered to the Fifth Conference of Irish Historians in Britain, Liverpool, Apr 1986. Louis [L. M.] Cullen, 'Catholics under the Penal Laws', *Eighteenth-Century Ireland*, I (1986), 23–36; id., *Emergence of Modern Ireland*, notably ch. 2, and his two chapters in *A New History of Ireland*, IV. 123–93. Lecky thought the laws in England more 'crushing' and less easily evaded. See his *History of England*, new imp., 7 vols. (London, 1913), I. 348.

[5] Patrick Rogers, *The Irish Volunteers and Catholic Emancipation, 1778–1793* (London, 1934), 58; PRONI, T.1722, John Byrne, *An Impartial Account of the Late Disturbances in the County of Armagh* (Dublin, 1792), particularly p. 8.

[6] Rogers, *Irish Volunteers*, 17–18; SPOI, 620/19/23, provides a good example of Catholic Committee submissiveness as late as Mar 1791.

[7] R. Dudley Edwards, ed., 'The Minute Book of the Catholic Committee, 1773–92', *Arch. Hib*, IX (1942), 3–172, and notably p. 40; *New History of Ireland*, IV. 201–2; M. Wall, 'Catholic Loyalty to the King and Pope in Eighteenth-Century Ireland', *Irish Cath. Hist. Comm. Procs.* (1961), 17–24; Eamonn O'Flaherty, 'The Catholic Question in Ireland, 1774–1793' (Nat. Univ. Ire., M.A. thesis, 1981).

[8] C. Litton Falkiner, *Essays Relating to Ireland, Biographical, Historical and Topographical* (London, 1909), 78.

[9] Rogers, *Irish Volunteers*, 64–6, 92–116; Hill, 'William Drennan' I. 66–9; *BNL*, 30 Sept 1783.

[10] Edwards, 'Minute Book of the Catholic Committee', 87; Grattan, *Life*, III. 116–22; Rogers, *Irish Volunteers*, 13–15, shows conflict between Catholic aristocrats and middle-class members of the Committee from the outset, the former preferring to sabotage the campaign rather than admit the leadership of their social inferiors.

[11] *Life*, I. 351.

[12] William Todd Jones, *A Letter to the Electors of the Borough of Lisburn* (Dublin, 1784); Patrick Rogers, 'A Protestant Pioneer of Catholic Emancipation', *Down and Connor Hist. Soc. Jnl*, VI (1934), 14–22.

[13] [Burrowes], *Plain Arguments*. R. B. McDowell, *Irish Public Opinion, 1750–1800* (London, 1944), 97–118.

[14] [William Drennan], *An Irish Helot Addresses Himself to the Seven Northern Counties who were not Represented in the Late Civil Convention, by Orellana* (Dublin, 1785—first pub., *BNL*, Oct 1784) [hereinafter *Letters of Orellana*], Letter V, 40; Hill, 'William Drennan', I. 78–84. On Charlemont see *Historical Collections relative to the Town of Belfast: from the Earliest Period to the Union with Great Britain*, ed. [H. Joy] (Belfast, 1817) [hereinafter *History of Belfast*], 308–10.

[15] [Drennan], *Letters of Orellana*, 39; McDowell, *Ireland in the Age of Imperialism and Revolution*, 315–26; Rogers, *Irish Volunteers*, 181; *Parl. Reg.*, III. 37, 43–85.

[16] O'Flanagan, *Lives of the Lord Chancellors*, II. 174–6.

[17] Hill, 'William Drennan', I. 86.

[18] J. S. Donnelly Jnr., 'A Contemporary Account of the Rightboy Movement: The John Barter Bennett Manuscript', *Cork Hist. and Arch. Soc. Jnl* LXXXVIII (1983), 1–50, also his 'The Rightboy Movement, 1785–8', *Studia Hib.* (1977–8), 120–202.

[19] Rowan, *Autobiography*, 126–33.

[20] Cullen, *Emergence of Modern Ireland*, 55–7; Marianne Elliott, *Partners in Revolution: The United Irishmen and France* (New Haven and London, 1982), 19–20, and id. 'The Origins and Transformation of Early Irish Republicanism', *Intl. Rev. of Social Hist.*, XXIII (1978), 413–15; A. T. Q. Stewart, *The Narrow Ground: Aspects of Ulster, 1609–1969* (London, 1979), 40–1.

[21] See, e.g., *NS*, 1–5 Dec 1792; Elliott, *Watchmen in Sion*, 23–4.

[22] Quoted in J. S. Reid and W. D. Killen, *The History of the Presbyterian Church in Ireland*, 3 vols. (Belfast, 1867), II. 31.

[23] PRONI, T. 3229/2/7, Cooke to Auckland, 6 Apr 1795; Peter Brooke, 'Controversies in Ulster Presbyterianism, 1790–1836' (Cambridge Univ. Ph.D. thesis, 1980), 29–30; W. Drennan, *Fugitive Pieces in Verse and Prose* (Belfast, 1815), 189–209. *Drennan Letters*, 72; *FJ*, 4 Jan 1792; *Parl. Reg.*, XII, 163–73, Grattan's speech; McDowell, *Irish Public Opinion*, 183–4. PRO, H.O. 100/34/45–49, 217v, 267 and 100/36/259, various correspondence on this point, Jan–Dec. 1792.; DDA, MS 161/5/79–81, Cardinal Antonelli to Troy, Apr–June 1792, expressing Rome's distaste for any alliance with the Presbyterians.

[24] Robbins, *Eighteenth-Century Commonwealthman*, 167–74; and see gradual recognition of this in *History of Belfast*, 274, 294–5, 297. See full discussion in Peter Brooke, *Ulster Presbyterianism: The Historical Perspective, 1610–1970* (Dublin, 1987), 81–92, 104, 112–29.

[25] *History of Belfast*, 297–8, reporting the Belfast Town Meeting of 8 July 1784; but see the Revd William Steel Dickson's sermon to the Synod of Ulster, June 1781, in *A Narrative of the Confinement and Exile of William Steel Dickson, DD* (Dublin, 1812), App., 1–30; Brooke, 'Controversies', 2–4, 20–1; McDowell, *Irish Public Opinion*, 105, 120–2.

[26] Cf. *Life*, I. 149–50, objections of the Revd William Bruce, Oct 1791.

[27] PRO, H.O. 100/34/3–4, MS letter headed 'A letter to a R.C. Gentleman from a dissenter of consideration and great alacrity', 10 Aug 1791.

[28] *FJ*, 12 Nov 1789, 14–19 Jan, 27 May 1790.

[29] *Charlemont MSS*, 96.

[30] H. Joy and W. Bruce, *Belfast Politics,... in the years 1792 and 1793* (Belfast, 1794), 341–2; *History of Belfast*, 334–42; SPOI, Westmorland MSS, I, 32; *Charlemont MSS*, II. 109–10, 114–22.

[31] *Charlemont MSS*, II. 119–20; *History of Belfast*, 343–8; Madden, *United Irishmen*, 2nd ser., I. 76.

[32] SPOI, Westmorland MSS, I. 32.

[33] [Drennan], *Letters of Orellana*, Letter V, p. 38. See also Brooke, 'Controversies', 24–5.

[34] SPOI, 620/19/12, Belfast Constitutional Compact, 1 Oct 1790. David W. Miller, 'Presbyterianism and "Modernization" in Ulster', *Past and Present*, no. 80 (Aug 1978), 80–1.

Chapter 8

[1] *FJ*, 14 May 1788, 24 Oct 1789, 1 Mar and 31 July 1790, and 15 Mar 1791.

[2] PRO, H.O. 100/33/81–2, Westmorland to Dundas, 11 July 1791; Lecky, *History of England*, VI. 46.

[3] See M. Wall, 'The Rise of a Catholic Middle Class in Eighteenth-Century Ireland', *IHS*, XI (1958), 91–115; Dickson, *New Foundations*, 120–1; Denis Gwynn, *John Keogh: The Pioneer of Catholic Emancipation* (Dublin, 1930); Francis Finegan, 'Was John Keogh an Informer?', *Studies: an Irish Quarterly Review*, XXXIX (1950), 75–86; *Dropmore MSS. The MSS of J. B. Fortescue Esq., preserved at Dropmore*, 10 vols. (London, 1892–4), II. 337, former Lord Lieutenant Buckingham's assessment of Keogh.

[4] *Life*, I. 63.

[5] Gilbert, *History of Dublin*, I. 354–5.

[6] O'Flaherty, 'Catholic Question in Ireland', 108–10; R. B. McDowell, 'The Personnel of the Dublin Society of United Irishmen, 1791–4', *IHS*, II. (1940–1), 12–53; SPOI, 620/19/22, 73, 107.

[7] Edwards, 'Minute Book of the Catholic Committee', 116–25.

[8] PRO, H.O. 100/34/33, Troy to Hobart, 29 Nov 1791; *FJ*, 28–30 Oct 1790, and SPOI, 620/19/23 for the deferential nature of Catholic addresses; and PRO, H.O. 100/33/97–8 [July 1791] for a characteristic response.

[9] See PRO, H.O. 100/33/235–41, 100/34/1–2; SPOI, 620/19/45; and Edwards, 'Minute Book of the Catholic Committee', 125 ff., for a full account of these proceedings.

[10] Grattan, *Life and Times*, IV. 40–1 (his son has some difficulty explaining this); *FJ*, 14 July 1791; Edwards, 'Minute Book of the Catholic Committee', 135.

[11] SPOI, 620/19/45, General Committee of the Roman Catholics, 14 Jan 1792.

[12] Russell's journal, SPOI, 620/15/6/3/98–106; MacGiolla Easpaig, *Tomás Ruiséil*, 35–6.

[13] *Charlemont MSS*, II. 136–7; Hill, 'William Drennan', I. 20–1.

[14] Russell's journal, SPOI, 620/15/6/3/19–20 and 23; also TCD, MS 868/1/40, and MS 873/70, Mary Ann McCracken on the impact of Paine on Ulster. McDowell, *Irish Public Opinion*, 164 and ch. ix generally. Ray B. Browne, 'The Paine-Burke Controversy in Eighteenth-Century Irish Popular Songs', in R. B. Browne, W. J. Roscelli and P. Loftus, eds., *The Celtic Cross* (Purdue, Ind., 1964), 80–97.

[15] *Drennan Letters*, 54; PRONI, T. 2541/IB1/2/27, Thomas Knox to Lord Abercorn, 17 [July] 1791; SPOI, 620/19/17, R. Johnston to J. Lees, 26 Oct 1790.

[16] PRONI, D. 591/303 and 305, McTier–Drennan correspondence, 9 and 11 July 1791; Hill, 'William Drennan', I. 22–33; *Drennan Letters*, 54–97; SPOI, 620/19/24, Drennan's printed proposal for a new society; PRO, H.O. 100/33/81–2, Westmorland to [Dundas], 11 July 1791, enclosing both Drennan's document and Tone's resolutions.

[17] MacDermot, *Theobald Wolfe Tone*, 59–62; Dunne, *Theobald Wolfe Tone, Colonial Outsider*, 12; MacGiolla Easpaig, *Tomás Ruiséil*, 40–9; A. T. Q. Stewart, *The Narrow Ground*, 102 and id., '"A Stable and Unseen Power": Dr William Drennan and the Origins of the United Irishmen', in *Essays Presented to Michael Roberts*, ed. John Bossy and Peter Jupp (Belfast, 1976), 80–92; TCD, MS 873/669, J. A. Russell to Dr John Gray, 16–22 Apr 1843; Madden, *United Irishmen*, 2nd ser., I (1843), 93, claims Tone as founder, but by 1860 he is denying this (see 2nd edn., 1st ser., 222, also his *History of Irish Periodical Literature from the end of the 17th to the middle of the 18th century*, 2 vols. (London, 1867), II. 227). For early claims that Tone was founder of the United Irish Society, see W. J. MacNeven, *Pieces of Irish History* (NY, 1807), 17.

[18] See *BNL*, 30 Sept, *FJ*, 10 Sept, 6 and 11 Oct 1791; O'Flaherty, 'Catholic Question in Ireland', 117–18; and PRO, H.O. 100/34/3–13, for talk of some alliance. Tone (Dickason) MSS, 'a copy of the association [UI] paper', 16 Sept 1791, shows a test for the Society already being devised before its inauguration.

[19] PRONI, D. 591/307, Drennan to McTier [5 July 1791].

[20] Unlike Drennan's declaration, Tone's resolutions are not printed; see PRO, H.O. 100/33/81–2, op. cit., and 91–3, copy of Tone's resolutions and covering letter; also RIA, MS 23 k. 53, Tone to Russell, 9 July 1791. *FJ*, 26–28 July, and *BNL* 19–22 July, print the Declaration of the Belfast Volunteers.

[21] TCD, MS 2046/41v; *Life*, I. 51–2.

[22] [T. W. Tone] *An Argument on Behalf of the Catholics of Ireland* (Dublin, 1791); *Life*, I. 341–66. Two further printings were ordered by the United Irish Society, (Belfast, 1791) and (Dublin, 1792). PRO, H.O. 100/34/41–2, unsigned, undated letter [Oct 1791] from a Belfast United Irishman to a Catholic friend. MacNeven, *Pieces of Irish History*, 15. The pamphlet is advertised in *BNL*, 9–13 Sept 1791. C. J. Woods, 'The Contemporary Editions of Tone's *Argument on Behalf of the Catholics*', *Irish Booklore*, II. no. 2 (1976), 217–26.

[23] See, e.g., Cullen, *Emergence of Modern Ireland*, 236; Marianne Elliott, 'Ireland', in *Nationalism in the Age of the French Revolution*, ed. Otto Dann and John Dinwiddy (London, 1988), 74, 78–9.

[24] PRO, H.O. 100/34/41–2, unsigned letter [Oct 1791].

[25] *Drennan Letters*, 59–60. Rumours to this effect were indeed circulating among the Catholics; see, e.g., *The O'Conors of Connaught: An Historical Memoir*, ed. C. O. O'Conor Don (Dublin, 1891), 300.

[26] O'Conor Don, *O'Conors of Connaught*, 301–2.

[27] *Declaration of the Catholic Society of Dublin* (Dublin, 1791). It was reprinted in *Tracts on Catholic Affairs* (Dublin, 1791), which also carries the resolutions of the United Irish Society and the letter of the Belfast Volunteers to the Catholics of Jamestown and Elphin, 4 Oct 1791. McKenna's declaration appears in PRO, H.O. 100/34/15–21 as *Declaration of the Society Instituted for the Purpose of Promoting Unanimity amongst Irishmen, and Removing Religious Pre-*

judices; also in Plowden, *History of Ireland*, III. App. no lxxiv, 156–61.
    [28] PRO, H.O. 100/31/318–9, Westmorland to Grenville, 6 Oct 1791, and 100/31/318–9, draft Whitehall letter to Westmorland, 26 Dec 1791; ISPO, 620/19/33, account of a meeting between the Catholics and Hobart, 26 Nov 1791; *Dropmore MSS*, II. 213–22.
    [29] Hill, 'William Drennan', I. 82, 96 and 99.
    [30] *Life*, I. 179.
    [31] SPOI, 620/19/28, resolutions of a general meeting of the Volunteer companies of Belfast, 4 Oct 1791, and see n. 26 above.
    [32] PRO, H.O. 100/34/10, [Sinclair] to [Russell], 4 Oct 1791, and 13, [Russell] to [?], 8 Oct 1791.
    [33] PRO, H.O. 100/31/209–12 and 227, Russell's resignation from and sale of his commission, June 1791.
    [34] PRO, H.O. 100/34/9, printed prospectus for the *National Journal*, 4 Oct 1791; *Drennan Letters*, 60–1; Brian Inglis, *The Freedom of the Press in Ireland 1784–1841* (London, 1954), 98–9; *DEP*, 7 Jan and 24 Mar 1792.
    [35] SPOI, 620/19/25–26, list of subscribers to the *Northern Star*, and resolutions of the 19 Sept meeting, also 620/19/42, replies from potential subscribers. Charles Dickson, *Revolt in the North: Antrim and Down in 1798* (Dublin, 1960), 192–4; W. T. Latimer, *Ulster Biographies Relating Chiefly to the Rebellion of 1798* (Belfast, 1897), 36–41; John J. Marshall, 'Old Belfast Signboards. With some notes on their Social, Historical and Literary Connections', *UJA*, XII (1906), 90–4, 110–17; Madden, *United Irishmen*, 2nd ser. I. 74–5, on Neilson; F. J. Bigger, 'The Northern Star', *UJA*, II (1895), 33–5.
    [36] PRO, H.O. 100/34/50, printed handbill *To the People*, announcing the *Northern Star*, 18 Nov 1791; SPOI, 620/19/40, agreement with the printer John Tisdall, Dec 1791.
    [37] *Drennan Letters*, 61.
    [38] *Life*, I. 53.
    [39] *Charlemont MSS*, II. 160.

Chapter 9

    [1] *History of Belfast*, 379; *New History of Ireland*, IV. 257.
    [2] RIA, MS 23. K. 53, Tone to Russell, 9 July 1791.
    [3] Tone's journal dates are very often a day out, as in this instance when he notes Wednesday.
    [4] A. Young, *A Tour in Ireland* (London, 1783), 126; *The Journal of the Revd John Wesley*, 4 vols. (London, 1895), II. 361, and IV. 120; W. Seward, *Topographica Hibernica* (Dublin, 1795), 'Belfast'; *New History of Ireland*, IV. 263; Joy and Bruce, *Belfast Politics*, 96.
    [5] *Life*, I. 143–4, 149; *BNL*, 21–25 Oct 1791.
    [6] *BNL*, 25–28 Oct 1791; *FJ*, 17 Oct 1791; J. C. Beckett and R. E. Glasscock, eds., *Belfast: The Origin and Growth of an Industrial City* (London, 1967); George Benn, *A History of the Town of Belfast from the Earliest Times to the Close of the Eighteenth Century* (London, 1877), 347–51; E. R. R. Green, 'The Cotton Hand-Loom Weavers in the North-East of Ireland', *UJA*, 3rd ser., VII (1944), 30–41; McNeill, *Mary Ann McCracken*; D. A. Beaufort, *Memoir of a Map of Ireland* (London, 1792), 17.
    [7] TCD, MS 2045/28; *Life*, I. 148–9; Young, *Tour*, 128.
    [8] *History of Belfast*, 225–7.
    [9] *Belfast Monthly Mag*. III (July–Dec 1809), 343–4.
    [10] Benn, *Belfast*, 527–64; C. E. B. Brett, 'The Georgian Town: Belfast about 1800', in Beckett and Glasscock, *Belfast*, 67–77; R. M. Young, *The Town Book of the Corporation of Belfast, 1613–1816* (Belfast, 1892); Emrys Jones, *A Social Geography of Belfast* (London, 1965), 37; *BNL*, 18–21 Oct 1791.
    [11] Benn, *Belfast*, 497–9; Jones, *Social Geography of Belfast*, 35; Wesley, *Journal*, IV. 300.
    [12] *BNL*, 25–28 Oct 1791; Edward Wakefield, *An Account of Ireland, Statistical and Political*, 2 vols. (London, 1812), II. 630; David W. Miller, *Queen's Rebels: Ulster Loyalism in Historical Perspective* (Dublin, 1978), 57. On the continuing troubles in Armagh, see *FJ*, 3 May, 15 Aug, 10 Sept, 11 Oct 1791.
    [13] TCD, MS 2045/29v; *Life*, I. 149–50.
    [14] *Charlemont MSS*, II. 160.
    [15] *BNL*, 25 Oct 1791; SPOI, 620/19/29–30, Tone to Chambers, 13 and 17 Oct 1791

(though in his journal Tone dates it Sunday night, the 16th); Tone (Dickason) MSS, 'association' paper, op. cit.; *Life*, I. 144.

[16] See PRONI, D. 1748, uncatalogued Tennent letters, notably Robert to Mary Tennent, 24 Apr 1800.

[17] *Life*, I. 367–8. The document appears also in *Dropmore MSS*, 160–2, and *History of Belfast*, 358–9. It was decided not to publish it in the newspapers. See PRO, H.O. 100/33/91–3, for the July version.

[18] *Life*, I. 55, 150–1.

[19] Tone (Dickason) MSS, Tone and Russell to Matilda, 20 Oct 1791, reproduced in *Life*, I. 153–4. The contrasting writing of the two friends is instructive, Tone's small, neat, flowing and right-slanting, Russell's an almost illegible scrawl. Flippant references to Dr McDonnell in the original letter are omitted in the *Life*. He was uncle to William Tone's wife.

[20] Around Feb 1791; see SPOI, 620/15/6.

[21] See *BNL*, 4 Nov 1791, for a description of one of these coteries, essentially a dance with tea.

[22] TCD, MS 2045/25, omitted from published *Life*.

[23] See, e.g., *Life*, I. 36.

[24] TCD., MS 873/669, J. A. Russell to Dr John Gray, 16–22 Apr 1843; but see TCD, MS 868/2/307–8, R. Simms chastising Russell for his drinking, 10 Aug 1797, also 207–8 and 262–3, other examples of Russell inviting such scolding.

[25] *Life*, I. 41–51, the Belfast journals. For the Belfast theatre see *BNL*, 14 and 25 Oct 1791, and Clarke, *Irish Stage in the County Towns*, 269–70.

[26] TCD, MS 2046/4v; *Life*, I. 15.

[27] Sean O'Faolain's 1937 edition of Tone's *Autobiography* was the first to restore some of the omissions.

[28] See, e.g., TCD, MS 2047/6 and 10v.

[29] *Life*, I. 545; TCD, MS 2041/10–14, and the titles of the essays are listed separately at the back of the notebook.

[30] Tone (Dickason) MSS, Matilda to Eliza Fletcher, 29 Apr 1827, also Mary Tone to Tone, 14 June 1797.

[31] SPOI, 620/16/3 Tone to Russell, 1 Sept 1795.

[32] T.W.T., 'An Essay on the Dramatic Character of Sir John Falstaff', *Universal Mag.*, II (Aug 1789), 122–6; *Remains of the Revd Samuel O'Sullivan*, II. 262; Tone (Dickason) MSS, Tone to Matilda, 18 Aug 1797, outdoing each other in their quotations; Madden, *Irish Periodical Literature*, II.113.

[33] *Life*, I. 54, 151–2; SPOI, 620/19/33, Westmorland to Grenville, 16 Nov 1791, enclosing the documentation of the new society.

[34] *Charlemont MSS*, II. 179.

[35] Tone (Dickason) MSS, 'Mirabeau' [Tone] to Mrs Tone, [Nov 1791]; also printed in *Life*, I. 152, but with many omissions.

[36] *History of Belfast*, 363–6.

[37] SPOI, 620/16/3, Tone to Russell, 1 Sept 1795, on Belfast as 'his adopted Mother'; also n. 29. In this letter he identifies himself with the Belfast rather than the Dublin United Irish Society.

[38] TCD, MS 2046/38v; *Life*, I. 48 and 183–4.

Chapter 10

[1] See PRO, H.O. 100/34/37–39, information on the United Irishmen and Catholic Committee; also SPOI, Westmorland Corr., I. 35, Westmorland to Pitt, 1 Jan 1792, and PRO, PRO 30/8/331/70–72, ditto, 18 Feb 1792.

[2] US Nat. Arch., T.199/3, William Knox to Thomas Jefferson, 17 Jan 1792.

[3] See L. M. Cullen, 'The 1798 Rebellion in Eighteenth-Century Context', in *Radicals, Rebels and Establishments*, ed. Patrick J. Corish (Belfast, 1985), 101–2, for the anti-Catholicism of those who advised Westmorland.

[4] SPOI, Westmorland Corr., I. 29, Dundas to Westmorland, 26 Dec 1791. For the exchanges between London and Dublin on this issue, see also I. 26–36, 41–51; PRO, H.O. 100/33/205–14, 100/36/32–36, 50–55; PRO 30/8/331/64–72 and 30/8/110/2/203–4, 210.

5 PRO, H.O. 100/34/273, Westmorland to Pitt, 17 Dec 1791; it was an argument which Richard Burke used with Dundas (H.O. 100/34/211).

6 *Dropmore MSS*, II. 214–15, 221, 237.

7 SPOI, Westmorland Corr., I. 36, Dundas to Westmorland, 5 Jan 1792.

8 PRO, H.O. 100/36/259, Westmorland to Dundas, 13 Mar 1792, also 100/37/5, Hobart to [?], 3 Mar 1792. DDA, Troy MSS, 161/5/55, for the hierarchy's opinion of the reforming Catholics.

9 SPOI, 620/19/37, account of meeting between the Catholic delegates and Hobart, 26 Nov 1791.

10 SPOI, Westmorland Corr., 1. 30, Westmorland to Hobart, 27 Dec 1791.

11 SPOI, 620/19/45, printed handbill of the proceedings; Edwards, 'Minute Book of the Catholic Committee', 144; *DEP*, 17 Jan 1792—also contains similar statements from a number of parish committees.

12 PRO, PRO 30/8/110/2/215, Auckland to [Pitt], undated. SPOI, Westmorland Corr., I. 49–50, letters from Dundas and Pitt, 29 Jan 1792.

13 SPOI, Westmorland Corr., I. 41, Westmorland to Dundas, Jan 1791.

14 *The Correspondence of Edmund Burke*, ed. J. W. Copeland et al., 10 vols. (Cambridge, 1958–78), VII. xviii.

15 *Dropmore MSS*, II. 192. Richard Burke's correspondence with ministers is voluminous, and their complaints about him many—see PRO, H.O. 100/33/245–9, 262–76, 100/34/205v–11, 214v and 218v, 100/36/44, 58–63; SPOI, Westmorland Corr., I. 49–50, 58, 62; NLI, MS 54/15, 45, 52, 55, 56; *Burke Corr.*, VII. 13–14, 18–20, 22–9, 32–7. Duke of Buckingham, ed., *Memoirs of the Courts and Cabinets of George III*, rev. edn, 4 vols. (London 1853–5), II. 203–4. See also Grattan, *Life and Times*, IV. 57 on R. Burke's character defects.

16 BL, Add. MS 35,933/45v extract from Hobart's account, 25 Jan 1792.

17 *History of Belfast*, 365–6.

18 PRO, H.O. 100/36/196–7, Westmorland to Dundas, 28 Jan 1792.

19 See W. J. McCormack, *Ascendancy and Tradition in Anglo-Irish Literary History from 1789 to 1939* (Oxford, 1985), 68–70, and for his corrective on the origins of the term, id., 'Vision and Revision in the Study of Eighteenth-Century Irish Parliamentary Rhetoric', *Eighteenth-Century Ireland*, no. 2 (1987), 15–17.

20 PRO, PRO, 30/8/110/1/203–4 and 2/215, Auckland to Pitt [undated].

21 *Parl. Reg.*, XII. 82–181; *FJ*, 26 Jan, 9 and 21 Feb 1792; *DEP*, 28 Feb 1792; PRO, H.O. 100/36/296; BL, Add. MS 35,933/44–54.

22 PRONI, T.2541/IB1/3/4: Knox to Abercorn, 19 Jan 1792.

23 Grattan, *Life and Times*, IV. 62; Kennedy, 'Irish Whigs', 167–95; O'Brien, 'Exercise of Legislative Power', 174–86; O'Flaherty, 'Catholic Question in Ireland', 135.

24 PRO, H.O. 100/37/3, Westmorland to [Dundas], 3 Mar 1792.

25 NLI, MS 394/63–4, Westmorland to Dundas, 27 May and 6 June 1792.

26 *NS*, 25–28 Jan and *FJ*, 22 Feb 1792; also PRONI, D.456/7, Tone to Sam McTier, 11 Feb 1792, and *Drennan Letters*, 80.

27 PRO, H.O. 100/38/245–8, Keogh to Hussey, 29 Mar 1792, also 100/36/63v, Hobart to Dundas, 17 Jan 1792 on the dispersal of Catholic Committee handbills; Edwards, 'Minute Book of the Catholic Committee', 56–7. Hill, 'William Drennan', 57. The *Digest* is reprinted in MacNeven, *Pieces of Irish History*, 122–42.

28 *Argument*, 5th edn. (Dublin, 1792), a reprint by the Dublin Society of United Irishmen, copy in RIA, Haliday Pamphlets, 609/5. See Woods, 'Contemporary Editions of Tone's Argument', 225–6.

29 O'Donoghue, 'Catholic Church in Ireland', 164–5; *Arch. Hib.*, 151–2 and 157–9; Plowden, *History of Ireland*, IV, App. XCI.

30 W. Todd Jones, *A Letter to the Societies of United Irishmen of the Town of Belfast upon the subject of Catholic Rights* (Dublin 1792), serialised in *NS*, 8 Feb–21 Mar 1792. See Elliott, *Partners in Revolution*, 7, 37–8 for Protestant fears about the landed establishment.

31 *FJ*, 4 Feb 1792; *Parl. Reg.*, XII. 143. See TCD, 2050/25v for Tone's opinion of the general mass of the Catholics. Archbishop Troy thought the middle-class leaders of the Catholic Committee went rather too far in their endorsement of this line of argument: see *Carroll Papers*, II. 25–6; DDA, MS 161/5/90, Dr Teahan to Troy, 8 May 1792; Revd Anthony Cogan, *The Diocese of Meath, Ancient and Modern*, 3 vols. (Dublin, 1862–70), III. 186–7.

32 MacNeven, *Pieces of Irish History*, 18–23.

Chapter 11

[1] MacNeven, *Pieces of Irish History*, 23 and 21–6 generally.

[2] PRONI, D.591/333, McTier to Drennan, 27 Mar 1792.

[3] *Drennan Letters*, 66.

[4] Hill, 'William Drennan', II. 64–5; SPOI, 620/20/71, report by the spy Collins, 16 Mar 1793.

[5] SPOI, Westmorland Corr., I. 30, Westmorland to Hobart, 27 Dec 1791; 620/19/76 and 122; *History of Belfast*, 262–3; *Life*, I. 55–6, 217–9; *Drennan Letters*, 68–9 and 72.

[6] Gilbert, *History of Dublin*, I. 71–89.

[7] SPOI, 620/19–20, the very detailed reports on members and proceedings by Thomas Collins; McDowell, 'Personnel of the Dublin Society of United Irishmen', 12–53.

[8] W. P. Carey, *An Appeal to the People of Ireland* (Dublin, 1794), i–vi, 4, 94; Carey was also refused membership at first, SPOI, 620/19/88 (6 July 1792).

[9] See SPOI, 620/19/69, 86, 97, 102, 104, 620/20/45, 48 and 60, for Tone's membership of the various committees.

[10] SPOI, 620/42/6, catalogue of pictures belonging to John Sweetman, 26 Nov 1798.

[11] PRO, H.O. 100/34/43–4, printed constitution of the Dublin Society of United Irishmen—defaulter's names were read out from the chair. See also SPOI, 620/19/84–85, 620/20/36, 57, 62 and 65 for such subscriptions and Collins's embarrassment at his inability to pay.

[12] SPOI, 620/19/62, proceedings of meeting, 25 Feb 1792; *FJ*, 28 Feb; *DEP*, 28 Feb; *Walker's Hib. Mag.* (Feb 1792), 192; *Drennan Letters*, 84. PRO, H.O. 100/36/196–7, Westmorland to Dundas, 28 Jan 1792.

[13] There was a marked decline in attendance at the Society at this time; see SPOI, 620/19/66 and 70.

[14] *Life*, I. 57–8; *FJ*, 25 Feb–3 Mar 1792; PRO, H.O. 100/36/331, Hobart to Scrope Bernard, 28 Feb 1792.

[15] R. B. McDowell, 'Proceedings of the Dublin Society of United Irishmen', *Anal. Hib.*, XVII (1949), 16–17.

[16] SPOI, 620/19/73, 84, 97, Collins's reports, Mar–Aug 1792; *NS*, 21 Apr; *FJ*, 19 Apr and 8 May.

[17] SPOI, 620/19/66 and 76, Collins's reports on UIS meetings of 2 Mar and 13 Apr 1792; PRONI, D.591/334, Drennan to Sam McTier, 25 Apr 1792.

[18] Reg. Deeds, Ire., 487/496/314272, transfer deeds, 20 May 1795; *Life*, II. 41 and 369. Local tradition sites Chateau Boue among the outbuildings of the Wolfe property at Blackhall. It was said to have survived there until about 1950. See F. MacDermot, 'Query: Wolfe Tone's house', *Jnl Kildare Arch. Soc.*, XIV (1964–70), 376.

[19] Tone (Dickason) MSS, Matilda to Eliza Fletcher, 29 Apr 1827.

[20] Tone (Dickason) MSS, Tone to Matilda, [Nov] 1792; also printed in *Life*, I. 52–3. The original shows haste, reflecting the new excitement of life. The use of playful synonyms in correspondence was a common practice of Tone's. This early admiration for the French revolutionary leader and noted polemicist Mirabeau was chiefly associated with his attack on the clergy—see RIA, MS 23. K. 53, Tone's copy of Mirabeau's address to the National Assembly, 14 Jan 1791, on the civil constitution of the clergy.

[21] Maxwell, *Dublin under the Georges*, 241–2.

[22] Ulster Museum, Tone to McTier, 28 Jan 1792, printed in *Ulster in '98*, ed. R. M. Young (Belfast, 1893), 96. I am grateful to Dr W. A. Maguire for drawing the original to my attention.

[23] Barrington, *Personal Sketches*, I. 278–9; TCD, MS 3805/41.

[24] TCD, MS 3805/1, 38 and 41.

[25] See SPOI, 620/19/62 and 73, for UIS resolutions of 25 Feb and 29 Mar 1792, which he drafted. They were legally unsound and lampooned in the *Freeman's Journal* of 8 May as emanating 'from the brain of some *simple-Tone*'. Ulster Museum, Tone to McTier, 28 Jan 1792.

[26] See MacGiolla Easpaig, *Tomás Ruiséil*, 54.

[27] *The Parliamentary History of England...to the year 1803*, 36 vols. (London, 1806–20), XXIX, 664.

[28] The intention seems to have been to attach his services to Lord Granard's borough in Longford (Johnstown). Granard had four members in Parliament and was married to Lady Moira's sister. My thanks to Colin Wisdom of the PRONI, for information on Granard. See also Plowden, *History of Ireland*, IV. App. 52–3.

[29] TCD, MS 868/2/122–3, John to Thomas Russell, 29 Mar 1796.

[30] *Life*, I. 212–17; Todd Jones was likewise closely connected with the Rawdon family, his father having been Lady Moira's physician and friend. See Rogers, 'A Protestant Pioneer of Catholic Emancipation', 15. See also Gilbert, *History of Dublin*, I. 392–400 and *Charlemont MSS*, II. 107–9 on Lady Moira.

[31] Trimleston, Kenmare and Fingal were seeking recognition of their titles; see PRO, H.O. 100/34/62–3, also *Burke Corr.*, VII. 95.

[32] *Life*, I. 373–6. This seems not to have been published.

[33] *Life*, II. 135; *NS*, 28 Jan, 15 Feb 1792. The articles were signed 'Nimrod', the biblical 'mighty hunter before the Lord', likewise used by Blackstone in his criticism of the unreasonableness of the Game Laws; PRONI, D.456/7, Tone to McTier, 11 Feb 1792; Ulster Museum, Tone to McTier, 28 Jan 1792.

[34] *Life*, I. 382–405. This critique was partially incorporated into his *Vindication* of October.

[35] *Life*, I. 394–5, also for signs of his rejection of parts of Locke.

[36] *Life*, II, 22 and 348; J. C. D. Clark, *English Society 1688–1832: Ideology, Social Structure and Political Practice during the Ancien Regime* (Cambridge, 1985), 307, 315–35; Gregory Claeys, 'William Godwin's Critique of Democracy and Republicanism and Its Sources', *Hist. of European Ideas*, VII, no. 3 (1986), 256–7; Jules Steinberg, *Locke, Rousseau, and the Idea of Consent: An Inquiry into the Liberal-Democratic Theory of Political Obligation* (Westport. Conn., 1978), 95–6, 109 and 139–40; Pocock, *Machiavellian Moment*, 462–75.

[37] Jean Jacques Rousseau, *The Social Contract*, tr. Maurice Cranston (Harmondsworth, 1968), Bk. II and p. 30; McDowell, *Irish Public Opinion*, 142, 154, 165, 168.

[38] *Life*, I. 342, 396–7; in this Tone is typical of the United Irishmen, and Rousseau is likewise absent from the *Northern Star*.

[39] *Life*, I. 219–20; *History of Belfast*, 369.

[40] TCD, MS 2050/1–2, Tone to Delacroix, 26 Feb 1796; for his appointment, see *Life*, I. 63–4, and Edwards, 'Minute Book of the Catholic Committee', 168–71.

[41] SPOI, Westmorland Corr., I. 57. Hobart to Westmorland, 25 June 1792.

[42] *Life*, I. 167, 209–12; *Burke Corr.*, VII. 126–38, 164–5, and 223, in which his father is still referring in October to Richard's 'Clients'; Edwards, 'Minute Book of the Catholic Committee', 170–1; and Richard Burke's letters in PRO, H.O. 100/34/213, 205v–211.

[43] Gwynn, *John Keogh*, 30–6; id., *The Struggle for Catholic Emancipation (1750–1829)* (London, 1928), 67–8; Finegan, 'Was John Keogh an Informer', 82–4; O'Donoghue, 'Catholic Church in Ireland', 171–2. See TCD, MS 873/381, and LC, Sampson MSS, Catherine Anne Tone to Grace Clarke Sampson, 13 June 1841, for similar accusations by McDonnell.

[44] *Life*, I. 63–5, 120–1.

Chapter 12

[1] TCD, MS 2050/1–2: Tone says that this was the reason for his appointment; PRO, H.O. 100/34/217v–8, Keogh to Thomas Hussey, 2 Oct 1792, holding out the threat of violence if the Catholics were not appeased.

[2] Belfast remained the centre of the Irish revival for over half a century: see Brian Ó Cuív, 'Irish Language and Literature, 1691–1845', in *A New History of Ireland*, IV. 413–14; *Bolg an tSolair* (Belfast, 1795). Russell was more interested in the revival than his friend. See TCD, MS 868/1/37, preface to an Irish dictionary, in Russell's hand.

[3] *Life*, I. 155–7; *NS*, 18 July 1792; McNeill, *Mary Ann McCracken*, 78–83; A. Milligan Fox, *Annals of the Irish Harpers* (Belfast, 1911), 97–107; and for the Gaelic revival of the period see Norman Vance, 'Celts, Carthaginians and Constitutions: Anglo-Irish Literary Relations 1780–1820', *IHS*, XXII (1981), 216–38; and P. Rafroidi, *L'Irlande et le romantisme: la littérature irlandaise de 1789 à 1805 et sa place dans le mouvement occidental* (Paris, 1972), 211–72.

[4] Drennan thought this 'prudent and proper', when Tone spoke of his intention in Dublin (*Drennan Letters*, 89). Keogh claimed credit for the moderate tone of the address (PRO, H.O.

100/38/266).

⁵ PRO, H.O. 100/34/207, R. Burke to [Dundas], 17 June 1792 and 100/38/266–7, Keogh to Hussey, 26 July 1792.

⁶ See Keogh's and Hobart's differing accounts in PRO, H.O. 100/38/266–7 and 100/37/180–1.

⁷ *Life*, I. 158–60; *NS*, 18 July 1792; *BNL*, 17 July; *History of Belfast*, 371–80; *Drennan Letters*, 89–90.

⁸ SPOI, 620/16/88a, 'Songs on the French Revolution. . .sung at the celebration thereof at Belfast, on Saturday 14th July, 1792'; also printed in *NS*, 18 July 1792 (which identifies Tone as its author).

⁹ *Life*, I. 155–63.

¹⁰ PRO, H.O. 100/34/66–7, letter enclosed in Lord Bayhem to Dundas, 25 July 1792.

¹¹ See PRO, H.O. 100/34/66–7, 100/38/41 and 72–85, corr. between Dublin Castle and London, July–Nov 1792.

¹² For reports about stockpiling of arms, see PRO, H.O. 42/21/159, 388, 435–442, 42/22/153, 169, 385, 42/23/205 and H.O. 100/38/3, 33–41, 69, 94; AAE, Corr. Pol. Ang. 583 fo. 119.

¹³ See, e.g., *FJ*, 6 and 11 Oct 1791, 17 and 24 July, 21 Aug 1792.

¹⁴ SPOI, Westmorland Corr., I. 68, Westmorland to Pitt, 3 Nov 1792; PRONI, D. 607/B/359–69, various reports on the south Down situation, May–June 1792.

¹⁵ PRO, H.O. 100/38/266–8, Keogh to R. Burke, 26 July 1792. See also Keogh's 'Common Sense to the Presbyterians of the Province of Ulster' (Sept 1792) in PRO, H.O. 100/38/5, a scurrilous broadsheet, which Drennan thought put men's lives in danger. *The Correspondence of the Rt. Hon. John Beresford*, ed. W. Beresford, 2 vols. (London, 1854), II. 13.

¹⁶ *NS*, 14 July 1792.

¹⁷ Seward, *Topographica Hibernica*, 'Rathfriland'.

¹⁸ *NS*, 28 July 1792; the address to the Defenders (reproduced in *Life*, I. 479–81) was printed by the *News Letter* on 24 Aug.

¹⁹ *A New History of Ireland*, IV. 667.

²⁰ O'Donoghue, 'Catholic Church in Ireland', 11–15, 159–60. Their main object in Drogheda was to secure the removal of Fitzsimons, 'a crack'd brained priest', supposed to have been responsible for much of the animosity of the Catholic side in the Down disturbances (PRO. H.O. 100/38/267, Keogh's letter cited above). Drogheda was then the seat of the Archbishop of Armagh.

²¹ *Life*, I. 186–8.

²² *Drennan Letters*, 96–102 and 106–7.

²³ The most celebrated example of this was the role taken by John Foster, Speaker of the Irish House of Commons, against the Defenders in Louth (*FJ*, 7 July, 8 and 15 Sept 1792)—i.e., those whom Tone was asked to defend.

²⁴ Hobart wrote suggestively to London about Keogh and 'the most violent of the Roman Catholic Committee' visiting the Defenders in prison and supplying counsel to defend them (PRO. H.O. 100/38/11–19); also *Report from the Secret Committee of the House of Lords. . .into the Causes of the Disorders and Disturbances which Prevail in Several Parts of this Kingdom* (Dublin, 1793).

Chapter 13

¹ See, e.g., PRONI, D.607/B/373, Lord Hillsborough to John Reilly [Aug 1792], for a description of the state of the roads between Newry and Hillsborough.

² *FJ*, 8 Sept and 15 Oct 1792; Plowden, *History of Ireland*, IV. App. p. 18.

³ The protest was printed repeatedly by the *Freeman's Journal* from 13 Aug 1792 through the remaining summer months; see also *Life*, I. 377–8. The Londonderry example was followed by grand juries all over the country; see *DEP*, 1 Sept–8 Nov, and *FJ*, 25 Aug–22 Sept for their resolutions and Catholic counter-resolutions, likewise from every part of the country.

⁴ *NS*, 15 Aug; *DEP*, 14 Aug 1792.

⁵ *FJ*, 13 and 30 Aug 1792.

⁶ *NS*, 18 and 22 Aug 1792. Tone was also writing on the defeat of Poland, likewise on the American constitution.

⁷ *FJ*, 15 Sept 1792.

⁸ See, e.g., MacCormack, *Ascendancy and Tradition*, 86–9.

⁹ See his 'Derry Farmer' and 'Petty Juror' letters in the *NS*, 18 and 22 Aug 1792; and his 'Protestant Freeman' and 'Senex' contributions to the *Hib. Jnl*, 24 and 26 Sept, and 8 Oct 1792.

¹⁰ See, e.g., PRONI, T.2541/IB1/3/35: George Knox to Abercorn, 13 Dec 1792.

¹¹ *Charlemont MSS*, II. 202; the reference is to Sterne's *Tristram Shandy*.

¹² *NS*, 26 Sept 1792.

¹³ *Burke Corr.*, VII, 238–9. *Dropmore MSS*, II. 327, 336–7; SPOI, Westmorland Corr., I 66–76, and PRO, H.O. 100/38/72–85, corr. between Westmorland and Pitt, Oct–Nov 1792.

¹⁴ *The Diaries of Sylvester Douglas, Lord Glenbervie*, ed. Francis Bickley, 2 vols. (London, 1928), I. 34.

¹⁵ TCD, MS 2044/12.

¹⁶ *Life*, I. 181, 185–9, 197–8, 203; Malcomson, *John Foster*, 206, 354–5, 406; PRONI, Abercorn MSS, T.2541/IB1/3/35.

¹⁷ A similar overture was made to the Ponsonbys, in which they offered to drop their immediate demand for the franchise (which they saw as the chief cause for alarm) if the Ponsonbys would introduce a bill granting their other demands. PRONI, T. 3393/15, Revd. T. L. O'Beirne to W. B. Ponsonby, 19 Sept 1792.

¹⁸ SPOI, 620/19/96, Collins's report of 27 Aug 1792; also Keogh's letters to Hussey in PRO, H.O. 100/34/213 and 217v–218, 31 July and 2 Oct 1792, and 100/38/11–19 and 70–71, for the Castle's view of Keogh as the leading agitator. See O'Flaherty, 'Catholic Question in Ireland', 145–6, and 152 for Keogh's 'experimentation with revolutionary politics'.

¹⁹ See PRO, H.O. 100/38/5, and McDowell, 'Proceedings of the Dublin Society of United Irishmen', 32–4, for Keogh's 'Common Sense'; *Drennan Letters*, 141. Byrne was fined £1,000 and imprisoned for two years for printing it; see Carey, *Appeal to the People of Ireland*, 37.

²⁰ *Remains of the Revd Samuel O'Sullivan*, II. 262; *Life*, I. 204.

²¹ *Life*, I. 178–9.

Chapter 14

¹ See, e.g., PRO, H.O. 100/37/146–50, Westmorland to [Dundas], 7 June 1792, transmitting the Catholics' electoral plan (signed by Byrne as secretary). Westmorland expressed his alarm at their 'electing a national assembly of Catholics upon the French principles of delegation'. He feared that such an assembly could not tolerate so aristocratic a Parliament as the present Irish House of Commons and would reform it. How then would England maintain its management of 'an Irish National Assembly'?

² Ryan's speech is printed in *DEP*, 8 Nov 1792.

³ See PRO, H.O. 100/34/60, Plowden, *History of Ireland*, IV. App. lxxxix, and *Life*, I. 62, 439–45, for the sub-committee's circular letter 'On the Manner of Conducting the Election of Delegates', 26 May 1792.

⁴ Cullen, 'Catholics under the Penal Laws', 31.

⁵ *FJ*, 25 Sept, 2 and 20 Oct 1792.

⁶ *Life*, I. 160.

⁷ J. W. Hammond, 'Thomas Braughall, 1729–1803, Catholic Emancipationist', *Dublin Hist. Record*, XIV (1956), 41–9.

⁸ TCD, MS 2043/16.

⁹ *Life*, I. 190–4.

¹⁰ James Dixon, a tanner and member of the Catholic Convention. See McDowell, 'Personnel of the Dublin Society of United Irishmen', 30, and SPOI, 620/54/18, Collins's list of United Irish readers, undated.

¹¹ TCD, MS 868/1/264–5; printed in *Letters of Tone*, Hobson, ed. 18–21.

¹² *Life*, I. 207, also TCD, MS 2044/35v.

¹³ *Life*, I. 208–9, and 181–90, 195–208 generally.

¹⁴ Tone (Dickason) MSS, Matilda to Catherine Anne Tone, 1 Aug 1829; *Life*, I. 182.

¹⁵ PROI, Betham's Abstracts: Prerogative Wills. Bet. 1/69/89.

¹⁶ The words are those of the *Northern Star*, 13 Oct 1792, but Tone expresses much the same sentiments: *Life*, I. 183.

[17] *FJ*, 9–20 Oct 1792; *DEP*, 30 Oct, describing the illumination in Dublin the night before; *Life*, I. 195.

[18] SPOI, 620/15/6/3/47–69, Russell's account of his father's death; MacGiolla Easpaig, *Tomás Ruiséil*, ch. viii.

[19] Carey, *Appeal to the People of Ireland*, 12–13; SPOI, 620/19/102, 104, 107 and 109, Collins's reports, 11 Oct–23 Nov 1792. *History of Belfast*, 385–6, and *Life*, I. 200 and 205; *Drennan Letters*, 95; *NS*, 7 Nov 1792.

[20] TCD, MS 2044/27v.

[21] *Life*, I. 202; *Drennan Letters*, 94; *Burke Corr.*, VII. 288 and 290; MacNeven, *Pieces of Irish History*, 30; PRONI, D.591/347B; *DEP*, 10 Nov 1792. The *Freeman's Journal* chose to ignore the meeting, except to comment on the assistance given by 'Barristers who have no other business' (8 Nov).

[22] *Burke Corr.*, VII. 293–4; O'Donoghue, 'Catholic Church in Ireland', 191–2. DDA, Troy MSS, 161/5/88, Troy to Bray, 8 Dec 1792.

[23] *Drennan Letters*, 102; *Life*, I. 222–4; *NS*, 5 Dec 1792.

[24] PRONI, T.2541/IB1/3/35 and 38, George Knox to Abercorn, 13 and 20 Dec 1792.

[25] *Life*, I. 75–86, 224–36; O'Flaherty, 'Catholic Question in Ireland', 148–64; *Drennan Letters*, 104; BL, Add. MS 35,933/63–64v, Westmorland to Dundas, 7 Dec 1792. Tone's account of the sittings of the Catholic Convention is the fullest we have, since meetings were in secret (MacNeven's speech alone being released to the press—*DEP*, 13 Dec 1792, also containing a brief outline of the proceedings—see also the 22 Dec issue). As secretary, his contemporaneous account consists of brief jottings on slips of paper. A fuller account was written afterwards, perhaps in America.

[26] This was a constant Catholic complaint: see PRO, H.O. 100/34/33–4, Troy to Hobart, 29 Nov 1791; also *DEP*, 13 Dec 1792, McNeven's speech to the Catholic Convention.

[27] *Life*, I. 205, and 411–86, for Tone's *Vindication*.

[28] See SPOI, Westmorland Corr., I. 79–82, and PRO, H.O. 100/34/234–7, for the December corr. between ministers in Dublin and London.

[29] O'Flaherty, 'Catholic Question in Ireland', 161.

[30] PRO, H.O. 100/34/233v–8, summary of corr. Dublin-London, Dec 1792.

Chapter 15

[1] *BNL*, 14 Dec; *NS*, 12 Dec; *FJ*, 11 Dec; *DEP*, 20 Dec 1792.

[2] Grattan, *Life and Times*, IV. 77–83.

[3] PRONI, T.2541/IB1/3/36 and IK/12/73–76, 80 and 82.

[4] *Life*, I. 88–9, 251–2; O'Flaherty, 'Catholic Question in Ireland', 164–5; PRO, H.O. 100/34/93–8 and *DEP*, 10 Jan 1792, Petition of the Roman Catholics of Ireland; SPOI, Westmorland Corr., I. 82 and 86, PRO, 100/42/57–8 and BL, Add. MS 35,933/64v, corr. Dundas-Westmorland, Dec 1792–Jan 1793; *NS*, 12 Jan 1793.

[5] See SPOI, Westmorland Corr., I. 87, PRO, H.O. 100/42/19–22, 65–6, 129–44, and BL, Add. MS 35,933/64v for this exchange.

[6] *Parl. Reg.*, XIII. 94–135; *FJ*, 15 Jan, 7 Feb 1792; PRO, H.O. 100/42/77–84, 98–9, 248–51, Westmorland and Hobart to London, 11 Jan–5 Feb 1792.

[7] *Life*, I. 242.

[8] SPOI, 620/20/6, communications between Hobart and the delegates, 18–25 Jan; also DDA, Troy MSS, 161/5/132, Troy to Bray, 19 Feb 1793; PRO, H.O. 100/42/274, Westmorland to Dundas, 9 Feb 1793, describing similar back-room negotiations between government and certain MPs. Grattan, *Life and Times*, IV. 95–6.

[9] NLI, MS 54A/74, 'Memorandum of the conversation which passed with Mr Dundas at Wimbledon on the 21 and 22 of January 1793'.

[10] *Parl. Reg.*, XIII. 253–5; PRO, H.O. 100/34/246, Hobart to Nepean, 26 Feb 1793; PRONI, T.2541/IB1/1012, George Knox to Abercorn, 6–14 Feb 1793.

[11] *FJ*, 5 Mar 1792; Malcomson, *John Foster*, 67–9.

[12] Plowden, *History of Ireland*, IV. 83; DDA, Troy MSS, 161/5/123, 133–5, corr. of Troy, Bray and Antonelli, 16 Mar–8 June 1793; *FJ*, 14 Mar 1793; O'Donoghue, 'Catholic Church in Ireland', 205–14.

[13] PRONI, T.2541/IB1/4/1–5, George Knox to Abercorn, 16–24 Jan 1793. Kennedy,

'Irish Whigs', 245–59.

¹⁴ Lecky, *History of Ireland*, III. 186. Outside Ulster, most 40s. freeholders were dependent on the land and tended to vote according to lines laid down by the local landlord.

¹⁵ PRO, H.O. 100/42/57–8, 'Substance of a communication made by Mr Secretary Dundas to Edward Byrne, John Keogh, James Edward Devereux and Christopher Bellew, 7 Jan 1793', and fos. 47 and 111 for a printed account of the negotiations circulated by the delegates in Ireland; TCD, MS 3807/40, handbill 'A full and particular account of the Delegates from the Roman Catholic Convention of this Kingdom to His Majesty', and 3806/2, Tone's notes on this issue, 27 Mar 1793 (printed in *Life*, I. 107–8). Dundas assured Cooke that the delegates had not asked for seats in Parliament: NLI, MS 54ᴬ/74, op.cit.

¹⁶ *Drennan Letters*, 154, 157 and 227; PRO, H.O. 100/43/234–5, Sackville Hamilton to Hobart, 22 Apr 1793.

¹⁷ TCD, MS 2045/1v.

¹⁸ PRONI, T.2541/IB1/4/10, Knox to Abercorn, 6 Feb 1793.

¹⁹ PRONI, T.2541/IB1/4/10, op cit.

²⁰ *Life*, I. 91–103, 106–8, 240–67; MacNeven, *Pieces of Irish History*, 40–1; SPOI, 620/20/63, Collins's information [16 Feb 1792].

²¹ Lecky, *History of Ireland*, III. 186.

²² *Life*, I. 265–7 in particular, but 252–67 gives details of these heated last sessions. Plowden, *History of Ireland*, IV. 52–6. *DEP*, 27 Apr 1793. See also SPOI, 620/20/57, an address from the United Irish Society, 19 Apr 1793, reminding Catholics that complete emancipation was not yet gained. See *FJ*, 23 Apr 1793, for the various Catholic addresses of thanks.

²³ *Life*, I. 100–1; see pp. 75–104 for Tone's lengthy analysis of events of these months and sense of shocked deflation at the outcome.

²⁴ I have examined this process in some detail in *Partners in Revolution*, 36–50.

Chapter 16

¹ *Drennan Letters*, 109 and 116; *FJ*, 22 Dec 1792; and PRONI, D.607/B/380–381, Hobart to Hillsborough, 9 and 18 Dec 1792.

² PRO, H.O. 100/38/118–25, letters of Westmorland and Hobart, 5 Dec 1792.

³ MacNeven, *Pieces of Irish History*, 35.

⁴ *NS*, 19 Dec 1792.

⁵ *FJ*, 30 Jan 1794, at the time of Rowan's trial.

⁶ PRO, H.O. 100/42/215–16, Hobart to Nepean, 28 Jan 1793.

⁷ PRO, PRO 30/8/331/98–100, Westmorland to Pitt, 1 Dec 1792.

⁸ *Life*, I. 208, 247 and II. 133; *Drennan Letters*, 105.

⁹ *Life*, I. 121–2; SPOI, 620/54/66: Collins's list of members [May 1794]; *Drennan Letters*, 123.

¹⁰ SPOI, 620/19/126 and 129, Collins's reports on the meetings of 21 and 28 Dec 1792.

¹¹ PRONI, T 2541/IB1/4/10, Knox to Abercorn, 6 Feb 1793.

¹² *Drennan Letters*, 193; *Life*, I. 183.

¹³ The Gunpowder Act placed heavy restrictions on the import, manufacture, movement and possession of arms and ammunition, and gave wide-ranging powers of entry and search to JPs and those appointed by them.

¹⁴ SPOI, 620/20/19 and 620/20/33/18–23, Russell's journal [Apr 1793], commenting on a letter of Tone's and making this very point.

¹⁵ *NS*, 2 Jan 1793; *FJ*, 29 Jan 1793.

¹⁶ PRO, H.O. 100/42/1–4, 9–14, 69, 104–5, 270–1, 289–92, 100/43/47–50, 67–8, 89, 97–8, 101–3, 145–56, 163–4, government corr. on the problem of Belfast and its containment, Dec 1792—Mar 1793; *Drennan Letters*, 143, 147–8, 152–6; *NS*, 6–13 Mar 1793; MacNeven, *Pieces of Irish History*, 54–8.

¹⁷ SPOI, 620/20/33/14, Russell's journal for 16–24 Apr 1793, and *Drennan Letters*, 165; and see PRO, H.O. 100/42/289–92, 100/43/47–50, 89, 103, 117, 145–51 and 154–6, and PRONI, D.607/B/384 on the loyalty of Belfast that summer. White's sense of having fought and won a major war was shared by the administration.

¹⁸ See *Charlemont MSS*, II. 213–14, on the riot, also the sense of Belfast having been

abandoned.

[19] SPOI, 620/20/1, the printed reform plan, and 620–20/44, 45 and 58, Society discussions on the proposals; R. B. McDowell, 'United Irish Plans of Parliamentary Reform, 1793', *IHS*, III (1942–3), 39–59; and the final plan of 1794 in PRO, H.O. 100/51/100, which reflects the changed circumstances from the preceding year.

[20] Claeys, 'William Godwin's Critique of Democracy', 260–1. The *Northern Star* serialised Godwin's *Enquiry*, Nov–Dec 1793; see also PRONI, D.591/449, Mrs McTier to Drennan, 16 Nov 1793; Russell called it 'a masterly book', though thought it said nothing new: SPOI, 620/21/23/53–4, his journal for Oct 1793. See also 620/20/44, UIS discussion of the ballot. Catholic members seem to have supported and Protestants opposed the ballot—see M. Wall, 'The United Irish Movement', *Historical Studies*, ed. J. L. McCracken, V (London, 1965), 133–4.

[21] MacNeven, *Pieces of Irish History*, 37, and Kennedy, 'Irish Whigs', 234–7; SPOI, 620/19/125, 'Association of the Friends of the Constitution, Address'.

[22] PRONI, T.2541/IB1/4/13, Knox to Abercorn, 20 Feb 1793; also *Charlemont MSS.*, 210; *DEP*, 21 Feb 1793; *FJ*, 10 Jan 1793.

[23] Kennedy, 'Irish Whigs', 245–60; *BNL*, 23 July 1793; *DEP*, 12 Dec 1793.

[24] *Drennan Letters*, 136; PRONI, T. 2541/IB1/4/16, Knox to Abercorn, 7 Mar 1793.

[25] *Life*, I. 269.

[26] *NS*, 20 Feb 1793; *DEP*, 14 Feb; *FJ*, 21 Feb; *History of Belfast*, 408–11; *Charlemont MSS*, II. 211 and 217.

[27] PRONI, D.591/369–70, Drennan to Sam McTier [Jan 1793], also *Drennan Letters*, 161–2; *FJ*, 21 May 1793; *DEP*, 4 Apr 1793.

[28] 'Report of a Committee appointed to enquire into the tendency of the war with France, of the raising of the Militia, etc.', by the United Irishmen of Dublin, 10 Feb 1793, printed in *NS*, 20 Feb, also in Madden, *United Irishmen*, 1st ser., II. 327–9.

[29] *FJ*, 7 Mar and 9 Apr 1793; *DEP*, 7 Mar 1793; PRONI, D.591/400, Drennan to Mrs McTier, 27 Mar 1793.

[30] SPOI, 620/20/33/3, 23, 31, Russell's journal, Mar–May 1793; *Life*, I. 108; PRONI, T.3391/96, Pollock to Forbes, 28 [June] 1793.

[31] *Report from the Secret Committee of the House of Lords*...(1793); also printed in *DEP*, 14 Mar, and *FJ*,12 Mar 1793.

[32] *Defence of the Sub-Committee of the Catholics of Ireland, from the Imputations Attempted to be thrown on that Body, Particularly from the Charge of Supporting the Defenders* (Dublin, 1793). *Life*, I. 475–86. See also John Sweetman, *A Refutation of the Charges Attempted to be Made Against the Secretary of the Sub-Committee of the Catholics of Ireland, Particularly that of Abetting Defenders* (Dublin, 1793), and Sweetman's letter in *DEP*, 9 Mar 1793.

[33] *FJ*, 26 Mar 1793.

[34] PRONI, D.591/416, Mrs McTier to Sam McTier [Apr 1793].

[35] SPOI, 620/20/49–62, Collins's reports, Feb–May 1793.

[36] PRONI, D.591/394 and 396, Drennan to Sam McTier, 4 and 9 Mar 1793.

[37] 'The Society of United Irishmen of Dublin to the People of Ireland', broadside dated 3 Mar 1793, in PRO, H.O. 100/34/111, also printed in Madden, *United Irishmen*, 1st ser., II. 333–7.

[38] PRO, 100/38/381–5, Pitt to Westmorland, 10 Nov 1792; NLI, MS 54^A/74, account of meeting between Cooke, Dundas and Pitt, 21–22 Jan 1793.

[39] PRO, H.O. 100/42/13–14, 'Memorandum on the state of the North of Ireland', enclosed in Hobart to Nepean, 29 Dec 1792.

[40] PRO, H.O. 100/38/361–5, extracts of information from Ireland, Oct 1792; Plowden, *History of Ireland*, IV. 52–3.

[41] SPOI, 620/21/23/70–77, Russell's journal, Jan 1794, speaking particularly of north Cavan; see PRO, H.O. 100/42/197–8, for Defender troubles in the region the previous year.

[42] See SPOI, 620/19/29, 33, 73, 101, 620/20/20 and 79, 620/21/27 and 35–7, 620/34/54, and PRO, H.O. 100/34/101–10 and 100/43/145–51, and *Drennan Letters*, 181, for the dissemination of United Irish literature. James S. Donnelly, Jr. 'Propagating the Cause of the United Irishmen', *Studies*, LXIX (1980), 5–23. See also Fitzgibbon's claims reported in *DEP*, 20 July 1793.

[43] SPOI, 620/20/12; also printed in *Life*, I. 369–72.

[44] T. Paine, *Rights of Man* (repr., Harmondsworth, 1983), 167–8.

[45] See PRONI, D.591/464, Drennan to Sam McTier [Jan 1794], also 461 for Emmet's 'plain, sensible, popular introduction' to their parliamentary reform plan.

[46] *FJ*, 9, 16, 26 and 30 Mar, 13, 20 Apr, 4 June and 17 Oct 1793; *DEP*, 16 Apr 1793.

[47] See, e.g., *FJ*, 30 May–1 June 1793, reporting from the *Sligo Jnl* of 28 May; see also PRONI, D.607/C/22 on this fear.

[48] *FJ*, 23–25 May 1793 (also extensive reports throughout May); PRO, 100/34/134–6, Hobart to Nepean, 8 June 1793, enclosing information from Wexford.

[49] PRO, H.O. 100/44/5–10 and 115–18, Westmorland to Dundas, 29 May and 8 June 1793, sending information on 'the late insurrections'.

[50] PRO, H.O. 100/46/264–5, Fitzwilliam to Portland, 15 Jan 1795, reporting Lord Fingall's assessment of lower-class Catholic discontent.

[51] PRO, H.O. 100/44/7–10, 'Extract of letters received respecting disturbances in Leitrim, Mayo, Roscommon and Sligo', in Westmorland to Dundas, 29 May 1793.

[52] *Parl. Reg.*, XIII. 254; see PRO, H.O. 100/42/15–17 also for Cooke's hope of using the Catholic leaders in such a role.

[53] *NS*, 29 May–1 June 1793.

[54] PRO, H.O. 100/44/184, Cooke to [Nepean], 17 June 1793.

[55] PRO, H.O. 100/51/154–6, Keogh to Nepean, 15 Apr 1794.

[56] See *Charlemont MSS*, II. 215–16; T. Bartlett, 'An End of the "Moral Economy": The Irish Militia Disturbances of 1793', *Past and Present*, no. 99 (May 1983), 58; PRO, PRO 30/8/331/105–10, Westmorland to Pitt, 1 Jan 1793, noting the same traits in disturbances the previous winter.

[57] PRO, H.O. 100/44/331–2, Cooke to Nepean, 30 July 1793.

Chapter 17

[1] PRONI, D.591/416, Mrs McTier, from Dublin, to Sam McTier [Apr 1793], suggesting the UIS was about to dissolve.

[2] Hill, 'William Drennan', II. 117–18; Carey, *Appeal to the People of Ireland*, 36.

[3] SPOI, 620/20/60–62 and 620/53/199, Collins's reports for May 1793; for printed copies of the two addresses see 620/20/20 and PRO, H.O. 100/43/162.

[4] SPOI, 620/20/33/13, 23, 31, Russell's journal; *Drennan Letters*, 164.

[5] Walsh, *Sketches of Ireland Sixty Years Ago*, 152–3; Morgan, *O'Briens and O'Flahertys*, I. 68–77; Gilbert, *History of Dublin*, I. 244–9.

[6] SPOI, 620/20/59, 62, Collins's reports, 3 and 31 May 1793; PRO, H.O. 100/42/225, Hobart to Nepean, 1 Feb 1793; TCD, MS 4833, Henry Sheares to Citizen Henry Flemming, 1 Dec 1792. The activities of this expatriate group in Paris are fully discussed in Elliott, *Partners in Revolution*, 51–63.

[7] Tone (Dickason) MSS, Matilda to Catherine Anne Tone, 22 Sept 1842; also *Life* I. 122.

[8] *Drennan Letters*, 153.

[9] *FJ*, 20 July; *DEP*, 20 July 1793; SPOI, 620/42/18, Henry Sheares's printed response, 21 July.

[10] PRO, H.O., 100/44/304–7, Hobart to Nepean, 21 July 1793.

[11] Tone (Dickason) MSS, Todd Jones to Tone, 20 Aug 1793, printed in *Life*, I. 275–7, see also p. 487; SPOI, 620/20/33/13, Russell's journal, 4 Apr 1793; TCD, MS 868/2/29v and 33, Margaret Russell to Thomas Russell, 11 May and 6 July 1793.

[12] Elliott, *Partners in Revolution*, 60–1.

[13] PRO, PRO 30/8/327/82–3, Fitzgibbon's private letter to Pitt, 14 May 1793; he also wrote the same day and to the same effect to John Beresford, then in London, *Beresford Corr.*, II. 13–14.

[14] *FJ*, 11 July 1793.

[15] *Life*, I. 286, Tone to Arthur O'Connor, 20 Oct 1795.

[16] Burrowes, *Select Speeches*, 32–8. Phillips, *Curran and his Contemporaries*, 390.

[17] PRO, H.O. 100/33/81–2, Westmorland to [Dundas], 11 July 1791.

[18] *DEP*, 1 and 8 Aug 1793; *Life*, I. 495–510, and see 'Table of contents', p.v, for William Tone's assertion that the letter was never published; PRONI, D.591/435, Drennan to Sam McTier, [July 1793].

[19] *Life*, I. 275–6; PRO, H.O. 100/46/73–5, damning criticism of Fitzgibbon from Limerick, sent by the admittedly biased Richard Burke, 30 July 1793.

[20] See also SPOI, 620/21/23/65–6, Russell's journal for Dec 1793, for Tone's continuing association with the opposition Whigs.

[21] *Life*, I. 513–17, also 511–12; despite the element of personal vendetta, Tone's charges against Fitzgibbon were substantially true: see *DEP*, 1 Aug 1793.

[22] *Burke Corr.*, VII. 509–11.

[23] *Life*, I. 275 for Moira's letter of 21 Sept 1793; *The Journal and Correspondence of William, Lord Auckland*, ed. the Bishop of Bath and Wells, 4 vols. (London, 1861–2), III. 125–6; F. O'Gorman, *The Whig Party and the French Revolution* (London, 1967), particularly 144, 154–5, 168, 175–80; MacDermot, *Theobald Wolfe Tone*, 110–11; Malcomson, *John Foster*, 388–9, 411; PRO, H.O. 100/43/97–8, criticism by the English Lord Chancellor, Thurlow [Mar 1793].

[24] *Life*, I. 275; *DEP*, 14 Sept 1794.

[25] *Life*, I. 273–4; SPOI, 620/21/23/68, Russell's journal for Dec 1793; PRO, H.O. 100/46/77–8, Hobart to Nepean, 27 Aug 1793; *NS*, 28 Aug; *FJ*, 21 Aug; *DEP*, 24 Aug 1793.

[26] *FJ*, 17 Oct; see also 16 July and 19 Oct 1793.

[27] See *Trial of Francis Graham for Attempting to Suborn Joseph Corbally, Taylor, to Swear that A. H. Rowan and J. Napper Tandy Esqs were at the head of the Defenders* (Dublin, 1794); *A Complete Collection of State Trials*, ed. T. B. and T. J. Howell, 33 vols. (London, 1809–28), XXV. 749–83, 'The Trial of James Bird, Roger Hamill, and Casimir Delahoyde...for conspiring to incite an insurrection in the Kingdom of Ireland...April 23, 1794'. Plowden, *History of Ireland*, IV. 99–100 (on Fay); PRO, H.O. 100/46/154–6, Keogh to Nepean, 15 Apr 1794.

[28] SPOI, 620/20/75, 78, 83, Collins's reports of Nov–Dec 1793.

[29] SPOI, 620/21/23/67–69, Russell's journal, Dec 1793; PRONI, D.591/519, Drennan to Sam McTier, 2 Aug 1794. A reconciliation was finally effected in February 1794; see Ann Arbor, Melville MSS, Douglas to Dundas, 17 Feb 1794.

[30] *FJ*, 5 and 14 Dec 1793.

[31] SPOI, 620/51/244, unsigned, undated letter of one of the Dublin members of the Catholic Committee; TCD, MS 868/2/24–5, Margaret Russell to Thomas Russell, 29 June 1793, also fo. 176, Margaret Tone to [Russell], 4 Feb 1796.

[32] SPOI, 620/21/23/65–77, Russell's journal, Dec 1793–Jan 1794. See PRO, PRO 30/8/325/124–5, Andrew M. Browne, a Mayo Catholic landowner, to [Pitt], 8 Feb 1794, for signs that many lower-class Irish would welcome the French.

[33] PRO, H.O. 100/52/90–92, Douglas to Nepean, 6 June 1794, on the ensigns John and George Lyster.

[34] *FJ*, 27 Jan–11 Feb 1794; *NS*, 3–10 Feb 1794; *DEP*, 30 Jan–8 Feb 1794; *A Full Report of the Trial at Bar...in which...A. H. Rowan Esq was Defendant* (Dublin, 1794); Rowan, *Autobiography*, 188–209; PRONI, D.591/464–8, Drennan to Sam McTier [Jan–Feb 1794].

[35] *Charlemont MSS*, II. 227–8; SPOI, 620/21/27–35, Collins's reports, Feb–Mar 1794.

[36] PRO, H.O. 100/51/76, Cooke to [Nepean] 23 Jan 1794.

[37] MacNeven, *Pieces of Irish History*, 70.

Chapter 18

[1] SPOI, 620/21/23/69–70, Russell's journal, 18 Jan 1794.

[2] SPOI, 620/21/27–37, Collins's reports, Feb–Apr 1794; the broadsheet carrying both the plan for parliamentary reform and the address to the people of Ireland is in 620/21/5–6 and PRO, H.O. 100/51/100.

[3] *FJ*, 3 Apr 1794.

[4] *Life*, I. 112; *Life of Curran*, I. 340.

[5] See *FJ*, 26 July 1794, trial of the Newgate gaoler, McDowell. For Newgate see Bernadette Doorly, 'Newgate Prison', in Dickson, *The Gorgeous Mask*, 121–31.

[6] Dagg, *College Historical Society*, 72.

[7] SPOI, 620/21/14, examination of Benjamin Vaughan, 9 May 1794. All Jackson's intercepted correspondence can be found in Howell, *State Trials*, XXV, 833–45, and PRO, T.S.11/1067/4935.

[8] This was Rowan's brother-in-law, Benjamin Beresford, a merchant operating out of the

Hanseatic towns and involved with John Hurford Stone and Nicholas Madgett in Paris, to whom he transmitted English newspapers.

[9] See, e.g., *Life*, I. 56.

[10] *Life*, I. 278. McNally declared Tone's statement 'very accurately drawn': SPOI, 620/10/121/27. The anonymous author of *Biographical Anecdotes of the Founders of the Late Irish Rebellion* (London, 1799), 6, thought Tone exaggerated the numbers of Catholics (3,150,000) and understated the number of Protestants (450,000 Established Church, 900,000 Dissenters). In fact the figures are relatively accurate, though inflated in the case of the Dissenters.

[11] See Rowan, *Autobiography*, 212, for the claim that he returned the statement to Tone. Tone's version is in *Life*, I. 277–9, Rowan's in PRO, T.S. 11/1067/4935 and in Howell, *State Trials*, XXV. 841–3.

[12] PRO, PRO 30/8/327, Cockayne to Pitt, 18 Apr 1794.

[13] *Life*, II. 533; Phillips, *Curran and his Contemporaries*, 206. See also PRONI, D.591/471 and 484, Drennan's letters of 19 Feb and 14 Mar 1794 on a possible French invasion.

[14] PRO, TS 11/1067/4935, copy of Jackson's letter of 24 April; Howell, *State Trials*, XXV. 749–83.

[15] PRO, H.O. 100/38/185–6 and 100/52/8–9, but in fraud cases only, where he was never called upon to testify.

[16] PRO, PRO 30/331/222–8, Westmorland to Pitt, 17 Apr 1794.

[17] *Life*, I. 111–12; PRONI, D.591/490, Drennan to Sam McTier, 3 May 1794.

[18] PRO, H.O. 100/52/46–7, Westmorland to Pitt, 12 May 1794.

[19] *Beresford Corr.*, II. 24–35.

[20] SPOI, 620/15/2/15, T. A. Emmet to Russell, [Nov 1798].

[21] Grattan, *Life and Times*, IV. 166–8.

[22] *Beresford Corr.*, II. 34

[23] PRO, PRO 30/8/331/238–41 and H.O. 100/52/46–7, Westmorland to Pitt, 8 and 12 May 1794; *Beresford Corr.*, II. 32–4; *Life*, I. 122. See also *NS*, 5 May 1794: report that Jackson had been sent from London 'with a view of entrapping such men as Mr Rowan'.

[24] *Drennan Letters*, 203. For the events described here see PRONI, D.591/485–587; PRO, H.O. 100/52/72–3; SPOI, 620/21/39 and 620/54/17 (Collins's reports), reproduced in McDowell, 'Proceedings of the Dublin Society of United Irishmen', 125–8; *FJ*, 29 Apr–17 May 1794.

[25] PRONI, D.591/486, Mrs McTier to Drennan [May 1794] and 517, Drennan to Sam McTier, 14 July 1794.

Chapter 19

[1] See *NS*, 10 July 1794; every issue thereafter carried reports of the expected changes. See also *Charlemont MSS*, II. 246–56.

[2] *FJ*, 19 Sept 1794.

[3] *Life*, I. 123, 288, and II. 135, 140, 172.

[4] PRONI, D.591/519 and 536, Drennan to Sam McTier, 2 Aug and [Dec] 1792; Kent AO, U.840/O.143/3–10, information of Francis Higgins, Apr–June 1795; Rowan, *Autobiography*, 216–18.

[5] PRONI, D.519/539, Drennan to Mrs McTier, [Jan] 1795; *FJ*. 17 Jan 1795; PRO, H.O. 100/56/143–4, address from the Catholics of Dublin [Jan 1795].

[6] PRO, H.O. 100/46/259–78, 100/56/39–40, 47–243, various corr. to and from Fitzwilliam during his viceroyalty.

[7] PRONI, T.3229/1/7, Fitzgibbon to Auckland, 24 Mar [1795] giving a full account and claiming, among other things, that Fitzwilliam waited a full month before seeing him.

[8] PRONI, D.591/544, Drennan to Mrs McTier, 6 Feb 1795; see also *FJ*, 15 and 29 Jan 1795.

[9] Ann Arbor, Melville MSS, Douglas to Dundas, 17 Feb 1794.

[10] PRO, PRO 30/8/102/2/208–9, 264–7, 30/8/103/600–609, 30/8/108/2/196–7 and 110/2/251–4, corr. to and from Pitt, particularly on Fitzwilliam's controversial ministerial changes.

[11] *NS*, 2 Mar; *FJ*, 28 Feb 1795.

[12] *History of Belfast*, 432–3.

[13] PRONI, D.591/551, Drennan to Sam McTier, 24 Mar 1795.

¹⁴ Plowden, *History of Ireland*, IV. 155–6; *NS*, 22 Feb–2 Mar 1795.

¹⁵ PRO, H.O. 100/56/399, Catholic delegates to [Portland], 10 Mar 1795; the letter is in Tone's hand.

¹⁶ *Burke Corr.*, VII. 195; see also 193–4 and 213. The Catholic delegates called on Burke and gave him a full account; he was also briefed by Sir Thomas Dundas, Fitzwilliam's brother-in-law, who was present at their meeting with Portland.

¹⁷ PRO, PRO 30/327/319, [McNally] to Downshire, 30 Mar 1795—it was of Downshire, their old enemy, that they most complained while in London (*Burke Corr.*, VII. 193–4).

¹⁸ *FJ*, 17 Mar 1795. PRO, PRO 30/327/319, op. cit., and *Burke Corr.*, VIII. 213. Tone also spent time with John Russell and his radical friends in London (notably Hugh Bell, an Irish wine merchant, friend of Sir Francis Burdett): see TCD, MS 873/330, Tone to John Russell, 13 June 1795.

¹⁹ *NS*, 9–16 Apr 1795; Plowden, *History of Ireland*, IV. 163. The Belfast Catholics had likewise declared their solidarity with their 'Protestant Brethren', SPOI, 620/22/3, printed account of their meeting, 29 Mar 1795. See also *Burke Corr.*, VIII. 245.

²⁰ AA Baltimore, Carroll MSS, 8M3, Troy to Carroll, 29 Apr 1795; PRO, H.O. 100/46/303, instructions to Camden, 1 Mar 1795.

²¹ PRO, H.O. 100/46/301–6, 'Instructions to Lord Camden. To be carefully kept at the office, but not entered in the book', Whitehall, 1 Mar 1795.

²² See e.g., MacNeven's 1798 statement in *Pieces of Irish History*, 206. J. P. W. Ehrman, *The Younger Pitt*, 2 vols. (London, 1969–83), II. 438; McDowell, *Ireland in the Age of Imperialism and Revolution*, 458. Background on the Fitzwilliam affair has been taken from Grattan, *Life and Times*, IV. 170–232; *Beresford Corr.*, II. 35–120; Plowden, *History of Ireland*, IV. 120–82; Philip Henry, 5th Earl Stanhope, *Life of the Rt. Hon. William Pitt*, 4 vols. (London, 1861–2), II. 281–310; Lecky, *History of Ireland*, III. 238–330; R. B. McDowell: *Ireland in the Age of Imperialism and Revolution*, 445–61, his contribution to *A New History of Ireland*, IV. 339–46, and his 'The Fitzwilliam Episode', *IHS*, XVI (1966), 115–30; E. A. Smith, *Whig Principles and Party Politics* (Manchester, 1975), ch. 7.

²³ PRO, H.O. 100/57/75, Pelham to Portland, 6 Apr; H.O. 100/56/239–43, Fitzwilliam to Pitt, 14 Feb 1795.

²⁴ See *NS*, 13–20 Apr 1795.

²⁵ Curran, *Sketches of the Irish Bar*, I. 85–7; PRONI, D.591/530 and 554, Drennan to the McTiers, [17] Oct 1794 and 25 Apr 1795; PRO, H.O. 100/57/3, Lodge Morris to John King, 28 Mar 1795 and 100/56/3–4, 155, 159 and 216, corr. concerning Cockayne, Jan–Feb 1795.

²⁶ Howell, *State Trials*, XXV. 880.

²⁷ Tone (Dickason) MSS, original of Tone's statement; *Life*, I. 114–15.

²⁸ PRONI, D.591/554, Drennan to Sam McTier, 25 Apr 1795.

²⁹ *Life*, I. 125–6.

³⁰ Kent AO, U.840/O.143/9; for the debates see *NS*, 11 and 14 May 1795 (this last issue carried a special pull-out supplement with Arthur O'Connor's speech), *FJ*, 9 May 1795, *Parl. Reg.*, XV. 208–361, and Marcus Beresford's account in *Beresford Corr.*, II. 108–9.

³¹ *FJ*, 9 May 1795; *Life of Curran*, II. 157.

³² *FJ*, 7 May 1795.

³³ SPOI, 620/51/244; this letter is unsigned and undated, but appears to have been written in 1794, by one of the committee appointed to superintend the subscription, i.e., Hamill, Braughall, Sweetman, Keogh, Byrne, McCormick and Denis O'Brien (see Plowden, *History of Ireland*, IV. 55).

³⁴ See Reg. Deeds Ire., 487/496/314272, various leases to the Donnellans, 297/347/195310 (1773) and 374/532/250721 (1786). For young Richard Tone, see Katherine Anne Tone Maxwell, 'Irish Family History; Tone of Bodenstown, Co Kildare', *Notes and Queries*, VII (Nov 27, 1920), 432–3.

³⁵ SPOI, 620/16/3, bill of exchange dated 19 May 1794 for £796. 2s. 11d., to be drawn in Tone's name on Philadelphia; also *Life*, I. 126.

³⁶ *Life*, I. 281–2.

³⁷ Montesquieu's influential *Spirit of the Laws* (1748) proclaimed monarchy, moderated by intermediary bodies, the most acceptable form of government.

³⁸ The letters are in *Life*, I. 280–3.

[39] LC, Madison Papers, ser. 1, reel 13, Matilda Tone to Warden, 8 Jan 1812; *Life*, I. 14–17. Matthew Tone was then about to leave France (where he had been since Aug 1794) for America. See AN, AF III 64 doss. 264 fo. 24, memoir of Tone on his brother, 1 Oct 1795.

[40] Tone to Russell, 12 Mar 1794, in *The Life of Wolfe Tone*, abr. and ed. Bulmer Hobson (Dublin, 1920), 23; Tone (Dickason) MSS, Matilda to Catherine Anne Tone, 24 Nov 1839.

[41] Hobson, *Life of Tone*, 21–3; TCD, MS 868/2/299, Tone to Russell, 12 Mar 1794; SPOI, 620/21/23/80–83, Russell's journal for Feb–Mar 1795.

[42] PRONI, D.591/478–9, 482–3, 533–4, 540, correspondence between Mrs McTier and Drennan, Mar 1794–Jan 1795, also 449 (16 Nov 1793).

[43] Carey, *Appeal to the People of Ireland*, i–iv, 46–8, 94. The evidence for this social mix in the north (and indeed for very advanced thinking among the skilled trades) is overwhelming: see, e.g., SPOI 620/20/33/48, 51, 63 (Russell's journal), 620/22/19, digest of information on Defenderism and the United Irishmen, July 1795; 620/22/7b, declaration of the 'Ballyclare Convention', 20 May 1795; PRONI, D.591/345 (reading societies); *NS*, 15 Dec 1792, and PRO, H.O. 100/38/183–4 (Irish Jacobins, Belfast); MacNeven, *Pieces of Irish History*, 76–8. Nancy J. Curtin, 'The Origins of Irish Republicanism: The United Irishmen in Dublin and Ulster, 1791–8' (Univ. of Wis.—Madison D. Phil. thesis, 1988), 463–5, 471–85, and her 'The Transformation of the United Irishmen into a Revolutionary Mass Organisation, 1792–4', *IHS*, XXIV (1984–5), 463–92, suggests that the Ulster societies were always more militant and that the change in 1795 may not have been as novel as once assumed.

[44] SPOI, 620/21/23/70–73, Russell's journal, Jan 1794.

[45] TCD, MS 868/1/15–20, Russell's journal, 3 Nov 1794.

[46] PRONI, D.272/39, Alexander Marsden to Gen. Nugent, 21 Aug 1798. Emmet's account is in MacNeven, *Pieces of Irish History*, 76–8. As late as 1798 Thomas Storey—the Belfast printer with whom Russell associated in late 1794—was still so little known to the Castle that it was having difficulty finding enough information to include him in the Banishment Act.

[47] Kent AO, U.840/O.146/3, reports to the Castle on Russell, May 1795.

[48] PRONI, D.591/552, Drennan to Sam McTier, 1 Apr 1795.

[49] PRONI, D.591/518–19, 523–4, 550–52, Drennan's accounts of the regrouping, and of the changed opinion of the Catholics after Fitzwilliam; D.607/C/56, J. W. [McNally] to Downshire, 8 Dec 1795; Kent AO, U.840/O.143/3–4, 10, information of 13–24 Apr 1795.

[50] PRO, PRO 30/8/326/1/16–21, Camden to Pitt, 21 May 1795.

[51] PRO, H.O. 100/57/21–7 and Kent AO, U.840/O.143/10, information reaching the Castle, Mar–Apr 1795.

[52] *Life*, I. 124–7, also 291–3, unsigned letter, evidently from Keogh, 3 Sept 1795. See Matilda's confirmation of this in Hobson, *Life of Tone*, 159–65. AN, AF IV 1671 plaq. 1 fo. 100, Lewins's account of these events [1797].

[53] SPOI, 620/16/3, MacNeven to Russell [Aug 1798]. The leading state prisoners were preparing a full statement of the progress of the United Irishmen. The confusion about origins was not simply an attempt to distance themselves from the atrocities of 1798 (though there was an element of that).

[54] Tone (Dickason) MSS, certificates dated 10 June 1795, testifying to Tone's admission to the Belfast Society of United Irishmen and the Belfast National Volunteers (i.e., those condemned in 1792).

[55] MacNeven, *Pieces of Irish History*, 176–7; *Report from the Committee of Secrecy of the House of Commons* [Ireland] (Dublin, 1798), 46–52, 307; see also R. R. Madden, *Antrim and Down in '98* (Glasgow, n.d.), 96–7, 108.

[56] *Life*, I. 127.

[57] TCD, MS 873/330, note attached to Tone to John Russell, 13 June 1795.

[58] SPOI, 620/16/3, Tone to Russell, 1 Sept 1795 (also printed in *NS*, 15 Oct 1795 and *Irish Press*, 5 Oct 1955).

[59] Kent AO, U.840/O.147/4/1, Rowland O'Connor of the Belfast stamp office to Sackville Hamilton, 7 June 1795.

[60] TCD, MS 873/330(1), Tone, Matilda and Mary to John Russell, 13 June 1795.

[61] See *Life*, I. 127–8; TCD, MS 873/381, Dr McDonnell to Madden, 6 June 1843; McNeill, *Mary Ann McCracken*, 104–6; *NS*, 18 June 1795.

[62] Kent AO, U.840/O.147/4/1, op. cit.

Chapter 20

[1] *Life*, I. 183, 535 and 546; Madden, *United Irishmen*, 1st ser., II. 340–1; *NS*, 8 Sept 1792, 20 Feb and 4 Sept 1794; *DEP*, 9 Oct 1794.

[2] See Kerby A. Miller, *Emigrants and Exiles: Ireland and the Irish Exodus to America* (Oxford, 1985), 169–72.

[3] See TCD, MS 868/2/151, letter initialled 'H.M.' from Philadelphia [July 1795], giving information on fares and conditions of trans-Atlantic voyages.

[4] PRO, F.O. 5/10/282–5, Edmund Randolph to George Hammond, 5 May 1795; US Nat. Arch., Dept. of State, Dispatches from US Ministers to GB, M.30 rolls 2–4, also General Records, Diplomatic and Consular Instructions, M.28 roll 3, contain numerous accounts of incidents and complaints. Also Free Lib., Philadelphia, McIntire Elkins Coll., Pickering to A.A. Deas, 15 Sept 1795.

[5] TCD, MS 868/2/2–3, Tone to Russell, 7 Aug 1795, extracted in the *NS*, 5 Oct 1795, and commented upon by the *FJ*, 8 Oct 1795. *Life*, II. 128–30.

[6] *Life*, II. 192.

[7] Thomas M. Doerflinger, *A Vigorous Spirit of Enterprise: Merchants and Economic Development in Revolutionary Philadelphia* (Chapel Hill, N. Car., 1986), 74–5.

[8] Michael J. O'Brien, *George Washington's Associations with the Irish* (NY, 1937), 48–9; *Aurora*, 7 Aug 1795.

[9] Eric Foner, *Tom Paine and Revolutionary America* (NY, 1976), 19–28.

[10] David J. Jeremy, *Henry Wansey and his American Journal* (Philadelphia, 1970), 107–12; Doerflinger, *Vigorous Spirit of Enterprise*, 23, 39–40.

[11] TCD, MS 868/2/2–3, Tone to Russell, 7 Aug 1795.

[12] Rowan, *Autobiography*, 273–314, contains a very full account of his residence in America. Tone's description resembles so closely much of what Rowan says that Tone may have been influenced by Rowan's opinions. For Rowan's activities in France see AAE, Corr. Pol. Ang. 588 fos. 184–8, 196, 262–4, 267–9, 274–80, 313–18 and Personnel sér. 1, 65 fos. 57–64.

[13] The documentation on the Jay treaty controversy and Monroe's involvement is enormous. This account based on US Nat. Arch., Dept. of State, M.34 roll 6 (dispatches from US Ministers to France, 1794–6), M.30 roll 3 (US Ministers to GB, 1794–5), M.28 roll 3 (diplomatic and consular instructions), especially fos. 13–67, M.23 roll 1 (French legation in the US), R.G. 84 (correspondence from the American embassy in Paris, 1794–6); Monroe Papers in NYPL and LC, also misc. Monroe material in LC (Madison Papers, ser. 1 reels 5–6), in Hist. Soc. Pa. (Gratz Coll. Case 2 Box 16), Univ. Va. Charlottesville (MS 5320), Free Lib., Philadelphia (McIntire Elkins Coll.). See also S. F. Bemis, *Jay's Treaty: A Study in Commerce and Diplomacy* (rev. edn., New Haven, Conn., 1962); Beverley W. Bond, *The Monroe Mission to France, 1794–1796*, Johns Hopkins Univ. Studies in Historical and Political Sciences, ser. XXV, nos. 2–3 (Baltimore, 1907); and James Monroe, *A View of the Conduct of the Executive in the Foreign Affairs of the United States 1794–1796* (Philadelphia, 1797).

[14] AAE, Corr. Pol. États-Unis 44 fos. 84–6, Adet to the Committee of Public Safety, 3 July 1795; F. J. Turner, ed., 'Correspondence of the French Ministers to the United States, 1791–97', *Amer. Hist. Assoc. Rep.* 1903, 2 vols. (Washington, D.C., 1904), II. 741; Philip S. Foner, *The Democratic Republican Societies, 1790–1800* (Westport, Conn., 1976), 36; *Aurora*, 29 June, 3 July 1795.

[15] Richard Buel Jr., *Securing the Revolution: Ideology in American Politics, 1789–1815* (Ithaca, NY, and London, 1972), 54–71; Marvin R. Zahniser, *Charles Cotesworth Pinckney: Founding Father* (Chapel Hill, N. Car., 1967), 24–5; Donald H. Stewart, *The Opposition Press of the Federalist Period* (Albany, NY, 1969), 143–235; J. Combs, *The Jay Treaty: Political Battleground of the Founding Fathers* (Berkeley, Calif., 1970); A. Young, *The Democratic Republicans of New York: The Origins, 1763–1797* (Chapel Hill, N. Car., 1967); Alan Lee Blau, 'New York City and the French Revolution, 1789–1797: A Study of French Revolutionary Influence' (City Univ. of NY Ph.D thesis, 1973), 455–520; Ronald M. Baumann, 'The Democratic-Republicans of Philadelphia: The Origins, 1776–1797' (Pa. State Univ. Ph.D. thesis, 1970), 512–22.

[16] Bernard Mayo, ed., 'Instructions to the British Ministers to the United States, 1791–1812', *Ann. Rep. Amer. Hist. Assoc.* (Washington, D.C., 1936), 83–9.

[17] See US Nat. Arch., Dept. of State Records, M.28/245, Instructions to Pinckney (Monroe's replacement), 14 Sept 1796, referring to Adet's distrust of the USA; Blau, 'New York City and the French Revolution', 520.

[18] Turner, 'Correspondence of the French Ministers', 734–83; US Nat. Arch., M.34 Roll 6 fos. 326–424 and M.53 Roll 1, for the frosty relations between Adet and the US government; Bond, *Monroe Mission to France*, 57–8.

[19] The report was written, Tone recalled, 'in the burning summer of Pennsylvania, when my head was extremely deranged by the Heat': TCD, MS 2048/17v; it was 92°F. in the shade: *Aurora*, 11 Aug 1795.

[20] P. C. Stoddart, 'Counter-Insurgency and Defence in Ireland, 1790–1805' (Oxford Univ. D. Phil. thesis, 1972), 86–91; PRO, H.O. 100/54/35, 'Proposed disposition of forces voted by Parliament for the service of Ireland, 1795'; BL, Add. MS 33,113/22, Pelham to the Duke of York, 18 Apr 1795 and fos. 66–70, 'Returns of the numbers of men furnished by Ireland for general service...1793–1 Nov 1796'.

[21] Elliott, *Partners in Revolution*, 138; R. A. E. Wells, *Insurrection: The British Experience, 1795–1803* (Gloucester, 1983), ch. 5; Lecky, *History of Ireland*, III. 515–17; and see Kent AO, U.840/O.143/6 and *NS*, 13 Apr 1794, for contemporary statements to this effect.

[22] AAE, Mém. et Doc. Ang. 19 fos. 378–88, memoirs by Madgett [1795].

[23] Tone (Dickason) MSS, copy Tone to Adet, 10 Aug 1795, likewise the various certificates presented as credentials.

[24] Tone assumed that the Jackson paper had reached the French government and indeed it had, via Rowan. Rowan never mentioned Tone, and Adet's communications perpetuated the confusion over the roles and identities of the two men. See AAE, Corr. Pol. Ang. 589 fo. 23. However, Tone's involvement with Jackson was already known: see AAE, Corr. Pol. Ang. 586 fos. 377–449, printed account of Jackson's trial, which arrived in May–June 1795.

[25] See AN, BB³ 107 fos. 180–90, for French interest in Scotland at this time; also PRO, H.O. 100/62/141, secret information 23 July 1796 on the follow-up to UI Scottish plans.

[26] Tone's memoir is in AN, AF III 64 doss. 264 fos. 17 and 20, which indicates that it did reach the Directory.

[27] AAE, Corr. Pol. États-Unis 44 fo. 334, Adet to the Committee of Public Safety, 1 Oct 1795, enclosing Tone's memoirs (fos. 335–6); copies of Tone's papers are also in Corr. Pol. Ang. 589 fo. 23 and AN, AF III 64 fos. 17 and 20. Adet's letter is also printed in Turner, 'Correspondence of the French Ministers', 786–7; see also pp. 800 and 806–8 for his complaints about lack of instructions.

[28] Rowan, *Autobiography*, 283, Rowan to his wife, 7 Sept 1795.

[29] SPOI, 620/16/3, Tone to Russell, 1 Sept 1795.

[30] Rowan, *Autobiography*, 289, 291, 294–5; *NS*, 10–15 Oct 1795, letter of either Reynolds or Rowan; TCD, MS 868/2/207–8, letter from Boston to Thomas Storey, 5 Feb 1796; Jeremy, *Wansey Journal*, 91; Doerflinger, *Vigorous Spirit of Enterprise*, 30; James T. Kloppenberg, 'The Virtues of Liberalism: Christianity, Republicanism, and Ethics in Early American Political Discourse', *Jnl Amer. Hist*, LXXIV (June 1987), 19.

[31] TCD, MS 868/2/13–15,, op. cit.

[32] TCD, MS 2046/66v–67, journal entry omitted from *Life*, I. 133.

[33] Bodl., Bland Burges Dep., 44 fos. 5–9 and 38, Thornton to Bland Burges, 31 Oct, 5 Dec 1791, 25 July 1792.

[34] Thomas Cooper, *Letters from America to a Friend in England* (London, 1794), 52 and 64. See also Richard J. Twomey, 'Jacobins and Jeffersonians: Anglo-American Radical Ideology, 1790–1810', in *The Origins of Anglo-American Radicalism*, ed. Margaret and James Jacob (London, 1984), 284–99; Bonwick, 'Joseph Priestley', 1–22; and Durey, 'Thomas Paine's Apostles', 681–8.

[35] TCD, MS 2046/66v–67, omitted from, *Life*, II. 133; in *Autobiography*, ed. O'Faolain, 86–7, but with omissions and several misquotes.

[36] *Drennan Letters*, 315.

[37] *NS*, 8 Sept 1792.

[38] Note the contrast with Cooper (*Letters from America*, 52–3), who admired in America the absence of tithes, game laws, poverty, religious animosity, crime and excessive rank and riches.

[39] *Aurora*, 22 Aug, 19 Oct, 23 Nov 1795; Maurice J. Bric, 'The Irish and the Evolution of

the "New Politics" in America', in P. J. Drudy, ed., *Irish Studies*, 4: *The Irish in America* (Cambridge, 1985), 143–67; E. C. Carter, 'A "Wild Irishman" under every Federalist Bed', *Pa. Mag. Hist. and Biog.*, XCIV (1970), 331–46; James Morton Smith, *Freedom's Fetters: The Alien and Sedition Laws and American Civil Liberties* (Ithaca, NY, 1956), particularly 23–6, 50, 163, 278–82.

[40] See in particular Lance Banning, *The Jeffersonian Persuasion: Evolution of a Party Ideology* (Ithaca, NY, 1978) and his 'Jeffersonian Ideology Revisited: Liberal and Classical Ideas in the New American Republic', *WMQ*, 3rd ser., XLIII (Jan 1986), 3–19, Joyce Appleby's response, 'Republicanism in Old and New Contexts', in the same issue, 20–34, and her *Capitalism and a New Social Order: The Republican Vision of the 1790s* (NY, 1984). But see the useful corrective by Kloppenberg, 'The Virtues of Liberalism', 9–33; Durey, 'Thomas Paine's Apostles', 661–8. See also Pocock, *Machiavellian Moment*, whose treatment of the development of classical republican ideas is at the centre of the debate.

[41] *Aurora*, 11 Aug, 8 Sept, 17 Oct 1795 (though every issue is an exercise in such Republican rhetoric); Buel, *Securing the Revolution*, particularly pts. ii and iii; P. S. Foner, *Democratic Republican Societies*; and for a still very full and clear account of the period, see John C. Miller, *The Federalist Era, 1789–1801* (NY, 1963).

[42] Even the British minister in America, Edward Thornton, was struck by Washington's monarchical tendencies and a greater degree of aristocracy in government than in 'monarchical countries': Bodl., Bland Burges Dep., 44 fos. 30–8.

[43] This is typical Democratic Republican rhetoric: see Doerflinger, *Vigorous Spirit of Enterprise*, 15–16, 23–6, 270–80.

[44] SPOI, 620/16/3, Tone to Russell, 1 Sept 1795; the incident described was that of the Philadelphia bankers procuring signatures to pro-treaty addresses by reminding creditors of their debts. See the *Aurora*, 22, 25, 27 and 31 Aug, also 21–2 Aug and 8 Sept 1795, for the growing attack on Washington. Adet was saying much the same thing; see, e.g., AAE, Corr. Pol. États-Unis 44 fos. 72–5.

[45] See Stewart, *Opposition Press*, 132–42, on the Anglophobia of the American Republican press.

[46] TCD, MS 868/2/13–15, Tone to Russell, 25 Oct 1795; most of the above comments are taken from Tone's letter of 1 Sept 1795, SPOI 620/16/3. See also *NS*, 8 Sept 1794, for Tone's admiration of cheap government in America.

[47] Edmund and Dorothy Smith Berkeley, *John Beckley: Zealous Partisan in a Nation Divided* (Philadelphia, 1973); Philip M. Marsh, 'John Beckley, Mystery Man of the Early Jeffersonians', *Pa. Mag. Hist. and Biog.*, LXXII (1948), 54–69. See NYPL, Monroe Papers (in particular letters dated 14 Dec 1795 and 2 Apr 1796), LC, Monroe Papers, Ser. 1, 23 June, 23 Sept 1795, Univ. Va. Charlottesville, Beckley Papers 2764a, for Beckley's correspondence with Monroe.

[48] *The American Gazetteer*, ed. J. Morse (Boston, 1797).

[49] Kenneth R. Rossman, *Thomas Mifflin and the Politics of the American Revolution* (Chapel Hill, N. Car., 1952); entry in *DAB*, XII. 606–8; Rowan, *Autobiography*, 283–4; TCD, MS 868/2/13–15, Tone [under pseud. William Penn] to Russell, 25 Oct 1795. Mifflin unfortunately left no private or personal letters.

[50] SPOI, 620/16/3, op. cit.

[51] Rowan, *Autobiography*, 291.

[52] Tone (Dickason) MSS, undated scrap of paper in Tone's hand concerning career and residence plans; also the originals of Todd Jones's letters dated 18 July and 20 Aug 1793 (reproduced in *Life*, I. 275–6, the latter printed mistakenly in the 1795 section, 282). Rowan, *Autobiography*, 283, Rowan to his wife, 7 Sept 1795. LC, Monroe Papers, ser. 1, Monroe to [Beckley], 1 and 5 Aug 1796, on Edwards.

[53] Bodl. Bland Burges Dep., 44 fo 38, Thornton to Bland Burges, 25 July 1792; Jeremy, *Wansey Journal*, 96, 112.

[54] The words are Rowan's—*Autobiography*, 282—but had clearly been related by Tone.

[55] Jeremy, *Wansey Journal*, 91–3, 125; *American Gazetteer*, 'Princeton'.

[56] 'Farmer' is substituted in the printed *Life*, I. 133, but 'boor' is used in the original: see TCD, MS 2046/66v–67.

[57] John F. Hageman, *History of Princeton*, 2 vols. (Philadelphia, 1879), I. 46, on the Leonard family property; and see Jeremy, *Wansey Journal*, 125, and *Aurora*, 17 and 21 Sept 1795, on property in New Jersey.

[58] Cooper, *Letters from America*, 51.

[59] The account is taken from Tone's letters to Russell, SPOI, 620/16/3 and TCD, MS 868/2/13–15, cited above, also *Life*, I. 133–4.

[60] The gentry he described in typical Democratic Republican language as 'speculating stockjobbers on the rights of the people': *Life*, I. 286.

[61] Letter to O'Connor, 20 Oct 1795, *Life*, I. 284–9.

[62] Letter to O'Connor, 20 Oct 1795, *Life*, I. 284–9.

[63] PRO, H.O. 100/62/149, J. W. [McNally] report on Tandy's corr., 26 July 1796; SPOI, 620/12/144, Tandy to his son, 1 Oct 1796.

[64] TCD, MS 868/2/13–15, Tone to Russell, 25 Oct 1795.

[65] *Life*, I. 283–4, 289–93, letters from [Keogh], Robert Simms and [Russell], 3, 18 and 21 Sept 1795, also from another unnamed Belfast United Irishman.

[66] Rowan, *Autobiography*, 266, 286–7, PRONI, D.591/461 and 484, Drennan on Mrs Rowan, 17 Jan and 31 Mar 1794.

[67] *Life*, I. 293.

[68] SPOI, 620/25/136, Matilda to Russell, 11 Sept 1796. See also TCD, MS 873/42, printed letter of Madden to Matilda, 21 Dec 1842, on the authorship of the letters; and MacNeven, *Pieces of Irish History*, 103–21.

[69] *Life*, II. 172.

[70] See SPOI, 620/25/136, Matilda to Russell, 11 Nov 1796; TCD, Dillon MS 6906/51, 58–60, Charles Hart's account of an interview with Matilda, 4 Mar 1849. I am grateful to Dr Chris Woods for drawing my attention to this document. I have also learnt much of Matilda's character from Mrs Katherine Dickason, whose grandmother remembered Matilda well.

[71] NYPL, Monroe Papers, Beckley to Monroe, 14 Dec 1795; Adet's dispatch of 2 Dec is printed in Turner, 'Correspondence of the French Ministers', 793–803; and see AAE, Corr. Pol. Ang. 589 fos. 111–15, Madgett to Delacroix, 29 Dec 1795.

[72] *Life*, II. 485; also Tone (Dickason) MSS, Tone to Matilda, 2 Sept 1798.

[73] *NS*, 18 Jan 1796.

[74] The travel notepad in which he signed is in TCD, MS 2047.

[75] Howell, *State Trials*, XXVII. 622.

[76] *Life*, I. 130–6, the account of his American residence.

Chapter 21

[1] Albert Mathiez, 'Le personnel gouvernemental du Directoire', *AhRf*, no. 59 (1933), 392, also 385–411, for an excellent portrait of the personalities of the regime; *Mémoires de La Révellière-Lépeaux*, ed. his son, 3. vols. (Paris, 1895), I. 332–55; R. Guyot, *Le Directoire et la paix de L'Europe* (Paris, 1911), 41–65.

[2] A full research analysis of the Directory remains to be written. Older works tend to be hostile: L. Sciout, *Le Directoire*, 4 vols. (Paris, 1895); A. Sorel, *L'Europe et la Révolution française*, 8 vols. (Paris, 1885), vol. V (whose damning picture was effectively contested by Guyot in *Le Directoire et la paix de l'Europe*); A. C. Thibaudeau, *Mémoires sur la Convention et le Directoire*, 2 vols. (Paris, 1824), vol. II. G. Lefebvre, *Le Directoire* (Paris, 1946, tr. NY, 1964), perhaps the most frequently consulted work on the period, perpetuated many of the nineteenth-century conclusions, and until the 1970s Albert Goodwin's call for a more balanced approach, 'The French Executive Directory—a Re-evaluation', *History*, XXII (1937), 201–18, went unanswered. Denis Woronoff, *La République bourgeoise: de Thermidor à Brumaire 1794–1799* (Paris, 1972; tr. Cambridge, 1984), Clive Church, 'In Search of the Directory', in *French Government and Society 1500–1850: Essays in Memory of A. Cobban*, ed. J. F. Bosher (London, 1973), Martyn Lyons, *France under the Directory* (Cambridge, 1975)—still the most comprehensive and accessible survey—and Jean-René Surratteau, 'Le Directoire—points de vue et interprétations d'après des travaux récents', *AhRf* (1976), 181–214, redressed the balance. The Goodwin approach has been the trend until lately (e.g. in the works of Clive Church, Colin Lucas and my own *Partners in Revolution*). In recent generalist works, however, there has been a return to the hostility of the nineteenth century (notably in D. M. G. Sutherland, *France 1789–1815: Revolution and Counterrevolution* (London, 1985) and Jacques Solé, *La Révolution en questions* (Paris, 1988). We must await Howard Brown's Oxford Univ. doctoral thesis, 'Power, Bureaucracy and the State Élite: The Revolutionary Politics of Army Control and Administration in France, 1792–1799', for an analysis of the operation of the Directory at the centre.

³ On the whole the Directory was popular at the outset, despite persistent criticism of its economic policies; see A. Aulard, *Paris pendant la réaction thermidorienne et sous le Directoire*, 5 vols. (Paris, 1898–1902), II. 351–3, 637, III. 224–36.

⁴ *Life*, II. 59. The playwright Ducis was forced to change the sharper aspects of Shakespeare for the Paris audiences; see Marvin Carlson, *The Theatre of the French Revolution* (Ithaca, NY, 1966), 140–2.

⁵ J. Godechot, *Les Institutions de la France sous la Révolution et l'Empire*, 3rd edn. (Paris, 1985), 493, also his *La Vie quotidienne en France sous le Directoire* (Paris, 1977), 161–4. Theatre managers were compelled to play the patriotic songs which so moved Tone and to suppress others. The most popular plays were those hostile to the Revolution.

⁶ TCD, MS 2048/20; and *Life*, II. 39 and 42, and for his comments on the theatre and opera, 3–4, 8–9, 11, 13, 47, 59, 74, 87, 88, 100, 102, 103, 111–12, 136, 148, 158, 162, 170, 173, 177, 180.

⁷ TCD, MS 2047/13v and 16, omitted from *Life*, II. 8. Tone's Paris journal for 1796 is printed, with many omissions, in vol. II. 1–180; the original, in three small notebooks, is in TCD, MS 2047–9.

⁸ TCD, MS 2049/51v; *Life*, II. 97–8.

⁹ TCD, MS 2049/55v; *Life*, II. 103. Tone was enraptured by Louise Contat, and with reason. She was one of Paris's most talented actresses, for whom Beaumarchais had created the role of Suzanne in *The Marriage of Figaro*; see Carlson, *Theatre of the French Revolution*, 4–5.

¹⁰ TCD, MS 2047/6, his drawing of such 'grotesque headdresses'.

¹¹ Godechot, *La Vie quotidienne sous le Directoire*, 131–2, 138–60.

¹² TCD, MS 2049/40; *Life*, II. 87.

¹³ *Life*, I. 246.

¹⁴ TCD, MS 2048/21; *Life*, II. 40–1.

¹⁵ TCD, MS 2049/116v; *Life*, II. 167.

¹⁶ TCD, MS 2049/72v (omitted from *Life*, II. 120).

¹⁷ TCD, MS 2047/20v; *Life*, II. 39–40.

¹⁸ TCD, MS 2049/34; *Life*, II. 79–80.

¹⁹ See TCD, MS 2047/21, 2048/17v, 2049/73v and 119.

²⁰ LC, Monroe Papers, ser. 1, reel 1, Monroe to Delacroix, 9 Dec 1795 and [Beckley], 1 Aug 1796, ser. 5, box 1, Monroe-Paine corr., 1794–6, also Madison Papers, reel 6, Monroe-Madison corr. Jan–Apr 1796; NYPL, Monroe Papers, Monroe to Thomas Pinckney, 7 Jan and to the French Police Minister, 29 Mar 1796.

²¹ *Life*, II. 32.

²² Frédéric Masson, *Le Département des Affaires Étrangères pendant la Révolution, 1787–1804* (Paris, 1877), 361–3; Godechot, *Les Institutions de la France*, 457–68; Mathiez, 'Le personnel gouvernementale du Directoire', 399–407; P. J. B. Buchez and P. C. Roux-Lavergne, *Histoire parlementaire de la Révolution française*, 40 vols. (Paris, 1834–8), XXXVI. 485–517; PRO, F.O. 27/47, royalist reports from France, May 1796, depicting the ministers as 'les valets du Directoire'; AN, AF IV 1597ᴬ plaq. 1 pᶜᵉ 10, Truguet's complaints about the Directory's attitude to its ministers.

²³ Sciout, *Le Directoire*, I. 427, is scathing on Delacroix; see also S. S. Biro, *The German Policy of Revolutionary France*, 2 vols. (Cambridge, Mass, 1957), 492 and 497–8; PRO, F.O. 27/47, royalist information from Paris, 9 Apr 1796, dismissing Delacroix as a nonenity.

²⁴ AAE, Corr. Pol. Ang., 589 fos. 111–15, Madgett to Delacroix, 29 Dec 1795; see also Elliott, *Partners in Revolution*, 60–3.

²⁵ The royalist-promoted uprising of Chouans, Catholic peasants in Brittany, against the Revolution at times deteriorated into sheer banditry and bloodletting.

²⁶ Guyot, 'Le personnel gouvernemental du Directoire', 173, 248–9; AN, F⁷ 7111–14 and 7151 doss. 4646.

²⁷ See PRO, F.O. 27/47, report by the English official in France responsible for prisoner-of-war exchange, to whom Madgett had been bragging, 25 Apr 1796.

²⁸ See Masson, *Le Département des Affaires Étrangères*, 380–2.

²⁹ See, e.g., AAE, Corr. Pol. Ang. 589 fos. 159–61, 'Notes sur l'Irlande', by Madgett, written during a working breakfast with Tone (*Life*, II. 53–4), also fo. 221; also AAE, Mem. et Doc. Ang., 53 fos. 240–6, two memorials on Ireland 1796, one in Madgett's hand, relating Tone's arguments almost verbatim.

[30] On Duckett, see Elliott, *Partners in Revolution*, particularly pp. 59–60, 139–42 and 218–20; a physical description of him is in PRO, F.O. 33/15/7 and 10 (he was well known to the British authorities); his communications with the French government during these months are mostly in AN, AF III 186[b] doss. 858–9 and AAE, Corr. Pol. Ang. 589. In his police file (AN, F[7] 7249 doss. B[3] 8073) he is described by Delacroix as having an 'esprit remuant' and as a danger to security.

[31] TCD, MS 2049/31; *Life*, II. 75–6.

[32] *Mémoires de Barras*, ed. G. Duruy, 4 vols. (Paris, 1896), II. 104 and 160; Biro, *German Policy of Revolutionary France*, I. 610–11; T. Aubin, 'Le rôle politique de Carnot, depuis les élections de germinal an V jusqu'au coup d'état du 18 fructidor', *AhRf*, no. 49 (1932), 37–51;A. Mathiez, 'Le personnel gouvernemental du Directoire', 397–9.

[33] M. Reinhard, *Le Grand Carnot: L'organisateur de la victoire*, 2 vols. (Paris, 1950), II. 216–20.

[34] TCD, MS 2048/10.

[35] TCD, MS 2048/11–12.

[36] TCD, MS 2049/47; *Life*, II. 92–3.

[37] See, e.g., E. Guillon, *La France et l'Irlande sous le Directoire* (Paris, 1888), 174; endorsement of the copies in AN, AF III 186[b] doss. 857 p[ce] 20; AN, BB[4] 103 fo. 134, AF III 205 doss. 949 p[ce] 9, and AF IV 1597[A] plaq. 1[1]; *Mémoires sur Carnot par son fils*, 2 vols. (Paris, 1861–4), II. 80–3.

[38] *Life*, II. 181–204; translated copies of the memorials are in AN, AF III 186[b] doss. 857 p[ces] 20–1, and AN, BB[4] 103/136–52; original copies by Tone in AF IV 1671, plaq. 1, fos. 88–98.

[39] MacNeven, *Pieces of Irish History*, 11; these claims are endorsed by the detailed compilation of information on the Defenders and the United Irishmen sent to the Home Secretary, 25 July 1795, SPOI, 620/22/19. See also AN, AF III 58 doss. 228 p[ce] 1, Irish parliamentary debates taken from the *Courier*. See also AN, AF III 186[b] doss. 858 and AAE, Corr. Pol. Ang. 589 fos. 155–7, for Duckett's memorials on Ireland, May–June 1796.

[40] SPOI, 620/22/29, Archbishop Troy to Robert Marshall, 8 Aug 1795.

[41] AHG, B[11]1, Hoche to the Directory, 28 Apr and 9 June 1796, also the Directory to the Minister of War, 19 Apr and undated [spring 1796] Chouan project by Humbert. Further details on the Chouan expedition can be found in AHG, B[1]173 fo. 6; ADSM (Hoche Papers) 1Mi/58/226/1614, Carnot to Hoche, 23 June; AN, AF III 362 doss. 1734, orders of 18–19 Apr (also in A. Debidour, *Recueil des actes du Directoire exécutif*, 4 vols. (Paris, 1910–17), II. 176).

[42] AN, AF IV 1671 plaq. 1 p[ce] 65 Tone to Clarke, 3 Apr 1796; *Life*, II. 80–2; see also AAE, Corr. Pol. Ang., 589 fos. 280–1, Tone's 'observations' on Aherne's instructions, 1 June (see TCD, MS 2050/11–14, Tone's copy of and observations on the instructions).

[43] See Col. H. Berthaut, *Les Ingénieurs géographes militaires, 1624–1831*, 2 vols. (Paris, 1902), II. 144–5; J. Godechot, *Les Commissaires aux armées sous le Directoire*, 2 vols. (Paris, 1937), I. 42–3; Reinhard, *Le Grand Carnot*, II. 169; Mathiez. 'Le Personnel gouvernmentale du Directoire', 408–9; Guyot, *Le Directoire et la paix de l'Europe*, 70–1.

[44] TCD, MS 2049/5v; *Life*, II. 50–1.

[45] These copies are in AN, AF IV 1671 plaq. 1 p[ces] 88–98, and 66, the covering letter to Clarke, 23 Mar 1796. They differ in small details from the original of February. TCD, MS 2049/16–16v; *Life*, II. 61–3.

[46] *Life*, II. 52. See also AAE, Corr. Pol. Ang. 589 fo. 395, Tone to Delacroix, 17 Sept 1796. See Delacroix's tetchy response of 27 Mar to Clarke's query about the memorials, in AN, AF III 186[b] doss. 859 p[ce] 3.

[47] Elliott, *Partners in Revolution*, 90–2.

[48] AN, AF IV 1671 plaq. 1 fos. 68–72, Tone to Clarke, 7, 15 and 17 May 1796; and see Sorel, *L'Europe et la Révolution française*, V. 140–1, on Clarke's manner.

[49] AN, AF IV 1671 plaq. 1 fos. 68–9, Tone to Clarke, 7 May 1796, and Clarke's reply in *Life*, II. 108.

[50] TCD, MS 2049/73v; *Life*, II. 58.

[51] TCD, MS 2048/24; the edited version is considerably milder: 'I also added that I had a strong objection to letting priests into the business at all; that most of them were enemies to the French Revolution' (see, *Life*, II. 45). Also omitted from *Life*, II. 59, is Tone's description of Ancien Régime France as 'under the yoke of popery and despots' (TCD, MS 2049/14v).

[52] See police file on Aherne, AN, F[7]7401 doss. B[5]3830; AAE, Corr. Pol. Ang., 589 fo. 182,

Madgett recommending him to Delacroix, 2 Mar 1796.

[53] AN, BB[3] 107 fo. 180, Aherne to the Minister of Marine, 25 May 1796.

[54] Tone's 'observations' in AHG, B[11]1 [20 Apr 1796], AAE, Corr. Pol. Ang., 589 fos. 280–1, and TCD, MS 2050/11–14.

[55] The instructions are in AN, AF III 186[b] doss. 859, and AAE, Corr. Pol. Ang. 589 fos. 267–9.

[56] Life, II. 94–7.

[57] See AAE, Corr. Pol. Ang., 589 fos. 264–6, AN AF III 57 doss. 224 fos. 7–8, and Debidour, Recueil des actes, II. 489–90, for the correspondence on the Aherne/O'Shee affair.

[58] Debidour, Recueil des actes, II. 660–2; AHG, B[11]1, the Directory to Hoche, 19 June 1796, and Hoche's reply of 23 June; ADSM, 1Mi/58/126/1593; E. Desbrière, Projets et tentatives de débarquements aux îles britanniques, 4 vols. (Paris, 1900–2), I. 107–9.

[59] See Maurice Hutt, Chouannerie and Counter-Revolution: Puisaye, the Princes and the British Government in the 1790s, 2 vols. (Cambridge, 1983), II. 358–9; Donald [D.M.G.] Sutherland, The Chouans: The Social Origins of Popular Counter-Revolution in Upper Brittany 1770–1796 (Oxford, 1982), 294–300.

[60] Debidour, Recueil des actes, II. 688–9, Carnot to Hoche, 22 June 1796.

[61] Debidour, Recueil des actes, II. 697–9, the Directory to Hoche, 23 June 1796; Life, II. 127.

Chapter 22

[1] See SPOI, S.O.C. 1015/3–15, and 620/10/121/26–9; PRO, H.O. 100/62–3, PRO 30/8/326/42–4 and Parl. Reg. XVI. 16–20, 42–53, for the disturbances, the Defender trials and executions, and the passage of the Insurrection and Indemnity Acts. See also T. MacNevin, The Lives and Trials of...Eminent Irishmen (Dublin, 1846), 314–479; Plowden, History of Ireland, IV. 185–211; Grattan, Life and Times, IV. 231–44.

[2] SPOI, S.O.C. 1015/21, Earl of Altamount, governor of Mayo, to [Cooke], 27 June 1796, on the plight of the Catholics forced to flee there. P. Tohall, 'The Diamond Fight of 1795 and the Resultant Expulsions', Seanchas Ardmhacha, III (1958), 17–50. McDowell, Ireland in the Age of Imperialism and Revolution, 464–71.

[3] PRO, H.O. 100/64/168–72, Camden to Portland, 6 Aug 1796, and H.O. 100/63/193–4 and 215–21, their correspondence of Feb–Mar 1796.

[4] PRO, H.O. 100/59/68–9 and 100/62/15–19, Camden to Portland, 6 Nov 1795 and 22 Jan 1796.

[5] See the heated exchange between Dublin and London on this extraordinary measure in PRO, H.O. 100/62/39–98, also 100/63/215–21, and PRO 30/8/326/72–5.

[6] Elliott, Partners in Revolution, 96; MacNeven, Pieces of Irish History, 117–20, 178–9; PRO, H.O. 100/62/135–8, secret information enclosed in Cooke to Pelham, 30 July 1796.

[7] See AN, AF IV 1671 plaq. 1 fos. 100–5, Lewins's account of these events. Keogh, also among the inner leadership, was then in England.

[8] AAE, Corr. Pol. Ang. 589 fo. 262, Delacroix to Reinhard, 31 May 1796, also fos. 249–53, Reinhard's letter of 18 May.

[9] AAE, Corr. Pol. Ang. 589 fos. 399–402, statement enclosed in [Barthélemy, French ambassador to Switzerland], to Delacroix, 6 July 1796, copy in AN, AF III 186[b] doss. 859 p[ces] 24–5.

[10] Life, II. 137–8. For a full account of the Fitzgerald/O'Connor mission, see Elliott, Partners in Revolution, 98–103. See also Barthélemy's later account of the mission in PRO, F.O. 27/54, in C. W. Flint to J. King, 13 July 1799, also in Hants RO, 38M49/1/56 (Wickham MSS).

[11] Tone (Dickason) MSS, Clarke to Tone, 12 July 1796.

[12] TCD, MS 2049/102v.

[13] AHG, B[11]1, Hoche to the Directory, 23 June 1796.

[14] Hutt, Chouannerie and Counter-Revolution, II. 448; E. Cuneo d'Ornano, Hoche, sa vie, sa correspondance (Paris, 1892), pt. 11, 249, 256, 259–62, 282.

[15] TCD, MS 2049/103–103v; Life, II. 152–4.

[16] AN, AF III 186[b] doss. 859 p[ce] 58, Hoche to the Directory, 16 July 1796.

[17] NLI, MS 704/19–23, 'Instructions pour le Général en Chef Hoche sur l'expédition d'Irlande', 20 July 1796, signed by Carnot and Letourneur (Carnot's only ally on the

Directory).

[18] *Life*, II. 168 and 159–62, also 42–4, 94, 160 and 309 on his fears of continuing French interference.

[19] TCD, MS 2049/105; *Life*, II. 155.

[20] Debidour, *Recueil des actes*, III. 111–12, 'Délibération[s] Secrète[s]', 16 and 20 July 1796; AN, AF III 147 doss. 694 fos. 116 and 205, Petiet to the Directory, 19 July and 14 Aug; AHG, B[11]1, arrêté of 20 July and Hoche's official acceptance, 6 Aug; AN, AF III 186[b] doss. 859 p[ce] 94, 'Inventaire des cartes données au Général Hoche', 22 July 1796.

[21] Debidour, *Recueil des actes*, III. 167; AHG, B[11]1, Barthélemy to the Directory, 30 July 1796.

[22] TCD, MS 2049/27; *Life*, II. 71.

[23] TCD, MS 2049/91; *Life*, II. 139, 157. The Légion de Police had mutinied in support of the Babouvists and had always shown a particular resistance to fighting at the front. See Jean-Paul Bertaud, *La Révolution armée: les soldats-citoyens et la Révolution française* (Paris, 1979), 315, 318, 319; Debidour, *Recueil des actes*, II. 697, Directory to Hoche, 23 June 1796, announcing Tone's appointment to the Légion de Police (he did not learn of it until 16 July). His commission is in Tone (Dickason) MSS, Petiet, Minister of War, to Tone, 17 July 1796.

[24] *Life*, II. 159–60, 176.

[25] TCD, MS 2049/105v.

[26] TCD, MS 2049/110; *Life*, II. 159, 162–4. He never drew his rations: see AN, AF IV 1671 plaq. 1 fo. 84, Tone to [Clarke], 5 Sept 1796.

[27] *Life*, II. 159–69; AN, AF IV 1671 plaq. 1 fo. 81, James Smith [Tone] to Carnot, 18 July 1796.

[28] TCD, MS 2049/121; *Life*, II. 172.

[29] AAE, Corr. Pol. Ang. 589 fos. 169–70, Tone to Delacroix, 26 Feb 1796.

[30] TCD, MS 2049/90; *Life*, II. 139.

[31] See, e.g., *Life*, II. 31.

[32] TCD, MS 2048/13–13v; *Life*, II. 29–30.

[33] *Life*, II. 139.

[34] TCD, MS 2049/121v; *Life*, II. 172.

[35] TCD, MS 2049/29; *Life*, II. 73–4.

[36] TCD, MS 2049/91; *Life*, II. 139.

[37] TCD, MS 2048/4v; *Life*, II. 18–19.

[38] AN, AF IV 1671 plaq. 1 fo. 82, Smith [Tone] to Clarke, 18 July 1796, also fo. 77; AF III 186[b] doss. 859 p[ce] 60, Smith [Tone] to Clarke, 21 July.

[39] TCD, MS 2049/97v; *Life*, II. 147 and 169.

[40] See J. C. Beckett in *A New History of Ireland*, IV. lx–lxiv; Claire O'Halloran, '"The Island of Saints and Scholars": Views of the Early Church and Sectarian Politics in Late Eighteenth-Century Ireland', unpubd. paper delivered to the 6th conference of Irish Historians in Britain, Durham, 1988; Jacqueline R. Hill, 'Popery and Protestantism, Civil and Religious Liberty: The Disputed Lessons of Irish History 1690–1812', *Past and Present*, no. 118 (1987), 96–129.

[41] Hist. Soc. Pa., Carey MSS, Emmet to Carey, 22 Apr 1819; see e.g., TCD, Mun. Soc. Hist. IV 5 May 1784.

[42] *Life*, II. 30.

[43] TCD, MS 2049/21; *Life*, II. 65–7, 97, 99, 295–316.

[44] The MS notebooks are in TCD, MS 2046, printed in *Life*, I. 11–69.

Chapter 23

[1] AAE, Corr. Pol. Ang. 589 fo. 395, Tone to Delacroix, 17 Sept 1796; *Life*, II. 179.

[2] *Life*, II. 179–80, 205–7; TCD, MS 2049/130.

[3] TCD, MS 2049/145; *Life*, II. 221, also 207.

[4] AN, AF III 186[b] doss. 860 p[ces] 55–6, Duckett's complaints to Gen. Dalton, 23 Oct 1796. *Life*, II. 219–21.

[5] AN, AF III 186[b] doss. 860 p[ce] 6, Hoche to Clarke, 2 Oct 1796.

[6] TCD, MS 2049/164–5; *Life*, II. 242.

[7] AHG, B[11]1, Directory to Hoche , 25 Oct and his reply, 1 Nov 1796.

[8] See Hutt, *Chouannerie and Counter-Revolution*, II. 233n., 437 and 458n.; Hoche on Quantin, 12 Nov 1796, in AN, AF III 186[b] doss. 860 p[ce] 85; and Debidour, *Recueil des actes*, III. 173, secret decision of 23 July on Quantin's expedition.

[9] TCD, MS 2049/162; *Life*, II. 239; AHG, B[11]1, Simon to Hoche, 27 Sept 1796, reporting local complaints about the legion's behaviour.

[10] Full details of Quantin's preparations are in AHG, B[11]1, notably the Oct–Nov dossiers; AN, AF III 186[b] doss. 859–60; and BB[4]99, Flotille de Dunkerque, 1796.

[11] AAE, Corr. Pol. États-Unis 44 fos. 109–10 and 431; Corr. Pol. Ang., 589 fos. 304–5, and AN, AF 186[b] doss. 859 p[ces] 62–3, Tate to Clarke and Delacroix, July–Aug 1796; BB[4] 103 fo. 33, Hoche to the naval commander, Morard de Galles, 25 Nov 1796.

[12] TCD, MS 163–4; *Life*, II. 240; also AN, BB[4] 112 fos. 120–3 on Tate's instructions.

[13] AN, AF III 186[b] doss. 859 p[ce] 108, Hoche to Clarke, 29 Aug 1796.

[14] AHG, B[11]1, Hoche's correspondence of October; and see Debidour, *Recueil des actes*, IV. 213, the Directory's reply of 5 Nov 1796.

[15] AAE, Corr. Pol. Holl. 595 fo. 3, the Dutch ambassador to Delacroix, 1 Jan 1797; AN, AF IV 1597[A] plaq. 1 p[ce] 10, Truguet's retrospective account; GSA, Archives of the Ministry of Foreign Affairs, 1796–1813, inv. no. 178, letters from Admiral De Winter, May 1796; also C. N. Fehrman, *Onze vloot in de Franse tijd: De admiraals De Winter-Verhuell* ('s-Gravenhage, 1969), 27–31. The Dutch subsidy was used for the Irish expedition.

[16] AN, BB[4] 102 fo. 67, Truguet to Villaret, 13 Oct 1796; he was still receiving instructions to prepare for India only weeks earlier: Debidour, *Recueil des actes*, III. 549.

[17] AN, AF III 186[b] doss. 860 p[ce] 5, Col. Shee to [Clarke], 26 Sept 1796; *Mémoires de Barras*, IV. 223.

[18] AN, AF III 186[b] doss. 860 p[ces] 6–7, Hoche to Clarke, 1 and 3 Oct; also AHG, B[11]1, Hoche to the Directory, 4 Oct, and Hédouville to the War Minister, 13 and 16 Dec 1796. See also G. Escande, *Hoche en Irlande, 1795–1789* (Paris, 1888), 127–35.

[19] TCD, MS 2049/151; *Life*, II. 227–8.

[20] AHG, B[11]1, ordre du jour, 2 Nov 1796.

[21] AN, AF III 186[b] doss. 860 p[ce] 82, Hoche to the Directory, 6 Nov 1796.

[22] AN, BB[4] 102 fos. 89 and 107, Villaret's dismissal and Morard de Galles's appointment, also fos. 85–6, Truguet's replies to Villaret's complaints; Debidour, *Recueil des actes*, III. 722.

[23] AN, BB[4]102 fos. 145–6, Morard de Galles to Truguet, 9 Nov; AHG, B[11]1, Hoche's protest to Clarke, 9 Nov 1796.

[24] AN, BB[4]102 fo. 109, Truguet to Morard de Galles, 7 Nov 1796.

[25] AHG, B[11]1, Hoche to the Directory, 3 Nov; AN, BB[4] 103 fo. 26, Truguet to Hoche, 7 Nov; *Life*, II. 225–6.

[26] Preparations were stepped up throughout November: see AN, BB[4]102; also AF III 186[b] doss. 860 and Debidour, *Recueil des actes*, IV. 228–9.

[27] Bodl., Curzon Coll. b.11/59, caricature dated 29 Oct 1796, 'The Messenger of Peace'. Malmesbury was annoyed that the Directory was publishing their negotiations in the press: PRO, F.O. 27/46, dispatch of 31 Oct, also *Moniteur*, 19 Nov. AAE, Corr. Pol. Ang. 590 fo. 31, Delacroix to Noel, [?] Oct 1796.

[28] ADSM, 1Mi/61/148/1956, Truguet to Hoche, 13 Oct 1796.

[29] Aulard, *Paris...sous le Directoire*, III. 613, 637, 667; PRO, F.O. 27/46, Malmesbury's dispatches of 13 and 28 Nov, 3 and 14 Dec 1796.

[30] AN, AF III 186[b] doss. 860 p[ce] 79, Truguet to [Clarke], 9 Nov 1796, also BB[4] 102 fos. 25–6, 'Instructions secrètes pour les commandans des vaisseaux et frégates' (printed), also fos. 40–1, blanks filled in 'Bantry' and 'Shannon' in Bruix's hand. AHG, B[11]1, Directorial decision of 25 Oct, giving Hoche full authority to decide the place of landing at sea.

[31] TCD, MS 2049/161; *Life*, II. 234–8, also 156 and 217.

[32] *Life*, II. 226; US Nat. Arch., dispatches from US ministers to Great Britain, M.30 roll 4, letters of Maj. Gen. Allen, 21 Nov and 14 Dec 1796, also Gen. Recs. Dept. of State, M.28 roll 4, Pickering to Rufus King, 6 Apr and 16 June 1797. See also PRO, H.O. 100/65/147–9, 223, and BL, Add. MS 33,102/273, 277, 283, corr. of Oct–Dec 1796.

[33] SPOI 620/18/3, list of arrest warrants, annotated by Under-Secretary Cooke, 17 Sept 1796; McCracken was arrested some weeks later and more arrests followed in November, see *NS*, 12–19 Sept, 11–14 Nov 1796.

[34] PRO, H.O. 100/65/136–7, Camden to Portland, 28 Nov 1796, also 100/62 and Kent

AO, U.840/0.149, 0.154/1, 0.156A/2, Camden's corr. with London, July–Nov 1796.

[35] *Life*, II. 222–4

[36] TCD, MS 2049/359, see also fos. 131v, 136v and 154 for similar complaints. None of these criticisms appear in the published *Life*. Matilda came to know MacSheehy well in Paris.

[37] Elliott, *Partners in Revolution*, 334–6.

[38] TCD, MS 2049/153v; *Life*, II. 230–2.

[39] These figures are borne out by PRO, W.O. 30/65/22, the army in Great Britain and Ireland, Oct 1796, also H.O. 100/64/129–35, Camden to Portland, 28 June 1796, on their scattered nature.

[40] See Elliott, *Partners in Revolution*, 107–8, for UI preparations in these months.

[41] AN, AF III 186[b] doss. 860 p[ces] 142 and 146, Hédouville to the Directory, 19 and 24 Dec 1796. Copies of MacSheehy's report are in AN, AF IV 1671 plaq. 1 fos. 128–9, AHG, B[11]1, and AAE, Mem. et Doc. Ang. 53 fos. 256–60. See also C. J. Woods, 'The Secret Mission to Ireland of Captain Bernard MacSheehy, an Irishman in French Service, 1796', *Jnl Cork Hist. and Arch. Soc.*, LXXVIII (1973), 93–108.

[42] TCD, MS 868/2/262–3, [Matilda Tone] to Russell, 9 Oct 1796.

[43] Tone (Dickason) MSS, Tone to Matilda, 30 Nov 1796; printed in *Life*, II. 329–36.

[44] See AN, AF III 186[b] doss. 860 p[ce] 82, Hoche to the Directory, 6 Nov 1796.

[45] TCD, MS 2049/253v and 172–3; *Life*, II. 245–51 and 417; Godechot, *La Vie quotidienne sous le Directoire*, 89–95.

[46] AN, BB[4] 103, fos. 122–3, Truguet to Petiet, 21 Nov 1796

[47] AHG, B[11]1, Hoche to Petiet, 8 Dec and Petiet to the Directory, 12 Dec 1796.

[48] Debidour, *Recueil des actes*, IV. 463, 476–8.

[49] AHG, B[11]1, letters of Hoche and Hédouville, 13 Dec 1796.

[50] AHG, B[11]1, Hédouville to Pétiet, 17 Dec, abstracting a letter just received from Hoche in the Baie de Camaret; also AN, AF III 186[b] doss. 860 p[ce] 139, Hoche to Dupont [Clarke's replacement], 16 Dec 1796.

[51] AN, AF III 186[b] doss. 860 p[ce] 146, also Debidour, *Recueil des actes*, IV. 523, correspondence of Hédouville, Truguet and the Directory, 24–25 Dec 1796.

Chapter 24

[1] Journal of the Voyage in TCD, MS 2049/168–87, in a separate booklet—he had inadvertently packed the current one in his trunk on 30 Nov—and printed in *Life*, II. 245–69; we are particularly well informed of events on board the *Indomptable* through journals also left by Vaudré and Chérin: NLI, MS 705 fos. 1–7 and 50–66; also fos. 9–13, journal of Gen. Spital, on the *Patriote*, 16–17, copy of letter of the captain of the *Révolution*, 36–48v, Bouvet's 'Mémoire justicatif', 20 Mar 1797, MS 704 fos. 36–49, partial journal of the frigate *Cocarde*; AN, BB[4] 102 fos. 173–204, Morard de Galles's journal and AHG, B[11]1, journals of Grouchy and Dumas (who sailed with Hoche on board the *Fraternité*).

[2] TCD, MS 2049/177; *Life*, II. 256; AHG, B[11]1, accounts sent by Chef de Bataillon Maubran and Gen. Hédouville, 17 and 19 Dec, also Laceron's account of 14 Jan 1797.

[3] AN, BB[4] 102 fos. 84 and 87, Truguet's dispatches of 24 Oct and 1 Nov 1796; 103 fos. 84–100, journal of Bouvet and Delmotte.

[4] AN, BB[4] 102 fos. 25–30, 40–1, 55, the instructions; Bouvet's 'Mémoire justificatif' of 20 Mar 1797 in NLI, MS 705, notably fos. 37–9. AHG, B[11]1, 'Journal du Général Grouchy sur l'Expédition d'Irlande', printed from MS journal in the Bibliothèque de l'Université imperiale de Strasbourg.

[5] AHG, B[11]1, Journal of the frigate *Surveillante*, Laceron, quartermaster.

[6] *Life*, II. 256–7; Laceron endorses Tone's complaints.

[7] The originals in Tone's hand are in TCD, MS 3807/15–17, that to the Irish sailors also in Tone (Dickason) MSS and *Life*, 258, 317–28. The printed addresses, accompanied by French translations, are in AN AF III 186[b] doss. 859 p[ces] 133–43.

[8] AHG, B[11]1, journal of the voyage of the *Fraternité* by Hoche's aide-de-camp Dumas.

[9] AHG, B[11]1, Grouchy to the Directory and to Petiet, 24 Dec 1796, also his notes attached to the proclamation to the army.

[10] French versions of the address are in B[11]1, dated 24 Dec 1796 and in Tone (Dickason) MSS. *Life*, II. 343.

[11] NLI, MS 705/16, the captain of the *Révolution* on the troops' restlessness, also Vaudré on their high spirits (a claim endorsed in most of the other communications).

[12] TCD, MS 2049/184v; *Life*, II. 264-5.

[13] See *DEP*, 17 Jan 1797, full account given by captured French prisoners, also NLI, MS 705/64, Chérin's journal.

[14] SPOI, 620/26/144, Nepean to Pelham. 21 Dec 1796; *Private Papers of George, 2nd Earl Spencer*, ed. J. S. Corbett, 2 vols. (London, 1913-24), I. 366, 368-71.

[15] Colpoys's reports are in PRO, H.O. 28/22/73-76 and SPOI, 620/18^A/5; Pellew's in 620/26/131. See also D. M. Steer, 'The Blockade of Brest by the Royal Navy 1793-1805' (Liverpool Univ. M.A. thesis, 1971), 54-75. AHG, B^111, Gen. Doraison to Petiet, 13 Jan 1797, shows French ships still moving in and out of Bantry unmolested on 6 Jan.

[16] See PRO, H.O. 100/62/190-201, 208-14, 100/64/168-76, 100/65/87-8, 97-8 for the exchange.

[17] PRO, W.O. 30/65/22, 'The Army in Great Britain and Ireland, Oct 1796.'

[18] PRO, H.O. 100/64/129-35, Camden to Pelham, 28 June 1796, outlining the problem; Stoddart, 'Counter-Insurgency and Defence in Ireland', 91-124; W. D. Griffin, 'The Forces of the Crown in Ireland 1798', in *Crisis in the Great Republic: Essays Presented to Ross J. S. Hoffman*, ed. G. L. Vincitorio (NY, 1969), 155-80.

[19] Some 17,800 had been raised by December (see English newspaper report of 9 Dec 1796 in AN, AF III 58 doss. 229 fo. 196).

[20] PRO, H.O. 100/62/171-83, Commander-in-Chief's report, 16 Aug; SPOI, 620/25/46, Gen. Smith, from Limerick, 10 Sept 1796; BL, Add. MS 33, 102/346 and 350, complaints by Gen. Dalrymple, 21 Nov and 1 Dec 1796.

[21] PRONI, T.3229/1/11-12, Clare [Fitzgibbon] to Auckland, 2 and 14 Jan 1797; SPOI, 620/26/115, 'Return of the number of troops that may be collected at Cork', Dec 1796; NLI, MS 809, defence measures on 'the proposed invasion of Ireland'.

[22] PRO, H.O. 100/62/393-4, Camden to Portland, 25 Dec 1796, enclosing Dalrymple's report of the 23rd. Initial reports exaggerated the numbers of French ships: see SPOI, 620/26/155-8.

[23] *DEP*, 27-31 Dec 1796; SPOI, 620/15/319, Peter Kenna to Arthur O'Connor, 27 Dec; PRONI, D.607/965-7, movement of Downshire militia from the north; NLI, MS 56/12-15, corr. with Brig. Gen. Knox, Dec 1796-Jan 1797.

[24] PRO, H.O. 100/69/29-31, Portland to Camden, 4 Jan 1797.

[25] SPOI, 620/28/23 and 35, reports of 3 and 4 Jan 1797; PRO, Adm. 1/3974, deposition of a seaman captured by a French brig, 22 Dec 1796.

[26] Aulard, *Paris...sous le Directoire*, III. 683-7, 698-704, 758; AHG, B^111, journal of the frigate *La Surveillante*, and NLI, MS 705/63, Chérin's comments.

[27] PRONI, T. 3229/2/12 and 14, corr. of Fitzgibbon and Cooke, [Dec 1796] and 12 Jan 1797.

[28] AN, AF IV 1671 doss. 2 fos. 166-73 and AAE, Corr. Pol. Ang. 590 fos. 217-23, accounts of Lewins and MacNeven, Mar and July 1797. For United Irish reactions see SPOI, 620/3/32/13, 620/15/3/9, 620/26/187, 190, 192, 202, 620/34/54, 620/36/226, also Kent AO, U.840/0.152/1.

[29] *History of Belfast*, 450-5; SPOI, 620/28/14, Pelham to Lt. Gen. Lake, 2 Jan 1797.

[30] Camden's complaints in Kent AO., U.840/C.102/2 and 0.156^A/7, also in *Spencer Papers*, I. 377-8, and *Auckland Corr.*, III. 375-7.

[31] *DEP*, 12 Jan 1797. See also T. C. Croker, *Popular Songs Illustrative of the French Invasions of Ireland* (London, 1845-7), 46-9, and SPOI, 620/28/61.

[32] *Parl. Hist.*, XXXIII. 5-127; *Parl. Reg.*, XVII. 159-66.

[33] AN, BB^4 102 fo. 14, Truguet to Villeneuve, 7 Jan; AHG, B^111, the Directory's reply to Grouchy's letter of 1 Jan 1797.

[34] Aulard, *Paris...sous le Directoire*, III. 672-718; SPOI 620/29/60, intelligence from Paris, 22 Jan 1797.

[35] Tone (Dickason) MSS, Tone to Tate, 19 Jan 1797.

[36] AN, BB^4 102 fo. 137, Truguet to Morard de Galles, 14 Feb 1797, and fos. 37-80, report to the Directory on the sinking of the *Droits de l'Homme*; NLI, MS 705/36, Bouvet to Barras, enclosing his 'Mémoire justicatif', 20 Mar 1797; AHG, B^111, article signed by all the generals for insertion in the papers, 18 Jan; ADSM, 1Mi/62/153/2069, account of various duels;

Moniteur, 15 Jan 1797.

[37] AHG, B[11]1 account by Gen. Dumas, Hoche's aide-de-camp, 16 Jan 1799; also NLI, MS 705/19–24, by Morard de Galles.

[38] *Mémoires de Barras*, II. 326 and 348; AHG, B[11]1, Hoche to Hédouville, 11 Feb, also to the Directory, 27 Jan, in AF III 186[b] doss. 860; and ADSM, 1Mi/62/152/2059, Grouchy to Hoche 7 Feb 1797.

[39] TCD, MS 2050/33.

[40] AHG, B[11]1, reports of Chérin and Doraison, 13 Jan 1797; NLI, MS 54[A]/96, estimate of enemy losses; *Mémoires de Barras*, II. 327–8, 352, 378–80, 390.

[41] ADSM, 1Mi/62/152/2037, Hédouville to Hoche, 30 Jan 1797.

[42] AHG, B[11]1, Hédouville to Petiet, 27 Feb 1797; and see Elliott, *Partners in Revolution*, 116–18.

[43] Tone (Dickason) MSS, Tone to Tate, 19 Jan 1797.

[44] Tone (Dickason) MSS, Tone to Hoche, 29 Jan 1797.

Chapter 25

[1] TCD, MS 2049/197; *Life*, II. 341–7, 388–92; Tone (Dickason) MSS, Tone to Matilda, 29 Jan and 11 Feb 1797; AN, AF III 437 doss. 2524 fo. 23, Tone's appointment as adjutant to Hoche, Mar 1797; A. Rousselin, *Vie de Lazare Hoche*, 2nd edn., 2 vols. (Paris, 1798), I. 321–2, 371, Hoche's resolution to return to the Irish business.

[2] P. Sagnac, *Le Rhin français pendant la Révolution et l'empire* (Paris, 1917), 134–41; T. C. W. Blanning, *The French Revolution in Germany: Occupation and Resistance in the Rhineland, 1792–1802* (Oxford, 1983), 100; Cuneo d'Ornano, *Hoche*, 294–6, and pt. II, 335–43.

[3] This undertaking to defray French costs was central to UI negotiations, as much to preserve their own independence as to attract French help. See SPOI, 620/18/14, information of Thomas Higgins, 17 Oct 1797; PRO, W.O. 1/396/399–401, report of a conversation with an unnamed United Irishman *en route* to Paris, 12 Nov 1797. On the disastrous state of French finances in 1797, see Albert Meynier, *Les Coups d'état du Directoire*, vol. I: *Le dix-huit fructidor* (Paris, 1927), 33; also reports reaching London in PRO, F.O. 27/51/265.

[4] *Life*, II. 416.

[5] R. Guyot, 'Le Directoire et Bonaparte', *Revue des Études Napoléoniennes*, I (1912), 321–34; *Mémoires de La Révellière-Lépeaux*, III. 31–3; Sciout, *Le Directoire*, II. 337–49.

[6] TCD, MS 2049/204; *Life*, II. 345.

[7] Tone (Dickason) MSS, Minister of War to J. Smith [Tone], 9 Mar 1797, his commission, with special attachment to Gen. Hoche.

[8] TCD, MS 2049/207–9; *Life*, II. 347–9.

[9] *DEP*, 22 Dec 1796; Tone (Dickason) MSS, Tone to Matilda, 11 Feb and 29 Mar 1797, likewise printed in *Life*, II. 388–92 and 397–8.

[10] TCD, MS 868/2/139–42, 160–61, 174–6, 189, 193, 202–3, the lengthy correspondence with Russell about Arthur, Feb–Aug 1796; Tone (Dickason) MSS, Tone to Matilda, 11 Feb 1797: *Life*, II. 310–12, 390.

[11] TCD, MS 2049/201, omitted from *Life*, II. 344.

[12] Tone (Dickason) MSS, Tone's letters of 13, 17 Jan, 11 Feb, 10, 25, 29 Mar and 18 Apr 1797; they are reproduced in *Life*, II. 381–99.

[13] Tone (Dickason) MSS, Shee (at Coblenz) to Tone, 22 Mar 1797; TCD, MS 2049/211v for his movements in Paris.

[14] TCD, MS 2049/213–14 and 212v; *Life*, II. 349–50.

[15] TCD, MS 2049/221–2; *Life*, II. 358–9; Tone (Dickason) MSS, Tone to Matilda, 10, 25, 29 Mar, on the problems of getting leave, and 18 Apr, 2 June and 2 July 1797—all printed in *Life*, II. 392–9, 401–2.

[16] *Life*, II. 355–8; Tone (Dickason) MSS, letters of Shee and Hoche to Tone, 8, 15 and 18 Apr, also his pass to Hamburg dated 15 Apr. For his letter to McCormick see AN, AF IV 1671 plaq. 1 fos. 158–9, memoir by Lewins, 31 May 1797, also AAE, Corr. Pol. Ang. 590 fo. 311, Reinhard to Delacroix, 19 May 1797.

[17] TCD, MS 2049/223, differing slightly from the edited version in *Life*, II. 223.

[18] TCD, MS 2049/236; the entire travel journal is in fos. 224–40 and *Life*, II. 360–80 (and 351–4, for journey Paris to Cologne). See also R. Fell, *A Tour Through the Batavian Republic*

During the Latter Part of the Year 1800 (London, 1801), which makes similar observations.

[19] *Life*, II. 353, 362.

[20] TCD, MS 2049/192; *Life*, II. 339.

[21] Tone (Dickason) MSS, Shee to Tone, 8 Apr 1797.

[22] SPOI, 620/36 and 620/10/121/123, McNally's information, 9 Feb 1797 and 14 Nov 1798; Elliott, *Partners in Revolution*, 175.

[23] *Life*, II. 344–6; *FJ*, 19 Jan 1797. For the internal Irish situation in these months, see Elliott, *Partners in Revolution*, 124–30.

[24] *Report[s] from the Secret Committee of the House of Commons [and House of Lords] in 1797*, cited as App. nos. II–III, in *Report from the Committee of Secrecy of the House of Commons of Ireland* (Dublin, 1798), 42–85.

[25] TCD, MS 2049/204.

[26] TCD, MS 2049/206.

[27] AAE, Corr. Pol. Ang., 590 fo. 311, Reinhard to Delacroix, 19 May 1797; Tone (Dickason) MSS, Tone to Matilda, 25 Apr 1797 (printed in *Life*, II. 400); ADSM, 1Mi/62/157/2091, Dupont to Hoche, 24 May; AHG, B¹★ 177 fo. 121v, the Directory to Hoche, 18 Apr, and B¹¹1, Hoche to the Directory, 30 May 1797.

[28] AN, AF IV 1671 plaq. 1 fos. 99–105, Lewins's account of his mission; PRO, H.O. 100/70/123–9, Camden to Portland, 30 Aug 1797.

[29] SPOI, 620/10/121/56, McNally, 16 May 1797; AAE, Corr. Pol. Ham. 111 fos. 148–50, Reinhard to Delacroix, 2 Apr 1797.

[30] AAE, Corr. Pol. Ang. 590 fos. 217–336 and Corr. Pol. Ham. 111 fos. 148–50, and 222, Reinhard's reports on Lewins, 30 Mar–1 June 1797; AN, AF IV 1671 plaq. 1 fos. 41–4, 99–105, later reports on and by Lewins. Many of these documents found their way to the British government; see *Memoirs and Correspondence of Viscount Castlereagh*, ed. 3rd Marquess of Londonderry, 12 vols. (London, 1848–54), I. 270–306.

[31] AHG, B¹¹1, Hoche to the Directory, 30 May 1797.

[32] Tone (Dickason) MSS, Shee to Citizen Smith, 7 June 1797.

[33] GSA, Archive of the Ministry of Foreign Affairs 1796–1813, inv. no. 49, Lewins to 'The executive committee of the united people of Ireland', copy in Tone's hand, 10 July 1797; Tone (Dickason) MSS, Tone to Matilda, 9 July 1797.

[34] See AN, AF III 51ᴬ doss. 118 fos. 34, 87, 216, AF III 57 doss. 223, AF III 59 (the divisions at Brest), AF III 58 doss. 228 fo. 1, newspaper reports on Ireland, and AHG, B¹¹1, copies of Reinhard's communications on Lewins, sent by the Directory to the War Minister.

[35] PRO, F.O. 27/50/24 Malmesbury to Grenville, 14 Aug 1797.

[36] *Life*, II. 408–9; ADSM, 1Mi/62/157/2094, Simon to Hoche, 7 June (copy in AN, AF IV 1671 plaq. 2 fo. 6).

[37] ADSM, 1Mi/62/157/2095, the Directory to Hoche, 9 June, also AHG, B¹★ 177 fo. 127v (minuted in AN, AF III 452 doss. 2685 fo. 18) and 2094, 2096–8, 2100, for the corr. of Simon and Dupont.

[38] AAE, Corr. Pol. Holl. 595 fo. 267, Noel (French minister in Holland) to Delacroix, 13 Mar 1797; AN, BB³ 108 fos. 14–15, Fouscuberte (French naval *commissaire* in Holland) to Truguet, 3 Mar and 27 Apr 1797, and BB⁴ 112 fo. 5, Truguet to Daendels and De Winter, 19 June. I. Mendels, *Herman Willem Daendels* (The Hague, 1890), pt. II, 24–5.

[39] *Life*, II. 409–15; AN AF III 463 doss. 280 fo. 42, Hoche to Truguet, 7 July. See Fehrman, *Onze vloot in de Franse tijd*, ch. 3, for the Dutch expedition to Ireland; also GSA, The Hague, Foreign Affairs, inv. no. 49, Gen. Dupont to Daendels, 13 June and Daendels to Hoche, 21 June 1797, also minutes of the meeting with the Batavian Committee on 28 June and Hoche's letter of the same date agreeing to abandon French participation in the expedition.

[40] ADSM, 1Mi/62/157/2100–2103, letters to Hoche from Simon, Dupont, Truguet and the Directory, 21–30 June; AN, AF III 463 doss. 2801 fo. 39, and AHG, B¹★ 177/130, corr. between Hoche and the Directory, June–July, also B¹ 173/36, Directory to Gen. Dejean, 27 June 1797.

[41] GSA, The Hague, Foreign Affairs, inv. no. 49, Hoche to Daendels, 1 July 1797—the letter presented by Tone on his return to The Hague, 5 July.

[42] *Life*, II. 416–17, his dates not quite accurate; Tone (Dickason) MSS, Tone to Matilda, 1 and 7 July, also Hoche's authorisation for his pay (1210 *livres*) to be made to MacSheehy and MacSheehy's signed receipt, 15 July 1797.

[43] GSA, The Hague, Foreign Affairs, inv. no. 49, resolution of the Committee of Foreign Affairs, 10 July 1797.

[44] TCD, MS 2049/258; *Life*, II. 422–3.

Chapter 26

[1] Meynier, *Les Coups d'Etat du Directoire*, I. 55–72, 97; AN, AF III 463 doss. 2800–2; Cuneo D'Ornano, *Hoche*, 325–35; *Mémoires de La Révellière-Lépeaux*, II. 120–5; Thibaudeau, *Mémoires sur la Convention et le Directoire*, 174–237, 367 ff.; *Life*, II. 415.

[2] AN, AF IV 1671 plaq, 1 fos. 99–105, Lewins's account of his mission, undated.

[3] See AHG, B[11]1, AN, AF III 463 doss. 2801 and Cuneo D'Ornano, *Hoche*, pt. II, 363–71.

[4] PRO, F.O. 27/50, Malmesbury to Grenville, 14 Aug 1797.

[5] AN, AF III 463 doss. 2801 p[ce] 49, Truguet to Carnot, 22 July 1797; he says the same in a long retrospective on his ministry, AF IV 1195 plaq. 1597[A] fo. 10. In fact Britain was already well informed: see PRO, F.O. 27/51/207.

[6] TCD, MS 2049/268v; *Life*, II. 432.

[7] See also AN, BB[4] 112 fo. 7, De Winter to the Minister of Marine, 2 Aug 1797, reporting that Duncan's force now greatly outnumbered the Dutch.

[8] TCD, MS 2049/270v; *Life*, II. 434–5, and for the period at the Texel, 417–42, also Tone (Dickason) MSS, letters of 20 July–31 Aug 1797.

[9] Tone (Dickason) MSS, Tone to Hoche, 31 July, also Hoche's reply, 20 Aug 1797. The latter is baffling. Hoche assures Tone he will join the Brest expedition as soon as the fleet is ready. It is difficult to tell whether he is just placating Tone, or whether in a calmer frame of mind than during the July crisis, he still considered leading an Irish expedition.

[10] Details on Tennent taken from PRONI, D.1748 (uncatalogued Tennent MSS). He was twenty-three at the time.

[11] The evidence for the progressive disintegration of the Ulster movement in 1797 is massive: see, e.g., Kent AO, U.840/0.196/2 (Turner's information); SPOI, 620/3/32/8 (John Conellan), 620/10/121/55–63 (McNally) and 620/34/54 (John Maxwell's notebook for 1797); PRONI, D.714/2/1 (Magin).

[12] PRO, H.O. 100/70/335–52, Turner's account, 8 Oct 1797; PRONI, D.714/2/3, Magin's information, 17 June 1797.

[13] *Life*, II. 428; AAE, Corr. Pol. Ham. 111 fos. 319–23, 353–4, Reinhard to Delacroix, 13 and 21 July 1797; *Report from the Committee of Secrecy . . . Commons* [Ireland] (1798), App. XIV, 138.

[14] MacNeven, *Pieces of Irish History*, 189, 196–7; SPOI, 620/10/121/62, McNally, 29 May, and 620/18/14, Higgins, 30 May 1797.

[15] *Life*, II. 428–9. On the division in the UI leadership, see SPOI, 620/18/14, Higgins's information, Feb–Sept 1797, 620/60/18, extracts from Kennedy's information; PRO, H.O. 100/70/335–52, Turner; *Report from the Committee of Secrecy . . . Commons* [Ireland] (1798), App. XIV–XV.

[16] MacNeven, *Pieces of Irish History*, 188–92, outlining the communications received in 1797. Tone's of May was the first since Bantry Bay. *Report from the Committee of Secrecy . . . Commons* [Ireland] (1798), App. XXXI; see PRONI, T.3229/2/22, Cooke to Auckland, 9 Feb 1797, SPOI, 620/10/121/62 and 620/18/14 (30 May, 8 July, 9 Dec 1797, 21 Feb 1798), 620/36 (25 Sept 1797), for effects of news from France.

[17] Tone (Dickason) MSS, Tone to Matilda, 27 Aug 1797.

[18] AAE, Corr. Pol. Ham 111 fos. 353–4, Reinhard to Delacroix, 21 July 1797; on complaints about Lewins, see Elliott, *Partners in Revolution*, 171 ff.

[19] AAE, Corr. Pol. Ham, 111 fos. 319–23, Reinhard to Delacroix, 13 July 1797; AN, AF IV 1671 plaq. 1 fos. 99–106, Lewin's account; GG[1]67 fos. 273–80, translation of MacNeven's memoir; MacNeven, *Pieces of Irish History*, 189–90, 194–6. PRO, H.O. 100/70/113–14, 123–9, Camden-Portland corr. 25 and 30 Aug 1797; *Castlereagh Corr.* I. 295–306.

[20] Tone (Dickason) MSS, Tone to Matilda, 31 Aug 1797.

[21] Tone (Dickason) MSS, Tone to Matilda, 7 and 20 July 1797.

[22] On the strained relations between the two countries at this time, see AN, BB[3] 108 fo. 32, French naval *commissaire* in Holland to the Minister of Marine, 3 Aug 1797; AAE, Corr. Pol. Ang. 592 fos. 48 and 69, Talleyrand to the Batavian *commissaires*, 5 and 23 Oct 1797; PRO,

F.O. 27/50, Malmesbury's reports from Lille, 22 Aug and 15 Sept 1797; S. Schama, *Patriots and Liberators: Revolution in the Netherlands, 1780–1813* (London, 1977), ch. 6–7, also traces French impatience at Dutch inability to settle its internal government and constitution, which was held to weaken the alliance. See also *Mémoires de La Révellière-Lépeaux*, I. 326, II, 192–8; *Dropmore MSS*, III. 347–52.

[23] Tone (Dickason) MSS, Tone to Matilda, 19 Sept 1797; also letter of 15 Sept; *Life*, II. 443–6; TCD, MS 2050/17, Tone to the Directory, 15 Oct 1797. NLI, MS 704/36, undated memoir on a Scottish invasion, in Tone's hand, probably that given to Hoche.

[24] TCD, MS 2049/281; *Life*, II. 448; Tone (Dickason) MSS, Tone to Matilda, 27 Sept 1797.

[25] Tone (Dickason) MSS, Chérin to Tone, undated from Germany.

[26] P. S. O'Hegarty, *A History of Ireland under the Union* (London, 1952), 219–20; John Stuart Mill, *England and Ireland* (London, 1868), 20.

Chapter 27

[1] AN, AF IV 1671 plaq. 1 fo. 104 and plaq. 2 fos. 175–6, Lewins's summary of communications with Barras [Dec 1797].

[2] Guyot, *Le Directoire et la paix de l'Europe*, 550–1; Tone (Dickason) MSS, Shee to Tone, 25 Dec 1797.

[3] Tone (Dickason) MSS, Simon to Tone, 28 Sept 1797. Tone was then *en route* from Brussels to Paris.

[4] TCD, MS 2049/282; *Life*, II. 450; Tone (Dickason) MSS, Tone to Daendels, 21 Oct 1797, enclosing a copy of the Scottish proposals which Tone had written for Barras and Debelle.

[5] *Life*, II. 451; Tone (Dickason) MSS, Shee to Tone, 25 Dec 1797; AHG, B[5] 41, arrêté of 26 Oct, setting up an Armée d'Angleterre, under the interim command of Gen. Desaix.

[6] See AN, F[7] 7293 doss. B[4] 2671, F[7] 7348 doss. B[4] 9145, F[7] 7440, 7417 and 7422; AAE, Corr. Pol. Ang. 592 fos. 65 and 139.

[7] Tone (Dickason) MSS, Daendels to Tone, 12 Mar 1798 and Tone's reply, 25 Mar.

[8] Tone (Dickason) MSS, Daendels's corr. 8 Sept, 3 Oct, 4 Nov, 12 Dec 1797.

[9] AN, BB[3] 108 fos. 35–9, reports of Fouscuberte, French naval *commissaire* to Holland, 9–15 Oct 1797; AN, AF IV 1597[A] plaq. 1[1] p[ce] 10, Truguet's bitter comments on the Texel expedition and Camperdown. GSA, Foreign Affairs, inv. no. 49, meetings of 7 and 9 Oct 1797. Schama, *Patriots and Liberators*, 281–3, PRO, H.O. 100/70/318–20, Portland to Camden, 3 Dec 1797, on the flag. Fell, *Tour through the Batavian Republic*, 322–4.

[10] Tone (Dickason) MSS, Tone-Daendels corr. 21 Oct–4 Nov and 12 Dec 1797; AHG, B[5] 41, Daendels to Desaix, Dec 1797—Jan 1798; AN, BB[4] 114 fo. 233, Pléville to the Batavian Committee for Foreign Affairs, 14 Dec and fo. 228, arrêté of 14 Dec 1797. For the Scottish plan see AN, BB[4] 103 fos. 171–5, Aherne to Lewins; F[7] 7401 doss. B[5] 3830, Aherne's application for travel documents, endorsed by Tone, and AHG, MR1420 fo. 26, Daendels to Bonaparte, 14 Jan 1798.

[11] *Life*, II, 458.

[12] F. Charles-Roux, *Les Origines de l'expédition d'Egypte*, 2nd edn. (Paris, 1910), 296–335; Guyot, *Le Directoire et la paix de l'Europe*, 567–92; Desbrière, *Projets et tentatives*, I, pt. IV; AHG, B[5] 41–2, Armée d'Angleterre, Oct 1797–Apr 1798; AN, BB[4] 120, Armements contre Angleterre, 1798.

[13] Tone (Dickason) MSS, Tone to Daendels, 3 Feb 1798.

[14] Guyot, *Le Directoire et la paix de l'Europe*, 601–13.

[15] TCD, MS 2049/296–8; *Life*, II. 464–6.

[16] TCD, MS 2049/290; *Life*, II. 458–60; Tone (Dickason) MSS, Daendels-Tone corr. 20 Dec 1797, 3, 16 and 25 Feb 1798.

[17] TCD, MS 2050/22, Tone to Talleyrand, 31 Mar 1798.

[18] SPOI, 620/10/12/66, McNally's information, 9 June 1797, and AN, AF III 59 plaq. 231 fo. 61, Lagau to Delacroix, 6 May 1797; PRO, F.O. 33/13/24 and 32, Frazer to Grenville, 23 May and 20 June—information which was then sent by Whitehall to Dublin Castle (SPOI, 620/31/61).

[19] SPOI, 620/10/121/32, 66, 69, 73, McNally's letters, July–Aug 1797, detailing the contents of Tandy's letters—69 tells of Tone's discussions in Paris and participation in the Bantry Bay expedition; also PRO, H.O. 100/70/93–4 and 139–41, details sent to Whitehall,

Aug–Sept 1797. See also his claims to the French authorities in AAE, Corr. Pol. Ang. 592 fos. 101 and 138; AAG, Personnel, 2nd ser., GB 755, Tandy, and PRO, F.O. 27/52/221.

[20] SPOI, 620/18^A/11, unsigned letter from Paris to Patrick Byrne [Mar 1798]. Tone (Dickason) MSS, Tone to Matilda, 13 June and 21 July 1797, the former likewise printed in *Life*, II. 402–3.

[21] Tone (Dickason) MSS, Tone to Matilda, 27 Aug 1797; *Life*, II. 417.

[22] TCD, MS 2049/293; *Life*, II. 460–2, 466–7; and for Muir's statements, the *Moniteur*, 7 Dec 1797, 4 Jan and 12 Feb 1798, the Dublin UI paper, the *Press*, 11 Jan 1798, AAE, M et D Ang. 2 fos. 153–72, Personnel 9 fo. 125, and AN, BB³ 125 fo. 54; C. Bewley, *Muir of Huntershill* (Oxford, 1981), 162–75.

[23] Tone (Dickason) MSS, Tone to Matilda, 9 Sept 1798, also his complaints of Bonneville in letters of 18 June and 2 Sept 1798. *Bien Informé*, 16 Fructidor VI. On Bonneville see David V. Erdman, *Commerce des Lumières: John Oswald and the British in Paris, 1790–93* (London, 1987), 75–6, 110–14.

[24] See copy in PRO, PC1/44/A.155.

[25] Tone (Dickason) MSS, Tone to Matilda, 2 Sept 1798. Paine was by now living in Bonneville's house at 4 rue du Théâtre français: see Audrey Williamson, *Thomas Paine: His Life, Work and Times* (London, 1973), 249–50.

[26] *Life*, II. 460.

[27] AAE, Corr. Pol. Ang. 592 fo. 43, memorial of Coigley and MacMahon, 4 Oct 1797, and fos. 161–6 and 220 for the arrival of the English republicans, John Ashley and Robert Watson; also AAE, M et D Ang 2 fos. 153–72, for Muir's memorial. Ashley sought and was given Tone's support for permission to reside in Paris (see TCD, MS 2050/20, Tone to the Minister of Police, 17 June 1798). The divisions were not always hard and fast.

[28] See claims of Lewins receiving a regular salary from Ireland in PRO, H.O. 100/70/335–7, and 100/75/7–9, and signs that he was receiving some funds, SPOI, 620/12/143, O'Connor to MacNeven [May 1802].

[29] *Life*, II. 502; see AN, F⁷ 7383^B, AF III 529 doss. 3460 p^ce 4, and AAE, Personnel 9 fo. 141, for Edward O'Finn in particular.

[30] AAE, Corr. Pol. Ang., 592 fos. 65 and 139, Talleyrand to the Minister of Police, Sotin, 20 Oct and 28 Dec 1797.

[31] See AN, BB³ 160 fo. 202, Talleyrand to the Minister of Marine, 1 Aug 1799; Kilmaine's conversation with Tone, in *Life*, II. 502.

[32] *Life*, II. 502 (Kilmaine); Tandy was fifty-eight, but looked much older, and all the French accounts speak of his 'great age'; see, e.g., AN, BB³ 145 fo. 177, also AHG, B¹¹ 2, Ameil's account, 22 Sept 1798.

[33] AAE, Corr. Pol. Ham. 112 fos. 178–9, Reinhard to Talleyrand, 18 Dec 1797; Tone (Dickason) MSS, Tone to Matilda, 12 June 1798.

[34] AN, F⁷ 7348 doss. B⁴9145, Tone to the Minister of Police, 8 Mar 1797.

[35] AN, F⁷ 7293 doss. B⁴ 2671, entire dossier of approvals by Tone and related documents, see also F⁷ 7422 doss. B⁵ 5933, 7417 doss. B⁵ 5396, and 7440 doss. B⁵ 7855; AAE, Corr. Pol. Ang. 592 fos. 65 and 139, Talleyrand to the Minister of Police, referring him to Tone, 20 Oct and 28 Dec 1797; TCD, MS 2050/20–21, 31, Tone to the Minister of Police, 16 Jan, 15 Feb and 12 June 1798. Tone (Dickason) MSS, Minister of Police to Tone, 26 Jan and 4 Feb 1797.

[36] AN, BB² 55 fos. 114–15, Turner to the Minister of Marine, 4 Mar 1799; *Castlereagh Corr.* I. 235.

[37] See PRONI, D.607/F/8, and 79; PRO, H.O. 100/75/7, 15–16, 42–3; Elliott, *Partners in Revolution*, 184 and 208; and *Castlereagh Corr.*, I. 227–8, for the Dublin-London conflict over the use of Turner's evidence.

[38] PRO, H.O. 100/70/339–48, information of 8 Oct 1797. See also his damning account in *Castlereagh Corr.*, I. 406–9.

[39] Turner's information during 1797–8 is in PRO, H.O. 100/70/331–3, 335–7, 339–48, 351–2, H.O. 100/75/5–9, 15–16, H.O. 100/76/271, H.O. 100/79/319, 321–23 and H.O. 42/43; *Castlereagh Corr.*, II. 264–309, gives a good idea of the scale and importance of his information. There are also copies or summaries in BL, Add. MS 33,105/258 and Kent AO, U.840/0.196/2. See also SPOI, 620/11/160/4, full account of his services upon retirement, 16 June 1803.

[40] See AAE, Corr. Pol. Ham. 112 fos. 20–2, Reinhard to Talleyrand, 20 Nov 1797.

[41] AAE, Corr. Pol. Ham. 112 fos. 178–9, Reinhard to Talleyrand, 18 Dec 1797.

[42] Tone (Dickason) MSS, Matilda to Tone, 14 June 1797.

[43] Tone (Dickason) MSS, Tone to Matthew 25 Apr 1798. For the Giauque's role in Hamburg see AAE, Corr. Pol. Ham., 111 fo. 339, 112 fos. 20–2 and 178–9; AN, AF IV 1671 plaq. 1 fo. 58, copy of Reinhard to Hoche, 21 May 1797; PRO, HO. 100/70/339–48 and 100/75/7–9, Turner's information, 8 Oct and 19 Nov 1797; PRONI, D.1748, T. Howard (John Tennent) to his brother William, 29 Sept 1797.

[44] Tone (Dickason) MSS, Tone to Kilmaine, 26 May 1798, also to Matilda, 18 Apr, 18 and 30 May, and Matthew, 25 Apr; TCD, MS 2050/30, Tone to Talleyrand, 12 June 1798; Life, II. 484–6; LC, Madison Papers, ser. 1, reel 13, Matilda to David Bailie Warden, 8 Jan 1812. On Arthur see also J. J. St. Mark, 'The Disappearance of Arthur Tone', Éire-Ireland, XX, no. 3 (Fall 1985), 56–70.

[45] Tone (Dickason) MSS, Tone to Matilda, 17 Jan 1797; printed in Life, II. 386.

[46] TCD, MS 2049/292; Life, II. 460–1, 473; Tone (Dickason) MSS, Tone to Matthew, 12 Apr, and Matilda 18 and 25 Apr, 22 May and 12 June 1797; PRO, H.O. 100/79/319, Turner's information, 8 Aug 1798.

[47] Tone (Dickason) MSS, Tone to Daendels, 12 Apr 1798.

[48] Life, II. 472; TCD, MS 2050/22, Tone to Talleyrand, 31 Mar 1798.

[49] Reproduced in Tone (Dickason) MSS, Tone to Matthew, 18 Apr 1798.

[50] Tone (Dickason) MSS, Tone to Daendels, 12 Apr 1798, enclosing letter to Delacroix, and Daendels's reply, 1 May.

[51] Life, II. 433–4; Tone (Dickason) MSS. Tone to Matilda, 12 June 1798.

[52] Life, II. 502. On Lewins in France after 1798 see Elliott, Partners in Revolution, 265–72.

[53] TCD, MS 2049/327; Life, II. 474–5.

Chapter 28

[1] Guyot, Le Directoire et la paix de l'Europe, 586–92.

[2] Tone (Dickason) MSS, Tone to Matilda, 6 Apr 1798.

[3] Tone (Dickason) MSS, Tone to Matthew, 12 Apr, and Matilda, 30 May 1798; TCD, MS 872/135, information from Matthew's court-martial in Ireland, 24 Sept 1798.

[4] Tone (Dickason) MSS, Tone to Matilda, 6 Apr 1798.

[5] Tone (Dickason) MSS, Tone to Matilda, 6 and 12 Apr, 18 May 1798.

[6] Tone (Dickason) MSS, letters of 9 Sept and 22 Aug 1798 respectively.

[7] Tone (Dickason) MSS, Tone to Matilda, 9 Sept 1798.

[8] Tone (Dickason) MSS, Tone to Daendels, 29 Mar 1798.

[9] Tone (Dickason) MSS, Tone to Matilda, 12 Apr 1798.

[10] AHG, B[5] 42, Tone's request for leave, sent 28 Apr 1798.

[11] Tone (Dickason) MSS, Tone to Matilda, 18 and 22 May 1798.

[12] Life, II. 492–505; TCD, MS 2050/26–7, copies of his reports, 29 May–12 June 1798; Tone (Dickason) MSS, Tone to Matilda, 30 May, 8 and 12 June, and Gen. Rivaud to Tone, 2 and 10 June; AHG, B[5]★ 115, Rivaud to Kilmaine, 28 May, and to Tone, 3 and 19 June; see AN, BB[4] 119–20, for measures taken by France to defend her northern coast against English attack.

[13] AAE, Corr. Pol. Ang., 592 fos.183, 194, 196, 204; Castlereagh Corr, I. 231–6.

[14] Tone (Dickason) MSS, Tone to Matilda, 12 June 1798, also 22 Apr and 22 May; TCD, MS 2050/31, copy of his letter to the Police Minister, 12 June.

[15] See Meynier, Les Coups d'état du Directoire, II. 29–109, for the coup of 22 Floréal (11 May) 1798.

[16] TCD, MS 2050/25, Tone to Dupetit Thouars, 24 May 1798.

[17] Tone (Dickason) MSS, Tone to Kilmaine, 26 May 1798.

[18] TCD, MS 2049/338; Life, II. 506–8; TCD, MS 2050/33, Tone to Grouchy, 16 June 1798.

[19] TCD, MS 2049/336v; Life, II. 506, also 491 and 502; Tone (Dickason) MSS, Tone to Matilda, 30 May 1798.

[20] TCD, MS 2049/304; Life, II. 471–2; Tone (Dickason) MSS, Tone to Matilda, 22 Apr 1798.

[21] TCD, MS 2050/30, Tone to Talleyrand, 12 June 1798; Tone (Dickason) MSS, letter to Matilda on same day; Life, II. 488–99.

[22] TCD, MS 2049/313, 315, 330; Life, II. 482–4, 504–9; Tone (Dickason) MSS, 18 June 1798.

[23] TCD, MS 2049/335; *Life*, II. 504.

[24] AN, BB⁴ 103 fo. 178, Lewins (he signs his own name) to 'Citoyen Directeur', [June 1798]; BB⁴ 122 fos. 302–4, Lowry, Orr, Hamilton and Teeling to the Directory, 16 June 1798, signing themselves members of the United Irish Directory.

[25] *Moniteur*, 16 July 1798; AAE., Corr. Pol. Ang. 592 fos. 190–93, the address of 14 July and the Council's reply; AN, AF III 274 p^ce 48, Address of the United Irish Society in Paris to the Directory, 21 June.

[26] *Life*, II. 510. TCD, MS 2049/339, for omitted comment on Digges.

[27] AN, BB⁴ 123 fos. 193–8, corr. of Bruix and Gen. Joubert, 1–18 July 1798. See also BB⁴ 122 fos. 7–32, for the rush of instructions and preparations June–July.

[28] AN, F⁷ 7505 doss. B⁶ 2874, the Commissaire du Directoire to the Minister of Police, 9 Aug 1798, and F⁷ 7480 doss. B⁶ 412, for passport irregularities of John Donavan. See also PRO, H.O. 100/78/160, 100/79/321, 100/87/318–22, 334–5 and H.O. 28/24/312, for information on the Dunkirk preparations reaching Whitehall.

[29] AHG, B¹¹2, Journal and report of Ameil, aide-de-camp of Gen. Desjardins, 9 and 22 Sept 1798, also official ministerial report of 11 Nov. See PRONI, D.3030/302 and PRO, PC 1/43/A152, Turner's report of 28 Dec, on the continued in-fighting; PRO, H.O. 100/77/222 and 100/79/63–4 on the informers.

[30] AN, BB⁴ 123 fo. 218, also 209, 212, 216, 217, 228, 230 and Desbrières, *Projets et tentatives*, II. 69–77, for Chérin's stream of letters and complaints.

[31] Tone (Dickason) MSS, orders from Bruix and Schérer, 1 and 15 July 1798; *Moniteur*, 6 July.

[32] Tone (Dickason) MSS, Tone to Matilda, 19 Aug. Grouchy had been sent to Italy.

[33] Sir Edward Crosbie, a liberal country gentleman of County Carlow, executed on trumped-up charges during the rebellion; Beauchamp Bagenal Harvey, Wexford landowner and leader of the rebellion in that county, convicted and executed under martial law; William Orr, a young Presbyterian farmer from Antrim, convicted and executed on dubious charges in Oct 1796. Orr was one of the first victims of the rebellion period in Ireland and his fate deeply affected many, Tone included. All but Coigley were Protestants.

[34] Tone (Dickason) MSS, printed and draft version dated 7 Aug (4,000 copies run off); TCD, MS 2050/15v-16, 37-8, copies of the addresses; BB⁴ 123 fos. 235–6, 244–5, Clarke sending the Bantry Bay addresses to Bruix, 31 July and BB⁴ 122 fos. 265–6, Hardy to Bruix, 3 Aug. See also 'Correspondance intime du Général Jean Hardy (de 1797 à 1802)', *Revue des Deux Mondes*, CLXI (Sept 1900), 98–9, 105.

[35] PRONI, T.3048/K/9; AN, BB⁴ 122 fos. 60, 69, 78, 100 and 103, corr. between Marine and War departments over pay, July–Sept 1798.

[36] *Mémoires de Barras*, III. 320.

[37] *Beresford Corr.* II. 173–4, 176–7.

[38] AN, BB⁴ 122 fos. 256 and 259, Bruix to Hardy, 10 and 26 Aug 1798; 'Correspondance intime du Général Jean Hardy', 103–4.

[39] AHG, B¹¹2, Chérin to the Director, Treilhard, 23 Aug, partly reproduced by Desbrières, *Projets et tentatives*, II. 77. Tone (Dickason) MSS, Tone to Matilda, 2 Sept 1798.

[40] AHG, B¹¹2, the rush of corr. for Sept; *Moniteur*, 15, 24–5, 28 Sept 1798.

[41] AN, BB⁴ 122 fo. 72, état de répartition des troupes, also fos. 11–12 on the overcrowding.

[42] Desbrière, *Projets et tentatives*, 141–5 and AN, BB⁴ 122 fo. 34, Bompard to the Minister of Marine, 20 Aug 1798; 'Correspondance intime du Général Jean Hardy', 101–3.

[43] SPOI 620/52/123, 'information of Michael Burke on the proceedings of the French at Castlebar', undated; PRONI, D.607/F/408, Annesley to Lord Downshire, 14 Sept 1798.

[44] Tone (Dickason) MSS, Tone to Matilda, 29 Aug and 9 Sept 1798.

[45] *Life*, II. 522.

[46] *Life*, II. 263–4.

[47] *Life*, II. 589.

[48] *Conseil des Cinq-Cents. Motion d'ordre . . . pour la veuve et les enfans de Téobald-Wolf-Ton*, 6–8, certificate signed by two Brest notaries, 1 Aug 1798.

Chapter 29

[1] AN, BB⁴ 122 fo. 4, cover page to file 'Expédition d'Irlande 1798—Bompard, Hardy'.

[2] PRO, F.O. 27/53, Bulletins from France, 24 Aug, 20 Sept 1798; F.O. 33/16/50,

information from Hamburg, 7 Aug 1798; H.O. 100/78/165–6, 223–4, 241–3, 258, reports on the Brest force sent by Whitehall to Dublin Castle, Aug–Sept 1798; *Castlereagh Corr.*, I. 249–50, 262–70, 306–9, 319, 334, 372–4, 380–2.

³ PRO, H.O. 100/70/331–7, Turner's reports advising additional defensive measures off Lough Swilly; NLI, MS 54ᴬ 135, 'Outline of the defence of Ireland', 28 Apr 1798; SPOI, 620/38/5, Wickham to Castlereagh, 1 June 1798; 620/52/119, information on Bompard's departure, 17 Sept 1798.

⁴ *Life*, II. 524. He is said to have 'harangued' Bompard when he expressed doubts about entering Lough Swilly: SPOI, 620/46/69, Cavan to Cooke, 10 Mar 1799, enclosing information of Waldryn, who had been on board the *Hoche*.

⁵ Desbrière, *Projets et tentatives*, II. 164–71; 'Correspondence intime du Général Jean Hardy', 108–12; Warren's account in *Annual Register* (1798), 144–7; PRO, H.O. 100/79/29–39, 53; *Courier*, 19–26 Oct 1798; AHG, B¹¹2, reports by the commander of the *Immortalité* (2 Nov), by Hardy (19 Nov); AN, BB⁴ 122 fos. 38, reports by Bruix (24 Oct), 41, 48–50, by Bompard (4 Nov), 241–7, by the captain of the frigate *Sémillante* (26 Oct), one of the ships which escaped; AN, AF III 206 doss. 943 fos. 9–11, Bruix to the Directory, 24 Oct, enclosing the *Romaine's* report; SPOI, 620/41/21, George Hill to Cooke, 6 Nov 1798.

⁶ *Life*, II. 545–6; also LC, Madison Papers, ser. 1, reel 13, Matilda to David Bailie Warden, 8 Jan 1812, relating Arthur's history. 'Correspondance intime du Général Jean Hardy', 117. See the account given by Hamilton in C. H. Teeling, *Sequel to the History of the Irish Rebellion of 1798: A Personal Narrative*, IUP repr. of 1876 edn. (Shannon, 1972), 337; SPOI, O.P. 47/28, Capt. R. Williams of the *Robuste* to Castlereagh, 2 Nov 1798.

⁷ *Life*, II. 525–6; *Courier*, 7 and 12 Nov; *Saunders's News Letter*, 12 Nov; *FJ*, 16 and 18 Oct, 3 Nov 1798; *Castlereagh Corr.*, I. 409; on Hill, see Madden, *United Irishmen*, 2nd ser., 2nd edn., 119–22.

⁸ SPOI, 620/51/239, Hill to Cooke, 3 Nov 1798. Another document has it that Hill recognised Tone on board the *Hoche*: 'Wolfe Tone, when he was recognized by Sir George Hill on board the Hoche, said, "Mr. Pitt is mad if he does not attempt an Union, and the French are mad if they do not attack Ireland before it can be affected"' (Cornwallis to Pitt, 31 Mar 1800, cited *The Later Correspondence of George III*, ed. A. Aspinall, 5 vols. (Cambridge, 1962–70), III. 330n.). This is endorsed by Simon in a letter supporting Matilda's pension application, 1 Sept 1799, in *Conseil des Cinq Cents. Motion d'ordre...pour la veuve et les enfans de Téobald-Wolf-Ton*, 8–9. See also PRONI, D.607/F/515, Robert Ross to Lord Downshire, 2 Nov 1798. The *Hoche* was renamed the *Donegal* and fought at the Battle of Trafalgar; see Seamus Brady, 'Wolfe Tone and Donegal', *Co Donegal. Hist. Soc. Jnl*, I (1948–9), 129–39.

⁹ SPOI, 620/41/21, Hill to Cooke, 6 Nov 1798, AHG, B¹¹2, Hardy to the Directory, 19 Nov 1798.

¹⁰ *Faulkner's Dublin Jnl*, 13 Nov 1798; SPOI, 620/41/23, Cavan to Cooke, 7 Nov 1798.

¹¹ PRONI, T.3048/J/3, copy of Tone to Castlereagh, [9 Nov 1798], enclosing, nos. 4–5, letters to Niou and the Directory. I have been unable to locate the latter in the French archives, although all others written by Tone to France eventually reached their destination.

¹² AHG, B¹¹ 2, Hardy's letters to Tone and Cornwallis, 4 Nov, and to the Directory, 19 Nov 1798, reporting the Lord Lieutenant's reply.

¹³ *FJ*, 22 Feb 1798; *Report from the Committee of Secrecy...Lords* [Ireland] (1798), 10–15.

¹⁴ PRO, H.O. 100/79/53, Sir John Borlase Warren to Castlereagh, 16 Oct, printed extract in *Annual Register* (1798), 145–6.

¹⁵ SPOI, 620/41/21, 23, and 25. Hill and Cavan to Cooke, 6–8 Nov; and for Boyd see MacManus, 'Bibliography of Theobald Wolfe Tone', 12, also his 'Man who Stole Wolfe Tone's Books'.

¹⁶ TCD, MS 6906, Dillon MSS, John Mitchel to J. B. Dillon, 17 Dec 1845; John Mitchel, *The History of Ireland from the Treaty of Limerick to the Present Time*, 2 vols. (Dublin, 1869), II. 68; 'Mitchel letter throws new light on capture of Tone', *Irish Times*, 30 May 1986.

¹⁷ PRONI, D.591/727, Drennan to Mrs McTier, 7 Nov 1798.

¹⁸ Madden, *United Irishmen*, 1st ser., 2nd edn., 482.

¹⁹ SPOI, 620/15/2/15, Emmet to Russell, undated. Russell was in dispute with the Kilmainham prisoners. He did not approve of their agreement with the government: see TCD, MS 868/1/124, undated draft of a letter by Russell complaining of the 'confession'.

²⁰ TCD, MS 868/2/279–80, Burrowes to Russell [*c.* 9 Nov 1798]; MacGiolla Easpaig,

Tomás Ruiséil, 128–9, Burrowes had likewise acted as legal counsel to Matthew Tone.

[21] *Life*, II. 564–5; TCD, MS 873/25, copy of Matilda to Margaret Tone, 11 May 1810.

[22] Phillips, *Curran and His Contemporaries*, 215; Finegan, 'Was John Keogh an Informer', 84; see partisan defence of Keogh in W. J. Fitzpatrick, *Secret Service under Pitt* (London, 1892), 163, 166, 193–4.

[23] TCD, MS 873/377–8, 380–81, 391, McDonnell to Madden, 1842–3; McNeill, *Mary Ann McCracken*, 142–3, 187, 216, 236; Sampson (Dickason) MSS, Catherine Anne Tone to Grace Clarke Sampson, 13 June 1841.

[24] *Courier*, 15 Nov 1798.

[25] Howell, *State Trials*, XXVII. 616.

[26] *FJ*, 13 Nov 1798.

[27] PRO, H.O. 100/79/95–97, enclosed in Taylor to Wickham, 10 Nov 1798; also BL, Add. MS 38,355/21–2; *Correspondence of Charles 1st Marquis Cornwallis*, ed. Charles Ross, 3 vols. (London, 1849), II. 434–5, differing slightly in spelling and punctuation from the H.O. version. The first line of the passage subsequently scored out was spoken by Tone, hence its appearance in Howell, although blocked out in the original copy.

[28] *Proceedings of a Military Court held in Dublin Barracks on Saturday the Tenth of November, for the Trial of Theobald Wolfe Tone* (Dublin, 1798).

[29] *Life*, II. 527–32—this version appears in *Conseil des Cinq Cents. Motion d'ordre...pour la veuve et les enfans de Téobald-Wolf-Ton*, 10–15.

[30] For reports of the trial and different versions of the speech, see Howell, *State Trials*, XXVII. 613–26; *Proceedings of a Military Court held in Dublin Barracks; Minutes of The Court-Martial held last Saturday. 10 November, at the Barracks of Dublin: with the Speech made upon that Occasion by Theobald Wolfe Tone Esq.* (Dublin, 1798); *Faulkner's Dublin Jnl*, 13 Nov (which nevertheless refused to print the speech as 'too inflammatory'); *Courier*, 12–14 Nov; *Walker's Hib. Mag.* (Nov 1798), 737–44; NLI, MS 8505, Allen Morgan to Revd Edward Berwick, 12 Nov 1798; TCD, MS 3365/69, Thomas Prior's notebook, 10 Nov 1798, and MS 872/152, court martials; BL, Add. MS 38,355/21–2, 'Tone's address to the court martial', sent by J. Blaquiere; see also Madden, *United Irishmen*, 1st ser., II. 354–6 and 3rd ser., I. 143–50.

[31] PRONI, T.3048/J/7, copy Tone to Emmet etc., 10 Nov 1798.

[32] PRONI, T.3048/J/8, original Tone to his father, 10 Nov 1798.

[33] PRONI, T.3048/J/9–10, copies Tone to Kilmaine and Shee, and TCD, MS 872/150, to Bruix, all dated 10 Nov 1798; the original to the Directory is in AHG, B^{11} 2, copies in TCD, MS 872/149–50, and PRONI, T.3048/J/15.

[34] TCD, MS 872/145, copies of 'Tone's Will', 10 Nov 1798, and receipts signed by Edward Witherington and Peter Tone.

[35] The ring was withheld from Emmet: see SPOI, 620/15/2/16, Emmet to Alexander Marsden, 3 Dec 1798.

[36] The pocket-book came into the National Museum's possession in the 1930s, on the death of Sweetman's great-great nephew. See *Irish Press*, 25 Nov 1936. I am grateful to Oliver Snoddy for bringing the pocket-book and press cutting to my attention. See also Madden, *United Irishmen*, 3rd ser., I. 156.

[37] The original in Tone (Dickason) MSS has the greeting to Lewins carefully cut out; but a copy in PRONI, T.3048/J/11, is complete. 'Wilkins' is Thomas Wilson, a Scottish radical businessman who befriended the Tone family *en route* from America at the end of 1796 and whom Matilda was to marry in 1816.

[38] Tone (Dickason) MSS; as with the first letter, there are changes in the versions printed in *Life*, II. 537–8, notably in the omission of the names of those whom Matilda felt had wronged her family, e.g., Harriet and Lewins.

[39] *An t'-Oglach* (June–July 1924); but see TCD, MS 872/151, for the sentence, minus aggravating clauses.

[40] PRONI, T. 3048/J/12, copy. On Sandys see Madden, *United Irishmen*, 1st ser., 2nd edn., 481–3.

[41] *Courier*, 19 Nov 1798.

[42] *Courier*, 16, 17 (Lentaigne appearing as Linton) and 26 Nov 1798, the last issue carrying an account of the inquest held on Tone, 19 Nov.

[43] MacDermot, *Theobald Wolfe Tone*, 274–5, thinks both eventualities unlikely.

[44] *Courier*, 16 Nov 1798.

[45] Howell, *State Trials*, XXVII. 624–6; *Faulkner's Dublin Jnl*, 13 Nov; *Courier*, 15–16, 19 Nov; *Saunders's News Letter*, 16 Nov; *FJ*, 13 Nov 1798.

[46] PRONI, T.3048/J/13, copy of undated letter Tone to Sandys, endorsed, 'Tone wrote the following letter to Major Sandys a few hours before his death; the letter is not dated, and was so badly wrote that it was with much difficulty so much of it could be made out.'

[47] TCD, MS 872/153, Castlereagh to Gen. Craig [20 Nov 1798].

[48] One bust is now in Trinity College, Dublin, and the other in the American-Irish Historical Library, New York.

[49] Tone (Dickason) MSS, Catherine Heaviside to Matilda, 30 Nov 1798, Matilda to Catherine Anne Tone, 22 Dec 1829; TCD, MS 873/31 and 41, Thomas Dunbavin to Dr Madden, 25 Mar 1847; Madden, *United Irishmen*, 3rd ser., I. 154–9.

[50] Bodenstown is not mentioned in contemporary documents, but Matilda confirmed that Tone was buried there; see Tone (Dickason) MSS, Matilda to Catherine Anne Tone, 22 Dec 1829; Madden, *United Irishmen*, 2nd ser., 2nd edn., 142–3; also *Courier*, 27 Nov 1798.

[51] Tone (Dickason) MSS, Matilda to Catherine Anne Tone, 4 Jan 1830. The receipts for the goods in TCD, MS 872/145, and see also MS 872/156 for Peter Tone's complaints about Sandys.

[52] *Courier*, 26 Nov; *FJ*, 20 Nov; *Saunders's News Letter*, 22 Nov; *Walker's Hib. Mag.* (1798), 812.

[53] Madden, *United Irishmen*, 2nd ser., 2nd edn., 139–41; also Charles Haliday, *Scandinavian Kingdom of Dublin*, 2nd edn. (Dublin, 1834), lxxix–lxxx. See *Dublin Evening Mail*, 8 July 1944.

[54] Buckingham, *Courts and Cabinets of George III*, II. 416; *Cornwallis Corr.*, II. 421–4, 434–5; *Castlereagh Corr.*, II. 7–8n.

[55] *Auckland Corr.*, IV. 67–8; see also PRO, H.O. 100/79/98–9, 108, Cooke-Wickham correspondence 12 and 17 Nov 1798; *Castlereagh Corr.*, I. 424–6, 445–8, and II. 14–15; and on the legal issue of competing jurisdictions, McDowell, *Ireland in the Age of Imperialism and Revolution*, 559–665, and *Parl. Hist.*, XXXV. 1233–4, Fitzgibbon in 1801, citing the problems posed by Tone's case.

[56] SPOI, 620/41/36, Hill to Cooke, 15 Nov 1798; *Auckland Corr.*, IV. 68.

[57] *Courier*, 17 Nov 1798; see also comments in less sympathetic papers such as the *FJ*, 13 Nov, and *BNL*, 13 and 16 Nov; *Castlereagh Corr.*, II. 7–8n.

[58] *Faulkner's Dublin Jnl*, 13 and 15 Nov 1798 (quoting from *Londonderry Jnl*); *FJ*, 13, 15 and 24 Nov, has a more sympathetic piece; *Courier*, 12 Nov; *Proceedings of a Military Court held in Dublin Barracks*, 5; Sir John Moore's account, cited in Madden, *United Irishmen*, 1st ser., II. 354–6.

[59] TCD, MS 3365/67, Thomas Prior's notebook, 2 Nov 1798.

[60] NLI, MS 8505, Allen Morgan to Revd Edward Berwick, 12 Nov 1798; *Drennan Letters*, 729.

[61] On Marsden's early days, see Burtchaell and Sadleir, *Alumni Dublinenses*, 554; *Records, Lincoln's Inn*, I: *Admissions, 1420–1799*, 513; TCD, MS Mun. Soc. Hist. 4, 3 Dec 1783; SPOI, 620/15/2/15, Emmet letter, cited above.

Chapter 30

[1] AN, BB[4] 122 fo. 38, AF III 206 doss. 943 p[ces] 9–11, AF III 45 doss. 162 p[ces] 253–4, Bruix's correspondence, 24 and 28 Oct 1798, and his leaked report of 20 Oct in PRO, F.O. 27/53, *Rédacteur*, 29 Oct 1798.

[2] *Life*, II. 542–8; AHG, B[11] 2, Kilmaine to the Directory, 17 Nov; Tone (Dickason) MSS, De Winter to Matilda, 10 Nov 1798.

[3] AN, AF III 206 doss. 943 p[ce] 108, Bruix to the Directory, 7 Mar 1799; AHG, B[11] 2, Hardy from Lichfield to the Directory, 19 Nov 1798; *Life*, II. 545–6; for precedents see AAE, Corr. Pol. Ang. 590 fo. 146 and 592 fo. 44, *Life*, II. 476, also AAE, Corr. Pol. Sardaigne 279 fos. 3–26, for the Piedmontese patriots in 1800; and AN, F[7] 3309 doss. 1, Prisonniers de Guerre français, Year VIII—1814. SPOI. 620/14/195, 620/18[A]/11, Wickham to Castlereagh, 5 Nov 1798, on the Irish prisoners.

[4] AHG, B[11] 2, Kilmaine to the President of the Directory, 17 Nov 1798; *Le Propagateur*, 20 and 27 Nov, 8 Dec, *L'Observateur politique, littéraire et commercial*, 4 and 6 Dec, *Le Messager des*

rélations extérieures, 6 Dec, *Gazette de France*, 4 and 6 Dec, *L'Ami des Lois*, 6 Dec 1798.

[5] AHG, B[11]2, annotated original of Tone to the Directory, 10 Nov 1798; Tone (Dickason) MSS, Bruix to Thompson [Lewins], 19 Mar 1799.

[6] *Life*, II. 547–65; Tone (Dickason) MSS, Shee's letters of 24, 28 and 31 Aug 1799 and 30 Dec 1801, Simon's of 1 Sept 1799, also all the supporting documents and the Napoleonic certificate granting the pension, 18 May 1804, and later letters of Matilda (e.g. 27 Dec 1834 and in Sampson (Dickason) MSS, 13 July 1843), to Catherine Anne Tone, about periodic declarations of her pension rights. For the case presented by Lucien Bonaparte, see *Conseil des Cinq Cents. Motion d'ordre...pour la veuve et les enfans de Téobald Wolf-Ton*, *Propagateur*, 31 Oct, *Gazette de France*, 31 Oct 1799, and *Life*, II. 550–6, also 564–5. A pension, originally of 1,200 *livres* for Matilda and 400 for each of the children, was doubled by Napoleon.

[7] AN, F[4] 1401 doss. P, 'Matilda Wolfe Tone' to [the Interior Minister], 3 Apr 1803.

[8] LC, Warden Papers, reel 1, Matilda to Warden, 22 Aug 1812. Through the personal intervention of Napoleon, the fees were reimbursed.

[9] *Life*, II. 546, 559–62.

[10] LC, Madison Papers, ser 1, reel 13, Matilda to David Bailie Warden, 8 Jan 1812.

[11] Elliott, *Partners in Revolution*, ch. 10.

[12] See *Memoirs of Miles Byrne*, ed. his widow, 2nd edn., 2 vols. (Dublin, 1906), I. 323. For examples of the esteem for Tone within French officialdom, see AAE, Corr. Pol. Ang. 593 fo. 173, Talleyrand to the Minister of War, 20 Mar 1800; AN, F[7] 8552 doss. 3922, favourable report on Matilda and William by the Minister of Police, 12 Dec 1807; AAG, Doss. pers., Lawless, 1807.

[13] Sampson (Dickason) MSS, Sampson to his wife, 5 Nov 1807, 19 July and 5 Sept 1808.

[14] Tone (Dickason) MSS, William's letters to his mother, 1813–17.

[15] See TCD, Dillon MSS, 6906/58, her comments to Charles Harte in 1849.

[16] *Life*, II. 564; this was in 1802, and the amount raised £787.

[17] *Life*, II. 570–6; AAG, classe. gén. alph., William Theobald Wolfe Tone, Matilda to the Duc de Feltre [Clarke], 17 Sept 1810. Matilda sought naturalisation for William shortly after this, and gained it after a typically intrepid encounter with Napoleon as he hunted in the woods of St. Germain (*Life*, II. 578–85). Tone (Dickason) MSS, William's naturalisation, 4 May 1812.

[18] Tone (Dickason) MSS, Matilda to William Sampson, 29 Mar 1813; also RIA, MS 23.K.53, her letters to Catherine Heavyside, Oct 1812–Dec 1814, for her protectiveness of William.

[19] *Life*, II. 221, 640, 674, and 595–674, for William's military career. Tone (Dickason) MSS, Gen. Dalton to William Tone, 30 Jan 1811, Dalton to [Clarke, Duc de Feltre], 14 June 1814, and certificate of Légion d'honneur, 17 Jan 1815.

[20] Tone (Dickason) MSS, William Tone letters to his mother, 1813–17.

[21] Tone (Dickason) MSS, copies from the National Library of Scotland of corr. between Charles Stuart, British ambassador to Paris, and the London and Dublin governments, 1815–16; *Life*, II. 671–2.

[22] LC, Warden Papers, vol. 22 fos. 4329–30, Matilda Wilson, from Edinburgh, to Warden, 25 Apr 1817.

[23] See RIA, MS 23 K 53, Matilda to Burrowes, 27 July 1816; *Life*, II. 591–3; also Hist. Soc. Pa., Poinsett Papers, vol. 2 no. 27, William Tone to Poinsett, 16 June 1819; *Nation*, 1 July 1848. See Tone himself on Wilson, in Tone (Dickason) MSS, letters of 2 and 9 Sept 1798. Wilson died in 1824.

[24] LC, Warden Papers, reel 3, William Tone to Warden, 7 Jan 1823, vol. 22 fos. 4329–50, Matilda to Warden, 25 Apr 1817; also Sampson (Dickason) MSS, Catherine Anne Tone to Grace Sampson, 26 Oct 1826.

[25] See below, Conclusion.

[26] Sampson (Dickason) MSS, Grace Georgiana Tone to Grace Sampson, 19 and 22 Mar 1849; *National Intelligencer*, 20 Mar 1849.

Conclusion

[1] Editions of Tone's *Life* (after the 1826 Washington edition) appeared in 1827 (London), 1828 (London—re-issued 1830, London), 1846 (Dublin), 1876 (Glasgow), 1893 (London—re-issued 1910 and 1912, both London), 1920 (Dublin), 1932 (Dublin, Irish language edn.), 1936

(London), 1937 (London), 1972 (Cork), 1973 (Tralee). None are full editions of the 1826 *Life*. Most omit the pre-1796 journals and the political writings, and nearly all the twentieth-century editions merely provide extracts.

[2] *New Monthly Mag.*, XI (1824), 1–11, 336–47, 417–23, 537–48, and XIII (1825), 267–72. *Life*. I. 2 and II. 589–93. How the journals fell into the hands of the author of the magazine articles is a mystery. There is no evidence that Tone kept copies, though he did of important correspondence. But Matilda was forever lending papers and the author may have seen them in this manner. Chris Woods suggests that the author was W. H. Curran, son of the famous barrister who defended Tone in 1798, and that he may have acquired the information from Thomas Emmet.

[3] Thomas MacNevin, *Select Speeches of the Right Hon. Richard Lalor Sheil* (Dublin, 1845), 1–7.

[4] Tone (Dickason) MSS, Matilda to Eliza Fletcher, 29 Apr 1827. She was reluctant to have a second printing 'at our expence', although abridged editions did appear in 1827, 1828 and 1830. *Autobiography of Mrs. Fletcher*, ed. by her daughter (Edinburgh, 1875), 142–3, 154, 354–5. For the reviews see also Tone (Dickason) MSS, Eliza Fletcher to Matilda, 19 July and 3 Aug 1826; *North American Rev.*, XXIV (1827), 321–45, by William Sampson; *Monthly Rev.*, new ser., IV (1827), 488–502; *New Monthly Mag.*, XIX (May, 1827), 483–90; *Westminster Rev.*, IX (1828), 71–98. Not all reviews, however, were so favourable. The swearing, 'amours' and drinking, to say nothing of the 'treason', offended English morality (see *Quarterly Rev.*, XXXVI (1827), 61–80, dismissed by Eliza Fletcher as 'a high Tory Review') while the *U.S. Literary Gazette*, IV (Apr–June 1826), 230–2, found the book too long and of little interest after a delay of 30 years.

[5] Tone (Dickason) MSS, Matilda to Catherine Anne Tone, 24 Apr 1836, 10 Apr 1837, 17 Mar 1841, 11 Aug and 11 Dec 1842; also the *Nation*, 1 July 1848, complaining of national ingratitude towards Tone. See Elliott, *Partners in Revolution*, 367–9, for reaction to O'Connell's attack on the United Irishmen.

[6] PRO, H.O. 100/158/461, W. Pole to the Rt. Hon. R. Ryder, 23 July 1810. also *DEP*, 17 July 1810; Fergus O'Farrell, *Catholic Emancipation: Daniel O'Connell and the Birth of Irish Democracy, 1820–30* (Dublin, 1985), 150–1.

[7] T. C. Croker found a third of the popular songs he was collecting for his *Researches in the South of Ireland* (London, 1824) were of a rebellious tendency (p. 329). G. D. Zimmermann, *Songs of Irish Rebellion: Political Street Ballads and Rebel Songs 1780–1900* (Dublin, 1967), 38–43; Elliott, *Partners in Revolution*, 366; James S. Donnelly, Jr., 'Pastorini and Captain Rock: Millenarianism and Sectarianism in the Rockite Movement of 1821–4', in Samuel Clark and James S. Donnelly, Jr., eds., *Irish Peasants: Violence and Political Unrest 1780–1914* (Madison, Wisc., 1983), 102–39; Tom Garvin, 'Defenders, Ribbonmen and Others: Underground Political Networks in Pre-Famine Ireland', and M. R. Beames, 'The Ribbon Societies: Lower-Class Nationalism in Pre-Famine Ireland', both in C. H. E. Philpin, ed., *Nationalism and Popular Protest in Ireland* (*Past and Present* pubs., Cambridge, 1987), 219–44 and 245–63 respectively.

[8] I acknowledge gratefully information gained from conversations with Tom Dunne and from his paper 'The Insecure Voice: A Catholic Novelist in Support of Emancipation', delivered to the Franco-Irish colloquium at Marseilles, Sept 1988.

[9] Tone (Dickason) MSS, Matilda to Eliza Fletcher, 29 Apr 1827. Moore, as a student, had become involved in the Catholic campaign of 1795, and would have known Tone—see Plowden, *History of Ireland*, IV. 164 and *NS*, 13 Apr 1795.

[10] Reg. Deeds Ire., 613/252/418/567.

[11] RIA, MS 23 K 53, Matilda to Catherine Heavyside, 10 Dec 1814; Fuller, 'The Tones: Father and Son', 100–1; *Cox's Irish Mag.*, VII (Jan 1814), 33–4; Madden, *United Irishmen*, 2nd ser. 2nd edn., 160. Mrs. Tone was also supporting a 'little girl', who may have been a natural child of Matthew; see TCD, MS 873/35, copy of Matilda to Mrs Tone, 11 May 1810.

[12] SPOI, S.O.C. 1031/36, information of W. Corbet, 28 Aug 1805.

[13] J[ohn] G[ray] to the editor, *FJ*, Sept 1873.

[14] NLI, MS 1791/24–7, copy of Matilda to Dr John Gray, 18 Dec 1843; *Nation*, 25 Nov 1843. I acknowledge with gratitude the help of Dr C.J. Woods on these points, and for permission to read his paper 'Tone's Grave at Bodenstown: Memorials and Commemorations', read to the Irland-Konferenz, Halle, GDR, Sept 1988.

NOTES TO PAGES 412–17

[15] See, e.g., NLI, MS 1791/2, Davis's frontispiece sketch for his proposed life of Tone: 'Liberty takes down the sword suspended from the ivied wall over Tone's grave and hands it to *me!*'

[16] Charles Gavan Duffy, *Four Years of Irish History, 1845–49* (London, 1883), 57–83, and its sequel, *Young Ireland* (Australian edn., 1881), 373, 387–8; T.W. Moody, 'Thomas Davis and the Irish Nation', *Hermathena*, CIII (1966), 5–31.

[17] *Uncollected Prose by W.B. Yeats*, ed. John P. Frayne and Colton Johnson, 2 vols. (London, 1970–5), I. 383. I am grateful to Dr R.F. Foster, who is currently writing a biography of W.B.Yeats, for information on Yeats's attitudes to the Tone tradition. 'Tone's Grave' appears in *Spirit of the Nation*, 2nd ser. (Dublin, 1845). See also Thomas Davis, *Historical Ballads, Songs and Poems* (Dublin, 1846), 171–2.

[18] NLI, MS 1791/3–30, the planned life and dedication to Matilda Tone (copy of latter also in TCD, MS 873/43); Duffy, *Young Ireland*, 680–3, and see, e.g., *Nation*, 8 July 1843 and 27 Sept 1845, also *Voice of the Nation* (Dublin, 1844), 146.

[19] Madden, *United Irishmen*, 3rd ser., I. 121–84.

[20] Tone (Dickason) MSS, Matilda to Catherine Anne Tone, 11 Dec 1842, 2 Feb and 11 Aug 1843; TCD, MS 873/42 and 310, also Madden, *United Irishmen*, 2nd ser., 2nd edn., 169–73. Matilda would have been well pleased with Madden's 2nd edn. of 1858, which included a detailed study of Tone; see 1st ser. 2nd edn., 222–7, 266–82, and 2nd ser., 2nd edn., 1–173.

[21] *United Irishman*, 12 Feb, 4 Mar and 20 May 1848; John O'Leary, *Fenians and Fenianism* (IUP repr. of 1896 edn., Shannon, 1969), I, 2–8, II, 147–8, 169. Mitchel drew heavily on Tone's *Life* for his *History of Ireland*, which was widely read.

[22] R. V. Comerford, *The Fenians in Context* (Dublin, 1985), 33–5, 37, 51–3. Miller, *Emigrants and Exiles*, 306–11, 334–40.

[23] Zimmermann, *Songs of Irish Rebellion*, 69–71.

[24] Comerford, *Fenians in Context*, 74–9; Alice Milligan, *Theobald Wolfe Tone* (Belfast, 1898), 113–16.

[25] The version of Tone's trial speech is that printed by his son in the 1826 *Life*.

[26] [T.D. and A.M.Sullivan], *'Guilty or Not Guilty': Speeches from the Dock or Protests of Irish Patriotism* (Dublin, 1867), 1945 edn., xix and xxxvii; 1968 edn., 27.

[27] Yeats, *Uncollected Prose*, I. 38–9, 340–1, 355–6, 386, and II. 34 and 289.

[28] *Irish News*, 20–22 June 1898.

[29] *Irish News*, 16 Aug 1898; Patrick Flanigan to James Short (chief marshal of the Tone ceremony), 5 Aug 1898, in commemorative pamphlet, *Wolfe Tone Memorial 1967* (Dublin, 1967), 18–19.

[30] Duffy, *Four Years of Irish History*, 232–3; T. Davis, *Letters of a Protestant on Repeal*, ed. Thomas F. Meagher (Dublin, 1847), v–vi, 34–5; Davis, *National and Historical Ballads* (Dublin, 1869), 84–6, 164–9.

[31] Milligan, *Theobald Wolfe Tone*, 34–7; and her 'The North is Up', under pseud. Iris Olkyrn, in the *Christmas Weekly Independent*, 1895; *United Irishman*, 27 June 1903.

[32] See, e.g., J.R.R. Adams, *The Printed Word and the Common Man: Popular Culture in Ulster 1700–1900* (Belfast, 1987), 143; R. Finlay Holmes, *Henry Cooke* (Belfast, 1981), 5.

[33] BNL, 20 June, 15 and 16 Aug 1898, and, for its dislike of O'Connell, 1 Mar and 2 Dec 1825, 21 July and 21 Nov 1826, 13 Feb 1827, 23 Apr 1830, 20 Jan 1832.

[34] P.H. Pearse, *Political Writings and Speeches* (Dublin, 1962), 168, also 53–63, 78–9, 112, 134, 169–71, 237–8, 240–2, 246–8, 251, 255, 263–93, 299, 303–4, 311–12, 317, 319, 323, 326, 344, 352—a token of Tone's impact on Pearse's imagination.

[35] *An Phoblacht. Republican News*, 27 June 1981 and 23 June 1983; Gerry Adams, *The Politics of Irish Freedom* (Dingle, 1986), 1–2.

[36] *Spirit of the Nation: The Speeches of Charles J. Haughey*, ed. Martin Mansergh (Dublin, 1986), 311, 572, 607, 672–3, 856, 939, 997–8, 1158–60, and press release of speech on 11 Oct 1987, kindly sent to me by Dr Martin Mansergh, Head of Research, Fianna Fáil. John Bowman, *De Valera and the Ulster Question, 1917–1973* (Oxford, 1982), 277, and 333 for similar views on Tone held by the Fine Gael party.

[37] *Wolfe Tone Annual* (1948), 18, 21–3, 36; *Wolfe Tone Weekly*, 19 Mar 1938; R. Jacob, *The Rise of the United Irishmen 1791–4* (London, 1937), 19; P. Walsh, 'Wolfe Tone and the Irish Catholics', *Irish Theological Quarterly*, XVII (1922), 167–8, 315–16. D.P. Moran, one of the

leading figures in the Gaelic League, held to be the creator of the philosophy of 'Irish Ireland', denounced Tone as un-Irish, with no conception of an Irish nation; see *The Philosophy of Irish Ireland* (Dublin, 1905), 8, 40; also F.S.L. Lyons, *Ireland since the Famine* (London, 1971), 230–3.

[38] Leo McCabe, *Wolfe Tone and the United Irishmen: For or Against Christ?* (London, 1937), 154–5; J.H. Whyte, *Church and State in Modern Ireland, 1923–1970* (Dublin, 1971), 67–8, 89–90; *Irish Independent*, 8, 19 and 22 May 1933.

[39] See, e.g., Aodh de Blacam, *Life Story of Wolfe Tone Set in a Picture of His Times* (Dublin, 1935), 164—also serialised in *Wolfe Tone Weekly* (1937–8); and Richard Hayes, 'The First Republican as Catholic Champion', *Irish Press*, 20 June 1932.

[40] J.W. Hammond, 'Tone's Throat Wound', *Dublin Evening Mail*, 8 July 1944. I am grateful to Dr C.J. Woods and Oliver Snoddy for information on this point. See also de Blacam, *Life Story of Wolfe Tone*, 208–9, Seán Cronin, *Wolfe Tone* (Dublin, 1963), 44–5, and Denis Ireland, *Patriot Adventurer: Extracts from the Memoirs and Journals of Theobald Wolfe Tone* ([London], 1936), 222, *Wolfe Tone Weekly*, 4 Dec 1937 and 18 June 1938, and *Wolfe Tone Today* (1963), 12, on the suicide.

[41] See the exchange between P.S. O'Hegarty and F. MacDermot in *Dublin Mag.*, XIV (1939), 66–72, and XV (1940), 60–3.

[42] *Wolfe Tone Weekly*, 19 Mar 1938.

[43] *An Phoblacht. Republican News*, 27 June 1981.

[44] Pearse, *Political Writings*, 283; Haughey, *Spirit of the Nation*, 939, 998; *An Poblacht. Republican News*, 27 June 1981; letter from the Workers' Party in *BNL*, 17 June 1986.

[45] See, e.g., Roy Bradford, 'Brits Out and Wolfe Tone', *BNL*, 11 Apr 1988.

[46] See *FJ*, 13 July 1793, Fitzgibbon describing Tone as 'the father of the Society of United Irishmen'.

Select Bibliography

Manuscript Sources

ENGLAND

London

BRITISH LIBRARY: Add. MSS 33,101–6, 33,113, 33,118–19 (Pelham MSS); 34,419 (Auckland MSS); 35,197 (Bridport MSS); 35,933 (Papers relating to Roman Catholics in Ireland, 1697–1798); 38,355 (Liverpool MSS).

LINCOLN'S INN LIBRARY: Red Books, vol. 3, 1753–93.

MIDDLE TEMPLE LIBRARY: Barristers' Ledger; Index to Minutes of Parliament, 1787; Middle Temple Receipt Books, 1787–8; Rentals, 1776–96; Students' Ledger; Treasurer's Accounts, 1782–1803.

PUBLIC RECORD OFFICE: F.O. (Foreign Office) 27/40–54 (France, 1792–8); 33/9–16 and 97/240–2 (Hamburg, 1794–8); 74/17–22 (Switzerland, 1796–8), H.O. (Home Office) 28/22–4 (Admiralty, 1797–8); 100/34–78, 101/2, 122/3 (Ireland, 1791–8). P.R.O. 30/8 (Chatham Papers). P.C. (Privy Council) 1/22–3, 43–4. T.S. (Treasury Solicitor) 11/55/1793 and 11/1067/4935. W.O. (War Office) 1/396 and 612 (intelligence, 1793–8) 30/63, 65 (defence, 1796–1804).

Maidstone

KENT ARCHIVES OFFICE: MS U.840 (Pratt Papers).

Nottingham

NOTTINGHAM UNIVERSITY LIBRARY: Portland Papers.

Oxford

BODLEIAN LIBRARY: Curzon Collection.

Winchester

HAMPSHIRE COUNTY RECORD OFFICE: MS 38M49 (Wickham Papers)

FRANCE

Paris

ARCHIVES DES AFFAIRES ÉTRANGÉRES: Correspondance Politique: Angleterre 582–93 and supplément 15, 21, 30; États Unis 44; Hambourg 107–13; Hollande 595; Sardaigne 279; Suisse 458. Mémoires et Documents: Angleterre 1^b, 19, 53, Fonds Divers, Angleterre 2; France et Divers États, 654. Personnel, 1ère série 1, 8, 9, 25, 39, 47, 55, 65; Arrêtés et Décrets, 8–9.

ARCHIVES DE LA GUERRE (Vincennes): B^{1}172–7 and B^1*177 (armées du Nord et de la Sambre et Meuse); B^{5}41–4 and B^5*114–16 (armée d'Angleterre); B^{11}1–2 (expéditions d'Irlande, 1796–8); Dossiers personnels (classified alphabetically). MR (mémoires historiques) 506 (journal of J.L. Jobit on Humbert's expedition), 1420 (various invasion proposals).

ARCHIVES NATIONALES: Pouvoir exécutif, AF II (Committee of Public Safety) 294, 468; AF III (Directory) 45, 51^a, 57–9, 64, 70, 147, 149, 186^{a-b} (the latter has been completely re-folioed by the AN since used for *Partners in Revolution*), 205–6, 268–9, 272, 274, 337, 362, 369–70, 373, 377, 400, 408, 437, 450, 452, 463, 505, 529, 579 and AF 111*20. AF IV (Consulate and Empire) 1195, 1597[A], 1671. Marine, BB[2]23, 55., BB[3]105, 107–8, 124, 143, 145–6, 160–2, BB[4]99, 102–3, 112, 114, 119–23, FF[2]137, GG[2]22–3 Comptabilité générale, F[4]1401. Police générale, F[7]3049, 3309, 4629, 7107, 7111, 7114, 7151, 7215, 7196–7, 7238, 7249, 7264, 7293, 7348, 7383[B], 7401, 7417, 7422, 7437–40, 7480, 8552. Hospices et Secours, F[15]3511.

Rouen

ARCHIVES DÉPARTEMENTALES DE LA SEINE ET MARITIME: 1Mi 54–71 (Hoche Papers).

IRELAND

Belfast

PRESBYTERIAN HISTORICAL SOCIETY: Sinclair MSS.

PUBLIC RECORD OFFICE OF NORTHERN IRELAND: D.272 (McCance collection), D.456, D.591 and D.729 (Drennan Letters), D.553 (Drennan-Bruce letters), D.607 (Downshire MSS), D.714 (Cleland MSS), D.1748 (Tennent letters, largely uncatalogued at time of use), D.2260 (Journal of Capt. Alexander Chesney) D.3030 (Castlereagh Papers), T.2541 (Abercorn MSS), T.3048 (McPeake Papers), T.3229 (Sneyd Papers), T.3393 (Rosse MSS).

ULSTER MUSEUM: letter, Tone to Sam McTier, 28 Jan 1792.

Dublin

DEPARTMENT OF IRISH FOLKLORE, UNIVERSITY COLLEGE: School MSS 458/24, 773/437, 776/338 and 1111/185, also MSS S.277/80–1, S.282/88, 132 and 222, S.935/6, S.936/174 and S.1405/237 (Tone in popular tradition).

DUBLIN DIOCESAN ARCHIVES: Troy MSS.

KING'S INNS LIBRARY: Admission Papers (T.W. Tone), Benchers' Minute Books, I, 1792–1803.

NATIONAL LIBRARY OF IRELAND: 54[A]-55 (Melville Papers), 394 (Westmorland Letters), 704–7 (French Invasion), 772 (Extracts from the Diary of Austin Cooper, 1782–1815), 809 (Defence), 1791 (Notes and Letters by Thomas Davis), 2245 (Michael Wycherly's notebook, 1781–2), 3212 (Tone Letters), 5181 (1898 Centenary Celebrations), 8505 (Allen Morgan to the Revd E. Berwick, 12 Nov 1798).

NATIONAL MUSEUM: Tone's Pocket Book, enclosing note of Peter Tone.

PUBLIC RECORD OFFICE OF IRELAND: Bet. 1/42/317 and 69/89 (Betham Abstracts, Prerogative Wills: John Lamport, 1747 and Jonathan Tone, 1792). Frazer MSS.

REGISTRY OF DEEDS: 225/38/144986, 236/228/154381, 315/399/213902, 337/17/ 224480, 341/388/228952, 342/359/230473, 346/109/230775, 348/557/235501 (deeds concerning Tone property in Dublin, 1762–83); 297/347/195310, 302/ 262/200020, 374/532/250721, 419/287/273989 (Tone property in Kildare); 487/ 496/314272 (Tone's transfer of Chateau Boue to Donnellan, 20 May 1795); 613/252/418567 (lease of house to Margaret Tone, 1805).

ROYAL IRISH ACADEMY: MS 23.K.53 (Burrowes MSS), MS 24.K.48 (Memoirs of A.H. Rowan); MS 12.P.13 (Journal of Daniel O'Connell).

STATE PAPER OFFICE, IRELAND: Private Official Correspondence; 620/1–67 (Rebellion Papers); Westmorland Correspondence.

TRINITY COLLEGE: MSS 868–9 (Sirr Papers); MS 872 (Courts Martial); MS 873 (Madden Papers); MS 2041–50 and 3805–9 (Tone MSS); MS 3365 (Thomas Prior's notebook); MS 6906 (Dillon MSS); Mun. Soc/Hist. 4–10, 40–1, 49, 50, 57 (College Historical Society MSS); Mun. V 5/3–4, 9, 16, 27, 35, 46, 47, 86 (College Muniments, including examination results, chamber lettings, bursars', deans' and proctors' books etc.).

NETHERLANDS

The Hague

ALGEMEEN RIJKSARCHIEF (GENERAL STATE ARCHIVES): Archives of the National Assembly, 1796–8; Archives of the Legations of the Batavian Republic, 1795–8; Archives of the Agency for Foreign Affairs, 1796–8, inventory nos. 49 (Irish expedition, 1797), 173 (letters from French and Batavian generals and officers, 1797), 178 (marine affairs, 1796–8); Collection Daendels, 1754–1862.

UNITED STATES OF AMERICA

Ann Arbor, Mich.

W.L. CLEMENTS LIBRARY: Melville MSS.

Baltimore, Md

ARCHIVES OF THE ARCHDIOCESE OF BALTIMORE: Carroll MSS.

Charlottesville, Va.

UNIVERSITY OF VIRGINIA: James Monroe Papers; Papers of John Beckley.

New York, N.Y.

NEW YORK PUBLIC LIBRARY: Monroe Papers

Philadelphia, Pa.

FREE LIBRARY: McIntire Elkins Coll.

PENNSYLVANIA HISTORICAL SOCIETY: Hampton L. Carson Coll.; Gratz Coll.; Edward Carey Gardiner Coll.; Cadwalader Coll.; Maria Dickinson Logan Family Papers; Irvine Papers; Poinsett Papers.

Short Hills, N.J.

Private Collection: Tone (Dickason) MSS; Sampson (Dickason) MSS.

Washington, D.C.

LIBRARY OF CONGRESS: Monroe Papers; Madison Papers; David Bailie Warden Papers; William Sampson Papers.

NATIONAL ARCHIVES: Microfilm: M.28 Rolls 3–5 (General Records of the Dept. of State, Diplomatic and Consular Instructions, 1795–98); M.30 Rolls 2–6 (Dispatches from U.S. Ministers to Great Britain, 1791–1800); T.1 Roll 1 (Dispatches from U.S. Consuls in Paris, 1790–1805); M.34 Rolls 6–7 (Dispatches from U.S. Ministers to France, 1794–7); M.53 Roll 1 (Dispatches from the French Legation in the U.S. to the Dept. of State, 1789–1805); M. 664 Roll 1 (Notes from Foreign Consuls in the U.S. to the Dept. of State, 1789–1826); T.199 Rolls 1–3 (Dispatches from U.S. Consuls in Dublin); T.211 Roll 1 (Dispatches from U.S. Consuls in Hamburg, 1790–1808); T.368 Roll 1 (Dispatches from U.S. Consuls in Belfast). Manuscripts: RG 84 (Corr. of the American Embassy in Paris, 1794–6).

Printed Material*

PRIMARY SOURCES

Newspapers and Periodicals

Ami des Lois	*Aurora*
Annual Register	*Bien Informé*
An Phoblacht. Republican News	*Courier*

---

* Only major works or those cited frequently are listed here. Full references to all sources cited are given in the Notes.

Faulkner's Dublin Journal
Freeman's Journal
Irish Independent
Irish News
Irish Press
Irish Times
Belfast Monthly Magazine
Belfast News Letter
Dublin Evening Post
Dublin Magazine and Irish Monthly
    Register
European Magazine
Gazette de France
Hibernian Journal
Irish Magazine

Messager des Rélations Extérieures
Moniteur
Morning Post
Nation
Northern Star
Observateur Politique
Propagateur
Rédacteur
Saunders's News Letter
United Irishman
Universal Magazine and Review
Walker's Hibernian Magazine
Wolfe Tone Annual
Wolfe Tone Today
Wolfe Tone Weekly

Parliamentary Papers

Archives parlementaires: Recueil complet des débats législatif et politiques des Chambres françaises, 1ère série; 1787–99, 91 vols. (Paris, 1879–1976)

Buchez, P.J.B., and Roux-Lavergne, P.C., Histoire parlementaire de la Révolution française, 40 vols. (Paris, 1834–8)

The Parliamentary History of England from the earliest period to the year 1803, 36 vols. (London, 1806–20)

The Parliamentary Register: or, History of the Proceedings and Debates of the House of Commons of Ireland, 1781–97, 17 vols. (Dublin, 1782–1801)

Report from the Committee of Secrecy of the House of Commons of Ireland (Dublin, 1798)

Report from the Committee of Secrecy of the House of Lords in Ireland (Dublin, 1798)

Report from the Secret Committee of the House of Lords . . . into the Causes of the Disorders and Disturbances which Prevail in Several Parts of this Kingdom (Dublin, 1793)

Other Contemporary Works

The American Gazetteer, ed. J. Morse (Boston, 1797)

The Journal and Correspondence of William, Lord Auckland, ed. the Bishop of Bath and Wells, 4 vols. (London, 1861–2)

Aulard, A., Paris pendant la réaction thermidorienne et sous le Directoire, 5 vols. (Paris, 1898–1902)

Mémoires de Barras, ed. G, Duruy, 4 vols. (Paris, 1896)

The Correspondence of the Rt. Hon. John Beresford, ed. W. Beresford, 2 vols. (London, 1854)

Memoirs of the Courts and Cabinets of George III, ed. Duke of Buckingham, 4 vols. (London, 1853–5)

The Correspondence of Edmund Burke, ed. T.W. Copeland et al., 10 vols. (Cambridge, 1958–78)

[Burrowes, Peter], Plain Arguments in Defence of the People's Absolute Dominion over the Constitution in which the Question of Roman Catholic Emancipation is fully Considered (Dublin, 1784)

Select Speeches of the late Peter Burrowes, Esq. K.C., at the Bar and in Parliament, ed. Waldron O. Burrowes (Dublin, 1850)

Carey, W.P., An Appeal to the People of Ireland (Dublin, 1794)

Mémoires sur Carnot par son fils, 2 vols. (Paris, 1861–4)

The John Carroll Papers, ed. Thomas O'Brien, 3 vols. (Notre Dame, Ind., 1976)

Memoirs and Correspondence of Viscount Castlereagh, ed. 3rd Marquess of Londonderry, 12 vols. (London, 1848–54), vols. 1–IV

Tracts on Catholic Affairs (Dublin, 1791)

Charlemont MSS. The Manuscripts and Correspondence of James, first Earl of Charlemont, H.M.C., 13th report, app. pt. VIII (London, 1894), vol. 11

Conseil des Cinq Cents. Motion d'Ordre faite par L. Bonaparte, pour la veuve et les enfans de Téobald-Wolf-Ton (Paris, 1799)

Cooper, Thomas, *Letters from America to a Friend in England* (London, 1794).

Debidour, A., *Recueil des Actes du Directoire exécutif*, 4 vols. (Paris, 1910–17)

De Lactocnaye, J.L., *A Frenchman's Walk through Ireland, 1796–7*, 2nd edn, ed. J.A. Gamble (Belfast, 1984)

[Drennan, William], *An Irish Helot Addresses Himself to the Seven Northern Counties who were not Represented in the Late Civil Convention, by Orellana* [*Letters of Orellana*] (Dublin, 1785)

——   *Fugitive Pieces in Verse and Prose* (Belfast, 1815)

——   *The Drennan Letters*, ed D.A. Chart (Belfast, 1931)

Dropmore MSS. The MSS of J.B. Fortescue Esq., preserved at Dropmore, H.M.C., 13th. report, append. pt 3, and 14th report, append. pt 5, 10 vols. (London, 1892–4)

Edwards, R. Dudley, ed., 'The Minute Book of the Catholic Committee, 1773–92', *Archivium Hibernicum* IX (1942), 3–172

Memoirs of the Life and Times of the Rt. Hon. Henry Grattan, ed. Henry Grattan Jun., 5 vols. (London, 1839–46)

'Correspondance intime du Général Hardy (de 1797 à 1802)', *Revue des Deux Mondes*, CLXI (Sept 1900), 98–117

Howell, T.B. and T.J., eds., *A Complete Collection of State Trials*, 33 vols. (London, 1809)

Jeremy, D.J., *Henry Wansey and his American Journal* (Philadelphia, 1970)

Jones, William Todd, *A Letter to the Electors of the Borough of Lisburn* (Dublin, 1784)

——   *A Letter to the Societies of United Irishmen of the Town of Belfast, upon the subject of Catholic Rights* (Dublin 1792)

[Joy, Henry, ed.], *Historical Collections Relative to the Town of Belfast: from the Earliest Period to the Union with Great Britain* (Belfast, 1817)

Joy, H. and Bruce, W., eds., *Belfast Politics, or, Collection of the Debates, Resolutions and Other Proceedings of that Town in the Years 1792 and 1793* (Belfast, 1794)

Keane, Edward, Phair, Beryl P. and Sadleir, Thomas U., eds., *King's Inns Admission Papers 1607–1867* (Dublin, 1982)

Mémoires de La Révellière-Lépeaux, ed. his son, 3 vols. (Paris, 1895)

MacNeven, W.J., *Pieces of Irish History* (New York, 1807)

Marriage Entries from the Registers of the Parishes of St. Andrew, St. Anne, St. Audoen and St. Bride, 1632–1800, ed. D.A. Chart (London, 1931)

The O'Conors of Connaught: An historical memoir, ed. C.O.O'Conor Don (Dublin, 1891)

Remains of the Revd Samuel O'Sullivan DD, ed. Revd J.C. Martin, DD, and Revd Mortimer O'Sullivan, DD, 3 vols. (Dublin, 1853)

The Life, Letters, and Speeches of Lord Plunket, ed. the Hon. David Plunket, 2 vols. (London, 1867)

Proceedings of a Military Court held in Dublin Barracks on Saturday the Tenth of November, for the Trial of Theobald Wolfe Tone (Dublin, 1798)

The Autobiography of Archibald Hamilton Rowan, ed. William H. Drummond (I.U.P. repr., Shannon, 1972)

Memoirs of William Sampson (New York, 1807)

Seward, W.W., *Topographica Hibernica* (Dublin, 1792)

Sketches, Legal and Political of the late Rt. Hon. Richard Lalor Sheil, ed. M.W. Savage, Esq., 2 vols. (London, 1855)

Private Papers of George, 2nd Earl Spencer, ed. J.S. Corbett, 2 vols. (London, 1913–24)

Thibaudeau, A.C., *Mémoires sur la Convention et le Directoire*, 2 vols. (Paris, 1824)

Tone, Theobald Wolfe [*et al.*], *Belmont Castle; or, Suffering Sensibility, containing the genuine and interesting correspondence of several persons of fashion* (Dublin, 1790)

—————— *A Review of the Conduct of Administration During the Seventh Session of Parliament Addressed to the Constitutional Electors and Free People of Ireland ... By an Independent Irish Whig* (Dublin, 1790)

—————— *Spanish War!: An Enquiry How Far Ireland is Bound of Right to Embark in the Impending Contest on the Side of Great Britain* (Dublin, 1790)

—————— *An Argument on Behalf of the Catholics of Ireland* (Dublin, 1791)

—————— *Defence of the Sub-Committee of the Catholics of Ireland, from the Imputations Attempted to be Thrown on that Body, Particularly from the Charge of Supporting the Defenders* (Dublin, 1793)

The Autobiography of Theobald Wolfe Tone, ed. S. O'Faolain (London, 1937)

The Letters of Wolfe Tone, ed. Bulmer Hobson (Dublin, [1921])

The Life of Theobald Wolfe Tone, ed. by his son, William T.W. Tone, 2 vols. (Washington, 1826)

The Life of Wolfe Tone, abridged and ed. Bulmer Hobson (Dublin, 1920)

The Journals of the Revd John Wesley, 4 vols. (London, 1827)

SECONDARY SOURCES

Ashcraft, R., *Revolutionary Politics and Locke's 'Two Treatises of Government'* (Princeton, N.J., 1986)

Ball, F. Elrington, *The Judges in Ireland, 1221–1921*, 2 vols. (London, 1926)

Barrington, Sir Jonah, *Personal Sketches of his own Times*, 2nd edn., 2 vols. (London, 1869)

Bartlett, T. and Hayton, D.W., eds., *Penal Era and Golden Age: Essays in Irish History, 1690–1800* (Belfast, 1979)

Bartlett, T., 'An End to the "Moral Economy": The Irish Militia Disturbances of 1793', *Past and Present*, no. 99 (May 1983), 41–64

Beckett, J.C., and Glasscock, R.E., eds., *Belfast: The Origin and Growth of an Industrial City* (London, 1967)

Benn, G., *A History of the Town of Belfast from the Earliest Times to the Close of the Eighteenth Century* (London, 1877)

Berthaut, Col. H., *Les Ingénieurs Géographes militaires, 1624–1831*, 2 vols. (Paris, 1902)

Bond, Beverley W., *The Monroe Mission to France, 1794–1796*, Johns Hopkins Univ. Studies in Historical and Political Sciences, ser. XXV, nos. 2–3 (Baltimore, 1907)

Boylan, Henry, *Wolfe Tone* (Dublin, 1981)

Brooke, Peter, *Ulster Presbyterianism: The Historical Perspective, 1610–1970* (Dublin, 1987)

Burtchaell, George D., 'Theobald Wolfe Tone and the College Historical Society', *Journal of the Royal Society of Antiquaries of Ireland* XVIII (1887–8), 391–9

Campbell, John, *The Lives of the Lord Chancellors and Keepers of the Great Seals of England*, 7 vols. (London, 1819)

Carlson, Marvin, *The Theatre of the French Revolution* (Ithaca, N.Y., 1966)

Clarke, W.S., *The Irish Stage in the County Towns 1720–1800* (Oxford, 1965)

Connolly, S.J., 'Religion and History', *Irish Economic and Social History* X (1983), 66–80

Corish, Patrick J., ed., *Radicals, Rebels and Establishments* (Belfast, 1985)

Craig, Maurice, *Dublin 1660–1860* (Dublin, 1969; repr. of 1952 London edn.)

Cullen, L.M., *The Emergence of Modern Ireland* (London, 1981)

—— 'Catholics Under the Penal Laws', *Eighteenth-Century Ireland* I (1986), 23–36

Curran, W.H., *The Life and Times of the Rt. Hon. John Philpot Curran*, 2 vols. (London, 1819)

—— *Sketches of the Irish Bar*, 2 vols. (London, 1855)

Curtin, Nancy J., 'The Transformation of the United Irishmen into a Revolutionary Mass Organisation, 1792–4', *Irish Historical Studies* XXIV (1984–5), 463–92

Dagg, T.S.C., *The College Historical Society: A History (1770–1920)* (Dublin, 1969)

Desbrière, E., *Projets et tentatives de débarquements aux îles britanniques*, 4 vols. (Paris, 1900–2)

Dickson, David, ed., *The Gorgeous Mask: Dublin 1700–1850* (Dublin, 1987)

Dixon, W. MacNeille, *Trinity College, Dublin* (London, 1902)

Doerflinger, Thomas M., *A Vigorous Spirit of Enterprise: Merchants and Economic Development in Revolutionary Philadelphia* (Chapel Hill, N. Car., 1986)

Donnelly, James S., Jr., 'Propagating the Cause of the United Irishmen', *Studies: An Irish Quarterly Review* LXIX (1980), 5–23

D'Ornano, E. Cuneo, *Hoche, sa vie, sa correspondance* (Paris, 1892)

Duman, Daniel, *The Judicial Bench in England 1727–1875: The Reshaping of an Élite* (London, 1982)

Dunne, Tom, *Theobald Wolfe Tone, Colonial Outsider: An Analysis of His Political Philosophy* (Cork, 1982)

Durey, M., 'Thomas Paine's Apostles: Radical Émigrés and the Triumph of Jeffersonian Republicanism', *William and Mary Quarterly*, XLIV (1981), 661–88

Elliott, Marianne, *Partners in Revolution: The United Irishmen and France* (New Haven and London, 1982)

—— *Watchmen in Sion: The Protestant Idea of Liberty*. (Belfast, 1985)

—— 'The Origins and Transformation of Early Irish Republicanism', *International Review of Social History* XXIII (1978), 405–28

—— 'Ireland', in *Nationalism in the Age of the French Revolution*, ed. Otto Dann and John Dinwiddy (London, 1988), 71–86

Escande, G., *Hoche en Irlande, 1795–1798* (Paris, 1888)

Falkiner, C. Litton, *Studies in Irish History and Biography, mainly of the Eighteenth Century* (London, 1902)

Finegan, Francis, 'Was John Keogh an Informer?', *Studies: An Irish Quarterly Review* XXXIX (1950), 75–86

Foster, R.F., *Modern Ireland 1600–1972* (London, 1988)

Fuller, J.F., 'The Tones: Father and Son', *Journal of the Cork Historical and Archaeological Society* XXIX (1929), 93–101

Gilbert, J.T., *A History of the City of Dublin*, 3 vols. (Dublin, 1859)

Godechot, J., *Les Institutions de la France sous la Révolution et l'Empire*, 3rd edn. (Paris, 1985)

Guillon, E., *La France et L'Irlande sous le Directoire* (Paris, 1888)

Guyot, R., *Le Directoire et la Paix de l'Europe* (Paris, 1911)

Gwynn, Denis, *John Keogh: The Pioneer of Catholic Emancipation* (Dublin, 1930)

Hutt, Maurice, *Chouannerie and Counter-Revolution; Puisaye, the Princes and the British Government in the 1790s*, 2 vols. (Cambridge, 1983)

Jacob, R., *The Rise of the United Irishmen, 1791–4* (London, 1937)

Lecky, W.E.H., *A History of Ireland in the Eighteenth Century*, new edn., 5 vols. (London, 1892)

McCabe, Leo, *Wolfe Tone and the United Irishmen. For or Against Christ?* (London, 1937)

McCormack, W.J., *Ascendancy and Tradition in Anglo-Irish Literary History from 1789 to 1939* (Oxford, 1985)

MacDermot, Frank, *Theobald Wolfe Tone and His Times*, rev. edn. (Tralee, 1969)

McDowell, R.B., 'The Personnel of the Dublin Society of United Irishmen, 1791–4', *Irish Historical Studies* II (1940–1), 12–53

—— *Irish Public Opinion, 1750–1800* (London, 1944)

—— 'Proceedings of the Dublin Society of United Irishmen', *Anal. Hibernica* XVII (1949), 3–143

—— *Ireland in the Age of Imperialism and Revolution* (Oxford, 1979)

McDowell, R.B., and Webb, D.A., *Trinity College Dublin 1592–1952: An Academic History* (Cambridge, 1982)

MacGiolla Easpaig, Séamus N., *Tomás Ruiséil* (Dublin, 1957)

MacManus, M.J., 'Bibliography of Theobald Wolfe Tone', *Dublin Magazine* XV, no. 3 (July–Sept 1940), 52–64

—— 'When Wolfe Tone Wrote a Novel', *Irish Press*, Christmas no., 1934

McNeill, Mary, *The Life and Times of Mary Ann McCracken 1770–1866: A Belfast Panorama* (Dublin, 1960).

Madden, R.R., *The United Irishmen, their Lives and Times*, 3 ser., 7 vols. (London, 1842–45), and rev. edn., 4 vols. (London, 1857–60)

Malcomson, A.P.W., *John Foster: The Politics of the Anglo-Irish Ascendancy* (Oxford, 1978)

Masson, Frédéric, *Le Département des Affaires Étrangères pendant la Révolution, 1787–1804* (Paris, 1877)

Mathiez, Albert, 'Le Personnel Gouvernemental du Directoire', *Annales historiques de la Révolution française*, no. 59 (1933), 385–411

Maxwell, Constantia, *A History of Trinity College, Dublin, 1591–1812* (Dublin, 1946)

—— *Dublin Under the Georges* (Dublin, 1946).

Meynier, Albert, *Les coups d'état du Directoire*, vol. I: *Le dix-huit fructidor* (Paris, 1927)

Miller, David W., 'Presbyterianism and "Modernization" in Ulster', *Past and Present*, no. 80 (Aug 1978), 66–90

Milligan, Alice, *Theobald Wolfe Tone* (Belfast, 1898)

Moody, T.W., and Vaughan, W.E. eds., *A New History of Ireland*, vol. IV: *Eighteenth-Century Ireland 1691–1800* (Oxford, 1986)

Morgan, Lady Sydney, *The O'Briens and the O'Flahertys: A National Tale*, 4 vols. (Paris, 1828)

O'Flanagan, J.R., *The Lives of the Lord Chancellors and Keepers of the Great Seal of Ireland*, 2 vols. (London, 1870)

Phillips, C., *Curran and his Contemporaries* (London, 1850)

Plowden, F., *An Historical Review of the State of Ireland*, 5 vols. (Philadelphia, 1806)

Pocock, J.G.A. *The Machiavellian Moment: Florentine Political Thought and the Atlantic Republican Tradition* (Princeton, N.J., 1975)

Reinhard, M., *Le Grand Carnot: L'Organisateur de la Victoire*, 2 vols. (Paris, 1950)

Robbins, Caroline, *The Eighteenth-Century Commonwealthman* (Cambridge, Mass., 1959)

Rogers, P., *The Irish Volunteers and Catholic Emancipation, 1778–1793* (London, 1934)

Sciout, L., *Le Directoire*, 4 vols. (Paris, 1895)

Stanford, W.B., *Ireland and the Classical Tradition* (Dublin, 1976)

Stubbs, T.W., *The History of the University of Dublin* (Dublin, 1889)

Suratteau, Jean-René, 'Le Directoire—points de vue et interprétations d'après des travaux récents', *Annales historiques de la Révolution française* (1976), 181–214

History of the Tone Family, comp. Frank Jerome Tone (Niagara Falls, N.Y., 1944).

Turner, F.J., ed., 'Correspondence of the French Ministers to the United States,

1791–97', *American Historical Association Report*, 1903, 2 vols. (Washington, D.C., 1904)

Wall, M., 'The Rise of a Catholic Middle Class in Eighteenth-Century Ireland', *Irish Historical Studies* XI (1958), 91–115

—— 'The United Irish Movement', *Historical Studies*, ed. J.L. McCracken, V (London, 1965), 122–40

Walsh, J.E., *Sketches of Ireland Sixty Years Ago* (Dublin, 1847)

Woods, C.J., 'The Contemporary Editions of Tone's *Argument on Behalf of the Catholics*', *Irish Booklore* II, no. 2 (1976), 217–26

Wyse, Thomas, *Historical Sketches of the Late Catholic Association*, 2 vols. (London, 1829)

Uncollected Prose by W.B. Yeats, vol. I, ed. John P. Frayne (London, 1970); vol. II, ed. Frayne and Colton Johnson (London, 1975)

Zimmermann, G.D., *Songs of Irish Rebellion: Political Street Ballads and Rebel Songs, 1780–1900* (Dublin, 1967)

Dictionaries, Guides, Indexes

Allibone, A.S., ed., *A Critical Dictionary of British and American Authors*, 3 vols. (London, 1870)

Burtchaell, G.D., and Sadleir, T.U., eds., *Alumni Dublinenses: a Register of Students, Graduates, Professors, and Provosts of Trinity College, in the University of Dublin* (London, 1924)

Foster, Joseph, ed., *Alumni Oxonienses, 1500–1886*, 4 vols. (Oxford, 1891)

Index to Dublin Grant Books and Wills, appendix to the 26th Report of the Deputy Keeper of the Public Records and Keeper of the State Papers in Ireland, 2 vols. (Dublin, 1895)

Phair, P.B., ed., 'A Guide to the Registry of Deeds', *Analecta Hibernica*, no. 23 (1966), 257–76

Raimo, J.W., ed., *A Guide to Manuscripts Relating to America in Great Britain and Ireland* (London, 1979)

The Records of the Hon. Society of Lincoln's Inn: Admissions and Chapel Registers, 2 vols. (Lincoln's Inn, London, 1896)

Roberts, R.A., ed., *A Calendar of the Inner Temple Records*, 5 vols. (London, 1936)

Sturgess, H.A.C., ed., *Register of Admissions to the Hon. Society of the Middle Temple*, 3 vols. (London, 1949)

Vicars, Sir Arthur, ed., *Index to Prerogative Wills of Ireland, 1536–1810* (Dublin, 1897)

Unpublished Theses

Atkinson, N.D., 'Sir Laurence Parsons, Second Earl of Rosse, 1758–1841' (Univ. of Dublin Ph.D. thesis, 1962)

Brooke, Peter, 'Controversies in Ulster Presbyterianism, 1790–1836' (Cambridge Univ. Ph.D thesis, 1980)

Curtin, Nancy J., 'The Origins of Irish Republicanism: The United Irishmen in Dublin and Ulster, 1791–8' (Univ. of Wis.–Madison D. Phil. thesis, 1988)

Hill, Colin P., 'William Drennan and the Radical Movement for Irish Reform 1779–94' (Univ. of Dublin M.Litt thesis, 2 vols., 1967)

Kennedy, Denis, 'The Irish Whigs 1789–1795' (Univ. of Toronto Ph.D. thesis, 1971)

O'Brien, M.G.R., 'The Exercise of Legislative Power in Ireland, 1782–1800' (Cambridge Univ. Ph.D. thesis, 1983)

O'Donoghue, P., 'The Catholic Church in Ireland in an Age of Revolution and Rebellion, 1782–1803' (National Univ. of Ireland Ph.D. thesis, 1975)

O'Flaherty, Eamonn, 'The Catholic Question in Ireland, 1774–1793' (National

Univ. of Ireland, M.A. thesis, 1981)

Phillips, James W., 'A Bibliographical Inquiry into Printing and Bookselling in Dublin from 1670–1800' (Univ. of Dublin Ph.D. thesis, 1952)

Stoddart, P.C., 'Counter-Insurgency and Defence in Ireland, 1790–1805' (Oxford Univ. D.Phil. thesis, 1972)

Index